Modern Marine
Weather

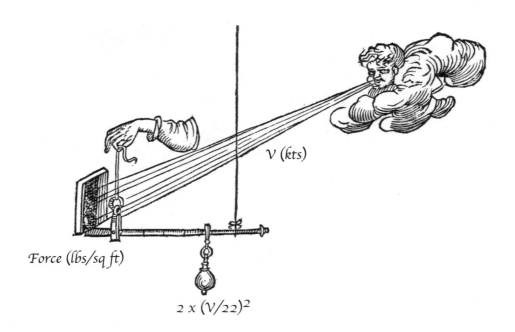

V (kts)

Force (lbs/sq ft)

$2 \times (V/22)^2$

We annotated this old engraving with an equation that is easy to remember.
It applies to wind perpendicular to the surface.

THIRD EDITION

Modern Marine Weather

— How to take weather into account for the planning and navigation of voyages, local or global, in any vessel, using the latest technologies as well as the time-honored skills of maritime tradition, so that your time on the water remains as safe and efficient as possible.

David Burch

STARPATH®

Seattle, Washington

ISBN 978-0-914025-58-0

Published by
Starpath Publications
3050 NW 63rd Street, Seattle, WA 98107
Manufactured in the United States of America
starpathpublications.com
10 9 8 7 6 5 4 3

"Starpath" is a registered trademark of Starpath Corporation.

News and resources related to this book, and contact with the author, can be found at www.starpath.com/wx

Contents

Preface to the first edition

The scope of this book is discussed in the Overview section of Chapter 1, as is the challenge of keeping up with the bold title *Modern Marine Weather*. In the last few weeks of production alone, the National Weather Service changed two important weather map conventions, and a valuable new complimentary software product became available. Each change called for last minute updates.

In an attempt to keep up with pertinent developments, we take a modern approach to the support of the book by creating a web page specifically for news and updates about this book. Please refer to starpath.com/wx for latest news on the book and its content. You can also make contact with the author through email links on that page. Your comments and suggestions will be much appreciated.

For those who want to review what they have learned in the book, there is a companion *Marine Weather Workbook* available that offers an extensive set of practical questions with full answers and related resources, organized according to the book chapters. It offers a way to structure your study and bring out relationships and practical points that might have been overlooked.

Preface to the second edition

New topics in this edition include the European ASCAT and Indian OSCAT satellite wind data and how to access it, barometer options, developments in numerical weather predictions, new weather resources for mobile devices, changes in NWS terminology and weather map conventions, new research that affects practical marine weather, and new data on ocean and coastal currents, among others.

A significant part of the update comes from use of the book in marine weather courses for five years in many different settings, from kayak clubs to Navy warships. We are grateful for the good reception and support of the text, and we acknowledge that by striving to improve it. Essentially every page includes some effort to enhance the clarity and precision of the explanations. And we will continue to do so. News, details, and updates are provided at starpath.com/wx.

Things are still changing, and getting more exciting as time goes by.

Preface to the third edition

A tremendous amount of the *modern* part of marine weather has changed in the past five years, which, with the addition of color, and all the benefits that brings, makes this a major update to the previous edition. We have greatly expanded the use of GRIB formatted forecasts, including overlays on weather maps and other images. High resolution rapid refresh models now make it possible to forecast local winds in digital format, which has a potentially revolutionary impact on day sailing in local waters—it's not just for ocean passages any longer. An overview of optimum weather routing has been added, along with expanded discussion of ASCAT scatterometer winds, which are now readily available in GRIB format.

We have emphasized obtaining weather data by email, including crucial details of the process. Now, with accurate barometers in our cellphones, the benefit of careful pressure analysis is more readily available, and has been stressed. The crucial practice of forecast management (map sequencing) has been improved, and new means of squall forecasting have been added. The entire book has been gone over to optimize descriptions, with major changes in many sections.

We did not shy away from including important internet links, well aware that they are subject to change. Updates as needed will be posted at starpath.com/wx. The links should be active in the ebook editions.

Acknowledgements

Over the years I have benefited from discussions of marine weather with several experts on the subject. In particular I would like to thank Lee Chesneau, (Ocean Prediction Center, retired) who kindly wrote the foreword to this book and provided valuable comments on several details, and Kenn Batt (Bureau of Meteorology, Australia) for ongoing discussions of Southern Hemisphere weather. Thank you both, again. I also wish to thank Joe Sienkiewicz of the Ocean Prediction Center for valuable suggestions.

I am pleased to thank Tobias Burch for his fine work on the graphics, layout, and design of the book and cover. Besides the processing of text and graphics in all forms and formats, he often turned rough sketches or ideas into informative, attractive vector products. It has been a pleasure working with him on this project and others.

Thanks also to the following companies who provided software, support, or services that helped in the production of this book: Expedition, Nobeltec Time Zero, Global Marine Networks, Memory-Map, Ocens, and Rose Point Navigation.

Mark Rowley and Jon Taylor provided valuable comments on the first edition. Ad Stofflen of the Royal Netherlands Meteorological Institute provided valuable comments on the ASCAT program.

———

For the second edition, I am especially grateful to University of Washington meteorologist Angeline Pendergrass, who provided a critical review of the manuscript, with many valuable improvements—especially in areas where explanations can cross the line between simple as possible, but not simpler. Needless to say, I take full responsibility for transgressions that remain. It has been a great pleasure working with her on this project and on our joint support for the ongoing second transatlantic expedition of the OAR Northwest rowers.

I am much indebted to my friend and colleague, marine weather and navigation instructor Larry Brandt. As with the first edition, he has gone over the book, cover to cover, with much good advice on precise expression and proper wording. The book has benefited from his great experience as both teacher and navigator.

———

For this third edition, we add our gratitude to these companies for their support: Great Circle/Squid-Marine, LuckGrib, Polar Navy, PredictWind, and Stentec WinGPS.

A special thanks to Craig McPheeters, developer of LuckGrib for Mac and iOS. Not only have we used his program for numerous images throughout the book, we have spent countless hours discussing numerical weather data and its application to practical sailing. His expertise in this subject and long ocean sailing experience have made his insights always productive and pertinent to the content of this book.

Thank you to Andrew Haliburton for valuable comments on sailing tactics. The book has benefited from several others on special topics, acknowledged in the book. For here, just a generic thank you again to all.

And I am pleased to add another note of gratitude to Tobias Burch, whose creation of all the graphics and technical production of the book have now been extended to editing. His requirement for clarity from the perspective of a non-mariner has led to numerous improvements.

You will notice very quickly in this new edition the key role played by the Saildocs program. They offer weather data by email at no charge to mariners around the world. Although there are free NWS options for much of the data, the convenience of the Saildocs process makes it the method of choice when possible. So I take a liberty here to thank Saildocs on behalf of the maritime community for the contribution they have made over the past 20 years.

Foreword

Modern Marine Weather—like a "Brave New World"—takes a bold step forward, and takes on today's challenges of the complexities of weather over the marine environment. This text is unique. It is a sorely needed and powerful upgrade to existing marine weather resources currently on the market! There are no hidden agendas with this outstanding text.

Author David Burch has provided the mariner with a balanced solution to this complex subject. From long standing traditional approaches to basic weather fundamentals (as one would find available in *Bowditch*), Burch then integrates discussions and examples of modern resources. He combines today's traditional human intelligence generated graphical weather charts and text forecasts with more newly available sources, such as Gridded Binary Data (GRIB) data, which is usually a singular weather forecast solution garnered from one of many computer generated forecast models. Both sources of weather data are now easily available to the mariner, as an integrated approach for marine weather forecasting and self-reliant decision making.

From the very beginning of the book, the reader is exposed to the words "National Weather Service" as being the provider of traditional weather forecast services. In practically the same breath, he also provides an overview of today's hot button issues where the reader is informed of the U.S. Coast Guard's recent abandonment of its latest attempt at eliminating long standing HF voice and single sideband radiofax signals, used by mariners to acquire weather information at sea. An action that defies logic! Right around the corner he mentions the importance of marine weather knowledge, the cornerstone of what I do for a living these days (teaching and training mariners on marine weather). After 33 years of hands on government and private sector forecasting and routing experience, I can tell you that the knowledge gained from *Modern Marine Weather* will stick to you as no other resource can do.

The detail of this text ranges from understanding all elements of charted ship reports (including subtleties of wind-feather symbols), conversion factors of meteorological parameters, time keeping (local times, valid times, GMTs, UTCs), to even the use of 10-point dividers—a handy tool to help determine wind strength on a surface pressure chart. Weather systems and navigation strategies... they are all there. The attention to detail in *Modern Marine Weather* reflects the integrity of the author, determined to get it right. I was really sold and literally overwhelmed with amazement that *Modern Marine Weather* is the only text I found that accurately covers the three cell theory—in my opinion, this is huge!

I strongly endorse this text as an invaluable resource that belongs in the wheelhouse along side of *Bowditch* as a mariner's reference on marine weather. The title alone suggests what today's mariner needs in this world of high technology—but do not forget the lesson learned from 2001 Space Odyssey. Hal must be monitored for good behavior. Only the weather-wise mariner is in a position to do so. *Modern Marine Weather* shows you how to become one!

Fair Winds.

Lee Chesneau

—retired senior marine forecaster at NWS's Ocean Prediction Center, popular lecturer and teacher, and co-author of *Heavy Weather Avoidance—Concepts and Applications of 500-mb charts.*

marineweatherbylee.com

"The most difficult problem of Astronomy becomes simplicity itself when compared with the extraordinarily complex agents that are in operation with the simplest meteorological phenomena."

— Sir Robert Stawell Ball, Royal Astronomer of Ireland, 1874.

CHAPTER ONE
INTRODUCTION

1.1 Overview

We admit immediately that *Modern Marine Weather* is a brave title. Of all technologies influencing marine navigation these days, those affecting weather preparation before a voyage and analysis underway, are changing as fast as any—partly because products and services are evolving rapidly, but also because the related technologies of wireless communications are changing so fast as well. Monthly we have new sources and improved technologies related to marine weather. New services and products from the National Weather Service (NWS) and commercial companies appear frequently.

Most mariners know about text messaging by cellphone, but fewer know their phones can access wind speed, wind direction, and pressure at a buoy or lighthouse along their route, whenever they might want it. We can also use our phones to get a live radar view showing precise locations of squalls in our waters, updated every 6 seconds! Aircards and cellphone hotspots offer broadband connection to the internet in most inland waters and many near coastal waters. The number of phone and tablet apps for weather and navigation work is growing exponentially.

There is also ongoing research into fundamentals that are "windfalls" to our trade. The demand for new energy sources has spurred much research into wind power generation, including where to locate the generators and how they interact with each other and with the local terrain. This has led to in-depth study of wind flow over and around barricades, directly applicable to predicting how close we can sail to an islet 20 ft high versus one 80 ft high, and still maintain our wind. This is a valuable resource for knowledge on sailing near land. Ocean modeling continually improves with better sea state and ocean current forecasts.

If we are to keep this book's title meaningful, we must stay on our toes and make every effort to keep the teaching materials and presentations up to date. Traditional book publishing procedures have a challenge here. If a book takes a year in production, it is destined to be out of date when it arrives. We need new means of publication and teaching to keep up with the topic. The solution is pretty obvious. The internet is the main source of revolution in marine weather content and services, and it also provides the way to keep materials and information up to date. Of all topics in modern marine navigation, it is fair to say that weather is affected the most by the internet. Updates on the content of this book can be found at starpath.com/wx.

There are also good reasons to get involved with modern sources of marine weather. The United States Coast Guard (USCG) will eventually discontinue the traditional high fre-quency (HF) broadcasts in voice and radiofax. In 2013 the middle frequency (MF) broadcasts were ended. High seas data in voice and radiofax—a longtime target for closing—are still available, but most sailors are already relying primarily on wireless connections to text versions of the reports and downloaded images of the weather maps. In contrast to the broadcasts, which are available at specific times only, these products can now be requested when needed by satellite phone (satphone) or HF radio. Check navcen.uscg.gov for the latest plans.

Needless to say, there are elements of weather work that do not change with time. What is changing are the types of data and how we receive them. What we do with the data in planning and navigation has not changed—what we watch in the sky and on the water, and how we choose our routes underway has not changed much since the great sailing days of the 1800's—though we do sail to weather a lot better! There is much to learn from knowledge gained in those days, especially from the works of pioneers such as Admiral Robert FitzRoy (1805-1865), the father of modern meteorology (and captain of Darwin's *Beagle*). We actually still use observations gathered by Captain Matthew Fontaine Maury (1806-1873) who compiled data from ship's logs into the forerunners of modern *Coast Pilots* and Pilot Charts. We rely daily when underway on the Beaufort wind force scale of Admiral Francis Beaufort (1774-1857). Its value has not diminished. We also touch on the work of George Hadley (1685-1768) who initiated the understanding of what causes the trade wind flow, the doldrums, and the great mid-ocean Highs.

We still need these basics of weather observation and respect for the sea, long-tested in maritime tradition. Modern tools are blessings that must be used thoughtfully. Global Positioning Systems (GPS), for example, has had a mixed influence on the practice of marine navigation. Certainly it is now a most valuable aid to navigation—to the point that it is essentially negligent to navigate without it. But with the advent of its (usually) great accuracy and extreme convenience has come a tendency to not study the basics of navigation. Whenever our GPS fails or is unavailable, or we make a cockpit error in using it, or when we are in some poorly charted area where having a digital position doesn't help at all, we must fall back on the basics.

Likewise, in modern marine weather, there are new and wonderful resources available now that are analogous to the arrival of GPS. We can push buttons now and end up with a full weather map laid out on the electronic chart we are navigating with. The overlays even include wind arrows plotted on the chart, showing wind speed and direction everywhere around us. Push another button and the predicted wave heights and directions are plotted as well. Push another button and we see how all of these change in the next hour, or the next day, or the next 5 days. We can obtain this data in a local bay or in the middle of the ocean. Just as when GPS was new, it is easy to ask, "Why do we need to study more?"

A main goal of this book is to answer that question. To explain just what we are actually getting with such a push-button system and how to use it safely. And of course to provide those basics we can fall back upon as needed. Continuing the GPS analogy, (which can tell us very nicely where we are, but does not tell us the best way to get to where we want to go) we also cover how to use the weather data we have, and how to interpret what we see around us in the water and sky. This helps to evaluate, and modify as needed, what we are told about the weather in order to choose the optimum course.

As for philosophy, a famous scientist once said that our goal in teaching practical science should be to make things as simple as possible—but not simpler. So a guiding principle has been to cover the theory of weather only insofar as it actually helps us make decisions in planning and navigation. There are many excellent books on meteorology that cover the background in more depth. Selections are listed in the References. But there are some nuts and bolts we cannot skip if we want to best apply what we learn. Our goal is to make the text a practical guide to the acquisition, interpretation, and application of marine weather data—not just tell you about it, but tell you how to use it.

Which brings up a thought that occurs more than once in the book. There will always be a forecast, and they are not labeled good or bad. At home we get 40% chance of rain, but at sea we do not get 40% chance of gale. So one of our ongoing goals underway and in our immediate planning of voyages is to develop those skills and resources that help us evaluate the forecasts we are given. We are not trying to outguess the professionals who gave us the forecast—that is not realistic. If they say the wind on the coast is going to be 20 kts, north of 38° 30' N, at midday tomorrow, then, *barring any immediate contrary evidence,* our best bet is to assume the wind is going to be 20 kts, north of 38° 30' N, at midday tomorrow. They have more knowledge on the subject and they have far more data than what we can see around us or download from our wireless sources.

But we can evaluate the timing of what they forecast when we are located in the forecast region—or when we have access to measurements from the forecast region. Weather systems are in motion, and their route and speed may change. In the ocean, we may only hear from the professionals every 6 hrs or so—although there are exciting new sources on the horizon that will change that. It could be things have changed since their last report. With trained observational skills, we may be able to detect changes in the timing of the event before the next forecast. We may be able to conclude that this system is early, and we should look for that wind much earlier.

More to the point, however, with learned techniques and observations we can assign some level of confidence to the forecast. If our study indicates that all signs point to this being a good forecast, then we carry on with more confidence. But, if our signs indicate this may not be such a good forecast, and if it is indeed wrong, our present plan may not be a good one. We are then better off just doing half of what we want to do, and wait for the next forecast to learn more.

In short, to do the best job with weather planning, we do not want to simply look at a map, read a text report, or listen to a voice broadcast, and say we are done—ready to make our decisions. Instead, we want to evaluate what we are told as carefully as possible. That evaluation process is another large part of the goal of this book.

Finally it might be valuable to point out early on that contrary to some images of marine weather study, it is not all about bad weather. In fact, if we do our planning properly and use our resources properly, we will avoid bad weather most of the time. As sailors, we will use our knowledge far more often to find *more* wind than to avoid too much of it. Find a route with 14 kts instead of 10 kts and you will get there faster. Find one with 5 kts instead of 3 kts, and the effect is even greater.

Practical knowledge of wind and waves is obviously not just the domain of sailors. The content of this book is equally valuable to all mariners. Just like the *Navigation Rules*, it applies to "every description of water craft used as a means of transportation on water."

1.2 Role of Marine Weather

When putting out to sea for an extended passage, the first and foremost concern is a sound and well prepared boat; next comes the basic health, fitness, and seamanship of the crew. With these basics in place, next priorities are fundamental navigation skills and knowledge of marine weather. There are those who sail around the world with only the most rudimentary knowledge of weather at sea, but there is a great deal of luck involved in these cases, and probably more anxiety than necessary. More important to the conscientious voyager, there is usually more risk and inefficiency than need be.

Bad weather is always a test of boat and crew, but it more often affects the progress of a trip without necessarily threatening the safety of a well prepared boat. Although bad weather is always recalled more vividly than fair weather, gales and worse are not common occurrences in most cruising. Knowing where and when bad weather is expected is fundamental weather knowledge every sailor should have. Avoiding it whenever possible is simply good seamanship. Weather statistics are available in *Coast Pilots* and *Sailing Directions*, presented on Pilot Charts, and discussed in standard references such as Bowditch's *American Practical Navigator* (nicknamed *Bowditch*). More detailed information can be found in the *Mariner's Weather Log*, published online three times a year by NOAA. The Climatology of Global Ocean

Winds (COGOW) data described in Section 10.6 have revolutionized sail route planning.

Weather and navigation cannot be separated at sea. To begin with, it is usually the same person tending to both matters, but more important, it is the weather that ultimately determines how fast and in what direction you proceed. In a sailboat, the sails are your engine and the wind your fuel. A car in the middle of a desert with no gas is in a bind. A sailboat in the middle of the vast calm of the Pacific High can be in a similar bind (remember the *Rime of the Ancient Mariner*!). Knowing about fair weather can be as important as knowing about bad weather. If it's too fair for too long, you won't get there.

The sensible elements of marine weather are temperature, precipitation, visibility, wind, and sea state. Of these, wind is by far the major concern, because wind makes the waves—the most immediate threat to a vessel—and wind can force you off course, creating delays or actual hazards in coastal waters. It takes extreme circumstances to create concern about the other elements of weather: deck icing or sun stroke can be real temperature threats; lack of water makes rain an important concern; and lack of navigation preparation can make fog a threat. But by and large, for the cruising sailor, anticipating the wind is the major goal of practical marine weather. The interplay of these sensible elements and how they relate to forecasting is covered in Section 1.3.

Feast or famine, wind is a constant concern to sailors. The driving force of the wind is what we care about, and it is important to appreciate that this force does not increase in direct proportion to the wind speed, but rather in proportion to the square of the wind speed. A 10-kt wind has twice the force of a 7-kt wind (since 10 × 10 is about twice as large as 7 × 7). A wind of 21 kts does not push on the boat 3 times harder than a 7-kt wind; it pushes 9 times harder. To appreciate the difference of a factor of 9 in force, imagine holding a large glass of water in each hand and then adding a gallon of water to one of them. Even small changes in wind speed have a big effect on boat speed. The difference between 7 kts and 10 kts of wind can mean a difference of many days in an ocean passage. On the other side of the concern, a gust from 15 to 22 kts of wind puts a tremendous additional force on the boat very suddenly. We must stay alert in gusty conditions.

Again, wind is just as important to power-driven vessels as it is to sailboats. In strong winds and big seas, optional routes are determined by the weather for all vessels.

The realistic challenge of wind prediction is not so much making a forecast completely on your own, but rather putting together what you can see and measure yourself, with what you have been told should happen by the weather services. Neither side of this information alone is as dependable as an educated combination of both. Consequently, there are two equally important aspects of learning weather: knowing the best sources of data for the region of interest and how to interpret them, and knowing what to look for from the boat and how to interpret what you see. As mentioned above, sailors

will find that knowledge of marine weather will be put to use much more often in finding more wind than in avoiding too much of it. If you find a route with 17 kts of wind rather than 14 kts you will have made a tremendous improvement to your voyage.

In the past, we spoke only of the "radio sources" of weather once underway. Nowadays it is best to use the phrase "wireless," since we are just as likely to be using a satphone at sea as we are a long-distance HF radio signal. Wireless sources available span the spectrum from full weather maps every few hours (from various sources) and satellite scans of the actual winds around us, to the abbreviated storm warnings incorporated into the National Institute of Standards and Technology (NIST) time broadcasts. The minimum radio sources one should consider for offshore sailing are the HF radiotelephone (voice) broadcasts of high seas weather, available every 6 hrs from U.S. Coast Guard (USCG) stations on any good short wave receiver. Most radio weather broadcasts are tabulated by time and frequency in a publication called *Radio Navigational Aids, Pub. 117*. The U.S. and Canadian versions (each cover the world) are available online and in print format.

The most relevant shipboard observations for forecasting include the existing wind, barometer, clouds, and sea swell. Temperature and precipitation can tell much about what is going on at that time (sometimes called "now-casting"), but these two factors do not help much with forecasting... except for the rain in some cases, as we shall see shortly. For each of the relevant factors mentioned, changes and trends always mean more than single observations. Furthermore, you need at least two of these factors to change in a consistent manner before the observations are relevant to forecasting.

Storms are usually preceded by the onset of a new swell because fully developed waves move faster than the storms that make them. Identifying a new swell within a confused sea, however, can be a subtle art. Also, with a few notable exceptions, strong winds replacing light winds nearly always are preceded by a dropping barometer. A drop of more than 4 or 5 millibars in 6 hrs is a pretty good sign that something is headed your way. We come back to details of shipboard forecasting later in the book.

A persistent gradual wind shift is often the best sign of approaching weather, although knowledge of the prevailing patterns can be crucial to the interpretation of the shift. Away from squalls and away from sea breezes in coastal waters, when the wind changes direction, the isobars (lines of constant pressure shown on weather maps) must have moved —or you moved to a new place in a stationary system—even though the pressure reading itself might not reflect this for some time.

Consequently, it pays to know that the wind has shifted, for example, from 280° in the morning to 260° at noon, rather than being simply aware that the wind has been westerly all morning. Often the wind speed changes when the wind direction changes, so to be sensitive to this sign requires that you separate the true wind from the apparent wind. When reaching across the wind, especially with the wind near the beam, it takes careful vector work or good electronics to spot a wind shift of this type.

And then there are the clouds. Every sailor's aspiration is to read the weather from the clouds. There is no doubt, it definitely pays to study the clouds, and we cover clouds in Chapter 5. The clouds will more often than not tell something of the truth about the approaching weather. With very few exceptions, there can't be strong winds well offshore without tall clouds. But it is very speculative business to forecast a particular wind from the clouds alone, without other supporting information. Textbook cases do occur, though. A halo around the sun or moon in previously clear skies is how shamans earn their keep; it is a very strong sign of an approaching warm front, especially in the summer. A cold front, on the other hand, is often visible approaching as a wall of tall cumulus, and you can count on increasing winds and a sharp veer when it passes. Headed south, the onset of trade wind cumulus is a good sign that the northeasterlies you experience are indeed the trades, and so on, in many special cases. We will go over details later and cover other dependable cloud signs.

For longer term forecasting, it is the high clouds that are important. Their direction and speed are valuable indicators of the winds aloft that must ultimately bring the surface weather to you. But as strong an indicator as they might appear, clouds in general must be treated in the same way as other shipboard signs: they must be interpreted in conjunction with other information, and it is always a sequence that is more significant than any one observation.

Both shipboard forecasting and the interpretation of weather broadcasts take practice. As with the study of navigation, a good approach is to treat it as a hobby. Do it better than you have to, when you don't have to, then you will be prepared. The more you know about marine weather, the safer and more efficient your cruising will be—plus a bonus: the more you know about weather, the more ways you have to explain why you were wrong, if things don't pan out the way you predicted.

1.3 Elements of Marine Weather

By way of an overview, let's look at the sensible elements of marine weather in perspective—meaning how do they relate to each other, what do they tell us about what is going on with the weather now, and what is likely to happen in the near future. We consider temperature, precipitation, visibility, wind, and sea state. These are on some level the end products we care about in marine weather. This discussion will bring up several topics covered in more detail later on.

Temperature

Temperature is certainly one of the key elements of weather for landsmen. It determines what clothes we wear and what activities we might plan outdoors. This is also about

its same significance for sailors on a daily basis in most cases; not much more. There are extremes of course. In high latitudes, the temperature is crucial to icing on the vessel that affects its stability, and in low latitudes bright sun and high temperatures could lead to sunburn and heat stroke. There are even certain estuaries where there is a strong correlation between local atmospheric pressure and the local temperature, in which case the wind speed can be predicted based on temperature differences.

And we certainly cannot forget that it is ultimately the heat of the sun that drives all of the weather on earth, and that very small changes in global average temperature can lead to catastrophic effects on the planet, but when it comes down to trying to figure out what might happen next with the local weather, the local temperature is not going to help much.

It can, however, tell us nicely sometimes what has just happened. When a cold front crosses over us at sea the temperature decreases maybe 10-15 °F, (somewhat less of a change than seen on land). This is nice "hind-casting," but as we shall see, we have other observations to confirm that a cold front is going by. Likewise, it should be no surprise that when a warm front goes by, the air gets warmer.

Another example might be when you experience the downburst winds from a squall. This air blasting down with the rain will be notably cooler than the local surface air because, first, higher air is cooler than lower air, and second, it cools further by rain evaporation as it descends. This observation tells us about what is taking place at the moment. In contrast to the cold front passage, however, this is a very localized patch of cool air—maybe just several miles in diameter or so, compared to a cold front that could stretch over several hundred miles or more.

So temperature is good at telling what is taking place or has taken place, but it is not much help with forecasting what will later take place. We are speaking about the temperature of the air. The temperature of the water is another matter altogether. Warm moist air is the fuel of all squalls and storms. Very warm water is the source of warm moist air. Thus whenever the water is warmer than seasonally expected, one should be on the alert for severe weather conditions. Cases like this have happened more than once in Cabo San Lucas, Mexico to the great chagrin of many yachtsmen. And we shall see that hurricanes do not form if the water temperature is less than 80 °F.

So how does temperature interact with the other sensible elements? It certainly affects precipitation. If the air is warm it rains and if very cold it snows. It is the very cold air aloft that generates the hail that comes with some squall downbursts. And certainly the air temperature (along with humidity) affects the visibility. If the air temperature drops to the dew point of the air, the moisture in the air will condense into fog. This is not the only cause of fog that might cross our path underway, but it is one of them. As we shall see, it can be very important to know that there is more than one source of fog.

The temperature of the air also affects the wind, but this is not well known except to scientists and high-tech sail makers. Cold air is more dense than warm air, so it packs a bigger punch. In other words the force on the boat from cold wind is some 30% or so higher than that of warm wind. The main reason we do not all know this as second nature is that cold wind comes in the winter when the wind speeds are on average higher than they are in the summer of warm winds. And since the wind speed itself is so much more important in determining the force of the wind, this seasonal difference in speed completely masks the relatively smaller effect of the seasonal difference in temperature.

For this same reason, cold wind makes bigger waves than warm wind, so air temperature also affects the sea state. And again, we do not notice this because the wind is stronger in the winter, and wind speed again is the dominant factor in building waves.

Precipitation

In contrast to temperature, precipitation can be both an excellent now-caster and an excellent forecaster. In other words, we need to pay much more attention to the type and duration of the rain than we do the temperature if we want to know what is going on and what might happen next, both on a large scale and on a very local scale.

Warm fronts bring light, steady rain for a long period before the front passes, whereas cold fronts come with short, heavy downpours that occur just as the front itself passes, lasting less than an hour or so. On a local scale, rain is also an excellent sign of the stage of squall development, as we shall later study in detail. The strong winds of a squall come with the rain. If the squall approaches without rain, the worst is yet to come. If it approaches already raining, the worst is past. These behaviors were summarized by 19th century mariners as:

> *Long foretold, long to last*
> *Short notice, soon to pass.*

Thus we will learn to keep an eye on the nature and duration of the rain to know what is taking place and what might follow. We have a section later on how to analyze old sayings about the weather.

Rain can also have a remarkable effect on sea state. A torrential downpour can tremendously dampen the waves by inhibiting the production of the small capillary waves that foster the larger ones. In the torrential rain of tropical squalls this effect can lead to an almost calm sea in 30 or 40 kts of wind, with only the prevailing swell remaining. This, in turn, also influences the measurements of wind by satellites, because they count on radar backscattering from the wind-ruffled wave surfaces.

Visibility

Fog has been a key factor in the minds of many navigators since recorded times, but it is much less a factor in these modern times of GPS and radar. In fact, navigation is generally safer in traffic in the fog, because most vessels tend to be more careful. As mentioned earlier, fog is clearly dependent on the temperature because one way it is formed is when the temperature drops to the dew point (radiation fog).

Visibility can also be related to the sea state in that one common source of sea fog is the upwelling of cold deep water along the eastern coasts of oceans (i.e., California coast), which can be enhanced by large westerly swells. Then, in turn, when the wind pushes the fog inland or along the coast, we have the wind affecting the visibility.

The wind also affects the production of radiation fog. Any wind above a knot or two stops its production since it mixes up the air at the surface before it gets a chance to cool. And sea fog—great thick patches of it—can move up and down the coast, onshore and offshore, and deep into estuaries along the coast. Visibility is often dominated by the local winds.

Visibility is also affected by precipitation. Snow can shut off visibility completely and a heavy rain can as well. Within intense tropical squalls, such as those that fringe a hurricane, or crop up on their own in extreme cases, the rain can be so heavy that you cannot see the bow of a 40-ft boat from the cockpit. And we all know that even patches of moderate rain can be seen on the water as obscuring the horizon behind it—a great value of radar is that you can often see traffic within such rain (with careful tuning), as well as monitor the actual motion of the squall itself. Target detection by AIS is not affected by rain or snow.

An interesting thing we will learn about visibility is that its forecast is usually very good. The official forecasts might be totally wrong about the wind, but spot on when they call for reduced visibility in the afternoon on the same day. The onset of fog depends on temperature and humidity, which are air mass properties, uniform over many miles around us and easy to measure accurately. But the wind is ultimately due to the pressure distribution, which changes easily when weather systems interact with land and each other. It is not uncommon to have a forecast calling for an afternoon high temperature of 64° (given to remarkable precision), and at the same time call for winds of "variable, 5 to 15"—i.e., we do not know the direction at all, and "5 to 15 kts" is another way of saying "0 to 15 kts," again meaning we do not know the wind speed either. But we can't be too critical here. We shall learn that in some confined areas, the isobars just have to rotate 10 or 20 degrees and a northerly turns into a southerly.

Wind

Except in high latitudes where icing is a threat, we can more or less accommodate whatever we get in the temperature, rain, and visibility departments. But this is not the case with the wind. We have come to the main thing that the mariner cares about. Wind is our engine in sail boats, and it is our primary obstacle in many classes of power driven and manually powered vessels. It is also the wind that makes the waves, and the sea state is usually the main safety concern for all vessels in most waters. So a study of *marine* weather is primarily a study of the wind. Essentially everything we do and all resources we call upon are for the purpose of understanding what wind we will get, where, and when. Chapter 2 is about wind and pressure. It is the main "theory" part of the book; essentially the only theory part. We need to know as much as we can about what causes the surface winds we experience or might experience.

Sea State

Waves and swells and the ripples on the surface of these make up the "state of the sea" we sail in. It is the road we travel. Is it flat, hilly, or mountainous? If the wind picks up, how long does it take the seas to respond? What happens if the wind shifts? How big will the waves get? What is the difference between waves and swells? What do we learn from the ripples or cat's paws we see? And so on.

These are not questions of "weather" to a landsman; these are oceanography. But they are part of marine weather according to the World Meteorological Organization (WMO). And we shall see that there are no simple answers to some of these questions. If we have wind, we have waves, but if we have waves of one height, we have waves of many heights—and many widths, and many lengths. The sea state is a statistical distribution of waves and swells. Thus we also have to learn what the NWS and the USCG mean when they say the wave height is 4 ft. It cannot mean that all the waves are 4 ft tall, and it does not mean that the average height is 4 ft either. We do not need an in-depth course on oceanography, but there are a handful of basic ideas and definitions that will serve us well underway, and in coastal and inland waters when planning our voyages or day sails around the weather. These topics are covered in Chapter 5.

We also might imagine other applications, such as landing in the surf or crossing the steep waves that build up at a river bar, both of which call for some understanding of wave behavior.

And ocean currents? Where do they fit in? They are really oceanography as well, but they are crucial to our planning, and just like the waves, they are for the most part driven by local or prevailing winds. So a marine weather book is also the logical place to learn about currents, and so we have a section on currents in Chapter 3, with an emphasis on the Gulf Stream—though techniques and resources learned there can apply to many other strong current systems around the world.

1.4 Terminology and Glossaries

There are several terminology sources that can be considered primary. These include:

(1) *The American Practical Navigator (Bowditch)*

(2) American Meteorological Society (AMS)

(3) National Weather Service (NWS)

(4) World Meteorological Organization (WMO)

The WMO "glossary" is a six-language database of terminology called Meteoterm; tips are included on how to search

Table 1.4-1. Marine Weather Terminology	
Bowditch Glossary	msi.nga.mil
AMS Glossary	glossary.ametsoc.org
NWS Glossary	w1.weather.gov/glossary
WMO Meteoterm	wmo.int
Starpath Glossary	starpath.com/glossary
Abbreviations	wpc.ncep.noaa.gov/html/contract.html

for specific terms. The International Maritime Organization (IMO) specifies how vessels are supposed to communicate with each other in *Standard Marine Communications (IA987E)*, but does not address weather terminology.

The Starpath Marine Weather Glossary is a compilation of the above references, often reworded to match our present usage, plus the inclusion of some modern terms or specialized sailing terms that are missing from the traditional sources. These sources are listed in Table 1.4-1.

1.5 Wind Terms and Symbols

In this section we get started on the fundamental terminology related to winds, and start looking at symbols used on weather maps for wind and related parameters. Throughout the book we talk about parts of weather maps, step by step, and soon you should be expert at reading weather maps, knowing what maps are there to help you, and how to use them for your planning.

Winds are named according to the direction from which they come. A north wind blows from the north, toward the south. A southwest wind is coming from the southwest, blowing toward the northeast. Thus when we record the direction of a west wind it would be 270. Wind directions are always considered true directions unless specifically stated otherwise. If we are told the wind direction is 135, we would look to the southeast to have our face into the wind. Winds have

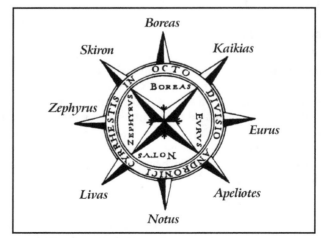

Figure 1.5-1. *Intercardinal winds defined on the Tower of Winds from ~200 BC in Athens. References to these winds can also be found in the writings of Homer, some six centuries earlier.*

been named this way since early civilization, as indicated in the Tower of Winds woodcut shown in Figure 1.5-1.

Keeping this definition in mind, it is easy to recall wind directions that might otherwise be more confusing. For example, a sea breeze blows *from the sea*, toward the land, just as a north wind blows from the north toward the south. Likewise, a land breeze blows *from the land*, toward the sea. Later on we study wind and terrain, and the concept of sea breeze plays a key role in that topic, since this is a wind specifically created by the land as it heats. Sea breeze is therefore blowing toward the shore and a land breeze is blowing away from the shore, toward the sea. See Figure 1.5-2.

Just as fundamental as wind-direction names are the names we use for wind shifts. We can barely get started talking about marine weather without knowing how to describe a wind shift. A wind shift to the right is called a *veering* shift. A wind shift to the left is called a *backing* shift, as shown in Figure 1.5-3. In other words, if you face the present wind, and then you have to turn right to face the shifted wind, the wind has veered.

A north wind that shifts to a northeast wind has veered; if it shifted to a northwest wind, it has backed. A southwest wind veers when shifting to the west and backs when shifting to the south. These definitions apply to all wind directions and to any location, both Northern Hemisphere (NH) and Southern Hemisphere (SH). The term "clocking" is the same as veering, but it is not as tidy a term and is more often misused. If you hear or read "the wind clocked around to the left," it's time to cringe. That is gibberish.

As an example of the use of this terminology in the NH, we note that as you rise in the atmosphere the wind speed increases and the wind direction veers—for reasons we will understand in Chapter 2. This fact has numerous consequences we can readily see.

If you face the surface wind, you will note that low clouds come from slightly to the right of the surface wind, because they are riding along in higher wind that is veered. Likewise, wind gusts well away from cliffs and other obstacles are usually caused by vertical instability of the air that just suddenly drops a patch of higher air down to the surface. Thus these gusts are higher in speed than the surface wind and veered in direction—the former is expected from the name "gust" itself, but the latter might not have been appreciated. Thus sailing to weather in these conditions you are better off on a starboard tack. Then every gust is a lift—which brings up even more terminology for wind shifts. A *lift* is a wind shift term used exclusively by sailors, unlike veering and backing, which apply to all mariners. When sailing, a wind shift away from the bow is called a lift, as illustrated in Figure 1.5-4. A wind shift toward the bow is called a *header*. A header on your tack is a lift for those on the opposite tack.

When sailing to weather, a header impedes progress while a lift enhances it. The opposite is generally true when sailing downwind. Note that a veer is a lift on a starboard tack, but a header on a port tack. A header is sometimes called a *knock*.

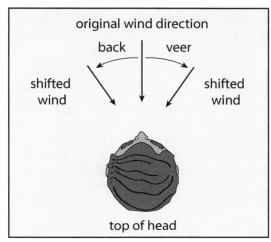

Figure 1.5-3. *Wind shifts defined.*

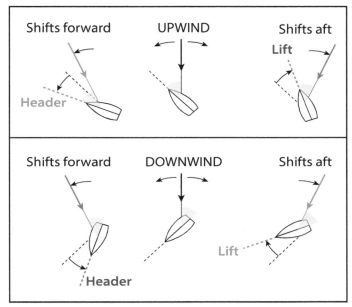

Figure 1.5-4. *Wind shifts on a sailing vessel, as seen from a boat with wind on the starboard side. The assumption here (not always true) is the destination is directly upwind or downwind, and the best progress is made with the same wind angle for a given wind speed, then lifts are favored upwind and headers downwind.*

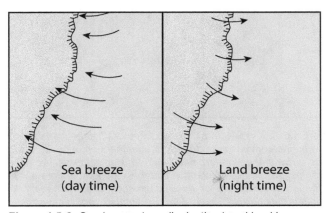

Figure 1.5-2. *Sea breeze (usually daytime) and land breeze (usually nighttime).*

There are still more key terms related to the wind direction. We have upwind and downwind, and windward and leeward. It is easy to overlook the distinction between these two sets of terms, but there is an important difference, which enters into official rules of sailing and of navigation in general.

Upwind and downwind are directions relative to a line perpendicular to the wind direction, whereas windward and leeward are directions relative to the centerline of the vessel. Windward and leeward are the opposite sides of the boat, unless you are going exactly downwind, in which case the *Navigation Rules* define windward as "the side opposite to that on which the mainsail is carried…"

Upwind and downwind, in contrast, are defined by a line through your vessel that is perpendicular to true wind direction. When you are tacking to weather with another vessel, that boat is ahead of you if he is upwind of you, regardless of where he is to windward or to leeward of you—and of course he can be ahead of you and to leeward. See Figure 1.5-5.

Moving on to symbols. Wind symbols are our starting point in reading weather maps. Figure 1.5-6 is an actual graphic definition given on an official NWS web site.

It shows the basic idea: half a feather is 5 kts; full is 10; a flag is 50. The arrow flows in the direction of the wind. Five knots is displaced from the end so as not to be confused with 10 kts. But other than those basics, this is a pretty poor defining graphic. First the winds marked NE are not from the NE according to these arrows; they vary from 014 to 024. If these were NE winds they should be oriented toward 045. The one labeled NNE shown at 008 is also wrong, it should be halfway between 000 and 045. Wind directions shown on maps and discussed in conversations and in writing are always assumed to be true directions unless specifically stated otherwise.

Secondly, the winds indicated in that defining graphic are not really what these symbols mean, though often stated that way. An arrow flowing from the NE with 1 feather means the wind at the arrow tip is anywhere between 7.5 kts and 12.5 kts. It does not mean the wind is specifically 10 kts. The force of the wind varies as the square of the wind speed, so 12.5 kts of wind is about 3 times "stronger" than that of 7.5 kts (12.5 × 12.5 ÷ 7.5 × 7.5 = 2.8). Likewise, one and a half feathers means winds of anywhere from 12.5 to 17.5 kts, spanning a factor of 2 in wind force. (See illustration opposite the title page.)

Figure 1.5-6. *Wind arrows from an official online source—an example of the sometimes poor definitions we run across.*

With this in mind, sailors would like to know forecasted wind speeds as accurately as possible, and indeed the predictions will be more *precise* than ± 2.5 kts. This does not mean the forecasts will be that *accurate*, but we certainly do not want to throw away precision that might be right.

Concern for these details is definitely a reflection on modern resources available. Standard weather maps generated by various weather offices around the world display the wind in this rounded format because (at least historically) they probably do not believe they were more accurate than that. And that is fair enough. But the NWS surface analysis maps that we use plot the actual ship reports of the wind, and these reports are received typically to a precision of ±0.5 kts (rounded to whole knots) and directions rounded to 10°.

Some years ago, all the winds in the world were typically reported as N, NE, E, SE, etc., at 15, 20, 25 kts, etc. But the Port Meteorological Officers (PMOs) at the NWS who coordinate the Vessel Observing Ship (VOS) program have done a good job over the years training the ship's officers who turn in the weather observations. Now we get more precise observations, corrected for vessel motion. We also now have satellite wind measurements that help identify actual winds on the ocean surface. Taking into account known limitations, accuracy standards for observations (human and satellite) are about ±2 kts in speed and ±20° in direction, but with

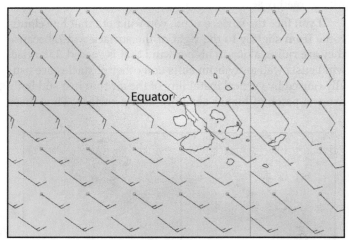

Figure 1.5-7. *Wind vectors near the Equator (Galapagos Islands), showing the convention of drawing the feathers on opposite sides of the arrow in the Northern and Southern Hemispheres. We get a better insight into this convention later on—the feathers are always on the low-pressure side of the wind direction, which is a reminder of what is called Buys Ballot's Law. Remember, too, in cases like this where the wind feathers span some 40 miles at this scale, that the report location is at the tip of the arrow.*

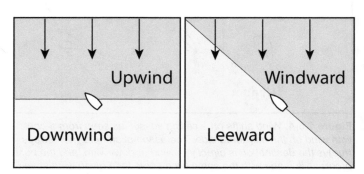

Figure 1.5-5. *Upwind - downwind; windward - leeward.*

care, human reports could be better. Ship reports periodically include wind speed precise to the tenth of a knot.

There is still another way to describe wind speeds in terms of the Beaufort force scale, which is used in the UK and Europe more than in the US. Force 5, for example, means wind speeds of 17 to 21 kts. This is a convenient, broad description of wind speed, but because it is based on the relationship between wind speed and sea state, we postpone this important concept to Chapter 5, which covers sea state.

We will also need to come back to the process of extracting the true wind speed and direction from the apparent wind speed and direction that we measure from a moving vessel. It is always the true wind speed and direction we care about in weather analysis and forecasting.

We will look at implications of these wind conventions shortly with specific examples, but there is another convention that is more subtle than crucial, namely, the feathers are drawn on the left side of the arrow in north latitudes and on the right side in southern latitudes. See Figure 1.5-7.

1.6 Quick Look at Resources

To best illustrate the points being made about wind symbols and forecast presentations we need to take a quick preview of resources that will be explained in depth in Chapters 7 and 8. This is also a way for readers to start experimenting with important sources as we proceed through the book.

Unfortunately, this must include note of the demise of the Marine Weather Services Charts (MSC) that were featured in our previous edition. Of the 16 charts that covered all U.S. waters, only the Alaska edition is left (MSC-15, Figure 1.6-1). Budget cuts prevented keeping them up to date, so they were discontinued. Among the many values of these free printed sheets were graphic maps of the forecast zones, broadcast

schedules, and local contact information. They included information on all sources of marine weather for use underway at the time. Granted, there are different sources now, but an organized, printed presentation remains valuable to many mariners. Losing them is not progress. See starpath.com/wx for an article on how to make an MSC on your own, using the latest obtainable resources online.

The Canadian counterparts of the U.S. MSCs are still available in print from some chart dealers and as a printable color PDF for download (Figure 1.6-2). These are especially useful to U.S. mariners sailing north, because conventions on zone identification, radio reporting sequences, and radio frequencies are different.

Another important source that recently changed is the NWS program called FTPmail. This is the way we can obtain *all* NWS products by email request. We come back to this service later and compare it to other options that apply in some cases. A description can be found at tgftp.nws.noaa.gov/fax/ftpmail.txt. Detailed instructions are found in Appendix B to a NWS document called *Worldwide Marine Radiofacsimile Broadcast Schedules*, which is a totally different subject we also cover later. This document is available at nws.noaa.gov/om/marine/rfax.pdf.

Getting back to the wind symbols, NWS surface analysis maps present several key ship reports right on the maps themselves. These are the reports that corresponded to the valid time of the map, and indeed, they contributed to the layout of the map itself. An example is marked "C" in Figure

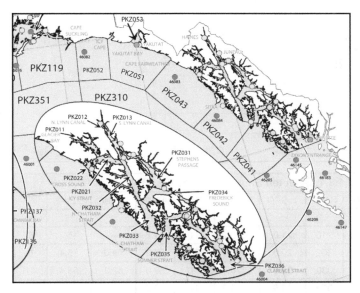

Figure 1.6-1. *Small section of MSC-15, showing boundaries of forecast zones. Much information on active sources is included on this last of the U.S. MSCs. Available also in JPG and PDF formats.*

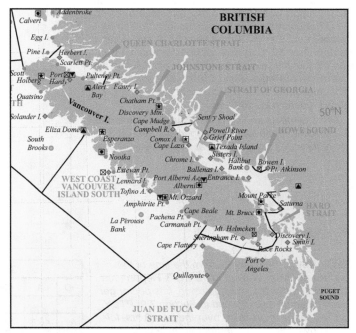

Figure 1.6-2. *Section of the* Canadian Marine Weather Guide: Pacific Coast, *with similar data as provided on the U.S. MSCs. Reporting stations are shown here, as well as the definitions of the forecast zones. Schedules, frequencies, and other valuable data are provided. Available as a PDF. The link at ec.gc.ca moves around, so find the latest at starpath.com/insidepassage.*

1.6-3—a ship report plotted as a nominal 20 kts (2 feathers) from the NNW. If we cared to study this map in depth, we could actually send an email request for the exact reports that it shows. A sample of such reports is shown in Table 1.6-1 below the figure. We see that this symbol plotted as a nominal 20 kts was actually 22 kts with a reported direction of 330 T.

Comparing the other samples, we see the reports and symbols are all fairly consistent with the map—except report "A," which clearly had a wrong pressure (report of 1030.2 when located just inside the 1024 isobar), but this type of discrepancy is rare. That wind report is also not consistent with the map, as we will understand better later in the book. We address maps and isobars throughout the book as we proceed; for now we are just looking at the use of wind symbols.

Another topic worth introducing early that we shall come back to in depth, is the use of vector wind forecasts in GRIB (GRIdded Binary) format. This system of GRIB data sources and GRIB data viewers is a primary tool for modern weather work. Working with GRIB forecasts as soon as possible not only helps with learning the basics behind them, it also puts live weather data in your hands at the same time.

Surface analysis and forecast maps provided by the NWS are often based on the Global Forecast System (GFS) numerical weather prediction model (discussed later). Mariners have ubiquitous access to GFS model data that the NWS uses, which provide wind and pressure forecasts every 6 hrs out to ten days, the first three or four of which can be fairly reliable. Most navigation software programs we use underway provide a way to request the data wirelessly worldwide, as well as a means of displaying it.

A sample is shown in Figure 1.6-4, which was chosen to match the weather map and reports from Figure 1.6-3. Wind data in GRIB format are fully digital, so wind, pressure, and other parameters, can be read directly from a mouse click or cursor rollover on the screen. The data are presented at specific grid points, but the software will interpolate values between grid points. The finest grid for GFS is one data point about every 15 nmi, so it is intended for global ocean naviga-

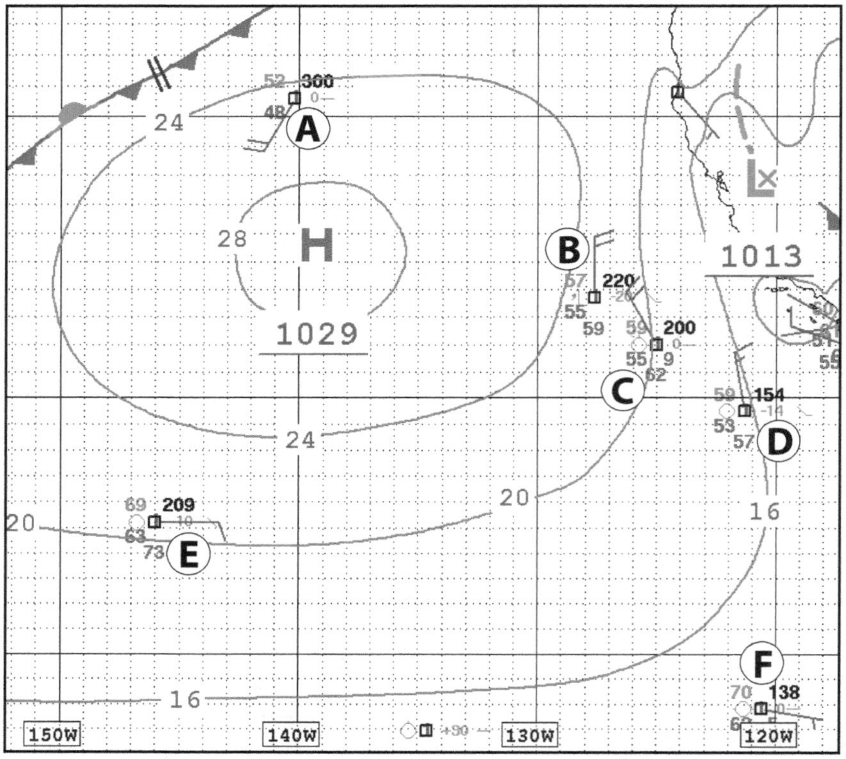

Figure 1.6-3. *Surface analysis map valid at 12z, May 18, 2017. Details of map reading are covered later, throughout the text. This type of map includes ship reports at the valid time. Selected reports are labeled on the map, with the corresponding actual reports in Table 1.6-1.*

Isobars are labeled by their last two digits: "20" means 1020 mb. The station-model format of the reports shown on the map is discussed in Section 7.7. The report at B shows a pressure of 1022.0 but the actual report was 1022.1, with a (pressure tendency, PTDY of decreasing 2.0 mb in the last 3h. The air temperature was 57.2, dew point 55.4, and water temperature 59. Compare reported pressures with the plots of the isobars, which were established by the model predictions and the actual reports.
The peak pressure at the center of the High (H) is shown underlined, 1029 mb.

Other symbols and conventions are presented as we proceed in the text. See especially Section 7.9. Weather maps are available at ocean.weather.gov.

Table Notes: *Ship reports from the time of the surface analysis map in Figure 1.6-3. Reports are obtained from ndbc.noaa.gov/ship_obs.php or get them by email as explained in Section 7.9. PTDY is the change in pressure over the past 3 hrs, followed by air and water temperature, dew point, and visibility. Full reports contain more data than shown on the maps.*

Table 1.6-1. Selected Ship Reports at 12z, MAY 18, 2017									
ID	LAT	LON	WDIR	WSPD	PRESS	PTDY	ATMP	WTMP	DEWP	VIS
			°T	kts	mb	mb	°F	°F	°F	nmi
A	40.6	-140.2	210	21.0	1030.2	0.0	51.8	—	48.2	5
B	33.7	-127.6	360	20.0	1022.1	-2.0	57.2	59.0	55.4	5
C	32.0	-125.0	330	22.0	1020.0	0.0	59.0	62.2	55.4	11
D	29.5	-121.3	350	15.9	1015.3	-1.4	59.0	57.2	52.9	11
E	25.2	-146.0	090	11.1	1021.0	-1.0	68.9	72.5	63.1	11
F	17.8	-120.6	100	7.0	1013.9	0.0	69.8	76.6	61.5	5

tion. For near coastal and inland work we need GRIB data from other sources, which can be at grid points as close as every 1 nmi.

In contrast to most weather maps, which show primarily the isobars with a few selected wind reports, these GRIB data files include complete wind field maps. They still use the conventional wind arrows in 5-kt incremental feathers, but these can also be labeled with the digital value of prediction at each arrow. Thus we easily tell what each 15-kt feather represents and we are not limited to 15 ± 2.5.

But with all this convenience and precision comes several important cautions to exercise when using this type of data—it is, for example, so fully automated that it has not had the scrutiny of professional meteorologists. We are looking at raw computer output that has not been vetted by human intelligence. The difference between the map of Figure 1.6-3 and 1.6-4 is, the former, though ultimately drawn by software, was created taking into account several numerical models, not just the GFS, with knowledge of how each has performed in the past under similar conditions. The NWS maps also include weather fronts (red and blue symbolized line) and local troughs of low pressure (red dashed line) which show up only indirectly in the GFS output. Figure 1.6-4 only uses the GFS data.

These days we face the challenge of making an intelligent interpretation of the combination of these two types of weather maps, so we can make our best weather routing decisions. One map is cruder than it needs to be and the other is more precise than justified. A goal of this book is to provide the background to make this evaluation and combine it with other resources available.

Weather maps we use underway and in planning come in two basic categories. One is the surface analysis that tells what was going on at the time the map was made, and the others are forecast maps valid at 24, 48 and 96 hrs into the future. Surface analysis maps, produced four times a day, only plot the winds that were reported by ships or coastal stations. Forecast maps show predicted winds only if they are greater than 33 kts.

GFS model forecasts are also made four times a day, at the same *synoptic times* as the surface analysis maps, namely, 00, 06, 12, and 18 UTC. These are the key times in marine weather. Worldwide observations are also taken at these times so they can be incorporated into the forecast calculations.

The primary source of NWS weather maps and other ocean data is the Ocean Prediction Center (OPC). A visit to their website shows the many resources available; we go over them in Chapters 7 and 8. Sources cited here are listed in Table 1.6-3.

The National Hurricane Center (NHC) provides data on tropical storms and hurricanes. We shall see that the text Advisories with associated text forecasts are crucial aids to tropical forecasts. The primary source for live and archived observations is the National Data Bouy Center (NDBC).

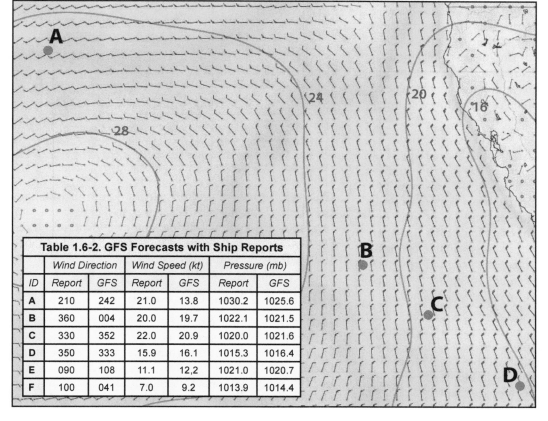

Table 1.6-2. GFS Forecasts with Ship Reports					
	Wind Direction		Wind Speed (kt)		Pressure (mb)	
ID	Report	GFS	Report	GFS	Report	GFS
A	210	242	21.0	13.8	1030.2	1025.6
B	360	004	20.0	19.7	1022.1	1021.5
C	330	352	22.0	20.9	1020.0	1021.6
D	350	333	15.9	16.1	1015.3	1016.4
E	090	108	11.1	12,2	1021.0	1020.7
F	100	041	7.0	9.2	1013.9	1014.4

Figure 1.6-4. *Section of a GFS forecast, to be compared to the surface analysis map and a list of actual ship reports (Table 1.6-1). This model output in GRIB format presents one wind vector every 0.25° (about 15 nmi). Note the calm or very light air in the center of the High inside the 1028 isobar.*

Table Notes: *Digital GFS values read from the screen compared to the actual reports. Both of these can in turn be compared to the surface analysis map issued by NWS at that time.*

Table 1.6-3. Selected Weather Sources	
Ocean Prediction Center (OPC)	ocean.weather.gov
National Data Buoy Center (NDBC)	ndbc.noaa.gov
National Hurricane Center (NHC)	nhc.noaa.gov
NOAA Weather Radio (NWR)	nws.noaa.gov/nwr
Index to NOAA marine weather sources	weather.gov/marine
FTPmail	tgftp.nws.noaa.gov/fax/ftpmail.txt
Environmental Modeling Center (EMC)	emc.ncep.noaa.gov
Popular source for a broad range of data	saildocs.com
Includes an annotated list of resources, with regional compilations to illustrate how they work together.	starpath.com/wx

VHF NOAA Weather Radio

NOAA Weather Radio (NWR) by VHF broadcast has been a dependable source of weather information for some 50 years for both inland U.S. and coastal waters. It remains a primary source for many mariners and a dependable backup to all. Coverage is essentially continuous along the U.S. coast (Figure 1.6-5), available 24 hrs a day, 7 days a week. The MSCs used to describe the frequencies and coverage, but with that source gone, we find this information from the NWR website.

With a handheld VHF you can listen to the local broadcasts at home for practice. There are also weather radios sold that receive the FM channels used, but they cost about as much as a handheld VHF these days. If you are located away from your sailing waters then you may not receive the short range FM signals for those waters, but you can still get all the information they include in text form online or by email request. NOAA has discontinued live streaming of these broadcasts, but several independent streaming sources for selected stations are online. Weather Radio apps for phones claiming this service are not dependable.

It pays to learn the format of the broadcasts and the sequence of the live reports, because the full broadcast can be some 10 min or so, which means missing a key report takes some time to correct. VHF broadcasts include observations updated every 3 hr, forecasts updated every 6 hr, a synopsis updated every 12 hr, and warnings updated as needed. See nws.noaa.gov/nwr for other information. Again, we shall see that all the data in these reports are available by email request, which is often a convenient method underway, although it is hard to beat the dependability and convenience of NOAA Weather Radio. See also Weatheradio Canada.

There are hundreds of websites with weather data, and dozens of commercial services, but the primary U.S. sources for these third party outlets are the same ones we have direct access to ourselves. They are listed in Table 1.6-3. More specific NOAA sources for model data, digital forecasts, satellite images, and satellite winds are covered in Chapter 8.

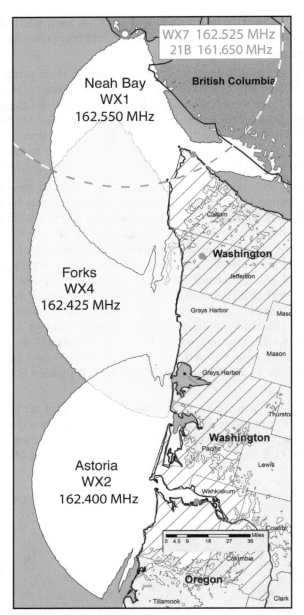

Figure 1.6-5. *An example of using data from the Coverage link at the NWR site to show where we expect to receive VHF weather broadcasts. We have manually overlaid these coverage regions for the illustration; top stations are from Weatheradio Canada.*

This is not to say that third parties do not provide useful service. Indeed, the remarkable services of saildocs.com, for example, are used worldwide, and even cited on official NWS sites. Saildocs is discussed in Section 8.3 and included in Table 1.6-3 to encourage early practice.

1.7 Units and Time Conversions

We can go through much of our domestic marine navigation life without many issues of units conversion. We use knots (kts) for speed, nautical miles (nmi) for distance, feet (ft) for elevation, and Fahrenheit (°F) for temperature. There is of course feet versus fathoms to deal with, and as we move on to electronic navigational charts (ENC) we get much more practice with meters, the international standard for heights, depths, and short distances. But generally we can set our navigation software and instruments to match our charts and not have to worry about making actual conversions. The Great Lakes and Intracoastal Waterway get our attention when they use statute miles for mile markers, and when we sail into Canadian waters we are confronted with consistent use of meters and Celsius temperatures (°C), all of which can be taken in stride.

This easy ride changes quickly in the field of marine weather. We can say good by to our innocence. No longer are the challenges limited to special cases or special locations. We are continually confronted with data values in different units, and it is not even so simple as saying let's just stick to the American or British system, or stick to the metric system, and so on, because typical marine applications mix up these systems frequently.

For example, if we go to the primary source for real-time weather observations, NDBC, they have wonderful displays of recent data histories, which let us display a graph or table of both wind and pressure on the same time scale, which is often a valuable comparison. But in looking at such data, we must always choose between two unfavorable options.

If we want wind in knots, we must take pressure in inches of mercury, and if we want pressure in millibars, we have to take wind speeds in meters per second. This is a sad state of affairs. Mariners want speed in knots and pressures in millibars (mb)—or hectopascals (hPa), which are the same as millibars. We do not want pressure in inches of mercury (inHg). That is for TV weather and aircraft navigation. And as mariners (as opposed to scientists), we do not want wind speeds in meters per second; we want knots. We also see some text reports of data that give pressures in mb from one source, with the same reports in inches of mercury when requested from a different source.

Here is another example. Wind and wave forecast maps from the OPC use feet for wave height on the 24h forecast, but meters for 48h and 96h forecasts. They have done so since the 1990s, with no plans for changing. Another intriguing example is U.S. surface analysis maps use °F, whereas maps for higher levels in the atmosphere use °C!

In short, even those accustomed to the metric system must make conversions when using U.S. sources. The U.S. government has had numerous laws passed, executive orders signed, and congressional board recommendations to make all NOAA products metric (cartography, meteorology, and hydrography), but this glacier hit a mountain wall some time ago. See U.S. Metric Association (us-metric.org) documents on the history and future of the transition.

Our training is best served by units we can think in, and we just have to pay the price of conversions for a while when confronted with units we are not familiar with. There are numerous apps that do this. With an internet connection you can request a conversion in the Google search field. Open Google search engine (or likely any other) and type "convert 59 f to c" to get 15 °C, or type "convert 5500m to feet" and get 18,044.6194 ft, and so on. You can also type in "12 + 45.6/pi" to get 26.5149308. Our tools change with time. With an internet connection, this is a fast way to make conversions or get math solutions. You can even type "plot y=2*(x/22)^2" to get a graph of our estimate of wind force in pounds per square foot.

The main conversions we run across in marine weather are listed in Table 1.7-1. The Appendix includes inspection tables for temperature and pressure that are often faster. Lapse rates do not come up often in practical marine weather, but we do discuss them in the

Table 1.7-1. Conversion Factors

Distances

feet, ft	x	0.305	=	meters
meters, m	x	3.281	=	feet
kilometers, km	x	0.540	=	nautical miles
nautical miles, nmi	x	1.852	=	kilometers
nautical miles, nmi	x	6 076	=	feet

Speeds

knots, kts	x	0.514	=	meters/second
meters/sec, m/s	x	1.944	=	knots
miles per hr, mph	x	0.869	=	knots
knots, kt	x	1.151	=	miles per hour

Pressures

inches of mercury	x	33.864	=	millibars
millibars, mb	x	0.02953	=	inches of mercury
millibars, mb	x	1	=	hectopascals

Lapse rates

C°/1 km	x	0.549	=	F°/1,000 ft
F°/1,000 ft	x	1.821	=	C°/1 km

Temperatures

°F = °C × (9/5) + 32
°C = (°F - 32) × (5/9)

Table Notes: *Example: 6 ft × 0.305 = 1.83 m.*

Table 1.7-2. Easy Temps

-40 C	=	-40 F	-4 × 18 + 32
-35 C		-31 F	
-30 C	=	-22 F	-3 × 18 + 32
-25 C		-13 F	
-20 C	=	-4 F	-2 × 18 + 32
-15 C		5 F	
-10 C	=	14 F	-1 × 18 + 32
-5 C		23 F	
0 C	=	32 F	0 × 18 + 32
5 C	=	41 F	
10 C	=	50 F	1 × 18 + 32
15 C	=	59 F	
20 C	=	68 F	2 × 18 + 32
25 C		77 F	
30 C	=	86 F	3 × 18 + 32
35 C		95 F	
40 C	=	104 F	4 × 18 + 32
45 C		113 F	
50 C	=	122 F	5 × 18 + 32

Table Notes: *Any temperature T in °C that is N × 10, with N an integer, will have a corresponding T in °F equal to N × 18 + 32, which are all whole digits, i.e., 10 °C is exactly 50 °F. Thus we have a handful of values that are easy. The values in between these, though not precisely whole numbers are very close, within a few hundredths of a degree.*

stability Section 3.4. Table 1.7-2 shows a way to think about temperature conversion that avoids division.

Timekeeping

And then there is timekeeping—local time versus Greenwich Mean Time (GMT), now called Universal Coordinated Time (UTC); valid times versus broadcast times on weather maps; watch times versus zone times; and so on. Weather work requires more care in timekeeping than any other area of navigation, including celestial navigation, which has a lot of focus on timekeeping.

Don't be surprised to find this a challenge when you begin work in marine weather—and it is, of course, crucial that it be done right. This will call for a whole section on sequencing of forecasts in Chapter 7, but for now we provide a preview of some issues involved.

First, all weather maps and many (not all) text forecasts are given in coordinated universal time (UTC), which is also called by some agencies universal time (UT), though there is technically a difference. This has been the proper name of Greenwich Mean Time (GMT) for quite a few years now, but we still see GMT used on some weather products. There is interesting history on how this name change came about, but this not significant to our subject.

UTC is often abbreviated with the letter "z" (zulu), because every zone in the zone-time system was at one time assigned a letter label, and "z" is the label for time zone zero. The synoptic times are therefore often listed as 00z, 06z, 12z, and 18z. In modern times, letter labels are not used for the other time zones. Again, there is interesting history behind these labels—they skipped the letter "j" for example—but we leave this for a Wikipedia project.

In marine navigation time zones are defined by their *zone description* (ZD), such that UTC = zone time + ZD. (This also applies to standard times and daylight times.) Pacific Daylight Time (PDT), for example, has a ZD of +7h. Suppose it is 2125 PDT on May 29. When we look at the radiofacsimile broadcast schedule online (ocean.weather.gov/fax_schedules.shtml), we see that available maps are sorted by their HF radio broadcast times, in UTC, labeled with a "z." At present, UTC = 2125 + 7 = 2825 = 0425z on May 30, and the schedule shows the most recent surface analysis map for the Eastern Pacific was available at 0331z, and that it is valid for 00z, on May 30. When we download and print out that map it will say that it is, "VALID: 00:00 UTC 30 MAY" which was 1700 PDT on May 29. The same time that is labeled "z" on the schedule is labeled UTC on the map.

Thus at the present time (2125 PDT), the most recent map available was valid for 1700 PDT, which is 4h 25m old. This is not quite as bad as it looks, because the earliest we could have got it was 0331z, so this map is already 3h 31m old at birth. It takes that long to compile all the 00z observations worldwide, feed them into a computer, get out the forecast, process it, and distribute it. Remember that 00:00 UTC is the first moment of the day, which is the same as 24:00 of the previous day, if we need to add or subtract times.

At this point we could look ahead on the schedule to see when the next analysis (06z) will be available. The answer is 0919z, which will be 0219 PDT tomorrow, or 4h 54m from now. This map will be 3h 19m old at birth. The times we can download the maps compared to the times they are broadcast vary with the maps. Some downloads are available earlier, some later. The relative age of the maps at birth vary from one map type to the next, but for specific map types they remain about the same.

When it comes to comparing the 00z analysis to our own observations, we have to look in our logbook for our recorded position, wind speed, wind direction, and pressure records at the valid map time, 00z, which would have been 1700 PDT today, 4h 25m ago. *We learn quickly that it is crucial to make a log entry at the synoptic times with position, wind, and pressure data.*

In short, we have no way around reckoning times forward and backward multiple times each day in different time systems. When we add to this forecast maps, which are available at different times still, and valid in the future not the past, things just get worse. And there are no shortcuts, such as choosing to work only in UTC. Everyone else on the vessel is working on ship's time, which is only fair. This nastiness is best kept in the nav station.

The trick is just go slow and label maps or printed reports with the ship's time. It will always be helpful on long passages to make up a time schedule of when various products are available and when they are valid. We have samples in Chapter 7 on map reading, where we also propose ways to store and organize weather maps. It is valuable to keep all the weather broadcasts on the same printed schedule: voice, text, and maps.

Also in these modern times, it is likely that you are not relying on HF radiofax broadcasts for these products, but are rather downloading them by satellite telephone or HF radio connected to a Pactor modem (Chapter 8). This has the big advantage of requesting the products when you want to, rather than having to listen to the live broadcasts at specific times, but we still have to know when they are first available, so the custom-made time schedule is still important. In fact, it is even more important, because many of the satphone weather services (such as GRIB data and compressed weather maps) add an extra time delay to the product distribution to account for the time it takes them to collect the data from the NWS and process them. This adds another column to our custom broadcast schedule.

2.1 What Makes the Wind

In Chapter 1 we learned the importance of wind in marine weather; now we take a closer look at wind and what causes it. The more we know about the forces that drive the wind, the better prepared we are to understand what is going on and make educated guesses at what might happen next.

Away from several important influences of land, the wind speed and direction we might anticipate (forecast) depends on where we happen to stand within a particular atmospheric pressure pattern. But knowledge builds upon itself. Often times, the best indicator of where we are in a pressure pattern is the actual direction of the present wind, and how this direction is changing with time. To understand this requires an understanding of how wind flows around high and low pressure systems, which we will get to after a review of atmospheric pressure itself. In the next section we cover the important use of barometers for reading the pressure when underway.

A 10-kt wind means the air—or a balloon riding along in this air—moves 10 nmi in 1 hr. Air is a fluid with mass, just as water is, although air is some 800 times lighter (less dense) than water and much more compressible.

Understanding the fluid nature of air and its interaction with fluid water and water vapor is helpful in describing much of practical marine weather. The fluid-fluid interaction between surface winds and the sea makes waves in the sea; a similar interaction between high-altitude winds and the water vapor of clouds makes waves in the clouds. Prominent cloud waves show the direction of the winds aloft just as well as water waves show the direction of surface winds—the direction of the winds aloft is extremely valuable to know, because it tells us the direction that storms move. Also, storms and frontal systems in the atmosphere behave much like eddies in rivers and waves in the ocean. We cover this in Chapter 3.

Air is held to the earth by gravity; if the earth were not heavy enough to provide this attraction, the air would spin off into space from the outward centrifugal force caused by the earth's rotation. Because air is compressible and the holding power of gravity decreases with increasing altitude, most of the atmosphere is compressed into a thin layer at the earth's surface, and this layer becomes less dense with increasing altitude above the surface.

Roughly 80 percent of the air is below 40,000 feet, with some 50 percent of the air below 18,000 feet. This altitude, which marks the halfway point through the atmosphere, is an important demarcation line in meteorology, because most of the atmospheric disturbances we experience as weather on the surface are confined to this first 18,000 feet of air. The winds above this altitude are stronger and much more persistent than those of the surface; also, the nature of clouds changes—from water vapor to ice crystals—at roughly this altitude.

Besides growing less dense with increasing altitude, the air also grows colder with altitude as less and less of the "atmospheric blanket" is above it to keep it warm. As a rough average, the air temperature drops about 4 F° per 1,000 feet of altitude as you rise through the atmosphere. Distinct cloud bases (ceilings) occur at the altitude at which the air temperature has dropped to the dew point of the air.

Although air weighs very little per unit volume, the total weights involved are still impressive. A typical room contains about 100 pounds of air. Over each square mile of the earth's surface there is some 30 million tons of air, and these massive amounts of air are not uniformly distributed over the surface. An uneven distribution of air is what causes the wind. If air flows across an entire state, for example, from the north at 20 kts, all day long, then there must have been very much more air to the north than there was to the south.

The amount of air at any place is determined by measuring the atmospheric pressure at that place. One way to describe atmospheric pressure is to simply state how much the air weighs that stands above a given area; a typical value would be 14.7 pounds per square inch, meaning a column of air, one square inch across, extending from the surface straight up to the top of the atmosphere weighs about 14.7 pounds. This is a perfectly valid unit of pressure, but it is more convenient and conventional for tires and scuba tank pressures than for atmospheric pressures—in these units, atmospheric pressures typically vary between 14.4 and 14.8 pounds per square inch.

Rather than pounds of air per square inch, atmospheric pressure is usually measured in either inches of mercury (14.7 pounds per square inch = 29.92 inHg) or in millibars (14.7 pounds per square inch = 1013.25 mb). The inches unit derives from the dimensions of a mercury barometer, an instrument used to measure pressure (Figure 2.1-1). The height of the mercury column rises or falls according to the atmospheric pressure exerted on

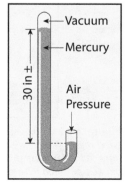

Figure 2.1-1. *Mercury barometer. Though not used in marine applications these days it remains the defining instrument for pressure measurement. The weight of the air over the open column is balanced by the height of the mercury on the sealed column, so the height of the mercury column is a measure of the pressure.*

MODERN MARINE WEATHER

the exposed mercury surface. This unit is used in aviation and in commercial radio and TV weather broadcasts.

In marine weather broadcasts and all weather maps, on the other hand, the common unit of atmospheric pressure is millibars (mb), and this is the best pressure unit to learn for marine applications. A millibar is a metric unit that derives from a weight of 1 kilogram per square meter of area. To convert inches of mercury to millibars use: mb = 33.864 × inHg, or start with 30.00 inHg = 1016 mb and correct this by 1 mb for each 0.03 inHg. For highest precision, the defining relationship is 1013.25 mb = 29.921 inHg; it will probably prove useful to know these numbers by heart. Units were reviewed in Section 1.7.

It is valuable to learn, for example, that pressures above some 1025 mb are high and those below some 1000 mb are low—although Highs and Lows are always relative in practice—and that a pressure drop of more than 2 mb per 3 hrs is a significant drop, implying the probable approach of strong winds, especially when this happens for two consecutive 3-hr periods. In severe storms and hurricanes, the pressure drops as fast as 10 mb per 3 hrs. Average monthly pressures in millibars along with extreme Highs and Lows for all coastal waters are listed in *Coast Pilots* and *Sailing Directions*.

The approximate average pressure worldwide throughout the year is 1013 mb. Common extreme values are 970 mb and 1040 mb. All-time record high pressure is 1084 mb at Agata, Siberia (Siberian High), on December 31, 1968, although most other world records by country are closer to 1060 to 1070 mb, also mostly over land. Record lows at sea level are in the eyes of hurricanes, and include Typhoon Tip in the Pacific, at 870 mb on October 12, 1979.

Areas of high and low pressure (called "Highs" and "Lows") are illustrated in Figure 2.1-2, which shows schematically the distribution of air over some 1 to 2 thousand miles of ocean. A High is a mound of air; a Low is a depression in the air. Someone at H measures a higher pressure (1022 mb) than someone at L (997 mb) because there is more air above them.

Since air is a fluid, the natural tendency of air in a pile is to fall down due to gravity, so the first force on air is simply gravity, which forces air away from Highs and into Lows—the piles want to fall down; the holes want to fill up. Consequently, air in Highs is always moving out of the High and descending, and air in Lows is always moving into the Lows and rising. (The vertical motion of air, descending in Highs and rising in Lows, will come up often as we progress in our understanding of wind flow.) Near the center of the 1013-mb region in the figure there would be no wind because the air distribution and resulting pressure is equal on all sides of the region.

The circles above the High and Low in the picture show how these areas would be represented on a weather map. The circles are contours of equal pressure, called isobars; by convention, they are labeled with the last two digits of the pressure they represent and are drawn at 4-mb intervals on most U.S. weather maps. Isobars are analogous to elevation contours on topographic maps, and in this schematic picture of the air distribution, they can be thought of as the actual heights of the air mass, although actual pressures are also influenced by the density (temperature) of the air as well as its height.

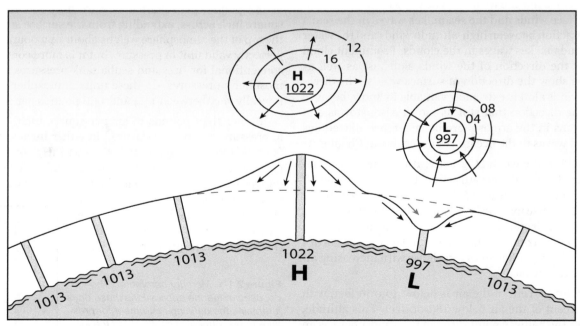

Figure 2.1-2. *Cross section (bottom) and plan view (top) of the atmosphere showing air distribution over a span of some one or two thousand miles. A plan view is like a topographic map of the air, which is the basis of weather maps. Lines of constant pressure are called isobars. A "16" means the pressure is 1016 mb. The peak values are always underlined and written as full pressures. In this analogy, gravity causes air to flow from higher to lower pressure, as marked by the arrows, diminishing the Highs and filling the Lows.*

Now, comes a twist to the problem. The driving pressure force is the same in all horizontal directions, but the actual motion of the air must be described relative to the spherical earth that is rotating below it. The result is called the Coriolis effect: anything that is moving in a straight line above a rotating surface traces out a curved path on the rotating surface. Think of the path of your footprints on the floor of a merry-go-round as you walk due north from its center as it rotates. You walked straight, but the path as seen by people living on the merry-go-round is curved. (This analogy is, unfortunately, only a poor description of the true Coriolis effect, in which the spherical nature of the earth is critical, but it does show the gist of what takes place.)

Because of the Coriolis effect, everything (winds, currents, ballistic missiles) in the Northern Hemisphere (NH) curves to the right as it progresses and everything moving in the Southern Hemisphere (SH) curves to the left. The extent of the curve depends on the speed of motion and on the latitude of the motion. The influence of the Coriolis effect is crucial to most of meteorology and oceanography. Since this effect accounts for a change in motion, it is often called the Coriolis force, even though there is not an actual force involved. Nevertheless, the concept is useful since this "force" can be balanced out by actual forces to account for the net motion of things on the earth.

As air in the Northern Hemisphere is forced out of a High or into a Low, the Coriolis force bends it to the right (Figure 2.1-3). At higher altitudes in the atmosphere, where no other forces act on the air, the wind continues to curve to the right until the Coriolis force bending it in balances out the pressure force that is trying to push it out. This leaves the air flowing parallel to the isobars around Lows and Highs (rather than into or out of them) with the wind circulating clockwise around Highs (as it descends) and counterclockwise around Lows (as it rises). The exact same forces are causing the wind to spiral one way around a High, and the opposite way around a Low.

This basic rule of how wind flows around Highs and Lows is fundamental to predicting winds, but before going on with that, note the rather curious circumstance that this represents. The only true force present (pressure gradient) is forcing the wind out of the High, yet in fact it is going around the High. It is like a ball rolling down an inclined plane, which then curves around and starts rolling parallel to the plane without reaching the bottom. This strange affair is the work of the Coriolis effect. If we did indeed have a gigantic *frictionless* inclined plane attached to the rotating earth, balls would not roll down it, but parallel to the slope. It is a fact to be appreciated without reliance on more common observations. (We shall also see shortly that the concept of "frictionless" is key to that story.)

The schematic description of the air distribution shown in Figure 2.1-2 implies the air is more or less uniform in density, but this is only an approximation to real air masses. Due to density variations, a High can have more air in it than neighboring Lows without its being piled higher than the Lows. Cold air is heavier than warm air, so a region of cold air will have a higher pressure than a similar region of warm air of the same height. Nevertheless, the flow from High to Low and the resulting circulation remains the same.

So far we have talked of the driving force of the wind as gravity pulling down piles of air, much as it pulls down piles of water (waves). But we can also think of the force on air purely in terms of the pressure on the air, as shown in Figure 2.1-4. The two concepts are based on the same principles, but when expressed in terms of pressures, we are no longer tied to the idea of piles of air. We can then understand wind in

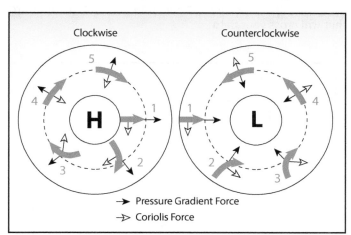

Figure 2.1-3. *Wind around Highs and Lows in the absence of friction. The pressure gradient force (PG) pushes the air from High to Low, then the Coriolis force (CF) bends it to the right. In the absence of other forces, it keeps bending until the Coriolis force balances out the pressure gradient force, leaving the air circulating around the systems parallel to the isobars—clockwise around Highs and counterclockwise around Lows. In the Southern Hemisphere the directions are reversed. (We shall see shortly that when friction is accounted for the flow is altered in a small but significant manner.)*

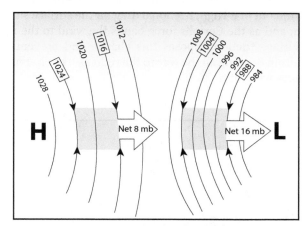

Figure 2.1-4. *Pressure gradient force. The shaded parcel of air in the High has an average of 1020 mb on each side, which cancel each other, but there is only 1016 on the leading edge compared to 1024 at the back. Thus the parcel is pushed from High to Low with a net pressure of 8 mb. This picture shows why the closer the isobars are the stronger the wind—the net pressure (force per unit area) is then higher. In the example here, the same region of air in the Low would be forced in the direction of low pressure with twice the gradient that a similar parcel of air experiences in the High.*

terms of pressures alone and do not have to consider what is creating the pressure—either piles of air, regions of cold air versus warm air, or some mixture of both.

The shaded parcel of air in the High has no net pressure difference on its sides, so there is no motion in that direction, but it has a greater force on the high-pressure side forcing it out than it does on the low-pressure side forcing it in. The net result is the air moves out—and then bends to the right. The same analogy shows how air is forced into Lows.

Although it is gravity that creates the pressure, the picture of pressure forcing the wind is more general, including both the effects of air temperature and altitude. Hence it is better to think of the pressure gradient as the basic driving force of the wind rather than the gravity that creates the pressure.

Because pressure is the ultimate driving force on wind, the effect of gravity on wind is usually called the *pressure gradient force*. As the name pressure gradient force implies, the steeper the gradient (slope) of the pressure, the stronger the force and the faster the wind. Just as a ball will acceler-ate faster down a steep slope than it will down a gentle slope, winds in a deep Low—or in the steepest part of a Low—will be much faster than those in a weak or shallow Low. Steep pres-sure gradients show up on a weather map as closely spaced isobars, just as a steep slope does on a topographic map, as shown in Figure 2.1-5.

So far we have discussed winds at higher altitudes, unaf-fected by the surface of the earth or ocean. As wind blows along the earth's surface, however, there is an additional fric-tion force acting on it that alters both its speed and direc-tion. Again, friction on air is an illusive concept, but recalling its fluid nature, think of how fast water might run down an inclined piece of sandpaper compared to an inclined piece of glass. Both fluids are affected by friction. Friction forces always resist the direction of motion. As the pressure forces the wind out of a High, frictional drag on the surface slows it down; and as the Coriolis force bends the wind to the right, the surface friction opposes this change and prevents the wind from bending all the way to the right as it does at higher altitudes without friction.

The result is that surface wind speeds are slower than those of higher winds, and the direction of surface wind does not exactly follow the isobars around the High but remains pointed slightly out of the High, as shown in Figure 2.1-6. The same thing happens with Lows; as the wind enters a Low, surface drag prevents it from bending completely to the right, so it ends up pointed slightly into the Low, rather than precisely around the Low. As a rule of thumb, the angle that surface winds point out of a High or into a Low is some 15° to 30° off the isobars, depending on the sea state and curvature of the isobars. The rougher the sea state the larger the angle. We nominally use 2 points (22.5°) as a typical value. On land where the friction is larger, this angle is more like 30° to 45°.

Although it might seem a minor point, this difference in wind speed and direction as a function of altitude—or more generally, as a result of friction—is fundamental in practical weather watching and forecasting. To best describe these ef-fects, we return again to the important definitions of wind shifts. A shift to the right is called a veer. A shift to the left is a backing shift. When we go up in the atmosphere the wind veers, as illustrated in Figure 2.1-7.

Another way to look at this is shown in Figure 2.1-8. The wind due east of a High would be a north wind of, say, 30 kts at the altitude of cumulus clouds, but a north-northwest wind of 20 kts on the surface, due to the frictional drag. El-evated winds are veered relative to surface winds, and this is true of all winds around Highs or Lows. One consequence of this is the motion of cumulus clouds. Because they are rid-ing along in the higher winds, they do not move in the same direction as the surface wind. If you face the surface wind, you should see cumulus clouds approaching from slightly to the right. For the same reasons, squalls or thunderstorms you see directly to windward are not actually headed your way. It is typically the guys some 30° or so to the right of windward that will cross your path.

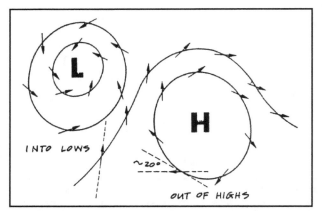

Figure 2.1-6. *Surface wind flow is slightly across the isobars, pointing some 15° to 30° into the Low or out of the High. At higher altitudes where the effect of surface friction is no longer felt, wind flow follows the isobars without crossing them. Friction gradually decreases with altitude, being essentially gone at some 1,000 to 2000 feet. We can consider the average crossing angle as "two points" (22.5°)—a well-known angle from the Nav Rules, because sidelights show two points aft of the beam.*

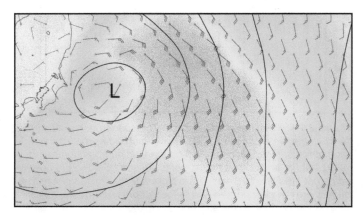

Figure 2.1-5. *When looking at a weather map, we expect the stron-gest winds where the isobars are the closest.*

Wind gusts are another example of this effect. Gusts well away from land and weather systems are often just large patches of higher air that have temporarily swooped down to the surface. Since the gust wind is coming from above where there is less friction, the gust wind is stronger in speed and veered in direction relative to the average wind you experience between gusts. In short, when the wind gusts, it will typically shift to the right—although as with any rule we might

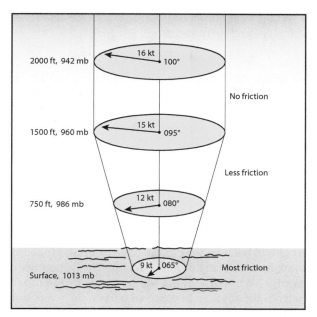

Figure 2.1-7. *As you rise in the atmosphere there is less friction, so the wind speed increases and it is bent more to the right (less friction resisting the Coriolis force), which means the wind direction veers with altitude. To see actual profiles of wind vs. altitude, go to* weather.uwyo.edu/upperair/sounding.html. *(In the Southern Hemisphere the wind backs with altitude.)*

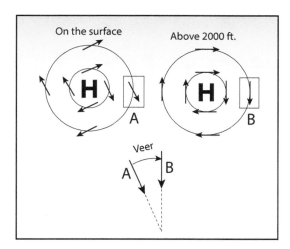

Figure 2.1-8. *Wind flow around a High on the surface (left) and at higher altitudes (right). With less friction aloft, the wind bends all the way around to flow parallel to isobars, but at the surface the friction retards the shift to the right, leaving the wind crossing the isobars. Comparing wind directions we see that the elevated winds are veered relative to the surface. Often it helps to decide if winds are veered or backed to put the arrow tips together as shown here. The same is true for winds around Lows in the opposite direction.*

come up with, we have to watch it happen for a few times before we can be confident on predictions.

Another consequence of friction is its contribution to the typical change in the wind near a relatively flat shoreline. Because water has less friction than land, winds are generally stronger over water than over land. It is not uncommon to have as much as twice the wind speed over a large body of water as you have at the same time over nearby land—an important practical point to keep in mind as you pull away from a sheltered or inland anchorage. When these frictional forces change at the shoreline, the wind direction also changes, and this wind shift usually starts gradually some distance offshore. With more friction on land, the wind is backed over the land relative to over the water, which means it is generally backed somewhat on the water just off a low flat shoreline as well, compared to farther offshore. We cover wind and terrain in Chapter 6.

Why Lows Have Strong Winds

Beside the fact that winds circle opposite ways around Highs and Lows, there is a much more important difference between these two pressure systems—low pressure brings bad weather and high pressure usually brings fair weather. More to the point, Lows have strong winds, Highs have weak winds. To see how this comes about requires a closer look at the forces involved—and a bit of arm waving.

As wind circles a High it has two driving forces acting on it in opposite directions; the pressure gradient force pushing it out of the High and the Coriolis force bending it into the High. If the air travels in a circle around the High, these two forces must be balanced, but they cannot be exactly equal in strength. If they were exactly equal, the wind would have no net force on it and it would move in a straight line, not a circle. "Balanced forces" has a special meaning when things move in a circle. To move in a circle, the inward, or center-seeking, force must be sufficiently larger than the outward force to keep bending it around in a circle. In any circular motion, the net center-seeking force is called the centripetal force; it is always equal to the inward force minus the outward force. For wind circling a High: Centripetal force = Coriolis force - Pressure gradient force.

This equation can be transposed to get an expression for the pressure gradient present when winds circle a High:

Pressure gradient (High) =

Coriolis force - Centripetal force.

When wind circles a Low, however, the inward force is the pressure gradient (pushing the wind into the Low) and the outward force is the Coriolis force. Or, for wind circling a Low: Centripetal force = Pressure gradient force - Coriolis force, and rewriting,

Pressure gradient (Low) =

Coriolis force + Centripetal force.

The important difference between these gradient equations for Highs and Lows is the sign (+ or -) of the centripetal force. In Lows it adds to the gradient; in Highs it subtracts. This difference is important because the curvature forces do not vary at the same rate. The strength of the Coriolis force increases in direct proportion to the wind speed, but the strength of the centripetal force required for circular motion increases in proportion to the square of the wind speed. Winds of low velocity can indeed circle Highs, but as the wind speed increases, the required centripetal force increases faster than the Coriolis force does, so it can't bend it into a circle. Since steep circular Highs cannot exist, there cannot be strong winds circling a High. The natural tendency of a circular High is to flatten out.

Lows, on the other hand, are just the opposite. Both terms in the gradient are positive, so the faster the wind goes, the steeper the gradient becomes. In the case of tropical Lows, whenever the wind starts moving in a circle, it accelerates. These Lows are destined to have strong winds. Once set in motion, they must run their course of continuing to deepen until they run out of fuel. Since their fuel is warm moist air, this happens whenever they run onto land where the air is drier or when they stop moving and consume all the warm moist air that is available. (Lows at higher latitudes have other important factors affecting their steepness as discussed in Chapter 4.)

As a rule, the faster a Low moves, the more intense its winds are. In the summer, Lows travel at some 10 to 20 kts on the average; in the winter they typically travel at 20 to 30 kts. In extreme cases, winter speeds can reach as high as 60 kts. In any season, Lows can stop (called stationary Lows). Throughout the midlatitudes (30° to 60°), Lows move eastward across the oceans. In the tropics, low pressure disturbances tend to move westward—a difference that can be traced back to the Coriolis effect.

All bad weather systems are low pressure systems. A storm is a large circular Low; hurricanes and other tropical disturbances are small, intense Lows; frontal systems are long narrow Lows; and squalls are very localized Lows beneath tall cumulonimbus clouds. Besides strong winds, Lows bring clouds and rain because the air is always rising in a Low. Clouds form when the rising air cools to the dew point and becomes saturated. When the weight of the water and ice in the clouds can no longer be supported by the updraft of air, it starts to rain. In Highs, on the other hand, the air is descending, so any clouds that happen into a High will evaporate as they heat on the way down. Highs are characterized by clear skies and light winds.

Lows and Highs Interacting

We conclude this discussion with two West Coast examples of wind behavior that are fully understandable on the basis of the way winds flow around Highs and Lows. Later chapters expand on these examples.

Figure 2.1-9 shows a typical weather pattern in the Pacific Northwest: a high pressure ridge along the coast with an offshore Low headed in. The dotted line is the path of the system that will pass eastward over the coastal mariner during a period of about one day. The expected winds can be figured by tracing this path to the west. The ridge provided clear skies and light winds from the northwest. As the Low approaches, the wind will back around to the west, southwest, and on to the south at the leading edge of the Low. The isobars are closer near the Low, so the winds will be strong by the time they arrive from the south. As the storm passes, the wind veers to the west.

Along this coast and in many other parts of the world, the first sign that bad weather is soon to replace fair wind from the northwest will be the onset of a backing shift in the wind. For this reason, it is valuable to log the precise wind direction when underway—say, from 285° in the morning, shifting to

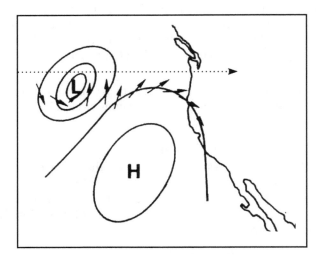

Figure 2.1-9. *A backing wind shift observed in coastal waters as a Low approaches along the dotted line. As the system moves in, the wind backs from NW to W to SW to S. Once the Low has passed, the wind begins to veer, going from S to SW to W to NW allowing for more fair weather and high pressure.*

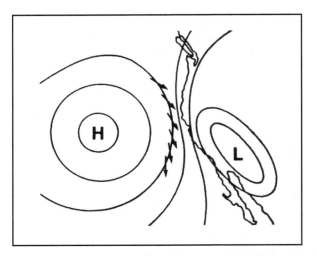

Figure 2.1-10. *Another example of High-Low interaction. A long lasting thermal trough develops over the deserts of CA and NV, and as the Pacific High drifts to the east it is blocked by the trough, which packs up the isobars along the coast. This pattern can give rise to strong winds and big seas that last for several days, due to the long fetch and stability of the patterns. It can also be a case of 30-40 kts of wind in crystal clear blue skies.*

265° by noon—rather than being aware only that the wind is generally westerly.

Farther south along this coast (Figure 2.1-10) the summer coastal winds are often enhanced by the interaction between a High and a Low. The figure shows a thermal trough of low pressure that builds up over the heated land (when land heats, the air above it grows less dense and rises forming a Low). The isobars between this trough and the prevailing Pacific High then pack up to form a steep gradient that brings strong north to northwest winds along the coast. Since both systems are stable, this pattern can last for several days. The long fetch involved produces large seas in this pattern. It is not uncommon to have steady 30-kt winds with 14-ft seas for several days when this pattern develops. Because it is on the edge of a High, this wind can come with clear skies, although it is just as likely to be in thick fog in this area.

2.2 Pressure and Barometers

Barometers are key instruments in practical marine weather. They help tell us what is taking place and what might be coming our way. When properly used they also offer a powerful way to evaluate the weather maps we depend upon.

There are three basic types of barometers, illustrated in Figure 2.2-1. Mercury barometers are the type used in the early days of sailing by the likes of Cook, FitzRoy, and Bowditch. After several corrections, they offer accurate pressures, but they are extremely difficult to protect and maintain underway, and they take up a large space. The broad peak of their usage is marked in a sense by FitzRoy's *Barometer Manual* of 1860. Early writings refer to them as "the glass," in reference to the glass tube that housed the mercury. We can remain very grateful to the early mariners who troubled with these devices, because with them they accurately mapped the pressure patterns of the world that were crucial to the development of global meteorology. It is a clear case of mariners contributing to the advancement of science.

Mercury barometers were pretty much completely replaced for underway usage by the late 1800s by aneroid barometers, first produced in the mid 1800s. The heart of the instrument is a partially evacuated, thin metal bellows called a sylphon. As the external pressure varies, the sylphon expands or contracts, and this motion is used to indicate the pressure.

Aneroid barometers are still the most common type used at sea, and the design of most units has changed little since they first appeared. Prices of common devices (from $50 to $500) primarily reflect the housing (how much brass is used) and brand name. Precision aneroid barometers (PAB) often do not look much different than common models from the outside, so they must be selected by brand name and reputation. They are in the $800 to $3,000 range. They come with a certificate of guaranteed accuracy over the range of the dial.

The third generic type of barometer is a purely electronic device. These have no moving parts and use various solid-state physics principles in microelectromechanical systems (MEMS) to measure the pressure. The technology of the sensors is well established. Working devices with various user interfaces for marine application are still changing a lot in the marketplace.

When electronic devices for marine application were first introduced they were expensive and no published testing was available. Now some 20 years later, we have tested many models extensively, both at sea and in the laboratory. Some have withstood the test of time, others have not. Several models that became popular during this period are no longer available, which must partly account for why they are still just catching on for routine use at sea after all these years. Electronic barometers have obvious advantages in ease of use and potential functions compared to aneroid barometers, but they carry with them uncertainty for longevity at sea and in the marketplace.

New since our last edition is the now ubiquitous presence of a dependable pressure sensor right in our cellphones, iOS and Android. These will typically be accurate to ±1.5 mb without adjustment, and can be improved with easy calibration. Strangely, the phones do not typically include native apps that read this pressure, but numerous free apps will do so. Thus most mariners have ready access to accurate pressure, maybe without even knowing it. It could well be your phone is the most accurate barometer on the boat.

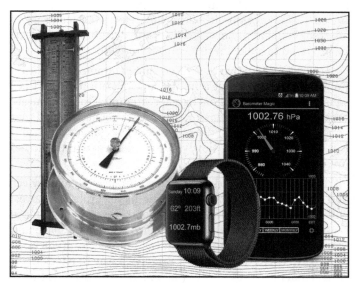

Figure 2.2-1. *Barometer types. Left is a Fitzroy mercury barometer, which were annotated with guidelines for interpreting pressure changes. About 30 inches tall, they formed the basis for early weather forecasting on land, as well as at sea. Middle is a Fischer precision aneroid. The scale is in mb and inches. Ships with helicopters use the inches scale for altimeter settings. This model is certified accurate to ± 0.7 mb. It has been used at sea for more than 50 years. About 6 inches in diameter, it is a popular choice of navies and weather services, worldwide. Right is a generic app for cellphones and smart watches, which reflect the modern revolution in barometry. The sensors they use are state of the art. Display and functions vary with app design, but the simpler the better. There are numerous free versions for iOS and Android. See starpath. com/marinebarometer/about.htm for free barometer app designed specifically for use in marine weather applications.*

Mariners care about accuracy *and* dependability. Our present state of affairs with barometers is analogous to electronics in navigation. We use GPS daily for its convenience and accuracy when functioning properly, but we always carry a sextant as backup. A good aneroid barometer is the equivalent to the sextant for a backup to a more convenient electronic barometer or cellphone, which requires power. Like a sextant, a high quality precision aneroid is a once in a lifetime purchase.

The key issue with all barometers is do they read the right pressure over the full range of pressures we care about at sea? We can always set a barometer to the right pressure at a single pressure, but how do we know it will remain right at other pressures?

Most quality electronic barometers, including the ones in our cellphones, are typically linear over the full range. Set them right once, and we can be confident that if they are working they are showing the right pressure. This may not be the case with a *common* aneroid, which might read high by say 2 mb at 1020 mb, then read low by 3 mb at 990 mb. Each barometer must be carefully calibrated to get accurate pressures. Once that calibration table or graph is in hand, then readings can be corrected as needed.

This is what distinguishes a common aneroid from a precision aneroid barometer (PAB); the latter generally does not need this special calibration, as they come with a factory certificate. The key issue in barometer selection (electronic or aneroid) is to have one with documented calibration data, or be prepared to make these tests on your own.

It is not well known these days that common aneroids are not dependable without a full range calibration, in part because historically mariners had not attempted to get accurate pressure from the barometer. Most teaching had argued that you just need to know if the pressure is going up or down and is it doing so rapidly or slowly. They did not care if the actual pressure is 1024.0 or 1022.5.

Things are simply different now. First, we have devices and procedures that can easily give us accurate pressures, with easy ways to verify them. Second, we now have more reasons to want accurate pressure. We are relying more and more on model outputs of wind and pressure predictions (viewed in GRIB format), so if we have a way to check them with actual pressures, we are that much better off. It is frankly a new way to look at the role of the barometer, and the value of this will become clear as we proceed through the book.

For completeness, a traditional *barograph* is a (typically good quality) barometer, with a strip chart that records the pressure as an ink trace, on a drum that rotates in response to a clock mechanism, electronic or manual. These are convenient on land, but require special dampening for use at sea to minimize the effect of vessel motion (Figure 2.2-2). On the other hand, if you record the pressure from a conventional barometer when you read it, you don't need the graph. Furthermore, we are likely to be more aware of what is going on with the pressure if we must read and record it in the log-

book on a regular basis, rather than having this done for us. A *microbarograph* is a barograph with extra bellows, precision movements, and expanded range used for more accurate measurements.

The automatic recording feature is not so crucial on an extended voyage, because someone is on watch all the time and can enter the logbook and record the pressure. On coastal or inland trips, however, the recording feature can be an asset for checking what took place over night while at anchor. Many electronic barometers include a history function that meets this need, either with a graphical display or a button to step back though the history. On the other hand, a good aneroid always has a *set needle* on the front. You can set it to present pressure at night, and check in the morning to see how the pressure has changed.

Value of a Good Barometer

In many cases, simply knowing that the pressure is rising or falling, and at what rate, is a sign that the weather is changing. This can be done with almost any barometer that you have actually seen go up and down in the past. But to get the most from a barometer, it is useful to know the right pressure, not just that it is going up or down. Furthermore, even those that do go up and down, might not do so at the right rate. I have seen barometers that go up and down beautifully within a narrow pressure range, and beyond this they just won't go. This type of imperfection would be seriously misleading in the vicinity of storms or when negotiating the corner of a High in a sailboat voyage.

A good electronic barometer, such as those we find in our cellphones, displays the pressure digitally to the tenth of a mb, and sometimes to the hundredth, although this last digit rarely has any value. This precision can give very early warning that the isobars are moving. If you see 1025.6 go to 1025.7 it is not reasonable to assume that the new pressure is really that accurate, i.e., known to the tenth, but you do have a first alert that it is going up. As the day progresses there is a cycle

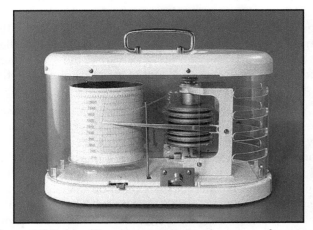

Figure 2.2-2. *A traditional barograph records pressure from an aneroid device for several days using a wind-up or quartz clock mechanism for the drum. The seven sylphons are clearly visible in this Fischer Navigator model, which includes extra dampening mechanism on the write arm for use at sea.*

(semidiurnal variation) to the pressure, which has to be taken into account in some cases (covered later), but you do know by 1025.8 that it is going up. In short, your cellphone barometer could be your first alert to changing conditions. A precision aneroid can be read, with care, to the nearest 0.2 mb.

Besides an early warning of changes, knowing the right pressure is especially useful for evaluating weather maps. You can read the wind speed and direction from your boat, and with a calibrated barometer you can add to that the observed pressure. With careful onboard measurements, you can then check to see if the surface analysis map is consistent with what you observed took place—maps are 3 or 4 hrs old when we first get them. If the map agrees with your measurements, you have more confidence that forecasts based on that map might be dependable. Also, if you are confident your pressure is right, you can sometimes judge the movement of systems by comparing your actual pressure with neighboring isobars on the maps. This is a very powerful analytic tool.

Suppose, for example, the pressure in a ridge (according to the map or another forecast you have) is increasing to the east, with the 1020 isobar plotted 200 miles west of you. If you have a calibrated barometer that shows you already have 1020 mb, then you might guess that the ridge has moved to the east faster than anticipated, or that the ridge is wider or higher than the maps think, etc. There have been cases like this where I could guess that such a ridge was moving about 12 hrs before this motion showed up on the maps. In some circumstances, such information can help with your decision making; but in all cases, such careful watching of the maps and your own pressure keeps you in tune with what is going on. Naturally, the more thorough your understanding of what you do know, the better your guesses will be about what you don't.

We address details of this type of routing tactic later, but just note for now that the center of a ridge (an elongated High) has light or calm air, whereas the wind can be in opposite directions on either side of it. Thus negotiating a moving ridge can be a key step in sailboat routing depending on our location within it, the size and motion of the ridge, and of course our potential speed in the conditions at hand.

At the end of Section 9.3 we explain how to use accurate pressure to confirm or anticipate the approach of tropical storms if you get caught without proper wireless communications—these systems are often well forecasted once formed.

The key to the above ideas is an accurate barometer, which does not necessarily mean expensive. Again, your cellphone barometer can do the job. Or, a barometer that has been on the boat for years might do the job just fine once it has been calibrated, as explained shortly.

The pressure should be recorded in the logbook every watch change, to a precision of a tenth of a mb. If using an analog scale on an aneroid device, then estimate the tenths. We should always use mb for the units. The barometer should be located somewhere clearly visible from the nav station where the logbook is filled in, ideally at eye level, and in easy reach if we have to shine a flashlight on it at night—some aneroid barometers have to be tapped to get a good reading (to overcome friction in the movement), but the better ones do not.

Also keep in mind that we will be comparing our observations with the surface analysis maps that are valid at 00z, 06z, 12z and 18z. Thus it is crucial to know what these local times are and to make a full logbook entry at these times.

When watching the barometer for specific weather changes it is best to record the pressure every hour to the nearest tenth of a mb. You don't have to do this very long before the instrument becomes a valuable aid to your forecasting and general awareness of what is going on with the weather.

How to Calibrate a Barometer at Home

The keys to properly setting a barometer at home, are knowing its elevation above sea level and having a reliable source of accurate pressures. We need to know the elevation because the density of the air decreases as we go up in elevation, which means there is less and less air overhead as we go up. Since pressure is the weight of the air above us, the pressure goes down as we go up. Weather maps, reports, and forecasts always give pressure corrected to sea level, so we have to know that elevation correction to compare what we read to reports at sea level. To remember the correction you can use our jingle

"Point four four per floor."

This means each elevation change of 12 ft (what we call a floor) corresponds to 0.44 mb. At home you could be at, say, 400 ft elevation, which would mean a correction of (400/12) × 0.44 = 14.7 mb. You will have to add 14.7 mb to your reading to get the corresponding sea level pressure (SLP) that you then compare to official reports, that in turn will have be interpolated for your location.

On the boat the corrections will be smaller. A barometer located 6 ft above sea level will read 0.22 mb lower than SLP, so the correction would be +0.22. When this correction is small, we can just offset the barometer reading itself so it reads directly in SLP. On a ship with the instrument 100 ft above the water, the correction would be: (100/12) × 0.44 = 3.7 mb. This, too, is small enough that you could just offset the instrument to read SLP directly.

With the barometer installed in its calibration location, start recording the pressure in a logbook every chance you get, trying to catch it on the hour if you can, but that is not crucial; you can interpolate the results as needed. If you have one, also record your cellphone pressure. Once you have a nice list of times, dates, and barometer readings (recorded to the tenth)—ideally spanning some reasonable pressure change—the next step is to find the closest source of archived accurate pressure online. If you have an internet connection, the best source is starpath.com/barometers. That site provides links to the ten closest official stations with accurate pressure along with range and bearing to each, typically with 36 hrs of past data. Detailed instructions are provided.

For pressure data further in the past, you can go to the the standard direct source of accurate pressure, the National Data Buoy Center, at ndbc.noaa.gov. If there is not a close reference station, then you can triangulate from a few nearby stations. If you are halfway between two stations, just use the average of them for your value. If inside the triangle of three stations, average all three. Airport data can be found at aviationweather.gov/metar.

Once you have a list of your measurements and the corresponding SLPs from one of these sources, make another column of the differences. A sample calibration is in Appendix 5. This table is then your barometer calibration (corrections) for the pressures you measured. If the corrections are all about the same with statistical scatter, you might just average them and consider that a single offset. If they change with pressure, then you will need to plot them out (correction vs. observed pressure) and use that graph for your corrections.

Once your barometer is calibrated, start testing your results, which is simultaneously practice with reading weather maps and doing a calibration underway, if that should ever be needed. Figure 2.2-3 illustrates the procedure using the unified maps which are available every 3 hrs, in contrast to the maps we get at sea every 6 hrs.

For another approach, if you live near any high hills you can take your barometer and cellphone for a car ride and record the pressure, Lat-Lon, and time, as you go up and down hills. (This also works in sky-scraper elevators.) You can use starpath.com/barometers to find ground elevation from Lat-Lon, as well as the pressure changes to expect—or use our jingle. Recording the times lets you check to see if the local pressure changed during your travels. One thousand feet is "83.3 floors," or a change of 36.7 mb. This does not help with high pressures, but it will show if your phone or other barometer is changing as expected. Google Earth can also provide ground elevation.

How to Calibrate a Barometer Underway

If you have already pulled away from the dock without having calibrated your barometer—i.e., missed an item on the departure checklist! (Section 9.5)—there are still ways to dial it in for present pressures. The basic idea is to regress a bit, and assume all the ship reports and weather maps are right, then set the barometer to match those. The trick is to use enough reports and maps to average out their fluctuations and our interpolation errors, till we have it generally agreeing with the maps. We can do this because maps are right far more often than they are wrong. Then after some period of this testing and setting, we will assume our barometer is right, and judge later maps relative to it. Indeed, you can practice this method at home, just as if you were in the middle of the ocean.

The method of using isobars for calibration underway is the same as just discussed for land. You can also get the official ship reports around you by email request. Send a blank email to shipreports@starpath.com with the word "help" in the subject line. This will return to you a set of instructions for obtaining all ship reports within 300 nmi of the position you request over the past 6 hrs. (This can also be a tactical tool for making routing decisions or map evaluation in that you can ask about any position; it does not have to be where you are located.)

With these two methods you can then effectively calibrate your barometer at sea the same way you would on land. Keep a record of your progress—i.e., date and time of the map,

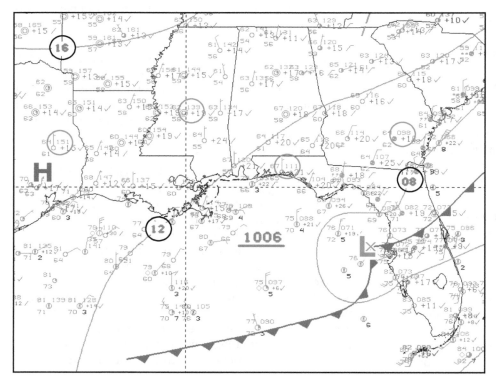

Figure 2.2-3.. *Using a unified analysis map from the Weather Prediction Center (WPC) to calibrate a barometer on land. These are available every 3 hrs from wpc.ncep.noaa.gov/html/sfc-zoom.php; the OPC shows these maps as well, but only every 6 hrs.*

To find a best pressure at the valid map time, plot your Lat-Lon on the map as carefully as possible and then look for closest report or interpolate the isobars. Circled bold blue numbers are the last two digits of the Isobar pressures; red circles mark the pressure reports from the stations used to make the map. In principle, interpolating the isobars would be more accurate than any one report. In the station model format, the red circled pressures from left to right are: 1015.1, 1013.9, 1011.1, and 1009.8 mb.

We strive to get our barometers accurate to the nearest mb, so we see this is quite doable with this map approach. This is the same method we would use at sea if our calibration becomes questionable.

what the interpolated map or report's pressure was, and what pressure your barometer read. Calibrating or navigating, this is the crucial step we have to do several times a day when underway if we want to do the best job of finding the best route. I cannot think of any exercise that is more valuable to good weather work at sea than this pressure comparison. If you note that you are almost always off by say +1.5 mb, then it might be time to consider going back and working on your calibration again. The pressure you read should be right more often than wrong.

Figure 2.2-4 shows an example of comparing a pressure from a surface analysis map with an onboard barometer. To do the best work here, it pays to plot the position carefully. If you are using the same map every day, you can make a Lat-Lon scale on a piece of cardboard for quick, precise position plotting on printed maps or on the computer screen, using the same zoom level each time. For Mac users, the app Pixel-

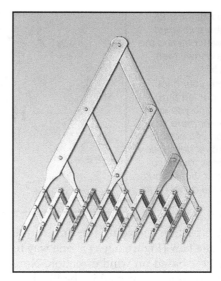

Figure 2.2-5. *For the navigator who has everything, there is this luxurious solution to your daily interpolation plotting. These so-called "10-point dividers" (!) divide any line segment into however many divisions you choose. The model shown opens to about 8 inches and sells for about $125. Every task they solve, however, can indeed be done with the simple interpolation trick shown in Figure 2.2-4 using any ruler scale. Nevertheless, it is a slick tool that would be used daily if available.*

stick is super convenient for reading distances and angles on a map or chart. Alternatively, we cover ways to georeference graphic weather maps in Section 7.4, which does away with the need to interpolate.

2.3 Properties of Highs and Lows

Table 2.3-1 summarizes properties of Highs and Lows itemized in this section.

Wind. Pressure gradients are weak in Highs and hence the winds are weak. More important, the dynamics of High circulation is such that circular Highs tend to weaken once formed, in contrast to circular Lows, which tend to deepen once formed.

Circulation. The directions stated in the table are for the Northern Hemisphere. They are reversed in the SH. The shift slightly out or slightly in (being some 15° to 30° off the

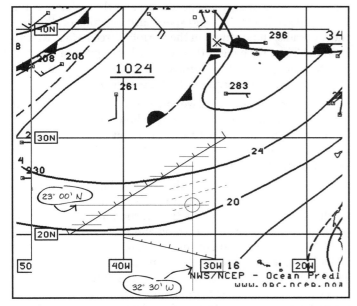

Figure 2.2-4. *Reading a pressure from a known location. Plot your position carefully on the map using the Lat-Lon scales provided, which can be interpolated as indicated. Then sketch in isobars proportionally or interpolate their spacing in a similar manner. Even a crude interpolation is better than a guess, and we want the best possible reading. Figure 2.2-5 shows a luxurious solution to the interpolation. At the time of this map, your vessel was located at 23° 00' N, 32° 30' W, from which we read a map pressure of 1021.0 If this was early in the voyage and we were still trying to calibrate our barometer, we would have to believe this and add this to our accumulation of calibration points. On the other hand, if we already have a well calibrated barometer, then we can use our own barometer pressure to evaluate this map. Suppose our calibrated barometer read 1023.6 mb. We would know then that the High is broader or higher than the computer models believe at the moment in this region, or the High has moved more SW than they think. Notice there are not any ship reports in this region, which means the isobars may be less precise.*

This observation is a crucial value of a calibrated barometer. It is always best to calibrate it before leaving. We only include notes on doing it underway if this important step in preparation was missed.

Table 2.3-1. Properties of Highs and Lows		
	Highs	Lows
Alternative names	anticyclones	cyclones, depressions
Wind	Light and Variable	Strong and gusty
Circulation	Clockwise and slightly out	Counterclockwise and slightly in
Sky	Clear, dry	Cloudy, rain
Vertical	Descending	Rising
Pressure	1020 to 1040 mb	1000 to 970 mb
Centers of Action	Pacific, Bermuda, Azores, Siberian	Aleutian, Asiatic, Icelandic
Elongated forms	Ridges	Troughs
Curved isobars	Sharper the curve, stronger the wind	Sharper the curve, weaker the wind

Figure 2.3-1. *Winds around Highs and Lows. Winds cross the isobars at about 15º to 30º, with smoother water having the smaller angle. This sample shows them crossing at 2 points, or 22.5º.*

Buys Ballot's Law is: place your back to the surface wind, raise your left arm, rotate it two points forward, and you are pointing to the Low center—or more specifically, toward the direction of lowest local pressure. The conventional description of Buys Ballot's Law assumes round isobars, with a Low in the center, but it works along any isobar, showing the direction to the next lowest isobar.

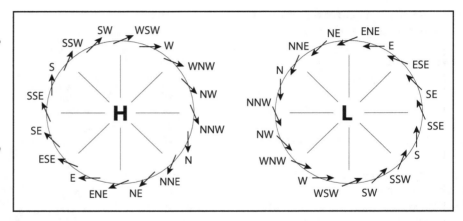

isobars) is due to surface friction retarding the turn of the Coriolis force. Buys Ballot's Law (Figure 2.3-1) is one way to locate the center of the Low based on wind direction. Note that though the circular direction is reversed in the SH, how the wind crosses the isobars is the same—into the Low and out of the High.

Sky. Air is descending in Highs so any clouds that happen into them are evaporated as they are pushed downward into warmer air. The air temperature cools at some 4 Fº per 1,000 feet going up, and warms at about the same rate going down (Chapter 3). In Lows, on the other hand, the air is rising, so the warm moist air from the surface cools to the dew point at some altitude and condenses into clouds. With enough water going into them, they eventually rain it back out.

Vertical motion. In Lows, air is converging at the surface and diverging aloft. In Highs this is reversed. If divergence aloft increases over a Low, more air is leaving than going in, so the Low deepens. Thus when a Low wanders into a location with stronger winds aloft that enhance the divergence it can deepen the Low, creating stronger surface winds, as discussed in Chapter 4.

Pressure. These are typical central values that one might see on weather maps. High and low pressures are always relative—1005 mb could be a High on one part of a map and a Low on another. Again, the table values are not definitions, just typical values, outside of typical extremes.

Centers of Action. These are semi-stationary locations of these pressure systems in certain seasons. All move around, form, and dissipate, but on average, at least in some seasons, you will find these systems in about these locations more often than not.

Figure 2.4-1. *Geostrophic wind speed (U) can be computed by setting the pressure gradient force (PG) equal to the Coriolis force (CF) and solving for U. The formula shown here assumes the isobars are 4 mb apart, and the distance between them (D) is expressed in degrees of latitude (separation in nmi divided by 60). This value is for straight isobars and assumes there is no friction acting on the wind. For curved isobars on the surface we must correct for the centrifugal force and for frictional drag. A value of 0.8 × U is a good approximation for winds on the surface as compiled in Table 2.4-1.*

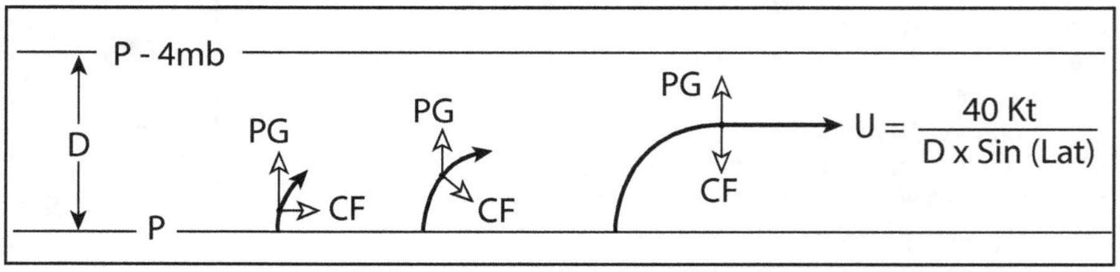

2.4 Figuring Winds From Isobars

We have learned so far that the closer the isobars the stronger the wind, and now it's time to be more specific on what spacings give rise to what wind speeds. Besides the isobar spacing (pressure gradient) the wind speed also depends on the latitude, because the strength of the Coriolis force increases with latitude. Thus we have it that, two isobars 150 nmi apart at 20º N, generate a surface wind of 38 kts, but this same isobar spacing at 45º N generates only 18 kts of wind.

When we look at a map, we can compare isobar spacing at two places on the map if they are at about the same latitude, but if one is much lower latitude, then that same spacing will generate much higher wind speeds. The mathematical result is summarized in Figure 2.4-1.

The basic driving force of the wind is the pressure gradient, which forces the wind from higher to lower pressures. As the air starts to move it is then turned to the right (NH) by the Coriolis force. This turning continues until the radial component of the gradient force is balanced out by the Coriolis force, leaving the wind flowing parallel to the isobars. The Coriolis force is proportional to the wind speed, so at lower latitudes (weaker Coriolis force) a higher wind speed is needed to make the Coriolis force large enough to balance the same pressure gradient force. Thus the same spacing of isobars at low latitudes creates much stronger winds.

The task now is learn how to figure these winds for various isobar spacings and latitudes, and show why we care to know this. Weather map reading is covered in more depth later on, but for now we just note that we will be working with two basic kinds of weather maps: surface analysis maps that compile all that is known about the weather at the synoptic times of 00z, 06z, 12z, and 18z, and surface forecast maps, which are projections into the future of what the isobars are expected to be 24, 48, and 96 hrs later.

$$U = \frac{40 \text{ Kt}}{D \times \text{Sin (Lat)}}$$

We should say right away that there are also maps of the winds (and waves) that correspond to each of these other maps of the isobars, so a cursory analysis might say we do not need to figure these ourselves. But that is not correct. First, winds given on the wind-and-wave maps do not cover all the locations we might care about on the maps, and second, they are often drawn with a very broad brush, if I might put it that way. We can often reasonably seek out much more specific data than are presented in these wind-and-wave maps.

Also the wind reports shown might not be consistent with the isobars surrounding them, and we have no way to know that without some procedure for judging what the wind should be. If they are not consistent, we are left with deciding which one is wrong, or what else might explain the discrepancy. Almost always, our routing decisions underway depend on the lay of the isobars, and if we are uncertain about their dependability we rely on the ship reports.

As noted earlier, on surface analysis maps, the OPC does not draw in wind arrows themselves, but they do show actual ship reports when available. If you want to know what the wind might be at a place where there are no ship reports, then you have to figure this yourself.

Figure 2.4-1 illustrates a point made in Section 2.1, that under equilibrium, without friction, the wind flows parallel to the isobars with a speed that can be calculated from basic physics principles. Thus the first guess at what wind should correspond to the isobars we see on a map comes from this geostrophic wind estimate for frictionless flow along straight isobars (Table 2.4-1).

In principle, the next step is to take into account the curvature of the isobars by making a correction for the centrifugal force (covered in Table 2.4-2) to yield what is called the gradient wind, and then we should reduce that wind by some amount for frictional drag on the surface—a factor that depends on the stability of the air (Table 2.4-3), because that mixes wind from different layers. But the right way does not lend itself to look-up tables, so we have an approximate method that should serve most purposes.

If we use the phrase "surface winds" to refer to the data from Table 2.4-1, which represent 80% of geostrophic wind speed for straight isobars, then we can compare these results to what we see on a map and then make approximate corrections for curvature as called for.

Let's look at a few examples from this one surface analysis shown in Figure 2.4-3. It would be instructive to carry out more examples on your own with other maps to see how the reports correlate with the isobars shown—keeping in mind that in some cases these isolated reports could have had an influence on where the isobars are drawn. For this type of comparison, we can consider ±2 or 3 kts in speed and ±20 or 30° in direction as essentially in agreement.

Table 2.4-1. Surface Wind Speed in Knots from 4-mb Isobar Spacing

		Isobar spacing (D) in degrees of latitude															
		0.4	0.6	0.8	1	1.5	2	2.5	3	3.5	4	4.5	5	6	7	8	10	12
Latitude	15°	310	207	155	124	83	62	50	41	35	31	28	25	21	18	15	12	10
	20°	234	156	117	94	63	47	38	31	27	23	21	19	16	13	12	9	8
	25°	190	127	95	76	51	38	30	25	22	19	17	15	13	11	9	8	6
	30°	160	107	80	64	43	32	26	21	18	16	14	13	11	9	8	6	5
	35°	140	93	70	56	37	28	22	19	16	14	12	11	9	8	7	6	5
	40°	125	83	62	50	33	25	20	17	14	12	11	10	8	7	6	5	4
	45°	113	76	57	45	30	23	18	15	13	11	10	9	8	6	6	5	4
	50°	105	70	52	42	28	21	17	14	12	10	9	8	7	6	5	4	3
	55°	98	65	49	39	26	20	16	13	11	10	9	8	7	6	5	4	3
	60°	93	62	46	37	25	19	15	12	11	9	8	7	6	5	5	4	3
	65°	88	59	44	35	24	18	14	12	10	9	8	7	6	5	4	4	3

Table Notes:

1. This table assumes the isobars are straight. For curved isobars, winds will be somewhat less around a Low and somewhat greater around a High. The effect of curvature can be up to some 30% depending on the radius of curvature, and even larger for small, fast storms. See Table 2.4-2

2. The table values (0.8 × U) assume the surface wind is 80% of the geostrophic wind (U), which can be computed from basic principles and reduced to U = 40 kts / (D × sin(Lat)), where D is the separation of 4-mb isobars expressed in degrees of latitude. To fine tune the results, the factor of 80% can be adjusted depending on the stability of the air if you have a guess of what that might be from nearby weather symbols at the reports or proximity to fronts. See Table 2.4-3

3. To find wind speed, measure 4-mb isobar spacing from a weather map in units of latitude degrees, then find wind from the table. Example: if at Lat 45° the 4-mb isobars are 120 nmi apart (2° on the Lat scale), then the expected surface wind is 23 kts, directed clockwise around the high pressure, pointed 15° to 30° out of the High, or counter-clockwise around a Low and 15° to 30° into the Low.

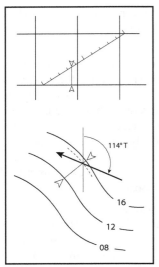

Figure 2.4-2. *Finding winds from isobars. The figure shows one way to interpolate the latitude scale using any ruler marked off in tenths—an approximation only, since the weather maps are Mercator projections, so the higher latitude degrees are slightly longer than the lower ones. The separation is measured perpendicular to the isobars and then transferred to the scale for measurement. Wind direction can be found by sketching in an isobar at the vessel's location at the time of the map, and then orienting the wind direction 15° to 30° into the low (we use a nominal 2 points = 22.5°). Then measure the wind direction relative to north. The example shows a wind direction of 114 T.*

Once the isobar spacing is known in units of latitude degrees (easiest unit since it can be read from the maps) then use Table 2.4-1 to estimate the wind speed. If the isobars are curved, a correction can be made from Table 2.4-2. Navigation programs Expedition and OpenCPN will load the maps with automatic georeferencing, then accurate values of latitude and isobar spacings can be read directly from the screen. We have also found that inexpensive micrometers are a convenient way to read distances from a map that are then going to be scaled—a big step up from a simple ruler. When working with graphics viewers of the maps, distances can be read with scaling tools. The Mac app Pixelstick is a neat solution. Since there are enough uncertainties in the theory of what the winds should be, it is valuable to at least have the distances and locations read as well as possible. We also need this practice for comparing our recorded barometer reading to map analyses.

An X on the map near an L marks the location of the minimum pressure for that Low. A second X at the end of an arrow marks the location of that Low 24 hrs later, labeled with

the expected new pressure underlined. Central pressures of Highs and Lows are always given in full and underlined.

Report of 30 kts at 51N, 156W. Predicted surface wind in that region from Table 2.4-1 is about 30 kts, but with a radius of about 5° the reduction is some 20% down to 24 kts. So the report of 30 is high for the spacing, so it must be influenced by the occluded front near by.

Report of 15 kts at 54N, 154W. Surface wind prediction is 20 kts, but with 20% curvature reduction we are to 16 kts which agrees.

Report of 15 kts at 40N 132W. Wind prediction is 17 kt, which essentially agrees, considering the location of the report.

Gale report at 39N, 127W. Surface wind from the table is 33 kts which agrees. (Gale is 34 to 47 kts.)

Report of 35 kts at 41N, 128W. The isobars here call for only 21 kts, so this report must be influenced by the front just north of it. But at 40N, 126 W, just below it, the gradient calls for 36 kts, so there is clearly strong wind within some 300 miles of San Francisco.

Report of 15 kts at 31N, 122W. Table winds predict 17 here, so this in in agreement.

Report of 15 kts at 30N, 150W. Isobars call for 13 kts here so this is consistent.

Report of 20 kts at 27N, 144W. Table winds are 15 kts here, so this is not consistent. Note the weather reported is rain in past hour, not at time of observation (see Section 7.7), so maybe the vessel was still in some influence of a squall.

Report of 20 kts at 30N, 130W. Here the table calls for just 10 kts. The isobar radius is about 6°, so no curvature correction (Table 2.4-2). The report is not consistent with the isobars. Either they were in a squall and did not report the weather, or the isobars are not right at this point.

Report of 10 kts at 31N, 158W. Surface wind is 8 kts. Curvature has a radius of 3.5°, but at

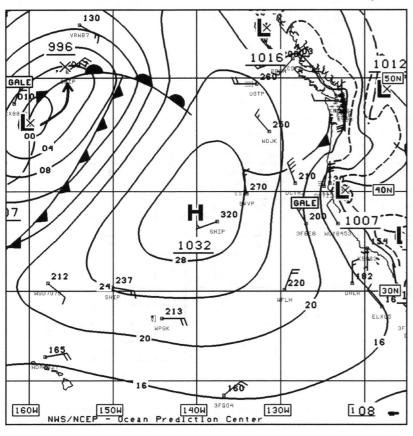

Figure 2.4-3. *Section of an Eastern Pacific surface analysis map. There are numerous ship reports on the SE side of the High but essentially none on the NW side. We can use Table 2.4-1 to find wind on the NW side and check those on the SE. Note that most reports show the wind crossing the isobars, but not every one, which means that either the report or the isobar is slightly off at those locations—or the report could be reflecting a local condition not apparent from the map.*

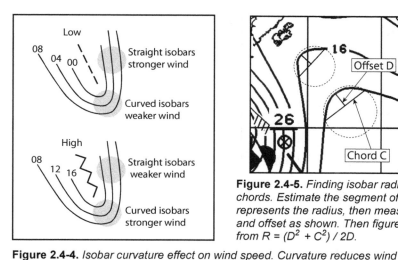

Figure 2.4-4. *Isobar curvature effect on wind speed. Curvature reduces wind speed around a Low or trough, but increases it around a High or ridge.*

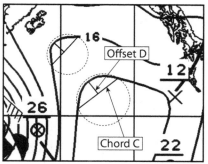

Figure 2.4-5. *Finding isobar radius from chords. Estimate the segment of the arc that represents the radius, then measure the chord and offset as shown. Then figure the radius R from $R = (D^2 + C^2) / 2D$.*

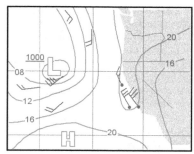

Figure 2.4-6. *Curvature enhancement of winds around a High. Here gradient winds of 20 to 25 kts are enhanced to 30 by a tight isobar radius of about 1.4°. The pattern is unusual in that it is normally "flipped over," with a High coming in and packing up against a Low over the deserts of CA and NV (see Figures 2.1-10 and 4.1-2).*

such a low wind speed there is only a 5% correction to 8.5 kts, which agrees with the report.

Report of 20 kts at 23N, 158W. The isobars call for 18 kts here, so this is consistent.

Again, it is instructive to practice a few of these on other maps online or in this book. This sample was chosen only because it was a simple map.

The isobar curvature correction comes from the centrifugal force needed to keep the wind moving in a curved path. This increases wind speed when the isobars bend around a High, but decreases the wind speed when they bend around a Low as illustrated in Figure 2.4-4. Chapter 4 explains how this behavior comes about. The correction depends on the square of the wind speed divided by the radius of curvature. Generally we can neglect this effect for winds less than 20 kts and for isobar radii greater than some 600 nmi.

Table 2.4-2 gives a simplified way to estimate this correction, which is generally not very large except for high wind speeds in tight circles. For midlatitude winds, it is generally just a 5% to 15% correction (with a few exceptions), but it is always an important correction for fast winds around tight tropical storms. Table 2.4-1 will overestimate those winds

unless curvature corrections are applied—Table 2.4-2 values would be a starting point, but those data were not intended for tropical storms.

To make any curvature correction you need some estimate of the radius of curvature of the isobars. Figure 2.4-5 shows one way to do that. Figure 2.4-6 shows an unusual situation where the curvature around a ridge had a big effect on wind speeds.

As mentioned earlier, we use a factor of 0.80 to scale the geostrophic wind to the surface wind. Other sources use 0.70 or 0.65 for this. Our choice is purely empirical. After comparing many ship reports with isobar spacings, we find that 0.80 does better on the average. It is also known that the stability of the atmosphere can make a difference in this factor, because unstable air mixes up the surface layer enough to end up with slightly stronger winds. A summary of these factors based on stability is shown in Table 2.4-3, which could be used to fine tune wind estimates—keeping in mind that if we get the winds right to within 10 or 15% we are doing well. There are a lot of uncertainties involved.

Table 2.4-2. Isobar curvature correction	
V^2/R	Correction
<25	none
25-50	5%
50-100	10%
100-200	15%
200-300	20%
300-400	25%
400-600	30%
600-1000	40%
1000-1500	50%
>1500	60%

Table Notes: *To find the curvature correction, first estimate R as explained in Figure 2.4-5, then compute the surface wind V from Table 2.4-1. Then figure the ratio V^2/R, where V is the wind speed in knots, and R is the isobar radius expressed in degrees of latitude, and from that value select the approximate correction. The correction diminishes winds around a Low, but increases winds around a high. These are approximate corrections for midlatitudes, adapted from Britton and Lilly, Sea State Forecasting*

Table 2.4-3. Effective surface wind = K × geostrophic wind			
Air Mass	Satellite photos	(Sea - air) temperature difference (F°)	K
very unstable	cloud sheets	> +8°	x 0.95
unstable	cell clusters	+4° to +8°	x 0.90
average	stratus	0 to +4°	x 0.80
stable	surface obscured	-4° to 0	x 0.65
very stable	low fog or stratus	< -4°	x 0.55

Table Notes: *Table 2.4-1 uses a factor K = 0.80 for average conditions. If you have reason to believe the air mass is more or less stable than average then you could adjust that factor with this table. Generally air within a High or within the warm sector of a frontal wave is stable, which would lead to less wind speed for the same gradient. Adapted from Britton and Lilly's Sea State Forecasting.*

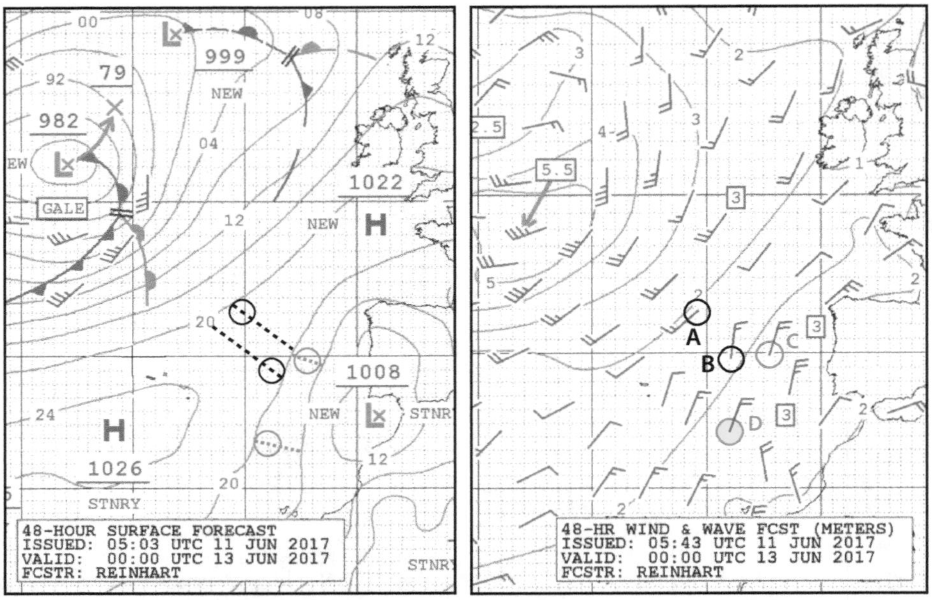

Figure 2.4-7. *A 48-hr surface forecast (left) and corresponding wind and wave map (right). Forecast maps only show winds greater than 33 kts, but others can be estimated using Table 2.4-1 Remember that lines on the wind maps are not isobars, they are lines of constant significant wave height in meters.*

Here we compare what we would predict from Table 2.4-1 with winds presented in the wind and wave map for the same time. For points A and B (black circles) on the edge of a ridge, we can assume the peak pressure in the ridge is about 1023 and use that to figure isobar spacings (D). All the examples shown agree with the wind map and the GFS predications of Figure 2.4-8 except point D, where the forecasted 20 kts on the wind map is notably larger than implied by the isobars on the surface forecast map. This discrepancy might be accounted for by different interpretations of how the "NEW" Low developing just west of the 1008 Low is affecting the isobars. We see in Figure 2.4-9 that the behavior of that new Low is evolving at the time of these forecasts.

Table Notes: *It is conventional when using decimal values of Lat-Lon to label S Lat and W Lon as negative. The Lat-Lon values and D lengths were measured digitally from these maps viewed in OpenCPN, as described in Section 7.4.*

48-HOUR SURFACE FORECAST
ISSUED: 05:03 UTC 11 JUN 2017
VALID: 00:00 UTC 13 JUN 2017
FCSTR: REINHART

48-HR WIND & WAVE FCST (METERS)
ISSUED: 05:43 UTC 11 JUN 2017
VALID: 00:00 UTC 13 JUN 2017
FCSTR: REINHART

Table 2.4-4. Wind Forecasts (48-hr) from Wind Map, Table 2.4-1, and GFS								
#	Lon	Lat	D nmi	D °	Table 2.4-1	W&W map	Map pressure	GFS WIND	GFS Pressure
A	-20.7	42.9	209.0	3.5	13.5	15.0	1021.0	11.0	1021.8
B	-17.8	39.6	253.0	4.2	11.9	15.0	1020.0	14.1	1021.1
C	-14.7	39.8	135.0	2.3	22.2	20.0	1018.0	21.7	1018.2
D	-18.0	34.3	209.0	3.5	16.3	20.0	1018.9	15.8	1018.7

The ability to estimate winds from isobars comes up in the forecasts as much as in the surface analyses. Figure 2.4-7 shows a 48-hr forecast of the surface map along with the corresponding wind and wave map. The wind map shows the winds that would be generated from the isobars shown on the surface map. Details of where winds might change direction or get stronger, however, are easier to detect on the isobar maps, so the challenge to figure associated winds comes up often when looking at these maps—even having the wind map right beside it, as illustrated in Figure 2.4-7. We also get some idea of the uncertainties involved. In the wind-and-wave map shown, we see a change in wind direction on each side of a long ridge, compressed between two Lows. The surface forecast helps explain that, but this is a case where the digital GFS data (Figure 2.4-8) is the best picture of the actual winds.

We made Table 2.4-1 for finding winds from mapped isobars because other solutions are not as convenient. One solution that is seen on some weather maps and in many textbooks is the use of a nomogram to figure the wind speeds. A sample is shown in Figure 2.4-10. This type of diagram is unique to the map it is on. We could make a diagram from Table 2.4-1, but the table is easier to use.

Digital forecasts viewed in GRIB format are an excellent way to learn the relationship between wind and isobars, which is the key to developing an understanding of how the pressure affects what we experience in the wind. Then the ba-

rometer becomes the key tool for monitoring what is taking place. If the wind shifts, the isobars rotated; if the wind speed increases, they got closer together; if the wind diminishes, they got farther apart.

At first glance, the details of this section may seem a lot to have in mind when we look at a weather map—and in a sense they are. But when that thought occurs, it pays to remember that it's all about the wind. And when it comes to figuring

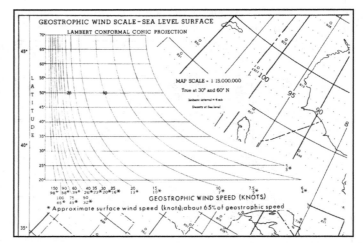

Figure 2.4-10. *A geostrophic wind scale. By transferring isobar spacings on this map to this diagram, geostrophic and surface winds can be estimated. This one assumes a friction reduction to 65% of geostrophic, whereas Table 2.4-1 uses a factor of 80%.*

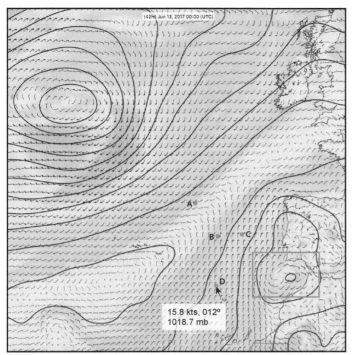

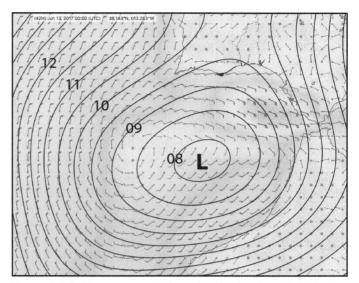

Figure 2.4-8. *GFS 48-hr forecast made at the same time of Figure 2.4-7, viewed in LuckGrib (luckgrib.com). This digital wind field is much easier to read than the corresponding NWS forecast map. Though more precise, in principle it may not be as accurate in some details. Fronts, for example, are not plotted in the GFS output, although the GFS precipitation data (not shown) sometimes offers a good indication of their location. The letters shown correspond to the data in Table 2.4-4. Wind speeds and pressures at these points are listed in Table 2.4-4. They are read from the screen with cursor rollover. GRIB viewers automatically scale the wind arrow density to match the display. Below shows a zoom into the region west of Gibraltar.*

Figure 2.4-9. *Zoomed view of the red region in Figure 2.4-8 to illustrate display options with the GRIB format. Notice the unusual wind pattern west of the Low, which marks the formation of the NEW Low shown in Figure 2.4-7. We expanded the isobars from the standard 4-mb spacing to 0.5 mb. The GFS output does not have any closed isobars around that region at this time. This is a case where the higher resolution regional models (discussed later) will be more valuable. GFS is a global model that does not account well for local terrain and it is only computed every 6 hrs.*

where the best wind will be, there is no easy way. It's all in the details.

Learning the use of GRIB viewers and the many varied sources of digitized forecasts is fundamental to modern weather work, and we develop these topics as the book proceeds. But there are basics we cannot do without, one of which is a proper measurement of the wind at hand.

2.5 Apparent Wind to True Wind

Keeping track of wind direction is quite a natural thing in a sailboat, maybe less so in a power-driven vessel. But when it comes to watching the weather, we have to watch the wind direction no matter what vessel we are in. The best way to do this is with electronic wind instruments—an anemometer to read the wind speed and a wind vane to read its direction (Figure 2.5-1). If your instruments fail, then you can rig a telltale to get the wind direction (read from the compass), and judge the wind speed from the sea state using the Beaufort wind force scale (Chapter 5). There is little reason, however, for not having these instruments, even on a power-driven vessel. They are relatively inexpensive. Wireless models sold for home use can also be applied to some vessels, and there are handheld units useful on even the smallest craft.

When installing wind instruments, keep in mind that they should be located well away from updrafts on the leading edge of sails or deck housings. An extension rod several feet long is a typical solution to getting the instruments out into "clean air" away from the structures on the boat.

Telltales or wind instruments show the direction of the *apparent wind,* as distinguished from the true wind. The apparent wind is the combination of the true wind over the water and the effective wind generated by the motion of the boat. The difference between the directions of the true wind and the apparent wind depends on how fast you are moving relative to the true wind speed. For boat speeds less than 10 or 20 percent of the true wind speed, the difference is negligible, and you can read the true wind direction directly from the wind vane or telltale.

When you are moving, the direction of the true wind is always aft of the apparent wind. If the apparent wind is on the beam, you must face this apparent wind and turn

Figure 2.5-1. *A simple apparent wind sensor and display unit. The apparent wind angle is shown on an analog dial, the apparent wind speed on a digital insert, specified to the tenth of a knot.*

somewhat aft to be looking in the direction the true wind comes from. This is true regardless of your point of sail. If the apparent wind is 45° on the bow, the true wind is closer to the beam. If the apparent wind is on the quarter, the true wind is closer to the stern as illustrated in Figure 2.5-2.

An easy way to remember this basic fact is to think of your boat dead in the water with a true wind of 5 kts on the beam. When stopped apparent wind and true wind are identical, but when you get underway and increase speed, the apparent wind will move forward and increase. In a speed boat going 30 kts the wind is straight in your face, dead ahead. Slow down and the wind will lower in speed and shift aft toward its true direction.

The exact number of degrees the true wind is aft of the apparent wind depends on your speed relative to the wind and on your point of sail. At any relative speed, the difference between the two is largest when you are sailing with the apparent wind on the beam. The difference is typically somewhere between 10° and 40°, where, generally speaking, the higher the performance of the sailboat, the bigger the shift can be.

When relying on the wind to monitor weather changes, it is the true wind direction we care about. When boat speed changes along with the wind direction, we can easily lose valuable information on wind shifts if we do not carefully make these corrections. It is common to many circumstances to have the first detectable sign of a change in weather be a backing shift to the true wind.

Definitions

True wind direction refers to the true wind blowing across the fixed earth. For wind conversions we need digital values of speed and direction. When a wind direction is less than 100, it is best to add a leading zero, i.e., the wind is from 050, said as "oh five oh" rather than "five-oh" or "fifty." In all wind discussions, wind *direction* is different from wind *angle*. The following definitions and abbreviations are used in Figures 2.5-3 through 2.5-6 for various true wind solutions. These solutions assume there is no current and no leeway, which

require special treatment. See Appendix 9 for a generalized solution and other nuances.

Apparent wind angle (AWA) is the direction of the apparent wind relative to the head of the vessel, usually listed as port or starboard. It varies from 0° (wind on the bow), through 90° (wind on the beam), on around to 180° (wind on the stern). Unlike wind direction, leading zeros are not used for wind angles. It is AWA = 30°, not 030. Since apparent wind angles are relative angles, it does not make sense to think of, or refer to, them as true or magnetic.

On some vessels, apparent wind angle is recorded in terms of an apparent wind direction (AWD), expressed in *relative bearings*, rather than using port and starboard. Thus AWA = 100 Starboard would be written as AWD = 100R, and AWA = 90 Port, would be written as AWD = 270R.

(Measurements of AWA and AWS below are affected by the heel of the vessel, so for most accurate data these must be accounted for as explained in Appendix 9.).

Apparent wind speed (AWS) is the speed of the wind in knots that we measure from a moving vessel. It is a combination of the true wind speed and the effective wind we create with our motion. Motoring at 8 kts straight into a 12-kt true wind, we would experience an apparent wind speed of 20 kts.

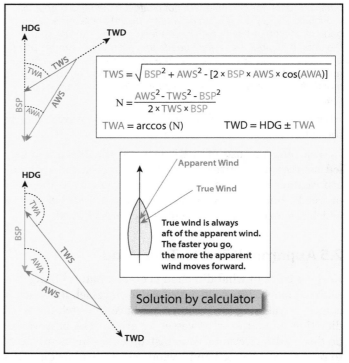

Figure 2.5-3. *Computing true wind from apparent using a basic trig calculator. From Figure 2.5-2 consider top-right example of AWS = 15 kts, AWA = 30°, and BSP = 6 kts. Then TWS = sqrt (6x6 +15x15 - [2x6x15xcos(30)]) = sqrt (261 - [180x0.8660]) = sqrt(105.11) = 10.25 kts. N = (15x15 - 10.25x10.25 - 6x6) / (2x10.25x6) = 83.94 / 123.0 = 0.6824, and TWA = arccos(0.6824) = 47°, which is 17° aft of the apparent wind. Notice that the wind vector generated by our motion is opposite to our heading, then following the vector arrows, we have true wind + motion wind = apparent wind.*

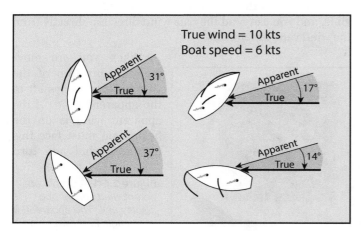

Figure 2.5-2. *True wind is always aft of apparent wind. The amount aft is marked by a shaded sector in each example. Telltales (orange) are shown on each flying in the apparent wind. A numerical example is solved several ways in following figures.*

Sailing dead downwind at 7 kts in a true wind of 12 kts, the apparent wind would be reduced to 5 kts. When sailing diagonal to the true wind direction, up or down wind, the resulting apparent wind speed cannot be determined from simple arithmetic, but instead vectors must be solved graphically or by direct computation using trigonometric formulas. Generally speaking, sailing into the wind, apparent wind speed is higher than the true wind speed; sailing downwind it is lower.

True wind angle (TWA) is the direction of the true wind relative to the head of the vessel, usually listed as port or starboard. It varies from 0° (wind on the bow), through 90° (wind on the beam), on around to 180° (wind on the stern). The true wind angle is always larger than (aft of) the apparent wind angle.

True wind speed (TWS) is the actual speed of the wind over the fixed earth. Generally it is expressed in knots (kts). 1 knot = 1.15 statute miles per hour = 1.85 km/hr = 0.514 meters per second.

Boat speed (BSP) is your boat speed through the water as measured by a knotmeter. For now we assume no current, which would mean BSP would be the same as speed over ground (SOG) measured by GPS. When these two speed values are notably different we have to use the methods of Appendix 9.

Heading (HDG) always refers to the *true* heading of the vessel. We need this when we convert from true wind angle (TWA) to true wind direction (TWD). When steering a compass course, it must be corrected for variation to get the true heading of the boat. Again, if your HDG is notably different from your course over ground (COG) from GPS, we need the methods of Appendix 9 to find TWD.

We covered all the traditional solutions in Figures 2.5-3 through 2.5-6 because mariners are typically self-reliant, but in response to "There ought to be an app for that" the answer is there are many such apps for iOS and Android. We can indeed solve this crucial step with our cellphones once we understand the basics of what we are solving.

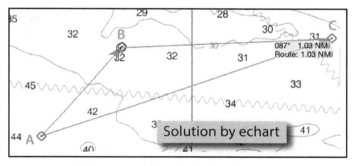

Figure 2.5-5. *Solving for true wind using an echart program. Each program has a slightly different best solution. With this approach we can solve for TWA, or go directly for TWD, i.e., if COG is 040, and AWA = 30°, the apparent wind direction (AWD) = 070. Here we use OpenCPN (opencpn.org). From any point A, draw a one-leg route to point B that is 0.6 nmi in direction 040. (Here we use a length scale of x0.1 for convenience). Then repeat from A, one-leg route to C at 1.5 nmi in direction 070 (040+30). Then use measurement tool or another one-leg route from B to C, to show TWS = 10.3 and TWD = 087, which is equivalent to TWA of 47. Any vector problem can be solved this way. You can also solve for AW from TW this way.*

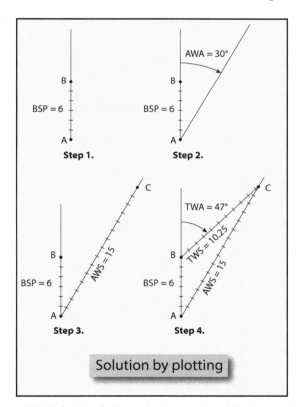

Solution by plotting

Figure 2.5-4. *Solving for true wind by graphic plot using a ruler and protractor. Given BSP = 6 kts, A = 15.0 kts, AWA = 30°, find True wind T and true wind angle TWA. Step 1. Mark off boat speed on a vertical line using any desired scale (line A-B). Step 2. Use protractor to layoff AWA as shown. Step 3. Use same boat speed scale to mark off the apparent wind speed (line A-C). Step 4. Draw in the true wind vector (line C-B). Measure the true wind speed as the length of this line (TWS = 10.2 kts), and the true wind angle it makes with the vertical line (TWA = 47°), and check that this is indeed aft of the apparent wind angle 30. See Figure 2.5-5 for a slick way to solve this triangle.*

Difference Between Heading and Apparent Wind Direction:	30	(degrees)
Apparent Wind Speed: (Specify Units)	15.0	○ Units of Ship's Speed ◉ Knots
Ship's Speed:	6	(knots)

Calculate   Reset

| Difference Between Heading and True Wind Direction: | 47.01 | (degrees) |
| True Wind Speed: | 1.708 (knots) | (units of ship's speed) 10.25 |

Solution by app

Figure 2.5-6. *Using an online navigation calculator to solve for true wind. These are available at starpath.com/calc. The webpage can be saved to your computer or phone for offline use. There are numerous mobile apps that solve for true wind. These can be very convenient, but we still need to know what they are doing.*

Tips, Tricks, and Special Cases

(1) With the wind on the beam, the true wind can be well aft of the apparent wind. For example, in 5 to 10 kts of true wind, a typical sailboat travels at some 0.6 to 0.7 times the true wind speed. At speeds of 0.65 times the true wind, when the apparent wind is on the beam, the true wind is 41° aft of the apparent wind.

(2) If the true wind speed changes and your boat speed doesn't, the apparent wind will shift, even though the true wind direction has not. For example, with the apparent wind on the beam, traveling at a hull speed of 7 kts in 10 kts of true wind, if the true wind increases to 15 kts but the boat speed stays at 7 kts, the apparent wind will shift aft some 20°, even though the true wind direction did not shift at all.

This effect can also be seen when there is a notable wind shear between the deck wind and the wind at the masthead where the wind is measured. If the wind is stronger at the mast head than on the deck it will show a different wind angle, even though it is from the same direction.

(3) Sailing downwind with the true wind well aft, a small change in true wind can result in a large shift in apparent wind direction. For example, at a boat speed of 6 kts in 12 kts of true wind at 170°, if the true wind shifts forward 20° and drops to 10 kts, the boat speed would likely remain about the same, but the apparent wind would shift forward some 40°. With only the apparent wind shift to go by, we could easily misinterpret this wind shift.

(4) When we *tack*, the bow crosses the true wind direction and moves through two times the true wind angle.

(5) When we *jibe*, the stern crosses the true wind direction and the bow moves through two times the supplement of the true wind angle (180° - TWA).

(6) Modern electronics can directly convert the apparent wind to true wind and display these values for you. Racing yachts usually use this equipment. The instruments require an input of your boat speed, and those that give out actual wind directions also need a digital compass input. When working well, these true wind instruments are a wonderful blessing, but it takes a lot of maintenance and tuning to get the output right. If any of the inputs is off just a little, the vector solution it provides for true wind can be off quite a bit. If you discover, for example, that the true wind direction or speed depends on what tack you are on, then the instruments are not tuned or calibrated properly.

Summary

We all need some well tested way to solve for true wind from the measured apparent wind. It is fundamental to practical marine weather. It must be learned so well that you would never put off doing it because you feel a bit uncomfortable about the process.

(In Appendix 9 we also note that sailing performance analysis typically uses a different definition of "true wind" that is relative to the boat's track through the water, which in turn calls for a new term "ground wind" for what is more commonly called "true wind" as discussed in this section.)

2.6 Getting Started on GRIB Files

As mentioned earlier, a predominant aspect of modern marine weather is the increasing usage of what are popularly called "GRIB files." This jargon needs immediate and distinct clarification. First, "GRIB" does not refer to the nature of the data in the files; it is a mathematical *format* for digitized meteorological and oceanographic data of widely varying types. These could be numerical weather or ocean model forecasts, or compilations of past satellite measurements of wind or wave height, or digitized versions of the NWS analyses and forecasts. So far we have illustrated only one type, the GFS numerical model forecasts of wind and pressure in GRIB format. The GFS model actually outputs over 100 distinct weather parameters at multiple levels (altitudes), including such things as duration of sunshine, or soil temperature one meter below ground—and of course other parameters mariners care about such as wind gusts, likelihood of convection, winds in the upper atmosphere, and others.

Basically, a GRIB file is a custom formatted dataset that includes weather parameters at each point on a grid. Think of a piece of transparent graph paper laying on a chart, with data available at each of the intersections of the lines. The spacing of the grid points depends on the dataset. The GFS has roughly one point every 15 nmi, updated every 6 hrs. This is adequate for ocean weather, but of limited use for coastal or inland waters—a bay 10 miles across could be skipped completely. It is what it says it is, a *global* forecast system. For finer details we need what is often called a *regional* forecast, which are presented on much finer grids, often updated hourly, that take into account terrestrial factors not present in a global model.

Another issue coming into play is the increasing use of a second GRIB format. The WMO standard for many years is what is now being called GRIB1. These files have the extension .grb (i.e., filename.grb). All navigation and weather software programs can read and display GRIB1 data. The new WMO standard format is called GRIB2 (extension .grb2); many programs can read and display this format, but not all. The distinctions between these and their significance is covered in Chapter 8

There are two aspects to the use of GRIB files. First we need a software program (an app) to view the files, and then we need to know where and how to download the files themselves. Many apps that can show GRIB files also include a way to download *selected* GRIB files, but we can also obtain data from other sources as well. Since the GRIB formats are standardized, a file downloaded from one source or app will typically be viewable in another.

Ways to View GRIB Files

Again, this is just an introduction so readers can start using these files as soon as possible. More examples and special

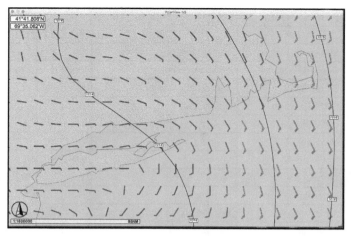

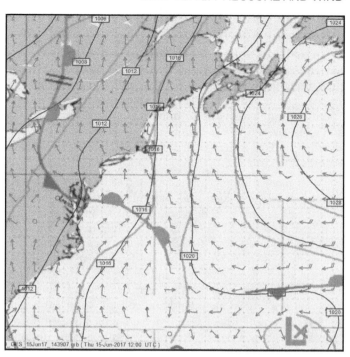

Figure 2.6-1. Top left. *A 24-hr GFS forecast shown in PolarView on a base map only display, without charts loaded. A color code for wind speed has been engaged. This is a common display option. This shows standard 4-mb isobars, but this can be changed as needed.*

Figure 2.6-2. Top right. *A 24-hr GFS forecast shown overlaid in OpenCPN onto a 48-hr surface forecast map issued the day before. The valid times are the same, but the GFS forecast is 24 hrs newer. Coordinating valid times and issued times using different resources is an ongoing challenge when evaluating forecasts.*

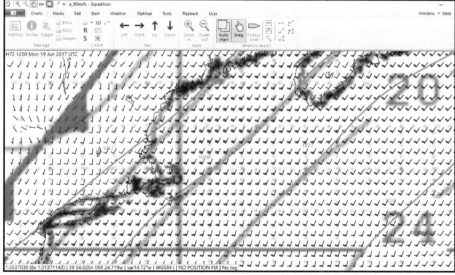

Figure 2.6-3. *A 72-hr GFS forecast valid at 12z on June 19 shown overlaid on a raster chart in Expedition. The GFS forecast was based on 12z on June 16. The GFS grid points are about 15 nmi apart (0.25°). In some programs, isobar colors and line thickness can be changed, as well as their spacing.*

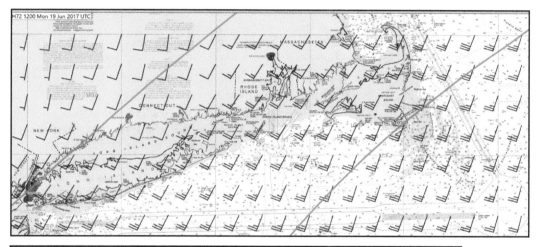

Figure 2.6-4. *Two forecasts for 12z June 19. One is the OPC 96-hr forecast map from four days earlier, and overlaid on that is the 72-hr GFS forecast based on data three days earlier. Except over land, where we do not count on the GFS, the model seems to be supporting the earlier NWS map so far, based on the lay of the isobars. Because latest issues of model forecasts and maps (both surface and wind-and-waves) are all at different times, we have to download in advance if we wish to later compare equivalent data.*

Expedition and OpenCPN each offer convenient ways to download and display georeferenced weather maps. Other navigation programs offer the option to load an image and then manually georeference it for navigation or weather work.

applications, such as optimum weather routing and unique datasets, are in Chapters 7 and 8.

In addition to dedicated GRIB viewer programs, most navigation software programs will display basic GRIB files, thus providing weather data overlays right on the charts you are navigating with, or on a base map if more convenient. Some programs allow us to import a graphic forecast map and then overlay GRIB winds and pressures right on the weather map for comparison or more detail. Examples are in Figures 2.6-1 to 2.6-4.

Most navigation programs have a free trial period to test various chart download and navigation functions offered. Looking ahead to weather work, we can add to that evaluation how they handle GRIB files, meaning display options, parameters shown, and direct download options. Almost all will show GFS wind, but we also need pressure, wind at 500 mb, sea state, ocean currents, and various other GRIB data. There are also several important sources for wind other than GFS that are crucial for inland and coastal work. Table 2.6-1 shows a sample list of GRIB viewers and navigation programs that show at least GRIB1 files with the basic options. (We postpone discussion of GRIB2 data, because there are several nuances to this format. Some programs in the Table 2.6-1 show all forms of GRIB2 data, some only specific forms, and some show none—furthermore, this is likely to change with new versions.)

It is fundamental to modern marine weather work to have a way to view GRIB files. If you do not have one already, you can select one or more from Table 2.6-1 to practice with. Each has unique features. Then you can practice downloading files from the services included in the apps, or with the direct email requests discussed below.

Most Electronic Display and Information Systems (ECDIS) used by commercial and governmental shipping offer the option to overlay weather and oceanographic data via GRIB files. Because this is not part of the official ECDIS standard, there is a wide variety of options in use. GRIB overlays of weather and ocean data are planned to be a more integral part of the next generation of ECDIS systems. Ships generally have better satellite communications than small craft, so there is much potential on the horizon. For the time being, prudent yachtsmen may have superior weather services onboard than ships that pass them.

Where to Get GRIB Files

Many GRIB viewer programs offer some level of GRIB file acquisition via the internet from within the program. Typical parameters are listed in Table 2.6-2. This can be either through a seamless direct link between the program and the source, or the program will generate a formatted email request that you then send manually to request the file, which is returned to you in several minutes as an email attachment. Needless to say, when requesting these over a wireless connection at sea (by either method) we must be aware of file size, and not ask for more than we need. We come back to this

Table 2.6-1. GRIB Viewers for Computers				
Name	Source	N1	N2	N3
Bluewater Racing	bluewaterracing.com	P	Y	Y
Coastal Explorer	rosepoint.com	P		Y
Expedition	expeditionmarine.com	P	Y	Y
GRIB Explorer	ocens.com	B		
LuckGrib	luckgrib.com	M		
MaxSea TZ	maxsea.com	P	Y	Y
Nobeltec TZ	nobeltec.com	P	Y	Y
OpenCPN	opencpn.org	B	Y	Y
PolarView	polarnavy.com	B		Y
Squid	squid-sailing.com	P	Y	
ViewFax	saildocs.com	P		
WinGPS	stentec.com	P	Y	Y
qtVlm	meltemus.com	B	Y	Y
XyGrib (ZyGrib)	opengribs.org (zygrib.org)	B		

Table Notes: *These are ones we are familiar with; there are many more. Each can import GRIB files from within the program. There is a wide range of functionality in these programs, both in weather and navigation applications. The common factor is the ability to load and display GRIB1 data on some level. Bright yellow background marks the free full or limited versions. Not all can view the various formats of GRIB2.*

N1: *M=Mac only, P=PC only, B= both.*

N2: *Optimum sailing route function: Y = yes.*

N3: *Includes nautical charts and GPS for full navigation: Y = yes.*

key point in Chapter 8. A GRIB file could be anywhere from a few kB to hundreds of MB!

When requesting a file from within a GRIB viewer (by either method), the first step is the user activates a tool to outline the region of interest on a base map. Then the type of data is selected from preset options, along with the resolution, duration, and step size. Then a button click either submits the request or creates an email to send. For typical files it takes just seconds to connect and download a file.

The primary sources of U.S. data files are the Environmental Modeling Center (EMC) for model forecasts, and the Digital Forecast Services branch of the Meteorological Development Laboratory for digital versions of the NWS forecasts (NDFD). We also have access to selected public GRIB data from several similar agencies in Europe.

It is possible, but not common, to request files directly from their primary sources, but this can be a complex pro-

Table 2.6-2. Weather Products Freely Available in Most Programs	
Parameters	Model
wind, pressure, precip, temp	GFS
waves and swells	WW3
ocean currents and SST	RTOFS

Table Notes: *There are many other parameters available from multiple sources worldwide, but these free products from the U.S. are built into most navigation programs that read GRIB files.*

cess, typically bringing much larger files than needed. The standard process is to rely on a third party to do the heavy lifting. These services download the primary data to their own servers and then parse out to the users the parts they request. They also process the data so they can be read in a typical mariner's GRIB viewer. The primary data are often in a different format.

There are commercial companies offering this service for a fee and there are a few others that offer the service at no charge to promote other products they offer. Notable among these is the popular saildocs.com, which has been in service since 1999; it is used worldwide. To learn about this email source for GRIB files send a blank email to gribinfo@saildocs.com. The retuned email explains the format and models available. We discuss this further in Section 8.3, which covers other data and services they offer. They also offer, for example, the High Resolution Rapid Refresh (HRRR) model, which is likely the most accurate model forecast for U.S. inland and coastal waters. See Figure 2.6-6.

For starters, install a GRIB viewer of your choice and then send an otherwise blank email to query@saildocs.com, and put this in the body of the message.

send GFS:36N,45N,75W,60W|0.25,0.25|0,6..48|PRMSL,WIND

Note no spaces. The vertical line (|) key is usually above the back slash (\) on the keyboard. You will get back the GRIB file for the region covered in Figures 2.6-1 to 2.6-4. This request will get two day's of forecasts, one every 6 hrs, starting with at the latest synoptic time available—details in Section 8.3.

Later we go over several commercial services that offer GRIB data. Some of them run their own models as well to supplement or improve on public sources. Expedition and Squid (Table 2.6-1), for example, offer GRIB files from both public and commercial services if you have the appropriate accounts. If you are new to both electronic charting and GRIB files, then OpenCPN is a way to have a look at both in either

```
To:     saildocs <query@saildocs.com> ˅

Subject:  send NAM, HRRR, GFS, NDFD, RTOFS, WW3 for Carib

From: Starpath Helpdesk – helpdesk@starpath.com

send NAM:36N,16N,86W,63W|0.03,0.03|0,3..72|WIND,MSLP
send HRRR:36N,16N,86W,63W|0.01,0.01|0,3,6|WIND,MSLP
send GFS:36N,16N,86W,63W|0.25,0.25|0,3..72|WIND,MSLP
send NDFD:36N,16N,86W,63W|0.09,0.09|0,3..72|WIND
send RTOFS:36N,16N,86W,63W|0.08,0.08|0,3..72|CUR,WTMP
send WW3:36N,16N,86W,63W|0.5,0.5|0,3..72|HTSGW,WVDIR
```

Figure 2.6-6. A sample email request to Saildocs for several model outputs. We must be careful with hi-res models like HRRR; the files can get very large, and even exceed Saildocs limits. There are other parameters that can be added, such wave period (WVPER) in the WW3 request. It would be rare to mix up hi-res regional models that extent out only a day or less, with the global models as shown in this example.

a Mac or a PC. Mac users will want to have a look at Luck-Grib; it represents the state of the art in public GRIB sourcing, graphic performance, and display options using its own data or imported files.

There is an increasing use of tablets these days for both navigation and weather work. Several tablet apps that show GRIB files from various sources are listed in Table 2.6-3. As with computer software, most navigation apps also include a weather overlay, although many of these are GFS only. They are not included in the Table, although the GFS could be a useful guide in some coastal waters. With products such as Iridium Go, tablets can be connected wirelessly to satellite communications directly or via email. In coastal waters, cellphone connections will often make the needed connections to data sources. Also new over the past year are tablet apps that offer some level of optimum weather routing for sailboats. We cover routing in Chapter 10.

Apps such as those in Table 2.6-3 show you either various model forecasts from their own sources, or they will import ones you downloaded yourself from other sources. A GRIB file on your computer can be transferred to the tablet by various means, depending on the tablet in use. One approach is just mail the GRIB file to yourself as an attachment, then when you open the mail in your tablet, select the GRIB viewer app you use to view it. Most have a more direct means of transferring files.

Summary and Perspective

The goal at hand is to start using GRIB files, and the GFS model forecasts are a good place to begin, in large part because they are so readily available in so many navigation pro-

Table 2.6-3. Tablet GRIB Viewers					
Name	Source		N1	N2	N3
Avalon Offshore	avalon-routing.com		B		
GRIB Explorer	ocens.com		A		
iGrib	mojoso.co.uk/igrib/		B		
LuckGrib	luckgrib.com		A		
OpenCPN	opencpn.org		G		Y
Pocket Grib	pocketgrib.com		B		
PredictWind	predictwind.com		B	Y	
qtVlm	meltemus.com		B	Y	Y
SailFlow	sailflow.com		B		
SailGrib	sailgrib.com		G	Y	Y
Squid	squid-sailing.com		B	Y	
WeatherTrack	weathertrack.us		A		
Weather4D	weather4d.com		B	Y	Y

Table Notes: These are ones we are familiar with; there are many more. Each can display or import GRIB files from external sources that include more than just GFS. There is a wide range of functionality in these programs, and options are certainly evolving.
N1: A = iOS only, G = Android only, B= both.
N2: Optimum sailing route function: Y = yes.
N3: Includes nautical charts and GPS for full navigation: Y = yes.

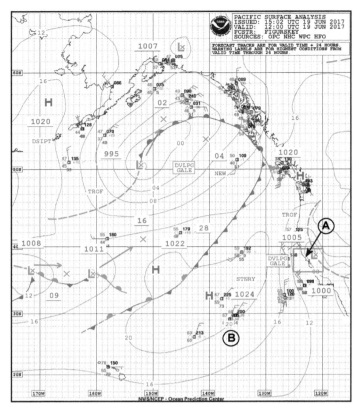

Figure 2.6-7. *A surface analysis map from the OPC. The GFS prediction for the area of the red inset is shown in Figure 2.6-9.*

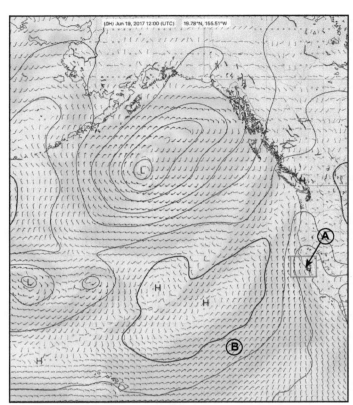

Figure 2.6-8. *The GFS h0 forecast valid at the same time as the OPC map in Figure 2.6-7. Both are based on the state of the atmosphere at 12z on June 19, 2017. The red insert marks the zoomed area shown in Figure 2.6-9. In this display, the 1020 isobar was set to be bold.*

grams. On the other hand, except for periodic ocean crossings, most of our sailing will be on inland and coastal waters, in which case the GFS is not at all our best source. Once we are comfortable using GRIB files for the basic GFS data, then we can move on to more specialized sources, which include regional models with higher resolution and more frequent updates, and we can start using digitized forms of the official NWS forecast, called the National Digital Forecast Database (NDFD), featured later in the book.

For now we have the two maps shown in Figures 2.6-7 and 2.6-8. The former is a product of human intelligence, based on the output from several different numerical models along with satellite data and images, and the knowledge of the professional meteorologists who put it together. The latter is a pure computer output from the GFS model alone. This is a good model, so we expect it to be right more often than wrong, and if we can be confident it is right, we see the great advantages of using it in Figure 2.6-8. Namely we have tremendous more detail on the winds and isobars. Generally we need to look at both products for the best picture of what is taking place, because the OPC map shows the fronts, and various troughs they can detect from satellite images. Moving fronts always raise a question in the pure model output data, because they complicate weather patterns.

We have several ways we evaluate the GFS forecasts (or any other model output); one is to compare its predictions to what was reported on the surface analysis map and the other is compare it to what we observed. Recall that both maps will

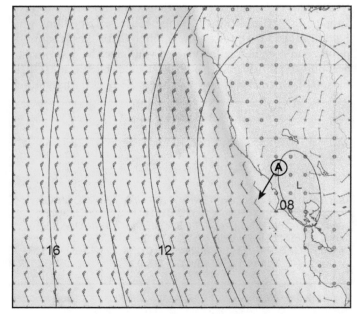

Figure 2.6-9. *A zoomed view of the area of Figure 2.6-8 marked in red. In this display, a color gradient is used to distinguish wind speeds, blue being lighter winds, red being stronger. The isobar spacing is set to 2 mb. The standard on NWS maps is 4 mb. This and similar images are from LuckGrib.*

be 3 or 4 hrs old when we first get them. As an example, we could look at point A, which is near Bodega Bay. Interpolating the distance between the 08 and 12 isobars, we would estimate the map prediction as 1008.7 mb. To get the wind from the OPC map we use Table 2.4-1 with Lat = 38 and isobar spacing d = 2.4°. This gives a wind speed of about 20 kts at about 315. The GFS value (Figure 2.6-8) was 10.1 kts at 320 with a pressure of 1008.3.

We can look up Bodega Bay Buoy (Station 46013) observations in the archives of the NDBC to find that they reported 11.6 kts at 330 with a pressure of 1009.0 mb at 12z, June 19, 2017. The pressures all agree, so we can assume the GFS is reasonable for this region at this time. We can't read much into the fact that the GFS winds were closer to the truth than the those we interpolated from the OPC map, because they did not actually forecast winds at that point. The goal here is just to show one type of comparison we can do. Underway in the ocean we would be using our logbook values for the truth, if there were no buoys nearby.

Likewise a check at point B on the OPC map (25N, 136W), we would interpolate the pressure as halfway between 16 and 20 or 1018.0 mb. The isobar spacing of 5.3° implies a wind speed of 14 kts (Table 2.4-1), and the direction would be about 040, crossing the isobars, out of the High by about 20°. From the GFS GRIB we can read digital values at that point and they are 16 kts at 038 with a pressure of 1017.1. In short, the OPC map and the pure GFS agree at this point, namely about 15 kts from 040 with a pressure of 1017.5±0.5 mb. The NE trades. We will find times when these do not agree so nicely, and when this happens, we need to exercise more caution when using the super convenient, high-precision pure model forecasts, such as the GFS.

To make a practice comparison like the one just done, send this request to query@saildocs.com with these three lines of text

send GFS:15N,65N,175W,115W

send https://ocean.weather.gov/P_e_sfc_color.png

send https://www.ndbc.noaa.gov/data/5day2/46013_5day.txt

This will bring back to you by email the latest GFS grib file; the latest Eastern Pacific surface analysis (color version); and a history of the data at Station 46013. The archived station data are in UTC, with wind in m/s. Later we go over more efficient ways to evaluate the GFS or other forecasts. Details of the Saildocs format are covered in Section 8.3.

Note on File Size

One of the beauties of the GRIB format is they are vector files, which are very much smaller than the comparable graphic (raster) files used for conventional weather maps. But we must still be aware of the file sizes we are dealing with, because the user has the opportunity to define what they want from the server that is providing them. If you take more than you need, and you are downloading by a satphone, you may be paying way more than you need to.

The first factor to consider is what region to cover. You typically do not need the whole ocean to figure out what is going on in your neighborhood. So step one is make a judicious choice of the boundaries. It will not take long to learn if you need more.

Next take just the products you need. Usually wind and pressure are the key factors, but precipitation can also help locate fronts and be of other interest. But if not, then don't take it. If you add precipitation you are increasing your file size by about one third.

Next there is duration. How many days do you need? Sometimes it is nice to look ahead 5 days, but the data are not very dependable out that far. So you might look at shorter periods most of the time, and just periodically take a longer look forward.

And how often do you need the data? The GFS, for example, is new every 6 hrs, but offers 3-hr forecasts. For some ocean sailing you may not need the intermediate data. When doing an optimum route, on the other hand, you might want as fine a step as possible. It pays to think on what you actually need. A raw data file of 20 kB can explode in size if you add a lot of intermediate data that you might not need.

Finally there is resolution. Different models provide data in different grid sizes and some providers offer optional resolutions. The finest step for GFS is 0.25°, but you can ask for lower resolution, i.e., 0.5°, 1° or even 2°. A factor of 2 increase in resolution will be a file of about four times the size of the same data in the lower resolution. A judicious choice here is important. A 1° × 1° resolution means one wind arrow every 60 nmi, but these are vector data, so you can still read the interpolated values of wind and pressure in between the plotted wind arrows.

The file size becomes a much more important issue when we look into high-resolution data that can have a resolution ten times finer than the GFS, with forecasts every hour. If we consider a "base file" as wind and pressure, for a 10° × 10° region, at 0.5° resolution, with 6-hr steps for one day, the file size will be about 12 kB. This then scales roughly proportional to the Area × Parameters × Forecasts / Resolution². In this example wind and pressure counts as three parameters, because models present the wind as X and Y components that the GRIB viewer then converts to vectors. Also a one-day's set of forecasts at 6-hr intervals would typically be 5 maps, called h0, h6, h12, h18, and h24. The h0 "forecast" is equivalent to a surface analysis at the most recent synoptic time. "h24" would be a 24-hr forecast.

For high resolution data, we would naturally limit the area covered. The HRRR wind and pressure forecasts in 1-hr steps for 18 hrs over San Francisco Bay is about 51 kB. This has a standard resolution of 1.62 nmi (0.027°), which is still completely manageable over a 4G cellphone network. At the synoptic times (HH=00z, 06z, 12z, 18z), the HRRR model is extended out to 36 hr, in which case judicious choices of parameters and region size are even more crucial.

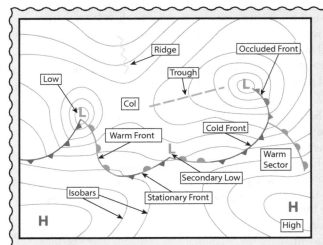

Summary of Map Symbols

Isobars are like elevation contours on a topographic map. H's mark the top of the Highs. L's mark the bottom of the Lows. From anywhere on a ridge, pressure decreases as you move away from it. From anywhere on a trough, pressure increases as you move away from it. A col is a saddle point in the pressure pattern. Fronts often mark discontinuities in the run of the isobars. Fronts are not shown on model forecasts, but may be obvious from wind directions or precipitation shown.

William Ferrel (1817-1891) American practical mathematician whose contributions to meteorology were as great or greater than his more famous contemporaries FitzRoy, Buys Ballot, and Maury. In 1856, he was the first to correctly explain global air circulation of the doldrums, trade winds, prevailing westerlies, and polar easterlies, creating his namesake Ferrel cell, correcting or replacing existing theories of the day. In the process he was the first to apply what we now call the Coriolis effect to global air flow, which was a crucial step to the future evolution of meteorology.

He also was also the first to present what we call Buys Ballot's Law for wind flow around a pressure pattern. His explanation of surface wind flow in 1856 was more clear and to the point than any other explanation had been before—or has been since!

Buys Ballot published his law of wind directions a year after Ferrel did, but Buys Ballot probably gets the credit because he presented it with actual data and had used it practically for many years. Ferrel's work, in contrast, was more theoretical, though based on known global wind patterns compiled by Maury—not to mention that Ferrel published his pioneering paper on global winds in *The Nashville Journal of Medicine and Surgery*!

Ferrel taught himself mathematics and astrophysics as a youth in Pennsylvania and Virginia, enough to become a teacher of the subjects, but then went on to the newly established Bethany College. Subsequently he worked for the Nautical Almanac Office and later for the U.S. Army Signal Corps, which eventually became the Weather Bureau in 1891. While at the Signal Corps he proposed for the first time the Plateau Correction still used to convert measured pressures at high elevations to the equivalent sea level values, crucial to the production of weather maps on land.

He made numerous other important contributions to meteorology, astrophysics, and hydrography, and especially in the areas where these fields overlap. He was, for example, the first to prove that the action of the moon on the tides tended to slow the earth's rotation. It appears he was a man with great physical insight into the mathematics he needed, unconstrained by rigorous formalism.

3.1 Warm Air Rises

The fact that warm air rises turns out to be a fundamental driving force behind much of the winds and weather we deal with. Warm air has a higher temperature than cool air, which means the molecules in it are moving faster. And since the air is not in a container with fixed dimensions, the air molecules bang about more, causing the air to expand as it gets warmer, so its density goes down. The same volume or region of air weighs less when it is warm, and thus it floats up in the mass of cooler air around it. So we now have a long way to say what we all know—warm air rises. If you want to dry your socks fast, you put them above the fire so they are heated by *convection*—transferring heat by the rising warm air. You could, of course, put them next to the fire and they would eventually dry as well. But this is heating by *radiation*. The heat itself is radiated from the fire; it is not being carried there by warm air. This type of radiation heating is how the sun heats the earth and oceans, but for now we look at the convective processes.

Consider an isolated desert island at night (Figure 3.1-1). The temperature and pressure are everywhere uniform, and no wind flows.

When the sun comes out in the morning (Figure 3.1-2) the land begins to heat, and it heats faster and more thoroughly than the water around it. This happens for several reasons. One, the light penetrates the water distributing its heat over more material, whereas on the land all the heat is absorbed in a relatively thin layer on the surface. Also, rocks, soil, and sand (earth) have a much lower specific heat capacity than

water does. The sun must add roughly five times more heat to water to raise its temperature by one degree than it does for the same amount of sand or rock. In fact, it is this property of water (its resistance to temperature change) that moderates temperatures on any midlatitude west coast compared to the corresponding east coast. On the west coast the incoming marine air is moist and thus it resists temperature changes, whereas by the time the air reaches the east coast it is dry, so east coasts have hotter summers and colder winters.

Returning to our island, when the land heats, it begins to heat the air in contact with the ground, and this surface air begins to rise.

As the day progresses, warm air rising off the island must be replaced by neighboring air, which starts to flow onto the island as a sea breeze (Figure 3.1-3). As this flow develops, the whole column of air above the island begins to warm. As the air above the island grows warmer relative to that over the water around the island, it progressively weighs less and less so the atmospheric pressure over the island begins to diminish relative to pressure over the water around it. Recall that pressure is just the weight of the air above us, so a low pressure area is developing over the island. This is the classic sea breeze pattern. Land heats, and air from the cooler water flows toward the land as pressure on the land drops relative to that of the adjacent waters.

As air rises in the atmosphere its temperature slowly decreases. The warm moist air rising over the island eventually cools to the dew point of the air, at which time the invisible

Figure 3.1-1. *At night with no weather pattern over the region, air temperature is everywhere uniform near the island and no wind flows. A calm night.*

Figure 3.1-2. *When the sun rises, it heats the land more than it does the water. The heated land in turn heats the air adjacent to it, and this warmer air starts to rise. Thus: sun heats the land, and then the land heats the air.*

Figure 3.1-3. *As more of the air column over the island is warmed, a local low pressure area develops, which pulls in air as a local sea breeze.*

Figure 3.1-4. *As the air continues to rise it eventually (midmorning) cools to the dew point and clouds are formed over the island. The process is common in tropic islands as it is on coastal mountain peaks. In Chapters 6 and 9 we will learn more from the observations of these thermal cloud caps.*

water vapor within it condenses into visible water that clings to the surface of dust and other particulates to form clouds (Figure 3.1-4). This heats the air somewhat by releasing the heat of condensation, so the air continues to rise. By this time there is an established air column flowing up that eventually fans out to either side flowing away from the island at higher altitudes.

The elevated air flowing away from the island eventually piles up against the neighboring air and starts to sink back to the surface forming a downdraft some distance off. Thus we have a High pressure area developing on the surface below this area of descending air. In the general case of a sea breeze like this, we end up with a circular cell of air flow from High to Low, converging into the Low on the surface and diverging out of the Low at higher altitudes (Figure 3.1-5).

This example illustrates general properties of all High and Low pressure systems. Wind converges into Lows on the surface and then rises, usually forming clouds as outlined. In Highs, on the other hand, air is always descending. So any clouds that happen into them get pushed down toward the surface, and as it descends it heats, which evaporates the clouds. Thus Highs are characterized by clear skies; Lows by cloudy skies.

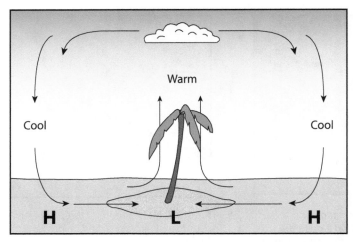

Figure 3.1-5. *By afternoon a well-established sea-breeze cycle is formed with clear skies over high pressures surrounding the low pressure of the island.*

3.2 Hadley Cells and Global Winds

The sun is the ultimate source of all weather on earth, because it heats the earth unevenly, adding more heat to the belt of the equator than to the caps of the poles. This comes about not because the equator is closer to the sun (that is actually not much of an effect), but because the sun is overhead in the tropics, whereas it is viewed at an angle from higher latitudes. See Figure 3.2-1. The energy per unit area deposited in the tropics is much higher than at the poles, throughout the year.

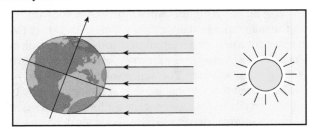

Figure 3.2-1. *Radiation density. When the sun is high in the sky, the energy density (per area) is higher.*

Thus we have unevenly heated fluids on earth (ocean and air) that strive for some level of equilibrium. That excess heat at the equator must be distributed around the earth so it can be dissipated, otherwise we would boil away the tropics. As it turns out, some 40% of this excess heat is transported away from the tropics by ocean currents, which we will come back to, but for now we are looking into the currents in the air that we call wind.

Recalling the discussion of warm island air in Section 3.1, the heated air along the latitude belt directly below the sun has a natural tendency to rise straight up to some high altitude, where it fans out to the north and south, headed toward the poles. Once it starts up it has no other choice. It can't come straight back down because there is a strong updraft of wind below it. So when the air has cooled and lost all its buoyant drive upward, gravity stops it from drifting on up and it is forced to flow toward the poles at a high altitude.

In this over-simplified model of the circulation on a non-rotating earth, the air would flow all the way to the poles where it sinks back to the earth, where it then is forced down the surface as a northerly in the NH and a southerly in the SH—a large single-cell cycle of continuous flow toward the poles at high altitudes and toward the equator on the surface, as shown in Figure 3.2-2. Then if we started the earth rotating, the Coriolis force would come into play to bend the flow to the right in the NH and to the left in the SH. So this would change the simple pattern into northeasterlies or easterlies throughout the NH and southeasterlies or easterlies throughout the SH.

Needless to say, this model is not quite right. It could more or less account for the trade winds, but does not do much at all to account for winds and weather at higher latitudes. The actual flow of the earth's atmosphere is more complex, the basics of which had been figured out in large part by the mid to late 1800s, but the details are still being sorted out today.

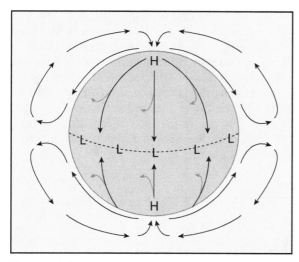

Figure 3.2-2. *A hypothetical single-cell circulation.*

The starting point of the simple model is still right. The air rises at the latitude where the sun is overhead and the air starts poleward at high altitudes. As it moves poleward, the longitude lines converge and the distance around a latitude circle decreases. The air must conserve angular momentum as it circles the earth moving north, so as it moves away from the equator it spins with increasing speed. By about latitude 30°, it is spinning so fast that eddies form instead of the air moving further poleward. Then the air piles up, forming subtropical Highs, and it sinks back to the earth.

This air descending at about 30° N and S runs back to the equator to create the *trade winds*. The Coriolis force turns the trades into E to NE in the NH and E to SE in the SH. This prominent cell of circulation is called the *Hadley cell*, named after George Hadley, an early proponent of the theory from the early 1700s.

Likewise at the polar extremes of the earth, the flow is also just about as simple as the one cell model. Cold air sinks to the earth's surface over the poles and heats as it flows toward the equator. But this air also only travels about 30° on average, and at roughly 60° latitude (N and S) it has warmed enough to begin to rise and flow back to the poles at a high altitude, forming the two Polar cells illustrated in Figure 3.2-3. Once the Coriolis force kicks in, the winds originally headed toward the equator, get bent to the west to become easterlies in the polar regions of both the NH and the SH.

The region on earth between latitude 30° and 60° is called the temperate latitudes or midlatitudes, or sometimes just "the latitudes," meaning any place on earth that is not in the tropics and not in the polar regions. The vertical profile of circulation in this region is called the *Ferrel cell* (after American scientist James Ferrel), and it's cellular flow is not as simple as that of the Hadley and Polar cells. Hadley cell air is descending at 30° and when it hits the surface it mostly heads to the equator to form the *trade winds*—the most steady and predictable wind system on earth—but some of it heads to the poles as part of the Ferrel cell, to eventually rise with the ascending air of the Polar cell at 60°. This north flowing surface

wind in the Ferrel cell curves to the right in the NH and to the left in the SH to make up the *prevailing westerlies*, which characterize the average wind direction throughout the mid-latitudes of both hemispheres.

Some of the wind aloft in this region does head back to the equator, but the majority of air aloft in this region is headed poleward as shown schematically in Figure 3.2-3, which under the influence of the Coriolis force is westerly. This brings up a key point in global circulation. At high altitudes, the wind (called the "winds aloft") is westerly at all latitudes (with a maximum in the midlatitudes), even though winds vary between east and west on the surface. These persistent strong winds aloft play a key role in the development and motion of weather systems on the surface, and we will come back to this important point later.

On the surface at around 60° N, where the warm westerlies coming up from the south collide with the cold easterlies of the polar cell, the air rises forming a semi stationary front called the *polar front*. This frontal region plays a pivotal role in the weather of the midlatitudes.

The descending cool air from the Hadley cell forms regions of High pressure around the globe at roughly 30° latitude, which in the early sailing days of the Western North Atlantic were called the *horse latitudes*, because of something to do with horses and mariners stuck in the Highs without wind. Either they ran out of water and could not care for the horses, or they pitched them overboard to lighten the vessels for better performance in light air. The term has come to mean that belt of the earth at about 30° to 35° where there is likely to be high pressure systems with no wind in their centers and typically only light wind circling them. On land these areas are typically both hot and dry. You will note that the great deserts of the world are located along this band. As

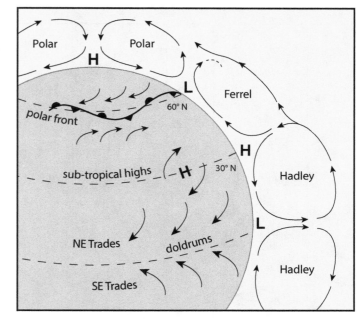

Figure 3.2-3. *Three cells of global circulation that lead to the formation of the polar front, the mid-ocean Highs, the trade winds, and the doldrums where the trades meet.*

seagoing mariners we will be continually confronted with these Highs, which tend to form in the eastern-middle of the oceans rather than span across them. All of our global sailing routes are designed to travel around them, clockwise in the NH, counterclockwise in the SH. Our goal will be to learn how close we can get to the center of such a High and still expect to find wind.

In the North Pacific the seasonal high is called the *Pacific High*. It is usually centered roughly due west of San Francisco (about 38° N) on the rhumb line between Hawaii and the Strait of Juan de Fuca that separates WA state and Canada. The High begins to form in June but is most stable in August. There is not really a single direct counterpart in the Atlantic, although we do sometimes hear the term "Atlantic High." More often, the dominant High in the Atlantic is to the SW near Bermuda and called the *Bermuda High*. Or, it is formed more to the NE and it is then called the *Azores High*. The stability from one day to the next of any of these subtropical highs depend on their shapes and the actual pressures, as well as the winds aloft.

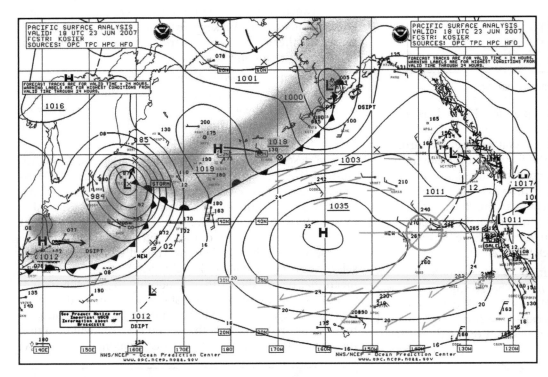

Figure 3.2-4. *Pacific High. Winds at the top (westerly barbs) are the prevailing westerlies; winds at the bottom (easterly barbs) are the trade winds. The location of the polar front is shaded in blue to mark the cooler air behind it. The normal location of the High is marked (green) at about 38N, 140W. This one is way west of the most stable location. The latitude at about 30N is shown as a typical northerly limit to the trade wind belt—see Figure 3.2-3. The dashed line from the Low at 50N, 130W is a trough of locally low pressure and rising air that could be seen in cloud images, but not yet affecting the isobars very much. We might later see a front develop along this trough. (In these older maps the vessel ID of ship reports were shown, which is no longer the case.)*

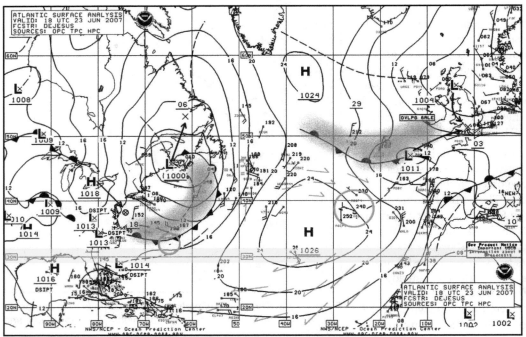

Figure 3.2-5. *Atlantic High. Winds at the top (westerly barbs) are the prevailing westerlies; winds at the bottom (easterly barbs) are the trade winds. Cold air (blue) above the frontal regions is shaded in. The locations of Bermuda and the Azores are circled in green, which are the more typical centroids of the High, which in turn give the High its name. This is rather rare example of an actual "Atlantic High." The latitude at about 30N is shown as a typical northerly limit to the trade wind belt. More generally, the bottom of the High will start the easterly or northeasterly flow, even though not part of a fully stable trade wind that would take place farther south.*

Figure 3.2-6. *Winds of the world on June 23, 2017 showing the much higher prevalence of strong winds in the high southern latitudes (Roaring Forties, Furious Fifties, Screaming Sixties) due to the absence of intervening land. The Pacific High is formed, but not yet fully developed, nor on station. The Atlantic High is trying to decide if it will be an Azores High or Bermuda High. Isobar spacing is 4 mb, with the 1012 mb marked in bold. Note that throughout the Pacific tropics the pressure is about 1012 mb which is often the case in the Atlantic as well, but this snapshot shows it a bit higher. If we looked at an animation of this map over several weeks (starpath.com/wx) we would see these tropical pressures remain fairly constant (± 2 mb), whereas the rest of the world pressures would vary 3 or 4 times as much as systems move around the midlatitudes. Later we use this known pressure invariance in the tropics as a very positive barometric indication of an approaching tropical storm. Note the winds flowing opposite directions around Highs and Lows, above and below the equator.*

Sample locations of the Atlantic and Pacific Highs are shown in Figures 3.2-4 and 3.2-5. Both of these sample Highs (selected at random at the time of the first edition) are rather off station, meaning not in their most climatically likely locations, and they are both rather larger than might be typical. The central pressures are about typical, though each could be even higher.

The wind flow along the bottom edges of these Highs (below about 30N) mark the top of the trade wind belt, and the flow over the top of these Highs makes up the prevailing westerlies.

As of 2018, the OPC no longer shows the motion of Highs on surface analysis maps, but they do show the present and 24-hr projected locations of Lows, providing the Low is not dissipating. This is done with two Xs, with an arrow between them. Central pressures of Highs and Lows are written out and underlined, often at some distance from the H or L.

Figure 3.2-6 contrasts the NH summer winds with those in the SH winter. Winter always brings stronger winds, but the difference seen here is dramatically enhanced by the open waters of the southern oceans. In the NH the global flow of westerly wind is interrupted by North America and Eurasia, so the SH always has much stronger winds in the higher latitudes. Sailors in the SH call these winds the *Roaring Forties, Furious Fifties,* and *Screaming Sixties*—although it is not so much that the prevailing westerlies themselves are always so

strong, but that they frequently bring with them fast moving systems with very strong winds.

ITCZ (Doldrums)

We turn back now to the starting point of this overall circulation, the equatorial belt of low pressure around the globe where the NE trades on the north side of it converge with the SE trades on the south side of it and the air goes straight up. Remember that in a Low air is always rising. This belt is called the Intertropical convergence zone (ITCZ) by meteorologists and called the *doldrums* by sailors. In this narrow zone there is very little or no horizontal wind (see blue area just north of the equator in Figure 3.2-6), but there is strong updraft, which in turn leads to clouds and rain—a global version of our island heating in the sun. Since this is very warm moist air, any slight change in stability can lead to major weather changes in the doldrums. Planning any sailing voyage from the NH to the SH, we must take into account the crossing of this belt of no wind. On the other hand, if you are looking for freshwater at sea, this would be your best bet since squalls are frequent.

The location of the doldrums is fairly constant in the eastern portions of the Atlantic and Pacific, but vary significantly with season in the western portions of those oceans and in southern Asia and the Indian Ocean. A sample is shown in Figure 3.2-8 which overlays a GFS forecast of precipitation onto a tropical surface analysis map from the NHC. The ITCZ

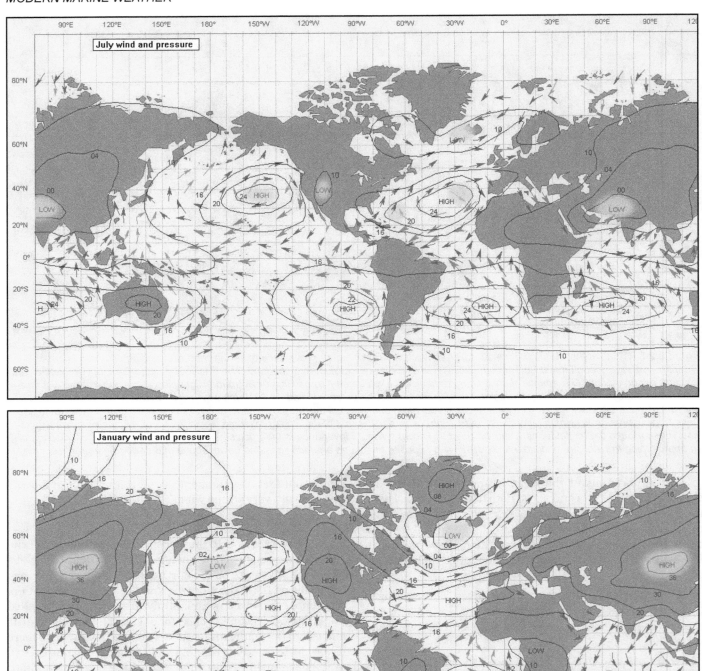

Figure 3.2-7. *Climatic world winds and pressures. The blue arrows are average winds; green are variable winds; and the red are steady winds, anticipated to flow as shown in two-thirds of all observations. Data from the Starpath Weather Trainer using multiple sources. See Pilot Charts or COGOW Data (Section 10.6) for more specific climatic predictions. Yellow marks the wintertime centers of action: Siberian High (driving the NE monsoon) and the Icelandic and Aleutians Lows, as well as the summertime centers of the Pacific and Atlantic (Azores or Bermuda) Highs and the Asiatic Low (driving the SE monsoon). A thermal trough over the U.S. West Coast is indicated as well, as a frequent source of enhanced coastal winds.*

(doldrums) is marked by a crosshatched double line where NE trades meet SE trades for the convergence. When these southern trades veer around to the SW, the line is called a *monsoon trof* (trough) and the cross hatch is removed. These are regions where tropical disturbances can develop, which might evolve into tropical storms. We cover tropical weather and more of these maps in Section 4.5.

The doldrums move north and south to favor the summer hemisphere, but they pretty much remain within in the NH, above the equator. This should be a surprise since the heating of the equatorial belt that drives these processes is fairly uniform between NH and SH on either side of the equator. The source of the discrepancy here are the ocean temperatures that control the location of the doldrums. The water is indeed warmer on average above the equator than below it. But that just transfers the question: why is that true if the heating is uniform north and south? The answer is not so tidy. It is a matter of the combined influences of the shapes and distribution of the land masses along the equator.

In other words, when it comes to the location of the doldrums we are dealing with another example of where the real world details simply do not quite match the idealized theoretical models. It is a bit like the behavior of tides. We have semidiurnal tides on the east coast of the U.S. (two highs of about the same height and two lows of about the same height each day) and on the west coast we have mixed semidiurnal tides (where the two highs and two lows are very different each day). But then, right in between the two coasts, the tides along the Gulf of Mexico are almost purely diurnal with just one high and one low each day. There is no simple explanation for this. It is a net result of the overall shapes of the continents and how they interact with the tidal waves in the fluid ocean. These are complex interactions. However, just like the tides pose no problem to us—we can look them up when we need them—we can also very accurately look up the location of the ITCZ when we need it. Tropical maps from the NHC and the unified maps from the OPC show these very nicely and they are accurate.

When there are options to our routes across the doldrums, it pays to study the model forecasts. Though often without wind, there are periodically regions we can reach that do carry light but steady air across them.

In the past, the NHC included outlined cloud symbols on the tropical maps indicating regions of thunderstorms. It seems they have discontinued that practice, but we can see them in aviation maps such as Figure 3.2-9, which we have access to underway. I want to stress that the cloud sketches on these tropical maps are not decorative. They are carefully drawn in to mark the boundaries of actual thunderstorms seen in satellite photos. I can verify from direct experience in these waters that they are remarkably good indicators of where you will enter the squalls and perhaps amazing lightning displays. On one occasion in about this region south of Tehuantepec the lightning in such a marked area was like sailing in a florescent light bulb. Lightning was going off continuously all night long in all directions and added light to the night sky, though no strikes seemed to be very close. A memorable experience.

The aviation prog chart of Figure 3.2-9 shows tropical storm Dora (with the conventional symbol) embedded in the regular thunderstorm cloud symbols. We could hope that this would have been more prominent, but this type of map

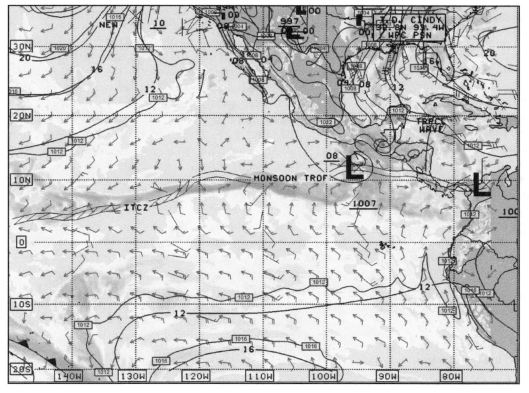

Figure 3.2-8. *GFS wind, pressure, and total precipitation (blue gradient) overlaid on a tropical Pacific surface analysis (PYFA90.TIF) from the NHC, valid 00z, June 23, 2017, viewed in OpenCPN. The lavender background is clear sky. The isobars agree fairly well (boxed labels are the GFS). Winds also agree reasonably well. In the ITCZ we see SE and NE trades meeting to rise and form rain. In the monsoon trof, NE trades meet SW wind created by local disturbance, and indeed two Lows have formed. We also see the intense local rain along the cold front in the SW corner. Using the GRIB viewer option to show wind streamlines is a good way to identify these convergence zones. Tropical waves as indicated here are discussed in Section 4.5. Displaying GFS total precipitation is often a good way to locate fronts and the ITCZ.*

Figure 3.2-9. *Section of an aviation prognostic chart valid at 12z, June 27, 2017. The Low forming on the monsoon trof in Figure 3.2-8 did form into a tropical storm. It was named Dora on the 24th, and moved to the location seen here on the 27th. CB (cumulonimbus) means tall thunderstorms. Numbers are cloud tops expressed in flight levels (hundreds of feet). XXX means their low cloud bases are not known. We also see abbreviations for* isolated, frequent, *and* occasional. *Interpretation and marine application of these maps is discussed in Section 4.6.*

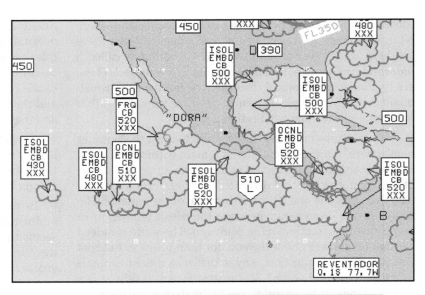

is not for navigation around tropical storms. We get much better information on these from other sources. This map is just a way to identify expected regions of thunderstorms, which do indeed tend to group up rather than be totally isolated.

Trade Winds

The "trades" are the most famous wind pattern on earth. They are the most steady, and the ones used historically to discover, explore, and trade around the world. When sailing your own vessel into the trades, the big question that always comes up is "When will we be in the trades?" or "Are these the trades?" It is not so simple a question, as you will likely be rounding a High and the wind may have come around to the right direction, but you are still not in the trades—you do not yet have steady winds you can count on.

The answer is essentially the same for the NH and for the SH. We discuss the NH here. As a rough guide we would expect the trades to start firming up somewhere about latitude 30°, but this can vary significantly with local weather patterns. The trades should bring winds somewhere between the NE and E, at speeds of some 10 to 20 kts. A NE wind of 15 kts, however, does not mean you are in the trades. This could be a temporary wind. Signs of the trades are schematically shown in Figure 3.2-10.

First, look for a steady wind lasting for some time, as well as seas that reflect this persistence. Trade wind seas are big, but well organized—that is, big without being steep, and running in the direction of the wind. Another good sign that you have reached the trades are the clouds you see, especially at night. These are called trade wind cumulus (cumulus humilis)—low, small, fluffy white cumulus, that fly by with the trades. At night, these clouds are often seen below a clear starry sky. It is a good sign you have reached the trades.

Here you can expect the wind to remain fairly steady, but it is not uncommon to have the trades drop to 10 kts (or less) on occasion or rise to 25 kts. There is often a diurnal variation to the wind speed, with stronger winds in the afternoon and lighter winds at night.

To summarize the dominant atmospheric circulation that dictates our global sailing routes—air rises in the doldrums near the equator and travels poleward at high altitudes to about the horse latitudes of 30° N and S. There it descends into the centers of large subtropical high-pressure zones. Air

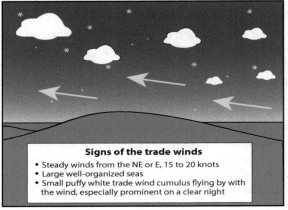

Figure 3.2-10. *Signs of the trade winds.*

flowing out of the equatorial sides of these highs flow into and make up the trade winds from the NE in the NH and from the SE in the SH. The flow over the tops of these Highs make up the prevailing westerlies that dominate the wind flow in the higher temperate latitudes. The interface between colder air at higher latitudes and the warm prevailing westerlies often leads to a semi-stationary polar front along the western side of the oceans that spins off many of the Lows and fronts that affect weather throughout the temperate latitudes. A typical graphic summary of climatic surface winds and pressures is presented in Figure 3.2-7.

An Impact of Global Warming

In the last couple years scientists have confirmed that the tropical belt has expanded some 3° to 8° of latitude between 1979 and 2010—increasing at a rate of about 1° to 1.5° per decade. This means the average location of the mid-ocean Highs are moving farther from the equator and the trade wind belts will likely grow wider. Storm tracks over the tops of the Highs (Chapter 4) are also moving poleward, which will gradually affect standard shipping and sailing routes in the higher latitudes. Tropical storms are also gradually reaching peak intensities at higher latitudes.

3.3 Winds Aloft

In the last section on global circulation we learned that in the region of the Ferrel cell that describes global wind flow at latitudes between about 40° and 60° there is poleward wind flow both at the surface and aloft near the top of the troposphere. Thus when the Coriolis effect turns these winds to the right in the NH and to the left in the SH, we end up with prevailing westerlies both on the surface and aloft in both hemispheres. (This is an oversimplified view of the complex wind patterns in the Ferrel cell, but the conclusion is correct.) This west wind aloft accounts for the fundamental rule that all weather systems move from west to east in the midlatitudes, both North and South.

The westerly winds on the surface are known as the prevailing westerlies. They make up the natural flow over the polar sides of the mid-ocean Highs, and they represent the average wind transport over the midlatitudes even when the Highs are not so prominent. In other words, if you were asked what is the surface wind direction somewhere between say 40° N and 60° N and you did not know anything more at all, your best guess would be westerly. The true answer at any specific time could be anything, but if all wind directions were plotted for all year, there would be a notable peak at westerly. Study pilot chart or COGOW wind roses (Section 10.6) for betting odds on specific dates and locations.

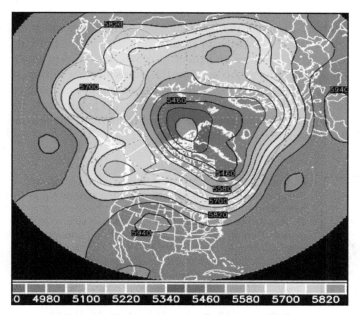

Figure 3.3-1. *Schematic view of the stream lines of the global wind flow at about 18,000 ft—about halfway up through the atmosphere where the pressure is 500 mb. The contours are the heights of the 500-mb surface. This view looks down to the North Pole in about the center of the flow pattern. Waves in this wind pattern are called Rossby waves. They slip very slowly to the east as they meander into various shapes of troughs and crests. We see a long wave over the Atlantic and a long wave over the Pacific, interrupted by a short wave trough over the Bering Sea, upstream from the common location of a surface low over the Aleutians—discussed later in Chapter 4.*

If you had to make the same guess of the surface wind from say 40° N to 30° N, then you might want to know if it is summer or winter. In the summer the right answer is likely calm (near the center of a mid ocean High), whereas in the winter you might still guess westerly, as the Highs are not so well established yet. From 30° N to 10° N, the easy answer is northeast trades, and again fairly easy, from 10° N to the equator being calm or very light doldrums. A climatic snapshot of these patterns is in the previous section (Figure 3.2-7).

The westerlies aloft, on the other hand, are another breed of wind pattern altogether. They are there for the same fundamental reason—part of the complex global circulation that balances out the heat distribution of the earth—but that about ends the analogy with westerly flow on the surface. Prevailing westerlies on the surface and the winds aloft that are also westerlies are two very different wind systems. Their properties and behaviors are quite different and the role they play in our marine navigation is quite different.

We care about the winds on the surface as they are the winds we sail in. We care about the winds aloft because they are the steering winds that guide the storms and other Low pressure patterns across the globe. These winds define the "storm tracks" we see on the TV weather each night, as illustrated in Figures 3.3-1 and 3.3-2.

The serpentine flow of these winds aloft drags cyclones (Lows) of wind along the surface of the earth much as a winding river carries eddies downstream. The long waves in this pattern are called *Rossby waves*, after Swedish-born American meteorologist Carl-Gustaf Rossby. When the winds aloft are from the SW, we look for storms to come from the SW; when they are NW, we look NW. There are typically 4 to 6 waves in the global pattern circling the earth, with wave lengths of 3,000 to 9,000 miles.

Figure 3.3-3 shows how the steering winds aloft slowly change the storm tracks as the Rossby waves in these winds slip slowly eastward. These winds are the reason we must

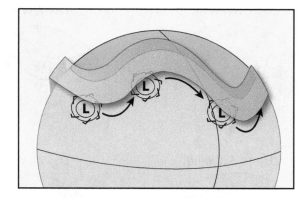

Figure 3.3-2. *Winds aloft creating storm tracks on the surface. A surface Low is shown schematically moving eastward along the storm track of the winds aloft. The total crossing time from trough to trough might be some 4 or 5 days. Surface Lows dragged along the path of the winds aloft bring surface winds from all directions as they pass, but the storm itself is moving easterly. The stronger the winds aloft, the faster the surface storms cross the oceans.*

look west to see what is coming next—or look southwest, or northwest.

We will come back in a moment to look more into the source and behavior of these winds aloft, but for now think more on their role as the steering winds or storm tracks that bring one weather system after the next to us.

Although Lows on the surface move eastward along these tracks—at speeds of some 0.3 to 0.5 times the speed of the winds aloft—the cyclonic circulation within the moving Lows result in surface winds from various directions as they pass.

In the 1740's, Benjamin Franklin was the first person to recognize that storms that cause the wind can move in a direction that is not the same as the way the surface wind is blowing. He was also one of the first people to study the Gulf Stream. He had a larger role in the early development of marine weather than many modern navigators realize.

Since the winds aloft are the steering winds for storms, and the path of the storm can determine the winds we experience, forecasting the flow pattern of the winds aloft is crucial to surface forecasting. We shall also see that these winds not only steer the surface Lows, but also have a great deal to do with their actual development. Strong winds aloft usually mean strong winds on the surface.

In later discussions of onboard observations and forecasting, we go over how you can determine the direction of the winds aloft from observations of waves and other patterns in cirrus clouds. These are the clouds located at the altitudes of these winds. The winds aloft create wave patterns in these clouds much as surface winds make waves in the sea. Then using tricks like the "crossed winds rule" (covered later) we can combine the observed surface wind direction with our determination of the direction of the winds aloft to anticipate whether the approaching Low will pass north or south of us.

The winds aloft are not at one specific altitude (they span a range of altitudes), but the steering winds can often be characterized by those at about 18,000 ft (5,500 m), which in terms of pressure is about halfway up through the mass of the atmosphere. The surface is at about 1,000 mb, so these winds are at about 500 mb pressure, recalling that pressure is simply the weight of the air above you. Most sharp distinctions in surface level air masses have disappeared at this altitude (no frontal boundaries remain) and the air is all cold this high, but these high-altitude winds are still determined by the temperature distributions of the air below them on the surface.

This comes about because the colder air at higher latitudes is heavier and thus the pressure drops faster with increasing altitude than it does in warmer air at lower latitudes, as illustrated in Figure 3.3-4. *This figure is the key to understanding the winds aloft.* If the air temperature were everywhere uniform, then the pressure surfaces at higher altitudes would all be parallel, as shown in the top part of Figure 3.3-5, and there would not be any horizontal gradient or enhanced winds at higher altitudes. But when there is a sharp distinction between air masses, as occurs around the globe at the polar front, then the pressure surfaces slope, and in fact have a sharp discontinuity in the vicinity of the polar front.

Thus the surface temperature difference leads to a sharp horizontal pressure gradient centered at about a 5,500 m altitude, which is usually expressed in this context as 550 dekameters. Note in the figure that at the 5,500-m line drawn there is a prominent pressure change of 700 to 200 mb at that altitude, but just a bit higher at 6,500 m or just a bit lower at 4,000 m, the horizontal gradient is very much reduced, i.e., the distance on earth between where the line cuts the 200 mb surface and the 700 mb surface is very much smaller at about 5,500 m. Thus the winds aloft are strongest at about this 5,500 m altitude, and since the 500 mb surface cuts through that altitude in many cases, the height contours of the 500 mb map are what is used to map out the flow of these winds, as we shall see shortly.

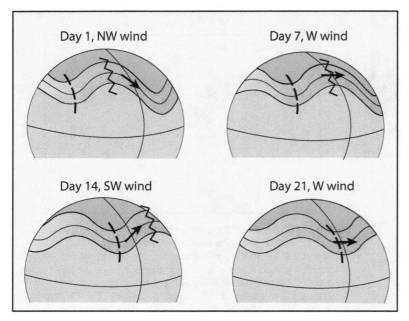

Day 1, NW wind

Day 7, W wind

Day 14, SW wind

Day 21, W wind

Figure 3.3-3. *Winds aloft. The Rossby waves in these winds at about 500 mb slide slowly to the east as shown here bringing our surface weather from slowly changing western quadrants, NW, W, SW, W and so on. Only extremely rarely do the wind patterns distort enough to reach us from the north or south. Note how the wind direction at the meridian shown changes with time. This picture is especially schematic in that the Rossby waves rarely hold their shape as they move across the globe, but rather tend to meander about like the Gulf Stream does as it starts its eastward trip across the Atlantic. This picture is just to show how the direction we look for storms to approach from varies slowly as the Rossby waves of the winds slip eastward. The time scale here is for the long waves, where schematically on average we might see quadrant changes (W to SW or SW to W, etc.) every week or two in this idealized pattern. Significant deviations from this rough average can be significant to forecasting as discussed later on. A short wave trough can cross more quickly. The shading reminds us the air north of the winds is cold. We also see upper level troughs and ridges moving east.*

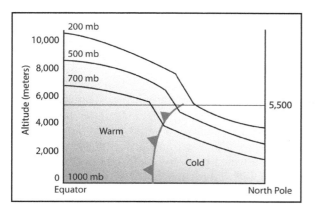

Figure 3.3-4. *Atmospheric pressure as a function of altitude in warm and cold air. In the region of the polar front there is a sharp change in the surface air temperatures, which leads to a discontinuity in the shape of the isobaric surfaces aloft because the pressure drops faster with altitude in the heavier cold air. This in turn creates a horizontal gradient aloft that drives these winds. Notice that this gradient is strongest at about 5500 m (18,000 ft), which explains why the winds are located at that altitude. The 500-mb surface passes through this region of strong gradient, so it is the contour map of that surface that is used by meteorologists to describe the wind flow aloft.*

Winds in this band have average speeds of some 35 kts in the summer to 70 kts or so in the winter. They can be even higher in areas near the polar front, where the winds become focused into the well known jet stream, which can have speeds of 150 kts or more. The overall winds aloft are sometimes referred to as the jet-stream winds, but that might be confusing because the jet stream is actually a narrow jet of wind embedded in the much larger overall flow pattern of winds aloft.

The jet itself is usually stronger than the winds around it (many consider that it must be 60 kts or so to be called a jet), and its axis is generally higher, at about 300 to 200 mb, near the top of the troposphere (Figure 3.3-6). The jet by definition is also a focused band of wind. It is some 50 to 250 miles wide and some 5,000 ft thick—a sample cross-section is 150 kts maximum at 25,000 ft (7,620 m), slowing to 50 kts above and below, at 30,000 ft (9,150 m) and 20,000 ft (6,100 m). The winds aloft, and the jet stream in particular, have a big influence on transcontinental or transoceanic air traffic, making eastbound flights significantly faster than westbound flights.

As seen schematically in several figures here, the winds aloft are shown in a serpentine path around the globe made up of long Rossby waves. It is fair to ask why this wind is waving; all we know so far is it started as pressure gradient flow toward the poles and was then curved to the right by the Coriolis force. For something to wave you have to have some balance between a driving force (such as wind on the surface of the ocean) and some restoring force (such as gravity in the case of water waves in the ocean). In the case of the Rossby waves, the driving force is the latitude dependence of the strength of the Coriolis effect: the higher the latitude the stronger the force.

Thus as the wind progresses to the north, the farther it goes the stronger the force to the right, until it bends enough to head back south again, but going south the force becomes weaker, so it heads back north again. And so on, making an irregular waving pattern as it proceeds east. Later in the section on cyclogenesis (formation of Lows) these Rossby waves come up again because the winds

Figure 3.3-5. *Isobaric surfaces on the earth. If we consider the altitude of all points above the earth's surface that are at some specific pressure, such as 500 or 250 mb, then a map of those altitudes is like a topo map of the earth. Here we have a cross sectional view of several surfaces under different temperature conditions on earth. In the top picture the air temperature is uniform over the earth and so the isobaric surfaces are all parallel. In the second picture the air temperature gradually changes from warm at the Equator to cold at the North Pole, so we see the isobaric surfaces uniformly compressing at higher latitudes. In the third picture we see the more common case of a frontal border between cold air to the north and warm air to the south. This leads to a discontinuity in the isobaric surfaces and thus to a large horizontal pressure gradient at about 500 mb, as discussed in Figure 3.3-4. The bottom picture shows schematically the winds aloft flowing eastward along this discontinuity. In Figures 3.3-1 and 3.3-6 we see actual global maps of these wind patterns. The concept of this figure is from the excellent online meteorology course from Lyndon State College.*

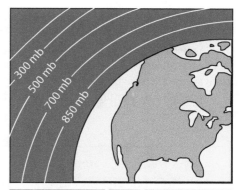

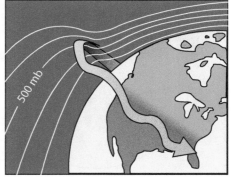

in them speed up and slow down as they turn corners along these waves, and these changes in speed in the winds aloft contribute to the development of Lows on the surface. Looking ahead, wind always rises in a Low, so if this rising air gets pulled away upstairs by fast moving winds aloft it will remove air from the system and thus deepen the surface Low—i.e., the divergence aloft is greater than convergence at the surface.

Figure 3.3-7 shows the type of map of the 500-mb surface that is used in marine weather. Also shown is the corresponding surface analysis map, with the cold and warm fronts indicated that separate cold and warm air masses.

The use of these 500-mb maps is presented in Section 7.8, where we discuss their value in understanding the surface analysis and forecasts, as well as how to use them to evaluate the surface analysis maps. It is important to remember there

will always be a forecast, and in marine weather these forecasts are not marked good or bad. In reality some are better than others, and these 500-mb maps can help us make this judgement ourselves.

In contrast, mountain weather and fire weather forecasts always come with some statistical evaluation of their dependability, much as the TV weather tells us there is an 80% chance of rain. In marine weather, we do not get "80% chance of gale." We either get a gale warning, or we don't, which is further affected by a reasonable tendency to be conservative. Probability forecasting, however, is gaining ground on all fronts, so we are likely to see it in marine weather at some point. Ensemble forecasting (discussed later) is a step in that direction, but really the same thing.

Special terminology is used when discussing winds at the 500-mb level. There is a broad classification of the flow as

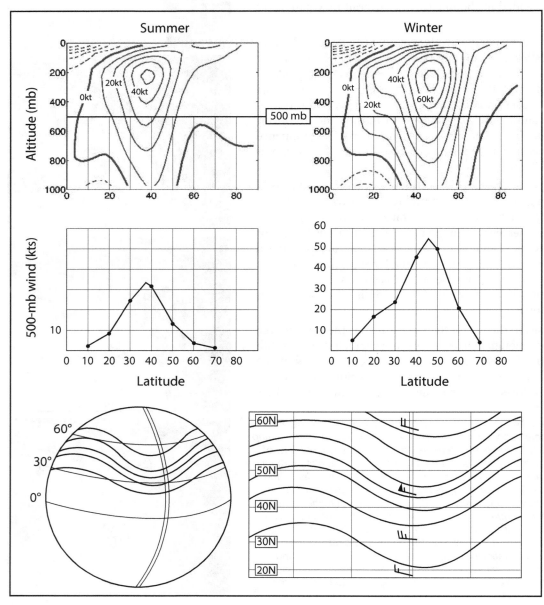

Figure 3.3-6. *The jet stream within the winds aloft. The top two figures show a profile of the winds aloft as a function of altitude and latitude. Imagine this as a cross section along some specific longitude line as illustrated in the bottom left sketch. Lines of constant wind speed are shown. The jet stream is seen at about 250 mb altitude—higher, stronger and more focused than the general flow of the winds at the 500-mb level. The jet is about 50 kts in the summer and 70 kts in the winter. Winds at the 500-mb level have been projected down and plotted in the middle two figures.*

The left side represents a summer situation, the right side a winter situation wherein the temperature difference between North Pole and Equator is about twice as large. A schematic 500-mb map of these winds is shown in the bottom right to show how these winds are represented. The top two figures are computations of Gerber and Vallis in the Journal of the Atmospheric Sciences, Volume 64, Issue 9 (September 2007), pp. 3296–3311

either *zonal* or *meridional* (Figure 3.3-8). Zonal flow means the Rossby waves have stretched out so the flow is mostly due east in a more or less straight line path. The winds can pick up a lot of speed in this pattern, which can bring one storm after the other across the ocean in quick succession.

Meridional flow means along a meridian, having a large north-south component to the flow. Steep waves can go due north or south, or even reverse for a sort of retrograde motion.

Within a meridional flow pattern there are several types of waves that occur often enough to have names, as shown in Figure 3.3-9. The uniform passage of a Low across the ocean

can be interrupted significantly by one of these perturbations in the flow. The omega block in particular can sometimes wrap around the mid-summer Pacific High and lock the High in place like a vise for a week or more—though this pattern is more often seen in the transitional periods of the spring and fall. Cutoff lows at the 500-mb level can have a significant influence on the surface weather.

The Rossby waves themselves are called *long waves* as they are the ones that can span full oceans or continents with one wavelength. Riding along on these long waves are *short waves*, (see Figure 3.3-10) that are the perturbations that lead to weather patterns on the surface below them. Chapter

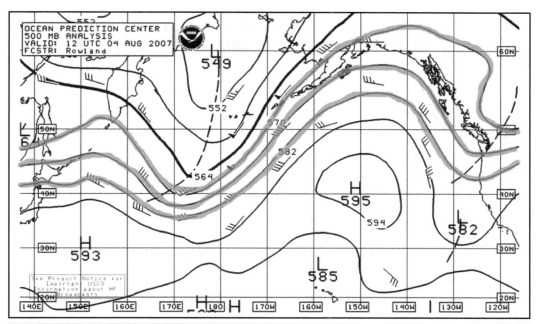

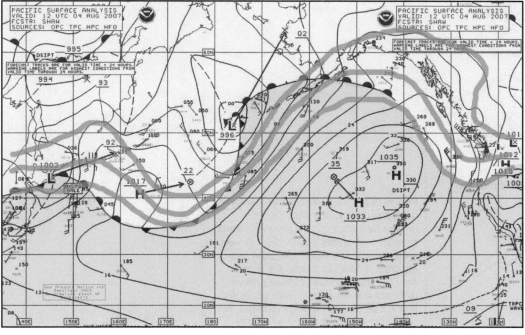

Figure 3.3-7. Top. *A 500-mb analysis map showing the altitudes of the 500-mb isobaric surface. These maps are used to map the winds aloft for marine weather applications. The lines are altitude contours, analogous to elevation contours on a topo map. The height units are dekameters; 564 dekameters = 5,640 m. This is a rare unit, essentially unique to this map.*

The 5640 meter contour is bold on these maps as it offers several guidelines to surface weather below it (Section 7.8). We have highlighted the three lines in purple that are overlaid below on the corresponding surface analysis map.

Bottom. *The corresponding surface analysis map, showing that the wind flow aloft often follows along the boundaries (fronts) between cold (blue) and warm (red) air on the surface, which has been marked here by shading. In the winds aloft we see a short wave (155E) creating a trough (175E) ahead of it in the long wave pattern.*

These are both maps from the first edition, but the style and content of these maps have not changed much, other than removing the vessel IDs from ship reports, and the 24-hr motion of Highs using circled Xs was discontinued in 2018.

The 500 mb maps are available from GFS in GRIB format, so we can now make overlays of this type underway at any time, as shown later in the book. Figure 7.4-8 shows more examples of this comparison.

4 covers the development of Lows and fronts and how the troughs and ridges created by these short waves in the winds aloft lead to storm development on the surface.

These short waves ride along on the long waves much as wind waves ride along on ocean swells. They can thus add or detract from the overall amplitudes of waves in the winds aloft in the same manner. In Figure 3.3-7, you can see a short wave in the winds aloft just entering into the trough of a long wave. The shortwave trough it is creating ahead of it is contributing to the development of the surface Low seen just to the east of it.

3.4 Atmosphere, Air Masses, and Stability

The Atmosphere

The part of the atmosphere we care about for surface weather is called the troposphere. It is the more or less uniform fluid of air surrounding the earth that is on average about 11 km (36,000 ft) high in the midlatitudes, but can reach some 17 km (55,000 ft) in the warm air of the equator and falls to some 7 km (23,000 ft) in the cold air of the poles. The density of the air is highest at the surface, decreasing with altitude. The air is roughly three times thinner at altitudes where commercial airliners cross the globe, and twice that high, it is essentially gone.

As we leave the surface and rise in the atmosphere at any latitude, the air temperature drops at a linear rate of about 3.6 F° per 1,000 ft till we reach the top of the troposphere (called the tropopause), which is defined as the altitude at

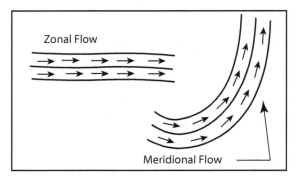

Figure 3.3-8. *Zonal versus meridional flow. Zonal flow means mostly due east, and often fast. Meridional means more of a north-south component to the flow. Figure 3.3-7 shows meridional flow all across the ocean.*

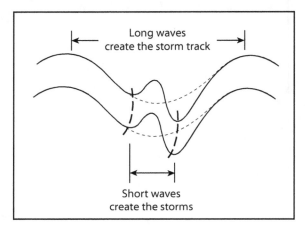

Figure 3.3-10. *Short and long waves in the winds aloft. See examples in Figures 3.3-1 and 3.3-7.*

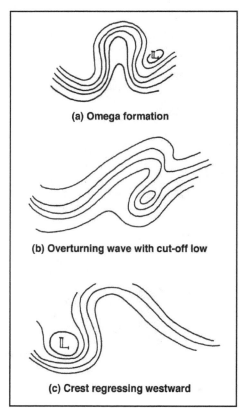

(a) Omega formation

(b) Overturning wave with cut-off low

(c) Crest regressing westward

Figure 3.3-9. *Perturbations in the flow patterns of the winds aloft. (a) The omega formation can be relatively small or span a complete ocean. (b) A forward crest leading to a cutoff low. (c) A receding crest leading to a potential cutoff low. The significance of these patterns to forecast evaluation is covered in Section 7.8 on use of the 500-mb maps. An actual omega block is shown later in Section 10.3.*

which the temperature stops falling and begins to rise. The temperature of the air at varying altitudes above the earth's surface is a complex balance of heat loss and heat gain.

Within the troposphere, the sun heats the earth and the earth heats the air. As the air rises away from its heat source, its temperature drops. Above the tropopause, the air contains an important band of ozone that absorbs energy from the sun, so the process reverses and the air gets warmer with altitude throughout what is called the stratosphere. Then this too changes farther up, and it gets colder again. For marine weather we care only about the troposphere, where the temperature generally drops with increasing altitude—except for the occasional temperature inversion, where it actually warms briefly.

The tropopause, however, is at a very high altitude, higher than we care about for most marine weather considerations. Although the narrowly focused jet stream does follow along just below the level of the tropopause, we care more about the much broader band of strong winds aloft at about the 18,000 ft level, where the pressure is about 500 mb (Section 3.3). Most of what we call weather is below 18,000 ft (or 500 mb).

Pressure drops as we rise in the atmosphere because there is less and less air above us, and pressure is simply a measure of the weight of the air above us. At the surface, the pressure is about 1000 mb (global annual average is more like the standard atmospheric pressure of 1013.25 mb, see Appendix 2), so at 500 mb we are halfway up through the mass of the atmosphere.

From there on up, the pressure continues dropping exponentially, such that after another 18,000 ft we are down by half of that to 250 mb and then after another 18,000 ft, we are down to about 125 mb. The jet stream at the top of the troposphere is at about 250 mb. About 75% of the mass of the atmosphere and nearly 100% of its water vapor is contained in the troposphere. Meteorologists also study higher layers of the atmosphere, but these do not affect our considerations.

The composition of the atmosphere is 78% nitrogen, 21% oxygen, and 1% of other gases, mainly argon and about 0.4% carbon dioxide. Mixed in with these gases is a few percent of water vapor by volume—near 0% for very dry air and some 4% for warm moist air. A global average is about 1%.

Needless to say, there are a lot of reasons to study and care about the atmosphere these days besides its effect on wind and waves, but they are beyond the scope of this study. There are many excellent online treatises on global warming, air pollution, alternative energy options, and related topics, often compiled under the broad heading of Earth Systems Science.

The density of air at the surface is about one thousand times lighter than water, but it is of course still a fluid with mass, like water, and thus has many similar fluid properties and interactions—just as does a fluid of water vapor condensed onto dust particles (low clouds) or a fluid of pure ice crystals (high clouds)... or a fluid of sand in the desert. Wind can thus make waves in the clouds, just as it does on water or

sand, and these cloud waves will prove useful to us.

For practical marine weather (wind!), we care primarily about just three specific altitudes in the atmosphere, illustrated in Figure 3.4-1.

First, there is the 500-mb level (discussed in the last section) at about 18,000 ft that is used to track the strong winds aloft that steer surface weather patterns across the globe and contribute to the formation of Lows on the surface. Maps of these winds offer a sometimes useful way to evaluate the dependability of surface forecasts.

Second, there is a level at somewhere around 2,000 ft where the frictional influence of the earth's surface no longer affects the flow of air. This is called the top of the *boundary layer*, or sometimes planetary boundary layer. Above this level (in the *free atmosphere*) wind flow is nearly geostrophic, parallel to the isobars. Below this level, the wind flows across the isobars as discussed in Chapter 2.

Finally, there is a thin layer of air just above the surface that can be useful for sailors to know about. Within this layer, the first 30 to 100 ft above the surface, the effects of friction on the air flow are strongest and sometimes erratic. This is called the surface boundary layer or sometimes just surface layer or ground layer. Above this layer the wind begins a more

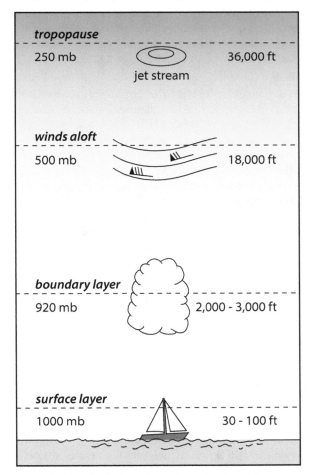

Figure 3.4-1. *Altitudes in the atmosphere of interest to mariners. All altitudes and pressures are approximate as they vary significantly with latitude, season, atmospheric conditions, and time of day.*

uniform increasing veer and increasing speed with increasing altitude, as it gets farther from the surface and feels less and less influence of surface friction. Within this shallow surface layer itself, however, it is more difficult to predict how the wind changes with altitude. The way the wind changes with altitude in this layer depends on the sea state, the stability of the air, and on the surface wind speed itself.

In light air (less than 5 or 6 kts), smooth seas, and stable conditions, wind speed will notably increase with altitude, rising just off the surface within the surface layer, but in stronger winds, speed and direction will be much more uniform within the surface layer. Most "surface-wind" reports are given as valid at 10 m (33 ft) above the surface, perhaps to avoid much of this variability.

We can often see from the cockpit what is taking place at each of these three distinct altitudes in the atmosphere. We visually see what is going on at about 18,000 ft in the motions and patterns of high clouds. Waves in cirrocumulus made by the winds around the 500 mb level show us which way these winds are blowing, and from this we can tell which way storms will approach. The procedure is similar to judging the true surface wind direction from the orientation of waves and whitecaps on the water surface. The NWS provides maps of these winds aloft that describe the wind flow in terms of the altitude of the 500 mb pressure surface expressed in dekameters on the 500-mb maps. Thus we have this one specific region of the atmosphere described in various contexts as either the 500 mb level, or 18,000 ft, or 5,500 m, or 550 dekameters.

We see visual effects of the boundary layer altitude by looking at the motion of low clouds. Face the true surface wind direction, and you notice that low clouds approach from some 15° to 40° to the right of the wind direction in the NH. The elevated winds moving these clouds (above or near the top of the boundary layer) are veered from the surface winds, because they are less influenced by surface friction. Likewise a building sea breeze will veer as the day proceeds in the NH, because it comes down to us from these higher altitudes as it builds. Gusts are also veered, because they are patches of higher air that have swooped down to the surface temporarily. These are all friction effects that we can understand knowing that elevated winds are stronger and veered.

We can see visual effects of the surface layer when we have different winds at the masthead than on deck in light air, but none or little change with height above deck in stronger air. Directional changes in wind at the masthead compared to on deck are harder to detect since an increased speed at the masthead (even without a veer) pulls the apparent wind aft at the masthead because the boat speed does not have time to change. We have to look for changes in sail trim on opposite tacks in light air to make conclusions about wind direction changes from deck to masthead. Or maybe compare our measured wind direction (which is at the masthead!) with the directions of ripples on the surface.

These visual observations of three distinct levels in the atmosphere are good reminders that the final wind we sail in on the surface is the result of three-dimensional interactions; it is not just high pressure one place pushing wind into lower pressure at another place. We will see more of this as our study progresses, and we learn how to picture what is going on at each of these levels to help us interpret surface winds and how they might change.

There is one notable exception to a statement made earlier that all weather we care about is below some 18,000 ft, and it is one that mariners care a lot about. Giant thunderstorms (squalls to mariners) can extend from a very low ceiling all the way to the top of the troposphere. Their clouds, called cumulonimbus, are an exception among clouds, not low and not high, but both. These huge convective cells are the largest things on earth, bigger than the pyramids, bigger than mountains. They can contain giant-lake-fulls of water at high altitudes.

Air Masses

In the midlatitudes, many weather patterns can be traced to the movements of large bodies of air, called air masses. They can be as large as 1,000 miles or more across and maintain their identity halfway or more up to the 500-mb level. They are characterized by uniform values of temperature and moisture content—sometimes with additional descriptions of their stability. The temperature is uniform horizontally across the air mass, but still decreases with altitude, but the moisture content is more homogenous in both directions. A region under the influence of an air mass usually experiences similar weather conditions throughout the air mass.

The formation of an air mass requires a large flat base area with uniform properties as well as atmospheric conditions that let the air remain stagnant over that location long enough for the air to assume the properties of the base, at least 3 to 5 days or so. The center of a large stationary High is a common source. Typical air masses that approach U.S. waters are shown in Figure 3.4-2.

Air masses are characterized by their temperature (relative to neighboring air) as warm (called tropical, labeled T) or cold (called polar, labeled P) and their moisture content. Moist air is called maritime (labeled m) and dry air is called continental (labeled c). All labels reflect their location of origin; maritime air is formed over the water, making it moist and continental air is formed over land, making it dry. Warm air comes from the tropics (or at least low latitudes) and cold air comes from higher latitudes, though not necessarily from the polar regions. There is also a classification for Arctic air, but this air mass has less common influence on marine navigation. Thus we have mT (maritime tropical) air meaning formed over warm water and mP (maritime polar) air formed over cold water.

When the air mass starts to move away from its source—which by necessity did not have much weather associated with it—the weather around it and within it begins to change. If cold air moves onto warmer water, it not only changes the local air temperature, but the warmer surface can now start vertical motion of air within the air mass. What happens then depends very sensitively on how much moisture is in the air and precisely how fast the temperature is dropping with altitude within the air mass (both are matters of stability, discussed shortly).

Thus the atmospheric engine has been turned on, and the weather we get will depend on the temperature, stability, and moisture content of the air mass at hand. When there is a distinct boundary between adjacent air masses, the two-dimensional surface between them is called a front, named during the era of the First World War when the concept of a battle-line front was well known to all. Figure 3.4-3 shows schematically how bordering fronts are represented on a weather map. Warm and cold fronts are potentially strong-wind systems, fundamental to marine weather.

Stability

Stability is a general term that describes how the state of a physical (or emotional!) system will respond to a small perturbation. A ball in the bottom of a bowl is in *stable equilibrium*—disturb it slightly and it will return to where it was, even though it may roll around a bit while returning to the old system. A ball resting on the top of an inverted bowl is in *unstable equilibrium*—disturb it slightly and it will roll off and be gone; the old system has changed and won't return on its own. A ball within a smooth indent in the top of an inverted bowl is in *conditional equilibrium*. Disturb it a little

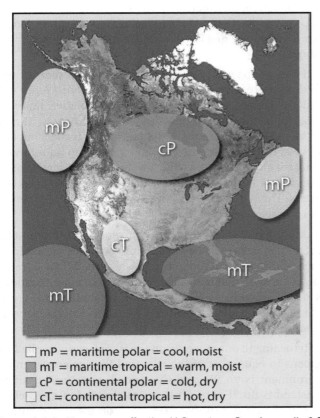

Figure 3.4-2. *Air masses affecting U.S. waters. See Appendix 6 for a world view of air masses.*

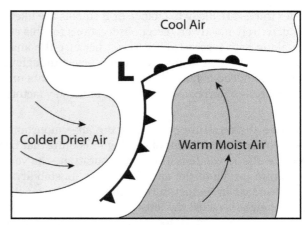

Figure 3.4-3. *Distinct boundaries between air masses are called fronts, which are depicted on weather maps with unique symbols, covered in Section 4.3.*

and it returns to its original position; disturb it more and it is gone. Figure 3.4-4.

Stable air is a state in which the *vertical* distribution of the atmosphere is in hydrostatic equilibrium (like the ball in the bottom of the bowl) so that an air parcel resists displacement from its original level. In these stable conditions, if an air parcel is forced up it cools more than the surrounding air, so it sinks back down. If it is forced down, it warms more than the surrounding, so it floats back up.

If the atmosphere is unstable, air parcels that start up keep going up. The stability of an air mass is determined by how its temperature varies with altitude, which in turn depends on how much water vapor is in the air. The stability factor is crucial to the development of squalls and Lows, and even without such a system nearby, it determines whether we have steady winds or gusty winds, and it determines what kind of clouds we see in the sky.

Stable air is characterized by stratiform clouds, or no clouds. If there are clouds, then just looking at them you can see there is little vertical action taking place. Unstable air is characterized by cumuliform clouds with vertical development, where just as obviously you can actually see vertical flow of the air, sometimes bubbling out at the tops. Stable air usually implies steady wind with no change expected, often a poorly defined cloud ceiling and maybe poor visibility, and if there is rain, it would be steady. Unstable air implies gustier surface winds with likely changes at hand, sharp cloud bases, often good visibility, and sporadic rain (showers).

It is valuable to be able to judge atmospheric stability from looking at the sky and present conditions to anticipate

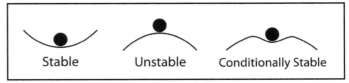

Figure 3.4-4. *Types of equilibrium.*

whether things are likely to change or if squalls are likely. In the end, we rely mostly on direct observations for this evaluation, along with forecast discussions, because the analysis of the related weather factors is complex—even though these days we can indeed obtain all the meteorological data underway. For present purposes, we just look at the key factors involved.

Besides the moisture content of the air—important because it controls the amount of heating or cooling that might take place due to condensation or evaporation—the vertical temperature profile of the air is crucial to its stability. The rate of decrease in temperature in the atmosphere with increasing height is called the lapse rate. The lapse rate of the International Standard Atmosphere (ISA) is 3.6 F° per 1,000 ft of altitude. It represents an average over the globe and seasons, but just like average pressures, it is not necessarily valid at any particular time or place. The ISA (Appendix 2) was developed to aid in the design of aircraft. To investigate atmospheric stability, however, we must consider other lapse rates.

The actual lapse rate at some place and time is called the *environmental lapse rate*, or ELR. This could be higher or lower than that represented by the ISA. It varies from place to place, and with time, and with altitude. It is essentially just a list of altitudes and the corresponding temperatures. The rate of decrease can change with altitude or even reverse, which is called a *temperature inversion*. The ELR (and other data) is measured several times a day with weather balloons—the instrument onboard is called a radiosonde; the data are called RAOB. The measurements are taken from as many locations as feasible, and the results are compiled and entered into the several computer models that are keeping track of the earth's atmosphere at various laboratories around the world. The models then predict how the ELR will change as the atmosphere evolves. Worldwide sounding data are available at 00z and 12z, which accounts in part for why the 00z and 12z forecasts using this data have special significance. Weather synopses are also published at these times.

The next step is to ask how a parcel of air is going to rise up through a particular ELR—which immediately brings up two key points to understanding the stability analysis used by meteorologists. What is this ubiquitous "parcel of air" used in every description of the process, and what exactly is meant by "rising up"?

Recall the little island with the palm tree in Section 3.1—Warm Air Rises. Before the sun came up, all the surface air around the island was the same temperature. Then the sun heated the island more than the adjacent ocean, and the heated island heated the lowest layer of air over the island itself, but not over the adjacent ocean. Thus we have sitting on the island surface a "parcel of air." It is not only warmer than the adjacent air, it is warmer than the air above it, and it may have a relative humidity different from adjacent air.

Because it is warmer (and lighter) than the air above it, it is going to start to rise. In this case it starts off by simply

floating up. But later in the morning, when the sea breeze develops, it will be pushed up by air coming in from all directions. So that is another way to force air to rise. Air can also be pushed up the side of a mountain by an onshore breeze, or bull-dozed up on the vertical edge of a moving cold front, or it can be pulled into a Low from all sides (convergence) and thus forced to rise. There are numerous mechanisms that cause air to rise. This is called *lifted air*. What happens then depends on the stability of the air mass the parcel is in, which in turn depends on how the ELR changes with altitude.

The next key point to understand is how air is considered to rise in this analysis. First, and foremost, it is assumed that the air in the parcel does not mix with the air it is rising through, and that it does not absorb heat or lose heat to the neighboring air. This is called *adiabatic* rising. All the action is within the air parcel itself. It will expand as it rises into lower pressures and as a result it will cool, but the cooling is all from within, not caused by the temperature of the environmental air it is rising through. The whole issue of stability is how much does this parcel cool as it rises compared to how much the temperature of the environmental air is changing. Both parcel and environment are typically getting cooler with altitude, but not at the same rate—and the environmental rate can also reverse (an inversion), at low or at high altitudes.

We don't know what the environmental lapse rate will be at any given time (it can change with altitude), but we can compute what the parcel rate will be from basic physics. If the air is not saturated (called "dry," meaning it contains less than the maximum amount of water vapor it can hold for its temperature, Section 3.5) the parcel temperature will drop at what is called the *dry lapse rate* (DLR), which is 5.5 F° per 1,000 ft.

If the air parcel is already saturated, it's temperature will drop more slowly, at what is called the *moist lapse rate* (MLR) of about 3 F° per 1,000 ft. The relative humidity makes this difference. As unsaturated (dry) air cools, its relative humidity just goes up, but as saturated (called "moist") air cools, it must condense its water vapor into liquid water, because it already holds as much water vapor as it can. When it condenses it gives off heat, which slows down its cooling process. Thus the MLR is lower (rising air cools more slowly; stays warm longer) than the DLR.

Unless we are in fog to begin with, most air starts up at the DLR until it cools to its dew point (and becomes saturated) at which time it starts to cool more slowly at the MLR—a transition, by the way, that marks the cloud base in most situations, because this condensed liquid water is what makes the cloud. Note that the ISA lapse rate (3.6 F°/1,000 ft) is in between the MLR (3 F°/1,000 ft) and the DLR (5.5 F°/1,000 ft).

Returning to our morning on the island, suppose the ELR happens to equal that of the ISA, and the surface air in the environment is 70 °F, and the heated, unsaturated air on the island is 80 °F. The air starts to rise and after reaching 1,000 ft the air parcel that originated on the island surface has dropped to 74.5° (80 - 5.5). At that altitude the air outside the island parcel is 66.4° (70 - 3.6), so the parcel is still warmer than its environment and keeps going up.

At 3,000 ft the parcel has cooled to 63.5° (80 - 5.5 × 3) and the environment has cooled to 58.5° (70 - 3.6 × 3), so it still rises. But by the time it gets to 6,000 ft the parcel will have cooled to 47° (80 - 5.5 × 6), whereas the air around it has cooled to 48.4° (70 - 3.6 × 6). Our parcel has overshot the equilibrium point and is now colder (heavier) than the environment, so it will sink back down. We leave it as an exercise to show that they will come to equilibrium with equal temperatures at 5,263 ft.

Consider next what happens when we take into account the moisture in the air. Suppose this 80° island air starts off with 70% relative humidity in the morning, corresponding to a dew point about 69 °F (Section 3.2). Now we have to take into account that as the air rises and gets cooler its dew point is going to get lower as well. Its relative humidity is going up and its dew point is going down. This takes place at a *dew point lapse rate* of about 1 F° per 1,000 ft until the air becomes saturated (temperature equals dew point), and from then on it cools at the MLR. As a parcel of air rises in the atmosphere its dew point drops by about 1 F° per 1,000 ft—actual values vary, but we use this value for now.

In the first 2,000 ft things progress as before, the island air is down to 69° (80 - 5.5 × 2) with its dew point down to 67°, and the outside air is down to 62.8° (70 - 3.6 × 2). Now, however we cannot make it all the way to 3,000 ft at the DLR, because the parcel temperature would be 63.5° whereas the dew point will only have dropped to 66°. We passed the saturation point. If you work out the algebra you see that at 2,444 ft the parcel air temperature has dropped to its dew point at that altitude, and moisture in the air will start condensing into clouds.

One way to estimate the condensation level in this example is to note that the difference between temperature and dew point is dropping at the rate of 5.5 - 1.0 = 4.5 F° per 1,000 ft, so we could estimate the condensation level (CL) in this example as: cloud base = 1,000 ft × (air temperature - dew point) / 4.5, where both temperatures are at the surface. In our example: $(80 - 69)/4.5 = 2.444$ thousand feet. This estimate of a cloud base would only be applicable to building clouds in the morning (lifted condensation level, LCL). Furthermore, actual dew point lapse rates vary significantly. The difference factor of 4.5 used here could range between 2 and 5. The LCL can be calculated more precisely from actual sounding measurements (or forecasted soundings based on numerical models), which measure (or predict) the air temperature and dew point as a function of altitude. Such data, presented as skew-T diagrams, are the primary means of predicting cloud levels, as well as the overall stability of the air. Sources for these diagrams are listed in Table 3.4-1.

Returning to the example, once the island air is saturated it will cool at the MLR of 3°/1,000 ft, whereas the environment is cooling at 3.6° per 1,000 ft (in this schematic example). In other words, from this point on, the environment is

Table 3.4-1. Skew-T Diagrams		
RAOB	GFS	Source
x		weather.uwyo.edu/upperair/sounding.html
x		weather.rap.ucar.edu/upper
x		spc.noaa.gov/exper/soundings
x	x	rucsoundings.noaa.gov/gwt (interactive)
	x	ZyGrib, XyGrib, and Expedition

cooling faster than the rising air, so the island air will keep on rising. It is completely unstable at this point unless something changes. In the air over islands in the trade wind zones, what usually happens is, at about 3,000 ft or so, the ELR changes to cap off these little puffy clouds into trade wind cumulus. If this does not happen and there are adequate amounts of warm moist air to rise, they will instead keep building into much taller squall clouds.

The lapse rates referred to are summarized in Table 3.4-2 with units conversions, because most actual data are presented in metric units. Figure 3.4-5 summarizes the relationship between stability and lapse rates, which forms the basis of a skew-T diagram, as shown in Figure 3.4-6.

As mentioned earlier, we are not going to be able to do much analytically with these concepts underway, which are beyond the scope of practical marine weather, but we can see the processes taking place. With a low ELR , or even an inversion (gets warmer going up, not cooler), we can experience calm air, with thin layers of radiation fog, which is common in periods of high pressure on inland waters. These are very stable conditions.

In some conditions of warm ocean waters, after the sun sets the air temperature can drop below the seawater temperature, which leaves a layer of very unstable air near the surface. What happens then depends on ELR. In squall prone waters, we can often judge, from cloud types forming and their vertical development relative to base height, what we might expect squall-wise for the evening. We pursue this idea later in Section 4.6 on squalls.

There are several numerical properties of the atmosphere that are derived from the skew-T profile (ELR curve) that we do have access to underway that could help determine the probability of squalls or increased convection in some circumstances. Two of these are the *lifted index* (LI) and the *convective available potential energy* (CAPE), which are measures of the instability of the air. Actual measurements are only available from land stations (at 00z and 12z), but

Table 3.4-2. Lapse rates		
Standard Atmosphere	6.5 C° / km	3.6 F° / 1,000 ft
Dry (DLR)	10 C° / km	5.5 F° / 1,000 ft
Moist (MLR)	5.5 C° / km	3.0 F° / 1,000 ft
Dew Point (approx.)	2-4 C° / km	1-2 F° / 1,000 ft
Conversion: (C°/km) × 0.549 = (F°/1,000 ft)		

Table Notes: *The MLR increases as the air cools and becomes drier, approaching the value of the DLR.*

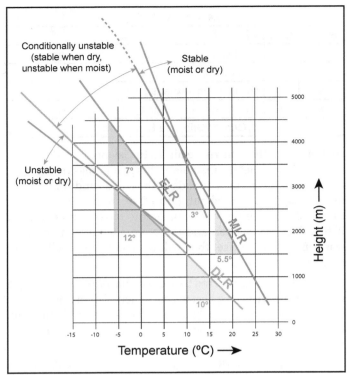

Figure 3.4-5. *Rising unsaturated air cools at the DLR (10ºC/1km), shown as an orange slope. (Skew-Ts always use metric units.) Once the rising air is cool enough to be saturated, it cools more slowly at the MLR (5.5ºC/km) shown as a blue slope. (At higher altitudes with temperatures below freezing, moist air becomes dryer and the MLR increases, approaching the DLR value, as indicated by the dashed blue line.)*

Red slopes indicate various possible ELRs. When rising air finds itself cooler than the environmental air, it stops rising, and becomes stable. Thus dry air is stable whenever its ELR ≤ DLR. The 7º and 3º ELRs are stable for dry air.

Likewise, moist air is stable whenever its ELR ≤ MLR. The 3º ELR is stable for moist air, as would be one with a 4º or 5º slope, not shown.

An ELR that is in between the DLR and MLR, such as the 7º example shown, is called conditionally unstable Its stability depends on the moisture content of the air. It is stable for dry air, but unstable for moist air. This condition also changes with decreasing temperature as the MLR increases. This picture is a key to understanding the skew-T diagrams (below), which rotate (skew) the temperature scale to the right so the ELR curve is nearly vertical over a large altitude range.

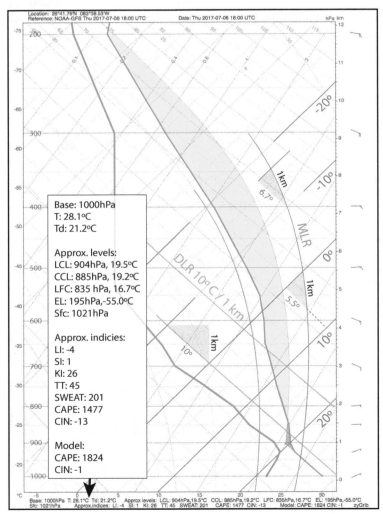

Figure 3.4-6. *A GFS forecasted skew-T diagram downloaded from ZyGrib; Expedition also offers these diagrams underway. These are complex diagrams of a tremendous amount of crucial information for forecasting. They are a Rosetta Stone for meteorologists, but more like a Tower of Babel when first approached by we mortal sailors! We annotated this one and added the insert of parameters derived from the curve, listed on the bottom edge. Altitude in km is on a linear scale on the right; pressure in mb is on a log scale of the left.*

The raw data plotted are the red line showing air temperature as the air rises (cooling at the ELR) and the green line showing dew point versus altitude. A cloud base would likely form at the altitude these two lines touch, but an accurate cloud base can still be found from this diagram when they do not touch. Multiple plots of the DLR and MLR curves are shown on the page so slopes can be compared to the ELR.

We see here air rising in a stable manner at the DLR (orange slope) until it becomes saturated at about 800 m, after which it rises at a lapse rate that is in between DLR and MLR, which makes it conditionally unstable for this now saturated air. (Note the MLR curving over to nearly match the DLR at subzero temperatures.)

The convective consequences of this unstable air (clouds only, squalls, or thunderstorms) depends on the specific shape of the ELR, which is characterized by several derived parameters (indices) listed in the insert. It takes a trained meteorologist to properly interpret these numbers, but the guidelines of Table 3.4-3 might offer a way for us to learn if any useful correlations can be made in the waters we sail. CAPE, LI, and CIN are GFS parameters that can be downloaded from many nav programs underway to assist with convective activity forecasts.

The yellow shading is the CAPE value of this ELR curve. It is area between the ELR and the MLR, between about 850 mb and 200 mb. The red shading is the CIN value. It is defined as the area to the left of the ELR between the surface and about 850 mb. This is more prominent when the ELR is smaller than the DLR at lower levels. See starpath.com/wx for links to more discussion of these diagrams.

Stability	Convection	LI	CAPE	SI	TT	SW
			Table 3.4-3. Stability Parameters Derived from a Skew-T Diagram			
Very stable	No activity	> 3	<0	>3		<50
Stable	Showers possible, TSTM unlikely	0 to 3	< 0	1 to 3		50 to 150
Marginally unstable	TSTM possible	-2 to 0	0 to 1000	-2 to 1	45 to 50	150 to 250
Moderately unstable	TSTM likely	-4 to -2	1000 to 2500	-3 to -4	50 to 55	250 to 300
Very unstable	Strong TSTM possible	-6 to -4	2500 to 3500	-6 to -4	55 to 60	300 to 400
Extremely unstable	Strong TSTM likely	< -6	>3500	< -6	>60	>400

Table Notes: *LI = lifted index; CAPE= convective available potential energy; SI = Showalter index, TT = total totals, SW (SWEAT) = severe weather threat. We also see in GFS data the parameter CIN = convective inhibition. NOTE these correlations apply only to local convective activity. Tropical and extra tropical storms once formed are characterized by other parameters. A hurricane can have zero CAPE. Convective activity correlated with these parameters have been developed mostly on land where surface heating is much different than at sea, so we must use these only as potential guidelines. Simulated radar reflectivity may likely be our best convection forecaster underway. See Table 4.6-3 and related text.*

these properties are computed in the GFS model, so we can get this data in GRIB format for any point on earth.

LI is obtained by computing the temperature that air near the surface would be if it were lifted to the 500 mb level, and then comparing that temperature to the actual temperature at that level. Negative values indicate instability—the more negative, the more unstable the air is, and the stronger the updrafts are likely to be with developing thunderstorms (Table 3.4-3).

CAPE is a measure of the buoyancy of the air. Both parameters are discussed extensively online as they are used by storm chasers around the globe who offer tables of thunderstorm probabilities based on these values. The NWS warns us, however, that there are no magic numbers or threshold values that can reliably be used to make these predictions on their own.

CIN (convective inhibition) is conceptually the opposite of CAPE. It represents the amount of energy needed to push cooler air up through warmer air above it. An area with high CIN is likely stable with little likelihood of squalls. CAPE is expressed as positive energy; CIN as negative.

One way to study the usefulness of these predictors for navigators is to monitor the coastal text forecasts for warm water areas prone to squalls (see Figure 4.6-5) looking for thunderstorm predictions. Then compare these parameters (CAPE, CIN, LI) available from GFS for zones calling for numerous (60-70%) and likely (>80%) thunderstorms, with nearby regions where no thunderstorms are forecasted. See also Table 4.6-1. The forecasters are using these data, among others, to make these forecasts. The simulated weather radar images discussed in Section 4.6 are very promising for forecasting squalls. They are a much more direct prediction than we can put together from these skew-T parameters.

3.5 Water—The Fuel of the Atmosphere

Just about every aspect of marine weather is dominated by water. The statement could be much stronger—life itself is dominated by the unique properties of this one molecule. But it is very specifically a controlling factor in marine weather. It is the surface we ride on (70% of the earth's surface) and the fuel for the wind that often dominates the navigation of all vessels, power, sail, paddle, and oar. A basic understanding of its properties is key to understanding the most important driving forces in the atmosphere.

Humidity is the amount of water vapor in the air; a property that has a crucial effect on the weather of that air. Water vapor is just water molecules in gaseous form (as opposed to liquid form). Water is the only substance that can exist in both liquid and gas forms at earthly temperatures—solid ice makes it even more unique. Not only does the likelihood of fog depend on the humidity, but so does the vertical stability of the air, which in turn determines the likelihood and fate of squalls and storms. Humidity is commonly expressed in terms of either dew point or relative humidity.

At most, there is only a few percent of water vapor in the air at any time, but these few percent often determine the winds and weather we observe. This small amount of water vapor is the fuel of the atmospheric engine. When air rises it cools, and when it cools the water vapor condenses into liquid water which gives off heat. This makes the surrounding air warmer and lighter than it was before, so the air rises more, eventually building huge convective cells of cumulonimbus clouds, which in turn lead to strong gusty winds on the surface as air rushes in to replace that which went up.

Whether we have little white puffy fair-weather cumulus skies with light air, or towering black cumulonimbus with 40 kts of wind, is often determined by differences of just a percent or so of water vapor in the air. Whether we have 20 miles visibility or fog so thick we can't see the bow, again can depend on differences of a few percent of water vapor in the air. To see how all this comes about, we take a closer look at how water behaves and how it interacts with air.

Water molecules, whether in the surface layer of the ocean or in a glass of drinking water, are in constant motion which causes them to periodically break loose from the surface and enter the air above it. The escaped water molecules make up an invisible gas of water vapor that mixes with the air molecules. When any of these water molecules in turn strike the surface, some of them stick and are re-bonded into the liquid water. Consequently, the boundary between liquid water and air is undergoing a constant exchange of water molecules back and forth from the liquid to gaseous stage. When there are more water molecules leaving the surface than returning to it, the result is evaporation. When more are sticking on the surface than leaving it, it is called condensation.

Whenever liquid water is placed in an enclosed container of pure dry air (0% water vapor in it), water vapor will begin to enter the air through evaporation. As time goes by, the percent water vapor increases, and as it does, the rate of condensation back into the liquid form increases with it. Eventually, the processes of evaporation and condensation balance out in a dynamic equilibrium condition, after which the amount of liquid water does not change nor does the amount of water vapor in the enclosed air. This equilibrium condition is called *saturation*, and it occurs at water vapor concentrations in the air of some 1 to 10 percent (by mass, at surface temperatures). The exact percent varies with the temperature of the air. Table 3.5-1 shows these limits as a function of temperature expressed in terms of vapor pressures. Also included in the table are the densities of water vapor expressed as the number of grams of water in each cubic meter of air.

One might ask why the saturation limit at, say, 68 °F, is 2.3% instead of, say, 23% or 46%? First—and this may seem surprising—it has nothing at all to do with the air. This limit is purely a property of water itself. Even if the water were exposed to pure neon gas rather than air, the equilibrium amount of water vapor in the neon at 68 °F would be the same. Even if liquid water were placed in an evacuated jar at 68 °F, eventually the pressure in the jar would rise to an equilibrium value (about 23 mb in this case) due to a gas of pure evaporated water, and the same number of water molecules would be in the previously empty container as there were when the container was initially filled with air. In other words, the actual amount of water vapor present in air is determined by the temperature of the liquid water present, not

the air surrounding it. When we say the air temperature is such and such, we make the tacit assumption that the liquid water in the air (which is condensed onto airborne particulates as mist, drizzle, cloud droplets, or rain drops) is also at this temperature.

Hence it might be helpful to clarify some terminology. We often speak of air "holding" water vapor, or we say "warm air can hold more water vapor than cold air," and so on, bringing forth the image of air acting as a sort of sponge. This is misleading in a sense. Air is not so much holding water vapor, as just coexisting with it. As stated above, the air itself has nothing to do with the amount of water vapor present; it is only the temperature of the water in the air that matters, which is for practical purposes the air temperature itself. In another sense, it doesn't matter how we say it as long as the concept is clear. Warm air can hold more water vapor than cold air, but it is a property of water we are referring to, not air.

The key property involved is called the vapor pressure of water, which is related to the molecular structure of its individual molecules and its surface. The fact that water has a vapor pressure of 23 mb at 68 °F is a fact of nature, much the same as saying it has a freezing point of 32 °F. Gasoline, for example, has a vapor pressure of some 170 mb at 68 °F and a freezing point of -70 °F. We could say that saturated air at 68 °F contains 2.3% (23.4 mb/1013.25 mb) water vapor, just as we would say that air saturated with gasoline contains some 17% gasoline vapor (170 mb/1013 mb)—note the gasoline values are rough guesses.

The saturation limits on water content in the air (or of any liquid in any gas) depend on temperature because the speed of molecules depends on the water temperature. The higher the temperature, the faster the surface molecules are moving which gives them more energy to break free of the surface bonding. In the enclosed container example, we assumed that the water and air temperature had equalized by the time saturation set in. Real air masses in contact with wa-

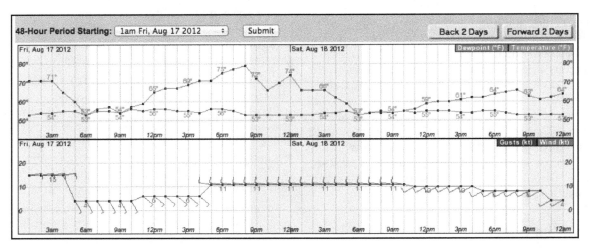

Figure 3.5-1. *Predicting fog by measuring or reading forecast temperature and dew point trends as a function of time. This type of plot is often called a* meteogram. *They are readily available online from the NWS and universities. Meteograms based on GFS or other model predictions are also available in several navigation programs. This forecast implies fog at sunrise (temp falls to dew point), burning off at 10 or 11 am, which adds much to the text and broadcast forecasts that simply called for "morning fog." Clear nights with large temperature drops overnight (characteristic of high pressure) often lead to morning fog.*

ter rarely reach saturation throughout the air mass, but they can do so in the thin layer next to the surface if the air is still. This layer is then mixed into the air mass by wind circulation, which increases the relative humidity of the air. Evaporation therefore also depends on wind because the wind mixes the surface layer of air, which keeps it from becoming saturated. Evaporation would be equal to condensation when saturation was reached.

The term *relative humidity* is used to describe the amount of water in the air relative to the maximum amount that can be present for that temperature of the air. At 77 °F, for example, a relative humidity of 80% means the air contains 80% of the water it can, which from Table 3.5-1 is 3.1% (or 23 grams of water for each cubic meter of air). In other words, 77 °F air with a relative humidity of 80% contains (0.8 × 3.1 or) 2.5% water vapor. Note from the table that this air would be saturated if it dropped to about 68 °F. Samples from a relative humidity table are in Table 3.5-2.

Once the air is saturated, no more water vapor can enter it, regardless of how much water is present. The air in between rain drops or snow flakes, for example, is saturated, as is the air supporting fog or clouds.

The amount of moisture in the air is a key factor to understanding the weather. But when considering the moisture content of air, it is usually the temperature that is more important than the relative humidity itself. Consider North Atlantic air in a snow storm with 100% relative humidity at 15 °F, compared to an off shore breeze in the Red Sea at 105 °F with only 10% relative humidity. Which has the most water vapor in it? See Table 3.5-1 for the answer. The very warm air, even at a very low relative humidity, has some 2.5 times more water in it than does very cold air at 100% relative humidity.

Summary: Air always contains a small amount of water vapor. It is typically about 1% (measured by weight or partial pressures), but it can be as high as 6 or 7% for saturated very warm air. Relative humidity is the ratio of the actual amount of water vapor in the air to the maximum amount

it can hold at that temperature. As the temperature of an air parcel drops, the relative humidity will rise since the amount of water vapor in the parcel is not changing, but the amount it can hold is going down with temperature. As the temperature is lowered further, it will eventually reach the dew point, which is the temperature at which the air becomes saturated. When the air temperature equals the dew point, the relative humidity is 100%, the air is saturated, and moisture becomes visible. Samples from a dew point table are in Table 3.5-3.

Once we know the air temperature, knowing the dew point is equivalent to knowing the relative humidity of the air as far as the moisture content is concerned, although there is not a simple conversion between them. Usually tables or special computations are required. Generally relative humid-

Table 3.5-1. Saturated air composition				
Dew Point/ Saturation Temp		Water Vapor Content		
°C	°F	%	mb	g/m³
100	212	100.00	1013.3	598.0
95	203	83.42	845.3	505.0
90	194	69.20	701.1	
85	185	57.05	578.1	
80	176	46.75	473.7	293.8
75	167	38.05	385.6	
70	158	30.80	311.7	
65	149	24.69	250.2	
60	140	19.70	199.3	130.3
55	131	15.54	157.5	104.4
50	122	12.20	123.4	83.1
45	113	9.80	98.9	65.5
40	104	7.20	73.8	51.2
35	95	5.50	56.2	39.6
30	86	4.20	42.4	30.4
25	77	3.10	31.7	23.1
20	68	2.30	23.4	17.3
15	59	1.70	17.0	12.8
10	50	1.20	12.3	9.4
5	41	0.86	8.7	6.8
0	32	0.60	6.1	4.8
-5	23	0.42	4.2	3.4
-10	14	0.28	2.9	2.4
-15	5	0.18	1.9	1.6
-20	-4	0.12	1.3	1.1
-25	-13	0.08	0.8	0.7
-30	-22	0.05	0.5	0.5
-35	-31	0.03	0.3	0.3
-40	-40	0.01	0.2	0.2
-45	-49	0.01	0.1	0.1
-50	-58	0.01	0.1	0.1

Table Notes: *Saturated water vapor content in air as percentages, pressures, and densities. This table has two distinct applications depending on what we call the temperatures on the left. If the temperature is that of the air, the data are for the saturated condition at that temperature, but if the temperature is the dew point, then the data are actual values for that dew point. (Values at temperatures below freezing are slightly smaller over ice, compared to the over water values shown.)*

Example 1: *at an air temperature of 77 °F, air can contain up to 31.67 mb of water vapor, which is 31.67/1013.25 = 3.1% water vapor, although it might at the time only hold 1 or 2%.*

Example 2: *if we have air with 1.7% water vapor in it, then the dew point of that air is 59 °F, regardless of its temperature. As the temperature of that air sample changes, its relative humidity will change, but its dew point won't.*

Example 3: *if the dew point is 50 °F, the table tells us that air contains 1.2% water vapor. We cannot know the relative humidity of this air until we know its temperature. If its temperature is, say, 77 °F, then the table tells us that air could hold as much as 3.1%. Hence its relative humidity would be 1.2/3.1 or 39%. Note that the density of liquid water is 1 gram per cc, so we can picture the water content by considering, say, 29 grams of water as 29 cc, which is equivalent to 1 fluid ounce. Use the units converter to figure how much water is included in a room of such and such dimensions if the air has a certain temperature and relative humidity.*

Dry	Dry bulb minus wet bulb																								
°F	1	2	3	4	5	6	7	8	9	10	11	12	13	14	15	16	17	18	19	20	21	22	23	24	...
...	...	...	...	...	...	...	...	...	...	...	...	...	...	...	...	...	...	...	...	...	...	...	...	...	...
60	94	89	83	78	73	68	63	58	53	48	43	39	34	30	26	21	17	13	9	5	1	—			...
62	95	89	84	79	74	69	64	59	54	50	45	41	37	32	28	24	20	16	12	8	4	1	—		...
64	95	89	84	79	74	70	65	60	56	51	47	43	38	34	30	26	22	19	15	11	8	4	—		...
66	95	90	85	80	75	71	66	61	57	53	49	44	40	36	32	29	25	21	17	14	10	7	4	—	...
68	95	90	85	81	76	71	67	63	58	54	50	46	42	38	34	31	27	23	20	16	13	10	7	3	...
70	95	90	86	81	77	72	68	64	59	55	51	48	44	40	36	33	29	26	22	19	16	12	9	6	...
72	95	91	86	82	77	73	69	65	61	57	53	49	45	42	38	34	31	28	24	21	18	15	12	9	...
74	95	91	86	82	78	74	69	65	62	58	54	50	47	43	40	36	33	30	26	23	20	17	14	11	...
76	95	91	87	82	78	74	70	66	63	59	55	51	48	45	41	38	35	31	28	25	22	19	16	14	...
78	96	91	87	83	79	75	71	67	63	60	56	53	49	46	43	39	36	33	30	27	24	21	18	16	...
80	96	91	87	83	79	75	72	68	64	61	57	54	50	47	44	41	38	35	32	29	26	23	20	18	...
...	...	...	...	...	...	...	...	...	...	...	...	...	...	...	...	...	...	...	...	...	...	...	...	...	...

Table 3.5-2. Sample Relative Humidity Table (%)

Table Notes: *Relative humidity table (selection). Relative humidity is given as a function of (dry bulb) air temperature and the dry-bulb minus wet bulb temperature difference, as measured with a sling psychrometer. Dots means further values are not shown; dash means values less than 1. At 70° if the wet bulb is suppressed by 7°, the relative humidity is 68%. From Figure 3.5-3, we learn that this corresponds to a dew point of 59°.*

ity is a better measure of how the air feels (muggy, dry, etc.), but dew point is more useful for predicting visible effects like fog or estimating cloud bases.

If the air temperature is 70 °F in near coastal waters and the dew point is 62 °F, then we could well expect fog on a clear night as we could expect the air temperature to drop at least 8° without the sun. As an exercise, show that these are conditions with a relative humidity of 77%. Figure 3.5-1 shows how a measure of dew point and air temperature can be used to predict when fog will set in.

We just have to practice to decide whether the difference between dew point and air temp or the relative humidity in percent is a better measure for practical evaluations of humidity. When the relative humidity is 100%, the air temperature equals the dew point and the height of the clouds (stratus) is zero. We are in fog. But what exactly does RH=50% mean to weather analysis? These numbers probably mean more to comfort and maybe good health on land.

It is rare to see tables that convert directly from dew point to relative humidity, since it would take one for each temperature. Most tables are designed to be used with measurements of the humidity and are expressed one way or the other in terms of air temperature and "suppression of the wet bulb temperature."

Humidity measurements usually involve measuring two temperatures: a *dry bulb* temperature (the normal air temperature) and a *wet bulb* temperature, which is a rather special temperature. The difference between these two temperatures is then used to look up either the dew point or the relative humidity. A sample is shown in Table 3.5-3

If you have only these typical tables available and want to convert dew point to relative humidity, you must first go to the dew point tables to work backwards to find the suppression of the wet bulb, and then use this suppression value in the relative humidity tables to find relative humidity.

It is easy, though, to see how the wet bulb temperature is just what we need to measure to get at the humidity in the air. The typical device used to measure humidity is called a sling psychrometer. It is two identical thermometers mounted on a handle with a pivot so it can be swung around in a circle. This slinging process is just a way of putting a good wind onto the instrument if it happens to be calm. One thermometer is a normal one called the dry bulb. The other is covered by a clean cotton wick, which must first be wetted in distilled water before slinging it (the wet bulb).

Wind on the wet bulb causes evaporation which cools it, so the wet bulb temperature is always lower than the dry bulb. The amount lower depends on how much evaporation takes place, which in turn depends on how much water vapor is in the air. If the air is already saturated, no evaporation occurs and the wet bulb equals the dry bulb.

The mathematical relationships that relate the amount of evaporation to amount of humidity, and amount of cooling to amount of evaporation, are complex and to some extent empirical. Hence the final analysis is usually done with tables of data rather than formulas.

Although a sling psychrometer may seem a handy device, there are some cautions to be noted. Accurate measurements are not as easy as they might appear. It is crucial that the wick and applied water remain pure in order to obtain good data. Salt spray is a serious wick contaminant that will invalidate the data, and it is difficult without extra care and extra equipment to insure that this is kept clean. Remember, you will always get a suppressed wet bulb, but whether it is suppressed the right amount is another question. You typically

Dry	Dry bulb minus wet bulb																								
°F	1	2	3	4	5	6	7	8	9	10	11	12	13	14	15	16	17	18	19	20	21	22	23	24	...
...	...	...	...	...	...	...	...	...	...	...	...	...	...	...	...	...	...	...	...	...	...	...	...	...	...
60	58	57	55	53	51	49	47	45	43	40	38	35	32	28	25	20	15	9	1	-11	-39	...	...	...	...
62	60	59	57	55	54	52	50	48	45	43	41	38	35	32	29	25	20	15	9	1	-12	-45	...	...	...
64	62	61	59	57	56	54	52	50	48	46	43	41	38	35	32	29	25	20	20	15	9	0	-13	-52	...
66	64	63	61	60	58	56	54	52	50	48	46	44	41	39	36	33	29	25	21	15	9	0	-14	-59	...
68	67	65	63	62	60	58	57	55	53	51	49	46	44	42	39	36	33	29	25	21	16	9	0	-14	...
70	69	67	66	64	62	61	59	57	55	53	51	49	47	45	42	39	36	33	30	26	21	16	9	0	...
72	71	69	68	66	64	63	61	59	58	56	54	52	50	47	45	43	40	37	34	30	26	22	16	10	...
74	73	71	70	68	67	65	63	62	60	58	56	54	52	50	48	46	43	40	37	34	31	27	22	17	...
76	75	73	72	70	69	67	66	64	62	61	59	57	55	53	51	48	46	44	41	38	35	31	27	23	...
78	77	75	74	72	71	69	68	66	65	63	61	59	57	55	53	51	49	47	44	41	38	35	32	28	...
80	79	77	76	74	73	72	70	68	67	65	64	62	60	58	56	54	52	50	47	45	42	39	36	32	...
...	...	...	...	...	...	...	...	...	...	...	...	...	...	...	...	...	...	...	...	...	...	...	...	...	...

Table 3.5-3. Sample Dew Point Table (°F)

Table Notes: *Dew Point table (selection). Dew point is given as a function of (dry bulb) air temperature and the dry-bulb minus wet bulb temperature difference, as measured with a sling psychrometer. Dots means further values are not shown. At 70° if the wet bulb is suppressed by 7°, the dew point is 59°.*

have to be up close using a magnifying glass to read the temperatures accurately, and in still air your own body heat can radiate enough to shift the thermometers.

To complete this general background on humidity, we have one last point to look at. Why does evaporation cause cooling and condensation cause warming and what exactly is cooled and warmed in the process? We will see that this question is closely related to the basic scientific concept of energy conservation and how atoms and molecules are bound together in solids and liquids.

Water molecules are bound together in chains and these chains are in turn bound together in the surface. The binding takes place in large part due to the electromagnetic attraction between negative and positive parts of neighboring molecules. Work must be done on the molecules to break them apart. Whoever does this work is going to lose energy in doing so. One way to look at the process is to imagine the air molecules continually bombarding the water surface and each time they hit it they impart a certain amount of energy to the surface. Some of the collisions might by chance hit a molecule that is already moving fast within its own statistical distribution of speeds. That collision then might significantly slow down the colliding air molecule while at the same time (since total energy must be conserved) giving an adequate kick to the water molecule it hit to set it free.

In other words, if a lot of evaporation takes place, then a lot of energy has to be transferred from air to the liquid water, which means the temperature of the air must go down. In the process of adding energy to water, two things take place. Some of the energy goes to raising the temperature of the water and some of it goes to breaking lose its molecules in evaporation. The part that caused evaporation is not raising the temperature of the water at all, but just changing its phase from liquid to gas.

Instead of thinking of water on the surface of the ocean evaporating, we can apply the same idea to clouds evaporating. Consider, for example, a cloud of water droplets (liquid water condensed onto a speck of dust), that happens into a high pressure region that pulls the cloud down into warmer air near the surface. As the cloud descends each of the water drops in it absorbs heat from the neighboring air (and from radiation from the earth), which warms some of them and evaporates others. The warm ones, on the other hand, now have an even higher probability of evaporation, and eventually they all evaporate, and in so doing cool off the neighboring air. Highs have clear skies for exactly this reason.

Condensation heating is just the opposite of evaporation cooling, but to understand it, we must carefully note who is heating whom. We have two gases coexisting, one made up of water vapor and the other air. While the water molecules are in a gaseous phase, they have much energy due to their motion, but when they condense into the liquid phase they have much less energy of motion. The difference is in a sense the energy they give up to the surrounding air. The over all temperature of the gas (water plus air) is due to the motion of all of its molecules, but if we remove the motion energy of the water molecules this difference must be picked up by the air molecules.

Pursuing the collision analogy, if two high speed molecules have glancing collisions, they would not slow down much, and nothing special would happen. But some collisions between air and water vapor molecules will leave the water molecule traveling at a very low speed while the air molecule leaves the collision at a higher speed. When this takes place near a water droplet, the vapor molecule is likely to make a slow collision with the water drop and stick. Hence the net effect of such interactions is to increase the average temperature of the air as it converts water vapor into water liquid.

Regardless of the details of the mechanisms, however, when water evaporates it cools the air and when it condenses it heats the air. And the amount of this heat transfer by these processes (called *latent heating*) is in fact very large. For each gram of water that undergoes this phase change, some 540 to 600 calories of heat is transferred, depending on the temperature of the water. For comparison, the complete combustion of 1 gram of gasoline yields some 11,000 calories.

When we consider the thousands of tons of water condensing in even a small squall, it is easy to see how latent heating can give rise to such violent winds, not to mention its contribution to the overall heating and cooling of the earth's atmosphere itself.

Heating and cooling of the atmosphere can take place by either conduction and convection (together called sensible heating) or by latent heating. Over land these two processes are roughly equal, except over dry deserts where there is only about half as much latent heating. But over the oceans (more than 70% of the earth's surface) latent heating is some 10 times more important than sensible heating. Warm moist air is not only the fuel of storms, it is the fuel of the entire atmospheric engine. It is crucial to the overall heat distribution on the planet and hence to our very existence.

Properties of Water

Liquid water is made up of two positive hydrogen ions and one negative oxygen ion arranged as a polar molecule with a positive and negative end. This polar structure gives rise to pure water's ability to withstand electrical conductivity (high dielectric constant) and to its high performance as a solvent, as well as to its relatively high freezing point.

Water ions form chains of up to 8 molecules, which require energy to form and thus accounts for water's ability to absorb energy and transport it around the globe. The circulation of the oceans contributes about an equal share with atmospheric circulation of the air in the overall distribution of heat from the tropics to the remainder of the globe.

Water is one of the few substances on earth that we can see or experience at reasonable temperatures in all its phases, solid, liquid, and gas. Its remarkable properties include: highest heat capacity of all common liquids and solids, highest latent heats of fusion and evaporation of all substances, highest surface tension of all liquids, dissolves more substances and in greater quantities than any other liquid, and highest dielectric constant of any liquid.

As distinguished from seawater, "fresh water" has a salinity of less than 0.5 parts salt per 1,000 parts of water. For comparison, typically pure river water contains 0.1 parts of salt per 1,000 parts of water. Brackish water is considered to have salinity of 0.5 to 17 parts per 1,000. Typical seawater has a salinity of 35 parts per 1,000, with variations over the oceans from about 34 to 36. Human taste buds can detect salt in water at about 1 part per 1,000.

Ninety percent of water vapor in the air comes from evaporation of surface water and 10% from transpiration of plants.

3.6 Primary Ocean Currents

Current flow and sea state are oceanography not meteorology, but to a mariner they are an integral part of the marine environment that we cannot separate from the broad topic of *marine weather*. Many decisions mariners make depend on currents and sea state as much as they do on the wind itself. And, as we shall see, wind, current, and sea state are intricately tied together in a way that is fundamental to our safety and efficiency underway.

We can describe current flow according to the navigation regions illustrated in Figure 3.6-1. These are not official geographic or oceanographic demarcations; they simply provide a way to discuss practical matters of current flow, which in broad terms is different in these regions.

Region 1. Inland

When sailing on inland estuaries, local currents (mostly tidal) can be a key factor to your navigation. Procedures and sources for predicting current flow are covered in standard navigation texts (see, for example, the author's *Inland and Coastal Navigation*, which has an extended coverage of currents). The main flow along the centers of channels is fairly well predicted in most cases. Along the edges, predictions are more difficult. The starting point is usually the *NOAA Tidal Current Tables*, or some electronic equivalent. Printable annual versions are online. The dramatic interaction of wind and current that determines wave steepness (discussed below) applies to these waters, as it does to all sources of current in any waters.

As a guideline you can assume that the current predictions right at (or very near) the point they are being predicted will be accurate in normal conditions to within about ±20% in speed and about ±20 min in timing. Things that cause variation from normal are persistent strong wind, unseasonal river runoff, and exceptional atmospheric pressures. The effects of wind, depth profile, and shape of the waterway are discussed in the navigation text cited above.

Inland currents are typically (not always) *reversing currents,* which mean they have only two primary directions, flood and ebb. The speed changes throughout each cycle, but the direction of flow within a cycle does not change much.

Region 2. Nearshore

Current flow within a mile or two of a coastline is typically the result of a complex set of forces. Contributing factors include tidal current, wind-driven current, prevailing offshore ocean circulation, and local currents running parallel and perpendicular to the shoreline caused by the surf. Near headlands, bays, or entrances to inland waters, the coastal flow also is strongly affected by the shape of the coastline.

Unusual *hydraulic currents* can also flow along a coastline with no wind or waves, nor any tidal changes. They are the result of a sloped water surface returning to level. For example, suppose there is a section of coastline (on the west coast) running due north for a hundred miles, which then curves prominently to the northwest, and runs for another hundred miles or so. This corner creates a geographic pocket of sorts that can influence current flow along the coast. If this corner were exposed to strong steady southwest winds for a day or more, the slope of the water would actually increase somewhat with a pile of water leaning against the corner—

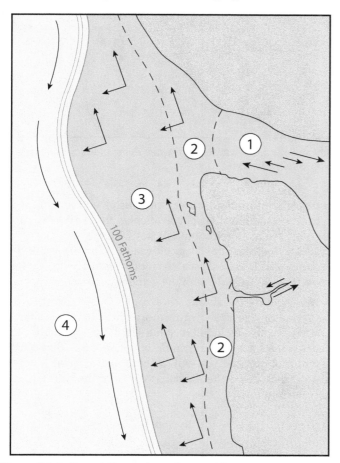

Figure 3.6-1. *Descriptive regions of current flow.*

Region 1: *Inland, represents inland waters with typically reversing tidal current flow, fairly well predicted in mid-channel from Tidal Current Tables.*

Region 2: *Nearshore, means a mile or two off the beach, generally a more complex zone with several different sources of current flow.*

Region 3: *Extends out to the deep water off the continental shelf. Current in this region is typically a combination of wind-driven and tidal. Tidal current in coastal waters rotates throughout the day. The arrows shown here indicate a time when the current was all flowing offshore and then 3 hrs later it is all flowing north. See Figure 3.6-2 for two samples of full cycles.*

Region 4: *Deep water, more the domain of global current flow resulting from ocean gyres. Climatic predictions in this region can be found in pilot charts and Sailing Directions. Real-time data comes from ocean model forecasts or HF radar measurements. Wind-driven currents, however, can be found in all waters, regardless of location. Ocean gyres are predominantly wind-driven on a global scale.*

and stay that way as long as the wind is blowing. When that wind dies off, the pile of water will seek equilibrium and create a significant south-flowing current along the shore for a day or so.

Because so many forces influence the flow, it is difficult to predict coastal currents without local knowledge. Nevertheless, these currents are important to nearshore navigation because they can severely hinder progress along routes that are exposed to sudden weather changes. The height and direction of swells also can change in a few hours with no change in local weather, as wave remnants of distant storms first reach the coast. Coastal currents can vary significantly in speed and direction at any one location and vary rapidly and irregularly from point to point along a coast. Although in many areas the currents farther offshore are fairly well understood by local mariners and documented in *Sailing Directions*, it is questionable whether much of the knowledge gained from extensive traffic of larger vessels farther offshore can be extrapolated shoreward into the nearshore domain.

Because there is so little data for the region that lies just outside of the surf zone, it is important to measure the current yourself using GPS as often as possible when transiting nearshore routes. (Current is the vector difference between your compass and knotmeter readings and your COG and SOG, read from the GPS.) It might then be possible to correlate this information with the state of the tide, wind speed and direction, lay of the land, and state of the surf, and gain some insight into the local current behavior that might help plan the rest of the trip. Nearshore current is a difficult subject in oceanography. When dealing with currents in these waters, your surprise threshold must be fairly high.

HF-Radar (HFR) Current Data

Luckily in many U.S. Coastal waters we have a wonderful resource based on HF-radar measurements (HFR). These stations measure the coastal currents in near real time, and they are readily available online and on smart phones (Figure 3.6-2). Each area will have to be checked to see how close to the shore the data are usable. Each station has resolution options that can affect this. The data extend 60 to 100 nmi offshore, depending on station and resolution, which means they can cover Regions 2, 3 and 4 in some cases. With one of these stations covering the waters you care about, you have accurate current information updated as often as every hour in some cases. You can also download a KML file, for use in Google Earth, that will show you the currents in your region of interest that are automatically updated. Each time you go to that page, you see latest values. Each data point also offers a detailed history of the current flow, which is helpful for making your own forecast. This resource provides actual measurements, but not forecasts. These HFR current data are a notable achievement of modern coastal navigation.

Current Region 3. Coastal Waters

Here we refer to waters more than a couple miles offshore out to the continental shelf. This area lies between the nearshore zone and the deep water off the continental shelf. There

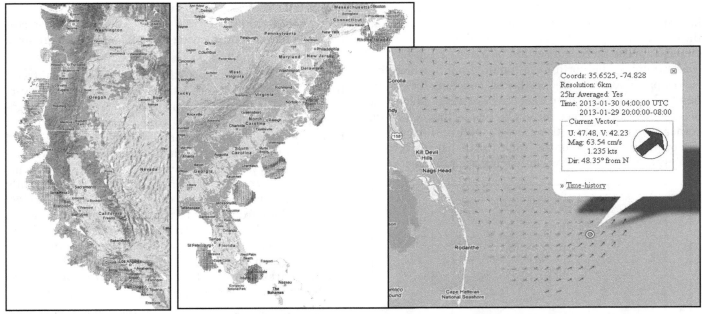

Figure 3.6-2. *HF-radar (HFR) current measurements. Left shows U.S. data locations; also available in Hawaii. Right shows sample data near Cape Hatteras. Data are presented at cordc.ucsd.edu/projects/mapping. See also hfradar.ndbc.noaa.gov.*

is no sharp distinction between this region and Region 2 inside of it, other than the flow is a bit simpler here, being primarily wind driven and tidal, whereas in Region 2 to the inside and Region 4 to the outside, there are other sources that might dominate the flow. Region 3 is covered well in many of the HFR measurements. The tidal influence shows up nicely in the "time history" of the data available throughout the region. For extensive regions, you will see where the tidal influence becomes dominated by the offshore flow. There is typically a notable rotary component in Region 3.

Rotary Coastal Currents

Within Regions 2 and 3, the tidal part of coastal current is typically rotary as opposed to the reversing currents found inland in Region 1. A pure rotary current changes directions without changing speed, so there are no slack waters. Current Tables, *Sailing Directions*, and some nautical charts provide diagrams that can be used to predict the speed and direction of rotating tidal currents based on the times of high and low tides at coastal reference stations. Rotary current behavior can often be spotted in the HFR data as well as in the ocean model forecasts discussed below.

Examples of rotary patterns are shown in Figure 3.6-3. Tidal currents in coastal waters rarely exceed 1 or 2 kts, and well away from the entrances to inland waters the average values are much smaller—although as with all currents, coastal currents accelerate near headlands as they converge and diminish at the mouths of bays as the flow diverges. The rotations are also not purely circular near long open coastlines. The current direction rotates (clockwise in the Northern Hemisphere) through 360° every 12 1/2 hrs or so, but the rate of rotation is not uniform, and the speeds are not exactly the same in all directions. Most tidal streams well removed

from inlets into inland waters flow faster and longer parallel to the coastline than perpendicular to it. Their rotation diagrams are not circles, but ellipses with the long axes lying parallel to the coastline. Near entrances to inland waters, on the other hand, the ellipses are more aligned with the inlet due to the flow in and out of the waterway.

Rotary current data are shown on some Charts (British and Canadian charts show this more often than U.S. charts), and they are also included in some Tidal Current Tables. It is a fact—sometimes less known than it should be—that coastal currents rotate, so if you sail in these near coastal waters it pays to track down the diagrams to make the best guess of likely current flow.

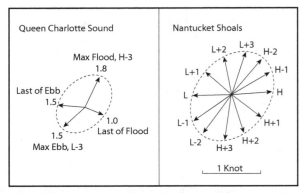

Figure 3.6-3. *Rotary current diagrams from two locations. The direction of the arrows show the set of the current, and the length of the arrows are scaled to the drift speed. The vectors rotate about once every 12.5 hrs. The notation "L+3" means 3 hrs past low water. The left data are from the British Columbia Sailing Directions; the right from the NOAA Tidal Current Tables.*

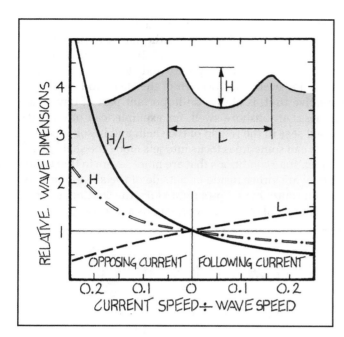

Figure 3.6-4. *Wave steepness as a function of current speed. Developed wind waves move in the direction of the wind at about 0.7 times the wind speed (average properties of the waves are given in Section 5.4). When they meet opposing current, they steepen according to the graph, where H is the height of the wave and L is the length of the wave. A wave in 10 kts of wind would be moving at about 7 kts with a length of about 25 times its height. If this wave traveled against 1.5 kts of current (0.2 times the wave speed), it would steepen by a factor of 3.5, according to the graph, making a wave whose length is only 7 times its height. Waves break at this steepness; so the gentle waves of a 10-kt wind in still water would be breaking in 1.5 kts of current. The graph also applies to swells from ships. These are already steep when produced and moving at the relatively slow speeds of the vessel. Those that are not breaking already will certainly break in opposing current.*

Graphic from Inland and Coastal Navigation, 2nd Edition, *Starpath Publications, 2016.*

See later Figure 5.4-4 to see how this effect can identify current flow patterns, even in fairly light air and weaker currents.

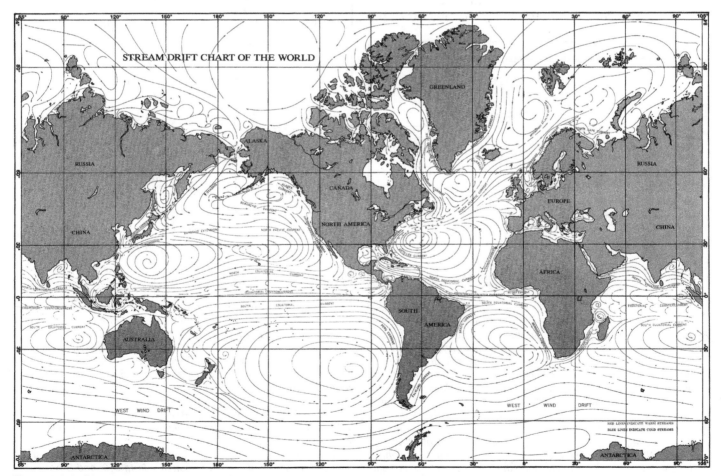

Figure 3.6-5. *Global ocean currents from 2002* Bowditch. *The 2017 edition does not include the graphic, but discusses the individual currents. These are good climatic averages, but satellite measurements and ocean models show that notable and irregular exceptions are common around the world.*

Wind-driven Current

In many areas rotary tidal flow is completely masked by wind-driven current whenever the wind blows steadily for half a day or longer. Expect this contribution to be approximately 2- to 3-percent of the wind strength, directed somewhat to the right of the wind direction in the Northern Hemisphere. If *Sailing Directions*, for example, predict north-flowing currents of 1 to 2 kts at a particular location expect the stronger end of the prediction when the wind blows toward the north and the weaker end of the prediction when the wind blows toward the south.

Wind-driven currents tend to be stronger in heavy rains because brackish water slips more easily over the denser salt water below it. All waters are subject to wind-driven currents, even land locked lakes.

Current Region 4. Offshore

As used here, we mean off the continental shelf, in deep ocean waters. The ocean currents discussed later in this section generally circulate around the main ocean basins much as the wind would flow around a large mid-ocean High, which should not be too much a surprise as they are basically large-scale wind-driven currents. These currents are strongest along the edges of the oceans, but the effective "edge" is often located along the continental shelf, rather than up against actual land—not always, but in many cases. Thus the best current reckoning on and off the shelf can be quite different in different parts of the world. In other cases the oceanic circulation does ride up onto and along the continental shelf. In any event, the location of the shelf, and where you are relative to it, is always an important part of navigation awareness. An onshore swell, for example, can often make confused seas in the region of the shelf, and in some regions currents can sometimes focus into jets along the shelf, giving rise to sea state conditions that are more severe in that region than they are either inside or outside of the shelf boundary. An ocean route that follows right along the continental shelf has the potential of being the worst possible choice!

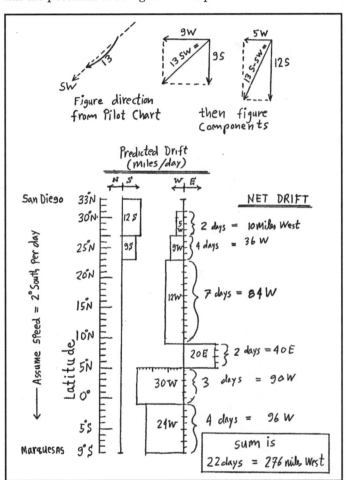

Figure 3.6-7. *A current log figured from a pilot chart. Pilot charts show currents as arrows flying with the set of the current, labeled with the drift in nautical miles per day (some use knots). First lay out your planned route on the pilot chart, and then record the currents and latitudes at which they change such as 13 nmi toward SW, or 13 to the S-SW, after the current changed. Then figure the components of the currents as indicated in the figure by drawing them to any chosen scale, and from these make a plot or table of the results. Then with an estimated speed, you can figure your net set over different legs of the voyage.*

This example is for a run from San Diego to the Marquesas at an average speed of 6 kts. The data are from U.S. and British pilot charts. In this example, you would want to make some progress east before you got to the southeast trades, to compensate for the large westerly set. Adapted from Emergency Navigation *by David Burch*

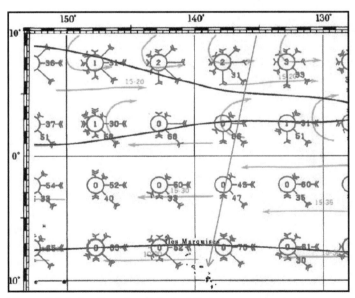

Figure 3.6-6. *Section of a pilot chart that shows current drift in nautical miles per day (green arrows). Notice that the predicted values can sometimes span a large range—15 to 35 as an extreme case in this section. Generally we might consider the values given as accurate to ± 50%, so 12 nmi per day could be anywhere from 6 to 18 per day. When the wind is strong and persistent, flowing with the current, then the higher end is likely; in weak or contrary wind, the lower end would be likely.*

We see the equatorial countercurrent affecting this route from roughly 2° N or 3° N to 7° N or 8° N. The U.S. and British versions of the chart do not agree exactly along this route. Recent data from an ocean model could be helpful. More aspects of pilot chart usage are covered in Chapter 8. Some pilot charts show double green lines marking the climatic borders of the countercurrent.

Offshore currents can be predicted by ocean models (discussed below) and incorporated into optimum route planning.

Current and Wave Steepness

A common but elusive current concern to all small-craft navigators is fast water flowing into strong wind. This is an ever-present concern in strong tidal waters, but it can be an equally serious matter in strong offshore currents such as the Gulf Stream. The waves are moving forward in the direction the wind is moving, and when they meet a contrary current they slow down. Their kinetic energy is converted to potential energy and they build in height and shorten in length. The rapid increase in wave steepness that accompanies these conditions can, quite literally, stop you cold. Sometimes we might go out of our way on a tack (sailing to windward) to get into strongly favorable current (flowing to windward), only to get there and find the waves are so steep that we made better progress without the aid of the current.

This is not a small effect, as shown in Figure 3.6-4. It applies to weak currents in just a few knots of wind where we notice it as just a roughness to the sea surface. When stronger current flows into stronger wind, we can see roads of whitecaps outlining the contrary current flow. In strong northerlies against the Gulf Stream you end up with big steep seas.

Always keep in mind the relative wind and current directions that lie ahead. These conditions can change suddenly where a waterway turns, and they always change when the tidal current reverses. Remember that current flowing with the wind actually smooths out the seas, so the potential sea state is deceptive before the current turns.

Ocean Currents

A general discussion of ocean currents is given in *Bowditch*, which remains an excellent overview of the climatic averages worldwide (Figure 3.6-5). The traditional climatic source for planning around ocean currents are the monthly pilot charts, as they are also a source of climatic winds and pressures. A sample is shown in Figure 3.6-6. Pilot charts are available online or in print. There are U.S. and British Admiralty versions. There are free georeferenced echart versions available at opencpn.org

The initial study of oceanic current flow was from Matthew Fontaine Maury, who compiled records from mariner's logbooks in the mid 1800s. Modern pilot charts are a direct descendent of his early work, and still include some of the original data. (A reminder, however, that for global climatic *wind* predictions, the COGOW data remains the best. See Section 10.6)

Refer to *Bowditch* for an introduction to the individual current systems. There are extensive data online about ocean currents. A good starting point is the Rosenstiel School of Marine and Atmospheric Science (RSMAS) at University of Miami (oceancurrents.rsmas.miami.edu). They not only have thorough, modern descriptions of the various world current systems, they also take part in the HYCOM Consortium (HYbrid Coordinate Ocean Model, hycom.org), which is devoted to computing ocean currents and other properties worldwide.

In the past few years, much of the ocean model data has become available online and in GRIB format and promises to be a valuable aid to mariners, as discussed shortly.

Planning with Ocean Currents

For a planned voyage, ocean model forecasts would likely be the best source, but even with those, we usually benefit by estimating the effect of currents on any planned route based on climatic averages, and that we can do with traditional tools such as printed pilot charts or an echart edition, after a general look at the global flow shown in Figure 3.6-5.

One approach is to plot your route on a pilot chart for the right month, and then make a list of the expected currents along that route. Then a convenient way to analyze it for navigation underway is shown in Figure 3.6-7. This procedure separates the current into North-South and East-West components, which helps much with the analysis underway. In areas where you have a large westerly set, for example, you know you need to make extra progress to the east whenever the wind allows it.

3.7 Ocean Current Models

An exciting development in global marine navigation is emerging in the field of oceanography. The advent of more sophisticated satellites and enhanced ocean modeling from several nations has given us a much finer look at global surface currents. Deep sea shipping can sometimes benefit from this knowledge to find optimum routes, but it can make a night and day difference to smaller vessels crossing the ocean.

Figure 3.6-4 showed the climatic averages of global current flow, but now we know this picture is only a coarse overview of the actual flow at any one time or place. Figure 3.7-1 illustrates the point clearly. The ocean surface is a very dynamic place, with meandering rivers of currents within their climatic boundaries and well outside of them. If we think of the climatic patterns as the highways of the ocean, we now know there are many arterials and byways along the way. And some of the byways are taking us 3 or 4 times faster than we thought they might, and indeed some byways are going the wrong way.

Any low-powered vessel can gain advantage by learning as much as possible about the currents before and during a voyage. Racing sailors crossing the Gulf Stream are well aware of this, but now we know that sailors anywhere in the world could experience *transient* currents of several knots in just about any part of the ocean—though some parts are more prone to these patterns than others (See Figure 3.7-2).

Luckily, we now have useful forecasts of ocean currents. The latest implementation of the HYCOM model is called the Global Real Time Ocean Forecast System (RTOFS). It is run by the U.S. Navy Research Laboratory and by NOAA at the National Center for Environmental Prediction (NCEP).

RTOFS data are available online as graphics at the OPC website. We can see where there is enhanced flow, but cannot learn numerical values of set and drift or precise boundaries. GRIB versions of RTOFS current and sea temperature predictions are readily available from several sources or direct from NOAA. Beyond the more or less uniform flow of the current, we are especially looking for areas of anomalous flow, either stronger than usual, or even in the opposite direction than expected. These anomalous, transient ribbons and eddies of current extend over distances of some 30 to 300 nmi, a size range called *mesoscale*. Knowing when to expect them, we can start looking out for them underway. We have so far only indirect evidence that predictions of such patterns might be accurate in remote parts of the ocean. The model has been optimized for the Gulf Stream and other selected regions, but we are slowly learning the dependability of the predictions inside and outside of those regions.

Sea water temperature, which is easy to measure accurately, can be a key guide to navigation in currents. Any navigation in regions of potentially strong currents is well served by a permanent way to measure and continually display the seawater temperature. This can also be valuable in tropical storm forecasting as well—warm water is the fuel of storms. Notable current boundaries in the ocean are usually indicated by notable water temperature changes. Properties of the RTOFS GRIB data are given in Table 3.7-1.

Other Ocean Models

There are public GRIB formatted ocean current data from Canada and several European nations that are discussed in Chapter 8. In several cases they are using regional models that would call for careful comparison with measured currents as they could be more accurate than the global RTOFS forecasts, which overlap each of those regions.

Commercial ocean forecasts are available from France, UK, and the European Union among others. These are pay

Table 3.7-1. Global RTOFS Model	
Coverage	Global
Resolution	0.08°, 5 nmi, 9.3 km
Products	Current set, drift; water temp
Forecast period	8 days (not available from all sources)
Time steps	3 hrs (not available from all sources)
Run time	00z, daily
Delay (data age)	16 hrs 20 min
Availability	Most GRIB viewers and navigation programs, or by email request from Saildocs

for use services that would not be usable in a yacht race, once the race has started. Likewise, several popular commercial sources of wind data, discussed in Chapter 8, also offer ocean currents and sea state data.

Likewise there are three other public U.S. model computations of ocean currents that might be considered in special cases. One is the Navy Coastal Ocean Model (NCOM), which offers higher resolution (1/36° compared to the 1/12° of RTOFS) forecasts for selected regions bordering the US. The NCOM model and links to data are at the OPC website. NCOM offers 3 days of data in 3-hr steps, but third party providers might limit this. There are data for the U.S. East Coast, the Gulf of Mexico and Caribbean, Hawaii, and Southern California. Comparisons between RTOFS, NCOM, and HFR are listed at starpath.com/wx.

Another source of global current information is from the Earth & Space Research Institute's program called Ocean Surface Current Analyses Real-time (OSCAR), which is described at esr.org/research/oscar. OSCAR provides a time-averaged look at global currents with a 1/3° resolution, but unlike the RTOFS and NCOM this is not a forecast; OSCAR currents represent a sliding average over 10 days that is updated every 5 or 6 days. OSCAR data are available by email request to Saildocs (Section 8.3). The file received identifies the valid time of the latest data, and from that you can anticipate when the next dataset will be available, typically at about 03z. OSCAR is an entirely independent depiction of the currents that is a lot closer to "satellite sensing" of the surface currents than a full ocean model can be. It is based on satellite measurements of seawater temperature and sea surface elevation, along with surface wind forcing from satellite wind measurements, supplemented by the GFS—all using simpler physics and analysis than possible with a full ocean model. The program has been active since 1992.

Because they are both global models, the RTOFS can be compared worldwide to the OSCAR averages. Current speeds from these 10-day averages are always lower than RTOFS, because varying current directions reduce the average speed in any one direction. There are extensive OSCAR validation data online for open-ocean locations. The predicted averages compare well with moored and drifting buoy data. In our own spot comparison of HFR measurements in coastal waters averaged over a 10-day period, OSCAR appears to underes-

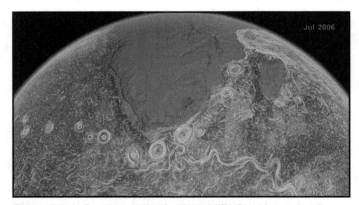

Figure 3.7-1. *Screen capture from the MIT/JPL video called Perpetual Ocean (NASA/Goddard Space Flight Center Scientific Visualization Studio). A dramatic illustration of the dynamic global current flow. Other parts of the globe are just as dynamic. The Cape of Good Hope is a breeding ground for large eddies that migrate across the ocean, as is the west side of Central America. Transient mesoscale eddies can create currents of several knots, over several hundred miles.*

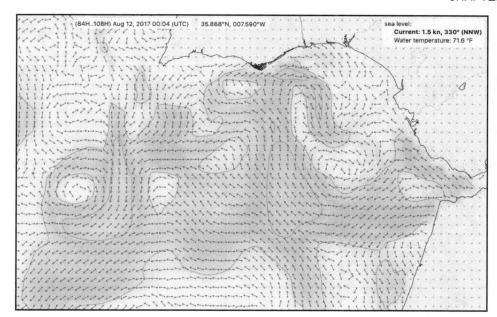

Figure 3.7-2. *Transient eddies west of Gibraltar that are common in this area, often even more pronounced and stronger. The lightest green is 1.5 kts, predicted by the RTOFS model. OSCAR averages often show persistent gyres in this region, but with peak currents of just 0.3 kts or so. Actual currents could be larger. Timely data are required to navigate the currents of these waters. Water temperature is always a guide to ocean currents. The strong southerly flow on the left is 7 F° colder than water to either side*

timate these stronger currents—the archived HFR data are available at each data point, so an average can be estimated. Likewise we might expect OSCAR to underestimate peak currents in mesoscale eddies or other transient current patterns.

OSCAR averages, however, serve as a good background for general planning, much as a pilot chart would, and then we can look to the RTOFS for prospects of more timely patterns. If you see a prominent eddy forecasted in your waters, chances are there is an eddy somewhere around there. The models do after all use measured water temperatures and sea level elevations that can mark these anomalies, and they watch them over time. The final (complex) analysis, however, might not yield precise locations and speeds.

Such forecasted eddies or rivers of current, call for careful measurements of current and seawater temperature underway. If you drive into one, watch how the current is changing as you proceed, and from that you can judge how to navigate to stay in it if favorable, or how to best get out of it. If you see one that you are not in, but could be favorable, then the layout of the forecast can illuminate the chances of reaching it. The time scale of these eddies and meandering bands of stronger currents are long enough to have initial planning done several days before getting to them. On the other hand, in coastal waters, we can see that finding the best current is a near real-time exercise.

Looking ahead, the Naval Research Lab (NRL) has released its new Global Ocean Forecast System (GOFS 3.1) model showing notable improvements over GOFS 3.0. The RTOFS forecasts from NCEP are based on the GOFS so we might expect overall improvements in current forecasting going forward. It could also be productive to compare the global surface current forecasts directly from GOFS 3.1 with those from RTOFS, as they do use different wind models and associated differences in arriving at a surface current forecast.

The GOFS 3.1 current forecasts are available online, but so far not in a convenient format for mariner's access.

The NRL ocean model data can be seen in graphic format starting at hycom.org, then select Ocean Predictions on the left, which leads to animations and stills of several models. To get to the latest GOFS 3.1 data as graphics and animations, select GOFS 3.1 on the left, then click the title link. The latest data at the present time is in Experiment 92.8.

Gulf Stream

The Gulf Stream (Figure 3.7-3) running from the Gulf of Mexico, around the tip of Florida, up the east coast along the continental shelf, and on across the North Atlantic is the most famous and typically strongest of all ocean currents. It often runs at 3 to 4 kts in places and greatly influences sea

Table 3.7-3. Navy Gulf Stream Features Abbreviations	
GS(N,S)	Gulf Stream boundary (north, south)
SHS	Continental Shelf Water, south edge
SFS	Secondary Shelf Front
SLS	Continental Shelf Slope Water, south edge
LBE	Labrador Current, east edge
NAN	N. Atlantic Drift, north edge
GEN	Gulf Stream Extension, north edge
AFN	NW African Upwelling
AZN	Azores Front, north edge
SGN	Sargasso Sea Water, north edge
LCN	Loop Current, north edge
WYYnn	Warm eddy (year, number, clockwise)
CYYnn	Cold eddy (year, number, counterclockwise)
———	Observed GS boundary
- - - - - -	Estimated GS boundary
——→	Direction of Flow

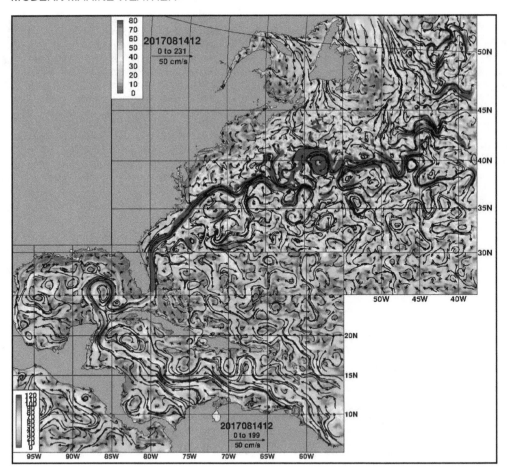

Figure 3.7-3. *GOFS 3.1 graphic depiction of the Gulf Stream. Two images from the NRL site (via hycom.org) have been combined here. The loop in the Gulf of Mexico can take various shapes, and sometimes cut off into a giant eddy. The view here is similar to that of May, 2010 at the time of the Deepwater Horizon oil spill, which led to much anxiety about the oil reaching the main flow around the south tip of Florida. This also explains in part why there is so much research on the Gulf Stream.*

state and progress along or across it. Benjamin Franklin gave it its name and provided the first map of it in the late 1700s. It remains the most studied ocean current system.

RTOFS and NCOM remain guides to planning routes across this current—the OPC site compares these two over these waters—but there are several other key resources that provide crucial support to those models. This includes known characteristics of the flow, which in turn relies on all important unique terminology, such as meanders, *north wall*, warm eddies, cold eddies, shelf water, and *Charleston Bump*, to mention just a few. For a concise yet thorough tutorial on the Gulf Stream see kingfish.coastal.edu/gulfstream. A valuable overview, list of sources, and instructive annual examples have been contributed by Frank Bohlen to the Bermuda Yacht Race website (bermudarace.com).

A working forecast starts with the Navy's graphic Gulf Stream Features Analysis. There is a north part (gsncofa.gif, gsnofa.gif) and south part (gsscofa.gif, gssofa.gif) in color or black and white. The latter has digital values of the water temperature. The file names have not changed for years, but latest versions do not include the legend of abbreviations shown in Table 3.7-3. Links to these Navy maps are at the OPC site.

The Navy maps are published every 36 hrs, but if the next map is due on the weekend don't expect it till Monday. GRIB formatted model forecasts can then be compared to or overlaid onto these graphic images (Section 8.8), as shown in Figure 3.7-4.

The Navy maps can then be brought up to date with near live sea surface temperature (SST) maps from Rutgers University measured by satellites, although the region of interest might be obscured by clouds. See rucool.marine.rutgers.edu. The Rutgers images are taken and enhanced for Gulf Stream temperatures every few hours. They are a way to see how the meanders and loops are moving in between available Navy features maps. There is also a chance to spot narrow bands of white clouds, just several pixels across, that mark the strong current flow (sharp water temperature changes)—a technique we discovered during the routing of the Transatlantic Rowing Race of June-August 2006. When the region you care about is covered by high clouds, just be patient and wait for a clear view of what you want.

Keep in mind that the actual strongest surface flow might not be correlated with the precise boundaries of warmest waters. The speed is mainly determined by the actual height of the surface, so this must be combined with the temperature boundaries, which as mentioned might be nicely marked by

Figure 3.7-4. *RTOFS currents for 12z on Aug 15 overlaid onto a section of the Navy Features map issued Aug 15 using the program Expedition. Cursor scans shows current speed in the lower left is about 4 kts, but farther on at the curve to the south the speed reduces to about 2 kts. RTOFS does not locate the warm eddy W1703 at exactly the same location at 12Z, but these two pictures of the current get closer in later RTOFS forecasts. The task underway for planning ahead is to view both descriptions to see what best describes what we actually see at the moment, supplemented by recent satellite images of the SST. Below is a zoomed view of part of the picture. SST color code is in °F.*

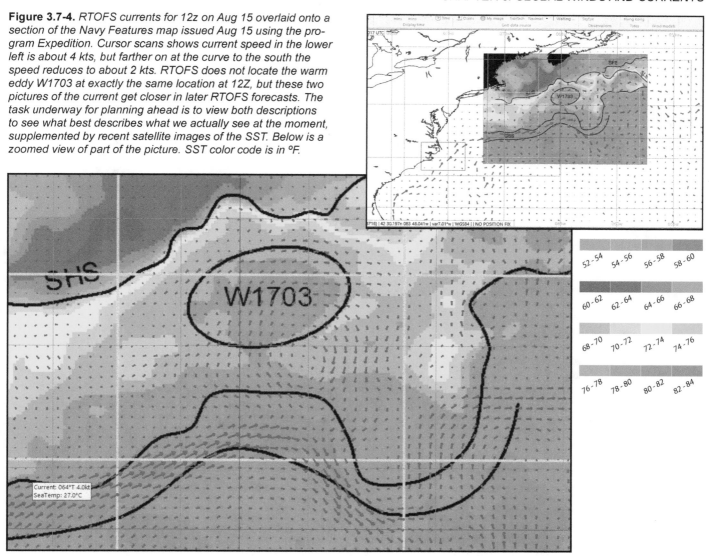

cloud bands that are easily identifiable from the vessel. Often the strongest flow is within some 10 to 30 miles of the north boundary of the stream, called the north wall.

Overlaying images from Navy features maps and Rutgers SST maps using a graphics program is a good way to understand what is going on—or do this directly within your navigation program as discussed in Section 8.8. The Navy features maps themselves are something like that. Johns Hopkins University also has valuable SST data for this application (see fermi.jhuapl.edu/avhrr).

The location of the north wall (heavy solid line) and south wall (heavy dashed line) of the Gulf Stream are marked on the OPC 24-hr wind and wave forecasts. (The north wall along the Florida Keys is given more precisely at weather.gov/images/key/gulfstream.png.) It is expected that Gulf Stream forecasts are reasonably accurate south of Cape Hatteras, but may be less so north of there. The Gulf Stream, like its counterpart in the Pacific, the Kuroshio, is a western

boundary current that then curves back to the east into the northern ocean. This *extension region* is where the computations are most difficult.

And to stress it once again, the key to efficient navigation is to be prepared to compute the actual current you are in by comparing your COG and SOG with your speed and heading. An accurate digital seawater thermometer is crucial equipment in these waters.

Robert FitzRoy (1805 - 1865), "Father of Marine Weather," was most famous as Captain of the HMS *Beagle* voyage (1831-1836) that carried Charles Darwin throughout the Pacific, but his accomplishments in marine weather were more than enough to guarantee his role in history.

After a successful career as ship captain, he devoted his time to sharing his knowledge of weather. He established weather stations around Great Britain and was the first to make weather forecasts (a word he invented) on eastern shores based on telegraph reports of observations to the west. He made the first synoptic charts (also his word) and compiled wind and sea state data collected from ship's logs, for which he invented the wind star system of plotting the statistics, similar to those used on pilot charts today. FitzRoy was also responsible for the idea of posting visual storm warnings at docks and marinas. In 1854 he was appointed head of the newly established national weather service, which evolved into the present UK Met office.

FitzRoy developed and standardized rugged marine barometers (mercury style, called FitzRoy barometers) and wrote the *Barometer Manual* (1856), which summarized their use along with other advice on practical forecasting. He was the first to champion the use barometric pressure in forecasting. His 340-page *Weather Book* appeared in 1862, which was the state of the art text at the time.

He was the first to argue in parliament for the licensing of merchant marine personnel, an institution that was eventually crucial to the development of maritime commerce worldwide. He also was the first to establish the convention of having the chief engineer dine with the captain and other officers on steam or auxiliary vessels—which further highlights his insight on maritime affairs.

Politicians and the press of the time, however, did not appreciate his work and often berated it. He also experienced conflict between his own religious beliefs and ideas coming from Darwin, of whose scientific basis he had played such a crucial role. In later life he suffered from severe depression aggravated by overwork that ultimately cost him his life. Original FitzRoy barometers are still available to collectors.

Matthew Fontaine Maury (1806 - 1873) contemporary and American counterpart of Robert FitzRoy in the UK. Maury has been called "Father of Modern Oceanography" and "First Scientist of the Seas." He had an active sea time career in the Navy from age 19 to 33, at which time a stagecoach accident prevented further sea duty. He then devoted his time to navigation studies and compiling wind and current data from ship's logbooks. The value of the work was recognized immediately. His early charts were used by the clipper Flying Cloud that set the New York to San Francisco sailing record in 1854, and held it until 1989.

He became the first superintendent of the newly established United States Naval Observatory in 1844 and held that position for the 16 years leading up to the Civil War, at which time he left (he was from Virginia) to serve in the Confederate naval establishment. During the war he developed torpedoes for the Confederacy that were "credited" with doing more damage to U.S. vessels than all other sources combined. After the war he became a Professor of Physics at Virginia Military Institute, sometimes called "the West Point of the South." His story is just one more example of how difficult it is to comprehend this tragic period of American history.

Before the war, Maury had issued his first Wind and Current Chart of the North Atlantic in 1847. Many more followed quickly. Some evolved into the Pilot Charts still in use today. Maury attended international conferences and proposed and promoted international cooperation on meteorology and oceanography. In 1855 he published his most famous work The Physical Geography of the Sea.

Like FitzRoy, he had other prominent maritime accomplishments away from meteorology and oceanography. Besides his weapons work, he studied whale migration and was one of the first to discuss the feasibility and a proposal for a submarine cable across the Atlantic. He was also a strong proponent of the Northwest Passage across the top of Canada, which led to much exploration, but none successful during his lifetime

4.1 Introduction to Strong Wind

June 1, 2007 marked a milestone in strong wind warnings for U.S. mariners. On that date the USCG *reinstated* the well known strong-wind visual warning signals that mariners had seen posted at yacht clubs, marinas, and port offices around the country for more than 100 years—prior to 1989, that is, when it was rather quietly discontinued. It is not clear why it was discontinued when it was. Perhaps it was an overconfidence in emerging communications technologies. Its revival after 18 years was likely tied to the tragic coastal weather experiences we had over those intervening years, and the desire to make every effort possible to alert an increasing coastal population of dangerous conditions. In any event, they are a welcome addition to our awareness of marine weather conditions. The warning signals and basic classifications of strong winds are shown in Table 4.1-1. We saw them in wide usage as hurricane Harvey came ashore in Texas in August, 2017.

There is a corresponding set of International Warning Signals, and many nations have their own unique warning signals. These are listed at the WMO website and in the *International Code of Signals, NGA Pub. 102.*

The terms of Table 4.1-1 are used mostly outside of the tropics. Within the tropics the wind names are more typically associated with their parent system as outlined in Table 4.1-2. Usage of the terms in Table 4.1-1 are in a transition of sorts

in modern times. When these visual warnings were discontinued, a storm warning outside the tropics meant any wind greater than 48 kts in regions where hurricanes did not occur. But also in those days the term "hurricane-force" winds did not appear very often on weather maps and forecasts. These days, however, hurricane-force winds is used frequently on maps and forecasts, so the meanings of these warning signs have evolved. When hurricane-force winds are forecasted, coast stations we checked with would show the "hurricane" signal, although official definitions online do not yet reflect this practice. Strong winds in the tropics usually come with very well localized cyclonic activity, meaning a small circular Low without associated frontal systems, such as a tropical depression, storm, or hurricane. Tropical disturbances can be more spread out and less structured (essentially a bunch of squalls), and the pattern called a *tropical wave* (formerly called *easterly wave*) is more like a trough oriented north-south moving from the east to the west. These latter two types of systems (discussed later) are similar to squalls and generally have winds less than 25 to 30 kts.

Another unique feature of strong winds in the tropics is they are usually very well forecasted. As with other parts of the ocean, there are daytime and nighttime work shifts of professional meteorologists in several weather bureaus around the world whose full time job is to watch the clouds and wind flow across the tropics. Whenever any specific activity is noted, they focus on it immediately and start making warnings and notifications. And most of these strong wind systems in the tropics—unlike larger counterparts outside of the tropics—do not generate strong winds over night. They take some time to develop as they go through fairly well predictable stages of intensification. If we are paying attention to our wireless sources underway, it is very unlikely that any such system will sneak up on us without plenty of warning. Hurricanes come in a broad range of sizes (Figure 4.1-1).

Table 4.1-1. Extratropical strong wind classification and warnings		
Visual display	Classification	Notes
	Small Craft Advisory 20 to 33 kts	1, 2
	Gale 34 to 47 kts	1, 3
	Storm Force 48 to 63 kts	1, 4
	Hurricane Force ≥ 64 kts	1, 4

Table Notes:

1. All wind classifications are sustained winds, meaning not just isolated gusts but the average wind over a 2-min period must be over the lower limit. The warnings, however, can be posted for either sustained winds or for anticipated frequent gusts in that range.

2. The lower limit varies with region in the U.S. and also can depend on sea state, with or without strong winds. There is no official definition of "small craft."

3. The Beaufort wind force scale (Table 5.4-3) subdivides this into: Near Gale 28 to 33 kts; Gale 34 to 40 kts; and Strong Gale 41 to 47 kts.

4. Outside of the tropics, storm winds could be anything over 48 kts, so an extratropical Low with 100 kts of wind would still be called a storm and not a hurricane, but with regard to names of winds themselves, even outside of the tropics, the name "hurricane-force" wind is now used commonly for winds 64 kts or above. The system itself is still called a storm, not a hurricane, if it is located and originated outside of the tropics. Beaufort scale divisions are: Storm 48 to 55 kts and Strong Storm 56 to 63 kts.

Table 4.1-2. Tropical strong wind categories		
System	Wind speeds	Notes
Tropical disturbance	< ~25 kts	1, 2
Tropical depression	~20 to 33 kts	1, 3
Tropical storm	34 to 63 kts	1, 4
Hurricane	≥ 64 kts	1, 5, 6

Table Notes:

1. Wind speeds are sustained, meaning average over a 1-min period, compared to 2-min average for extratropical definitions.

2. No official wind ranges, but localized convective identity that lasts at least 24 hrs.

3. An advanced disturbance with at least 1 closed isobar and circular wind flow. Often the precursor to a tropical storm.

4. Note the wind definitions are different for extratropical storms.

5. "Hurricane" is a tropical cyclone in the North Atlantic, Caribbean Sea, Gulf of Mexico, or eastern North Pacific. In the western North Pacific ocean they are called "typhoons"; in the western South Pacific and Indian Ocean they are called "cyclones."

6. Hurricanes also have categories (Saffir-Simpson scale) defined by wind speed: 1 = 64 to 82 kts, 2 = 83 to 95 kts, 3 = 96 to 113 kts, 4 = 114 to 135 kts, and 5 = >135 kts. These categories are used more on land than in marine applications. They are based on potential property damage by the wind.

Outside of the tropics, on the other hand, life is actually much more complex with regard to strong wind systems. Besides being tremendously larger systems outside the tropics, they often intensify much more rapidly. Extreme cases are called *meteorological bombs*. They have central pressure drops of more than 24 mb in 24 hrs. (The process at any latitude is called *rapid intensification*.) But even common extratropical systems generally pose more widespread threat to mariners than do typical tropical storms and hurricanes. First and foremost, the regions of strong winds are very much larger in higher latitude storms—over 1,000 miles across in some cases—compared to hurricanes that are often as small as a couple hundred miles in diameter. Small craft can often maneuver around tropical storms and hurricanes, but there is essentially no such maneuvering around something that spans huge portions of the ocean.

Frontal systems are another distinction between weather at higher versus lower latitudes. Though frontal systems do periodically reach down into the tropics, it is rare. Fronts are, nevertheless, probably responsible for most of the strong wind experienced on the globe if we average over all times and places; but not necessarily the main source for all mariners. Statistically, for example, a mariner on the southeast coast of the U.S. is more likely to get strong wind from a front than from a strong Low without a front, whereas this is not the case on west coast waters, where Lows as much as fronts are likely to bring strong winds. We

will learn more of how this comes about shortly. Waters off of southeast Australia is another place where strong winds are more likely the result of fronts than of Lows alone—estimates from local sailors make it as high as 80 percent more likely.

There are many other differences between strong wind systems within and outside of the tropics. We will come back to specific comparisons between tropical and extratropical systems once we have some background on each. Hurricanes have caused tremendous damage and loss of life *on coastal lands*—often from storm surge and flooding—but when it comes to threats to mariners at sea, storms at higher latitudes have caused far more destruction *at sea*, especially to fishing vessels who are forced to work in all conditions. On the other hand, if we were to look up what system overall causes most damage to humans and property worldwide, we would probably find that it is not hurricanes nor extratropical storms, but isolated thunderstorms (and associated tornadoes and flooding) that are the big culprit in the long run. There are simply more of them, more often, and in more locations.

The maritime equivalent of tornadoes are waterspouts, but these are not in practice a very common threat to marine navigation. They are even more rare over water than tornadoes on land, more easily avoided, and on the average much less intense and shorter lived. Table 4.1-3 summarizes sources of strong winds at sea. Individual sources are covered later in this chapter.

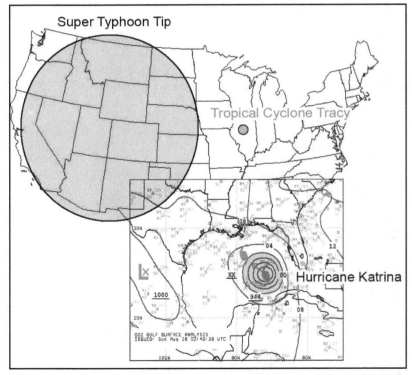

Figure 4.1-1. *Relative sizes of hurricanes. The world's records for big (Tip) and small (Tracy) tropical systems with hurricane force winds are shown over the U.S. for comparison—although the former was in the Philippines and the latter in Australia. The size of Katrina shown is a more typical hurricane size, although it was stronger than average in wind strength by the time it made landfall. At the stage shown storm force winds were limited to a diameter of about 200 nmi. See also related notes in Table 4.1-3.*

Table Notes:

1. Individual squalls are rarely forecasted, but likelihood of squalls is well forecasted in local waters. Regions of enhanced convection (numerous thunderstorms or tropical disturbances) are shown on tropical maps often with dependable boundaries marked, though severity is not given. We have to now say "rare" and not "never" for individual squalls, because new hi-res, rapid-refresh models (Chapter 7) can forecast large individual squalls, which is part of their goal.

2. These are rare and transient systems that are difficult to forecast, but they do create relatively long lasting strong winds.

3. Cold fronts are usually more severe than warm fronts. Boundaries are clearly marked on maps

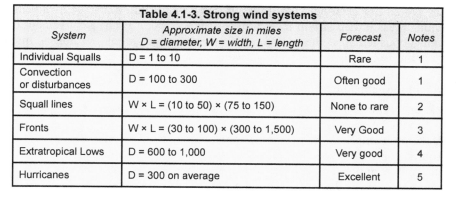

Table 4.1-3. Strong wind systems			
System	Approximate size in miles D = diameter, W = width, L = length	Forecast	Notes
Individual Squalls	D = 1 to 10	Rare	1
Convection or disturbances	D = 100 to 300	Often good	1
Squall lines	W × L = (10 to 50) × (75 to 150)	None to rare	2
Fronts	W × L = (30 to 100) × (300 to 1,500)	Very Good	3
Extratropical Lows	D = 600 to 1,000	Very good	4
Hurricanes	D = 300 on average	Excellent	5

4. Location and extent of central areas well marked on maps, though conditions along the edges are more variable and harder to predict. Shapes become irregular at larger distances from the center.

5. Recorded extremes were typhoon Tip (1979, 1200-nmi diameter) and cyclone Tracy (1974, 52-nmi diameter), both way outside the average size distribution. See Figure 4.1-1.

Keeping in mind that a front is always a trough of low pressure, we can say that strong winds usually come from regions of low pressure of one kind or another. There are, however, notable exceptions. As discussed in Chapter 2, wind speed is driven by the pressure gradient. If the isobars are close, the wind is strong; if they are well separated the wind is weak. Any weather pattern that pushes the isobars together can cause strong wind.

It is valuable to remember this fundamental point about the gradient being the driving force and not the pressure itself. We can otherwise get so accustomed to associating strong wind with falling barometer that we might forget the potential for even stronger winds to build once the barometer starts back up—all we need is a pressure gradient that is tighter on the back side of the system than it is on the front side that caused the initial drop. A well known example of this type of pattern ("the sting in the scorpion's tail") is covered in Section 4.4. It is actually a fairly common situation in certain parts of the world.

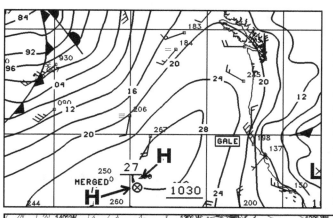

Figure 4.1-2. *A stationary trough over California and Nevada compressing isobars along the Pacific High. This pattern can bring 30 or 40 kts of wind over a long stretch of the coastline and last for several days. It is unique in that it can come with crystal clear sunny skies, but since this area is a breeding ground for sea fog, it can also come in pea soup fog. In either case, the winds are strong without low pressure, 1020 mb or higher is not uncommon. The top shows an OPC surface analysis; the bottom shows it in a GFS model prediction (GRIB data). See also Figure 2.1-10 and related discussion.*

These maps are for the same valid time, and are a good example of how the GRIB data can agree or maybe disagree with the analyzed maps from the OPC that include actual ship reports. Notice the reports (20 kts and 15 kts) off WA and OR are not predicted by the GFS model data in the GRIB map. The strong winds near San Francisco are predicted well, as is the wind pattern below the frontal system in the NW part of these maps. The isobars near the top of the ridge, however, do differ and thus give different values of the weaker winds in that region.

In making these comparisons it is important to use the same base valid times, in this example, 00z, May 12. The grib file is the h0 "forecast," which is effectively a surface analysis. It would not be as productive to compare the 00z OPC map of May 12 with the h06 forecast based on the 18z GFS run the previous day, May 11, even though the valid map times would still be the same, 00z May 12.

79

We do not even need low pressure for strong wind. Although it is rather rare in most waters of the world, a High can get pushed up against a Low, or vice versa, in such a way that the isobars between them get compressed and lead to strong winds along a narrow band between the two systems, where the actual pressure is relatively high.

But we don't need rare events like that to get strong winds without a Low in some locations. Along the west coast of the U.S., for example, we have an occasional, though significant, summertime circumstance of the Pacific High getting pushed up against an unmovable prominent trough of (thermal) low pressure over the deserts of CA and NV (Figure 4.1-2).

When this happens, the isobars of the High stack up along the coast building strong winds (easily 30 kts, sometimes 40 kts) over a very long fetch. This can lead to strong winds far into the ocean, and right along the coast the result can be chaotic seas along a long stretch of the coast, especially in the vicinity of the continental shelf, some few to a dozen miles from the coastline. What makes these conditions almost unique worldwide is the weather is otherwise quite beautiful, because you are sailing in a high pressure system—though it could also be in pea soup fog in this region as well.

Many Pacific Northwest sailors returning to Seattle after a circumnavigation of the world report that their biggest challenge with wind and seas worldwide were off the coast of CA and OR getting past one of these "California trough" events—usually meaning getting south of Point Conception, where the coastline turns sharply in to the SE.

Richard Henry Dana records his amazement at these gale force winds in a cloudless sky in *Two Years Before the Mast*, published in 1840. Sailors like himself from the U.S. Northeast had never seen such wind and waves in perfectly clear, sunny skies, because there is no counterpart in the Northeast waters.

4.2 Satellite Winds

In the first edition of this book we discussed satellite winds from the QuikSCAT satellite, a U.S. instrument that was the primary source of satellite winds for marine application. That instrument failed in 2009, after a long and very productive career, contributing much to the development of numerical weather prediction. It was also the source of data for the CO-GOW project (Section 10.6) that we continually benefit from. For a while there was no U.S. replacement, but then the RapidSCAT instrument on the International Space Station (ISS) provided valuable data, but that only lasted from 2014 to 2016; conflicts with crucial missions of the ISS contributed to that discontinuation. Now we rely on the well established and dependable European satellites Metop-A (Figure 4.2-1) and Metop-B and their onboard scatterometers called AS-CAT. They are operated by the European Organization for the Exploitation of Meteorological Satellites (eumetsat.int). Metop-C is planned for 2018.

Although ASCAT has been operational since 2007 with convenient data online from the Royal Netherlands Meteorological Institute (KNMI), the existence of QuikSCAT GRIB data overshadowed this resource while operational. The AS-CAT data have been available to U.S. meteorologists since 2009, and the data became available in convenient format in 2011 from the Ocean Surface Winds Team (OSWT) of the Center for Satellite Application and Research, a division of NOAA.

Another source of data was available starting in 2009 from the Indian satellite OceanSat2, and its scatterometer called OSCAT, but that instrument expired in 2014, approaching its design lifetime. It served well in mitigating the loss of QuikSCAT over those years.

The ASCAT satellite winds are very similar to the earlier QuikSCAT, but there are important differences to cover. Since the resulting winds and how we use them are essentially the same, we kept several examples of QuikSCAT winds from earlier editions of this book. These examples were selected over a long period of time to match other sources of data and we do not gain by starting that long process again.

Metop-A circles the earth continuously measuring actual wind speeds and directions over approximately 90% of the ice-free ocean on a daily basis. The radar instrument (scatterometer) doing the measurements on Metop-A is called AS-CAT for Advanced Scatterometer. It measures wind speeds in the range of 2 to 30 m/s (4 to 60 kts) with an accuracy of ± 2 m/s (4 kts) or 10% of the wind speed, with a direction accuracy of ±20°. It has a spatial resolution on earth of 25 km, which implies one wind arrow every 13 nmi.

The satellite is in a low-earth, sun-synchronous polar orbit, with a height above the earth's surface that varies from 822 to 850 km. In sync with the sun, it crosses any latitude at the same *local mean time* (LMT) each day. The ascending node (satellite headed north) crosses the equator at 2131 LMT. The orbital period is 1 hr 41 min (101.3 min), so the descending node (satellite headed south) crosses the equator on

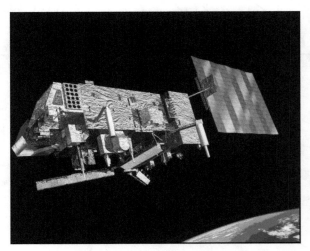

Figure 4.2-1. *Metop-A satellite that carries the ASCAT scatterometer. Photo compliments of eumetsat.int.*

the other side of the earth 51m later, about 2222 LMT. There are 14.2 orbits per day, and as the earth rotates beneath the satellite's orbit, it measures ocean surface winds below it.

As the earth rotates under the satellite, it covers progressively more western swaths of the surface, ascending on one side of the earth and descending on the other side (Figures 4.2-2 and 4.2-3). Each swath is about 950 nmi wide, centered on the satellite's geographic position as it moves, but we do not get data from directly below the satellite because the AS-CAT instrument cannot sample the ocean directly below it. This leads to what is called the *nadir gap*. It extends 190 nmi either side of the path. This data gap is the main user distinction between ASCAT and QuikSCAT, which had a different design and could sample the ocean beneath it.

Although the satellite makes a near-overhead pass on a specific point only every 4 or 5 days, it measures winds over a swath of ocean below it, so we get useful data more often than that, usually about once a day or every other day, depending on our latitude—higher latitudes get more frequent data. Furthermore, the winds some distance from us could still be useful for evaluating the weather maps and forecasts at our location. Figure 4.2-4 shows sample data

Satellite-borne scatterometers transmit microwave (radar) pulses to the ocean surface and measure the backscattered signal received at the instrument. Since wind itself does not substantially affect the radiation emitted and received by the radar, scatterometers use an indirect technique to measure wind velocity over the ocean. Wind stress over the ocean surface generates ripples (cat's paws) that roughen the sea surface. These wavelets modify the radar cross section of the ocean surface and hence the magnitude of backscattered signal. As you might know from experience with navigation radar, a rough surface scatters more than a smooth surface, and thus we can see very generally how this works. The stronger the wind, the rougher the surface and the more radar signal is scattered back to the satellite.

Roughness in this case is essentially defined by the wavelength of the radar. ASCAT uses 5.7-cm radar, which is between x-band (3-cm) and s-band (10-cm) radar used on vessels. So any perturbation of the surface on the order of 5 cm is very rough for this wavelength.

In order to extract wind velocity from these measurements, the computers doing the analysis must understand how wind makes waves and how radar scatters from these wave surfaces. It is not the waves themselves doing the scattering here but the wavelets on the surface of the waves. There is clearly a lot of analysis involved, but the results are then scaled to match buoy observations.

A hindrance to any microwave radar system is the presence of rain. As we know from navigation radar, rain drops are great radar reflectors and thus they interfere with all radar measurements. Another point to be aware of as we see more satellite wind data from various sources (including oceanographic sources) is the convention for wind direction can depend on the source. Oceanography sources sometimes

present wind arrows reversed. Check wind flow relative to isobars if in doubt. Satellite winds reported to mariners are always normalized to those valid at 10 m above the surface (as are GFS and other model forecasts), which means actual surface winds could be slightly less than reported in satellite data

Satellite wind measurement is a wonderful technology and a key to modern weather analysis worldwide, not just for marine weather. Data from the satellites are used to seed the computer models that go on to generate worldwide forecasts over land and water. As a mariner, and particularly a sailor, these near real-time measurements are precisely the data we care about the most: not a forecast nor model prediction, but the actual measured winds around us. Look carefully at these data and you will spot squalls not shown on the weather maps and you will spot lulls that could not be anticipated from the maps as well. You can also tell precisely where fronts create shear lines in the wind that can be crucial to tactics. Generally we have access to the data some 3 hrs after the satellite has gone by, with usually one or two tactically useful passes per day.

How to View ASCAT Winds Onshore and Underway

Since we get data only for the times of satellite passes, it is crucial to know the time of the latest data pass over your location and to have a means of estimating the time of the next useful pass, which is a bit complicated by the nadir gap of missing data below the satellite.

There are two ways to access satellite wind data: graphic images posted online that are available to everyone, and GRIB formatted versions available in specific GRIB viewers. The primary sources for the online graphic data are KNMI and OSWT, given in Table 4.2-1. Viewed from a computer onshore with high-speed internet, we can compare the two sources at leisure, and perhaps get complimenting information from each. KNMI data, for example, are overlaid on a cloud image that often helps interpret the source of the winds, but this sometimes makes it harder to read wind speeds. Once underway and limited to satphone communications, however, the OSWT data becomes the clear preference because of the way the data are stored online.

Samples of ASCAT data are shown in Figure 4.2-3 (and throughout this section). An internet connection is required, but this is becoming more and more a practical reality at sea. Data in image format can also be freely obtained underway by email, which most vessels have these days, although a special procedure is required.

Beyond providing the truth on actual surface winds at specific times, ASCAT data are ideal for evaluating model

Table 4.2-1. ASCAT Data by Graphic Image	
Source	Link
KNMI	knmi.nl/scatterometer/ascat_osi_25_prod/ascat_app.cgi
OSWT	manati.star.nesdis.noaa.gov/datasets/ASCATData.php

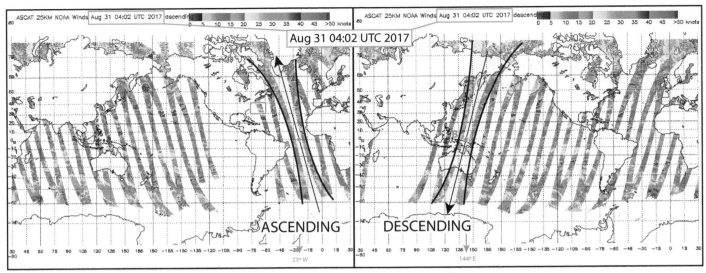

Aug 31 04:02 UTC 2017

ASCENDING   DESCENDING

Figure 4.2-2. The two graphic index pages of ASCAT winds from the OSWT website, showing the last 12 passes (up and down), with a gap (about 4,000 nmi wide and 3.5 hrs in time) between the newest pass on the right of the gap and the oldest one they choose to show us on the left of the gap. This thoughtful display convention can be used to estimate the time of subsequent passes. Clicking a point on the index brings up an image of wind vectors at that location in a fixed Lat-Lon window (10° × 15°). The red square on the latest ascending pass is an example shown in Figure 4.2-3. Each index is updated every hour; this one was updated at 0402, Aug 31. The black borders we added mark the edges of a single swath of data for a complete orbit, showing the nadir gap of no data along the satellite track. This pass would be about 101 minutes older than the newest to its left. The satellite moves due north and south in a polar orbit, but its track on the globe bends to the west as the earth rotates to the east below it. The widening of this swath at higher latitudes is an artifact of the map projection, which leads to adjacent tracks overlapping at Lat ≥ 49°, with newest data being part of the western-most pass.

At any longitude, Metop-A crosses the equator ascending (northbound) at 2131 local mean time (LMT) and then descending (southbound) half a cycle later (51 min) at 2222 LMT. The observed time of crossing in UTC will be this LMT plus the observer's longitude converted to time at 1 hr/15°. The satellite then proceeds away from the equator at about 3 min/10° of Lat (101.3 min/360°), a correction we can usually ignore. For passes shown on the index, we learn the valid time from the data images (Figure 4.2-3). The longitude of the descending path (point B) after ascending at 23° W (point A), is 23° W + 180° = 203° W = 157° E, but in 51 min the earth rotates east 51 min × (15°/60 min) = 12.75°, so we get 157° E - 13° = 144° E, which is farther west!

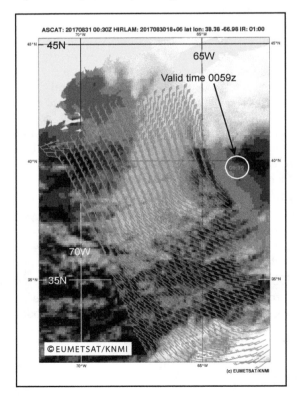

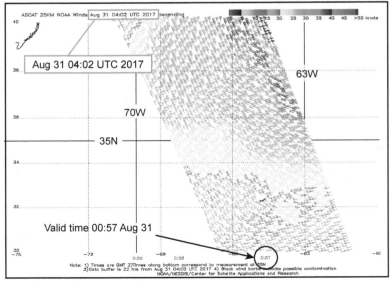

Figure 4.2-3. ASCAT winds as presented at KNMI (left) and OSWT (right). The data have 25-km resolution in each, but the Lat-Lon grid size of the data windows and the presentation styles are different. These data at about (35N, 65W) are valid at 0100z on Aug. 31, which we read from the images in tiny numbers, but we could figure that as follows: ASCAT crosses equator at 50W at 2131; correct for LMT: 50W/(15°/hr) = 0320; then add 0009 to get to 30N, which gives 0100. NOTE: pass date same as index date, because it is between 00:00 and 04:02. Had the indicated pass time been, say, 06:57, then the valid pass time would be 06:57, Aug 30.

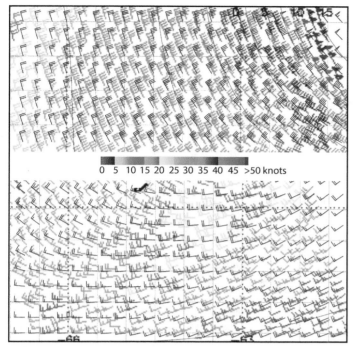

Figure 4.2-4. *GFS wind forecast (black barbs) in GRIB format overlaid onto the ASCAT image of Figure 4.2-3 using Expedition. The agreement is exceptionally good, verifying the value of this model data at this time and place, both close to the storm (top) and 480 nmi away (bottom). Note the value of the ASCAT colorbar in the middle section; yellow over 20; green under 20. GFS arrows all nominal 20 in the display, but a cursor shows these vary from 17.5 to 22.5 kts confirming this detail of the ASCAT data. Overlaying GRIB data on images is discussed in Section 8.8*

forecasts as shown in Figure 4.2-4. The task in doing that is to find the model forecast at the corresponding time (or closest possible time) of the satellite data. The comparisons shown are fortunately very close in time and indeed the GFS model did an excellent job reproducing both wind speed and direction, both close and some distance from a major storm. This comparison does not always lead to such good validation, but either observation is useful to us. (Another example is shown later in Figure 4.2-9).

ASCAT wind data can also reveal details of the wind flow that we could not have learned from other sources. An example is in Figure 4.2-5 showing an isolated area of squalls. Occasional thunderstorms in this area were forecasted earlier in the aviation progs, but this did not show up on the OPC maps nor in the GFS forecasts, nor any regional models available for that area. This is a conspicuous example, but there is *almost always* information in the ASCAT data on some level that is helpful—think of a radiologist studying an X-ray! We see more examples as we proceed.

A second satellite, Metop-B, also provides ASCAT data available at OSWT. Metop-B follows Metop-A in the same orbit, about half a cycle (51 min) behind. In this time period, the earth rotates 12.5°, so this pass does not typically add new wind information but expands the swath to the west by 12.5° of Lon, which means more at lower latitudes than higher.

Getting Graphic ASCAT Data Underway

On land (or sea) with internet, we get the data as just described, but once underway and relying on email, there

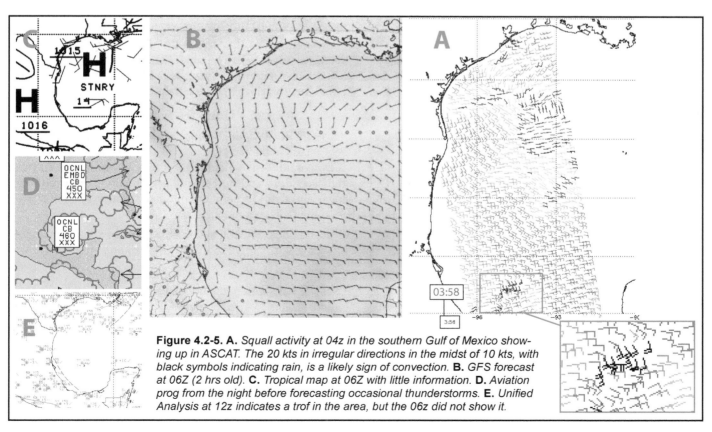

Figure 4.2-5. A. *Squall activity at 04z in the southern Gulf of Mexico showing up in ASCAT. The 20 kts in irregular directions in the midst of 10 kts, with black symbols indicating rain, is a likely sign of convection.* **B.** *GFS forecast at 06Z (2 hrs old).* **C.** *Tropical map at 06Z with little information.* **D.** *Aviation prog from the night before forecasting occasional thunderstorms.* **E.** *Unified Analysis at 12z indicates a trof in the area, but the 06z did not show it.*

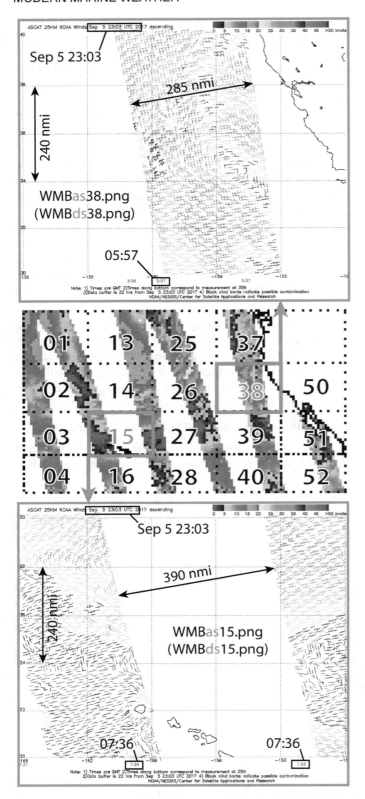

Figure 4.2-6. *Learning ASCAT file names from the OSWT graphic index. Viewing the whole earth index online, click a point of interest to call up the (10º × 15º) Lat-Lon data image for that region. The link to that image will then show in the URL field. Samples shown here are for the ascending pass. Change "as" to "ds" for the corresponding URL of the descending pass.*

is more involved. The procedure is to determine the image file name and then ask for this by email from Saildocs. We can do this with the OSWT data because the file names do not change for specific points on earth; they are just updated when new data are available. (This is not possible from KNMI as each file has a unique name and they are not stored in an accessible location online, in part due to the copyright they maintain on every image.) We can learn the OSWT file names from a right-click on the graphic index page, as shown in the middle section of Figure 4.2-6, from which we can create the series of maps that span a specific voyage as shown in Figure 4.2-7.

The valid UTC of the data is given in very small purple letters at the base of the swath in data image for that region (top and bottom sections of Figure 4.2-6). This is the hour of the pass; we must figure the date from the time of the index, given at the top of the data image. Since each index contains 22 hrs of data, the date of a specific swath will be the same as that of the index, or the day before. See note in Figure 4.2-3. A specific data image can contain parts of two swaths. These could be from the same pass, thus having the same time (within minutes) or they could be parts of two successive passes, in which case the two times will differ by 101 min.

In Figure 4.2-6 top, the index was valid at 2303, Sep 5, and the swath of data was valid at 0557, on this same date. If we assume we just downloaded the index (i.e., present time within an hour of 2303) then this data is now 17 hrs 06 min old (2303 - 0557), which in turn implies we can expect new data for this region in the next few hours, because any data on the index page is never more than 22 hrs old, no matter where it is located on the index. Note that even though, at 2300, this data would be old, it is nevertheless at a very convenient time, almost exactly 06z, a synoptic time when surface analyses are available. For data that does not match a synoptic time, we can use the previous GFS run and interpolate the forecasts to match the ASCAT pass time.

ASCAT images from Saildocs

Without a broadband connection at sea (which allows direct access to the index), once we know the file names for the region of interest, we can request these (keeping in mind that the ascending and descending are equally good candidates for useful data) by sending an email to query@saildocs.com with the following message:

send https://manati.star.nesdis.noaa.gov/ascat_images/ cur_25km_META/zooms/WMBas15.png

or

send https://manati.star.nesdis.noaa.gov/ascat_images/ cur_25km_META/zooms/WMBds15.png

Use plain text email and capitalization matters. This should return to you within a few minutes the requested image. They are 30 to 35 kB, which is well within reason for satphone or HF-radio connections.

Bear in mind, however, that not only are the OSWT and Saildocs websites not official NWS sources, they each specifi-

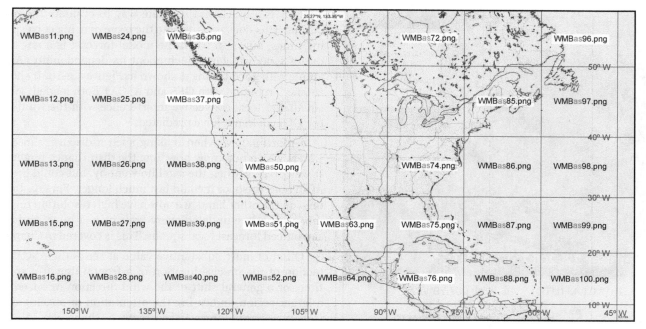

Figure 4.2-7. *ASCAT (Metop-A) file names from OSWT. The ascending (as) and descending (ds) are equivalently good data; it is a matter of chance as to which will be most timely at the moment needed. The files can be requested from Saildocs. They are 30 to 35 kB each. Similar filename maps for other oceans are at starpath.com/wx.*

cally warn that they may not be available at all times. (With that said, they have both been remarkably dependable for very many years.)

ASCAT in GRIB Format

Raw ASCAT data are collected from the satellites and analyzed by KNMI, who in turn share this data worldwide in a scientific format called NetCDF (network common data format). A tremendous amount of model and measurement data in meteorology and oceanography are shared this way among scientists, but this format is not readable by common navigation and weather apps for mariners; they need GRIB format. On the U.S. side, the OSWT converts this data to images and distributes them as discussed earlier, and the NCEP converts this data to GRIB2 format, which is available to the public at ftp.ocean.weather.gov/data/ascat_ab. Hourly files are stored for six days, then overwritten. Each file (300 ± 50 kB) represents a specific reference time and contains all new data swaths (ascending, descending, A, and B) since the previous file. Each grid point (at 25-km resolution) includes the wind vector and the valid time of that wind vector expressed as the time interval prior to the reference time.

There are several programs now, and likely more in the future, that will download and display ASCAT winds in GRIB format. These include the WeatherNet-GRIB Explorer system for PCs and GRIB Explorer Plus for iPad (ocens.com) and the LuckGrib products from luckgrib.com. Ocens converts the data to GRIB1; LuckGrib maintains the GRIB2 format. Expedition is one navigation program that can display these data from either source now, and likely others will follow. Until then, we can view the data on the viewers of the two providers and compare those displays with maps and model

forecasts shown in other programs. These two GRIB sources use different approaches to what is downloaded and how it is displayed, but both let the user select the Lat-Lon range of interest, which means the files can be very small. When using the direct download from NCEP, we must take the full span of latitudes for the longitude band covered in the most recent pass. Figure 4.2-8 shows a local region of ASCAT winds in GRIB format. A broader view of the pass is in Figure 4.2-9.

The GRIB format offers a precise digital presentation of wind that is much easier to read than the graphic images. Comparing digital ASCAT data with a corresponding model

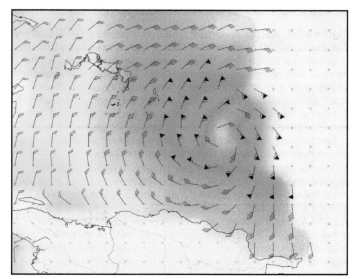

Figure 4.2-8. *ASCAT wind measurements at 0132z on Sept. 22, 2017 (hurricane Maria) displayed in GRIB format using LuckGrib. Figure 4.2-9 shows this data segment in the larger perspective of the data swath.*

analysis is a quick and accurate way to evaluate the model output. This does not alleviate the issue of using corresponding times, but even when the model forecast is a few hours out of sync, we learn much about its dependability. An example with good timing is shown in Figure 4.2-10. It shows a zoomed in region with GFS and ASCAT both loaded. We see squall and local convective interference with the winds that the GFS could not have predicted.

Unfortunately, when making such a discovery in ocean waters we do not know how long the disturbance might last. It was present when the satellite went by, but could be gone in an hour or so, or it could last much longer. For coastal waters, on the other hand, we now have high resolution regional models that are updated every hour or half hour, and these can indeed forecast local squalls. This is covered in Chapter 7.

Often of more substantive value at sea is the ASCAT detection of the precise location of a frontal line at a specific time, or a general shift of the wind direction or speed over a larger region, indicating the orientation or spacing of the isobars were not forecasted correctly by the model.

When loading both ASCAT and model forecasts into the same navigation program we might need to combine the GRIB files externally as explained in Section 7.5. Typically we use a model forecast that precedes the ASCAT pass time so we can then interpolate the model time to match the unique ASCAT pass time.

Throughout the rest of the book we have several examples of using scatterometer data to evaluate forecasts or learn more about the winds around us. It is an important, definitive tool.

Predicting next ASCAT pass time

If we find that latest data at a location of interest is too old to be useful, then there are several ways to anticipate when the next usable pass will occur—keeping in mind that

Figure 4.2-9. *ASCAT in GRIB format from dedicated GRIB viewers. Top from Ocens; bottom from LuckGrib. Ocens presents all passes over the past 22 hrs (from the time shown on their screen) in one window, with newer data overwriting older. Find the valid time for any location with the cursor over a wind arrow. LuckGrib downloads all passes over past 3 days, and shows them individually in 2-hr steps, selected by the time bar at the bottom. Valid time at the cursor is given relative to the time window being displayed. Both presentations can be zoomed in to show wind arrows at the native 25-km resolution (see red section in Figure 4.2-8).*

Downloaded files from either can be used in other navigation programs set up to view ASCAT data. The cross marks a common point in each, reporting (within cursor width at this scale) winds of about 8 kts from 085 at about 0135z. The two left swaths are one ASCAT-A pass; the swath on the right is the eastern half of the previous ASCAT-B pass. In these displays, the colorbar shading was applied to wind speed. Changing the color coding to valid time helps identify individual passes. In the top we see overlays of descending and ascending passes. Each program requires practice adjusting the display to optimize a valid time or wind speed emphasis. Zoomed into a region of interest, the valid time is easier to discern. Note these are real observations in GRIB format; not like the model predictions we see in other GRIB products.

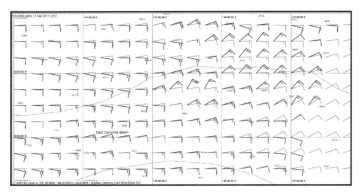

Figure 4.2-10. *Section of an ASCAT pass in GRIB format valid at 2347, September 10, (black arrows) loaded into Expedition along with a 00Z, September 11, GFS forecast (red arrows). We see excellent GFS agreement with ASCAT throughout this broader region (map height shown is 150 nmi), but there are notable differences seen here in a localized region. Satellite images at the time show many cumulus clouds in that region implying likely squalls. Squalls can also be indicated by displaying precipitation, but this depends on viewer options. See section 7.5.*

in many applications we only need it to be close enough to evaluate the GFS in the region, or other model we might be using.

The simplest approach, which could be adequate, is just look at the index graphic (for both ascending and descending) to identify the area you care about. This point will either be within the 4,000-nmi gap between newest and oldest passes (see Figure 4.2-2) or outside of the gap under, or between, one of the plotted passes. If your location is in the gap—good and bad news—you have no data at the moment, but you know you will get data within the next 3.5 hrs. This gap will be filling in with a new pass, every hour or two, as the oldest pass to the left of the gap is erased. The reasoning applies to ascending and descending passes.

If your location is near a plotted pass shown, you can check the time of that pass, and estimate the time of the next nearby pass based on where you are on the index of passes relative to the gap between newest and oldest. That gap is effectively 2 passes wide, so you can count passes for a rough estimate. If you are on the west side of the gap, you will get data earlier than on the right side of the gap.

Suppose your location is 2 passes to the left of the gap. The newest is on the right edge, so you are about 4 passes away from new data, or 4 × 101 min or about 6 or 7 hrs away, which will be in the next synoptic cycle. The latency of the ASCAT data (about 3 hr) is about the same as the GFS model data, so if you catch a most recent pass near a synoptic time, there should be a model forecast to go with it, approximately.

With a good internet connection there are online satellite tracking services that show where each satellite will be over their next several passes. (You will need a Metop ID number from Table 4.2-2). An example is in Figure 4.2-11. There are also mobile apps that provide a list of passes for any location. An example is the Android app SatOrbit by Silvioitaly. These run without internet connection, but periodically they will call for updating the orbital constants.

IMPORTANT SUMMARY TO THIS SECTION

You may fairly observe that there are many nuts and bolts to this section. These can be safely skipped by those who do not plan to use this resource.

We go to this detail to emphasize that the clean, crisp digital precision of model forecasts in GRIB format might mislead us into thinking this implies a level of accuracy. It does not. We have the choice to just move on, and keep in mind there are uncertainties, or we can use methods presented here and elsewhere in the book to cross check the model forecasts when we need to do the best we can, or a crucial decision must be made.

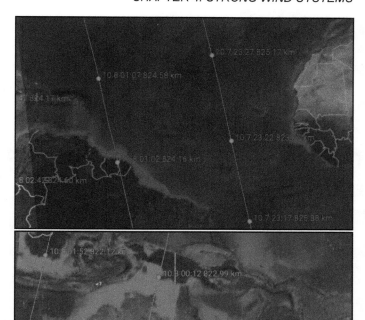

Figure 4.2-11. *Samples of tracking Metop A with an online app from* lizard-tail.com/isana/tle/plot/?terminator=true&catalog_number=29499*. Another with a different format is at* ssec.wisc.edu/datacenter/METOP-A*.*

Just as we learn in basic navigation not to rely on any single source for crucial decisions, so it is in weather work. To sail by any one forecast model alone, could indeed be worse than navigating by GPS alone. Likewise, sailing by custom weather reports alone prepared for you by a third party is about the same. There are communication factors in such arrangements that can confound the best prepared advice. Prudent navigation calls for having the basic knowledge needed to spot check all of our sources. There are numerous examples historically and recently to support these precautions.

4.3 Fronts and Low Formation

Chapter 3 tells how the sun's uneven heating of the earth creates warm air over the tropics and cold air over the polar regions, and further shows that this is not a static situation. As the earth's atmosphere strives for thermal equilibrium, giant three-dimensional cells of circulation bring tropical air into direct contact with colder midlatitude air along the polar front, located around much of the globe at higher midlatitudes (Figure 4.3-1). The polar front (broadly speaking) is made up of cold eastward wind on the north side and warm westward wind on the south side, but all fronts no matter where they are located are to some extent a shear line between warm air flowing one way and colder air flowing the opposite way. As the name "front" (from battle front) implies,

Table 4.2-2. Metop Satellite IDs for Tracking Apps			
Name	*NORAD ID*	*Int'l. code*	*Launch date*
METOP-A	29499	2006-044A	2006-10-19
METOP-B	38771	2012-049A	2012-09-17

this is a band of continuous conflict, which ultimately leads to many of the strong wind systems we see in the temperate latitudes around the world.

We also saw that descending air from the Hadley cell gives rise to large areas of high pressure around the globe, such as the Pacific and Atlantic Highs, as well as vast areas of high pressure over Russia and Canada. When these Highs sit stagnant for a period of time, the properties of the air within them homogenize to form distinct air masses of cold or warm air. Cold air masses tend to form on land under ridges in the winds aloft, whereas warm air masses tend to form in the subtropical Highs (see Appendix 6). There are no fixed definitions, but maritime tropical air is generally considered to have temperatures greater than 65 °F and dew points greater than 60 °F, which forms a benchmark for the other classifications (Section 3.4). When these air masses do eventually start to move away from their places of origin, warm air moving into colder or cold air moving into warmer, we again have frontal boundaries between adjacent air masses developing that can lead to increased wind and changes in the weather.

Below we show how moving fronts can evolve out of perturbations in the polar front, but we can also have fronts forming anywhere on the weather map whenever specific configurations of pressure patterns occur, as shown in Figure 4.3-2. Once a stationary front develops in one of these ways, it too can get underway leading to a moving front or fronts, which in turn could spawn new Lows.

Fronts are important not just because they can present a strong wind pattern on their own, they are also significant as an important source of deep Lows we experience in the midlatitudes. We shall see below that perturbations in a stationary front not only lead to moving fronts, but air circulation around and over them can lead to circulating wind patterns that can build into extratropical cyclones. In short, they are a source of our storms and Lows in general. In the midlatitudes, cyclone development is a natural by-product of the conflict between cold and warm air as the atmosphere struggles for thermal equilibrium. (Storm development in the tropics, on the other hand, takes place within a single warm air mass by quite different processes.)

But it is easier to understand the processes of front and Low development (frontogenesis and cyclogenesis) once we learn more of the properties of the fronts themselves. The leading edge of a moving mass of cold air is much different than the leading edge of a moving mass of warm air, primarily because the cold air is heavier.

Shape and Properties of Fronts

Warm air is lighter than cold air, so when it moves into regions of cooler air it slides up and over it, forming a long

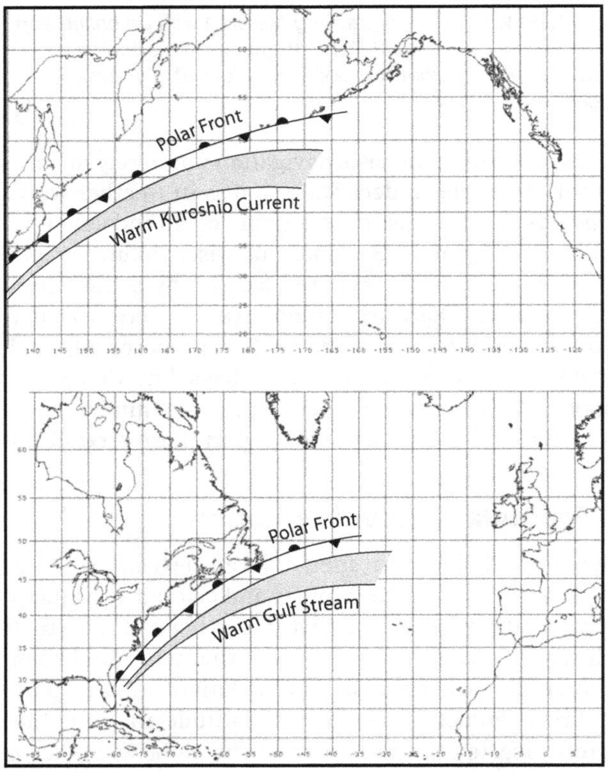

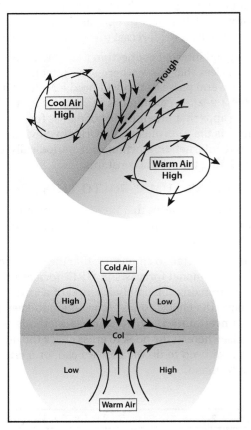

Figure 4.3-1. *Common locations of the semi-stationary polar front, which spawns many moving fronts and Lows that cross the ocean. There are cold easterlies north of the front and warm westerlies below it. The polar fronts are commonly found in these locations because of the warm ocean currents that flow northward along the continental coasts (western boundary currents). The sharper the air temperature contrasts, the more active the front. See also Appendix 6.*

Figure 4.3-2. *Ways fronts can form. Besides the large scale movement of air masses whose leading edges are fronts, any pressure pattern that brings warm and cold air into contact can create a frontal zone. A* col *is a saddle point in the pressure distribution.*

gentle slope. The rising warm air can extend some 400 miles or more from its contact with the surface, to the point overhead in the cooler air where we might first see the indications of a warm front approaching in the high clouds above. The strongest, gustiest winds and heaviest rain, however, are usually found in the 50 miles or so from the surface location of the front, as plotted on a weather map. (Figure 4.3-3).

Warm fronts are characterized by stratus clouds. As the mass of warm air rises up the slope of the frontal surface it cools and condenses into stratus clouds, and this continues all the way up to the top of the front that we see overhead at a long distance from it. By then the high cirrostratus is beginning to break up to leave just patches of cirrus clouds. (Cloud types are covered in Chapter 5). Looking at it from the other end, if we are in clear blue skies, the first signs of an approaching warm front will be the appearance of new cirrus clouds. They will then just dissolve into high stratus that continues to lower in the sky (cirrostratus, altostratus, and then nimbostratus). It is not so much a transformation of the clouds we see, but a sequence of clouds that is passing by. When the surface front is about halfway to us, it will start to rain—a long, slow, steady rain, that continues till the warm front passes by.

A cold front, on the other hand, is more of a wall of cold air moving into warmer air. Its surface curves back over the cold air as it moves forward at a slope some 4 or 5 times steeper than that of a warm front. The cold front comes in more like a snowplow, pushing the warm air straight up at its steep

surface, which gives rise to a relatively narrow band (again 50 miles or so) of cumulonimbus clouds (very tall, raining cumulus). Generally the winds are stronger and gustier at a cold front passage than they are at warm front passage, and the rain is usually very different. Ahead of the cold front there could be no rain, or just scattered showers, but at the cold front surface itself there are immediate downpours of heavy rain, as the strong winds set on very quickly.

Oftentimes, warm and cold fronts come in pairs (a day or two apart), as we discuss below, with the warm front approaching first, replacing cooler air, followed by what is called the *warm sector*, followed by a cold front. Either type of front can occur on its own without this pattern, but the *frontal wave* pattern of both emanating from a central low at the crest of the wave is more common in many parts of the midlatitudes, as shown in Figure 4.3-4.

When you are in the warm sector ahead of a cold front you can see it coming on the horizon. It appears like a long continuous row of squalls, tall dark clouds with low bases (cumulonimbus), often horizon-to-horizon wide. On the other hand, we can't really see a warm front approaching on the horizon. We just know it is happening, because of the long steady rain (for a day or so) as we watch the stratus cloud ceiling lower over us, as the wind slowly builds in strength. The properties of warm and cold fronts are summarized in Tables 4.3-1 and 2. The temperature change across a frontal boundary can be as much as 15 F° within an hour or so.

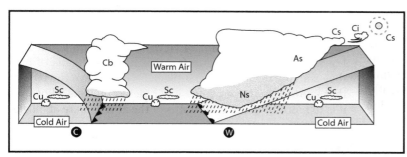

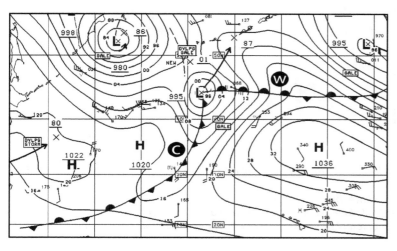

Figure 4.3-3. *Schematic profiles of a cold and warm front, both moving to the right. The scale shown here (and in all textbooks) is very greatly distorted. The slope of the steeper cold front is only about 1:30 or so, meaning a rise of only 2 or 3°, and the warm front is even much flatter than that. This sketch represents the cross section view of C—W in Figure 4.3-4, below. Notice that the warm front rain starts about halfway from first signs overhead to the actual passage of the surface front, which could be some 400 to 600 nmi away. The most active weather at the cold front spans about 50 nmi at the surface front. Clouds and abbreviations are discussed in Chapter 5. A ring around the sun or moon (scattering in transparent cirrostratus) are strong first indicators of a warm front (see Figure 9.4-5). The warm sector can sometimes be covered by stratus (overcast skies), which hides its location in satellite photos.*

Figure 4.3-4. *A moving frontal wave in the polar front in the mid-Pacific, consisting of warm front followed by cold front. The stationary parts of the front are marked with symbols on opposite sides of the front. Symbols on one side only means the front is moving. In this example the polar front has moved east of its typical formation zone along the coast (Figure 4.3-1). The isobars in the warm sector are parallel to the winds aloft, which mark the direction of motion of the system, as shown by the arrow marking its location 24 hrs later. The large Low to the NW of the wave was dropped off there several days ago by an earlier wave that went by, as illustrated in Figure 4.3-6.*

When the fronts come in pairs, the cold front is usually moving faster than the warm front, up to twice as fast. Everything is faster in the winter than summer, and surface system speeds usually depend on the speed of the winds aloft, but average speeds of cold fronts are some 15 to 25 kts, whereas warm fronts move at more like 10 to 15 kts. We can always learn these speeds in specific cases at hand by comparing the surface analysis map with the 24-hr forecast map, or the 24-hr forecast to the 48-hr forecast, and so on. Just note how far they moved in what period of time. You will note when doing this, however, that not all parts of a front move at the same speed. Sometimes the top end near the peak of the wave tends to move faster than the tail end of the front, which just gets stretched out across the ocean, sometimes almost stationary at one end.

	Warm	Cold	Occluded	Stationary
Weather	Steady rain, then mist or fog	Heavy rain at front, then showers	Steady rain, then squally	Intermittent rain and clearing
Principal clouds	Stratus (St)	Cumulonimbus (Cb)	Stratus then Cb	Lowering stratus then Cb
Temp. changes	Slow rise	Sudden drop at front passage	May rise or fall	Slow rise
Avg. speed Summer Winter	10 kts 15 kts	15 kts 25 kts	10 kts 15 kts	Slow or stopped Slow or stopped
Symbols				

Table 4.3-1. Fronts (see Table 4.3-2 for details)

Table Notes: *Cloud abbreviations are in Appendix 1.*

Cold fronts move faster than warm fronts in a frontal wave primarily because they are heavier *cold* air pushing the lighter *warm* air of the warm sector, whereas the warm sector air has to push heavier *cool* air ahead of it to make the warm front move.

The main consequence of this difference in frontal speeds, is that the cold front very quickly (a day or two) catches the warm front, which has the effect of diminishing the area of the warm sector as it lifts its warm air aloft. It can do this in one of two ways, depending on the relative temperatures of the cold air behind the cold front, and the cool air ahead of the warm front that it is replacing, as shown in Figure 4.3-5. The intersection of these two fronts is called an *occluded front*, which, more specifically, can consist of a cold occlusion (the most common type) or a warm occlusion. Properties of occluded fronts are included in Tables 4.3-1 and 2. Most fronts reaching the Pacific Northwest coast are occluded by the time they arrive, bringing with them simply a period of bad weather (rain, strong gusty wind, poor visibility). A cold occlusion

approaches like a warm front, and you can't see the cold front coming, but the rain just gets heavier and the winds stronger. The weather just gets bad for a while, then it clears after the front passes, just as it would were a cold front to go by.

Since air temperature changes at the frontal surface, the isobars will have a prominent kink in them as they cross the front, giving rise to a sudden veer in the wind direction as the front passes. The sharper the kink (V-shape), the larger the veer, and usually the stronger and gustier the winds. If the isobars flow right across the front on the map with little kink or even bend in them, then it is a weak front, with perhaps little more than some clouds and rain representing the trough it is in.

How Fronts Can Create a Low

From a practical point of view we care more about how Lows behave once they are formed than the details of how they actually form in the first place. We can leave the bulk of that knowledge to the professional meteorologists whose job it is to monitor the overall status of the atmosphere at all ele-

Figure 4.3-5. *Warm and cold occlusions. Both systems close off the warm sector and raise the warm air aloft, lowering the center of gravity of the system, causing it to accelerate. The deepest warm air marks the location of the pressure trough, which is shifted off the frontal surface in these systems. Thus, there would typically be no wind shift at the passage of a cold occluded front, but rather some 50 miles or so behind it, and the shift might not be so prominent as it is for a cold front. For warm occlusions, the shift would be some 150 miles in front of the occluded front and these could be more prominent, but again there would be no shift at the front itself.*

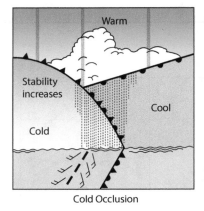
Cold Occlusion

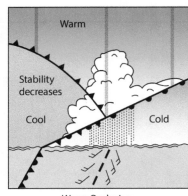
Warm Occlusion

It is usually hard to tell the type of an occlusion from the clouds you see and its plot on a map. But if the map shows an occluded front going by and the air gets colder after the passage, then it was a cold occlusion, otherwise it was a warm one. An exception might be a cold occlusion bringing in a wall of uniform stratus descending from an obvious line across the sky of cumulus forms—a reflection of the increased stability of the air mass.

These systems are characterized by the three frontal surfaces shown, but in practice at least one of them is poorly defined. Thus this typical textbook picture is rarely what these complex systems actually look like. In fact, some models of their formation do not rely on the concept of the cold front catching the warm front at all, but rather different processes that occur when the central Low separates from the crest of the frontal wave.

Table 4.3-2. Warm Front

	Before Passage	During Passage	After Passage
Weather	Continuous rain or snow	Precipitation usually stops	Possibly a light drizzle or fine rain
Clouds	In succession: Ci, Cs, As, Ns; sometimes Cb	Low Ns and scud	St or Sc, sometimes Cb
Winds	Increasing speed and backing	Sudden veer*, sometimes decreasing	Steady direction and speed
Pressure	Steady fall	Levels off	Little change
Temp.	Steady or slow rise	Steady rise, usually not sudden	Little change or very slow rise
Visibility	Fairly good except in precipitation	Poor; often mist or fog	Fair or poor; mist or fog may persist
Dew point	Steady	Slow rise	Rise, then steady

Table 4.3-2. Cold Front

	Before Passage	During Passage	After Passage
Weather	Usually some rain, possible thunder	Heavy rain, possible thunder and hail	Heavy rain, then scattered showers or fair
Clouds	Ac or As, Ns, followed by heavy Cb	Cb with Fs and scud	Lifting rapidly, followed by As or Ac
Winds	Increasing and becoming squally	Sudden veer*, very squally	Gusty, continual veer or steady
Pressure	Moderate to rapid falls	Sudden rise	Rise continues slowly
Temp.	May drop slightly in pre-frontal rain	Sudden drop	Continued slow drop
Visibility	Usually poor	Temporarily poor, improving rapidly	Generally good, except in showers
Dew point	High and remaining steady	Sharp drop	Lowering

Table 4.3-2. Occluded Front

	Before Passage	During Passage	After Passage
Weather	Continuous rain or snow	Heavy rain; possible thunder & hail	Possible heavy rain; then scatter showers
Clouds	In succession: Ci, Cs, As, Ns; sometimes Cb	Cb with scud	Lifting rapidly, followed by As or Ac
Winds	Increasing	Sudden veer*, squally	Gusty
Pressure	Steady fall	Moderate rise	Rise continues slowly
Temp.	Steady, or slow rise	May rise or fall depending on occlusion	May rise or fall depending on occlusion
Visibility	Fairly good except in precipitation	Temporarily poor, improving rapidly	Generally good, except in showers
Dew point	Steady	Slight drop, especially if cold-occluded	Slight drop, but may rise some if warm-occluded

Table Notes: *Cloud abbreviations are in Appendix 1.*
In the Southern Hemisphere wind backs at a frontal passage.

vations and thus come up with their predictions of where and when the Lows and fronts will form, which we learn about in the 48-hr and 96-hr surface forecasts. Nevertheless, it is valuable to understand the basic components of one such process in so far as they help us interpret what we see around us and on the maps—especially if we happen to be sailing in a region where Lows and fronts are actually forming at the time, or we somehow end up without professional forecasts. We should keep in mind, however, that there are other mechanisms for Low formation that do not require a front at all.

Wind speeds aloft, for example, can sometimes be estimated from patterns in high clouds, and when they are faster than usual, it generally means stronger winds (deeper lows) on the surface and faster moving systems. Fast fronts or fast Lows as a rule mean stronger surface winds. When we identify fast winds aloft we expect an approaching system to be more severe, even if we don't have maps or forecasts to confirm this. Or, as early mariners put it, "Mackerel sky and mare's tails *[signs of fast winds aloft]*, make tall ships set low sails." A quick look at Low formation helps us understand the basis of this observation.

The process can be thought of in two steps. What starts the wind flowing counterclockwise in a circle (Northern Hemisphere), and then what makes it accelerate once it does. The last step is the same as what makes the Low deepen.

We already know something basic about the second step. Recall from Chapter 2 that we outlined a fundamental point about the underlying science of circular wind flow. When wind starts to flow counterclockwise around circular isobars (a Low), the sum of all the forces involved tends to increase the pressure gradient that is driving the wind, whereas when wind starts to flow clockwise around circular isobars (a High) the sum of forces is just the opposite—it tends to reduce the gradient driving the winds. Thus Lows once formed have a natural tendency to deepen and give rise to strong winds, whereas Highs have a natural tendency to weaken, giving rise to light winds. In this section we are looking at the processes that can enhance that natural tendency for Lows to deepen once formed.

The key point is that frontal lines are usually associated with some level of wind shear—cold air flowing to some extent against warm air. Wind shear is a general term meaning the wind speed or direction changes abruptly. It does not have to actually flow in opposite directions as it does at some fronts. In many contexts, wind shear refers to changes in wind speed with increasing elevation, but it can describe horizontal changes as well. The polar front is an example of shear.

Tidal current flow offers a good analogy. Tide rips are shears in the current flow near prominent points of land or shoaling where contrary currents collide or scrape past each other. Prominent current eddies can form at this boundary, sometimes a foot across, sometimes a mile across. We can see sticks spinning that are caught along such an eddy line as we sail by. When a prominent eddy fills an entire bay, it can meander out of the bay, still spinning, at the change of the tide. As this eddy moves out and is captured by the current flow in the main waterway, it moves downstream much as a surface weather low is pulled along the surface by the winds aloft. The edges of the large eddy are essentially fronts of contrary current flow, and again, secondary eddies can develop along this shear line. An easy way to imagine how a circular eddy might be formed at a shear line is just to roll a pencil between your outstretched hands. One hand pushes it one way, the other hand the opposite way, and it spins.

There are close analogies in the behavior of wind and water, especially when it comes to the formation of waves. Because of this analogy, several common weather patterns are referred to as "waves." This should not be too much of a surprise, because in both cases we are dealing with fluid-fluid interactions. In one case it is air creating waves in the more dense water; in the case we will look at here it is warm air creating waves in the more dense colder air.

Although we often think of fronts as two-dimensional curves on a weather map, they are of course three-dimensional surfaces extending vertically between the two air masses, as indicated in Figure 4.3-3. The polar front, for example, is a stationary front, with the vertical surface leaning northward over the colder, heavier air. Rising straight up through the cold eastward flow, one would eventually punch through the surface of the front into the warm westward flow. Thus there

is a very distinct fluid-fluid shear taking place all along this three-dimensional frontal surface just as there is with wind blowing over the surface of water. We just have to imagine our water surface stood straight up and sloped back a bit.

Early models of Low and front formation are based on the idea of this warm wind creating a wave in the colder air below it. The process is outlined in Figure 4.3-6. It is usually referred to as the Norwegian cyclone model, in respect to the Norwegian meteorologists who first proposed the idea shortly after World War I. These days it is known that the basic ideas they proposed do not on their own account for the full range of cyclone formations we observe across the midlatitudes, but elements of the model still remain fundamental to newer concepts and help us picture the process taking place.

One of the newer concepts is that of "conveyor belts" of air that circulate around the wave linking the surface structure to the winds aloft, as shown in Figure 4.3-7. This is a key concept from the mid 1980s that shows just how the surface lows

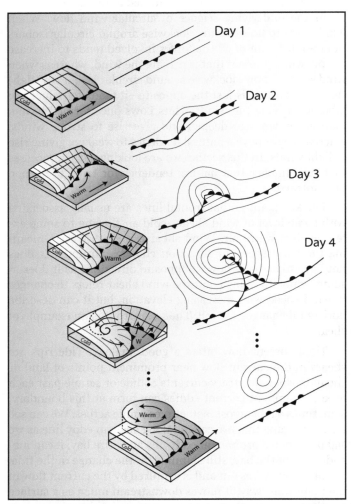

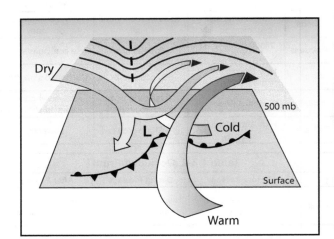

Figure 4.3-7. "Conveyor belts" of air. These are the typical wind flow patterns that link winds aloft to surface systems. Thus when the winds aloft move east they drag the surface systems with them. The dominant warm air conveyor brings the warm moist air (fuel for latent heating) from the surface up to the winds aloft over the gentle slope of the warm front. Cold air flowing along behind the warm front (originally running parallel to the polar front) is forced aloft on the cold conveyor when it interacts with circulation around the central low at the crest of the wave. Dry air descends in the higher pressure behind the cold front via the dry air conveyor, clearing the sky behind the cold front, and sometimes reaching the surface with enhanced gusty winds (see "sting jet" in Section 4.4). The extent of this descending dry air is often visible in satellite photos, clearing out a path in the cloud pattern to form a comma shape (Figure 4.3-11). Lows often form just downstream of a trough aloft (Figure 4.3-8) because of the divergence in that region.

Figure 4.3-6. Norwegian cyclone model, showing how a wave in a stationary front can generate moving fronts and one or more surface cyclones (Lows). Imagine the wave moving up the frontal line to the NE, rather than cut apart and stacked as shown here.
A modern competing model of cyclone formation is called the Shapiro-Keyser model, from 1990. It differs mainly in that the surface cold front fractures off of the wave and moves through the warm sector perpendicular to the warm front, which itself is then more like a warm occlusion (Figure 4.3-5). The result of this process in a mature system is not a bent-back occlusion, but a bent-back warm front, surrounding a core of warm air, called a seclusion. I am told that some 40% of extratropical cyclones can be described by this S-K model.

are dragged along the surface by the winds aloft. It is a good analogy to think of surface cyclones as eddies in the river of winds aloft. We use this continually to know where the Lows are going and how fast they are moving. The conveyor belt concept shows how action on the surface is directly linked to winds that are some 18,000 ft above the surface. See Figure 4.3-8.

Figures 4.3-9 and 4.3-10 show how the surface winds respond when a Low passes by, north or south of us, with or without an associated front. Note the veer at the front and the behavior in the warm sector.

Figure 4.3-11 shows a satellite image of a wave cyclone where the belts of air are clearly discernible. It is in fact pic-

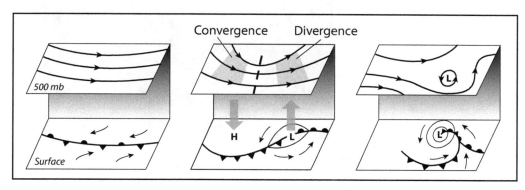

Figure 4.3-8. *Lows often form under the divergence zone just downstream of a trough aloft in the 500 mb winds. Compare 500-mb maps with the corresponding surface analysis maps to see the effect. The important concept of divergence is illustrated in Figure 4.3-12.*

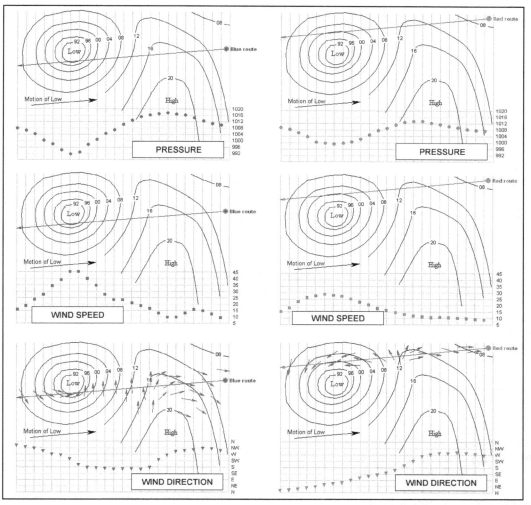

Figure 4.3-9. *Winds and pressures on various routes crossing a weather pattern as seen on a surface analysis map. You can think of your vessel being stationary or slow somewhere on the right, and the weather pattern crossing you as it moves to the right in the pictures, or think of the patterns as stationary and your vessel crossing it as you move to the left. The time scale from one side to the other of each picture is about 2 days if the system were moving. The top routes show passage through the top of the ridge and then north of the Low center, whereas the lower routes pass south of the Low center. Once past the ridge, on the right side of the Low and facing its direction of motion, the wind veers as the Low approaches, but on the left side it backs (see Section 4.7).*

Notice you can expect a slight rise in pressure as the ridge is passed, or pushed below you, and that in every case the approach of the Low is signaled by backing winds. In many cases the backing of the winds can be an earlier signal than the pressure drop, because the winds will still back even as you ride along a near constant isobar on the top of the ridge. Somewhere along the line, you would see the clouds start to thicken and lower, but this could be rather late in the sequence without a warm front involved. Adapted from the Starpath Weather Trainer Live software program.

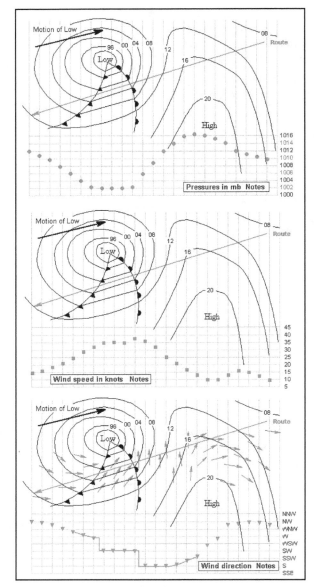

Figure 4.3-10. *Same data as Figure 4.3-9, but now including passage of a frontal wave. Notice there is a sharp veer in the wind at the frontal boundary, usually larger at the cold front than the warm, and larger when the temperature drop across the front is larger. The system moves in a direction parallel to the isobars in the warm sector, which has typically steady winds and stable pressure.*

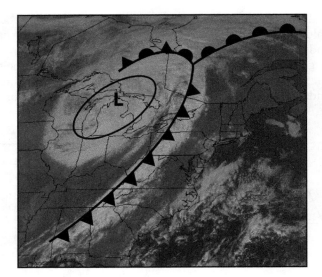

Figure 4.3-11. *"Comma cloud." The shape of mature frontal wave clouds in satellite photos often look like a large fuzzy comma. A prominent gap in the comma behind the cold front indicates the intrusion of a strong dry-air conveyor (as was illustrated in Figure 4.3-7).*

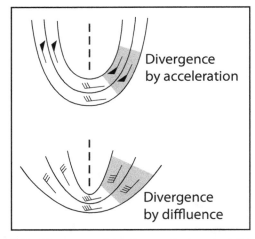

Figure 4.3-12. *Divergence downstream of a trough aloft by an increase in speed (acceleration) and by a spreading out of the elevation contours (diffluence).*

tures like this that help meteorologists understand what is taking place on the surface.

Finally we come back to the basics of an idea mentioned in Chapter 2. For a low to deepen, the amount of air leaving the system aloft (divergence) has to be larger than the amount of air entering the system on the surface (convergence). When more goes out than goes in, there is increasingly less air in the column and thus the pressure drops. A trough in the winds aloft offers the ideal situation. When the winds aloft flow down into a trough they converge at the turn, and then diverge as they accelerate out of it. When a surface wave happens to be just below this region of divergence downstream

of the trough line, it sucks the air out of the cyclone and deepens the surface low. If you compare the 500-mb maps of the winds aloft, you will nearly always see a trough line (marked by a dashed line) just upstream (to the northwest) of the surface low.

The Life of a Low

• A wave develops in the elevated surface of a stationary front, which starts wind circulating counterclockwise around its intersection with the surface. (Straight isobars initially parallel to the front line on the surface close at the crest of the wave, because the front is a trough at the surface. Once the front forms the S-shape of the wave, the pressure rises in all directions away from the inflection point of the "S," which forms the closed low.)

• An upper level trough wanders over the fledgling surface low to offer the needed divergence aloft to deepen the Low (Figure 4.3-12). Air is transferred between the surface and the winds aloft via the conveyor belts. The warm air conveyor taking the warm moist air aloft is the primary driving force, since it brings in the fuel. As the warm moist air rises to colder elevations the water vapor condenses, giving off heat that further drives the winds upward, deepening the surface low. The source of fuel and the fortuitous location of the upper level trough providing the divergence are the key factors to Low development.

• As the system contracts with higher winds, it gets deeper and smaller, so its moment of inertia is reduced, and to conserve angular momentum it has to rotate faster—like an figure skater pulling in her arms to increase her spinning rate. Thus the smaller the Low gets the faster it rotates.

• As the cold front occludes the warm front, it forces the warm sector aloft, replacing it with heavier cold air. This lowers the center of gravity of the entire system, which lowers its potential energy. This must be compensated for by an increase of kinetic energy, achieved by accelerating the rotating wind speed of the colder air below it. When the warm air is gone from the surface, the system is rotating at maximum speed. For this reason, Lows associated with these frontal waves are generally near their peak intensity at the time the fronts occlude, which is something we can see on the weather maps and follow in the subsequent forecasts.

Details of the surface system evolution described here depend on the flow pattern of the winds aloft. Some patterns favor evolution more like the Norwegian model, others more like the Shapiro-Keyser model, but nevertheless, this very general description should still help you interpret what is shown on the maps, which is the goal at hand.

• And then with the warm air gone (its source of fuel for latent heating) and the upper level trough moved on to the east or dissolved, the main system on the surface begins to dissipate. It just spins off the top and slows by friction. We see this on the map as the isobars expanding and eventually the annotation DSIPT (for dissipated)—which does not prevent a new system developing along the occluded front if another trough aloft comes along overhead, and in fact such *secondary lows* formed in that manner can turn out to be much worse than the original one.

With this background we can look at a weather map and have a better understanding of what is represented by all the curves and lines we see, and anticipate and understand what we see in the forecasts of their behavior. Certainly not all Lows and fronts behave in these simplified scenarios. In fact, the massively complex processes involved are still only slowly becoming understood. No two storms are ever the same in their formation details, but looking at surface analysis maps you will easily identify, every day, in every ocean, similar frontal waves folding and unfolding over periods of several days. You will also see waves start to build and then simply fall back into the front, which often means the needed trough aloft did not show up.

On a personal note, years ago I attended a NWS conference on weather forecasting where a speaker gave a talk that touched on the Norwegian model of cyclone formation. It all seemed to make sense, except I could not understand why the wave formed in the first place. So I boldly raised my hand to ask, "But what starts it off? Why does a wave form in the frontal surface in the first place?" The room became dead silent. The speaker, a well known expert in meteorology, paused with a perplexed look on his face for a few moments, and then said, "I don't know. Maybe a goose flew through it," which gave the audience of professional meteorologists a good chuckle at my naivety. I should have just asked myself why is it that some sticks are spinning and some just riding along the eddy lines we see on the water.

Divergence and Convergence

We pause briefly before ending this section to discuss two fundamental terms in Low formation that might be more subtle than suspected. Without this understanding the key role of the trough aloft might not be clear, and sometimes appear inconsistent when viewed on 500-mb maps.

Divergence means the air is spreading out. When air diverges you can add more air to the region and it will be carried away. When air converges, on the other hand, it is packing up, which inhibits air from entering the region. Convergence aloft forces air down to the surface, which feeds Highs on the surface. Divergence aloft carries rising air away from the region, which deepens Lows on the surface.

Divergence and convergence come about two ways, either by a change of speed or a change in flow pattern (Figure 4.3-12). If the leading members of a marching band slow down when crossing the 50-yard line, but keep marching in a straight line, the band will converge. Pretty soon you won't be able to put anymore band members in the pile. This is convergence by deceleration. On the other hand if the front of the band speeds up as it crosses the line (accelerated), the band spreads out, which is divergence by acceleration.

Likewise, if the right side of the band turned somewhat to the right at the line, and the left side turned somewhat to the left at the line, then the band would still diverge, even if it stayed at the same speed. This is divergence by diffluence, meaning simply the flow spreads out. If they all turned in at the line they would converge by confluence and make another pile. These two terms (diffluence and confluence) apply to water flow as well, which is another non-compressible fluid that behaves in a similar way—"Pittsburgh is located at the confluence of the Allegheny and Monongahela rivers."

On surface maps, wind flow along isobars is determined by the closeness of the isobars and their curvature—a point that was discussed in Chapter 2 on wind flow. The closer the isobars the faster the wind. The same is true for wind flow aloft, but on 500-mb maps we are looking at elevation contours, not isobars. But the rule is the same, the steeper the 500-mb surface the faster the wind. Thus close contours mean fast wind; wider spacing means slower wind.

So what do we have after that bit of background? If two *straight* isobars spread apart, the wind flow spreads out (diffluence), so we should have divergence. But when the isobars spread apart, the gradient is reduced and the wind speed slows down, so we should have convergence. What we end up with is neither one. They cancel each other—or maybe one effect is slightly larger, but no significant effect overall.

The key issue here is the contours in the winds aloft are not straight lines. Their wind flow is analogous to gradient wind along curved isobars, as opposed to geostrophic wind along straight isobars (Chapter 2). When two parallel isobars change from a straight-line to curve to the right around a High, the gradient force (out from the High, into the Low) is in the same direction as the centrifugal force (out from the center of curvature; in this case out from the High) and thus the wind speed increases. But when these same parallel isobars curve to the left to go around a Low, the same gradient force into the Low is now opposed by the centrifugal force pointing out of the Low, and thus the wind speed decreases.

Thus we have the basic behavior that when uniform wind (parallel contours) flows down the side of a trough and reaches the curve to the left it slows down, and then when it leaves the curve and straightens out it speeds back up again. This latter acceleration leads to divergence just downstream of the trough. In those cases where there is confluence into the trough, there is often a comparable diffluence on leaving the trough, which again gives rise to divergence just downstream of the trough.

In short, most troughs aloft, regardless of their shape and the wind arrows that are shown on the 500-mb maps, give rise to some level of convergence upstream of the trough (driving cold air down to the surface) and some level of divergence downstream of the trough pulling warm air up from the surface. The rate at which surface Lows develop depends a lot then on the speed and evolution of the trough above it with regard to these factors that control the level of divergence it offers.

4.4 Types of Lows

As mentioned in Section 4.1, strong winds come from tight pressure gradients, which show up on weather maps as close isobars. Low pressure itself is not required. Nevertheless, most cases of strong winds are in fact usually associated with low pressure. This section provides an overview of the types of low pressure patterns that give rise to strong winds. For want of a better title, it is called "Types of Lows"—the goal is to provide some ways to characterize the pressure patterns so we can talk about them, and understand the terms as they come up later. These are not unambiguous classifications of Lows, however, nor are they formal terminology in some cases. This section could have been called "Types of Gales."

Fronts and Lows

Not counting local squalls that can generate strong winds over a very small area, an initial distinction we might make for sources of strong winds on larger scales is between strong winds from Lows versus strong winds from fronts. In this sense, we are thinking of Lows as more or less round, closed isobars surrounding a central low pressure (sometimes called a *depression*), whereas fronts are located in long expansive troughs of low pressure. On a worldwide average, frontal zones are likely the most common source of strong winds simply because they cover and influence so much of the earth's surface, extending as they sometimes do clear across oceans and continents.

Most fronts are associated with a parent Low, but often it is difficult to determine whether the formation of the front led to the formation of the Low or the formation of the Low led to the formation of the front. There is much overlap in the concepts of frontogenesis (the formation of fronts) and cyclogenesis (the formation of Lows or cyclones). Thus we come to what might be considered a first distinction among low pressure systems, that of Lows with associated fronts versus Lows without associated fronts.

In Section 3.1 we discussed one type of Low without a front—the low that developed over an isolated island that heated more with the rising sun than did the surrounding waters. This type of *thermal low*, however, is not restricted to small scales. The large thermal low that develops over California and Nevada can have a major influence on the coastal winds of Oregon and California. An even larger such low develops over India in the summertime, which is a major contributor to the world famous monsoon winds that completely reverses the wind flow seasonally along continents and is responsible for much of maritime and cultural histories of both Asia and Africa.

Tropical and Extratropical Lows

In the midlatitudes, most Lows have fronts associated with them—but not all, by any means, as shown below—whereas in the tropics, the reverse is true. It is very rare to see a Low with a front in the tropics. Lows in the tropics, however, have many other distinguishing characteristics besides the absence of fronts, and thus one of the major distinctions between Lows is whether or not they are tropical or extratropical systems. They are both circular depressions in the atmospheric pressure, with winds flowing round them, counterclockwise in the Northern Hemisphere, clockwise in the Southern Hemisphere. In both cases the wind crosses over the isobars near the surface as it converges into the center of the Low, which forces the air to rise to higher altitudes in their centers. But other than that, these are distinctly different types of low pressure systems. They are formed differently, they behave differently, and they are much different in size. Distinctions between tropical and extratropical Lows are listed in Table 4.4-1.

As the names imply, these two types of systems are generally restricted to the waters they are named for, but like all weather patterns on earth they are steered along the globe by stronger winds at higher altitudes. As we have seen in Section 3.3, these higher winds meander around the globe, and periodically they can wander off their normal routes enough to carry an extratropical Low right down to the tropics, fronts and all. Perhaps even more often—though still not at all common—tropical storms can find their way well into higher latitudes, especially along the east coast of the U.S. where the warm waters of the Gulf Stream provide a trail of fuel (warm moist air) all the way up to Canada. About 4 tropical systems each year make it all the way to the latitudes of Canada.

As a tropical storm leaves the tropics it generally evolves to look more like an extratropical system—meaning primarily that it gets bigger and perhaps less purely circular, and often picking up a frontal system along the way. One of the worst Pacific Northwest storms in modern times (the Columbus Day storm of 1962) was the remnant of Typhoon Freda that had wandered unusually far north of the tropics along about 165° E, till it got captured by a southern dip in the winds aloft and carried east. It was diminishing as it moved north and then remained steady as it moved east, but then rejuvenated with a fury as it crossed under the axis of the winds aloft over unseasonably warm northern waters closer to the coast. Its central pressure dropped by more than 30 mb in less than a day, reaching a low point of about 958 mb. It made landfall from California to Canada with winds of over 80 kts. The record setting winds in the north (over 100 kts in some places) were still less than its tropical typhoon peaks, but the region covered by them was ten times the size of its tropical parent. Needless to say, this was an extreme event, in some categories it is considered the worst of the 20th Century, but numerous similar events have occurred over the years from the tropics to the Pacific Northwest.

Another more recent example of a tropical storm wandering north was tropical storm Alberto on the East Coast, which showed that it is not unheard of for the extratropical offspring to be even stronger than its tropical parent. Tropical storm Alberto formed in the Yucatan Channel on June 10, 2006 and moved across the Gulf of Mexico to go ashore at the panhandle of Florida with winds of just under hurricane force. Thirty-six hours later it crawled offshore at Cape Hatteras, NC with winds of barely 30 kts after a 600 nmi trip overland. But once over the warm waters of the Gulf Stream it took less than 24 hrs to build back all the power it lost and more. It proceeded on to the N-NE to pass directly over the fleet of the transatlantic rowing race in the early hours of June 15 with hurricane force winds, significantly stronger than it had as a tropical system.

There are on average about 5 tropical systems per season that reached above 40° N in the Atlantic—some more severe, some less severe than the Alberto remnant. Tropical systems moving north are more common on the east coast because of the Gulf Stream.

Table 4.4-1. Comparison of Tropical and Extratropical Cyclones	
Tropical	*Extratropical*
Form in the tropics	Form outside of the tropics
Primarily oceanic, forming and maturing only over warm oceanic waters. If they cross over large land areas, they weaken quickly and eventually die.	May develop and intensify over water or land.
Develop primarily in the summer and autumn months of their hemispheres.	Occur at any time of year, but are most powerful during the winter.
For some portion of their lives, most tropical cyclones move in a westerly direction.	Generally head eastward and rarely travel toward the west.
Mature tropical cyclones are generally much smaller than extratropical cyclones. A typical tropical storm, for example, is 200 to 500 miles in diameter.	A North Pacific winter cyclone, on the other hand, may span 1500 miles or more. Typical extratropical storms are some 700 to 1,000 miles in diameter.
Do not have fronts.	Usually have associated frontal systems.
Mature tropical cyclones have a central calm area called the "eye".	Do not have an eye.
Strongest winds near the center.	Strongest winds usually near the periphery.
Can have sustained winds of 120 to 150 kts—a "super typhoon" is one with winds over 130 kts.	Almost never this intense, although very severe ones can generate winds up to 100 kts and often over 64 kts which defines hurricane force.
Relatively rare. In a typical year, about 70 tropical storms of hurricane strength will form worldwide.	Very common. In the same year, there would be some 1,500 or more extratropical storms developing.
Forecasted tracks notably more dependable than forecasted intensities.	Uncertainties can vary between location and intensity, but not systematically. Varies from storm to storm.
GFS model winds are often underestimated, sometimes by a lot.	GFS model winds usually meet specified accuracies.

This latter storm was a good example of modern marine weather in action. By the end of the same day the storm was identified in the Yucatan Channel, it was announced on the NHC website that there was a 5 to 10% chance of 50-kt winds off the coast of New York five days later. From then on, the predictions from both the NHC and the OPC just got better as time progressed. The subsequent minimum pressure recorded in the OAR Northwest row boat from Seattle matched to within a millibar the 48-hr prediction and subsequent surface analysis for their location. With their computer and satphone (both charged by solar panels) they had a weather data collection and analysis system onboard (with shore-based support) that would match that of deep-sea commercial vessels, forty times their size, with orders of magnitude more funding. With the communication options, products, and services now available, every vessel can have state of the art marine weather support regardless of size and budget.

Meteorological Bombs

The Columbus Day example of tropical storms turning extratropical shows how rapidly the pressure can drop in an extratropical low in some circumstances. But it does not have to be a post-tropical system to deepen so rapidly. In fact it happens more likely outside of the hurricane season in the cooler weather (October to March), when there is a larger temperature gradient between the high latitudes and the midlatitudes. There is a name—more of a nickname—for the result of such explosive cyclogenesis. It is called a *bomb*. A meteorological bomb is any system whose central pressure drops rapidly, according to Table 4.4-2. They occur in both the Northern and Southern Hemispheres. (To research the subject, a more general term would be *rapid intensification*.). Many of the famous Nor'easters in the northwest Atlantic have resulted from this type of development, aided by the interaction of warm Gulf Stream air and the cool air of the polar front. The storm that overtook the tragic 1979 Fastnet Yacht Race is also attributed to such a system. The "Queen's Day Storm" in the SW Pacific between Fiji and New Zealand in early June of 1994 is another. Many famous storms are in this category.

Bombs are of course again extreme cases, but they reflect a general distinction between the formation of extratropical and tropical systems. Tropical systems are formed in one air mass of uniform temperature and humidity, whereas extratropical systems are generally formed at the interface of two distinct air masses. Cold air essentially kills off a tropical system, whereas cold air interacting with warm air is crucial to the formation of most extratropical systems, which is why

most have fronts associated with them, at least in their formative stages.

From a practical point of view, a key distinction is there are many fewer bombs in the tropics. There are of course horrendous storms and hurricanes almost guaranteed in certain places at certain times, but these do not sneak up on us. They develop along a more or less well defined sequence, and usually take several days at least to build into deep systems. And though it is true that tropical cyclone intensities are more difficult to predict than their tracks, the potential of this behavior and the possible extent of strong winds, seems to be covered very well in tropical forecasts. As a further contrast, hurricane season is summertime, whereas "bomb season" is mostly wintertime.

Secondary Lows

A secondary low is one that develops with or in association with a primary low. It is a common event, and oftentimes the secondary lows evolve very rapidly and end up more intense than the primary low they are associated with. When an extratropical wave pattern of warm and cold fronts evolves, it is common that the system will spawn new Lows as the low center of the wave begins to dissipate. These are referred to in discussions as secondary lows. They occur at both ends of the system—at the tip of the occluded front and at the tail end of the cold front trailing behind. Over half of these waves systems develop a secondary low at the end of the occlusion. When the occluded front is prominent and bends backwards to resemble a scorpion's tail it can become very intense as discussed below.

The other type of common secondary low develops on the tail end of the cold front as shown in Figure 4.4-1, which shows several types of lows. These can also evolve to be more severe than their parent or primary low. These latter kind can occur with or without the first type of secondary low. Both cases of secondary low formation occur when there is a fortuitous alignment of the surface systems with the winds aloft that provides the extra divergence aloft needed to cause them to deepen. Secondary lows developing in sequence at the tails of their respective cold fronts (as many as 3 or more) are called a family of lows. Besides understanding the terminology, a key significance to these secondary lows is their potential to develop rapidly and to become severe.

Sting in the Scorpion's Tail

The secondary low that often develops at the tail end of a bent-back occluded front is a notorious strong wind system that was first identified by Norwegian meteorologists in their original proposal of the cyclone wave theory itself. They spoke of the "poisonous tail" of the bent-back front. These are important systems to keep an eye on because they often develop explosively (bombs) and can be difficult to forecast. They also often, if not usually, present the mariner with the experience of much stronger winds once the barometer starts back up. Notice in Figure 4.4-1 the common result that the gradient is tighter on the aft side of the system. Thus if we grow accustomed to having winds start to diminish as a more

Table 4.4-2. Meteorological Bomb	
Lat	mb drop per 24 hrs
60	> 24
50	> 21
40	> 18
30	> 14

conventional low passes by and the barometer rises, we will be sadly disappointed in these cases. The "sting" of even stronger winds comes with a rising barometer.

In rare occasions of an intense bent-back occlusion, the conveyor belt of cold dry air (shown in Figure 4.3-7) that swoops down from the winds aloft can give rise to very strong gusts (80 kts or more), which are significantly higher than would be expected on the basis of the normal gust ratios found in comparable strong winds in other systems. These enhanced winds are referred to as a *sting jet*, with the same reference to the shape of the occlusion and the jet of wind descending from above. Several of the worst storms ever in the Pacific Northwest and the British Isles have been characterized by this effect.

Upper-level Lows

In covering the terminology of low pressure systems we frequently mention upper level lows as they often come up in weather discussions. It is what it sounds like. A specific low pressure system at higher elevations, with or without a counterpart on the surface. They are usually of interest to mariners when they show up at the 500 mb level, since this domain is the only upper level we commonly have maps of when underway. Needless to say, professional meteorologists are watching and analyzing low pressure patterns at all levels of the atmosphere, not just the 500-mb level.

The winds aloft that flow along and around these lows were discussed in Section 3.3. In these winds aloft we can have troughs of low pressure, closed lows (meaning one or more closed lines of constant height) that are still within the flow aloft, or cutoff lows that have separated from the main flow, and hence the name *cutoff*—they are cut off from the main flow of the winds aloft. All three of these upper-level low pressure patterns (Figure 4.4-2) affect what is taking place on the surface.

Cutoff Lows

Cutoff low can refer to a low aloft or a low on the surface. When a cutoff low in the winds aloft finds its way down to the surface it creates a type of low of special interest to mariners because it happens fairly frequently and it can be difficult to forecast. It is also another way to get a prominent circular low in the midlatitudes that may not have fronts associated with it. As noted above, most midlatitude lows have fronts associated with them and indeed they relied on these air mass distinctions to build their own enhanced circular flow in the first place. Cutoff lows can be an exception because of the way they are formed.

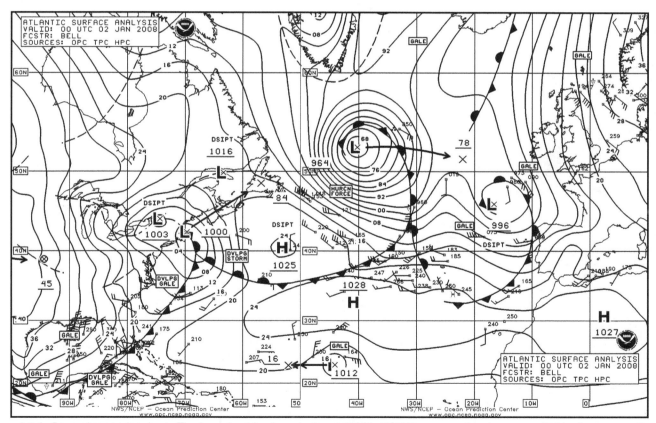

Figure 4.4-1. *Several secondary lows. The large bent-back occlusion at 52° N, 40° W is a secondary low generated by the wave pattern of an original parent low (no longer there), centered at the peak of the wave below it. That parent low started off much as the one at 42° N, 70° W, which is itself another secondary low to the original one. Another is likely to develop at the end of its cold front, to form a family of 3 lows. Notice how the gradient of the large occlusion is much stronger on its aft side (the arrow shows it moving east), which will bring hurricane force winds with a rising barometer. This is the "sting in the scorpion's tail." The cutoff low at 25° N, 45° W is actually moving west, which is more like the behavior one would expect of a tropical system, but this one was in fact a cutoff low formed 5 days earlier and still pretty much in the same location, but now moving "backwards."*

The usual process is a lobe is formed in a deep trough in the winds aloft, which then just closes off and leaves the low isolated from the main flow, as shown in Figure 4.4-2. This leaves a closed low of circulating cold air aloft. When this structure is prominent enough or lives long enough, its circulation is translated down to the surface to create a surface low. Since it is now detached from the normal westerly flow of the winds aloft it can remain in the same location for several days, and maybe even drift backwards in some cases.

Cutoff low behavior during and after formation is difficult to forecast, other than they are likely to remain in the same place for some time. Cutoff lows subsequently dissipate on their own, or get recaptured by the winds aloft and taken to the east.

In the Northern Hemisphere there are about 100 cutoff lows formed each year, more or less uniformly distributed across the midlatitudes of northern waters. In the Southern Hemisphere, cutoff lows are a prominent component of the marine weather patterns off the southeast coasts of Australia, Africa, and South America.

In Section 7.8 on the use of the 500 mb maps, we propose that the development of a cutoff low aloft implies we might be more conservative on our interpretation of the surface forecasts, because their behavior can be difficult to predict. We can be fairly certain they will stay more or less where they develop on the surface because they have escaped the main flow aloft that usually pulls the lows along the surface, but it is less certain how they will develop or how they might influence neighboring isobars.

A cutoff low is like a drummer who has fallen out of the line of a marching band. We can guess he will hang around a while, but we don't know if

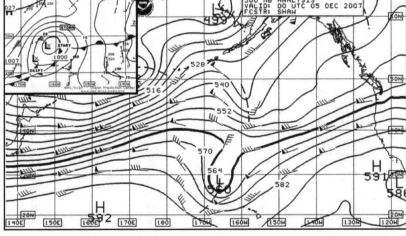

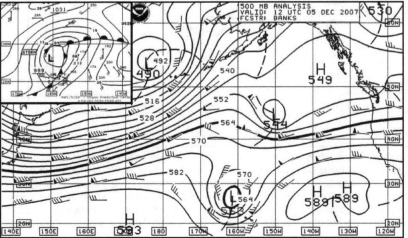

Figure 4.4-2. *Cutoff low formation. The left side shows three stages in the development of a cutoff low, 12 hrs apart. This low does not end here fully cutoff aloft, but is certainly a closed low aloft, that acts much like a cutoff low—the terms are sometimes used interchangeably.*

Inset on each of these is a segment of the corresponding surface analysis in the region directly below the upper level low.

In the top left, the surface low started to develop just east of the trough aloft as described in Section 4.3, moving east with the flow as marked by the arrow in the surface insert.

In the middle picture, the upper level low starts to form and the surface system stops moving east. At that time, the 48-hr forecast (top for Figure 4.4-3) shows it staying in the same place, just north of Hawaii, for another 2 days, while the rest of the surface systems above it (not shown) keep marching along with the flow aloft.

In the bottom left we see the surface low system still developing, but essentially stationary. Note in the surface analysis at the valid time of the 48-hr forecast (bottom of Figure 4.4-3) the properties of the surface cutoff low are pretty well predicted, as is the rest of the region between southern CA and HI—but maybe not as precise as it might be if that low were not there.

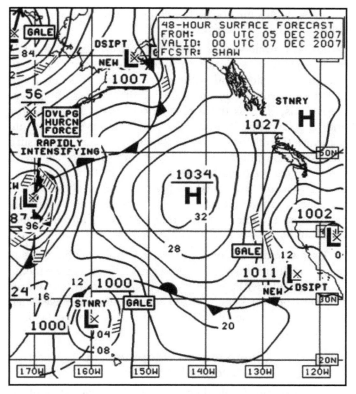

Figure 4.4-3. Top. *A forecast made at the time of the middle panel of Figure 4.4-2.* Bottom. *The surface analysis at the time of this forecast, so it can be checked. The map style on the bottom is different as it was obtained from archives (ncei.noaa.gov/thredds/ model/ncep_charts.html), and that is the form they use. The others were taken live, at the time they were first published in their original format.*

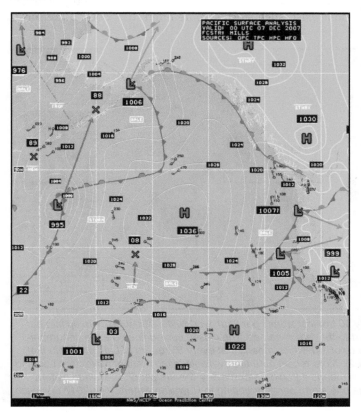

he will get mad, or just go away, or step back in line with the band and move off again. Luckily we have professional meteorologists telling us what they think is likely to happen, and their judgement will be better than ours. An example is shown in Figure 4.4-3, where the forecasts were actually quite good. Forecasts for a similar one in Figure 4.4-1 were not so good.

4.5 Tropical Storms and Hurricanes

Summary

If your goal is to sail in a hurricane, you can indeed do just that. They are frequent enough, last long enough, and are located well enough that you could look up when and where they are, and then go there and sail into one, or wait for one to come to you. These data are presented in Figure 4.5-1 and Table 4.5-1.

On the other hand, if your goal is to not sail in a hurricane, then you can equally well succeed at that. Look up the same information you did before, but then don't go there.

In one sense it is that simple, but in another it isn't. Hurricane distribution in time and space is a statistical one, and they do wander out of the norms. To strictly rule out the interaction with hurricanes would rule out a vast amount of ocean for many months of the year. So if we are to do any sailing in or near these zones, we are obligated to know the basics of their behavior in order to safely manage their appearance in our space—which is to imply we did our homework and have not willfully or accidentally ventured into their space.

We are much assisted in this by the great amount of data that has been collected on these things over the years, as well as by the large number of trained people whose very occupation it is to watch them (via satellite, aircraft, and other special observations), forecast their behavior, and report it online and over the radio. With any shortwave receiver we can get current and forecasted data on their location, intensity, and motion. The National Hurricane Center (NHC) is the main resource for this data in waters adjacent to the United States. Regional Specialized Meteorological Centers (RSMC) for tropical storm forecasting in other parts of the world are discussed in Chapter 8. The first one to our west is the Central Pacific Hurricane Center in Honolulu. Hurricanes headed to HI are covered by NHC till about 140°W and then switched to Honolulu Center—they do not drop off the face of the earth, as might appear from the NHC graphics at times!

Regardless of the source or detail of reports, we are still left with the task of interpreting the information usefully and taking proper actions. Remember that even when the storm itself is in clear sight visually, there is often still the chance that proper maneuvers will greatly reduce its impact. And when it is still far off and approaching, the proper maneuver can have an even larger effect on minimizing the interaction.

Remember, too, that 150-kt winds and chaotic 50-ft seas are not the sort of thing we survive solely with good seamanship, intelligence, and will power. It also takes a great deal of luck, which as prudent navigators we are reluctant to rely upon. It is the gravest mistake to not maneuver away from them when you have the knowledge and ability to do so. The NHC recommendation is to avoid the region of winds greater than 34 kts that surround the center of the system.

Tropical Cyclones

The term "cyclone" refers to any area within which the atmospheric pressure is low in all directions relative to its surroundings. Such systems are generally circular and exhibit counterclockwise circulation in the Northern Hemisphere (clockwise in the Southern Hemisphere). Tropical cyclones are cyclonic storms which originate in the tropics and subtropics of both hemispheres. First appearing as minor atmospheric disturbances over warm oceanic waters, they can develop into the most destructive storms on earth. Fully mature tropical cyclones are relatively rare compared with other types of storms, but they are exceedingly violent and must be regarded with the utmost respect. Avoiding a tropical cyclone should be the primary consideration for any mariner planning or conducting a voyage through areas where such storms occur.

Mature tropical cyclones are known by various names throughout the world: in the western North Atlantic, central and eastern North Pacific, Caribbean Sea and Gulf of Mexico, they are called *hurricanes*; in the western North Pacific, they are called *typhoons*; in the Bay of Bengal and Arabian Sea, they are called *cyclones*; in the southern Indian Ocean and the western South Pacific, they are called *tropical cyclones*. Colloquially, they are called *willy-willies* off the coast of Australia; and off the Philippines, *baguios*. In this section, we generally refer to them as tropical cyclones, or hurricanes.

Regional names may be used when referring to a specific locality.

Tropical cyclones are one variety of cyclone. The other major group of cyclones includes those which originate outside of tropical and subtropical regions and hence are called *extratropical cyclones*. The familiar Lows of temperate regions, such as the winter storms of the North Pacific and North Atlantic Oceans, are extratropical cyclones. While both varieties of storm share the traits of low central pressure and cyclonic winds, there are important differences between them. Properties of each were compared in Table 4.4-1. The most important distinguishing feature of tropical cyclones is the concentration of large amounts of energy into a relatively small area. For the mariner, this translates into very high winds and heavy seas.

Despite much use of the phrase in public media, there is no official definition of a "superstorm." It is used in the media (not the NWS) without discretion to mean an intense extratropical storm that could or did cause a lot of damage. Such storms are often the midlatitude remnant of a tropical storm, but not always.

Origin and Development of Tropical Cyclones

There are no simple theories that adequately account for the complex origin and behavior of tropical storms. There are, however, large amounts of observational data that scientists and sailors have used to determine the general conditions under which tropical storms develop, which assist the model forecasts. Mature tropical storms require very specific atmospheric and oceanic conditions. Even when the proper conditions exist, such storms, more often than not, do not form.

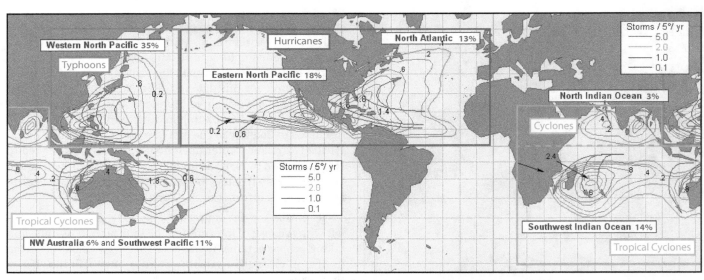

Figure 4.5-1. *Tropical systems. As of 2010 statistics, there are roughly 90 tropical storms per year, worldwide. About 50 develop into hurricanes, cyclones, or typhoons—percentages by region are shown next to the region names. The closed curved lines are the geographical distributions. The solid blue line, for example, represents a frequency of 1.0, which means that every 5° square of Lat-Lon within that line experiences 1 tropical cyclone per year on average (Bowditch 2002). More recent data are available in the* Mariner's Weather Log *and websites of several RSMC. Hawaiian waters are bounded by 0.2, which means a tropical storm every 5 years per 5°; the island waters span some 5 of these zones, so we expect and indeed see on average one storm per year getting to Hawaiian waters. The 2017 Bowditch has a newly expanded section on tropical systems.*

Only 10 percent of tropical disturbances, the first stage of a tropical cyclone, eventually develop hurricane force winds.

Hurricanes form only over warm water. A good rule of thumb is the seawater temperature must be at least 80 °F (26.7 °C). The maximum possible intensity of hurricanes increases as the water temperature increases. Hurricanes derive their energy from the latent heat released as water vapor condenses. As long as the center remains over warm water, a hurricane has a large supply of heat energy. This heat energy is converted into the kinetic energy of motion, which is what drives the winds. Since hurricane paths often follow that of warm water, weather maps showing water temperature might help interpret their paths.

We used to think that over warm water a hurricane had *limitless* supply of warm water, but recent research is showing that if a hurricane stops long enough it will consume the warm surface water and initiate mixing of cooler water from below. So to some extent it has to keep moving to keep building.

Hurricanes form most commonly in late summer and early autumn when tropical waters are at their warmest. When planning voyages, remember not to overlook the basic fact that the seasons are reversed in the Southern Hemisphere.

Most hurricanes form between 5° and 25° latitude, especially between 10° to 15° latitude. Hurricanes do not form within 4° or 5° of the equator because they require the Coriolis effect to initiate cyclonic circulation and the Coriolis effect is insignificant close to the equator.

Hurricanes always develop from a pre-existing disturbance in the tropical atmosphere. This disturbance may be moving, but only slowly, less than 10 kts or so. Obviously when traveling in these waters we should be alert to any such disturbance to the east of us. The probability is low that it evolves into a storm or hurricane, but it does have that potential much of the year.

Tropical storms generally develop in a region of below-normal pressure (less than 1004 mb) in low latitudes. Heavy rain or rain showers are usually present. (Average pressures in hurricane zones are 1012 to 1014 mb; Section 9.3)

The Intertropical Convergence Zone (ITCZ) is that belt of light winds, showery squalls, and ascending air currents which lies between the converging NE and SE trade winds near the equator. Commonly known to mariners as the doldrums, the ITCZ exerts a primary influence on all weather in the tropics, and is an important element of tropical storm formation. When the ITCZ migrates across the equa-

tor, the trade winds follow it. Those winds are then subject to the Coriolis effect which can transfer sufficient spin to the converging winds to cause the formations of a large vortex. If such vortices are reinforced and sustained, they can develop into storms and hurricanes.

One of the situations in which a hurricane is most likely to develop is the conjunction of a tropical wave with an ITCZ that bulges across the equator, as shown in Figure 4.5-2. Tropical waves are troughs of low pressure moving west with the trade winds. They can impart a cyclonic pattern to the NE trades, which can be reinforced and closed by the deflected trades. A closed cyclonic circulation is the crucial step in organizing a tropical storm.

Hurricane formation also requires the wind to be vertically uniform throughout the atmosphere. In the easterly trades, hurricanes do not form where winds aloft are westerly. Even when they are easterly, if they are very strong they will not be uniform with the surface flow. Near Hawaii, for example, the trades are northeasterly, but the winds aloft are typically

Table 4.5-1. Tropical cyclone statistics													
NORTH ATLANTIC													
Jan	Feb	Mar	Apr	May	Jun	Jul	Aug	Sep	Oct	Nov	Dec	Annual	
----	----	----	0.1	0.1	0.6	1.0	3.2	4.1	2.1	0.7	0.1	12.1	S
----	----	----	----	----	0.1	0.5	1.6	2.6	1.2	0.5	----	6.4	H
WESTERN NORTH PACIFIC													
Jan	Feb	Mar	Apr	May	Jun	Jul	Aug	Sep	Oct	Nov	Dec	Annual	
0.4	0.2	0.4	0.7	1.2	1.6	3.7	5.8	5.0	3.8	2.6	1.4	26.6	S
0.2	----	0.2	0.4	0.7	1.0	2.2	3.5	3.4	2.9	1.6	0.7	16.7	H
EASTERN NORTH PACIFIC													
Jan	Feb	Mar	Apr	May	Jun	Jul	Aug	Sep	Oct	Nov	Dec	Annual	
----	----	----	----	0.7	1.9	3.5	4.3	3.7	2.2	0.3	0.1	16.6	S
----	----	----	----	0.3	0.8	1.8	2.1	2.5	1.3	0.2	----	8.9	H
NORTH INDIAN OCEAN													
Jan	Feb	Mar	Apr	May	Jun	Jul	Aug	Sep	Oct	Nov	Dec	Annual	
0.1	0.1	----	0.2	0.8	0.6	0.1	----	0.3	1.0	1.3	0.6	4.9	S
----	----	----	0.1	0.4	0.1	----	----	----	0.1	0.6	0.2	1.6	H
SOUTHWEST PACIFIC AND AUSTRALIAN REGION													
Jan	Feb	Mar	Apr	May	Jun	Jul	Aug	Sep	Oct	Nov	Dec	Annual	
3.5	3.8	3.2	1.7	0.3	0.1	----	----	----	0.2	0.5	2.2	15.6	S
1.5	1.9	2.0	1.0	0.1	----	----	----	----	----	0.3	1.2	8.0	H
SOUTH INDIAN OCEAN													
Jan	Feb	Mar	Apr	May	Jun	Jul	Aug	Sep	Oct	Nov	Dec	Annual	
2.7	2.5	2.0	1.2	0.4	0.1	0.2	0.1	0.3	0.5	1.2	1.4	12.5	S
1.5	1.5	1.3	0.7	0.2	----	----	----	----	0.1	0.6	0.6	6.6	H

Table Notes: *On the far right, S is the total number of tropical storms per month; H is number of those storms that develop into hurricanes or similar systems. These are averages from 1981 to 2010 (from 2017 Bowditch). Any one year could be different. A value of 0.2 would mean that every 10 years there would be 2 in that month, or 1 every 5 years. Checking NHC for years 2010 to 2017 we get for North Atlantic S=13.8 (4.6), H=9.4(3.0) and Eastern Pacific S=15.9(4.6), H=7.1(3.4), where (SD) are the standard deviations. and See Tropical Cyclone Climatology section of the NHC website. Other recent data can be found at the respective RSMCs. See also Figure 4.5-1.*

westerly, so this is an unlikely place for hurricane formation. Hence with maps of the winds aloft available, one could probably improve on the statistical estimates of the probability of hurricane formation from tropical disturbances. The steadiness of the winds (needed for hurricane formation) is enhanced where the air temperature near sea level is relatively constant over a wide area.

Tracks and Movement

No two tropical cyclone tracks have ever been identical. They do, however, follow trends that might help us understand what we might expect. Typical tracks were shown in Figure 4.5-1. The best source of recent tracks for specific storms, regions, or seasons is the history section of the NHC website. A printed annual summary (including extratropical systems) is given in the *Mariner's Weather Log*.

After formation, while still in lower latitudes, the tracks of tropical storms tend to be sinusoidal. That is, they swerve back and forth, while maintaining a generally westward (and somewhat poleward) direction. During this period, their speed is slow, some 4 to 13 kts, and erratic. They may stop and start in fits, and may even go backwards for short intervals. See Figure 4.5-3.

At some point in their westward progress, tropical storms usually curve poleward. After they curve poleward, they tend to "recurve" on around to the east—that is, to a poleward track with an eastward component. This happens when they come under the influence of the westerly winds aloft. During the process of recurvature, the speed of the storm is usually very slow (2 to 8 kts) and erratic.

After recurvature, the track of a tropical cyclone is much straighter and its speed increases dramatically—some 15 to 20 kts typically, but speeds as high as 40 or 50 kts have been observed. Since it is moving poleward, it may rapidly leave the area of warm seas from which it draws it energy. The storm will then begin to decay, though it can continue to carry potent winds and precipitation. At this stage it can evolve into an extratropical cyclone.

When attempting to project the future course of a tropical cyclone, keep in mind that superimposed on the general behavior discussed above, there are more than a dozen generic patterns to these tracks that have been identified over the years, including many twists, zigzags, loops, and so forth. It is unlikely one could out-guess them. Wireless reports of forecasted positions from the NHC are the best bet. These get more accurate every year, but they still strongly recommend all mariners keep in mind what they call the 1-2-3 Rule for estimating the uncertainty in the forecasted positions. This safety factor is added to what the NHC calls the 34-kt Rule:

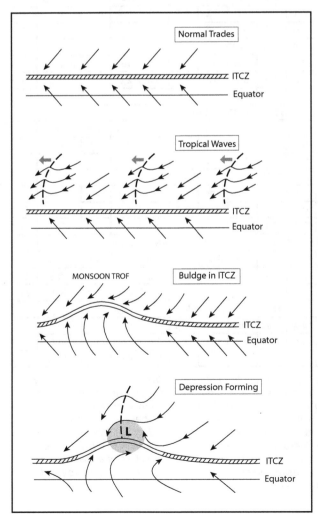

Figure 4.5-2. *One method of tropical depression formation. Top shows normal trade wind flow meeting at the Intertropical convergence zone (ITCZ), which is typically just north of the equator, but close enough that no Coriolis effect occurs—the Coriolis force is zero at the equator and increases with strength at higher latitudes. This normal flow can be distorted two ways.*

A longitudinal trough moving west called a tropical wave can shift the NE wind to the E and SE as shown. They bring clouds and rain for 2 to 3 days as they pass, travelling at some 9 to 18 kts. Gusty winds can occur as the trough line goes by. About 70% of Atlantic hurricanes begin in this manner. Tropical waves are often visible on satellite photos and always clearly marked on tropical maps. They appear as waves in the trade winds with a wavelength (distance between them) of about 1,000 nmi.

Another distortion of trade wind flow can come from the random oscillation of the ITCZ (doldrums). It does not remain at a fixed latitude but waves about in irregular patterns in response to local disturbances. When this region bulges far enough north, as shown, the Coriolis force starts to kick in and bend the wind to the right. As of 2012, the NWS now distinguishes between the ITCZ region (double line with crosshatch) with NE winds above and SE winds below, and a monsoon trough (double line, no crosshatch) whenever there are SW winds below it. This is often a good way to guess wind flow when none is marked on the map. Trough is spelled trof on most weather maps. Both lines are troughs, in that pressure increases as you move away from the line in either direction. See Figure 10.2-1 on Monsoons to learn the origin of this name.

When a tropical wave meets one of these northern excursions of the ITCZ conditions are set up for formation of a circular low, as shown on the bottom. Once this Low starts circulating, if the water is warm (80 °F or more), and the air unstable enough, with the right winds aloft, conditions are right for the newly formed Low to deepen into a tropical storm and perhaps hurricane.

"For vessels at sea, avoiding the 34-kt wind field of a hurricane is paramount. Thirty-four kts is chosen as the critical value because as wind speed increases to this speed, sea state development approaches critical levels resulting in rapidly decreasing limits to ship maneuverability." (See Figure 4.5-4.)

The only thing we might count on when planning routes around these, or to minimize likely contact should one develop, is the bigger picture that they move generally west and then curve poleward. They rarely move toward the equator.

Classification of Tropical Systems

In successive stages of development, the tropical cyclone may be classified by form and intensity. The four primary stages are known successively as tropical disturbance, tropical depression, tropical storm, and hurricane, cyclone, or typhoon, depending on location.

Stage 1. Tropical Disturbance

A tropical disturbance is a migrating system of convection, generally 100 to 300 miles in diameter. It does not have fronts and may or may not alter the local prevailing winds. It does not have strong winds or closed isobars, i.e., isobars that completely enclose the low. To be classified as a tropical disturbance, a system must have maintained its identity for 24 hrs or more. About 20% of identified tropical disturbances further develop into a tropical depressions.

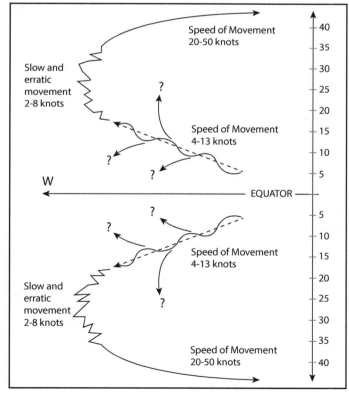

Figure 4.5-3. *Typical motions of a tropical cyclone. The scales shown are all broad averages that can be kept in mind if no data are available to you. The NHC does a very good job on predicting actual tracks and their uncertainties. Refer to their website for archived real tracks.*

Stage 2. Tropical Depression

The next stage in the development, a tropical depression, has one or more closed isobars, some rotary circulation at the surface, and sustained wind speeds up to 33 kts. They can be spotted in satellite photos of clouds, and sometimes by scatterometer wind patterns, even when telltale lower-cloud patterns are obscured by higher clouds.

Tropical depressions are assigned a number to aid in tracking and disseminating information about individual cyclones. The regional hurricane center assigns the numbers, beginning with the number "01" at the start of each new calendar year. The label may also include a letter. The label is used on advisories until the depression develops into a tropical storm, at which time it gets a real name and the number is no longer used on maps.

A tropical depression has a roughly 70% chance of developing into a tropical storm. Once identified, the NHC assigns a more specific percentage to further development.

Stage 3. Tropical Storm

A tropical storm has closed isobars, a distinct rotary circulation, and sustained winds over 34 kts but still less than 63 kts. There are about 100 tropical storms formed on a typical year worldwide. All tropical storms are assigned a name. A tropical storm has about a 70% chance of maturing into a full-fledged hurricane.

Stage 4. Hurricane, Cyclone, or Typhoon

A hurricane has closed isobars, strong and very pronounced rotary circulation, and sustained wind speeds of 64 kts or higher. Hurricanes are one of the most wondrous products of the earth's atmosphere. They are, in essence, huge heat engines that convert the thermal energy of warm water into the kinetic energy of wind and waves. And despite the fact that they are a major threat to coastal towns and to unfortunate mariners that happen into their path, they are in fact a crucial element of the earth's heat distribution process. Though always different in details, they share certain common features, described below.

Wind

To be classified as a hurricane, a tropical storm must have maximum sustained winds of over 64 kts. Many hurricanes, however, have much higher winds—as do, by the way, many extratropical storms. Super typhoons of the Western North Pacific have sustained winds as high as 140 to 150 kts at some point during their lifetimes. To make matters worse, gusts in a hurricane may exceed the sustained winds by as much as 30-50%. Gusts in a 150-kt hurricane could conceivably reach 225 kts.

The wind in a hurricane crosses the isobars at an average angle of 20-30°, with the angle decreasing nearer the center. At the wall cloud of the eye, there is no longer any inflow and the winds are tangential to the isobars. Typical wind patterns in an intense cyclone are shown in Figure 4.5-5. Real data compiled by the NDBC are presented in Appendix 10.

Figure 4.5-4. Top. *The 1-2-3 Rule refers to forecast uncertainties of 100-200-300 nautical miles at 24-48-72 hrs, respectively. The danger area to be avoided is the shaded area inside the indicated cone, which is defined by the forecasted maximum radii of winds over 34 kts, extended by a safety margin derived from ten years of forecasted track error analysis. The 34-kt radius and its extension is easy to plot using the latitude scale. Each 60 nmi = 1° of latitude. Forecasted tracks are becoming more accurate yearly, but the sizes and intensities of the storms remain a challenge that leads to these larger safety margins.*

Bottom. *A 3-day verification of Hurricane Sandy forecast. OSCAT winds at 1700 on Oct 28, 2012 with overlay of the 72-hr forecast made on Oct 25, showing radius of maximum 34-kt wind and the 1-2-3 Rule extension (dashed arc). Also shown is the predicted 50-kt wind radius, which is not part of the 1-2-3 Rule, but shows here that the 50-kt forecast was very good. The actual storm center was just 30 nmi NE of predictions, and the storm did increase in size, as was forecasted. The 34-kt radius prediction was good, but there was in fact a much larger field of this wind range than predicted, which shows the value of the 1-2-3 Rule.*

See nhc.noaa.gov/prepare/marine.php and nhc.noaa. gov/marinersguide.pdf for a detailed discussion from the NHC on use of the 34-kt Rule and the 1-2-3 Rule and other safety matters near tropical storms.

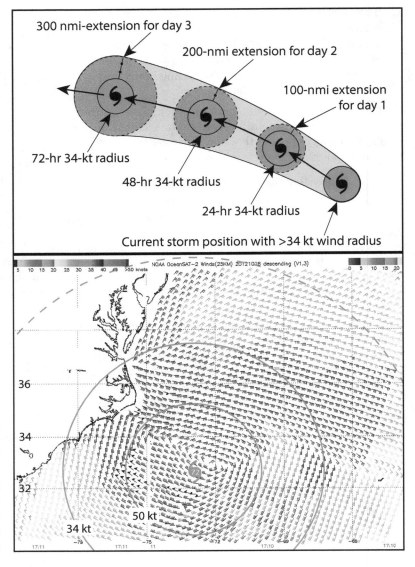

In the Northern Hemisphere, wind speeds are typically greatest on the right side of a tropical cyclone looking in the direction of movement. In this sector, the forward movement of the storm is added to its internal wind velocity, resulting in a higher net wind. On the left side the forward movement of the storm is subtracted from the observed wind velocity. In the Southern Hemisphere, the left side of the storm has the more powerful winds. The distinctions between the right and left sides of a cyclone, however, are much more significant with more complex origins than covered here. (Section 4.7 covers details on the sides of a storm.)

Pressure

The high winds of a hurricane are the result of extremely low pressure at the center of the storm compared with that in surrounding areas. In simplest terms, this low pressure results as warm air rises out of the center of the system. The intense winds occur as external air rushes inward to replace the ascending air.

The barometric pressure at the center of a typical hurricane may be 60 or 70 mb below the mean value at the outer edge of the closed isobars. Very intense storms can have pressures 100 mb lower. Because the wind strength is related to the difference in pressure over a horizontal distance (the pressure gradient), the pressure at the center of a storm is a measure of its intensity. A formula for estimating the maximum sustained winds of an intense tropical cyclone is

$$\text{Max Wind} = 16 \text{ kts} \times \text{square root (dP)},$$

where dP is the pressure difference in mb from the periphery to the center of the storm—but we must keep in mind that there are broad variations in this relationship, depending on storm size and stage of development, as shown in Figure 4.5-6.

A hypothetical barograph trace for a typical hurricane is shown in Figure 4.5-5. In that sample, the periphery is about 1000 mb and the central pressure is 920, so dP = 80 mb, which would estimate a max wind of 143 kts, which would make it a category 5 hurricane with a *relatively* high central pressure.

The Eye

The center of a hurricane is like no other meteorological phenomena on earth; the *eye of the storm*. The eye is a circular or elliptical area, 10 to 20 miles in diameter, of relatively light winds and clearing skies. The eye is often depicted as a welcome brief respite for those caught in a hurricane, but this is a seriously flawed conception. Waves within the eye are mountainous and very confused, as they are converging from all surrounding parts of the storm. As the eye passes, the winds return with their previous ferocity, but from the opposite direction.

Wall Cloud

Surrounding the eye of a hurricane is an immense structure of rapidly ascending and rotating air called the wall cloud. The wall cloud is the area of most violent winds and heaviest precipitation in the entire hurricane. Depending on eye diameter, the wall cloud zone extends some 5 to 30 miles beyond the eye. See Figure 4.5-7.

Size of Hurricanes

Based upon the extent of their associated clouds, winds and barometric pressure perturbations, tropical cyclones average 400 to 500 miles in diameter. This is the size of the cirrus pattern that would be seen in a satellite photo. In weather discussions and publications, however, the diameter of a hurricane can be expressed in several ways:

(1) Area of hurricane-force winds (≥ 64 kts)

(2) Area of tropical storm winds (≥ 34 kts); or

(3) Diameter of the outermost closed isobar.

The latter is well defined and clear in surface maps and roughly coincident with the circular pattern of cirrus clouds seen in satellite photos. The forecast descriptions of tropical storms, on the other hand, provided in voice and text forecasts, are very specific and unambiguous. They tell the winds in the four quadrants about the storm, along with the radii of the various quadrants. (Examples are given in Figure 4.8-4.)

When a storm first reaches hurricane intensity, the diameter of 64-kt winds can be relatively small (under 100 miles, though the range is broad). But as the storm ages, it expands laterally. A typical Atlantic hurricane has an area of hurricane-force winds of about 100 miles in diameter, with gale-force (34 to 64 kts) winds over an area up to some 400 miles in diameter. Super typhoons of the Western Pacific may have hurricane-force winds to a radius of some 300 nautical miles or more, with gale force winds spanning an area over 1500 miles in diameter. Tropical storms in other oceans, however, are generally much smaller than this. Record sizes were illustrated in Figure 4.1-1. A cross section of typical hurricane dimensions is shown in Figure 4.5-5. Remember that "tropical storm winds" (34 to 63 kts) is a different definition than "storm winds" (48 to 63) used outside the tropics.

Review

Hurricanes are steered by the winds of the upper atmosphere. As they develop, they move slowly away from the equator, curving toward the pole when they enter the easterly trade wind belts. While in the tropics, their path can be very erratic. They may even stop and reverse direction. Occasionally, a vessel may be struck twice by the same hurricane.

Eventually, the storms slide further poleward and out of the trades. The path of any individual storm is influenced not

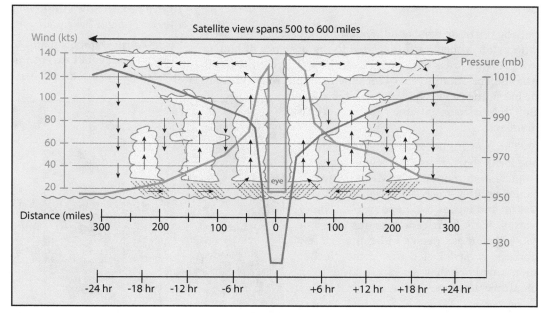

Figure 4.5-5. Cross section of an intense hurricane. No two hurricanes or typhoons are the same, but they do have similar general properties. This picture is intended to represent average values for a large system. Note the correlation in clouds, squalls, wind, and pressure, shown here very schematically.

Here we see winds at 100 miles off of 50 to 70 kts; in weaker systems, which may be more typical (peak wind 100 kts), the winds could be as low as 40 kts or so at 80 to 100 miles off, when the systems are still below roughly 30° latitude. At higher latitudes, after recurvature, the region of strong winds often expands considerably. The very strong winds are concentrated near the wall cloud within about 50 miles of the center. It is obviously prudent to keep alert early and put as much distance as possible between you and the center. The time scale on the pressure trace assumes a storm motion of 300 miles in 24 hrs (a relative speed of 12.5 kts). The dotted line along the clouds represents roughly the outline that would appear as the cloud bar on the horizon. This could be in clear sight while conditions at your position are still relatively normal, with still adequate time to maneuver out of the path of the most intense winds and seas. Within this schematic picture, once the barometer starts down (5 mb below normal for the region, season, and time of day, after perhaps a slight rise) then it is clear sign of the presence of a tropical cyclone, even if a cloud bar is not discernible. See Appendix 10 for several measured wind and pressure profiles.

Figure 4.5-6.
Tropical cyclone maximum winds and central pressures. The Saffir-Simpson categories are indicated (circled numbers), along with the pressure ranges often associated with them. These correlations, along with the dotted lines marking average correlations at lower speeds, are consistent with an early prediction procedure called the Dvorak method. Notice that even though the average initial tropical storm (34 kts) might correspond to a pressure of 1005 mb, there could be depressions with half or twice that wind speed with this same central pressure. Likewise, the implication of the graph would be that a 960-mb central pressure would on average have winds of 100 kts, but they could be anywhere from 95 to 115 kts, or even a broader range on the fringe of the statistics. Climatic wind speeds in the tropics can be seen in the COGOW (Section 10.6) website; average pressures and their standard deviations are in the Starpath Mariner's Pressure Atlas.

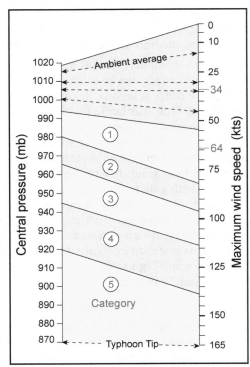

only by the trade winds and westerlies, but also by the circulation aloft, which itself is related to the presence of high or low pressure areas in the region. A strong High in the North Atlantic, for example, may block the recurvature of an Atlantic hurricane to the NE and force it into the Gulf of Mexico or onto the North American mainland.

The average life span of a hurricane is about 10 days, from its recognition as a tropical disturbance to its death. A hurricane dies after it leaves the region of warm waters and moves over land or over colder waters. If the hurricane remains in tropical waters, it can persist indefinitely; a few hurricanes have lasted over a month. But sooner or later they get blown away from the tropical waters.

There are sometimes two or more hurricanes present simultaneously in one region. If the two hurricanes approach each other, they may revolve around one another, with the smaller hurricane moving more rapidly—known as the Fujiwara effect.

Important details on forecast sources for these systems are in Chapter 8. The text Advisories are a key component.

4.6 Squalls

Squall is the name mariners use for thunderstorms similar to those so common on land in the Midwest and in Florida, though at sea one does not always hear thunder from these nor do we seem to get as much hail as on land. But we do get rain and we do get wind, sometimes a lot of wind.

Here we take a look at squalls at sea and on inland waters—how they work, how to judge their intensity, and what to expect when they hit. Have you ever noticed, for example, when tacking into the wind that squalls seem to always bring wind from the wrong way? If such things are true often enough we should know about it. We will be safer and faster if we do. Sample pictures are in Figure 4.6-1.

To get value from weather tactics, though, we need rules of thumb. If we try to qualify every circumstance with all possible exceptions we end up with such a hodge-podge of information that we forget how to guess what's going to happen. With a rule of thumb we at least have an easy way to later remember what actually did happen; the rule worked or it didn't work. Here is an example of a rule we covered in the section on fronts. Wind shifts at any weather front will be permanent veers. Face the surface wind before the front passes and the new wind will be to the right of it, some 30 to 60°, after the front passes.

Here's another example of a rule of thumb that is exactly on the topic of squalls. When the strong gusts of cold wind from a squall (called the downburst) first hit they will be from the direction of the squall.

In warm waters, squalls are more common at night than during the day, but except for the darkest nights, this direction is usually easy to spot because the squalls are usually easy

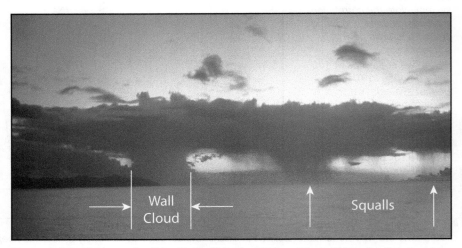

Figure 4.5-7. *Photograph of Hurricane Klaus in 1984, courtesy of Charles Brown, who was taking part in NOAA's Voluntary Observing Ship program at the time he took this photo, less than 200 nmi from the wall of the storm, uniquely visible in the picture centered over the headland on the left. On the right are several squalls. Notice how calm the water is at this distance off and how clear the sky. Klaus Lasted from Nov 5 to 13, with peak winds of 80 kts at 980 mb on Nov 9.*

to spot—by definition they must be isolated storms. Even if they are already raining and you can't see under them, you can usually see rather well-defined boundaries to the rain. At sea, during the day or twilight, you can watch them form on the horizon, and sometimes even maneuver away from them or into them as you see fit. With radar they can be seen very clearly, night or day.

You can decide if you are on a collision course with one just as you would a large ship—more like a mountain in this case. Watch the angle on the bow to the center of the thing. If the center of the cloud or rain area moves forward, it will pass in front of you. If it moves aft, you cross in front of it. And if it doesn't change with time you are headed for it, or it's headed for you. Remember to use the angle to the center of it for this. As it gets closer this is important—if you just use one edge, the other edge might end up on the other side of the boat while you are working through the theory. With a good hand bearing compass you can do even better, since it is not sensitive to your own heading, as the bow angle is.

With radar, just set the electronic bearing line (EBL) on the center of the squall and watch it. It can also help to use an overhead projector marker (semipermanent, yet water soluble) and draw an outline of the squall on the radar screen as you first see it. This tells a lot more about what it is doing in time. Remember, though, this is a relative motion problem. The radar is telling us just what we want to know, its motion relative to us. But once we leave the radar screen and want to figure actual courses and speeds for the squall, we must first unfold our own course and speed, just as we do in collision avoidance. In radar terminology this is called solving the relative motion diagram. There are more notes on radar later in this section.

In any event, once you can point to the center of the squall area, you are pointing to the direction the winds will shift toward when they hit, regardless of the surface winds you have at present. This direction changes as the squall's relative position changes, so it must be watched and the squall's motion anticipated if some action is considered. This discussion refers to the strong winds from a new downburst. Winds before and after the downburst behave differently.

It's not hard to see where this rule comes from if we take a look at the nature of squalls. Squalls are local thunderstorms with heavy rain and strong gusty winds associated with one large pile of cumulus clouds. The actual cloud column may only be some 6 miles across at the surface, but the strong winds will come a couple miles before the cloud is overhead (Figure 4.6-2). Squalls can be moving or stationary, but at sea with any wind at all they are likely to be moving at some 10 to 20 kts. Generally the stronger the surface wind the faster they move—though they don't necessarily move in the direction of the surface wind, and they nearly always travel faster than the surface wind. If the surface wind is very strong (anything approaching 20 kts or so) they are not likely to form in the first place, because strong wind mixes the atmosphere and prevents the convective cells from forming.

Figure 4.6-1. *Samples of squalls at sea, from various waters, but all below Latitude about 35°.*

Squalls are cumulus clouds that went out of control. Their formation starts with a normal cumulus cloud as warm moist air begins to rise. As the warm air rises it cools, and when it cools to the dew point the invisible water vapor condenses to water droplets which form clouds. Near the base and sides of the cloud, the rising warm air causes the local pressure to drop which attracts more air toward and up into the column. Generally a developing cumulus cloud has a well defined base, which shows up as a flat-bottom, being the height at which the air temperature has dropped to the dew point of the rising surface air. If the air is cooling fast enough as it rises, and there is sufficient warm moist air to be pulled in from the neighborhood, then the cloud continues to build.

Details of the process, however, are fairly complicated. One ingredient, for example, is the heat released when the water vapor condenses into clouds—since we must add heat to water to vaporize it, we get this heat back when it condenses. This heats the inside of the cloud column and allows the air to rise still higher and form taller clouds. The process continues until it runs out of warm moist air, in which case you are left with nothing more than a big cumulus cloud. But if the building process continues the cloud eventually gets so tall and heavy with water and ice slush (called *graupel*) that gravity overtakes the upward force of the fast rising air. Then it all starts to fall back down and you have a mature squall underway.

Once the water, ice, and cold air dragged with them start back down, all the tremendous energy that has been sucked up into the thing starts to pour back out. Air heats by compression as it descends, just as it cools by expansion when it rises. But this downdraft is not normal in this sense, partly because it starts down being pushed by the rain and hail. As the descending air heats by compression it evaporates rain and ice, and the evaporation cools it back down again.

The result is descending air which is actually getting cooler and denser than the air it falls through. And since the only force retarding its motion down is the buoyancy of the air below, the denser the downdraft gets the faster it falls. The result is an accelerating, gusty downdraft that can blast the surface at some 50 kts or more.

The cloud can build in 20 minutes or so, or it could take considerably longer. Once it starts down, though, the dissipation time is more predictable. The period of strong winds could be as brief as 20 minutes or so, and would rarely last more than an hour. The average life cycle of a thunderstorm inland is just over an hour, but at sea it seems they occasionally last longer—though it's often hard to tell if you are in just one squall or a series of them. And of course the total time you are actually in the squall depends on your relative courses and speeds.

As for wind strength predictions, the rain is the signal of the stage of the squall. The strongest winds come with the first heavy rain. As the rain dies the winds weaken. If you find the well-formed cloud approaching and it's not yet raining, you can look forward to getting whatever it has to offer as soon as the heavy rain starts. If it comes already raining

lightly, you have missed the worst of it. The wind-shift rule (toward the squall), though, should also work on the fringes of the thing even if you don't actually get into its rain.

The predicted wind shift comes about because the downdraft fans out in all directions from the center of the squall when it hits the surface. See Figures 4.6-3 and 4.6-4. But the resulting wind strengths on the surface are not the same on all sides of the squall. The diverging downdraft winds must be combined with the wind that comes from the motion of the squall itself. In front of the squall (in the direction of its own motion) the two sources of wind add, and at the back of the cloud they subtract.

The strong winds of a squall are at it's leading edge, in a large protruding region called the cold dome which extends some 2 miles in front of the squall (Figure 4.6-2). If it comes straight toward you, you will get its strongest winds a couple miles in front of the cloud—some minutes before the cloud is overhead or it starts to rain. On the other hand, at the back side of even a severe squall the winds can go very light and fluky until the previous surface wind fills back in.

Typical moderate ocean squalls might have winds of some 20 to 30 kts with gusts to 40 kts or so. Smaller squalls have weaker winds, and rare super squalls may have even stronger winds. As a rule of thumb, once you have sailed through a few to establish a reference, you can use their height, base, and color as guidelines for what to expect from the next. The taller they are, the lower their base, and the blacker they are the worse they will be. Blacker means the rain is still in it and there is a lot of it; taller means there is more energy in the thing and the downdraft has a longer time to accelerate; and the low base implies the air is cooling faster with elevation than normal, which means the updraft that built it was probably stronger and pulled more fuel up into this one than the one you recall that had a higher base.

Despite how mean it looks, once an anvil top appears on the squall (a cloud feature called incus) it is typically past its worst stage. This top comes when the cloud builds so high

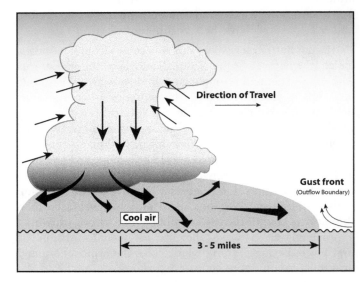

Figure 4.6-2. *Dome of cold gusty air leading a squall.*

that it reaches the strong winds aloft that simply blow its top off. But generally the downdraft has started before this happens, and the squall begins to dissipate as soon as the downdraft starts.

The use of squalls in racing tactics is tricky business at best—meaning if it works you can be proud, but if it doesn't, you have plenty of reasons why. On inland or near coastal waters it's especially hard since the probability of squalls moving rather rapidly along a course diagonal, or even contrary to, a light surface wind is much higher than in the ocean.

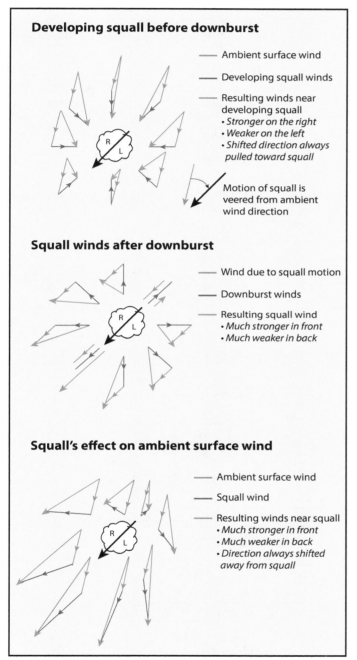

Figure 4.6-3. *How squalls can affect the ambient winds around them. No two are the same, so this is a rough NH average.* Top. *Moving or not, squalls pull wind in when building.* Middle. *Downburst winds are enhanced in front due to the motion of the squall itself.* Bottom. *Downburst winds dominate the nearby ambient wind.*

The above rule on the cold-dome wind shift still applies and might save you from getting knocked over, but other factors may well out-weigh any advantage that comes from that.

In the ocean it's rather different, or so it seems to me. There the squalls, or at least moderate squalls, are more likely to move in the direction of the surface winds, or more precisely, just veered some from the surface winds. In this case a collision course with the squall will usually produce a header at the cold dome. By collision course I mean you are sailing toward its path but hit the cold dome before you cross the path of the squall. These conditions produce a header most of the time regardless of point of sail or tack, and if this can be counted on, it might be used to a tactical advantage when racing, which we shall come back to in a later note.

Squall Guidelines

#1. Squalls to weather are not the ones you care about. They will miss you. It is the ones to the right of the true wind some 30° or so that are headed toward you.

#2. If they are not yet raining, their strongest winds are yet to come.

#3. Before they start raining, they are pulling air into them, which bends the local winds toward them to some extent.

#4. The strongest winds come with the first rain.

#5. If they are already raining, their worst is past, but gusty, increased winds can still occur.

#6. The dome of downburst winds can extend a mile or two in front of the cloud and rain edge.

#7. The strongest winds are in front and just to the sides, and they emanate from the squall at this point, i.e., they bias the local winds as shown in the Figure 4.6-3.

#8. Behind any squall is death warmed over for a sailor—a long period of light fluky wind, as if the squall sucked all of the air out of the ocean as it went by. It could take as much as an hour or more for the wind to fill back in.

#9. Benchmarks for comparing squalls are their height, base, and color.

#10. Regions of intense or numerous thunderstorms (TSTM) used to be marked on NHC tropical analysis maps as cloud outlines. They were good for predicting locations of intense convection, but they seem to have discontinued that practice. We can see these convection forecasts on the 24-hr aviation progs as noted in Section 3.2. See Figures 3.2-9, 4.2-5. We might also estimate squall likelihood from model forecasts as discussed below.

#11. Specific squalls are not covered in typical forecasts because they are so transient, but in coastal waters, the likelihood of thunderstorms is given VHF reports or zone forecasts available by email—terms used are in Tables 4.6-1,2. Squalls can also be spotted periodically in ASCAT data that happened to see one in action. Some of the wind data might be corrupted by rain in these cases, but that rain corruption does a nice job in outlining squall boundaries at that snapshot in time. See Figure 4.2-5.

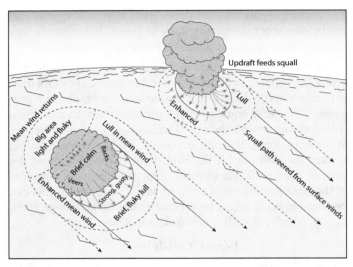

Figure 4.6-4. *Typical squall wind patterns. Squall on the right is before the rain; left is after the initial downburst. These are starting points for identifying winds around isolated squalls. Actual patterns may differ depending on the proximity of other squalls.*

#12. The key to successful tactical use of squalls is to keep careful records as you go to school on the first few. Generally they will behave in a similar manner, so knowing what happens when one approached from a given relative direction at a given place in its life time (raining, not raining) will likely tell you what the next similar one will do. But one coming up the other side of the boat may behave differently, so note what it does. A night of good record keeping could take you clear across the ocean with a knowledgeable footing.

A good way to start school is to make a note in your log when you altered course for a squall, then your track on an echart program is a record of what took place. A cellphone camera snapshot of the radar screen for records could also help.

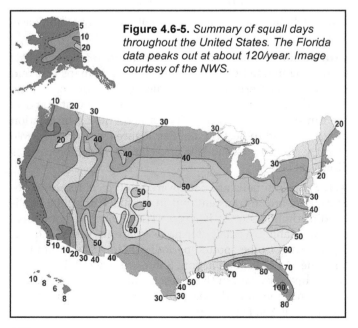

Figure 4.6-5. *Summary of squall days throughout the United States. The Florida data peaks out at about 120/year. Image courtesy of the NWS.*

Probability of Squalls

Squalls require the right amount of warm moist air and adequate vertical instability of the air. When these conditions are met we get a lot of squalls. If the conditions are not met, we do not get squalls. At sea they occur mostly in warm water and then mostly at night when the air temperature drops below the water temperature. They also do not like much ambient wind. If there is more than 15 kts or so of steady wind, then that seems to mix up the air and prevent the convective cells from developing. Normally when we get a lot of squalls the ambient winds are fairly light, meaning about 10 kts or less. The probability varies a lot across the U.S. as shown in Figure 4.6-5. In Puget Sound we have only 6 or so days a year with squalls; parts of Florida have 120 or more.

Though we expect a lot squalls rather than isolated ones, that is totally different from an organized system of squalls called a mesoscale convective system (MCS). Here they are working together to make a typically much more serious event, sometimes prominent in satellite cloud images.

Squalls on Marine Radar

Samples of squalls on (navigation) radar are shown in Figures 4.6-6. How to evaluate these for true speed and course of the squall is covered in the author's book *Radar for Mariners*, which is the source of these illustrations. Within warmer waters, your radar will be used more often for squall tactics than collision avoidance and navigation, and it will be tremendously valuable for the job. A stabilized radar using an integrated heading sensor helps much with the analysis.

Weather radar images (radar.weather.gov/Conus) sometimes highlight TSTM with yellow outlines, but we can spot these ourselves in real weather radar images or model forecasted simulated radar, as explained at the end of this section.

Table 4.6-1. Thunderstorm Forecast Terms		
as Coverage	*Percentage*	*as Probability*
isolated (few)	10 to 20%	slight chance
scattered	30 to 50%	chance
numerous	60 to 70%	likely
categorical	> 80%	categorical

Table 4.6-2. Squall (TSTM) Categories	
NWS Term	*Estimated Description*
just "TSTM"	< 20 kts, < 2 nmi dia, < 2hr.
moderate TSTM	20 to 30 kts, < 6 nmi, 2 to 4 hr
strong TSTM	> 30 kts, ≥ 6nmi, ≥ 2 to 4 hr
MCS	> 30 kts, 60-100 nmi, > 6 hr

Table Notes: *The forecast distribution terms (Table 4.6-1) are official NWS terms, but the descriptions given for the TSTM categories in Table 4.6-2 <u>are not official.</u> They are only estimated, working guidelines, to more complex criteria used in the forecasts, including REFC values discussed in the text. All values are approximate. The term severe TSTM used on land means winds > 50 kts. MCS is mesoscale convective system, an organized group of squalls.*

CHAPTER 4. STRONG WIND SYSTEMS

Squall Lines

A squall line is a line of thunderstorms that have a common lifting mechanism. So unlike a common isolated squall that is the result of an isolated source of lift, these have an external source that is forcing the air upward, and thus they can last longer and become more severe. Whereas a typical isolated squall may have winds of 25 to 30 or even 40 kts in extreme cases, a severe squall line could commonly generate 40 kts and sometimes as much as 80 kts of wind.

Squall lines can be up to several hundred miles long and 15 to 50 miles wide, and in some cases the downburst from front of the line can feed the updraft ahead of it, making them to some extent self-perpetuating once set into motion. And whereas normal squalls last 20 minutes or so, these can last many hours or even a day or more as they move eastward across the water or land at 10 to 30 kts. Very serious ones have been documented over waters from the Great Lakes to the Tasman Sea. At starpath.com/wx we include two case histories, one from the Great Lakes (a special class of squall line called a *Derecho*) and another well studied example that capsized HMS *Eurydice* off the Isle of Wight on March 24, 1878.

Aircraft pilots played a large role identifying squall line systems on land, but they have also been long known to mariners. They are rare, but pose a special hazard at night if they are not recognized as such and thus may be confused with a simple isolated squall because their full extent could not be seen. During daylight hours they would not be mistaken, appearing as a very nasty cold front stretched clear across the horizon. Radar is extremely valuable. The goal of the mariner is to avoid them if possible, and if not, to move perpendicular to them to minimize the encounter.

Figure 4.6-6.
Squalls on radar (adapted from the author's book Radar for Mariners, McGraw-Hill, 2013). The top row shows range rings at 2.0 nm; the bottom row, from another vessel, has ring spacing of 1.0 nm. Both vessels are on starboard jibe running before relatively small squalls. The high-contrast areas are reflections from water drops; the lighter tones are plot trails of past squall positions. Both sequences are in head-up mode.

The times (T) of the screen shots are shown relative to the left figure in each row. The apparent squall motion to the right in the top middle image is artificial, due to a left turn of the ves-

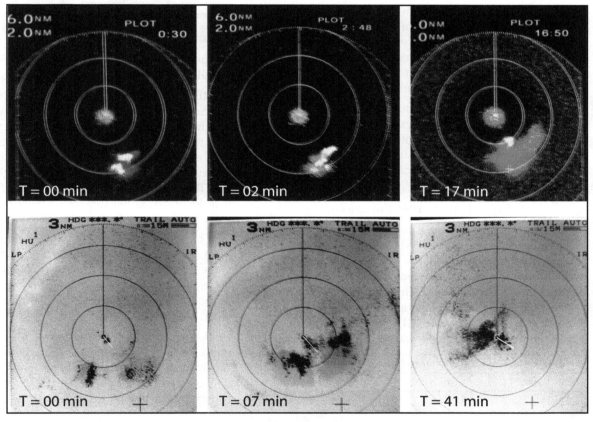

sel heading. Likewise, the large smear of the plot trails at T = 17 minutes is also due to heading changes during this time, as well as squall development, dissipation, and motion. A stabilized display mode would remove much of this uncertainty. Note that the squall did not catch the boat, which picked up speed when the advancing edge of the squall winds reached the boat, in this case at about 3 miles in front of the rain echoes. This is downwind sailing at about 10 kts. In 17 minutes, the squall has only gained about 1 mile on us. The size of the rain pattern has reduced. The gain had been increased to emphasize the last of the rain pattern.

In the bottom sequence at T = 0 the wind was calm, but it picked up at T = 7 minutes to about 9 kts true, when the rain echoes were about 0.5 mile from the boat. In this sequence, however, there was no apparent rain on the horizon nor over the vessel. The wind increased to as much as 15 kts, but this was not enough to keep this vessel ahead of the squall, and by T = 41 minutes it was forward of the beam and the wind was nearly calm again. The squall on the right developed and then dissipated. In the bottom sequence we have marked with a short line the direction of the center of the sea clutter, which is toward the face of the waves; when there is wind, this is usually the true wind direction.

In both examples, the squalls were effectively running as parallel radar targets, which is consistent with them approaching from some 30° to the right of the true wind direction, since we were sailing with the true wind at about this angle off the stern on the starboard quarter.

You will often see long lines of individual squalls at sea, with one squall after another formed in a distinct line, but these do not make up a squall line. A squall line is not a line of squalls. A line of squalls has some level of gap apparent in the radar image of the row of squalls. But real squall lines are different systems. They will draw a bright white smear across your radar screen as far as the radar can see. These are not like normal squalls, and they do not move like normal squalls.

I confronted a real squall line once not far from the Bahamas. In that case we could clearly see one end of the system visually, and what appeared to be the other end, but it wasn't. The true extent of it was awesome on radar. We put the pedal to the metal and actually managed to scoot around the end of it, pushing a big bow wave and burning up a lot of fuel. We later learned of the great damage it did to several vessels that did not escape it.

A fast moving cold front, snow-plowing air in front of it as it proceeds, is often the source of extra lift needed to form a squall line, but there are also other rarer conditions of instability that can create these. The mechanisms are complex and diverse. Squall lines formed by fast cold fronts are typically some 100 miles ahead of the front and parallel to it.

Squall lines can sometimes be seen in satellite images or ASCAT measurements in which case they could be forecasted, but more often than not these powerful systems are not forecasted at sea. On land they are usually spotted and tracked in weather radar images and wind warnings announced in advance.

Squalls in Model Forecasts

A new development in marine weather is the availability of *simulated radar* forecasts, which is just what it sounds like—digital forecasts of what the weather radar will look like in the future; in a sense, the ideal way to forecast squalls or convective activity of any kind. This parameter, composite reflectivity (REFC), is available in any of the WRF based models, such as HRRR, NAM, and NBM, and, as of June 12, 2019, it is in the new GFS for global waters. Models are discussed

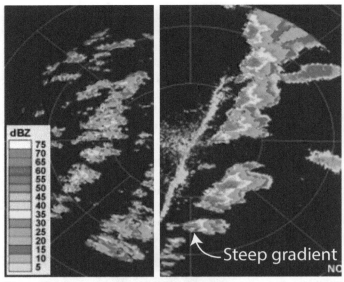

Figure 4.6-7. *Samples of weather radar observations. Small squalls on the left and large ones on the right. Compliments of NWS.*

in Chapter 7. We can anticipate that REFC will be a valuable squall forecaster, at least out to several days.

REFC units are dBZ (a logarithmic scale of reflectivity); we can interpret them the same way we interpret actual weather radar measurements. Appendix 7 discusses this application to rainfall, but now we focus that idea onto squalls with estimated values shown in Table 4.6-3, which includes corresponding precipitation rates we might see looking at the PRATE parameter in the model forecast. Squalls will generally be identified as isolated regions with peak dBZ > 40, with a steep gradient of reflections, as shown in Figure 4.6-7.

These forecasted model parameters along with the stability parameters list in Table 3.4-3, primarily CAPE, which we also have access to underway, offer the opportunity to anticipate squalls when we might not have official forecasts of them. This can be crucial for planning underway, or even when anchored.

A system of strong squalls (MCS), unsuspected by several anchored vessels, formed rapidly on Aug 9, 2017 over the Spanish islands Ibiza and Formentera. It has been nicely documented by sailor scientist David Gal, who provides European mariners with his own WRF forecasts at openskiron. org. Images from the incident are shown in Figures 4.6-8, 9,

Table 4.6-3. Rough REFC Correlations to Forecast Terms			
dBZ	(mm/h)	*"showers"*	*"thunderstorms"*
65	421		severe (>50 kts)
60	205		strong / severe
55	100		strong tstm
50	48.6		moderate tstm
45	23.7		tstm probable
40	11.5	heavy	tstm possible
35	5.6	moderate	
30	2.7	moderate	
25	1.3	showers (unspecified)	
20	0.6	showers (unspecified)	
15	0.3		

Table Notes. *Guidelines only; these are not official definitions.*

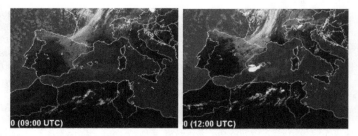

Figure 4.6-8. *Satellite images of squall development. At 09z August 9, there was no indication; by 12z, the MCS was obvious, which developed further in later hours. Satellite images are available by email request (See Section 8.3). Squalls show up as bright spots.*

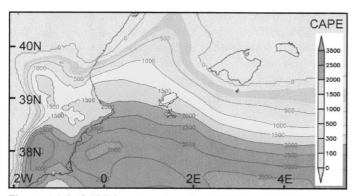

Figure 4.6-9. *CAPE from the openskiron WRF model at 18z on August 9. CAPE values over 2000 indicate an instability susceptible to squall development (Table 3.4-3). From openskiron.org.*

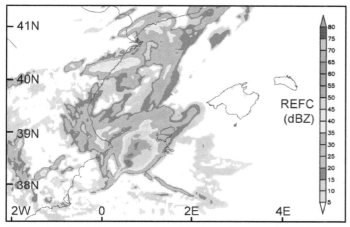

Figure 4.6-10. *RECF forecast for 23z from the openskiron WRF model run at 18z on Aug 9. RECF values over 50 indicate strong convection. From openskiron.org.*

and 10, compliments of David Gal. These data are after formation of this system, but he has shown that such rapidly exploding MCS can be spotted this way up to 36 hrs in advance. See the full story at wild-silk.org/storm-in-formentera.

Besides the WRF data, openskiron offers convenient access to GRIB files from the ICON model (DWD, Germany) and Skiron model (University of Athens). This is a pubic service, well worth supporting.

4.7 Sides of a Tropical Storm

Most storms are asymmetric to some extent, having conditions more severe on one side than the other. But when it comes to practical matters of what we are going to do about it, the subject of asymmetry is pretty much restricted to dealing with tropical storms. Tropical systems are relatively small and well localized, with relatively well predicted short-term tracks, so in many cases they can be maneuvered around to great advantage, because the left-right distinctions are much more pronounced in tropical systems. It would be rare that any smaller vessel could maneuver to one side or the other of an extratropical storm spread a thousand miles across the ocean.

On the other hand, modern weather routing services with good long range forecasting and knowledge of individual vessel performance data can direct the routes of fast deep-sea vessels to avoid the worst conditions, even in extratropical systems. This type of ship routing can even be more generally useful with these larger extratropical storms than they are with tropical storms—though usually the gain is mainly from getting to the side that puts the wind and seas aft or reduces them, and not so much an issue of the distinctions in severity on the two sides.

Thus the discussion of this section is essentially limited to tropical systems. In the Northern Hemisphere, wind and sea conditions on the right-hand side of storms (called the *dangerous* side or semicircle) are more severe than those on their left-hand sides (called the *navigable* semicircle). In the Southern Hemisphere, the situation is reversed. Right and left are defined as when facing in the direction of motion of the storm center as shown in Figure 4.7-1. There are several reasons that lead to conditions being different on the two sides, having to do with wind speed, wind direction relative to the storm's path, the sea state produced, and to its general location on the globe.

In the Northern Hemisphere, storm winds circulate counterclockwise around the center of a Low. Thus, when facing in the direction the storm is moving, the left side has wind blowing aft, the right side has wind blowing forward (Figure 4.7-1). If the storm were stationary, the wind speed on either side would be about the same if we sailed into it. Once the storm starts to move, however, this is no longer true.

Consider a cylinder of still air, the size of the storm, moving east at 20 kts. If this moving air passed over you, you feel a west wind of 20 kts, regardless of what side of the cylinder you are on. A 20-kt westerly, after all, is just air moving east at 20 kts.

Now consider this cylinder of air a revolving storm with winds circulating counterclockwise at 30 kts. While the storm

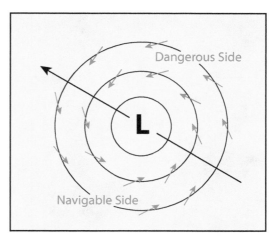

Figure 4.7-1. *Sides of a NH tropical storm. Winds and seas are bigger on the right hand side, and first winds of the storm, as they approach, tend to push you into the path of the storm. Buys Ballot's Law locates the low center: back to the surface wind, left arm out, and slightly forward, to point to the Low center.*

remained stationary, there would be a 30-kt easterly north of the center, with a 30-kt westerly south of the center. When the storm starts to move west at 20 kts, however, its own motion adds to the surface winds it carries with it. North of the center, we get 30 + 20, or 50 kts of easterly, whereas south of the center we get 20 kts of easterly + 30 kts of westerly, which leaves a 10-kt westerly. In this idealized example there is dramatic difference in wind between right and left side of the storm, especially when we recall that the force of the wind is proportional to the wind speed squared—the force of the wind is 25 times stronger on the dangerous side in this (idealized) example.

Thus, in the Northern Hemisphere, a storm's motion adds wind to the right side (dangerous semicircle) and reduces the wind on the left side (navigable semicircle)—the vector addition of winds, however, is never quite so simple as indicated in this example at the peak location right on the beam of the storm. The overall flow pattern of the wind is more complex and subject to other influences, so the distinctions, though still very important, are not this drastic.

Another independent factor can enhance wind speed on the right side in some cases. Tropical storms tend to move westward through the northern tropics (contrary to the direction of midlatitude storms that move easterly), which leaves the subtropical Highs on their right hand side. As the storms approach the isobar pattern around a near stationary High, their own isobars are compressed giving rise to stronger winds on the side closest to the High (Figure 4.7-2). A similar type of isobar compression takes place when a High moves up against a stationary thermal low over land. A

prominent example on the California coast was mentioned in Section 4.1. Thus there is this additional factor that can contribute to winds on the right in some cases. The situation is exactly symmetric in the Southern Hemisphere.

Statistics of hurricane landfall in southern Florida and the Gulf Coast show the prominent distinction in wind speed on the two sides of the storm—we can also see this in ASCAT wind measurements at sea—but when it comes to interactions with the system underway, the name "dangerous side," often has more to do with wind direction than wind speed.

When a storm approaches so as to pass you on its dangerous side, its increasing winds tend to push you into the path of the storm (north or south of the equator), whereas on the navigable side the building wind pushes you away from the path of a storm. Keeping in mind that tropical storms and hurricanes are often relatively small in size, this wind direction can be the dominant factor in your overall experience of the event. Recall that just some 80 to 100 miles from a typical hurricane center (that might have 100 kts of wind), winds could be down to 40 kts or so. Sailing against the wind in big seas on the dangerous side can mean no progress at all, versus accelerated progress away from it on the navigable side.

Still another factor is tied to typical paths of the storms themselves. They move generally westward in both hemispheres, and then tend to curve poleward—rarely do they move toward the equator once formed. Hence the dangerous side is also the side the storm is likely to turn toward as it progresses. It is, however, difficult to stress any tactical advantage to this propensity. First, the motions are erratic and only statistically go poleward, and second it could wrongly imply some virtue in crossing over an anticipated path based on its likelihood of curving to the right. Remember, when it comes to actually meeting the storm, distance from its center is the key issue. It would be hard to reckon giving up good separation for being on one side or the other when it actually passes. Most experts do not recommend crossing the path of a tropical storm if there is any risk in reducing your closest point of approach (CPA). Forecasted behavior and the NHC's 1-2-3 Rule for predicting the storm position uncertainty are key components to the analysis (Figure 4.5-4).

Finally there is the all important state of the sea. Winds on the dangerous side are stronger, so they make bigger waves. Waves are also bigger on this side because those made in the aft dangerous quarter are the least affected by the changing wind direction as they move through the front part of the storm—the waves generally move faster than the storm. Waves on the navigable side, though still very serious, are actually diminished by this effect.

The dangerous-side waves can be especially enhanced for fast storms (>15 kts) traveling in a straight line for half a day or more. This can lead to what is called a *trapped fetch*, meaning the waves from the dangerous stern quarter travel at about the speed of the storm, and riding along with it experience effectively very large fetch and duration. Waves built by tropical storms and hurricanes reach phenomenal heights,

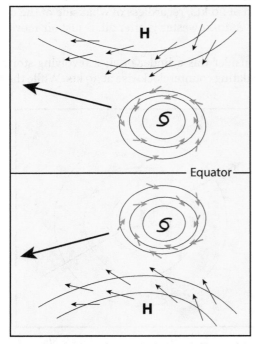

Figure 4.7-2. *Interaction of a tropical storm with a subtropical High can increase the gradient on the dangerous side in either hemisphere. The same effect can persist when a tropical storm heads north along the Gulf Stream with the Atlantic High on its right.*

so any maneuver to avoid the worst of them by staying on the navigable side is crucial to the best handling of the situation.

How you might be able to take any of this knowledge into account in negotiating specific situations, however, is another matter. This clearly depends on where you are relative to the storm, how big it is, and most importantly how fast you can move in the prevailing wind and seas. Section 4.8 on storm avoidance does not offer any more advice on this, but it does show how to maximize the separation once you make your choice.

A key issue in choosing your best route will always be knowing precisely where you are relative to the storm's present location and to its forecast track. Storm data are available hourly on even the most rudimentary shortwave radios—improve reception with a long wire for an external antenna. The storm position is given in decimal degrees along with its true course and speed. It's best to keep an ongoing plot of the storm location. Use a small scale plot to show both you and the storm, and then maybe a larger scale plot of the storm

region so you can plot the course of the storm and then subsequent positions to see if it is doing as predicted or to watch how its course might be changing.

If you get caught in the fringes of the storm circulation or have lost your contact to the forecasts, then you have the clouds, barometer, and wind to watch. The clouds and barometer and maybe sea state can tell you it is coming, but it is the wind that tells what side you are on, or more specifically, how the *wind shifts* tells you. In the Northern Hemisphere, on the right side it shifts to the right, and on the left side it shifts to the left. But these are not jingles to remember and apply. There is too much at stake to make a mistake (that's a better jingle). Draw a circular low and mark its direction of motion and then draw in the wind arrows to be sure it all makes sense. Note the wind arrows on the leading edge of the Low. The side with wind pushing you into the path is the dangerous side.

If you are on the dangerous side, the wind veers as shown in Figure 4.7-3. If it is not clear which shift is a veer, put the

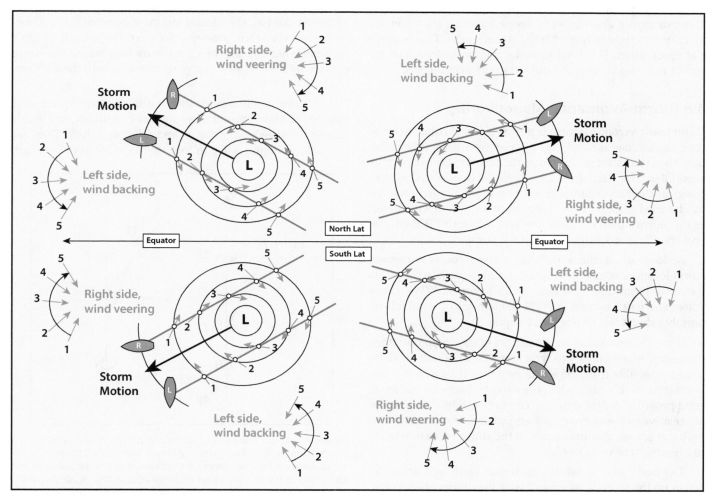

Figure 4.7-3. *Sides of a storm. On the dangerous side (red), winds and seas are bigger, and the first winds of the storm as they approach tend to push you into the path of the storm. The wind shift history (veer or backing) establishes your location within the closed isobar circulation pattern. You must use true wind only (stopped, or corrected for your motion) and away from squalls to record the trend. The inserts put the wind arrowheads together to help identify the shift direction. From farther off, before entering the closed isobar pattern, wind shifts may not behave this way.*

117

arrow heads together (as shown) and you will see if the shift is to the right or left.

Remember these shifts all refer to true wind directions, so it is crucial to convert the apparent wind to true wind to correct for your motion, or stop completely to get good data on the true wind direction and speed. Also these are expected shifts when within the organized circular flow around the fringes of the Low. Outside of that range, the wind and wind shifts could be doing anything, so the plot of reported positions is the main source of relative locations if available.

Bear in mind that if it is a well developed hurricane or intense tropical storm, then that system will be circled by rings of squalls, or squall lines, and these bring typical squall winds related to the squalls themselves, so you have to be well away from these to evaluate the wind of the main system. If you have to start running before a local squall, keep in mind what direction you would ideally be going to keep away from the main system. You may have the opportunity to benefit from such a squall, or may be better off to heave to and avoid losing ground on the direction you want to go.

If the wind direction remains steady, but the barometer keeps dropping and the wind keeps building, then you are more or less right in line with the storm's path. This is a crucial observation. It is time to make way as best you can toward the navigable side as outlined in the next section.

4.8 Storm Avoidance Maneuvering

If you know a tropical storm is posing a risk of collision some days or distance off and you are not yet within its circulation, then the safest thing is to go out of your way to avoid the encounter. The NHC and other Regional Specialized Meteorological Centers (RSMC) give storm-track predictions that can be used to guide your choice of route, which will change as the storm's path changes. The text Advisories (Chapter 8) give specific storm dimensions and motion.

Besides all of the standard weather sources, tropical storm location, course, and speed, are also given in the storm warnings broadcast each hour at h+8 min on WWV (male voice) and h+48 min on WWVH (female voice), available on portable shortwave radios (see Chapter 8).

If you do get caught on the fringes of its circulation, then the goal is to act quickly to set a course that takes you as far away as possible from the storm center as it passes. It is important to do this early while the wind and seas let you make good progress. A first step is to carefully establish where you are relative to the storm center and what side of its projected path you are on. A running plot of the storm's location is key to keeping track of its motion.

The best route to take to maximize your separation depends on the storm's speed and your maximum speed—and, of course, on the storm track, which is likely to change, maybe even frequently. The optimum course can be determined from a plotting technique using a maneuvering board that is explained in *Bowditch* (*Pub. 9, American Practical Naviga-*

tor), but it is not a very intuitive procedure, unless you work a lot with relative motion diagrams in radar.

To simplify the solution we have made a table and procedure that tells you the course that will maximize your distance from the storm as it goes by. It is easy to use. It also tells you the benefits of choosing the optimum course.

If you are faster than the storm, you have several options, in light of past discussion, based on likely storm paths and where you are relative to possible shelter. But if you are very slow compared to the storm, the best route is one perpendicular to the storm's track, obviously favoring the navigable side, if that is safety achieved. If you are faster you have more freedom to choose your positioning; much less so when you are slower.

For any speed lower than the storm speed, the optimum course is somewhere forward of the perpendicular route by an angle that depends on the ratio of your two speeds. (In this usage, "forward" always means toward the direction of the storm's track—away from the storm.) By heading forward of the perpendicular, you give yourself more time to increase the separation from the track of the storm. If you take the optimum course, the closest point of approach (CPA) occurs when the storm crosses your stern (Figure 4.8-1). On a perpendicular course, the CPA occurs well before the storm crosses your stern, so you give up much in both the CPA and the time to CPA.

To figure optimum course, estimate your speed over ground (SOG) in present wind and sea conditions, and divide that by the speed of the storm, and call that ratio R. Then use the table in Figure 4.8-2 to look up the value of the angle a,

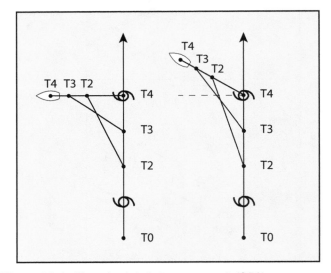

Figure 4.8-1. *Closest point of storm approach (CPA) on perpendicular course (left side) versus optimum course (right side). Tx-Tx is the distance between storm and vessel. A vessel traveling at half the speed of the storm has an optimum course that is 30° forward of the perpendicular (Figure 4.8-2). In this case the CPA occurs as the storm crosses its stern, at time T4, whereas on a perpendicular course (left side) the CPA occurs much sooner (T3) and it is closer than on the optimum course. The storm is moving straight up the diagram. The vessel departs from the storm track (at T0) at the place where the storm will be at T4.*

which is how much you would point forward of the perpendicular to achieve the optimum course.

The table in Figure 4.8-2 also shows the advantages in time and CPA of choosing the optimum course. Every mile counts when interacting with well-localized tropical storms and hurricanes. Also note that even though the CPA of the optimum course is not always increased a lot over the perpendicular course, the time to CPA is increased significantly. The more time you have, the more the chances are the storm will deviate to a course that gives you more separation, in addition to giving more time to prepare. Notice that the closer your speed is to the speed of the storm, the more you might benefit from an optimum diagonal course.

This shortcut solution gives the optimum course to take but does not offer numerical values of the CPA and time to CPA. The maneuvering board solution does offer this data if done properly, but it seems a better solution to plot the routes on a chart or universal plotting sheet and just measure the values you want directly, as outlined in Figure 4.8-3.

This plot should be ongoing in any event so you can update your choice of course and monitor your progress. An echart program is a convenient way to make the plot and analyze it. Draw the lines as routes between waypoints, if the program does not offer a specific way to draw range and bearing lines.

Needless to say, every circumstance in such conditions will be unique and no fixed proposal is the answer to all the challenges that might arise. This procedure just provides a way to figure the route that would offer the best separation if that is what it boils down to. There are numerous books on heavy weather seamanship that describe more specific actions to consider in these conditions.

Remember this maneuver only works when done early enough that you have some choice in route. Once the storm

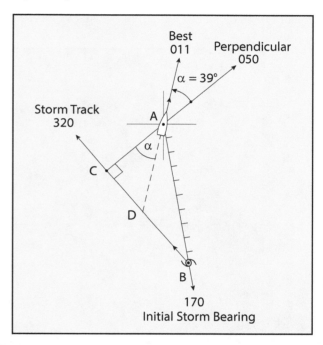

Figure 4.8-3. *Storm avoidance plot. A storm is reported 200 nmi off in direction 170, moving toward 320 at 19 kts. Your max speed is 12 kts. Find maximum CPA and time to CPA. This is the example given in* Bowditch *that they solve by the maneuvering board method.*

The optimum course is 39° forward of the perpendicular to the storm track (Figure 4.8-2), from which we figure the optimum course: 320+90 = 050, and 050-39 = 011.

Plot the storm location at 200 nmi off (A-B) using any convenient miles scale.

Draw in the storm track (B-C) and project your course back (A-D) to see where the storm crosses your stern. Time to CPA (T) is how long it takes the storm to get from B to D, so T = (B-D) / 19kts. The value of the CPA is distance D-A plus the distance you travel in that time, or CPA = (D-A) + 12 × T.

Plot this out at a scale of your choice to learn that CPA = 187 nmi and time to CPA = 4h 52m.

You can use tracks like those shown in Figure 4.8-4 (online throughout the hurricane season) for storms in progress to practice hypothetical maneuvers. Figure storm speeds from projected daily positions.

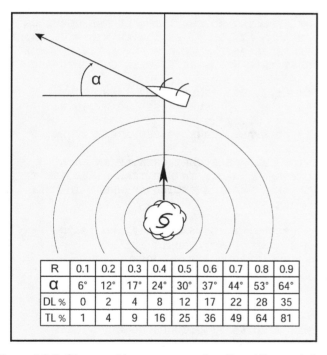

R	0.1	0.2	0.3	0.4	0.5	0.6	0.7	0.8	0.9
α	6°	12°	17°	24°	30°	37°	44°	53°	64°
DL %	0	2	4	8	12	17	22	28	35
TL %	1	4	9	16	25	36	49	64	81

Figure 4.8-2. *Storm avoidance maneuvering. To put the most distance between yourself and an approaching tropical storm—or to achieve maximum CPA with another vessel or squall—head forward of the perpendicular to the target's true path by an angle alpha (α), where α depends on the ratio (R) of your speed in present conditions (SOG) to the storm speed. If your speed is 12 kts and the squall's speed is 19 kts (R = 0.63), choose α = 37°, or interpolate for a more accurate value of 39°, or if you have a trig calculator compute the angle: α = arcsin (your speed / storm speed).*

DL and TL are the percentage distance lost (in CPA) and time lost (in time to CPA) if we choose a perpendicular course versus the optimum diagonal course. In the example above, our CPA would be 17 percent smaller and the time to the CPA would be 36 percent shorter if we went perpendicular to the path rather than forward by the optimum amount. When on the optimum heading, the CPA occurs when the squall crosses your stern, which is not the case on any other heading.

gets closer, your options for increasing separation and minimizing contact with the system are more limited.

NHC Projections

The National Hurricane Center offer remarkably accurate predictions for the location and wind speeds of tropical systems. I am sure they would not put it that way, and they are continually striving for more improvement, but the fact is the predictions are usually very good and they are very easy to use and interpret. They acknowledge that the tracks are more dependable than the intensity forecasts.

The data are available from the website nhc.noaa.gov (see also Section 8.7). As soon as clouds start moving in a circle or satellite winds show some organization, they are right on top of it. The disturbance is marked on a map and easily followed. They are also updated every 6 hrs or so, if not more frequently. Samples of the predictions are shown in Figure 4.8-4. The tropical weather discussions they provide are very informative.

Similar information for other tropical storm regions around the world can be found at the several Regional Specialized Meteorological Centers (RSMC). Links are provided at the NHC website.

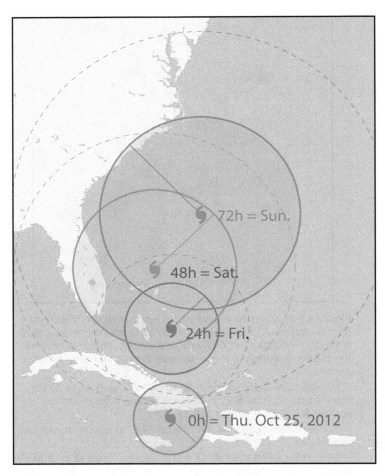

```
NWS NATIONAL HURRICANE CENTER MIAMI FL.
0300 UTC THU OCT 25 2012
HURRICANE CENTER LOCATED NEAR 19.4N 76.3W
AT 25/0300Z. POSITION ACCURATE WITHIN 20
NM. PRESENT MOVEMENT TOWARD THE NORTH OR 10
DEGREES AT 11 KT. ESTIMATED MINIMUM CENTRAL
PRESSURE 954 MB. EYE DIAMETER 20 NM. MAX
SUSTAINED WINDS 80 KT WITH GUSTS TO 100 KT.


64 KT....... 25NE   20SE   20SW   20NW.
50 KT....... 50NE   60SE   40SW   40NW.
34 KT.......110NE  120SE   70SW   60NW.
12 FT SEAS..120NE  300SE  120SW  120NW.


WINDS AND SEAS VARY GREATLY IN EACH
QUADRANT. RADII IN NAUTICAL MILES ARE THE
LARGEST RADII EXPECTED ANYWHERE IN THAT
QUADRANT.


FORECAST VALID 26/0000Z 24.4N 76.2W
MAX WIND 70 KT...GUSTS  85 KT.
64 KT... 20NE   20SE    0SW    0NW.
50 KT... 70NE   70SE   40SW   50NW.
34 KT...150NE  120SE   70SW   90NW.


FORECAST VALID 27/0000Z 27.6N 77.2W
MAX WIND 65 KT...GUSTS 80 KT.
50 KT...120NE  100SE   90SW  120NW.
34 KT...250NE  160SE  100SW  230NW.


FORECAST VALID 28/0000Z 30.5N 74.5W
vMAX WIND 60 KT...GUSTS 75 KT.
50 KT...120NE  120SE  120SW  100NW.
34 KT...300NE  270SE  180SW  300NW.
```

Figure 4.8-4. *Application of the NHC's 34-kt Rule and Mariner's 1-2-3 Rule to Hurricane Sandy as it passed over Cuba on its way north. Plot the present and forecasted locations of the storm, and then use the maximum 34-kt radii to plot the areas to be avoided (colored circles). These radii are given for each quadrant. They are marked in the picture and color-coded in the report shown here (we added the color). Then extend these radii by 100, 200, and 300 nmi for days 1, 2, and 3, shown here as dashed circles.*

This storm grew in size rapidly. In the tropics the 34-kt radii could be smaller and change less, but tropical storm sizes vary significantly, so there is no rule on this. At the beginning of the report they say the storm course is 10 degrees. This should have been written 010T, but they do not follow maritime tradition on this detail. The 1-2-3 Rule is not a reflection of simply the track uncertainty, which is known better than this, but it includes that along with uncertainty in size and intensity.

This type of study can be carried out for any time using archived hurricane data at the NHC. The ASCAT winds are also archived, which can be used to verify the value of the safety Rules.

5.1 Cloud Notes for Mariners

We care about clouds because they can often tell us where we are relative to a known weather pattern and tell us the degree of development of other systems when we do not have any forecasts or reports. In this sense, clouds can be a sign of the coming weather, but they are not a guaranteed sign. Clouds plus barometer is better; clouds, barometer, and a wind shift is better still; and all of these plus an official forecast is best. Usually a progression of cloud changes in a specific trend is better than any one cloud type or formation for forecasting.

It is not always easy to identify cloud types. Usually there are several types in the sky at once, and clouds change form with time. During these transitions the formally correct label for the cloud can be unclear—even professional meteorologists might disagree on the precise label for clouds in many cases. Also, some clouds that look identical have one name when at a high altitude and another name when at a lower altitude. For shipboard forecasting, however, these fine distinctions are not important. There are just a few basic types of clouds that can help with forecasting, and they are easy to recognize.

Cloud Categories

Clouds are characterized by the height of their base and their shape (Figure 5.1-1). There are high clouds, middle clouds, and low clouds; and within these height ranges there are puffy, heaps of clouds (cumulus types), wispy tufts of clouds (cirrus types), and monotonous layers of clouds (stratus types).

From a practical point of view, it is often useful to categorize all clouds as either those in layers (stratiform), which represent stable air, versus those that are puffy individual units (cumuliform), which represent vertical motion and instability in the air. For forecasting, it is valuable to establish this property of the air mass from the nature of the clouds we can see.

It is also useful to recognize the significance of clouds with waves in them (a *cloud species* called undulatus) and to be aware of the distinctions between what high clouds are telling us versus what low clouds indicate.

Clouds are even further characterized by their composition as either made of water droplets (the low clouds) or ice crystals (high clouds) or some mixture (mostly in the middle range). These distinctions are important in squall formation and the production of lightning, rain, snow, etc.

High Clouds

High means in the upper half of the atmosphere, above some 18,000 ft, well above Mt. Rainier, for example. Cloud altitudes (all referenced to sea level) depend on latitude because the atmosphere is much taller at the equator than at the poles, but here we refer to typical heights in the midlatitudes. This is the region of the winds aloft, whose path around the globe, projected down onto the earth's surface, is called a "storm track" on TV weather. This is the domain of the jet stream, although not all winds aloft are jet stream winds.

Since the air temperature drops with increasing altitude (at the rate of about 4 F° per 1,000 ft), the high-cloud domain is more importantly characterized by temperature. All water vapor is frozen at high altitude, so high clouds are made of ice crystals; lower clouds are made of water droplets. High clouds are always cirrus types: either individual wisps or tufts (cirrus); continuous layers, patches, or thin translucent veils (cirrostratus); or puffy clumps (cirrocumulus). The word *cirrus* in a cloud name always implies it is a high altitude cloud, whereas words derived from *cumulus* or *stratus* can apply to clouds of all altitudes.

Low Clouds

Low clouds are those below some 7,000 ft. Altitudes at sea are not so easy to judge, but on land you may have mountain peaks with known heights above that reference. These peaks would then always rise above low clouds. *Fair weather cumulus* clouds typically ride along at the upper half of this lower level—that is, at about 3,000 to 6,000 ft high. When you see these well formed, relatively small and smooth-sur-

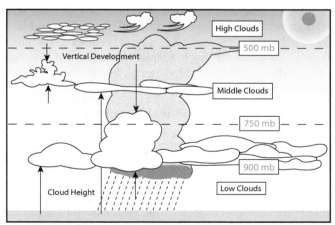

Figure 5.1-1. *Cloud classification by base height. Middle clouds are those with bases between 7,000 and 18,000 ft, but these are not rigorous boundaries. Other dimensions of interest are the cloud top heights, and the vertical extent of a cloud.*

faced, white cumulus clouds in the sky, they can be used as the reference altitude. Clouds at their height and below are low clouds; clouds above them are middle and high clouds. Low clouds can also be on the ground. These would be stratus clouds, which on the ground we call fog. Cumulus clouds are rarely lower than about 1,000 ft.

The height of the cloud base can be estimated for building clouds from the dew point, since by definition the dew point is the temperature at which invisible water vapor condenses to form visible clouds (see Section 3.4). On dry days, cumulus clouds are higher than they are on wet days. A meteorologist would use the skew-T diagram to find the low cloud base, called the lifted condensation level (LCL). A typical value in the trades would be about 3,000 ft, at a pressure of about 900 mb.

The direction of motion for low cumulus clouds is nearly the same as that of the surface winds. The cloud direction will be slightly veered from the surface winds because winds above 1,000 ft or so are less influenced by the frictional drag of the air along the surface. Friction is greater over land than over water, so the veer is about 15° over smooth water, and 30 to 45° over land. If you face the true wind direction, without the influence of hills, mountains, buildings, etc., you should observe low clouds approaching from about 30° to the right. Over smooth water, the direction is closer to the wind, over rough land it is farther to the right.

Middle Clouds

Middle-height clouds are everything between high and low. They have the prefix "alto," which—though implying "high" in other contexts—we must think of as meaning "middle" for cloud terminology. There is some rough logic to the terminology. There are only two types of middle clouds, altostratus and altocumulus. In the low-cloud domain we have stratus and cumulus, thus the altostratus and altocumulus are the higher forms of these types. We don't confuse them with the high-cloud domain, because these are always cirrus or cirro-type. Then we see the middle-cloud concept in these sequences: stratus, altostratus, and cirrostratus, and cumulus, altocumulus, and cirrocumulus. Stratus looks like stratus, high or low. When low it is called plain stratus, mid-level it is called altostratus, and when high it is called cirrostratus. Likewise, cumulus drifting higher in the sky are called altocumulus, although they could look much like their lower counterparts called plain cumulus.

Clouds with Vertical Development

The one unique cloud form with regard to height classification is the cumulus with vertical development, usually cumulonimbus or towering cumulonimbus. They can reach from a very low base, all the way up to the high cloud region where the winds are strong. These are called low clouds because their base is in the low-cloud region even though their tops can be very high. Another that fits into this category is a regular cumulus with extensive vertical development even though it is not yet a thunderhead. Tall cumulus congestus species can be in this category.

Modern Cloud Study

The internet and powerful search engines have changed how we can study clouds. Clouds are categorized into *genera*, and each genus has *species*, and any of these might have specific *features*. It is a complex system, but now very easily studied with the image search from an online program like Google. Do an image search on the species "cumulus congestus," just mentioned, and you will get pages of images of this cloud. Or image search for a cloud feature like "arcus cloud," and you get another amazing presentation of hundreds of samples of the cloud. We mention several clouds here as we proceed with a sketch or picture, but an internet image search is a way to really see what these look like and how they can vary.

A particularly good source for mariners is the remarkable WMO Cloud Atlas.

wmocloudatlas.org

It has excellent images, searchable by all criteria, and many examples include associated weather maps and skew-T diagrams, with implications to forecasting.

Rain Clouds

It is sometimes useful to make a further distinction in clouds, beyond height and shape, by distinguishing whether or not the cloud is actually producing rain. Any cloud that is raining or threatens imminent rain is called a "nimbus" type cloud. Technically the cloud must be raining (or snowing) to get this name, but the rain may not be falling on you. It could be off in the distance. Any raining or snowing cumulus is called cumulonimbus, while any raining or snowing stratus is called nimbostratus. Cirrus clouds are so high and have so little ice content that when their ice crystals fall, they evaporate before reaching the ground, and so there is no "cirronimbus"—although we can indeed see ice crystals falling from cirrus clouds into the slower winds below them, streaming back as *mare's tails*.

If a rain cloud is not raining on us, we must judge the presence of rain from its color or the color of the sky just under it. Rain in a cloud usually makes it dark, sometimes black, at least on the bottom surfaces. A crystal-white cumulus is

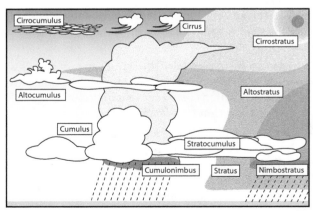

Figure 5.1-2. *The ten basic cloud genera. Mariners benefit from knowing these distinctions, but finer details are not often called for.*

not a rain cloud. The rain first shows up as the shading on the surface structure of the cloud becomes more pronounced. The bases of cumulus clouds tend to flatten out as the rain accumulates in them, and then get ragged again after they rain. If you see tall cumulus clouds without flat bottoms they may have finished their raining elsewhere.

The distinction between stratus and nimbostratus is not as easy to make if it's not raining on us. Dark, overcast skies approaching are probably nimbostratus; light gray or white overcast are more probably just stratus. Nimbostratus are deep clouds: their bases are at low altitude but they stretch into middle heights. Rain from cumulus clouds is heavy and short and in isolated patches. It is called *showers* in forecasts. Stratus rain is lighter and lasts longer, and is spread uniformly over large regions. In forecasts it is called *rain!* A typical rain storm may include both types of rain and clouds.

There are ten basic cloud genera, which all mariners benefit by knowing, as they each tell us something about the weather. They are discussed individually below. See Figures 5.1-2 and 5.1-3.

Cumulus Clouds

Cumulus clouds are the best known clouds. Cloud clouds. Puffy, white, with well defined boundaries, they can be fairly smooth, with regular surfaces, round or globular, or very ir-

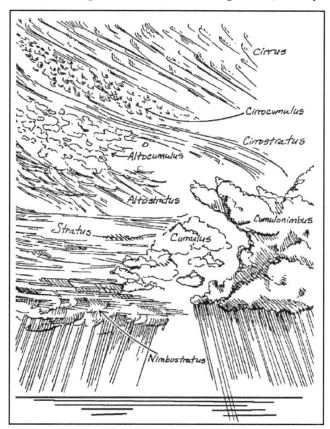

Figure 5.1-3. *Schematic of basic cloud genera. Even with such a rough schematic, the types should be identifiable from their elevation and shape. The most common cloud seen in the sky, stratocumulus, is missing from this presentation, from the* NWS Observing Handbook No.1.

regular in shape. They can be all sizes from huge, covering the whole sky, or small like cotton balls. Small cumulus clouds typically reside at the upper edges of the low-cloud domain (5,000 to 7,000 ft). Larger ones with vertical development can extend all the way to the top of the troposphere.

Small and medium sized cumulus clouds that are well formed into regular shapes in a clear sky are signs of fair weather. These are called fair-weather cumulus. When the clouds are ragged and torn by strong winds it can be a sign that the weather will deteriorate.

Cumulonimbus

Cumulonimbus are also easy to recognize. They are the tall thunderheads. Cumulus clouds that are tall, though not yet raining, but building up to it, are called cumulus with vertical development (cumulus congestus). This is a good name for any cumulus cloud that is obviously getting taller and not just bigger. They can still be quite white; though they will darken and their shadowing will become more pronounced as they get closer to raining.

When cumulus clouds reach the upper atmosphere where the winds are strong, they fan out into an anvil shape (incus) and sometimes blow off into strips of cirrus. Sometimes the anvil is swept off into the direction of the winds aloft.

Thunderheads at sea (squalls) are often well-localized; you can sometimes steer around them. These squalls show up prominently on the radar. See Section 4.6 on squalls.

Thunderheads mean strong, gusty winds and rain, although usually not severe seas, since the fetch of the waves is limited to the size of the squall. The winds may gust to 30 or 40 kts (in very severe ones), but the wind passes fairly quickly—a few minutes to an hour or so. The winds can set on rapidly from light air once the cloud is near. Generally, the higher the clouds, the blacker the clouds, and the lower the base below them, the stronger the winds will be. Typical squall clouds, however, bring winds more like 20 to 25 kts from light air conditions.

If the clouds show smooth mammary shapes (mammatus) hanging from the base, be especially cautious. These are signs of the severe vertical winds at the region of the clouds. They are often seen associated with tornadoes (on land) and waterspouts (at sea), although some authorities argue that the formation of these clouds takes place after the most severe surface winds have occurred. An analogous cloud is the roll cloud, or arcus, that forms on the leading edge of severe squalls. These are more consistently an imminent threat.

Plain cumulus and cumulonimbus clouds are easy to recognize. The distinctions among the other cumulus-type clouds, however, can be more difficult without some practice. These are the altocumulus, cirrocumulus, and stratocumulus.

Stratocumulus

Stratocumulus are low cumulus clouds in a layer or large flat patches of cumulus. Remember the name: stratus—there must be a layer of them, and cumulus—they must show some lumpy, or puffy structure; or at least some distinction of individual clouds, even though they are compressed into a layer. If you see low clouds that are not well defined cumulus then they are either stratus or stratocumulus. If they show no structure, they are stratus; otherwise they are stratocumulus. Cumulus clouds often have a flat bottom. When several of these join together they can form a layer of stratocumulus.

Stratocumulus are often seen at sunset. Cumulus formation requires an updraft from a warm surface, like the ground during the day. At the end of the day, as the air cools, this updraft weakens, and the cumulus settle down into narrower layers of stratocumulus. These may even further fade into stratus and then disappear at night.

Most books show their example photo of stratocumulus at sunset, since these clouds are so common then. Often the morning clouds over land are thin stratocumulus. It is interesting to watch these clouds build into cumulus as the day warms up. This process is an obvious sign of fair weather—alternatively, they could deteriorate into stratus and nimbostratus.

At night in the tropics, the water remains warmer than the air. So the updraft normally restricted to land takes place over water at night. This gives rise to the famous trade wind cumulus. Small, puffy cumulus that fly by with the trade winds between you and a crystal-clear night sky—one of the more memorable aspects of sailing in these waters. I think these clouds contribute to the iconic image of the moon over Miami, one of the few places in the U.S. where they are often seen.

Stratocumulus can form into bands and waves that show the winds at higher altitudes, but these clouds are still low (by definition) so the wind direction you get this way will be closer to the surface winds than to the steering winds aloft. Higher clouds are better for reading the direction of coming weather. Persistent waves in stratocumulus, however, do indicate that conditions are fairly stable.

Generally stratocumulus are fairly easy to distinguish, with the only likely confusion being with altocumulus. Layers of altocumulus are not called strato-alto-cumulus, but just altocumulus. Hence the only distinction is the altitude. If they are low, about the same height you would see or expect to see low cumulus, then they are stratocumulus, otherwise they are altocumulus.

Altocumulus

Altocumulus clouds are high cumulus, though they often may appear more similar to high stratocumulus than to high cumulus. That is, they are usually characterized by layers or patches of layers or sheets of individual small clouds. Altocumulus is the typical well defined layer of clouds that we often rise and descend through on an aircraft. These clouds are often formed into rows (streets or bands) of clouds with a short wavelength pattern running across them. The winds aloft run parallel to the bands and perpendicular to the waves.

When altocumulus are not in regular rows, they often still form a cobblestone pattern of small white clouds that look like sheep backs or tuffs of wool or cotton.

Altocumulus alone are not an indicator of coming weather. But when they are followed by cirrus above or thickening cumulus below, it may be a sign of coming weather. About the best indications altocumulus can give, come when the regular cobblestone pattern breaks apart into chaotic patches of isolated, small cumulus clouds with irregular shapes. This is a sign that the winds aloft have increased sharply and a thunderstorm may be imminent. This form of altocumulus is short lived.

Cirrocumulus

Cirrocumulus are very high cumulus, made of ice crystals. They are similar to altocumulus, but the individual clouds that make up the overall pattern are smaller. Generally speaking, cumulus clouds have the largest individual cloud elements, stratocumulus the next smaller, very roughly fist sized with your arm outstretched; altocumulus are next at about thumb size, and cirrocumulus are the smallest with individual cloudlets of about the size of the nail on your little finger.

Cirrocumulus show little if any shading. When they don't have the cobblestone pattern, they form larger, thin patches of cloud. When these patches also show the cobblestone pattern, it looks like scales on a fish, and the sky is called a *mackerel sky*.

Cirrocumulus can also show well defined ripples running across the upper wind direction. These are one of the best indicators of the winds aloft, but unfortunately, cirrocumulus are not a very common type of cloud. Cirrocumulus waves look like ripples in sand, which distinguishes them from altocumulus waves which look more like sheep lined up in rows—a coarser structure compared to the more delicate cirrus patterns.

At first it may seem difficult to distinguish cirrocumulus (high) from altocumulus (middle) and from plain cumulus (low). Until one has a feeling for the altitude of clouds when looking at them, just bear in mind the size of the individual puffs. Individual puffs of cirrocumulus are much smaller than those of altocumulus, which are in turn much smaller than typical plain cumulus. Actual angular widths are given in Section 5.4, from official NWS descriptions.

Also, cirrocumulus, being clumps of ice crystals at high altitudes, rarely show the pronounced shading we see in lower cumulus clumps of water vapor. Cirrocumulus remain snow-white and not very tall vertically, so they never really appear ominous, as the other forms of cumulus can. Without the shading, cirrocumulus do not often appear as billowy as lower cumulus.

Cirrus

Cirrus clouds are the high, thin, wispy clouds of ice crystals that often look like feathers or mare's tails. They occur typically in isolated patches, often in an otherwise clear sky.

When they thicken they form cirrocumulus or cirrostratus. The mare's tail shape comes when the ice crystals fall from the strong winds aloft into the weaker winds below.

Cirrus can be the first signs of a coming warm front; but this is not an infallible sign—these clouds sometimes appear as the last high remnants of a passing cold front when the weather is clearing. A warm front is better indicated when cirrus appear from clear skies and then thicken and lower into cirrostratus and altostratus.

Since warm air is lighter than cool air, when a moving mass of warm air runs into a region of cooler air, it rides up and over it, as shown schematically in Figure 5.1-4. Consequently, when a warm front approaches, the first thing that we notice is the cool dry air way above us is invaded by the warm moist air riding up on the approaching wedge of the warm front, while we remain in essentially unchanged conditions below it. We can see this taking place because this new moisture above us freezes into cirrus clouds. If we are in clear skies to begin with, we can often tell from the first appearance of cirrus clouds that a frontal system is approaching. New cirrus can be one of the early warnings that things might deteriorate in the next 12 to 24 hrs.

> "Mackerel sky and mare's tails
> make tall ships set low sails."

This is a forecast based on the transition of cirrus into cirrocumulus, or a combination of both clouds. Together they make a better forecast than either one alone.

Stratus

All stratus-type clouds are characterized by their lack of character. They are veils of uniform cloud cover without structure. This type of cloud can exist at any altitude. When low, these clouds are called simply stratus; at middle heights they are altostratus; and when very high they are called cirrostratus. When this type of sky is raining, the cloud is called nimbostratus. Stratus clouds often appear as a background for other cloud forms, and when any cloud form thickens into a continuous layer it becomes a stratus form.

Stratus clouds are low overcast, usually extending down to the horizon, at least in some directions. When right on the ground, stratus clouds are called fog or haze. They come in various shades of gray depending on how near they are to raining and the time of day. The sun or moon usually does not show through stratus clouds. Strong winds sometimes tear stratus into shredded bands called stratus fractus (or *scud*), but typically the presence of low, light-colored stratus clouds is not a threat of stormy weather.

Dark nimbostratus, however, can accompany long periods of strong winds which are a hazard since they cover a large area over a long time so the seas can build under them. It is the long steady storms that are the most dangerous because of the seas.

Altostratus

Altostratus are stratus clouds at higher levels, which means, since we can't see the tops of them, that they have higher bases. A high overcast sky is probably altostratus, but there are other ways to help identify this important type of cloud. Remember that altostratus are stratus clouds, so they don't show any structure.

The sun and moon can sometimes be seen through altostratus, though only faintly—as if through ground glass. These clouds do not show rings (halos) around the sun or moon, whereas the other type of high stratus cloud, cirrostratus, nearly always do.

Altostratus are the most reliable sign that hazardous weather is possible—strong winds and long periods of high seas. These clouds can indicate an approaching low-pressure area long before the barometer begins to drop. Look for a "watery" sun or moon with no halos and a high ceiling of stratus clouds about half a day or so before the bad weather. Be even more confident of your forecast if the high overcast thickens and lowers as it approaches. Do not confuse the sometimes prominent glow surrounding a translucent sun or moon with the specific halos discussed below.

Cirrostratus

Cirrostratus clouds are the very high, thin and light colored (milky) overcast which sometimes results from thickening cirrus clouds. All clouds at this altitude are made of ice crystals, which gives them their light color. Thin transparent layers of these clouds show halos around the sun and moon.

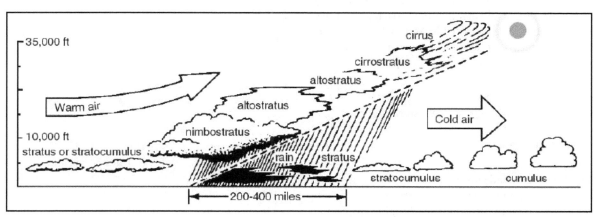

Figure 5.1-4. *Clouds at a warm front. See Chapter 4 for more details.*

The radius of the halos will be 22° in most cases, because of the way light refracts through ice crystals. You can check this with a sextant. The radius of the ring will be just less than a hand's width, thumb to little finger, with your arm outstretched. These are large patterns, covering some one quarter of our full view in their direction. See Figure 9.4-5.

Again, cirrostratus are stratus clouds, so they show no structure. If patches do show some formation into clouds, they are probably cirrocumulus. The sky can be made up of large areas covered with cirrostratus, which break up on the edges into cirrus and cirrocumulus. The sun always shines through cirrostratus—at least enough to cast shadows.

Increasing amounts of cirrostratus can be the sign of an approaching warm or occluded front, especially if they thicken and lower into altostratus. Consequently, a ring around the sun or moon is a sign that bad weather is approaching (Figure 9.4-5). This is a better indicator in the summer, however, than it is in the winter. In the winter, the average altitude of ice clouds is lower so more clouds enter this region and show this sign. In the summer the clouds must be high to show this, which makes it more likely that the air was pushed up there by the leading edge of a warm front.

Essentially all examinations for mariners on knowledge of weather require the identification and distinction of these ten basic cloud types. Further details on cloud species (fractus, humilis, congestus, etc.), and cloud varieties (opacus, undalatus, etc.), and cloud features (arcus, mammatus, incus, etc.) are usually not required. What we can learn from the clouds for our own practical observations are covered adequately by an understanding of these ten cloud types. If you care to know more of this genealogy, see the WMO Cloud Atlas cited earlier.

5.2 Sample Cloud Pictures

The samples shown in Figure 5.2-1 are from the *NWS Observing Handbook No.1* (vos.noaa.gov). The WMO Cloud Atlas has many more examples. See also Section 8.4 on Buoy-CAMs to see live pictures of clouds at sea.

Low Cloud Types (CL)

Stratocumulus (Sc). Gray or whitish patch, sheet, or layer of cloud which almost always has dark parts, composed of tesselations, rounded masses, rolls, etc., which are non-fibrous, and which may or may not be merged; most of the regularly arranged small elements have an apparent width of more than 5°.

Stratus (St). Generally grey cloud layer with a fairly uniform base, which may give drizzle, ice prisms, or snow grains. When the sun is visible through the cloud, its outline is clearly discernible. Stratus generally does not produce halo phenomena.

Cumulus (Cu). Detached clouds, generally dense and with sharp outlines, developing vertically in the form of rising mounds, domes, or towers, of which the bulging upper part often resembles a cauliflower. The sunlit parts are mostly brilliant white; their base is relatively dark and nearly horizontal.

Cumulonimbus (Cb). Heavy, dense cloud, with considerable vertical extent, in the form of a mountain, or huge towers. At least part of its upper portion is usually smooth, fibrous, or striated, and nearly always flattened; this part often spreads out in the shape of an anvil or vast plume.

Middle Cloud Types (CM)

Altocumulus (Ac). White or gray patch, sheet, or layer of cloud, generally with shading, composed of laminae, rounded masses, rolls, etc., which are sometimes partly fibrous or diffuse, and which may or may not be merged; most of the regularly arranged small elements usually have an apparent width between 1° and 5°.

Altostratus (As). Grayish or bluish sheet or layer of striated, fibrous, or uniform appearance, totally or partly covering the sky, and having parts thin enough to reveal the sun at least vaguely, as through ground glass. Does not show halo phenomena.

Nimbostratus (Ns). Heavy cloud layer, often dark, the appearance of which is rendered diffuse by falling rain or snow, which in most cases reaches the ground. It is thick enough to blot out the sun or moon. These are classified as middle clouds, but can be present at lower altitudes as well.

High Cloud Types (CH)

Cirrus (Ci). Detached clouds in the form of delicate white filaments, or mostly white patches or narrow bands. These clouds have a fibrous appearance (hairlike), or a silky sheen, or both.

Cirrocumulus (Cc). Thin white patch, sheet, or layer of cloud without shading, composed of very small elements in the form of grains, ripples, etc., merged or separate, and more or less regularly arranged; most of the elements have an apparent width of less than 1°.

Cirrostratus (Cs). Transparent, whitish cloud veil of fibrous (hairlike) or smooth appearance, totally or partly covering the sky, and generally producing halo phenomena.

5.3 Fog

Although some frontal systems and low stratus from any source can generate fog, as a practical maritime guideline we can say that, in a nutshell, there are two kinds of fog: sea fog and radiation fog. Radiation fog is formed on land during clear calm nights, when the temperature drops to the dew point. Such clear nights are often associated with high pressure systems and otherwise fair weather. The incidents of this fog that we care about are those that can spill downhill to flow out over the surface of the water. A sample is shown in Figure 5.3-1. Radiation fog is characterized by very light air, and often burns off by midday. It can't be formed in winds over 5 kts or so, because this mixes the air near the surface and prevents the necessary cooling. On the other hand, a dead

CL=1 *Cumulus with little vertical extent.*

CM=3 *Altocumulus, semitransparent, cloud elements change slowly, one level.*

CH=9 *Cirrocumulus alone, and/or cirrus and cirrostratus*

CL=4 *Stratocumulus from the spreading cumulus.*

CM=6 *Altocumulus from the spreading of cumulus or cumulonimbus.*

CH=1 *Cirrus filaments, strands, hooks, not expanding.*

CL=7 *Stratus fractus and/or cumulus fractus of bad weather.*

CM=2 *Altostratus, dense enough to hide sun or moon, or nimbostratus.*

CH=7 *Cirrostratus covering whole sky.*

Figure 5.2-1. *Sample pictures of clouds used for cloud coding. These are from NWS Observing Handbook No. 1—Marine Surface Weather Observations, which is available online from the VOS web site. Each cloud layer (Low, Medium, and High) is divided into 9 types, which the Handbook describes as above. Here we show only 3 of each level. The VOS cloud coding does not correlate with specific genera or species, but rather to cloud patterns that assist with weather interpretation.*

calm is not good for radiation fog formation. This leads to just patchy, knee-deep fog. One or two knots of breeze is ideal; just enough to transport the fog along the surface. Cloudy night skies keep the earth warm and prevent the formation of radiation fog.

In waters exposed to radiation fog, the forecasting of reduced visibility is usually very good—even when the corresponding wind forecast is totally wrong! Wind speed and direction depend sensitively on the spacing and orientation of the isobars. Slight changes can cause dramatic differences in wind, especially in valleys. Fog on the other hand is determined by relative humidity and temperature, which are air mass properties, uniform over large areas, and easy to

Figure 5.3-1. *Radiation fog. This midmorning photo from a seaplane shows radiation fog spilling out onto the eastern end of the Strait of Juan de Fuca from Whidbey Island. From the air this looks like clouds, but it is in fact fog, on the surface, as you can see it wrapping around the trees.*

measure. By monitoring dew point and air temperature it is easy to predict when fog will set in (see Figure 3.5-1). In some areas we might get a wind forecast of "Variable, 5 to 15 kts," whereas the temperature forecast is for 64 to 66°. We are getting a temperature forecast to within a few percent, whereas "Variable" means they do not know the wind direction at all, and "5 to 15" is another way of saying "0 to 15," which effectively means the speed is also not known. In short, when we hear a call for reduced visibility, chances are it will be right, even if the wind might be wrong.

Sea fog, on the other hand, forms when warm, moist air blows over cold water. It comes in from the ocean, even though it may have been formed originally along the coast. Once formed, it moves with the prevailing wind. It can cover vast areas, and unlike radiation fog, it can be present with strong wind or in calm air. It could be found in mid-ocean or along the coast, and well into bays and sounds. It does not burn off, but may recede temporarily as the wind shifts offshore. Sea fog is readily apparent on satellite photos and usually well forecasted.

It is important to understand the nature of the fog we are in before guessing what the wind might do on the basis of the fog, or upon guessing whether or not it will burn off. There was a case of experienced inland kayakers who, paddling along the Pacific Northwest coast, assumed the onset of fog implied calm air ahead, as that was their sole experience on inland waters. They ventured on into a shocking encounter with 30 kts of wind in pea soup fog. All made it to safety, much wiser for the experience.

We must likewise be careful on assumptions about sea fog clearing. It can leave the scene and then turn and come back later on the same day. Two prominent sea-fog episodes are illustrated in Figure 5.3-2.

Coastal statistics on fog are available in the appendices to the *Coast Pilots*. Sea fog is often formed along the California coast. A deep onshore swell brings cold water to the surface, and then, when warm moist air moves onto the cold water, sea fog is formed. Once a patch of sea fog finds its way into near coastal waters it can be pulled onto the beach by a building sea breeze, which then relaxes at night letting the fog slip back out to sea in a light land breeze.

Sea fog is sometimes referred to as advection fog, which is not incorrect, but sea fog is the better term for our application. There are types of advection fog that are not sea fog. Scientific papers that study the subject use the term sea fog, as do most mariners.

Even though sea fog often comes with strong wind, it is not required, nor it is part of the formation process. It simply happens that many parts of the world that have frequent sea fog also have frequent incidents of strong wind. Thus off the coast of California in the summertime, you can have 40 kts of wind in crystal clear skies *or* in pea soup fog—as well as in the normal situation of storm cloud conditions.

As mariners we care about fog in large part because of its affect on visibility. The formal definition of "fog" however,

Figure 5.3-2. *Two sea fog episodes, facing page. Left. Visible satellite photos of fog in the Pacific Northwest off the coast of Vancouver Island BC, WA, and OR, shown twice a day for 3 days, June 17 to 19. White areas over the water are fog; dark areas are clear. North winds around the offshore High push the fog south, clearing the Washington coast by the 18th. The thermal Low onshore, however, starts to move inland, which, with a decreasing offshore High, causes the coastal winds to become more westerly and southwesterly, pushing the fog back into WA waters. By 8 AM on June 19 we see a new patch of fog moving SE along the coast of Vancouver Island, which then mixes with the batch coming up from the south. Right. Sea fog entering the Strait of Juan de Fuca, lingering a day, and then dissipating, on August 9. The dominant weather patterns in place at the time are shown next to the fog sketches. Notice there was 20 kts of wind with this soup fog in the Strait. It penetrated 80 miles into the Strait and then 50 miles more down to Seattle in Puget Sound. Later pressure patterns pushed the ocean fog to the north and the inland fog onto land where it dissipated.*

From Marine Weather of Western Washington by NOAA Commander Kenneth E. Lilly, Jr., (Starpath Publications, 1983.)

implies more restriction than we might normally think of. According to the IMO (and WMO) definitions shown in Table 5.3-1, the visibility must be below 1 nmi to be called fog, otherwise we are technically dealing with haze, though many mariners might still call it fog.

If you sail in areas with Vessel Traffic Services (VTS) such as Puget Sound, New York Harbor, San Francisco Bay area, Houston, and others listed in Table 161.12(c) in the back of the *USCG Navigation Rules Handbook*, then you have a unique source of information on visibility. Besides the regular VHF Weather Radio broadcasts, you can monitor the VTS traffic control channel to hear what they have to say. Generally in times of restricted visibility, there is much discussion of it. The controllers will frequently ask the reporting vessels what visibility they have. Thus you can learn these de-

Table 5.3-1. International Visibility Codes		
Code	Description	Range
0	Dense fog	visibility < 50 yds
1	Thick fog	50 ≤ visibility < 200 yds
2	Moderate fog	200 ≤ visibility < 500 yds
3	Light fog	500 ≤ visibility < 1000 yds
4	Thin fog	0.5 ≤ visibility < 1 nmi
5	Haze	1 ≤ visibility < 2 nmi
6	Light Haze	2 ≤ visibility < 5.5 nmi
7	Clear	5.5 ≤ visibility < 11 nmi
8	Very Clear	11.0 ≤ visibility < 27 nmi
9	Exceptionally clear	27 nmi ≤ visibility

Table Notes: *These categories of visibility are the same ones used in the U.S. and International Light Lists for figuring luminous range from the charted nominal range of navigation lights. Visibility is usually meant to be how far you can see an unlighted conspicuous dark object in daylight with the naked eye. We can measure visibility very accurately underway using radar as we scan the horizon visually. Simply note the radar range to land just in sight, or note the range to a buoy as it leaves or enters visible range. It is a valuable exercise. The WMO equivalent uses m and km for units.*

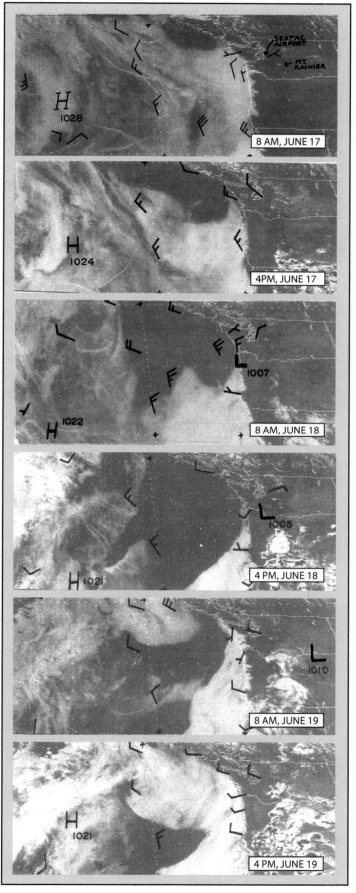

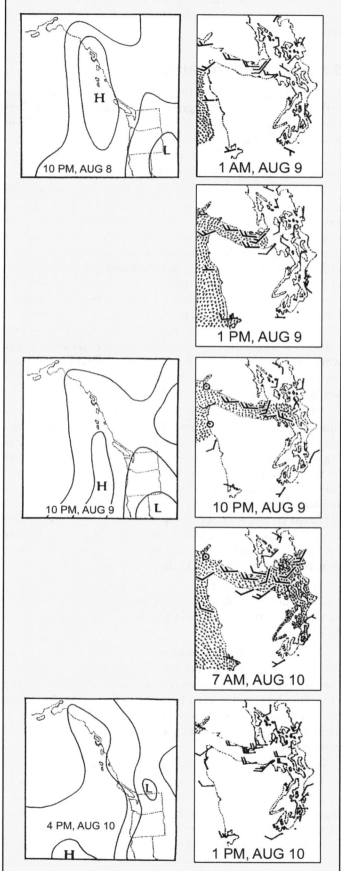

tails throughout the waterway and not have to wait the 3 hrs typical for updates to the observation reports on the NOAA Weather Radio.

5.4 Wave Notes for Mariners

This section is a guide to the practical interaction we have with waves. A good background reference would be Van Dorn's *Oceanography and Seamanship, Second Edition* (Cornell Maritime Press, 1993). Here we cover just a few basics and rules of thumb. Wave forecasting is introduced at the end of this section, with details left to Chapters 7 and 8.

It is usually possible to distinguish three types of wave motion on the surface of the sea: ripples, wind waves, and swells, as illustrated in Figure 5.4-1. Ripples are the cat's paws (wavelets) on the surface of waves that show the instantaneous wind direction. Ripples are just tiny waves with very little inertia. Without inertia to keep them going, they disappear the instant the wind stops, or they change direction the instant the wind changes direction. The direction of ripples can change instantly in response to gusts or small wisps of wind. They respond fast because they are *capillary waves*, whose restoring force is surface tension, as opposed to larger waves restored by gravity. Ripples are usually riding on wind waves, and the wind waves are often riding on a gentle, rolling motion of the sea called swells.

The distinction between swells and wind waves is sometimes difficult to make, especially when the wind waves are bigger than the swells. But when the swells are at least as big as the wind waves, they are prominent. There can also be swells without wind waves. It is not uncommon to see a calm, waveless sea rolling like a giant corrugated-tin roof or washboard. In the more general case, though, the seas are a confused combination of waves and swells. For orientation from the seas, we must distinguish swells from wind waves because prominent swells can provide persistent reference directions despite changes in the wind and waves.

If we clarify our terms, we can call wind waves just "waves," but it requires that declaration. The word "waves" can mean anything in various contexts. Going forward here, "waves" means wind waves.

Waves are caused by local winds. They grow or subside with the wind, and they advance in the general direction of the existing wind. The direction and size of swells, on the other hand, are not related to local winds. Swells may move with or against the local wind, or at any angle relative to it. The origin of swells is usually a long distance from the local conditions.

Swells are the remnants of waves that are no longer driven by the wind that created them. Either they outran a storm, or the winds died or changed direction. Swells persist purely from their own inertia, which is immense. When unopposed by counteracting winds, swells may run for a thousand miles or more and persist for several days or longer. In some areas and seasons, there are prevailing swells that reflect the prevailing storm or strong wind patterns of some distant region.

To distinguish swells from waves, recall how waves are defined (Figure 5.4-2). Wave height is the vertical distance from trough to crest. Wavelength is the horizontal distance between successive crests, measured in the direction of the wave's motion. And finally, *wave width* is the transverse extent of the wave in the direction perpendicular to the wave's motion.

The height of waves depends on the strength of the wind, the size of the wind pattern (fetch), and the duration of the wind. Regardless of the factors controlling the wave heights, there is always a statistical distribution of wave heights. A fixed wind speed blowing in a steady direction over a given fetch for a given duration of time generates waves of many heights, lengths, and periods. The distribution of heights at any time is characterized by its *significant wave height* (SWH), which is the average height of the highest one third of all waves in the distribution.

Starting from a flat sea, the onset of a new wind starts wave development, the SWH of which increases with time (duration), but even if the wind blows forever, the SWH can be limited by the fetch of the wind, meaning the distance over which the wind blows at constant speed *and direction*. The equilibrium wave distribution of a given wind speed when not limited by fetch nor duration is called the *fully developed seas* for that wind speed. The required conditions for various wind speeds are shown in Table 5.4-1.

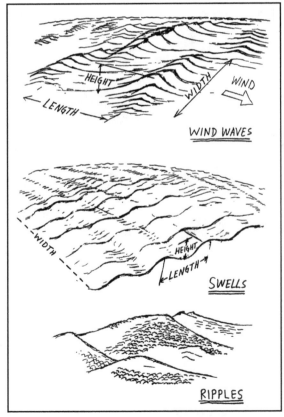

Figure 5.4-1. *Types of waves. Ripples are little wavelets riding on the surface of wind waves, which in turn ride on a rolling surface of swells. The combination is called the sea state or just the seas. Adapted from the book* Emergency Navigation.

If a 20-kt wind blows for a half a day or so, over a distance of about 80 miles, it makes waves with a SWH of some 8 ft. Limit any one of these factors and the SWH will be lower. It is not often we see fully developed seas for 20-kt winds, though we often do see 20 kts of wind. The seas we commonly see are limited by either fetch or duration.

The height of swells we meet depends on the height of the waves they evolved from and on the distance they traveled from their source. As swells move away from their wind source, their height slowly decreases and their length increases. They become less steep. In general, the biggest swells are not as steep as even the smallest waves. A description of the combined seas (wind waves and swells) is given by the Douglas Sea State Scale (Appendix 3). The relationship between wind and sea state is given by the Beaufort wind force scale (Section 5.5).

Though swells are not as steep as waves, their primary distinction is their shape. Swells have smooth, rounded crests, whereas wave crests are sharp and cusp-like. Waves can break, open-water swells do not. And swells are very much wider than waves. The width of swells can appear to be unlimited. The troughs of well-developed swells on calm water can look like highways extending out to the horizon—and they can be just as good a reference direction. The widths of waves, on the other hand, are typically only a few times their length, and they appear even narrower because their height is peaked near the center of the wave. Also, successive swells are remarkably uniform in height, like the ridges of a washboard, whereas wind-driven wave patterns are very irregular. If we have waves at all, we have waves of many heights.

Graphic Wave forecasts

For a quick look at real wave data, check the bottom of the Atlantic or Pacific Products pages at the OPC website. They show forecasts for wave period and direction from the Wave Watch model, WW3. Then print the forecasts or save the images. (Wave heights would be more interesting, but they are not shown there. We can get heights at another site.) Then on the next day or so, compare these forecasts with actual measurements from the NDBC website. There, we must find

a few buoys that provide wave data. Not all offer this, so it is click and check. These live data can then be compared to the graphic forecasts as shown in Figure 5.4-3.

Wave and swell directions are defined like winds, namely the direction they come from. Arrows on the graphics point in the direction they flow toward. We do not often refer to the direction of waves, since they are presumed to be in the direction of the wind, but we do refer to swells as, say, "westerly swells," meaning they are coming from the west.

To see graphic wave forecasts for other times and parameters, google "NCEP model guidance," then click WW3 to show regions available, select a region, then the model runtime, then the time span of interest. There are three parameter combinations to choose from. Watching how these wave patterns change with time provides an excellent way to see how wind waves evolve into swells and how the properties of swells change as they cross the ocean.

For practical wave work underway—we need the wave data for optimal routing—the WW3 digital forecasts in GRIB format are the most useful. There are also more parameters available to choose from to help develop a working vision of the sea state. There are also other ocean models with wave forecasts. Chapter 7 discusses details of using GRIB files, and Chapter 8 lists sources for this data underway.

List of key points, rules, guidelines, and approximations

In no particular order; numbered only for cross reference.

#1. Wave dimensions are defined in Figure 5.4-2

#2. Wind waves always come as a statistical distribution of heights and lengths. If we have waves at all, we have waves of many different heights. So when speaking of wave height it *always* refers to a statistical property, such as average wave height, height of the highest one third, most likely wave height, etc. (Swells are different; they can have a specific height.)

#3. For *individual* waves or swells: L = 5 T^2, where L is wavelength in feet; T is period in seconds.

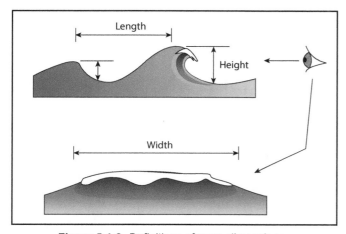

Figure 5.4-2. *Definitions of wave dimensions.*

Table 5.4-1. Properties of fully developed seas			
Wind speed (kts)	**SWH (ft)**	**Duration (hr)**	**Fetch (nmi)**
10	2	2	10
15	4	6	34
20	8	10	75
25	14	16	155
30	22	23	280
35	32	32	460
40	50	47	830
45	60	56	1030
50	78	69	1420

Table Notes: Adapted from *HO Pub. No. 602, Practical Methods for Observing and Forecasting Ocean Waves,* by WJ Pierson, G. Neumann, and RW James, 1971.

Figure 5.4-3. *Comparing a wave period and direction forecast from 24 hrs earlier with live buoy data. This is a corner of the full Atlantic forecast from the OPC. Arrows point in the direction the waves are moving, but the buoy reports tell us the direction they come from. The reports are for 12z Oct 13; wind and pressure data were removed. The agreement with period and direction are very good. The parameter shown is called "dominant" wave by the OPC and NDBC; the NCEP graphic output calls this "peak" wave; the corresponding WW3 GRIB parameters (DIRPW, PERPW) are called "primary" wave—my comments on this practice have been censored!*

For ocean sailing we would be counting more on the 48-hr forecast, this one being of most use for understanding the waves in terms of wind patterns on the corresponding maps. For practical use, the GRIB format from WW3 is more useful. Note that the pop-up buoy reports from the index page at NDBC show only the wave parameters shown here, but clicking the more info link gives more wave parameters. These are discussed, along with use of WW3, in Chapter 7.

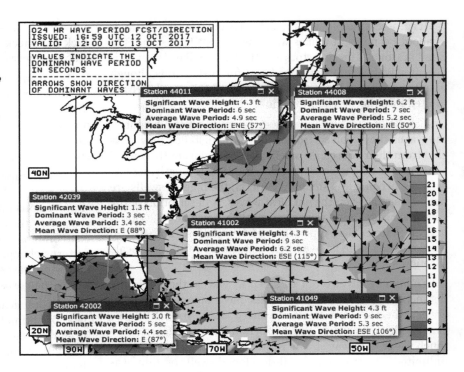

#4. Wind waves move in the direction of the wind—or about that. When a new wind fills in, it can take a while for the seas to adjust to the new direction. Look carefully to the surface of the waves to see if ripple direction and wave direction are the same.

#5. Swells can move in any direction relative to existing wind, because they come from storms that are far off or long gone. The direction swells come from marks their origin, where the storm was or is coming from.

#6. "Westerly swells" means swells come in from the west, and so on.

Table 5.4-2. Wind wave height distribution relative to significant wave height (SWH)	
Wave description	*Wave Height*
Most probable wave height	0.5 × SWH
Average height of all waves	0.6 × SWH
Average of the highest one-third of all waves	1.0 × SWH
Average of the highest one-tenth of all waves	1.3 × SWH
About 1 out of 2,000 waves	2.0 × SWH

Table Notes: *If a forecast calls for "6-ft waves," it means SWH is 6 ft. In this pattern you would expect the average of all waves to be about 3.6 ft (0.6 × SWH). About 1 in 2,000 would be 12 ft high (2 × SWH). This latter wave is not a "rogue wave," it is just a wave at the less-probable end of the normal wave-height distribution.*

#7. A long, low swell can be the first sign at sea or along a coast of an approaching storm. Swells may precede a storm by a full day or longer. On the other hand, new swells might appear and the storm never does. It changed direction or dissipated.

#8. All big waves start out as ripples. Oil or soap on the water makes a slick that prevents ripples from forming, and hence inhibits the formation of larger waves—to some extent, in some cases.

#9. "Seas" is often used to mean the combination of waves and swells, but sometimes "seas" is used to describe wind waves alone, and then we hear of "seas and swells." To be safe, distinguish waves as either *wind waves* or *swells* and avoid "seas" when referring to just one type. To mean both, use *combined seas*. To mean either, use *waves*. Terms like wave speed, wave height, wavelength, wave period, must be interpreted in context of wind waves, swells or combined seas, thus this must always be clarified.

#10. Fetch is the upwind range of water over which wind is constant in both speed *and* direction. It is NOT the sea room in the direction of the wind.

#11. Duration is the length of time the wind blows at a steady speed *and* direction.

#12. Significant wave height (SWH) is the average height of the highest 1/3 of all wind waves. Radio and text reports of wave height are in SWH, although they rarely mention that. Table 5.4-2 shows how the rest of the wave-height distribution is related to the SWH.

#13. Wave height depends primarily on wind speed, duration, fetch, but it also depends on rain fall, air temp, and water depth. Of all of these, wind speed is the most important factor. The others are complex. See Oceanography References.

#10. "Fully developed seas" for a given wind speed means the wind waves have reached their ultimate height, length, and speed, and they are not limited by fetch or duration.

#14. Waves are made by wind, earthquakes, breaking glaciers, volcanoes, or passing vessels. They could also be made from an intense downdraft of a severe squall line. On rare occasions I have seen a single large swell wave cross the vessel at sea from no apparent source at all. And of course, waves can be made by the sun and moon—the tidal bulge is indeed a wave crossing the oceans and estuaries.

#15. In wave motion, water is not moving with the wave, but rather is traveling in a circle beneath the crest; at the crest the current of the circular motion is in the direction of wave motion; in the troughs, the wave current is opposite to the wave motion. The higher the waves and the faster they are moving (more developed), the stronger the circular motion is and the faster this wave current is. In big waves, water can be circulating at 2 or 3 kts or more. This factor can contribute to boats rounding up going down big waves.

#16. Wind-wave speed slowly builds to about 0.9 × wind speed for fully developed seas.

#17. The average height of combined seas can be figured from a right triangle: the two sides are wave and swell heights; the hypotenuse is height of combined seas. Or use:

Combined-h = SQRT [(Wave-h)^2 + (Swell-h)^2].

#18. Wave steepness = height/length. All waves break at a steepness of 1/7, but most break earlier at 1/10. (They begin to look steep at 1/18.) Steepness increases dramatically when wind and current are in opposite directions; steepness diminishes when wind and current are in the same direction. This is a huge effect in places like the Gulf Stream. See Figure 3.6-4.

#19. At sea, waves look bigger than they are since we tend to concentrate on the big ones. Waves always look smaller in photographs than they are, both relatively and absolutely.

#20. When approaching a river bar or island cut from seaward with a following swell, remember you are looking at the back side of the waves in front of you, so you may not see how steep they are, or even note that they are breaking at the bar or cut.

#21. Wave height builds whenever waves are slowed down—it is a transfer of kinetic to potential energy. Waves are slowed when they enter shallow water, meet opposing winds, or opposing currents.

#22. Waves are affected by the land when the water depth diminishes to about one half the wavelength, at which time they slow down and they steepen—the period does not change. This is referred to as the *depth of the wave*, meaning below this depth there is no wave associated motion of the water.

#23. Most damage and deaths attributed to hurricanes are caused by storm surge and other sources of water coming ashore, i.e., extreme rain. Surge comes from an extreme wind-driven current riding on a rise in the sea level due to exceptionally low pressure, exacerbated at low tide. (Climatically rising sea level will make this worse eventually, but it is not a significant factor in surge height at present—which is not to say that climatically increased frequency, intensity, and latitude range of storms does not contribute to the likelihood of surge.)

#24. Rogue or freak waves (*extreme storm waves*) are much higher and steeper than average waves; have much longer widths; are usually deeper (relative to surface level) rather than taller than typical big waves; are possibly caused by downdrafts along squall lines that happen to hit the trough of a larger than average wave moving at about the same speed as the squall, or possibly the result of constructive interference of large wave patterns. They are perhaps more likely in strong winds in strong adverse current such as north wall of the Gulf Stream or Agulhas Current. They are rare, poorly understood phenomena.

#25. A cubic meter of water weighs about one ton, which accounts for the force of waves and their potential destructive power. (One might read that sentence twice. The safety harness of a mariner on deck has to be very strong.)

#26. As a guideline to predicting wave height, SWH (in ft) for fully developed seas reaches about 2% of the (wind speed)^2 for wind speeds less than about 30 kts, and 3% of (wind speed)^2 for higher wind speeds. Thus 20 kts would yield about 8-ft seas; 40 kts would equal about 48 ft seas. This guideline can be tested with buoy data from the NDBC, after confirming that fetch and duration minimums have been met. It is rare to see fully developed waves for winds greater than 20 kts or so.

#27. To estimate duration required for fully developed seas, it takes a duration in hours equal to one-half the wind speed in knots to develop seas to most of their potential for winds less than about 30 kts, but a duration in hours equal to the wind speed for higher wind speeds. Thus 20 kts would take about 10 hrs to develop; 40 kts would take about 40 hrs to develop.

#28. Confused or chaotic seas occur when waves and swells are running in crossed directions.

#29. The Beaufort scale (Table 5.4-3) is used to relate sea state to wind speed. When the seas are not consistent with the wind, it is most likely current that is the cause. Remember it takes some time for seas to develop when the wind changes.

#30. Whitecaps are first seen on still water when the wind speed is about 10 kts; in a contrary current of 1 or 2 kts, whitecaps will be seen at some 8 kts; with a following current, whitecaps are not seen until some 12 kts. Even relatively low-speed current can be detected in light air by a change in the texture of the water surface, as illustrated in Figure 5.4-4.

#31. Squalls may have strong winds, but they never make waves as big as the wind speed might indicate, because the fetch and duration are very limited.

#32. Trade wind waves are much larger than might be guessed from the wind speeds, because the fetch and duration are extremely long.

#33. Tsunamis are not a threat at sea, where they are barely detectable, but they are a major hazard in shallow waters near shore or in bays. They are usually well forecasted these days, but we have numerous tragic historic cases to show that in some oceans this was not always true.

#34. The center of a hurricane has an eye of calm wind, but the seas (already big anywhere near the system) in the eye are steep and chaotic. The eye is not a nice place at sea.

#35. Sea state along the edge of the continental shelf is often rougher than it is well away from this transition, offshore and inshore. It pays to be aware of the shelf location on coastal routes. It will typically drop off about 100 fathoms. On coastal passages, it is always valuable to find and mark that drop off with a highlight pen.

#36. Just as waves have many heights, they also have many periods, lengths, and speeds. The distribution is shown in Figure 5.4-5. Note that we can relate period, length, and speed, but there is no such relationship of any of these with height.

#37. Use of sea state for orientation when steering without a compass is covered in the author's book *Emergency Navigation* (McGraw Hill, 2008). Parts of this section have been adapted from that book.

Wave Speed

The usual concern in waves is maintaining control of the vessel. This is true at all times, and a major concern when crossing a bar or other opening to enter a harbor in a high following sea. When ocean yacht racing, negotiating the waves to maximize the time spent surfing is usually the key to winning downwind races. In all cases, it is valuable to have a good feeling about wave speeds and what affects them.

Figure 5.4-4. *Reading the current from the water. The texture of the surface is often enough to spot the direction of current flow. Wind against current makes steep waves and wavelets, just as wind with the current smooths out the seas as well as the wavelets.*

At the helm, waves moving faster than you pass under the vessel, whereas you run over the slower ones. To keep on or off the face of a wave, the vessel speed must be adjusted, either with more or less power, or by coming up into the wind to pick up speed.

The relationship between wind speed and wave speed is just as complicated as it is between wind speed and wave height. Any given wind speed (no matter how constant or steady) will create many heights and lengths of waves, as well as many different periods of wave motion. Since a wave period is the time it takes one wave to pass, meaning crest to crest, or one wavelength of distance, the velocity of a wave is just

wave speed = wavelength / wave period.

This is the fundamental definition of speed (distance/time), but note the units. If length is in meters and period in seconds, the speed is m/s. Starting from basic physics of waves restored by gravity, and adjusting the length to feet, we can express the relationship between period and length as $L = 5 T^2$, which means the wave speed (adjusting units to knots) depends only on period, namely:

Wave speed (kts) = 3 T (sec).

When we are moving as well, an accurate period measurement is not so easy, so estimating the length may be more accurate. On the other hand, forecasts always give period, never lengths. From these forecasted periods you can determine the speed and length. Also it remains easy to note if the waves are faster or slower than we are.

The height or steepness may have some small effect, but the primary factor in wave speed is the wavelength. Long

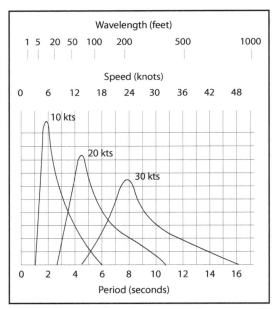

Figure 5.4-5. *Statistical distribution of wave periods as a function of wind speed (10, 20, and 30 kts) for fully developed seas, with corresponding scales for wave speed and wavelength, though these data serve only as a rough estimate of speed and length distributions. It is natural to be aware of wave speed relative to boat speed when sailing downwind.*

waves move faster than short waves. You can have a very low swell traveling faster than a more menacing-looking steep wave that is much higher. Indeed, the fastest waves are the very long low tsunami waves created by underwater earthquakes. These may only be some inches high traveling at 100 kts or more! On the other hand, in a typical seaway, the biggest waves are also the longest waves and hence travel faster than the little ones.

Since a low swell that has long ago outrun its driving wind can be faster than higher waves in the thick of a storm, it is clearly not possible to make a direct relationship between wave speed and wind speed in a given seaway. Viewed from within a given wind pattern, the crucial factor to wave speed is how long the wind has been blowing. All waves start out small, moving slowly, and gradually increase in height and length and consequently speed. It is the *relative speed* of

Table 5.4-3. Beaufort Wind Force Scale				
B	Wind Speed in kts	Wave Height* in ft	WMO Description	Effects observed at sea
0	< 1	0	Calm	Sea like mirror.
1	1 - 3	< 0.4	Light air	Ripples with appearance of scales; no foam crests.
2	4 - 6	0.4 (1)	Light breeze	Small wavelets; crests of glassy appearance, not breaking.
3	7 - 10	2 (3)	Gentle breeze	Large wavelets; crests begin to break; scattered whitecaps.
4	11 - 16	2 (5)	Moderate breeze	Small waves, becoming longer; numerous whitecaps.
5	17 - 21	4 (8)	Fresh breeze	Moderate waves, taking longer form; many whitecaps; some spray.
6	22 - 27	8 (13)	Strong breeze	Larger waves forming; whitecaps everywhere; more spray.
7	28 - 33	13 (19)	Near gale	Sea heaps up; white foam from breaking waves begin to be blown in streaks.
8	34 - 40	18 (25)	Gale	Moderately high waves of greater length; edges of crests begin to break into spindrift; foam is blown in well-marked streaks.
9	41 - 47	23 (32)	Strong gale	High waves; sea begins to roll; dense streaks of foam; spray may reduce visibility.
10	48 - 55	29 (41)	Storm	Very high waves with overhanging crests; sea takes white appearance as foam is blown in very dense streaks; rolling is heavy and visibility reduced.
11	56 - 63	37 (52)	Violent storm	Exceptionally high waves; sea covered with white foam patches; visibility still more reduced.
12	64 and over	> 45	Hurricane force	Air filled with foam; sea completely white with driving spray; visibility greatly reduced.

Table Notes: *B = Beaufort force number. The wave heights shown are conventionally included in this scale, described as "probable" ("highest"), but these are broad estimates, not consistent with typical wave statistics terminology—effects of likely fetch and duration limits are accounted for in some manner. It is important to remember that wave height is not an integral part of this important concept of relating wind speed to the appearance of the sea. Beaufort's original version (early 1800s) did not even include wind speed (added 1903) nor sea state description (added 1906). The scale so corrected (still without wave height) was adopted by the WMO in 1939. Wave heights were added in about 1960—possibly to accommodate discussion of waves for those who express wind speed in Beaufort Force numbers rather than knots. Since wave height does not help with the primary goal of the scale, their inclusion is more distracting than beneficial. They are included here because they appear in the Bowditch and the NWS versions without adequate explanation.*

Table 5.4-4. A Personal Beaufort Scale
1 or 2 knots. See wind with light smoke (incense), but can't feel it
4 knots. First feel the wind on face or neck
10 knots. Can first see isolated white caps in still water. Not immediately obvious, but if you look you will see some. Change to 8 knots in a contrary current of 1 or 2 kts; change to 12 kts when wind and current are same direction.
20 knots. Sustained 20 makes sea surface appear as bed spread of white caps. It is the first thing that catches the eye.
15 knots. In between 10 and 20! That is, white caps are easy to see, don't have to look for them (10 kts), but they do not dominate your vision of the surface (20 kts).
30 knots. First see spindrift. Usual first clear signs of spindrift (blowing foam or spray) are in gusts of 30 in winds of 25+ or so. Also seen flying off of wave crests. It's a good way to judge the gust speed, for gusts seen away from your location.
40 knots. Need goggles if it is raining and sustained. What looked like fish scales on wave surfaces at lower speeds now looks like deep gouged out roof tiles. Big waves occasionally break. Surface dominated by spray.
Shortcut to remember the scale (B>2): **Mean wind (kts) = 6 × B - 10.**

Table Notes: *In a sense, it has to be personal to the individual to be useful.*

wind and waves that builds the waves. As soon as the wave speed approaches the wind speed they stop building. They are fully developed.

A common formula for the speed of an individual wave is familiar to many mariners, since it is just this relationship that determines hull speed, meaning the speed at which you begin to climb over the vessel's bow wave:

Wave speed = 1.34 kts × SQRT (wavelength).

A wave (or waterline) that is 49 ft long will be traveling at 9.4 kts (1.34 × 7). Recall wave speed = 3T, and L=5T², so the mysterious 1.34 is just an approximation of 3/SQRT(5).

Table 5.4-5 uses *average* wavelengths as a function of wind speed to compute *average* wave speed as a function of wind duration. Looking for empirical patterns in these data, we find that after the wind has been blowing for a period of time in hours equal to the wind speed in knots, the wave speed will be about 0.9 times the wind speed. This is similar to the duration criteria we discussed earlier for achieving fully developed seas, or nearly so for practical purposes. In other words, when the seas have nearly matched their full potential for the present wind speed, the waves are on average traveling at about 0.9 times that wind speed.

This table is based on average values. The length criteria still applies to individual waves. The longer waves will be faster than the shorter waves. The distribution data displayed in Figure 5.4-5 shows more what an actual distribution of speeds would be like—though this too is a only a rough picture of the distributions. In short, in every seaway there will be varying speeds.

From a practical point of view, these are just guidelines to gauging the approximate wave speeds to be expected, and even this is only useful in wind and seas you have watched develop. In many cases of interest, this won't apply at all. On crossing bars in a following swell, the local wind has nothing to do with the wavelength of the swells and hence their speeds. Likewise, when sailing in the trades, the seas, long and fast, are developed over many days over many hundreds of miles of fetch. They may have developed in an average wind of 20 kts but it is only blowing 12 kts at the moment. These waves will reflect their average development for a half a day or so.

Hence we are left with just looking and judging the length. Or better still, keep the mind on the size of the waves relative to your own speed. If one passes you when your knotmeter

Table 5.4-5. Wave Speed (kts) vs. Wind Speed and Duration					
	10 hr	*20 hr*	*30 hr*	*40 hr*	*50 hr*
10 kt	9	12	14	15	15
20 kt	14	18	20	22	24
30 kt	17	22	26	29	32
40 kt	20	27	31	35	38

Table Notes: *These are average values of broad distributions (see Figure 5.4-5). A sample is: in 20 kts of wind, the average wave is moving at 14 kts after the wind has been blowing for 10 hrs.*

reads 9 kts, then you know that every wave that long or longer will do the same. Likewise, by watching this it helps develop that intuition as to what waves you can catch or how soon you have to set up to get on one as it approaches. Keeping an eye on wave speed keeps you in better tune with the sea.

Wave Forecasts

The primary U.S. global ocean model for wave forecasting is the Wave Watch model (WW3). There is also a Great Lakes forecast. See graphic displays of some parameters (as in Figure 5.4-3) and more at polar.ncep.noaa.gov/waves. We can request various parameters, organized as wind waves, swell waves, and combined seas (Table 5.4-6).

The Deutcher Wetterdienst (DWD) also has excellent global and European regional wave forecasts, as well as weather maps (opendata.dwd.de)—Google's Chrome browser offers a convenient auto translate service. DWD uses different abbreviations for the wave parameters, but the parameters themselves are established by WMO (Table 5.4-6). Details on the use of, and access to these GRIB formatted data are in Chapters 7 and 8, including how to incorporate the forecasts into optimum routing.

Table 5.4-6. WW3 Wave Parameters	
Abbreviation	*Meaning*
Wind waves	
WVDIR	Direction of wind waves
WVPER	Mean period of wind waves
WVHGT	Significant height of wind waves
Swell waves	
SWDIR	Direction of swell waves
SWPER	Mean period of swell waves
SWELL	Significant height of swell waves
Primary and Secondary	
DIRPW	Primary wave direction
PERPW	Primary wave mean period
Combined seas	
MWSPER	Mean period of combined wind wave and swell
WWSDIR	Direction of combined wind waves and swell
HTSGW	Significant height of combined wind waves and swell

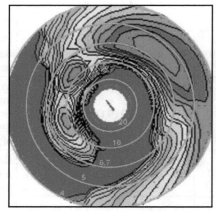

Figure 5.4-6. *WW3 wave spectrum of energy (colors), period (green rings), and direction at a buoy. Two swell patterns show up as narrow period spreads at about 9 seconds; the wind waves to the NE at about 6 seconds are the primary or dominant part of the wave pattern containing the most energy. They have a broad range of periods. You can view wave spectra at polar.ncep.noaa.gov/waves. Use Product Viewer; check Spectra; then click a buoy on the map.*

6.1 The Varied Effects of Land on Wind

Throughout the book we have stressed that wind is the ultimate concern in marine weather for all mariners and we have discussed how the wind behaves in the presence of various weather patterns. All wind theory presented so far made the tacit assumption that wind flow over the water was not influenced by the presence of nearby land.

Most boating by far, however, is done in near coastal or inland waters where land can have a strong influence on both the speed and direction of wind. Indeed, often what we experience on the water is so dominated by the influence of land that it is more important to understand this influence than it is to understand details of the primary weather pattern covering the region. Nevertheless, the presentation here is not backwards. To learn about boiling water, the first step is to learn to put heat to the pot, then we learn the important detail that putting a lid on the pot greatly speeds up the process.

Wind and terrain (micro-meteorology) is a difficult subject, in both theory and practice. The height, shape, slope, extent, texture, location, temperature, and even the color of all surrounding lands are each potentially crucial to their influence on the wind. With so many variables, there are often conflicting influences in the same area—some trying to strengthen the wind, others trying to diminish it. Some features of a shoreline and nearby terrain might tend to make the wind flow parallel to the shore, others perpendicular to the shore. Furthermore, the same land features usually behave differently with different initial wind directions.

The best that can be done to prepare for educated guesses is to learn about wind behavior in isolated idealized circumstances, and then look for examples underway to reinforce your learning. When you find an example you understand, explain it to someone else as a "classic example of such and such," and when you find an example that does not seem consistent with the theory you know, spend some time pondering the lay of the land and the wind around it to see if you might figure out what is going on. This will be much more productive than simply concluding that all such theories are useless.

Now, with a brief rest from all that back pedaling, we can get on with some principles and guidelines. The various influences of land can be thought of in two categories: large-scale regional effects that are well known and forecasted routinely, and local effects that are not at all presented in official forecasts—keeping in mind, however, that prominent local wind behavior is often presented in the *Coast Pilot* and *Sailing Directions* descriptions, even though not covered in weather broadcasts. It is also useful to distinguish effects caused by

the temperature of the land from those caused by the geometry and texture of the land.

Sea Breeze

Land heats and cools in response to the sun much faster than any body of water does. There are several reasons for the difference in heating. They were discussed in Section 3.1 along with other aspects of a building sea breeze, which is shown schematically in Figure 6.1-1. When land heats, the air in contact with it heats, which causes it to expand. The expanded air is less dense than the air above it, so it rises. Atmospheric pressure measures the weight of the air, so as

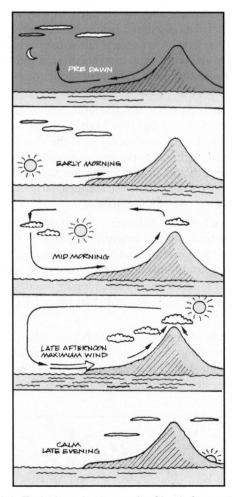

Figure 6.1-1. *Typical sea-breeze cycle. Clouds form over land as the low pressure builds (rising air), while clouds over water tend to dissipate (descending air). We show an example with mountains because they accentuate cloud formation, but sea-breeze cycles do not require coastal mountains.*

the air column over the land becomes increasingly less dense, the pressure over the land drops relative to that over the adjacent water. In this manner, the uneven heating of land and water creates adjacent high and low pressure systems, with a resulting wind flow from High to Low.

The rising air in the low pressure over land is replaced by an onshore flow of air from the higher pressure over the water. The developing onshore wind is called a sea breeze, in keeping with standard wind terminology (a north wind is from the north; a sea breeze is from the sea; a land breeze is from the land). The development and behavior of sea breezes is a fundamental part of the interaction of wind and terrain. This process can generate significant winds in the complete absence of moving weather patterns.

The classic sea breeze occurs in near coastal waters, mostly on clear summertime days, along straight, featureless coastlines—again, this is an idealized situation, not necessarily a common one. In the idealized case, the breeze starts around mid morning, gradually builds to peak speeds of some 10 to 12 kts in early afternoon, and dies off by late afternoon—unless there is some element of channeling of the winds, and then they last longer and die off fairly rapidly after sunset. When channeled as discussed below, sea breezes can be very much stronger. The breeze is first felt within only a half mile or so of shore, as a light wind blowing directly onto the shore, and it may even start more parallel to the shore, coming from the left side looking offshore.

As the day progresses and the land heats more, the wind builds and usually (in the Northern Hemisphere) veers as it builds to blow more diagonally onto the shore. On a west coast, an initial light westerly or southwesterly would fill in as a northwesterly; on an east facing coast, an initial easterly or northeasterly would fill in as a southeasterly. A veering sea breeze is illustrated in Figure 6.1-2.

Looking at two past America's Cup sites, in San Diego the breeze starts typically mid morning, light, from some 240 or so, and then veers around and builds to some 12 kts from as high as 280 or so. In Valencia, Spain, the sea breeze typically starts around 11 AM from the NE, then by midday is due east perpendicular to the shore, and then more like SE by race time in the afternoon.

During late afternoons, the sea breeze might extend out some 10 miles from shore. Sea breezes are usually included in the radio forecasts for areas where they occur regularly, although they are not usually referred to as "sea breezes" in the reports.

A land breeze is just the opposite. Whenever the land is cooler than the water, the relative pressure over land is higher and the breeze in near-coastal waters comes from the land. Land breezes are most common at night, where they occasionally fill in after a sea breeze dies off. On flat shorelines, land breezes are typically much weaker than the corresponding sea breeze, and are too light to be included in forecasts. Where there are tall hills or mountains along the coast, however, the nighttime land breeze can be significantly stronger because it is enhanced by cool air falling down the slopes of the hills—the cool air from the peaks could not fall down during the day because of the sea breeze blowing up the slopes.

If the implications of land and sea breezes were nothing more than this (a moderate onshore breeze in late afternoon followed by a gentle offshore breeze at night), it would not be a major concern to mariners in any craft. The real importance of land and sea breezes arises when you combine these temperature effects of land with the geometry of the land, which can enhance these winds significantly—not to mention a fortuitously placed passing High or Low that can enhance it even further.

Air is a fluid that flows over and around the terrain of land as water flows around the terrain of the waterway. Winds behave much like currents in this regard. Wind flowing through a narrow pass accelerates, sometimes to very hazardous speeds, and downwind of obstructions, the wind forms eddies and becomes very turbulent (gusty).

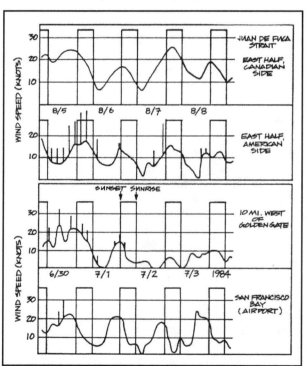

Figure 6.1-3. *Funneled sea breezes in the Strait of Juan de Fuca and San Francisco Bay. Winds typically start to build midday (halfway between sunrise and sunset) and then die off fairly rapidly at sunset. These are typical speeds, although 30 kts is not uncommon in either area. Gust winds when reported are shown as vertical lines. (Adapted from* Marine Weather of Western Washington *by Kenneth E. Lilly, Jr., Starpath Publications, Seattle, 1983.)*

Figure 6.1-2. *Sea breeze over Long Island, NY, showing how the wind veers as it builds. (Adapted from* Weather at Sea *by David Houghton and Fred Sanders).*

A sea breeze in confined waters (such as a bay, sound, or river bordered on two sides by high land) becomes a *gap wind* which can reach 20+ kts on a regular daily basis. Examples from the Strait of Juan de Fuca between Washington state and Vancouver Island, BC, and from the San Francisco Bay are shown in Figure 6.1-3. Such special cases are usually well forecasted, but they are still important to know about when it comes to planning. You can count on these winds in these areas long before specific forecasts are available and plan trips around them. Knowing there will most likely be strong afternoon winds, you can plan your crossing of these waters during early morning—although this might require setting off in fog, so it's important to check that the fog is indeed a radiation fog that will burn off before the winds develop. Along an ocean coast, the fog could be sea fog, which might not burn off but actually grow thicker as the sea breeze develops (see Section 5.3).

When it is not possible to avoid the wind, you can plan around the currents, which are known a year in advance. Tidal currents change direction every 6 hrs and the times of peak flow vary slowly throughout the month. Try to avoid currents flowing against the wind if you must traverse an area with strong afternoon winds. In most cases where there are strong sea breezes there are also strong currents—the land constrains the water as well as the wind—and generally, in these cases, the prevailing wind directions are the same as the flood and ebb directions. As a rule, whenever winds and currents are both strong as a result of land constraints, they generally flow in the same or opposite directions.

Strong sea breezes are confined to the constricted region, so you typically won't feel them till you get there. As you approach the mouth of a channel, valley, or narrow bay, be prepared and expect the winds to increase very rapidly when you reach the exposed part of the waterway. Such channels also, of course, enhance normal weather pattern winds in the same way, as, for example, when approaching channels between islands in Hawaii. The trade winds might nearly double as you turn into a channel.

When sailing along a coastline in 10 or 15 kts of wind—from onshore or offshore—be prepared for up to twice that wind at the entrance to a large constriction. *Sailing Directions* and *Coast Pilot* descriptions of these bays and entrances usually include warnings of this wind behavior, but the same process can occur on a smaller scale without specific references in these guides. Look ahead for white caps as you approach any turn or inlet. This is true for any wind pattern, not just sea or land breezes.

This brings up a footnote on terminology. The terms sea breeze and land breeze are in one sense defined by the direction of the wind, but in common usage, these terms are usually reserved for *winds created by the land*, i.e., thermal winds in some form. If the overall pressure pattern is just making the wind blow onto the shore, then this would not be called a "sea breeze." It is just an east wind, west wind, etc. If we call it a sea breeze, we expect it to behave as a sea breeze, i.e., build and veer in the morning and go away at night.

Returning to channel winds, if you are already in the enhanced winds of a channel and proceeding along it, as you approach a large bay or any other opening onto the channel, you can expect the wind to lighten as it diverges at the junction.

Storm and frontal forecasting is also notably different in channels with restricted wind directions than it is in open water. When winds are so constricted that they can flow only up or down a waterway, an approaching storm will not be foretold by a gradual shift in wind direction, as it often is on the open coast. In a confined waterway, the existing wind just dies off and then rebuilds, sometimes rapidly, from the opposite direction when the storm approaches. Fronts (and isobars in general) crossing channels are covered in Section 6.2

Knowledge of sea breezes can help a lot with onboard forecasting in coastal waters, and inland waters as well in some cases. When there is no afternoon wind—under clear or partly clear skies—when sailing in an area well known for sea breezes, chances are there is low pressure offshore (bad weather of some kind) that is preventing its development.

With low pressure offshore, the thermal low developing on land can't get low enough to pull in the air and start a sea breeze. Even earlier in the day you can spot the beginnings of sea breeze development (or the lack of it) from the clouds over land. When the sea breeze circulation first starts, the updraft of wind on coastal peaks will create small cloud caps over them—the moist onshore flow of air cools as it rises and when it cools to the dew point, water vapor in the air condenses into clouds. If you do not see any cloud caps by mid morning, the sea breeze is not getting started, and there might be low pressure offshore. This could be an early sign of bad weather. Once the storm gets closer, the clouds in general will have thickened and lowered and you wouldn't expect the sea breeze anyway—the land can't heat when it's blanketed by clouds.

In special areas, *katabatic* land breezes can be as hazardous as funneled sea breezes. Katabatic wind can be any wind

Figure 6.1-4. *Cold katabatic winds sinking to the surface from hill tops during the night. These winds do not require a driving force other than gravity, but they would be much accelerated in the presence of the pressure patterns shown in the insert of Figure 6.1-6, in which case they might be called* fall *winds. With strong katabatic winds, there is often a frontal surface separating the cold and warm winds over the water.*

flowing downhill (the name is from Greek for descend), but the usual implication in a katabatic wind is that it is from cooling alone, meaning the air at elevation is cooler and denser than the air below it, thus it falls down the hill (Figure 6.1-4). Other names for this wind are "drainage wind" or "gravity wind," which is meant to distinguish them from cold, downslope winds that are forced down the slope by local weather patterns—these latter winds are called *fall winds,* which is confusing terminology as they must be forced down, whereas the katabatic winds come down without extra force. Winds flowing uphill are called *anabatic wind.*

The steep ice coasts of Greenland and Antarctica are famous for frigid storm-force winds pouring down off the land, but these are exceptional cases. More generally we can think of katabatic wind as the downslope wind that runs down any high slope without the need or assistance of a special weather pattern. Then "fall wind" is reserved for those that require a unique weather pattern (and often a related season) to be prominent. Most of the famous downslope winds with names are actually fall winds. In Europe, the *Bora* is a cold northeast fall wind on the Dalmatian coast of Croatia and Bosnia; the *Mistral* is a north fall wind that blows down the Rhone valley south of Valence, France, and into the Gulf of Lion; the *Papagayo* is a violent northeasterly fall wind on the Pacific coast of Nicaragua and Guatemala; and the *Vardar* (or *Vardaris*) is a cold fall wind blowing from the northwest down the Vardar valley in Greece to the Gulf of Salonika.

Squamish is a town at the head of Howe sound in BC. The name means "Mother of the Wind" in Coast Salish. The sometimes violent wind emanating from Howe Sound (Figure 6.1-5) is a channeled fall wind that has given the name "Squamish" to all such outflow winds in fjords at other locations around the world.

Gap winds in the Columbia River Gorge at the Washington-Oregon border can be of either variety. In summer, the west wind can howl in at 40 kts as a funneled sea breeze; in winter, the east wind can howl out at 40 kts as a *Squamish* wind.

As another example of the complexity of land-wind interactions, note that mountain winds pouring down onto the water are not always cold. Many places located at the base of mountains periodically experience strong downslope winds that are very much warmer than the ambient temperature.

In Germany, Switzerland, and Greenland such a wind is called a *foehn;* in Southern California, it is called a *Santa Ana;* on the eastern slopes of the Rocky Mountains, it is called a *chinook.* These are weather pattern winds that are dramatically modified by the high terrain. Often in these cases, the warm dry air coming down the mountain started out as moist cool air forced up the other side by the prevailing weather pattern. Persistent strong Highs over the CA desert can lead to dramatic *Santa Ana* events resulting in devastating wildfires.

In the lifting process, the air is dried out by condensation (leaving fog, rain, or snow on the up-wind slopes), which also warms the air when the heat of condensation is released (Figure 6.1-6). Then with proper conditions present, this air is forced down on the other side where it arrives at the base both drier and warmer than it went up. As the air descends it heats even more—descending air of any kind heats by compression as it descends. Cold katabatic winds only appear to

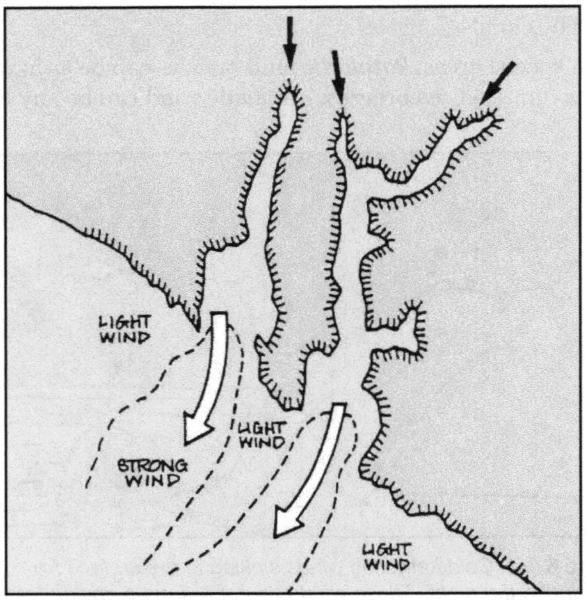

Figure 6.1-5. *Squamish-type winds (channeled fall winds) pouring out of coastal inlets. In cases like these at Howe Sound, BC, there is often a sheer line which marks the sudden onset of very strong winds. (Adapted from* Marine Weather Hazards along the British Columbia Coast, *Environment Canada, 1987.)*

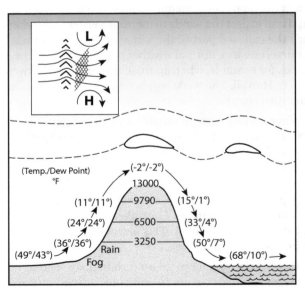

Figure 6.1-6. *Development of a warm dry* foehn *wind. The dry air warms more on the descent than the moist saturated air cooled on the ascent. The warm air must be forced down the shoreward side by strong winds aloft by either a low pressure to the left or a high pressure to the right of the downwind slope, as shown in the inset. Mountain wave clouds often indicate the strong winds aloft. (Adapted from* The Science and Wonders of the Atmosphere *by Stanley David Gedzelman, 1980.)*

be an exception—they are so very cold to begin with that the warming that occurs as they descend is not noticed.

Foehn winds, however, can be distinguished from katabatic winds by more than just temperature. Whereas cold katabatic winds might occasionally be accelerated by the local weather pattern as they descend, they more typically occur without any driving force other than the gravity pulling the cold dense air down to the surface. Foehn winds, on the other hand, are warm and thus lightweight, so they will not sink unless forced to. They require special conditions, typically including strong winds at the mountain peaks, to carry the wind over the top and low pressure downwind of the mountain base to pull the air down. Thus foehn winds are warm fall winds, as we are using the terminology. Mountain wave clouds (pictured in Figure 6.1-6) are often a sign that these conditions are present. Foehn winds can be hazardously strong and they always create unseasonably warm, dry conditions.

It is not so common, but plain and simple flatland gap winds can also become famous and get a name of their own, such as the *Tehuantepecer* in the Gulf of Tehuantepec off Salina Cruz, Mexico. This wind can be very strong and can only be predicted by looking at pressure differences. The atmospheric pressure on the Atlantic side of the isthmus has to be significantly higher than on the Pacific side. The usual decision for cruisers transiting the coast is to cut across the Gulf to save time when no strong winds are present, or follow the beach when they are strong. This does not get you out of the wind, nor out of the blowing sand, but the fetch close in

is small, so the waves are manageable. Off shore the winds *and* seas are a challenge. A sample of this wind seen in satellite data is shown in Figure 6.1-7, which coincidentally also shows a Papagayo event.

Wind Shadows

The geometry of the land, however, does not always create hazardous winds; it can be a blessing. Large obstructions provide shelter from the wind in the obvious way of just blocking it (*wind shadow*), but they can also provide shelter in less obvious ways. An offshore wind coming over a steep cliff does not come spilling directly down to the water, but flows over the edge, only reaching the surface some distance offshore, as shown in Figures 6.1-8 and 6.1-9. The exact distance off as a function of the height of the obstruction is hard to predict and depends on the nature of the obstruction—height, width, porosity, and roughness. You can be confident, however, that you will get out of an offshore wind when you approach a high shoreline, and you typically do not have to go all the way to the beach to do so.

As a rough guideline, you should feel the wind diminish when you get close enough that one hand width (4 finger widths) at arm's length will span the height of the obstruction. This is also a rough guideline you can use to judge how close you must get in behind a large rock or island to use it for shelter. Or better still, this is a proposed way to judge relative distances off so you can make your own measurements for future use. See Figure 6.1-10.

An onshore wind behaves the same way to some extent. It will not blow all the way to the base of a cliff and then go up and over it, but it will rise some distance off to flow smoothly over it. In this way, a very steep leeward shore (cliff) offers shelter from the wind just as a steep windward shore does. Again, use hand widths to monitor your approach and hopefully get some insight into wind behavior in various conditions. A kayaker or other small craft traveling close to the shoreline can take advantage of this shelter more often than larger vessels might dare to. (This effect can be seen on the deck of some large, fast vessels underway. The most wind is at the bow and as you walk aft toward the superstructure the wind lifts and offers shelter.)

Downwind shadowing has been studied extensively by wind power engineers. The Danish Wind Industry Association website includes an online wind shade computer that lets you set height, width, porosity, and roughness of a barrier and then lets you choose a wind speed to see how the barrier perturbs the downwind flow. It is not exactly analogous to wind on the water, but is a good check of the basic ideas. See sample data and links in Figure 6.1-11.

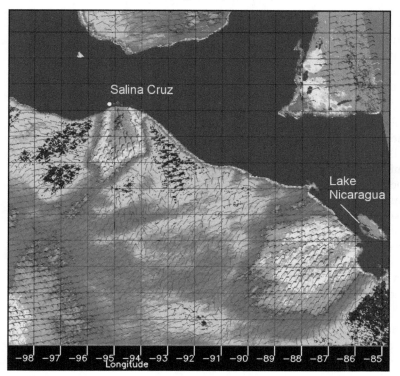

Figure 6.1-7. *Two famous wind patterns,* Tehuantepecer *in the Gulf of Tehuantepec, Mexico (94-95°W), with winds over 35 kts, and the* Papagayo *off of Lake Nicaragua (86-87°W) with winds up to 30 kts, viewed in satellite wind data (Chapter 4). On average there are 12 gale events and 7 storm events per season (Nov to Mar) at Tehuantepec. GFS forecasts may miss these winds (about 50% in one study), but regional models (Chapter 7) should be OK. Text forecasts (human intelligence) should fill in what models might miss.*

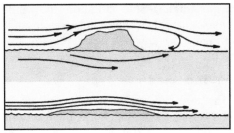

Figure 6.1-8. *Wind flow around tall and low obstructions. Tall obstructions such as a cliff or timbered shoreline can provide shelter on both the windward and leeward sides. Shelter on the windward shore (wind rising) does not extend as far offshore as it does on the leeward shore. When headed for windward shore shelter, be prepared for gusty winds where the wind first hits the surface just before getting into the sheltered region. This region is often marked by white caps or prominent cat's paws.*

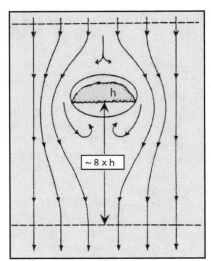

Figure 6.1-9. *Wind flow around a tall obstruction. As a rough guideline, the wind pattern returns to its normal flow pattern at a distance downwind equal to about 8 times the height of the obstruction. Shelter should be available near the center of the obstruction when well within this distance.*

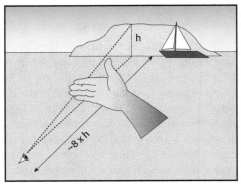

Figure 6.1-10. *A way to estimate ranges using fingers, which are typically about 2° each at arm's length. This hill and mast are about 8° high. Wind shadows or lifting or dirty air begins at a distance off of about 8 × the height of the object disturbing the air. This is a rough guideline. It could be anywhere from 6 to 10 depending on the details (see Figure 6.1-11). For those who like trig, the tangent of this average value angle is h/8h, so the angle is 7°, which is roughly 4 × the typical finger width. Think of this as a starting point to fine tune your own hands and observations.*

Edge and Corner Effects

Recall that Section 2.1 explained why wind veers as you go up in the atmosphere where there is less and less friction. The same effect can take place on the surface if the wind flows from an area with more friction to one with less. Whenever wind flows to an area with less friction, the wind veers. There is much less friction over water than over land, so when wind flows off the shoreline onto the water it will veer. And vice versa, when it flows from water onto a low flat shoreline it will back. And since wind is a fluid, it does not make this change abruptly, but will do so gradually as it crosses the shoreline, as shown in Figure 6.1-12.

Thus we anticipate a result that every sailor knows about. The wind along the shoreline—for one reason or another—is likely to be different from the wind in mid channel. It is not uncommon to be tacking back and forth down the middle of a channel, just to note that boats near shore are reaching right down the beach. But it is not so simple as just assuming the mid-channel wind will back as it approaches a low shore. How low is low? If it is a cliff, the wind will flow along the cliff, following the shape of the shoreline. We can only keep in mind the basic mechanisms in idealized conditions and see if one makes sense for the particular wind direction. Then note that if it behaves the same way next time, you are ready to predict what will happen the third time!

Figure 6.1-13 illustrates how this friction effect can change the nature of wind flow over a point of land, or corner of an island in a manner that is opposite on opposite sides of the wind direction. It is called the *corner effect*. It is actually fairly common, and may well explain some local knowledge you have about your own sailing waters. Think of a point that you round to the right going downwind and get routinely knocked

on your ear—often to blast right into a relatively calm shadow just around the point. It is one of those things that makes sense once you analyze it, but you might not have thought of it that way— it is well known to those who know it well!

When setting off in the morning, remember that wind over the water is always stronger than it is over nearby land (by as much as a factor of 2) and that in most places, wind in the early morning implies some moving weather system approaching. If the skies are still partly clear, consider the eventual effects of a building sea breeze. It might cancel what wind you have, or it might enhance it considerably. Even on calm mornings, it pays to plan around known sea breezes—to have the building sea breeze at your back on the way home from a round trip, for example, might suggest an obvious choice of routes. Remember that even in a power-driven vessel, it is more comfortable and fuel efficient to travel downwind, with the waves rather than against them.

Figure 6.1-14 shows just one example of how you might take advantage of known wind behaviors. This is essentially an element of local knowledge. If you are tacking up a long channel with points on both sides, it can make a huge difference if you are in phase or out of phase with the points.

6.2 Isobars Crossing Channels

One day while working on this book we noted the office barometer was on a plummet. The barometer had dropped almost 9 mb in the previous 6 hrs (Figure 6.2-1)—way more than our "4-5-6" guideline, which says a drop of 4 or 5 mb in 6 hrs is a significant change. This was about twice that rate. If this continued for another half day or so we would be in meteorological bomb territory—meaning a very serious, ex-

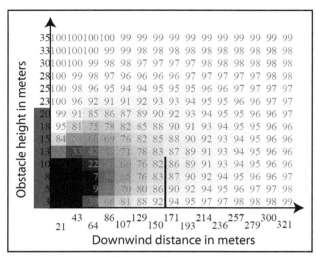

Figure 6.1-11. *Numerical values of wind speed in percentage of unperturbed speed downwind of a 20-meter-tall, full-blocking obstacle, 20 m wide. Note vertical and horizontal scales are different. The guideline of 8 × height (160 m downwind) for back to unperturbed air is not bad in this case. See line between 150 m and 171 m. The worst disturbance is at about half the obstacle height. Data computed from the shade calculator at* windpower.org.

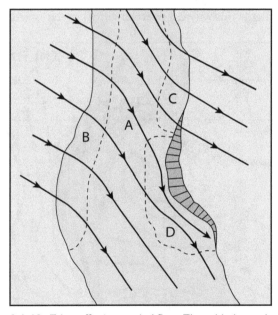

Figure 6.1-12. *Edge effects on wind flow. The mid-channel wind is near N-NW, but near the windward shore it is more westerly as it bends to the NW on the land. Put another way, the NW wind on shore veers toward the N-NW over the channel. Thus if you are sailing in region A, you will find region B and region C more backed, so long as the land is fairly low and flat. In region D, on the other hand, the cliff just bends the wind around to follow the shoreline.*

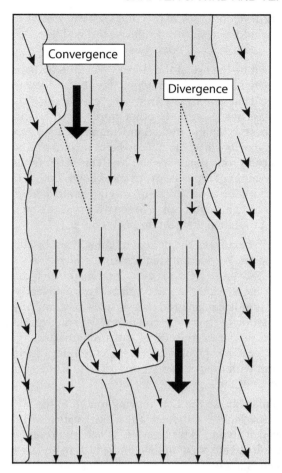

Figure 6.1-13. *The Corner Effect. Wind flow over and around a large low island (bottom) and over similar flat points of land (top). Frictional drag backs the wind over the land, which focuses it on one side and diminishes it on the other. When sailing downwind (in the NH), "Flat points on your right have the might."*

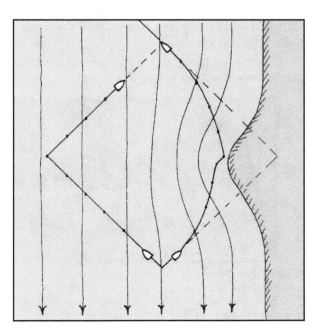

Figure 6.1-14. *The advantage of tacking at a headland when the wind follows it around the bend. Two boats start off at the bottom on opposite tacks but sailing at the same speed. The one headed to the point is continually lifted going in, and then with a judicious tack at the point, is lifted on the way back out, to gain considerably on the boat staying in unperturbed air.*

plosively developing storm (Section 4.4). But when we looked out the window, it was dead calm, and it had been so for the past few hours at least. What was going on?

Could it be the eye of the storm? We did have some wind in the early hours of the previous day. But we know better than that. That would be a pretty big "eye" at the rate winter storms pass over Seattle. In other words, a calm Low center (rare at best in high latitudes) moving at an average winter-time speed of 25 kts would have to be some 600 nmi across to create a calm zone that lasted 24 hrs. This is ten times larger than the center of typical extratropical Lows, even if they did have such a calm zone. Guessing was not going to help. It was time to look at a weather map to see what was taking place. A section of that map is shown in Figure 6.2-2.

At a first glance of the map, it might still not be clear what was going on. We see a strong pressure gradient over our location in Seattle at 47° N, 122° W, and might therefore wonder even more why it is dead calm. The map clearly shows the Low that is causing the pressure we saw, and the direction of motion of the Low is consistent with an expected drop in pressure. The magnitude of the strong easterly gradient is about 4 mb per 55 nmi across Puget Sound, which is also consistent with the pressure drop recorded if we account for the motion of the Low.

The map shows the Low moving inland to the NE with a 24-hr arrow length of about 7° (420 nmi), which corresponds to a speed of about 17 kts to the NE, which would very roughly give us a drop rate of (17 nmi/hr) × (4 mb/55 nmi) = 1.2 mb/hr, which is about 7.2 mb per 6 hrs. This is essentially consistent with what we observed as we do not know the Low's speed very well. Notice that the 24-hr end point is not marked by an × as usual, but just the words "Inland"— this map does not attempt to account for the effect of coastal mountains. Also, we can compute the speed of the next Low behind this one more precisely, because both end points are marked. It will cover 12° (720 nmi) in 24 hrs, so it is moving at 30 kts. If our Low was actually moving faster than we can tell from the map, or if it was deepening, we would get the larger drop rate that we actually detected.

So we can understand the pressure drop we observed and the pressure itself, but why still no wind?

The reason there is no wind in Puget Sound is the orientation of the isobars. There is a huge gradient across Puget Sound, east to west, but essentially no gradient at all along Puget Sound in the north-south direction. And since the Sound is between two mountain ranges, there is no driving force to the wind. The circular motion around the Low center created by the Coriolis effect is completely blocked in a mountain valley. The geostrophic wind speeds we compute based on the isobar spacing discussed in Chapter 2 no longer apply. It is just the pressure difference from one end of the valley or channel to the other that creates the wind. In Puget Sound, for example, we can often estimate the wind solely on the pressure difference between the north end and the south end of the Puget Sound waterway, a distance of some 80 nmi. We can look at the maps on the National Data Buoy Center web site to choose reference points at each end. The guideline is then:

Puget Sound wind speed = 10 kt ×
(North-end pressure - South-end pressure, in mb).

Thus a 2-mb difference gives rise to 20 kts, with wind direction northerly if the north end has higher pressure, or southerly if the south end has higher pressure. This prescription works fairly well for winds below 30 kts or so. For stronger gradients this will way overestimate the wind speeds. Also

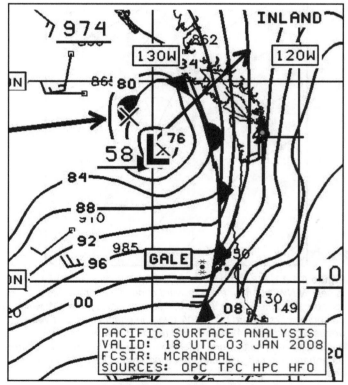

Figure 6.2-2. *Section of a surface analysis map at 18z on Jan 3rd. The pressure over Seattle (47° N, 122° W, red dot) is about 998.5 at this time (just inside the 00 isobar), and it would later drop to 993.5 at 00z on the 4th (4 PM local time on the 3rd), as can be seen more clearly in Figure 6.2-5. The barometer in Fig. 6.2-1 at 160 ft elevation (-5.8 mb) was reading station pressure, which implies 991.8 mb at sea level. The time of the barometer photo is a couple hours after the map time here.*

Figure 6.2-1. *Barometer showing 986 mb, dropping fast. The trend symbol on the right means the pressure is dropping at 2 mb per 3 hrs or faster. This effective design is unique to this instrument, which was sales stock, hence the wrapping.*

we need to keep in mind that in most valleys and channels, the wind speed builds going downwind along the channel. The downwind end will have stronger winds than the upwind end ("Speed = force × time" is a form of Newton's Law).

At map time the pressure difference between Bellingham and Olympia (top end to bottom end) was essentially zero (Figure 6.2-3), and consequently we had no wind. If you look outside the mountain range (Figure 6.2-4) you see over 30 kts of wind at this same time. In the region west of the mountains they were essentially in open air, unaffected by terrain.

Using the guideline mentioned above for Puget Sound winds, if the easterly gradient we had at map time of 4 mb/55 nmi had been rotated so the isobars ran across Puget Sound, rather than parallel to it, then we would have had gale force winds instead of a calm—we can't be more specific because that speed is beyond the realm of the guideline. The Strait of Juan de Fuca, which did experience the full gradient along its prominent channel, had winds over 40 kts much of the time.

The fact that winds in large valleys or channels can often be predicted based on pressures alone can often be used to tactical advantage by sailors. In Puget Sound, for example, there are many days that sailors end up drifting around in the Sound waiting for wind, not knowing if it will fill in from the North or from the South. By monitoring the pressures at both Seattle and Bellingham or Seattle and Olympia, they can answer that question as soon as the pressures are different. More often than not, the pressure will change before the wind develops (or is forecasted), so a navigator can impress

the crew with their shaman-like insights as to which direction the wind will fill in from and at about what intensity.

In some cases there are pressure reports from airports over the VHF radio (such as Bellingham airport) that are not on the NDBC site, or we can use *dial-a-buoy* with a cellphone (Section 8.3) to get the pressures. The NDBC data are typically updated every hour or so, whereas on VHF we get reports only every 3 hrs and synopses and forecasts only every 6 hrs. More details and examples of this type of channel wind analysis are available at starpath.com/local.

In a sailboat race, knowing which way and when the wind will fill in from a present calm gives you the advantage of having the right sails ready to be rigged, as well as time to start planning the route. Thus when sailing in any prominent

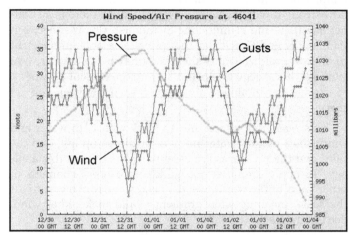

Figure 6.2-4. *Wind speed and pressure just offshore of Cape Elizabeth, WA at weather buoy 46041. The wind at 00z on Jan 4th (far right) is over 30 kts at this exposed location, but at the same time inside the mountain range in Puget Sound the wind is essentially calm (Figure 6.2-5). This graphic and the one below are from the NDBC. The are called "combined plot."*

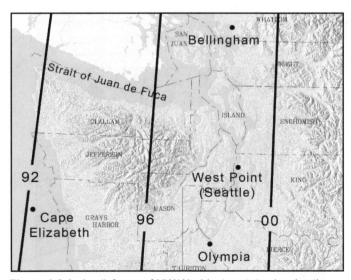

Figure 6.2-3. *A relief map of NW Washington state showing the isobars from Figure 6.2-2 overlaid on it. Two wind reporting stations are shown. West Point Lighthouse in Seattle on Puget Sound lies within the mountain valley between the Olympics to the west and the Cascades to the east, whereas the buoy station offshore from Cape Elizabeth is in open water. The easterly pressure gradient across Puget Sound is about 4 mb per 55 nmi (see Figure 6.2-6 on gradient names), but there is essentially no gradient at all in the north-south direction, and hence no wind in the Puget Sound. In contrast, there are gale force winds on the coast at the same time. Figures 6.2-4 and 6.2-5 show winds and pressures inside and outside of the channel.*

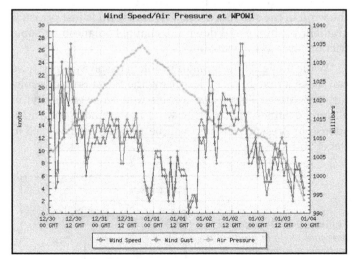

Figure 6.2-5. *Wind speed and pressure at the West Point Lighthouse on Puget Sound in Seattle, WA. Inside the mountain range we see that the wind at 00z on Jan 4th (far right) is essentially calm, whereas outside the mountain range (Figure 6.2-4) the wind is strong (note different wind speed scales).*

channel, it could well be useful to monitor and plot the reported pressures at each end of the channel. You may spot trends that will help predict the winds faster than those you get over standard NOAA Weather Radio. You can also use your observations to confirm regional model forecasts, discussed below.

It is rather like some of those special channels in tidal estuaries where it seems there is no way in the world to predict when the current will change and when it will be flowing in what direction. Such places are not listed in tidal current tables, but you can often learn what you want by plotting the actual tide height at each end of the channel, and then making a graph of the difference between the tide heights as a function of time. This plot will often serve well as a means of telling when the current will change directions and relatively how strong it will be. North of Puget Sound there is a channel like that—the 11-mile long Swinomish Channel between Padilla Bay and Skagit Bay that provides a popular shortcut to Anacortes along a more sheltered route by La Conner, WA. Without this special tide computation, the current flow of up to two knots will almost always be a surprise when you get there.

This reasoning almost has to work with both water and wind, since neither water nor wind will run up hill, and the tides and the pressures are essentially the hills in this analogy. To apply this pressure guideline to other channels in other parts of the world, we just need some rough way to set the scale, meaning what gradient would make what wind. See Figure 6.2-6

Recall that we discussed something very like this in Chapter 2, where we presented a formula for surface wind based on geostrophic wind (friction free) reduced by 20% to account for surface friction. That procedure actually comes out fairly close to the Puget Sound results, but it is not directly applicable. It has in it, for example, a latitude dependency from the Coriolis force, which is not a dominant force driving the wind in the situation here. Channel wind is just pressure gradient pushing wind down the channel balanced by some friction force as the wind builds.

While it might be a complex problem to solve properly, we can make a first guess by just using the Puget Sound results for everywhere. That is, we make a first order guess that in all long channels that restrict wind flow, wind speed in response to pressure changes will be roughly what we see in Puget Sound:

Channel wind (kts) = 800 × pressure gradient,

where the gradient is in mb per nmi. Thus a 1 mb per 80 nmi gradient gives rise to 10 kts; as would 2 mb per 160 nmi.

This is not quite so outlandish a proposal as it might seem, because we have another piece of data. Wind in the Strait of Juan de Fuca, between Canada and Washington state, also follows a wind speed versus pressure gradient guideline almost the same as this one. And that waterway, 12 miles wide and 80 miles long, is far more of a channel than is Puget Sound. Thus we have two rather different channels, one running east-west and the other running north-south that both behave in about this manner. So for now we will call this the "800 rule for channel winds" and wait to collect more data from around the world to see how helpful it can be. Remember that it does not work for winds stronger than about 30 kts.

Thus the wind in a mountain valley or long restricted channel depends very sensitively on the orientation of the isobars and subsequent pressure gradient along the long axis of the channel. We shouldn't be too critical of the weatherman who has to predict this wind when a front approaches. First the incoming front hits a mountain range, which is usually a big jolt to its predicted motion. Then as it crosses the mountains, the orientation of its isobars relative to the channel controls the wind flow in the channel. Sometimes the rotation of just a few degrees can have a huge effect.

What we should expect when sailing in such conditions also depends on which way the front is moving across the channel. In Figure 6.2-7 we see a front crossing a channel with steep hills or mountains on either side. In this case there is a very weak gradient and thus light air north of the front,

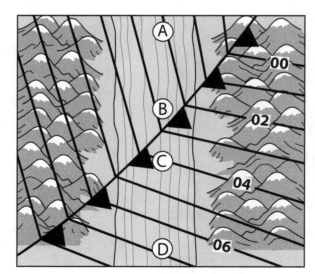

Figure 6.2-7. *Schematic of a front crossing a mountain valley, channel, or gorge, and associated isobars. The pressure gradient is weak from A to B, giving light or no wind north of the front, but strong from C to D giving rise to strong southerlies. The key practical issue is which way the front is sliding across the valley. As the front moves to the east, it slides down the valley, but other motions could bring the front line up the valley. What you experience with time depends on where you are in the waterway.*

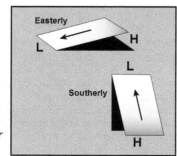

Figure 6.2-6. *Definition of pressure-slope or gradient directions. It is the same as that of the wind if the wind flowed directly from high to low pressure. Figures 6.2-2 and 6.2-3 show an easterly gradient over Puget Sound.*

but strong gradient and strong wind south of the front. The whole question of what wind we get depends on where we are relative to the front line, and which way the line is moving. This is always true to some extent anywhere you are, but the difference can be night and day in a channel.

If this schematic front is moving north, the wind is light ahead of it and then suddenly strong when it passes over. If you are already in the strong wind of such a front and it is moving south, then expect it to potentially go flat calm in a few minutes when the front passes over. Setting out for a sail or a race in such a channel on a day you know a front is going to pass over you, the key issue is to think of how the isobars will look when crossing the channel during your sail. This may tell you which side of the waterway to favor, or when to cross sides, and so on.

Remember, if you are on the windward side of the waterway when the wind is strong, the waves will not be so large as on the leeward side, where the wind has more fetch to work with.

6.3 Wind Forecasts Near Land

One of the most important recent developments for inland sailors is the availability of high-resolution wind forecasts in GRIB format that take into account local terrain. For several years now, a few lucky regions in the U.S. have had locally run Weather Research and Forecasting (WRF) regional models that continue to do an excellent job of wind forecasting in local waters, but these data are typically graphic products, not in the GRIB format we can load and navigate with.

Data from University of Washington Atmospheric Sciences is just one example. Their forecasts for the complex Puget Sound and connecting waters remains as good as it gets, but these data are only available in graphic format, and often many hours later than we would hope for.

But now we have, throughout the U.S. inland and coastal waters, very high resolution forecasts, updated hourly or half-hourly with the latest observations. These data now give us hope of forecasting on a level that might even be used in optimum routing programs that previously were only useful in coastal or ocean waters. Practical details are in Chapter 7; here we just introduce two sources, the High Resolution Rapid Refresh Model (HRRR), based on WRF, and the National Digital Forecast Database (NDFD).

The HRRR (pronounced "her") data covers the region shown in Figure 6.3-1. It provides wind, pressure, and precipitation, among other parameters, every hour, out to 18 hrs, except at the synoptic times, when it extents out 36 hr. There is one data point every 1.6 nmi, which means we have relatively good insights into waters as narrow as 4 or 5 miles across. The model is updated every hour, to account for observed winds at buoys, as well as seen by radar, and other measurements. Now, for the first time, we actually have forecasts for local squalls on the water or thunderstorms on land. This can be used not just in the coastal waters shown in the

figure, but also for boating on inland lakes and rivers, and indeed for weather forecasting on land. With these tools in hand, your favorite navigator is now the best person to ask about conditions for the picnic next weekend or a hiking trip.

These new developments were in large part motivated to predict severe thunderstorms on land. The forecasts are available to mariners from several sources and can indeed be seen updated every hour on your cellphone (Figure 6.3-2), as well as incorporated into a computer or tablet for routing. The HRRR model actually provides wind forecasts every 15 minutes, but we have not seen this available yet from third party providers.

The NDFD data are in another category altogether. This is not strictly a *model* forecast such as GFS or HRRR, it is the product of the interplay between observations, numerical modeling, and the crucial addition of input from the regional office forecasters around the U.S., which includes those of the national centers such as OPC and NHC. These are the digitized format of the official NWS forecasts, which are now available to mariners in GRIB format. We have had one sector of this data, called Oceanic, for some years, but this sector is more of a global coverage with resolution of 5.4 nmi, updated every 6 hrs. Now mariners are beginning to get access to the high resolution coastal and inland forecasts in GRIB format. NDFD is a complex program, and we leave the details to Chapter 7.

For now I want to stress the NDFD sectors called CONUS (continental U.S.) and Regional (AK, HI, PR&VI). The CONUS and HI data have a resolution of 1.35 nmi, with wind and waves forecasted out 7 days. The PR&VI data has the amazing resolution of 0.7 nmi! The CONUS data are updated every 30 minutes, so there is not much call for the far end of the forecast period. On the other hand, a three-day race could not be planned with HRRR (out only 18 hrs) but could be with the NDFD CONUS sector, which has slightly better resolution. It is not clear, however, without further testing, which data source will be best for which waters or for which application. These issues are addressed in the next chapter. The NDFD CONUS coverage is the same as the HRRR (Fig-

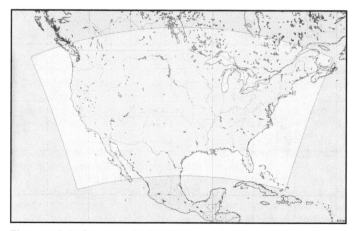

Figure 6.3-1. *Coverage for HRRR model forecasts. Note extended coverage outside of the U.S. Image from LuckGrib. NDFD CONUS coverage is the same, but no land coverage outside the U.S.*

ure 6.3-1), except there are no data on land outside of U.S. borders.

Since we are all on a learning curve with the value of these regional models for inland sailing, we must test them before relying on them. One way to do this is on the night before a sail, request forecasts for overnight, and the next morning compare the forecasts with what took place at a few buoys along the route. One procedure is to load the GRIB files in your viewing program and then in the morning spot check buoy data (Figure 6.3-2) at specific times in the forecast.

Alternatively, if your GRIB viewer or navigation program displays *meteograms*, you can see timelines as shown in Figure 6.3-3. This sample covers just a 9-hr period, because we need the forecast times to overlap to compare them, which should be enough to see which one does best. The sample shown provides a tough test, with light wind falling off, then filling in with a large wind shift—common behavior on confined waterways. Compare the detail these forecasts offer with a typical VHF zone forecast over some 20 square miles: "FRI NIGHT: W wind 5 to 15 kt. SAT: SW wind 5 to 15 kt in the morning becoming light." With that said, the digital forecasts must obviously add to our knowledge to be useful.

If an overnight test of past forecasts shows encouraging results, we have more confidence in using the actual forecasts for the day ahead of us. The National Blend of Models (NBM) discussed in Chapter 7 is a very promising solution for mid-range, hi-res forecasts. See Appendix 8.

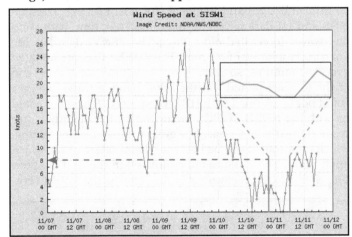

Figure 6.3-2. *Wind speed at Smith Is. station (SISW1) from the NDBC. Red lines mark the section shown in Figure 6.3-3—the green wind direction arrows in that figure are also from the NDBC data. The NDBC shows these plots, and also includes digital values back for 45 days, which can be copied into a spreadsheet and plotted. The green observations are compared to the red forecasts in Figure 6.3-3.*

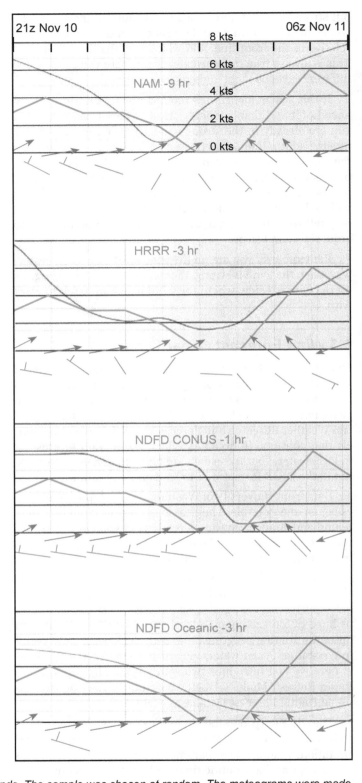

Figure 6.3-3. *Several numerical forecasts compared to measured winds. The sample was chosen at random. The meteograms were made in Expedition. The NAM (a WRF based model, Chapter 7) example is 9 hrs old at the time of this forecast window. It was pretty good considering its age and resolution. This was 12-km resolution. There is a 3-km NAM available from some sources. The NDFD Oceanic is readily available, 10-km data. The HRRR and NDFD CONUS should have done the best, but this is not clear from this sample. It is impressive that all predicted the speed to go lighter or calm and rebuild in another direction at about the right time ± 1 hr. The pressure forecasts (not shown) were good in all four. Forecasted wind speeds were all higher than observed in this time slot, but all knew when winds were light. It was a time of a steep drop in the wind, which is tough to forecast, and certainly not a conclusive test of any source. It is intended just to show the process of comparing forecasts to observations. This isolated example is encouraging. All of these model data are available from Saildocs, except the NDFD CONUS. The NBM (Appendix 8), not used here, has a very convenient way to spot check forecasts at buoys.*

7.1 Overview of Weather Maps

We have used weather maps throughout the book, so they are not a new topic at this stage. We are now fine tuning and expanding applications and discussing map types not yet covered. We also address details of GRIB formatted products and numerical weather models.

The OPC document called *Radiofacsimile Charts User's Guide* (ocean.weather.gov) lists all of their maps with an explanation of each. It is the starting point for learning weather maps. The name is a bit old fashioned, as fewer vessels are using radiofax to receive their maps. This is still a viable method, but many HF radios are being replaced by satellite phones (satphone), and fax maps are now more often downloaded as needed, rather than having to tune in at exactly the right time to receive the HF fax broadcast. Also the digital versions yield sharp map images all the time, whereas HF fax reception varies with weather, time of day, and tuning of equipment. A sample of a fax map received with poor HF reception is shown in Figure 7.1-1.

The radiofacsimile broadcast schedule, however, still serves a good purpose, even when we do not use that delivery method, because this document tells us when the products are available. As a rule, map products might be available on the internet a few minutes earlier than on this schedule, but not much. Interactive HF-radiofax schedules are available at tgftp.nws.noaa.gov/fax/marine.shtml that provide links for direct download.

Surface analysis and forecast maps are pretty standard internationally. Some European countries use a 5-mb spacing of isobars instead of 4, and some maps from UK and elsewhere (including other branches of the NWS) are on an azimuthal projection instead of the Mercator used by the OPC. But weather symbols and other conventions are the same. When downloading maps via the internet, be sure to check the altitude of the maps to be sure you have surface maps, sometimes just labeled MSLP (mean-sea-level pressure). One thing that is universal are the valid times. For surface analysis, these are always 00z, 06z, 12z, and 18z; forecast maps are typically valid at 00z and 12z. Sometimes the abbreviation "HH" is used to mean one of the synoptic times, thus one might say that OPC maps (valid at HH) are typically *available* at HH + 3.5 hrs.

Section 7.2 covers surface analysis and forecast maps. There are also several maps of waves and swells, which we might use as presented or compare with more specific WW3 model predictions.

The OPC does not do much with ocean currents other than mark the edge of the Gulf Stream on 24-hr wind and wave forecast maps in the Atlantic. We discussed this and ocean models in Chapter 3.

Section 7.3 explains a valuable way to learn more about weather maps by comparing the maps with the text forecasts. It is like having a professional meteorologist tell you what the map means. It is an excellent exercise both in the learning process and underway.

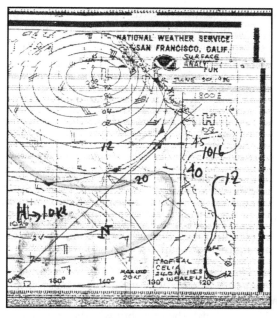

Figure 7.1-1. *How lucky we are! A map received underway by radiofax (in 1986) in conditions of poor reception, which can happen today as well as then using HF radiofax—and they can be worse than this. Digital maps, in contrast, are always sharp and clear.*

Here we see a very basic use of the map. The sailing vessel position (45° N, 130° W) is marked along a rhumb line to the destination. We are sailing (to weather) right along the edge of a cold front, and even though no winds are shown in the region, we know to expect a prominent veer to the west when the front crosses. One isobar around the High is marked with a highlight marker for a quick reference on how things change, map to map (every 6 hrs), and a note that the High is moving east—which shows why the rhumb line is not a route we can follow under sail very long on the way to Hawaii from the Pacific Northwest. This boat is going to have to head south at this point to stay in wind along the edge of the High. The large "N" drawn by hand at 30° N, 140° W marks the former location of the ocean station November (long gone), which still serves as a key waypoint for sailors experienced in this crossing. Most winning routes on the Victoria to Maui Yacht Race pass within a hundred miles or so of this point.

Several navigation programs let us load weather maps just as we would a chart. With this functionality we can read lat and lon, measure distances, set waypoints, and so on, relative to our vessel's GPS position displayed on the map. Section 7.4 explains these options, including overlaying model forecasts right on the NWS graphic maps for comparison.

Numerical weather prediction from computer models presented in GRIB format was introduced in Chapter 2. These are often referred to as "GRIB data" or "GRIB forecasts," but this is misleading. GRIB is just the format of the data, not a description of what it is. There are many kinds of weather data presented in GRIB format besides model predictions of wind and pressure. It is rather like referring to a piece of writing as "PDF data," not distinguishing between a James Joyce novel and an ad for used tires. ASCAT satellite winds (Chapter 4) can be presented in GRIB format and these are actual measurements. Sea surface temperatures (SST), wave and swell data, are also available in GRIB format.

In Section 7.5 we explain unique benefits of model data along with the potential hazards of using model output that are not vetted by professional forecasters. It can be valuable to keep in mind what these data represent since they are now so readily available online (one impressive presentation of several models is at windy.com) and via mobile apps, including direct downloads into most navigation programs. With these ECS (electronic charting system) options, you see predicted winds, waves, and currents overlaid on your present charted GPS position.

Although there are occasional drawbacks, the wide distribution of this "GRIB data" is bound to lead to safer and more efficient boating in general, simply because mariners who previously never looked at weather data at all (because frankly, they were harder to get and interpret in the past), now have this information readily available, and it is bound to help far more often than it might lead astray.

An underlying theme of this book, however, is to help those navigators who want to make their very best weather decisions—not just safe and efficient, but safe and most efficient. Not just finish the race, but win the race. We emphasize avoiding even rare mistakes, by catching those few cases that might not be right in the data, when looking at just one source alone. We follow that tenet of good navigation that says we should not rely on only one source. Thus we discuss in Section 7.6 ways to check the model data with official forecast products from the OPC and similar agencies. Once we have confirmed that the models are consistent with what the professional forecasters recommend, then we are in a position to take advantage of the great convenience of the GRIB format with the confidence that we have double checked our sources.

Obviously, it is not just yacht racers who want the best in weather analysis. Many mariners who work on the water daily depend on accurate forecasts, and as such can benefit from knowledge of how to check the forecasts when crucial decisions are at hand. Section 7.6 follows up on that ap-

proach with a way to use the 500-mb maps to evaluate the confidence level of a surface forecast.

In Section 7.5 we briefly describe several specific models and point out the role of regional models in particular, which are updated hourly and take into account the local terrain when making forecasts—they are one of the major new developments in modern marine weather.

7.2 Using Weather Maps

We often benefit from looking at weather maps, even sometimes for day sails on inland waters. They can explain a forecast we don't understand, or shed light on the dependability of the forecast. For ocean and coastal sailing, on the other hand, they become the primary tool of our navigation. We are speaking now of professionally analyzed map products (either graphic or digitized) from agencies like the OPC and their counterparts around the world—the use of direct model output is covered more in other sections.

The key question when it comes to applying what you learn from weather maps is: how fast is your vessel? Even more specifically, how fast will it be in the conditions of wind and sea that are forecasted? You might, for example, make 8 or 10 kts in flat water, but only half that or less into 6-ft seas. It all depends on the vessel and the details of the conditions. The progress of a sailing vessel obviously depends on the wind as well as the waves. The tactical use of map information (weather routing) always requires projected dead reckoning through the proposed conditions to see where you will be when forecasted conditions apply. This boils down to having in mind, if not in graphics and tables, some form of *polar diagram*, that describes how your vessel, power or sail, makes progress in various wind speeds and directions.

It is much like taking the current into account when planning a longer voyage through areas with strong, varying tidal currents. The crucial leg could be though a pass with very strong currents that are only favorable at 0800 tomorrow, but the weaker currents between here and there will vary with and against you twice during your route to the pass. Hence to figure when you will be at the pass, you have the more complex job of figuring the net influence of the changing currents on the way to the pass. Good weather tactics are always tied closely to good navigation—which usually means good dead reckoning skills and good knowledge of your vessel.

Another determining factor that enters the decision making is the nature of the voyage itself. An ocean sailing race is clearly governed by different tactics than a vacation cruise. Likewise, a delivery (of vessel or goods) often involves balancing out cost factors between time underway and the risk of damage to cargo and gear. Needless to say, however, on any voyage on any vessel, the master ultimately has to decide where the line is between safe and fast. Knowledge of marine weather and reading weather maps in particular is often a key element in this decision process.

The following notes apply to all vessels, but the examples tend to be more oriented to slower vessels, and in some cases specifically to sailing vessels. In all cases, the tactical use of weather maps comes under the heading of *weather routing*.

Surface Analysis Maps: Step by Step

These maps are offered every 6 hrs, valid at the synoptic times of 00z, 06z, 12z, and 18z. They show isobars, fronts, Highs and Lows, areas of fog, along with scattered ship reports of wind, pressure, and temperatures (air, dew point and water). For winds at other locations you have to use a geostrophic wind table, formula, or diagram to convert isobar spacing to wind speed and the orientation of the isobars to get wind direction (Section 2.4). The OPC offers maps of the North Pacific and North Atlantic, in two parts each, east side and west side, referred to respectively as Part 1 and Part 2 (Figure 7.2-1). Other sources of maps divide up the oceans differently. Environment Canada maps cover, on a larger scale, the higher latitudes off of both their east and west coasts.

Step 1. Get the latest map (by radiofax or satphone), and plot your position on it. This map will be valid at one of the synoptic times, but will not be available until about 3.5 hrs later (HH + 3.5 hrs). Thus to plot your position on it, you have to check your logbook and hope you have a DR position at the right time—if not, then DR to get one, and write yourself a reminder or set an alarm clock to remind yourself to record a DR position at the synoptic times in the future. This is fundamental to good weather tactics. We want logbook records of Lat-Lon, wind, and pressure at each synoptic time.

Plot the position carefully, which means choosing some way to interpolate the Lat-Lon scales on the weather map—that is, if you do not have the weather map loaded into your ECS, which does all this for you. Some programs download the map and georeference it with a button click (Section 7.4).

Step 2. Interpolate the isobars for map pressure at your charted location and get wind speed and direction from the spacing and orientation of the isobars (Section 2.4). Compare your logged observations with the map reports. If they agree you can have more confidence in the map and upcoming forecasts than when they do not. Obviously, your instruments must be calibrated so your observations are correct.

If they do not agree, see if you can figure out why. Usually it means a system is moving toward or away from you at a different speed than anticipated. Or it could be simply that the isobars are not drawn properly. If the wind speed and direction are right, but the pressure is off, then that could imply a displaced system, meaning the timing is off, but shape is right. If wind direction is right and pressure is right, but you have more wind, then the isobars are oriented properly, but they are closer together than predicted. If everything is right except the wind direction, then the orientation of the isobars is wrong, and so on.

Step 3. From your position on the map, draw in your past and intended track. Usual plotting tools won't work without a compass rose, so use a Weems plotter or simple protractor. This track shows what weather (wind) you are sailing toward. Then figure and plot your anticipated position 24 hrs and 48 hrs from now.

Besides a general synoptic overview of the weather pattern, this is about all that can be done with the surface analysis itself, as this map is already at least 3 or 4 hrs old and you can't move fast enough to get into other parts of it.

This picture of essentially present weather conditions, however, might be helpful to explain what clouds you see in the sky or it could account for wind shifts or pressure changes you have observed, but did not understand, or it will more generally show why you have the weather you have, or what you missed. But we must ultimately rely on the forecasts for shaping our future courses.

The extent that this analysis properly reflected our recent observations is the extent to which we can have faith in the upcoming forecasts. Often discrepancies we note in one surface analysis will be repaired in the next one, 6 hrs later. Remember that in routine ocean sailing we are generally sailing around the Highs, and these are often bordering on light air regions where the ship reports might be less accurate, and consequently the isobars they help generate may not be so accurate, though this is getting much better these days as mariners realize how valuable accurate data is. In the past, reports of good weather were not as accurate as those of bad weather. In other words, mariners took the attitude that who cares if this 12 kts is from the NW or the N-NW, etc. Now with the

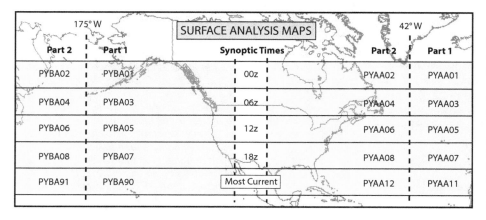

SURFACE ANALYSIS MAPS						
Part 2	**Part 1**	**Synoptic Times**			**Part 2**	**Part 1**
PYBA02	PYBA01		00z		PYAA02	PYAA01
PYBA04	PYBA03		06z		PYAA04	PYAA03
PYBA06	PYBA05		12z		PYAA06	PYAA05
PYBA08	PYBA07		18z		PYAA08	PYAA07
PYBA91	PYBA90		Most Current		PYAA12	PYAA11

Figure 7.2-1. *Pacific and Atlantic surface analysis maps, with FTPmail file names: add .gif or .TIF to get the format of choice. To get maps by internet use:* ftp://tgftp.nws. noaa.gov/fax/PYAA02.gif. *The gifs open in a browser; TIFs need a special viewer. The TIFs are notably smaller files, and Saildocs (Section 8.3) reduces those by another factor of two, which makes them the source of choice when they have what we want. FTPmail, however, has a larger selection of weather products, essentially anything that NWS offers.*

guidance of the Port Meteorological Officers and improved instruments, ship reports continue to improve.

On the other hand, the route around the corner of a High that a sailor might follow is rarely the shortest route between any two points for commercial ships. Thus the actual number of ship reports is lower than along great circle routes, which is another reason the isobars in these regions might be off. In short, an accurate description of the winds at the corner of a High might take a couple of reports to home in on once things have changed much.

This is still true even though the model predictions are seeded with wind speed observations from satellites. These data definitely help, and the isobars are much better with satellite data than without it, but actual measurements at sea at synoptic times are still crucial to the best results. Satellite wind measurements are also not optimized for light air, which is often the case in these regions.

Step 4. To learn the most about your present conditions, keep this most recent surface analysis map and study it as you listen to the latest voice broadcast of high seas weather for the same UTC. Or if you are downloading the text version of the high seas report, then you can use that, which makes this process very much easier. The key point is we need to have the times of the report and the map be the same.

For example, consider the Eastern Pacific high seas weather at 00z. We get the surface analysis map by radiofax or internet (via satphone or HF radio) at 0331z (ocean. weather.gov/shtml/pacsch.php). It is three and a half hours old when we first get it. We get the HF voice broadcast from the USCG Communications Area Master Station Pacific at 0430z (nws.noaa.gov/om/marine/hfvoice.htm), and we can get the text report valid at 00z at 0541z (tgftp.nws.noaa.gov/data/forecasts/marine/high_seas/). This last report is the text version of what is read by voice. It is not broadcast as a text fax by the USCG, so we need to use FTPmail or Saildocs to get it (Section 8.3). The UTCs of the HF-radio broadcasts (map and voice) are the only guaranteed times. The internet products (map and text) could be a little before or after these times.

Details learned from the voice or text reports can be noted directly onto the map. Often you will learn things not apparent from the map alone. The map also makes it easier to interpret the voice or text report, since you can see what they are talking about. It also saves you recording a lot of information that interests you, which is difficult to know without the map in front of you. Some times the voice may be available before the maps, in which case it still helps to use an older map when listening to the reports, or better, record the report and play it back when you get the map in hand. This is not an issue when using text versions. This powerful way to learn about weather maps is covered in detail in Section 7.3; it can be practiced on land before your voyage.

Using Surface Forecasts

Surface forecast maps from the OPC show the lay of the isobars, locations of fronts, Highs, and Lows, and wind ar-

rows, whenever the wind is expected to be ≥ 34 kts. The forecast maps (progs) are the key maps for setting your course. We first emphasize the OPC maps, as if we had no other resources. In practice we will be using the maps to verify the model forecasts, which are easier to navigate with, so there will be cross checking at various stages—covered in more depth in Section 7.6 on evaluating the model forecasts.

A sample OPC map sequence as accumulated underway is shown in Table 7.2-1. The available times shown are the HF-fax broadcast times, which are roughly the same in the Pacific and Atlantic, constant from year to year. (Maps received by email request could be an hour or so earlier or later than these times.) We start on the morning of the first day, with a 12z surface analysis (SA) that we got at 1531z, which would be 0831 PDT, the local time for the West Coast in the summer. This is called map (1) in Table 7.2-1. We then plot our 12z position on the map and compare our logged wind and pressure from 3.5 hrs ago (12z) to check this map.

At about this time we can also download the 12z-GFS forecasts. These include a forecast every 3 hrs for 48 hrs, then every 6 hrs till 96 hrs, labeled h0, h3, h6... h48, h52... . They extend further, but those are too uncertain to be of interest. These GFS forecasts from the earlier 06z run (06z-GFS) are likely what we had used to plan our route so far. The h0 forecast of the 12z-GFS sequence will be very similar (if not identical) to the 12z SA, and chances are our wind and pressure measurements will be pretty close to both forecasts well—but we note any discrepancies as an early indication that the map or GFS might be off where we care about. Note there are now more frequent GFS forecasts (Table 7.5-1), but these do not match the map times.

	Table 7.2-1. Weather Map Sequencing							
PDT	UTC	#	Day 1	#	Day 2	#	Day 3
0831	1531z	01	12z SA	10	12z SA	19	12z SA
1233	1933z	02	12z 24H	11	12z 24H	20	12z 24H
1303	2003z	03	12z 48H	12	12z 48H	21	12z 48H
1343	2043z	04	12z 96H	13	12z 96H	22	12z 96H
1424	2124z	05	18z SA	14	18z SA	23	18z SA
2031	0331z	06	00z SA	15	00z SA	24	00z SA
0108	0808z	07	00z 24H	16	00z 24H	25	00z 24H
0138	0838z	08	00z 48H	17	00z 48H	26	00z 48H
0219	0919z	09	06z SA	18	06z SA	27	06z SA

Table Notes: *Sample schedule for a summertime Pacific voyage. This does not show other important maps such as wind and waves or 500-mb winds. "12z SA" means surface analysis valid at 12z; "12z 48H" means a 48-hr forecast, valid at 12z, and so on. Forecast valid times are paired by color with corresponding SA. The UTC times are those of the HF-fax broadcasts. The maps are available by email request somewhat earlier. You can use the map #s to layout a few practice runs at home over a few days. It is best to figure out the organization at home than to develop it underway. The OPC promises 72-hr forecasts beginning in 2018; this process could then be adapted to include them—FTPmail versions are available now; rfax versions not yet available.*

As the day progresses, we collect OPC forecasts 24H (02), 48H (03) and 96H (04), so by 1343 PDT we have an overview of what to expect for the next two days, plus an educated guess of day 4 (96H). We can now decide if our intended route is viable or do we need to make changes. At this stage we can also compare the 12z-GFS h24 to 12z 24H (02) and 12z-GFS h48 with 12z 48H. Recall, we are assuming the professionally vetted OPC maps are more dependable than the pure GFS model data, so we are checking to see if the GFS might be right in the forecasts, because we prefer to use them if so.

One hour later at 1424 PDT, we get an OPC 18z SA (05), which is our first check to see if the OPC still agrees with their earlier assessment. Namely are the isobars at 18z (05) intermediate to the 12z analysis (01) and the 24z forecast (02)? Or usually more useful, is this 18z SA (5) a logical step between the 12z SA (01) and the 12z 48H forecast (03)? Historically, the 24H maps have not been very detailed, but they seem notably improved in the past months, hopefully marking a new policy. Nevertheless, we essentially navigate by the 48H forecasts, just keeping in the back of the mind what the 96H calls for.

And we can start again with an 18z-GFS sequence. The GFS forecasts become available at about the same time as the OPC SA maps. We don't have new OPC forecasts yet (these come in the early hours of tomorrow), but we can check the 18z-GFS h0 with 18z SA (5), and we get a new look at the GFS forecast for our existing OPC forecasts 24H (02) and 48H (03), but now we must be careful to check the valid times of all the maps we are comparing. The 12z 24H map (02) will now correspond to the h18 forecast of 18z-GFS, and the 12z 48H map (03) will be h42 in the GFS sequence.

While it is still daylight, we get at 2031 PDT the 00z SA and 00z-GFS, and can repeat the process, still without any new forecasts from OPC. Now we look at 00z-GFS h12 and h36.

In the early hours of Day 2 we get new OPC forecasts 00z 24H and 00z 48H, along with a 06-GFS run, which is the first really new routing data of the voyage, and the process starts again. The navigator relying on HF fax got to sleep from 9 PM to about 1 AM; work till about 3 AM or so; then nothing new with these basic maps until 830 AM. On the other hand, when using FTPmail or Saildocs to get the maps by email, there is much more freedom, as you can choose a time and just download all you need up to that time in one request. The file names are shown in Figure 7.2-1 and Table 7.2-2.

When making the GFS to OPC comparisons we soon appreciate another feature of the GFS model data: all maps are in the identical format, whereas the OPC maps SA, 24H, and 48H each has unique format and conventions (the 96H is the same as the 48H). We have presumed so far that we are comparing the two forecasts by inspection, looking at them side by side or screen by screen. In Section 7.4 we show a more precise method that overlays the two. When set up and practiced, this can be faster as well as more precise.

Philosophy

In following sections we go over various tactical routing decisions we confront underway, which in turn determines the details we are looking for in these forecasts. This careful study of analysis and forecast sequencing is serving in effect three purposes. One is we want to evaluate NOAA's confidence in the forecasts, signaled by a consistent evolution of the maps, rather than abrupt changes. A simple example would be a place with W wind now that is forecasted to be NW in 48 hrs, we might expect to be W-NW in 24 hrs. Later we add another way to evaluate the forecasts by looking at the winds aloft (500-mb) and their progs to see if they are stable with good flow or in a pattern with less dependability.

The second goal is learning how well the GFS forecasts *on their own* can reproduce the full-fledged OPC forecasts. If successful, we can confidently use the convenient GRIB format as is, otherwise we may have to consider digitally rotating the GFS isobars and maybe scaling the wind speeds up or down by some amount. These digital manipulations are possible in modern ocean routing programs discussed later.

And then finally we can look at the weather pattern details we care about for our tactics, and be prepared to adjust. It is like looking up the tidal currents in a complex waterway, planning around them, but then continually measuring them to see that they are what was forecasted, and adjust as needed if not. On weather maps we watch the corners of Highs, behavior of fronts, or look out for a new Low pushing isobars around that calls for major route rethinking, and so on. And to be sure, although we shape routes largely by the 48-hr forecasts, we still have to keep in mind what is happening even farther out in some key parts of a voyage or race. Specific examples are in the following sections.

A key point to the philosophy of this process is that to do your best, you cannot just look at the latest map and the latest forecast and go by those alone—even if you update on each new forecast. When you do that, you have not learned anything about how they are changing and if they might be

Table 7.2-2. Forecast Map File Names			
Forecast	Atlantic	Pacific	Pacific Tropics
00z 24H	PPAE00	PPBE00	PYFE79
12z 24H	PPAE01	PPBE01	PYFE80
Latest 24H	PPAE10	PPBE10	PYFE10
00z 48H	QDTM85	PWBI98	PYFI81
12z 48H	QDTM86	PWBI99	PYFI82
Latest 48H	QDTM10	PWBI10	PYFI10
12z 96H	PWAM99	PWBM99	
0z 72H	——	——	PYFK83
12z 72H	PPAK98*	PPBK98*	PYFK84
Latest 72H	——	——	PYFK10

Table Notes: *See caption to Figure 7.2-1 for details and Table 7.2-1 for forecast name conventions. *72-hr maps available in 2018.*

dependable or if they might just as well change again on the next round.

Using only the latest map and forecast is like just looking at the radar without the target-trails option turned on. You see where all the targets are now, but you have no idea how they got there, and thus you don't know how to predict what will happen next. It is also analogous to recording only your GPS data (position, COG, and SOG) in the logbook without any DR info such as course steered and knotmeter speed. You know where you are now, and what you are doing now, but you do not know how this relates to what you were actually doing to get here. If you lose your GPS data you will not have any idea how well you can do pure DR when you have to, and you will not be able to predict your position into the future with much accuracy.

With that now said, we should quickly add that in many cases of radar use and GPS navigation you can indeed *get by* with shortcuts, just as in many cases of weather tactics you can *get by* with just looking at the latest forecasts. But if you want or need to do the very best you can, then it is the sequence you must study, not just a single snapshot. There will always be a forecast, and they are not marked good or bad. When you have a crucial maneuver to make and do not have full confidence in the forecast, then you might consider doing just half of what you want, and wait six hrs for the next map to complete the maneuver, or go back to the earlier route.

Unless dramatic things are afoot, in a slow moving vessel we are mostly trying to decide if we are to sail above or below some desired course. In other words, the route starts out as a series of waypoints along the climatically best route, or one we have set up initially for some reason. Then we watch the weather evolve to decide if we can take this route, or if we need to sail a course to the right or left of it for some reason. The following are a few examples of general course set-

ting based on maps. Although we emphasize sailing, some of these tactics can significantly enhance the comfort and efficiency of power-boat passages as well.

Sailing Around Highs

Most summertime transoceanic sailing routes involve going around a large mid-ocean High. The reason for going around is there is no wind in the middle of the High. The situation is shown schematically in Figure 7.2-2. You can flip, mirror, or rotate this picture for other oceans or routes.

The fundamental step is to know you have to go around, and start off with that climatic knowledge. In other words, regardless of what the forecasts say about the wind at the location of the High when you depart, it takes too long to get there, and the map could be different by then. Statistically it is even likely to be so—meaning if you see wind there now when you are not supposed to, then chances are it will be gone by the time you get there. We are looking here some 600 miles ahead, which could be 4 or 5 days away.

The usual tactical decision then is how close can you cut the corner and not run out of wind. The key is judging the stability of the High—from its surface shape and location, from the 500-mb maps, and from a good barometer! The challenge is also raised because the corner typically has lighter air, often with a ridge to cross, and not likely on any main shipping routes. The few, if any, ship reports could be uncertain—but not necessarily! You could compute winds of 4 or 5 kts from what you see on the map, but then see *more than one* report of 10 kts! That would be encouragement that there is some wind there. See details on sailing around Highs in Section 10.3

On the other hand, when it is not a sailboat race you might not always want to avoid a High. It could be that you are just tired after a long hard sail through bad weather north

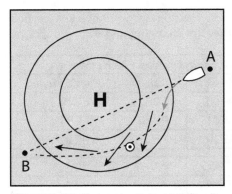

Figure 7.2-2. *Going around a High to preserve your wind. Tactics are covered in Section 10.3. Generally staying 2 isobars off the peak pressure when it is seasonable is a conservative route to keep your wind. You can get closer to higher than average Highs. Forecasts and ship reports are good guides. The white and black dot shows the target pressure that should mark the peak pressure at the corner if nothing changes.*

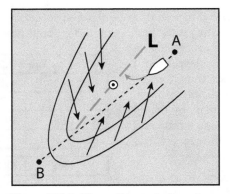

Figure 7.2-3. *The sailing route from A to B will be fastest in the following winds above the trough line. The trough line will be at the local minimum in the pressure so it should be detectable underway. This maneuver would work best when the trough is moving toward you. The target pressure marking the minimum pressure expected at the trough line is shown.*

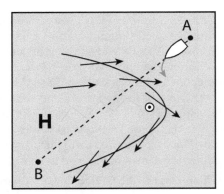

Figure 7.2-4. *This sailing route from A to B will be fastest in the following winds below the stationary ridge line. Anticipate stronger winds at the sharp bend in the tip of the ridge. By recording a target pressure of the crossing from a weather map you can use your own barometer to keep track of where you are relative to the ridge top. If the wind veers around as you proceed and the barometer remains steady, you know you are following an isobar around the corner.*

of the High or strong trades below the High. In these cases you could easily look forward to some calm air for a while, to rest and clean up the boat and fix anything that might have broken. It is also the place where you might find Japanese glass fishing floats! For those driving a trawler across the ocean, the Highs are the obvious best routes. Right straight through the middle so you stay in flat water and calm seas as much as possible.

Crossing a Trough

The best laid plans, however, can still get invaded by some low pressure system where we don't want it. As discussed in Chapter 4, you are not going to maneuver around giant extra-tropical Lows, but you might just end up on the wrong side of a much more localized trough. You might, for example, be headed down the east side of a near stationary trough in head winds for several days, whereas if you fell off for a while and crossed the trough you would bite the bullet for a day and then get into downwind conditions (Figure 7.2-3). Look at the progs to see if your speed and position on the alternative courses pans out with this reasoning. Watch the pressure to judge your progress. The pressure will be a minimum as you cross the trough line. You should be able to just plot it out to monitor your progress and know when you are across it. If the trough is sliding toward you this could be a very efficient maneuver. If it is slipping away from you, on the other hand, this might not work at all.

Sailing Across Ridges

A similar choice can be confronted when approaching the top of a ridge (Figure 7.2-4). It is effectively going around or across an elongated High. One side is down wind, the other

side is to weather. When on a route across the top of it, you might have the opportunity to get from wrong side to right side, or to stay on the right side if you are already doing well. Again, due to the slow speed of a sailboat, it is not feasible to make major adjustments, but sometimes you can maneuver enough to make a difference. The progs plus your DR are the only way to evaluate this.

Sometimes the corner of a High we are rounding can extend out to form a ridge of lighter air that we must cross, and the tactical decision will be where to cross the ridge, looking ahead to jibe angles once the wind veers around the corner.

Isobar Curvature at the Corner of a Ridge

When sailing right near the corner of a ridge, you might run across the effect of curvature on the isobars. Winds at sharp bends in ridge isobars are stronger than those in the straighter sections. Sometimes you can alter course for just a day or so to keep in the stronger winds. Check the progs, and use your basic knowledge here. Forecast maps will usually not give any indication of this enhanced wind at a sharp corner in a ridge (they only show winds ≥ 34 kts), but you can count on an enhancement there, and it may be to your tactical advantage to know about it.

Course to Meet New Wind

Shaping the best course to meet the trades or other wind patterns some days ahead is another common challenge on ocean crossings. It is also one that can be easily overlooked, often to much detriment. If your destination is still another several hundred miles down the trades once you enter the trades, then it can be crucial that you plan ahead to enter

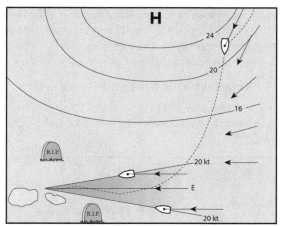

Figure 7.2-5. *Approach cone. Sailing at a true wind angle of 165 to 150°, we are sailing roughly parallel to the isobars on starboard jibe, since the wind crosses the isobars at 15 to 30°. The approach cone tells us when to jibe to line up with one of the laylines defining the cone. To draw the cone, look ahead to the trade wind forecasts and draw that line in to your destination (NE 12 kts on the left with a true wind angle of 160; E 20 kts on the right with a true wind angle of 170). Then draw in your two laylines for the best wind angles for your boat, which depend on the wind speed. Strong winds call for higher true wind angles (sailing more downwind) than light winds. The safest route is to jibe back and forth across the central wind line, if the trades are steady. If they are predicted to change to strong, then favor the bottom half of the cone, but don't redraw the cone till you see the reports—again, doing "half of what we want to do," till we know for sure it will happen. Trade winds are accurately forecasted and frequently reported in observations. It is important to keep the cone updated and to stay within its boundaries. It can be a big mistake to get caught outside of it. Also due to wind and wave matching, it is likely that one jibe will meet the waves better than the other, so that is something to keep in mind as you blend out of the High circulation and into the trades. A universal plotting sheet as used in celestial navigation is convenient for drawing the cone on any lat-lon scale you choose. If the wind shifts on you or for any reason you end up too close to the edge, you might have to go to a head sail for a while to get back in position.*

and sail the trades in the optimum manner, which will depend on the speed and direction of the trades, and on your boat performance. If you end up, for example, having to go a long distance dead downwind in light-air trades (10 kts or less) you will be going very slowly and rolling about the seas if they have not settled down yet. Had you approached from farther downwind, you could be reaching across them with a faster, more comfortable ride.

On the other hand, if you come in on your destination too far downwind on the trades and they are strong (approaching 20 kts), then you end up on your beam ends trying to claw your way across them to keep from overshooting your destination. If you choose the better course in these circumstances and come in at a lower course, you are ready to surf downwind at a large wind angle.

The solution is to plan well ahead when you can still make small adjustments to your course so you end up at the right place down the line. The procedure is outlined in Figure 7.2-5. It starts by knowing your boat's performance (Section 10.7 on polar diagrams), meaning, in this application, what your best downwind sailing angle is for different wind speeds, modified by the practical knowledge of how the boat behaves in the waves you have. Typical values might be, for a true wind speed of 10 kts, the best true wind angle is 150°, but for 12 kts it moves aft to 160°, and for 20 kts it is back to 170° or so. If you do not know these values now from an earlier ocean passage, you will learn them fairly quickly underway on an ocean crossing, sailing night and day in varying wind and sea conditions. The key is to record this data as you learn it, so route planning improves with time. The yacht designer's polar diagrams are the starting point that you then modify with your own experience.

The next key step is to actually draw the approach cone as outlined in the Figure 7.2-5 and keep your position plotted on that diagram. It is the truth meter that will keep you out of trouble. Sketch in the tombstones as a stark reminder!

Tropical Analyses and Forecasts

Tropical maps from the NHC show the locations of the ITCZ (doldrums) as well as easterly waves (labeled TRPCL WAVE) and monsoon trofs. They cover the breeding grounds of the tropical storms, which can actually affect your sailing quite a ways north of them. Watch these maps for the motion and effects of tropical storms. Sometimes a tropical storm can form and expand, and then push the corner isobars of a High way off of their climatic locations. This can cause the gradient to tighten up and suggest good wind along a route closer to the High center that might not otherwise have been chosen. But be careful with this. Tropical storms can dissipate or move off very quickly, and when they do so the High can expand equally quickly and come and sit on top of you leaving no wind over vast regions of the ocean. Sections of tropical maps are shown in Figures 3.2-8. Tropical map file names are shown in Figure 7.2-6.

Crossing the Doldrums

Any long route that takes you across the equator usually involves crossing both trade wind bands and their associated wind-driven equatorial currents, in addition to crossing the light airs of the doldrums with a section of equatorial counter current flowing back to the east. Figure 3.6-7 showed one way to evaluate the net drift of the current as a function of your boat speed. There can easily be a large net drift to the west that must be accounted for.

A typical route of this type is the nearly due north-south one between Hawaii and Tahiti. The issues are about the same going either way. The net drift to the west must be compensated by making some miles to the east, but the normal trade wind directions of NE and SE mean that we are essentially close hauled on the rhumb line for roughly half of this trip. Which brings up a point that applies to this circumstance, as well as to many others in ocean sailing.

The trade wind directions are not rock stable from the NE and SE. They actually vary quite a bit, often swinging clear to the East. The message here is whenever the wind allows it, regardless of our point of sail, we should take that opportunity to put some easting into the bag. It does not hurt to bank as much as we can, so if the winds do pick up from forward of the beam, we then have some freedom. If they don't go unfavorable, we just fall off and spend our money.

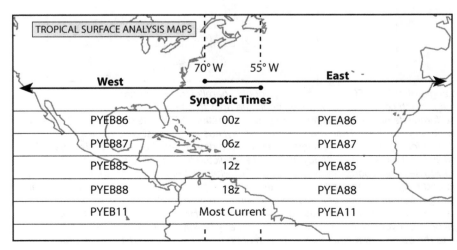

Figure 7.2-6. *Tropical surface analysis maps from NHC, with their FTPmail file names indicated. Just add the ".gif" or ".TIF" extension to get the file type you prefer. (Note one is lowercase, one is uppercase). The .gifs open directly in any browser; the .TIFs will download automatically, to be opened in a separate image viewer. To get maps by internet, use this URL: ftp://tgftp. nws.noaa.gov/fax/PYEA11.TIF. These "tropical" maps extend to 50° N, offering a view of how the OPC maps blend into the NHC tropic regions. The wind reports on tropical maps are the same ship reports seen on the corresponding OPC maps, but not in station model format. See Section 8.3 for email requests.*

West	Synoptic Times	East
PYEB86	00z	PYEA86
PYEB87	06z	PYEA87
PYEB85	12z	PYEA85
PYEB88	18z	PYEA88
PYEB11	Most Current	PYEA11

Defining a Course to Steer

Many ocean routes will be defined as a desired course, with some suggestion on how to bias it for best long-term progress, such as, make some miles to the right whenever you can. Or it could be, steer this course, but try as hard as you can not to go south of it. Or, sail as low as you can without losing control of the sails or going slower than a particular speed—and definitely do not just heat it up to go fast. On the other hand, I have seen circumstances in which the best "course" can be described simply as "go as fast as you can" without being any more specific on the actual heading. This can happen when sailing to weather on a lifted tack, or sailing downwind in oscillating winds, when the set of the sails provides natural limits to the course.

This last circumstance, however, is not common. Normally there is something you want to do, but you can't quite do it for one reason or another, so you have to compromise, and work for it. Then the key issue becomes, when do you tack or jibe for the best results? This choice depends on whether or not you just want to be on the favored jibe to a given waypoint, or are you trying to put some money in the bank for anticipated conditions farther down the route.

The favored jibe is easiest to evaluate using your GPS. Just put the next waypoint in as your destination and monitor your velocity made good (VMG) *to that waypoint.* Thus recording a VMG in the logbook, along with SOG and COG, can serve as a good truth meter for staying on the favored jibe. But you still have to compare that to true wind speed, because if that is down, your VMG will go down with it.

When you are positioning yourself for the next leg, such as working your way over to an approach cone, then you are more likely headed for a layline or course line than an actual waypoint. Or maybe you are just headed off to find the new wind—across a trough or front for example. Then the task is to decide when you have gotten there, and be sure you are far enough into it that you will not sail right back out when you jibe or tack, or the wind shifts a little. Good logbook records help with that, as well as a GPS echart track (the value of these for tactical analysis cannot be overstated). Some echart programs let you go back over a track to read not just where you were at what time, but also what your speed was at the time. Target barometer pressures are the best way to monitor your location relative to the isobars.

7.3 Practice Reading Weather Maps

The following exercise teaches how to interpret weather maps and, additionally, provides a protocol for combining weather maps and voice or text reports, that can serve you well in actual weather analysis underway. It teaches the symbols and conventions used in preparing surface analysis weather maps. Most of this information also applies to forecast maps.

The best way to learn what a weather map means is to let a professional describe it to you. This is easily done, over and over again, by simply comparing a surface analysis map with the corresponding high seas text report that covers the region at that time. Like the maps, these are produced four times a day, around the world. By studying these, you soon learn what the maps mean. *At home or underway, you will always learn something about the map from the text report, and something about the text report from the map.*

To see how this works, we provide a sample map and the corresponding text report, and later show where you get these live to carry on with the practice. This example was chosen at random. Some are more instructive than others. This one, for example, does not have much interesting taking place in the subtropics. In the hurricane season you will have more activity there, with tropical systems, easterly waves, etc. You can also do this comparison with tropical maps.

Instructions for Map-Text Comparison

On the following pages we present a surface analysis map of the North Atlantic that is a combination of Part 1 and Part 2, since these are published and broadcast separately. In practice you would normally use just one or the other part, unless you happen to be near the dividing line, in which case you would need to look at both of them.

The map is on one side of the page and the corresponding high seas text report is on the facing page. Both sets of data are from the OPC. The text report is the same report that is read over the HF high seas radio by the USCG, four times a day. It is also distributed by NAVTEX as a text message to vessels with that capability on board.

This exercise is a self-guided tour. Just read through the text description and look around on the map to see the section it is discussing. You will have to use the Lat-Lon scales to locate the sections.

When doing your comparison, note in particular how they describe the winds and how the winds appear on the map. Close isobars, high winds, etc. How close is close? Check it out. Compare the wind flow direction with the lay of the isobars. Note the use of the X's to mark the 24-hr forecast locations of Lows that are remaining significant. Refer to the OPC *Radiofacsimile Charts User's Guide* to see what the symbols mean, along with other notations. You can also refer back to Section 2.4 on reading winds from isobars.

Note the frequent use of "quadrants" and the radii of wind regions around the Lows. A "western quadrant," as an example, spans bearings of 225 to 315 True from the center of the Low. How are fronts described? Cold fronts have pointed symbols, warm fronts have round symbols. Observe how actual ship reports of wind speeds compare with the text descriptions of the winds in various zones, etc. Take your time; hunt around.

Interpreting the Text Report

We have not made an effort to simplify the visual presentation of the text reports by fixing the word spacing or getting rid of all caps, which are so hard to read. We leave it this way since this is what you get when you download or receive it by NAVTEX, so you might as well practice with that now.

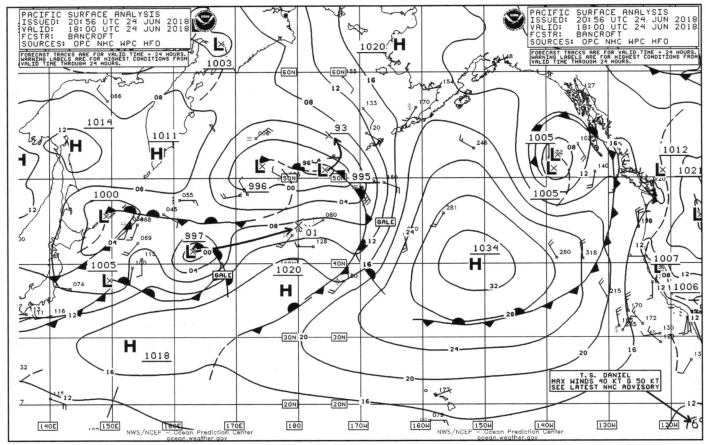

Figure 7.3-1. *Surface analysis map of the North Pacific, Part 1 and Part 2, to be compared to the high seas text report provided on the next page. For practice in map reading, compare descriptions in the text report with this map. The text report excerpt given here only covers the eastern side. The full Metarea XII text covers to 160E. It is presented in three sections.*

Refer to the list of abbreviations in Appendix 1 as needed. Read the valid times carefully and do not confuse them with the times that state when the map was actually published. Those will be later than the valid time.

SECURITE (say-cur-e-tay) is a standard radio alert implying information related to navigational safety. Sometimes they will use PAN PAN (pahn-pahn) here to indicate a more severe condition at hand. All reference to SEAS usually means significant wave height in feet, which is the average of the highest one third of all waves. SW SEMICIRCLE means bearings from 135 to 315 True from storm center. FRONT FROM 48N 140W TO 45N 130W TO 38N 125W means plot these three points on the chart and draw a line between them to see the lay of the frontal line. Expressions like WITHIN 240 NM N OF THE FRONT N OF 48N means draw in the frontal line, use dividers to mark a line parallel to it on the north side, and then look to this region above Lat 48 to see the region in mind. RAPIDLY INTENSIFYING is an officially defined term meaning pressure dropping at 1 mb/hr (or more). If it does this for 24 hrs it is called a "meteorological bomb." FORECAST WATERS means the region covered by this report. See boundaries at the introduction to the text report. CONVECTION means cloud cover, usually cumulus, usually indicates locations of convergence. These regions are

specifically marked in aviation progs, but rarely shown in the surface analysis. Sometimes regions of heavy thunderstorms will be noted. FORECASTER = name of individual who prepared the report.

Now you can begin your self-guided tour of the weather maps. Try to make sense of all words in the report.

How to Proceed with Live Practice

One way to get the surface analysis and the corresponding high seas forecast is to use the *briefings* option from the OPC website at:

ocean.weather.gov/shtml/briefing.shtml

Briefings provide all maps and all text reports available, updated 4 times a day. They are separated into "Marine Charts" and "Text Forecast" packages for each ocean. The packages are simply a long vertical presentation of all relevant maps and texts. This is a quick way to access all OPC products. For direct access to the surface analysis maps and corresponding text, bookmark the following links.

Atlantic: tgftp.nws.noaa.gov/fax/PYAA12.gif (map) and tgftp.nws.noaa.gov/data/forecasts/marine/high_seas/north_atlantic.txt (text).

Selections from METAREA XII HIGH SEAS FORECAST
issued 2345 UTC SUN JUN 24 2018

<u>PACIFIC N OF 30N AND S OF 67N E OF A LINE FROM BERING STRAIT TO 50N 160E</u>

SYNOPSIS VALID 1800 UTC JUN 24. 24 HOUR FORECAST VALID 1800 UTC JUN 25.

GALE WARNING

LOW 51N176W 995 MB MOVING NE 10 KT NEXT 6 HOURS THEN TURNING MORE N. FRONT EXTENDS FROM LOW TO 46N169W TO 41N170W TO 35N178W. WITHIN 180 NM E AND SE OF FRONT FROM 39N TO 47N WINDS 25 TO 35 KT. SEAS 8 TO 13 FT. ELSEWHERE WITHIN 300 NM NE SEMICIRCLE AND 240 NM S QUADRANT AND WITHIN 360 NM NE AND E OF FRONT WINDS TO 25 KT. SEAS TO 10 FT.

SYNOPSIS AND FORECAST

COMPLEX LOW WITH MEAN CENTER 52N139W 1005 MB MOVING SE 15 KT. BETWEEN 120 NM AND 420 NM S QUADRANT AND BETWEEN 90 NM AND 240 NM W QUADRANT WINDS 20 TO 30 KT. SEAS 8 TO 15 FT...HIGHEST IN S QUADRANT. ELSEWHERE WITHIN 600 NM S...240 NM E...300 NM NW AND 420 NM W QUADRANTS WINDS TO 25 KT. SEAS TO 12 FT...HIGHEST S OF LOW.

24 HOUR FORECAST LOW 50N129W 1014 MB. WITHIN 420 NM SW AND W QUADRANTS WINDS TO 25 KT. SEAS 8 TO 12 FT.

24 HOUR FORECAST OVER FORECAST WATERS BETWEEN A LINE FROM 37N123W TO 30N128W AND A LINE FROM 43N124W TO 30N144W AREA OF N TO NE WINDS 20 TO 30 KT. SEAS 8 TO 12 FT.

DENSE FOG. VSBY OCCASIONALLY LESS THAN 1 NM WITHIN 240 NM E AND SE OF A LINE FROM 48N171W TO 40N171W TO 34N177E AND OVER FORECAST WATERS FROM 39N TO 45N W OF 171E.

24 HOUR FORECAST DENSE FOG WITHIN 180 NM E AND SE OF A LINE FROM 52N157W TO 40N160W TO 38N170W...WITHIN 360 NM E AND SE OF A LINE FROM 47N176W TO 43N178E TO 40N176E TO 34N176E AND FROM 36N TO 45N W OF 166E.

HIGH 40N151W 1034 MB MOVING E 15 KT.
24 HOUR FORECAST HIGH 40N143W 1033 MB.
48 HOUR FORECAST HIGH 41N138W 1031 MB.

<u>E PACIFIC FROM THE EQUATOR TO 30N E OF 140W AND 03.4S TO THE EQUATOR E OF 120W</u>

TROPICAL STORM WARNING

TROPICAL STORM DANIEL NEAR 16.9N 116.4W 1003 MB AT 2100 UTC JUN 24 MOVING NNW OR 340 DEG AT 10 KT. MAXIMUM SUSTAINED WINDS 40 KT GUSTS 50 KT. TROPICAL STORM FORCE WINDS WITHIN 40 NM S SEMICIRCLE...30 NM NE QUADRANT AND 0 NM NW QUADRANT. SEAS 12 FT OR GREATER WITHIN 0 NM W SEMICIRCLE...75 NM NE QUADRANT AND 90 NM SE QUADRANT WITH SEAS TO 15 FT. ELSEWHERE WITHIN 90 NM NE...120 NM SE...120 NM SW AND 15 NM NW QUADRANTS WINDS 20 TO 33 KT. SEAS TO 10 FT WITH SW SWELL. REMAINDER OF AREA WITHIN 240 NM SE SEMICIRCLE OF DANIEL WINDS 20 KT OR LESS. SEAS TO 9 FT IN SW SWELL.

SYNOPSIS AND FORECAST

N OF 27N BETWEEN 121W AND 132W WINDS 20 KT OR LESS. SEAS TO 9 FT IN NW TO N SWELL.

24 HOUR FORECAST NW OF LINE FROM 30N126W TO 27N130W TO 25N140W WINDS 20 KT OR LESS. SEAS 8 TO 9 FT IN MIXED NW AND NE SWELL. REMAINDER OF AREA WINDS 20 KT OR LESS. SEAS LESS THAN 8 FT.

CONVECTION VALID AT 2045 UTC SUN JUN 24...

TROPICAL STORM DANIEL...SCATTERED MODERATE TO STRONG OCCURRING IN BANDS WITHIN 210 NM SE AND 30 NM NW SEMICIRCLES.

LOW PRESSURE NEAR 16.5N105.5W...SCATTERED MODERATE ISOLATED STRONG WITHIN 180 NM S AND 120 NM N SEMICIRCLES.

<u>NORTH PACIFIC EQUATOR TO 30N BETWEEN 140W AND 160E</u>

SYNOPSIS AND FORECAST.

TROUGH 30N170E 27N167E 25N165E MOVING NE SLOWLY. 24 HOUR FORECAST TROUGH 30N174E 25N160E.

WINDS NE 20 TO 25 KT FROM 15N AND 28N BETWEEN 175W AND 155W. 24 HOUR FORECAST WINDS NE 20 TO 25 KT N OF 20N E OF 170W.

WINDS 20 KT OR LESS REMAINDER OF FORECAST AREA.

OTHERWISE ISOLATED MODERATE TSTMS FROM 17N TO 23N BETWEEN 170E AND 180W...AND FROM 12N TO 18N BETWEEN 160W AND 170W.

Figure 7.3-1 continued. *Selections from Metarea XII text report to compare with the surface analysis. Metareas are defined in Chapter 8. Wave heights are SWH. This is an abbreviated sample to study the analysis maps. Much more forecasting is included in the full report. It is crucial to keep in mind the Lat-Lon boundaries of the regional sections (underlined) when interpreting the statement "remainder of the forecast area."*

Pacific: tgftp.nws.noaa.gov/fax/PYBA90.gif (map) and tgftp.nws.noaa.gov/data/forecasts/marine/high_seas/north_pacific.txt (text).

Or even more automated, send this email to nws.ftpmail.ops@noaa.gov. Red is Atl; green is Pac; delete unwanted.

```
open
cd fax
get PYAA12.gif
get PYAA11.gif
get PYBA90.gif
get PYBA91.gif
cd ../data/forecasts/marine/high_seas
```

```
get north_atlantic.txt
get north_pacific.txt
quit
```

Or we can use Saildocs, which when possible has typically easier commands than FTPmail. In this case, send email to query@saildocs.com with this message:

```
send PYAA12.TIF
send PYAA11.TIF
send PYBA90.TIF
send PYBA91.TIF
send Met.4
send Met.12
```

With the same color conventions, although actual email should be standard black text.

The Next Step

Once you have practiced map-text comparisons, the next step is to make your own map from text reports alone. This is an excellent exercise to prepare you for the circumstance when you might have voice or text only without a graphic or digital map. You can make your own base maps using universal plotting sheets (used in celestial navigation), or download the master base maps from the OPC for the waters you plan to analyze. You can find these at ocean.weather.gov/base-maps. They are blank Mercator maps of the oceans as GIF files, conveniently marked off in 1° intervals. To use these we need to print some to take along, or have a portable printer onboard—there are numerous options, very small, some inkless, and most with 12-volt adapters. On an extended voyage, other uses of these printers will emerge. Bound booklets of base maps are available online and at some navigation suppliers (see starpath.com/wx).

When underway you could plot the information on the ocean chart you are using for navigation (paper or digital), although universal plotting sheets remain an attractive option as they can also be used to lay out an approach cone, discussed earlier. It pays to buy a pad of these for the nav station (14" × 14" sheets, printed on both sides).

To make your map, plot the storm location, and then draw in the quadrants forecasted and sketch in the winds. The fronts are also given as a series of points you can plot, as are areas of fog, and so on. It is another good exercise to get you more involved with the forecast.

7.4 Georeferencing Image Files

Georeferencing means adding digital coordinates to an electronic image of a weather map or other image so you can load it into a navigation program just as you would a nautical chart. With that done, your live GPS position shows on the weather map, and you can read Lat-Lon from a cursor,

as well as measure ranges and bearings on the maps, such as isobar spacings and orientation. There are several commercial products that provide this functionality, but the ones that stand out for practical use are actual ECS programs that we use to navigate. These then offer the added feature of letting you overlay GRIB formatted wind and pressure forecasts on top of the georeferenced maps or other images. It is especially valuable for overlaying ocean current forecasts onto actual sea surface temperature measurements. The ready availability of this function is a key development since the previous edition of this book.

Several examples of georeferenced images were shown earlier: Figures 2.6-2, 2.6-4 (GFS on OPC forecasts); 3.2-8 (GFS wind on tropical analysis); 3.7-4 (RTOFS currents on Navy Analysis); and 4.2-4 (GFS winds on ASCAT image).

Figure 7.4-1 shows a WW3 wind and wave forecast on top of the OPC forecast, which shows that these OPC data appear to be taken from that model. The WW3 winds are typically very similar to the GFS winds. In these displays we may have to customize the GRIB wave height contour intervals (meters) to match the OPC forecasts given in feet.

Most weather data are on a Mercator projection and these are easy to georeference. Several navigation programs accomplish this with just two button clicks to calibrate corners of the map, which is especially easy since the coordinates are clearly printed on the maps. Once this short step is completed, that configuration can be saved to use with subsequent views of that map, because OPC map images always have the same graphic dimensions. Some programs, Expedition and OpenCPN (plugin weatherfax_pi) are two examples, have gone beyond that convenience and provide links to download important image products directly, which then appear automatically georeferenced for display and overlay. These are

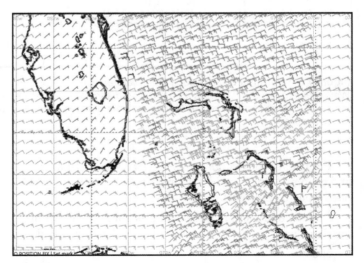

Figure 7.4-2. *GFS winds overlaid onto an ASCAT measurement at 03z Nov 28—a corner of image WMBas75.png shown in Figure 4.2-7. The color coding of the GFS winds was selected to match the colorbar of the ASCAT image, with blue turning to green at 17.5 kts. We see the GFS has done a fine job in reproducing these winds in speed and direction. GFS winds have about the same resolution (27 km) as the ASCAT (25 km).*

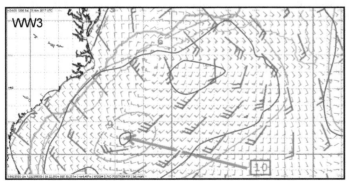

Figure 7.4-1. *A 24-hr OPC wind and wave forecast overlaid with the WW3 model predictions (red wind) at the same time. The purple WW3 contours are all 6 ft, except the inside one is 9 ft, with a peak at 10 ft, which is pointed to on the OPC map. It appears these are the same data, even though the 9-ft contours do not align. The green lines on the OPC map mark the Gulf Stream boundaries.*

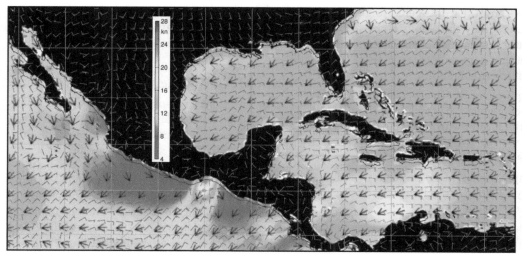

Figure 7.4-3. *COGOW winds for Nov 16-30, overlaid with a GFS h0 forecast on Nov 28 (red barbs). The comparison will vary during this period, but mostly above 30 N. In lower latitudes the agreement is pretty good throughout this two week period, or likely any other. We even see in the GFS a 35-kt Tehuantepecer active (as expected) with large patches of lighter air on either side. The flow and strengths are dependable enough to plan a route in advance across these waters. It could be different on a specific date, but the statistics are good, as expected from COGOW, being averages of real measurements.*

00z	pyba02ir.gif
06z	pyba04ir.gif
12z	pyba06ir.gif
18z	pyba08ir.gif

00z	pyba01ir.gif
06z	pyba03ir.gif
12z	pyba05ir.gif
18z	pyba07ir.gif

00z	pyaa02ir.gif
06z	pyaa04ir.gif
12z	pyaa06ir.gif
18z	pyaa08ir.gif

00z	pyaa01ir.gif
06z	pyaa03ir.gif
12z	pyaa05ir.gif
18z	pyaa07ir.gif

Figure 7.4-4. *Surface analyses overlaid on satellite cloud photos available from the OPC website; two images for each ocean, with a 10° Lon overlap. Individual maps are available underway from Saildocs:* send https://ocean.weather.gov/shtml/pyaa02ir.gif, *inserting the file name of choice at the end. Images are about 350 kB. The clouds images are infrared (ir), which means the brighter ones are higher (meaning colder) clouds.*

remarkable and forward-looking resources; we hope to see more navigation programs adopt this functionality.

Figure 7.4-2 shows an example of using ASCAT measurements to test the GFS model. This overlay of model predictions and actual measured winds remains the ultimate validation of any model. This example turned out to not only verify the GFS, but also revealed winds almost identical to the climatically expected values (COGOW) for this time of year.

Questions about actual winds versus climatic predictions can be evaluated by overlaying a current GFS forecast onto the COGOW predictions for the time, as shown in Figure 7.4-3. This comparison brings up the valuable point that in lower latitudes climatic wind predictions are more likely to be correct than they are at higher latitudes, where more large-scale wind systems are in play throughout the year. In the tropics there are occasional *easterly waves* and seasonal tropical storms moving by, so we are never guaranteed to see the climatic averages at any specific time and place, but these systems are localized enough in size and duration that they do not have much affect on climatic averages.

Overlays are also helpful for comparing cloud patterns with fronts, surface winds, and isobars. We can do this for general study to understand correlations to be applied later, or we might use near-live data to correlate what we see in the sky with what we might expect with the winds. There are several approaches to this. For learning, or when we have an internet connection underway, we can use the very nice overlays on the OPC website, as shown in Figure 7.4-4. They offer several options, including animations (in the Product Loops section) over up to 17 days—a remarkable resource for learning weather maps and associated clouds. It is interesting to compare the idealized frontal cloud patterns discussed earlier with actual cloud images over real maps.

With regard to overlays on clouds, the OPC versions are especially convenient, as they have converted the satellite images from their native *polar stereographic projection* to the Mercator projection we are accustomed to in weather maps and charts. Expedition offers the option of loading and georeferencing a polar image (i.e., tgftp.nws.noaa.gov/fax/evpn06.jpg) *without changing the projection* as shown in Figure 7.4-5. This sample shows GFS 500-mb heights over-

161

laid on a cloud image, which shows how the fronts get strung out under the winds aloft as witnessed by the clouds above them. Satellite images in Mercator format are available at aviationweather.gov/satellite, but they have dated file names, which makes then less convenient for email request.

OpenCPN takes a different approach; the weatherfax_pi plugin facilitates the polar image conversion to Mercator with a set of georeferencing manipulations, after which GRIB data *or other images* can be overlaid upon it. The Mercator cloud image can also be exported for use in other programs.

The UK Met Office, for example, uses a polar projection for their ocean maps (available by FTPmail), which makes an overlay a tremendous asset for comparing with GFS. An example is shown in Figure 7.4-6.

Although the most common application of overlaying images might be comparing a local section of the GFS forecast with an OPC map, we do not always need images for productive overlays. As pursued later on, it is often instructive to view the relationship between winds aloft and the surface analysis below, to evaluate the surface forecast itself. This can be accomplished overlaying two graphic images (from OPC) as shown in Figure 7.4-7 top, or we can accomplish this much

easier with GFS GRIB files alone, as shown in Figure 7.4-7 bottom. Essentially all nav programs allow this type of display. We can show both the surface heights and wind speeds at 500 mb.

Why Care About the Whole Ocean?

This is a fair question. In a small boat at sea we are sailing just a few hundred miles every day or two. And as noted earlier, in many cases we can just look at that section of the forecast, and go by that. But in special cases such as a sailboat race or crucial scheduling for any reason, we want to put some level of confidence onto the forecast before making decisions that risk a loss of time if the forecast is uncertain in the details we care about. To make an evaluation of this certainty generally requires looking at the shape of the entire atmosphere around us—that is after all what the numerical models are doing to come up with the forecast.

Thus we can benefit by looking at the shape of a High or the movement of a front, or other features well removed from our actual location. Animation resources at the OPC are a tre-

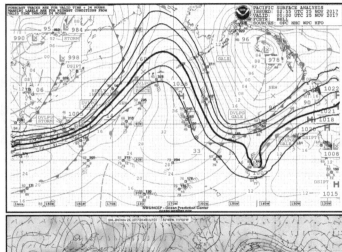

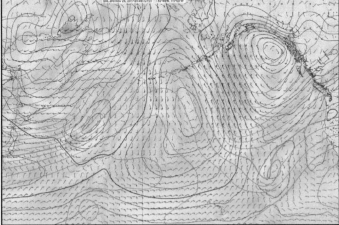

Figure 7.4-7. Top. *An OPC surface analysis with a graphic plot of a few selected 500 mb surface heights overlaid—the black lines, which are similar to elevation contours on a topo map. Only a few lines are shown to simplify the picture. Features of this comparison are discussed later. Bottom. The same comparison, but using only GRIB files from the GFS model. This is a quick, easy comparison to make underway, which often tells us much about the surface analysis.*

Figure 7.4-5. *Cloud image overlaid with 500-Mb heights that mark the flow of the winds aloft. Cloud patterns are often better correlated with winds aloft than they are with surface winds.*

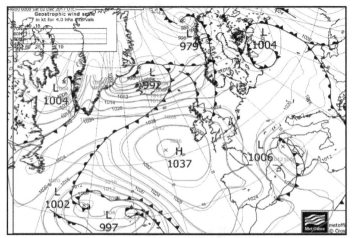

Figure 7.4-6. *A UK Met Office polar plot of surface analysis compared with U.S. GFS model. Agreement is very good for these two independent numerical predictions, which is not always the case.*

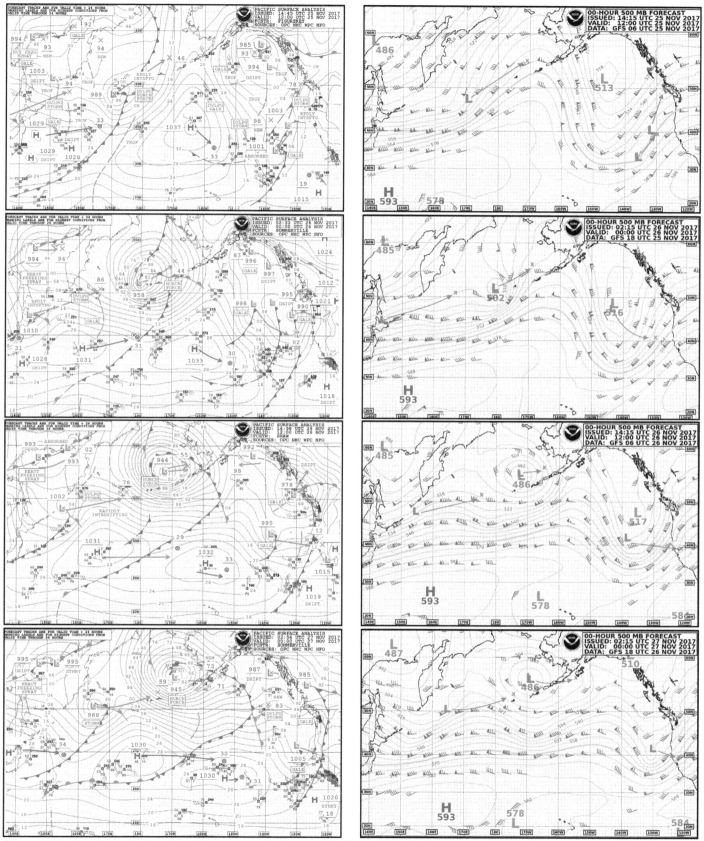

Figure 7.4-8. *Sample evolution of weather maps, skipping over the 06z and 18z surface maps, which do not have 500-mb counterparts. Instructive animations of both are available at the OPC. Choose any point on the surface to see how it is affected by motions of larger features, long distances off. We can display this type of evolution of both maps in the GFS GRIB forecasts, but they do not show the fronts, or other annotations. We come back to this figure in Section 7.6—we added the surface Low motions (purple) to the 500-mb maps.*

mendous aid to understanding how weather maps evolve. A short sample of surface analysis and 500-mb maps is shown in Figure 7.4-8.

Wind and Wave Maps

Besides the surface and 500-mb analyses and forecasts, the OPC also produces graphic forecast maps called "wind and waves forecasts." These are available by HF-fax, email request, or direct internet download. These products, however, seem to be very similar if not identical to the WW3 model numerical forecasts that are available in GRIB format (see Figure 7.4-1). The Atlantic map includes Gulf Stream boundaries on the 24-hr forecast. To the extent they are the same content, they are less crucial to practical work because the WW3 data are included in essentially all navigation programs.

Unified Surface Analysis Maps

The NWS offers weather maps of the oceans in two styles. One is what we have called the "OPC maps," produced by the OPC in conjunction with the Environmental Modelling Center (EMC), which are designed for marine application, with only limited coverage on adjacent lands. The other style covers land and ocean equally; it is called the *Unified Surface Analysis*—unified in that they are a joint product of the WPC, OPC, NHC, and HFO in the Central Pacific. They include essentially the same content over water as the OPC maps, but they differ in a couple important ways. See a comparison in Figure 7.4-9.

First, the OPC maps are on a Mercator projection accustomed to navigators, whereas the unified analyses are on an equirectangular projection, which distorts bearings relative to the meridian, especially at midlatitudes and higher. The unified analyses are also updated not just at the synoptic times (HH), but also HH + 3 hr (i.e., 03z, 09z, etc), potentially offering new information in near coastal waters relative to the OPC maps, which update only at HH. The *Unified Surface Analysis Manual* (online) gives an informative description of their production.

OPC maps use smaller pressure labels that are less intrusive on the content, rendering the maps easier to read in some places. Ship and station reports on unified maps can include more data, but they do not include SST, as the OPC maps do.

Occasionally there are more ship reports on the unified maps, with other minor differences (See Section 7.7).

Another distinction, for those sailing in the Gulf of Mexico, Caribbean, and Central America, is the coverage of the unified map (ocean.weather.gov/UA/Mexico.gif) offers a broader perspective of the region than the OPC counterpart, which could help understanding weather in that region. That, along with updating every 3 hrs, makes it worth checking the unified maps for coastal sailing.

National Digital Forecast Database (NDFD)

For some years now the NWS has generated digital versions of the their analyses and forecasts, but only recently has the full range of this data become readily available to mariners in GRIB format. The data are produced in several sectors called *Oceanic* (covering specific ocean waters); *Regional* for selected areas (AK, HI, etc.), and *CONUS* (continental US), which includes a wide range of coastal waters as well. Resolution and update times vary. Details for accessing these data are included with the numerical models overview (Section 7.5); this source of data, however, is not pure model output as are, for example, the GFS forecasts. The NDFD products are a coordination among various numerical predictions and the forecasters at the OPC, NHC, and the local weather offices covered in the sectors.

In principle, the NDFD products are the best the U.S. has to offer, updated hourly, or even half-hourly, with latest observations and at resolutions capable of forecasting individual squalls. Nevertheless, we have to gain more experience with the data to evaluate its maritime application. The dynamic nature of the forecasts can lead to irregularities in the presentation that do not distract from use on land, but can interfere with its use in optimized weather routing. A goal of the NDFD program is to eliminate such variations, but there are many facets to the development of the final product, so we stand by to see how this resource fits into marine applications.

We would expect, for example, that where the NDFD oceanic sector overlaps the OPC maps we would get identical agreement, in which case we could digitally compare pure GFS with OPC using GRIB files alone. For regional applications, the input of the local offices should be an improvement

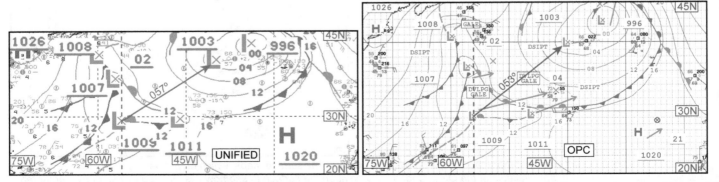

Figure 7.4-9. *Left is a unified analysis map; right is the same ocean coverage from OPC on a Mercator projection, meaning correct true bearings can be read relative to a meridian. The green bearing (057°) on the unified map is not correct, and would be worse at higher latitudes.*

over the regional models alone, which we will learn as more mariners use the NDFD in local waters. Ways to compare NDFD and the HRRR and NAM models was described in Section 6.3.

Looking ahead: GIS, KML Files, and S-412

In a 2017 OPC website update, a new section called "GIS" became prominent. It is a common abbreviation we see around the internet that stands for Geographic Information System. It is a concept that began with precision GPS and related software developments that allows for various layers of information to be displayed, interactively, over a map of some form. The form of the map can be switched among streets, topographic, nautical charts, and others. It is an ideal format for presenting social, political, economic, as well as climatic and hydrographic data, to best visualize and interpret the relationships among them. It is now used in essentially all industries, agencies, and organizations.

GIS enters into the realm of navigation and marine weather in part because of anticipated changes to the IHO standards for electronic navigational charts (ENC) and the electronic chart display and information system (ECDIS) that professional mariners use for routine navigation. Even the more basic electronic charting systems (ECS) used by all classes of vessels are already a form of GIS. We can, for example, click a point and ask for tide height, tidal current, magnetic variation, and so on at that specific point. These are data layers on a nautical chart.

Overlaying weather maps, ship reports, SST images, and model forecasts in GRIB format is another example. The IHO is planning to standardize this process. In short, they see the great value of these weather overlays (as we have tried to stress in this book), and want to incorporate these into a sys-tematic procedure with common standards for the products, be they graphic images, GRIB files, tide data, ship reports, or so on. At present, each of these overlays have separate procedures in different navigation programs, some with more options than others.

The OPC is working with various international communities to develop a new standard called "S-412 Weather Overlay," which will meet the requirements of S-100 (Universal Hydrographic Data Model), the next generation of IHO S-57 (Transfer Standard for Digital Hydrographic Data).

A sample of this idea can be seen with existing features of Expedition in Figure 7.4-10. Eventually such data as well as hazard grids (marking high winds and sea state) will be digitized in a common vector format so they can be displayed as a layer on an ENC. Then we can interact with the weather map just as we do with navigation objects on the chart, i.e., click a light symbol or a rock to learn it various properties. Based on the already extensive list of weather objects in S-412, we have a lot to look forward to with this implementation. (Use of objects and attributes in ENCs is covered in detail in our book *Introduction to Electronic Chart Navigation.* See References for more on the S-412 Weather Overlay.)

The OPC have gotten a start on introducing this concept to the public with their links to KML files for many of their weather maps in the GIS section of their website. Keyhole Markup Language (KML) is just one of several digital formats that can be used in GIS. It is popular with Google Earth (GE) as a way to overlay georeferenced images onto a globe. To use the OPC versions, you need to install the free GE app, download one of the OPC's KML files to your computer, and double-click it to open it in GE. Then save this GE "place" before quitting, after which the map will be updated each time you turn it on from your list of saved places. No further connections to the OPC must be specified.

The maps used are still georeferenced raster images, not the vectors we anticipate with S-412, but we see the GIS con-

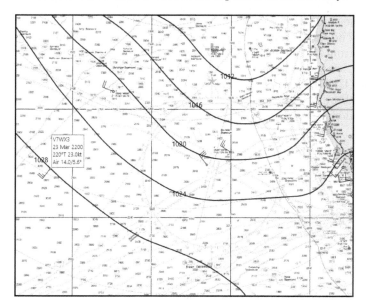

Figure 7.4-10. *GFS isobars and live ship and buoy reports overlaid onto a raster navigation chart (RNC) in Expedition. Each of the reports can be mouse clicked for fuller details. In the S-412 concept, all available weather data will be accessible in this manner using any compliant navigation program.*

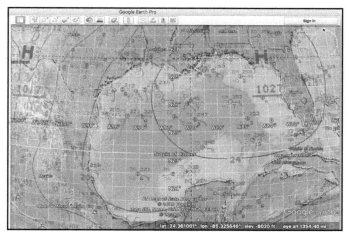

Figure 7.4-11. *A homemade Google Earth overlay (starpath.com/ wx). Just click the GOM.kml file and it will open in GE and then update automatically every 6 hr. Control transparency with the slider on the bottom left (not shown). The OPC KML samples all function as intended, but the graphics are a bit coarse. The system is new.*

cept. Cloud overlays and buoy locations to check conditions can be added. Figure 7.4-11 shows a KML file we made ourselves to illustrate the principle. It is fairly easy to do.

7.5 Global and Regional Models

Vectorized model forecasts are certainly weather maps, so we include them in this chapter. Numerical weather prediction (NWP) has been the backbone of meteorology for many decades. The various atmospheric models in use get better every year and now we have access to even more model data in GRIB format. Nevertheless, it remains fundamental to compare any pure model output with the human intelligence of the official OPC forecasts. As noted earlier, this is easier now that we have digital versions (NDFD) of the official forecasts in GRIB format, not just their graphic products.

To reiterate the reason: We want to use the model GRIB (gridded binary) format whenever we can, because it is on a fixed grid, which means it can be interpolated in time and space. It is easy to read and interpret for any application, not to mention its use with optimum route planning. So in large part, our use of OPC forecasts is primarily to confirm the model forecasts before we depend on them. There are, for example, special circumstances with any model that lead to known weaknesses (discussed later), and sure enough, the models do not always agree with each other.

A valid question would then be, why not just use the NDFD GRIB format, which is the official forecast to begin with? The answer is, in some cases we can indeed do just that, and end up with what could in principle be the best solution— still falling back on our ultimate test that it reproduces what we see now and saw in the recent past (Section 6.3 outlined ways of making that check on inland waters). If it does not do that, then regardless of the source it is wrong, and our job is to hunt around the models, or our own modifications of the models, to find what is truly best—we can scale the winds and rotate the isobars of a GRIB forecast, if that is all it takes to achieve better agreement.

But there is more to the answer. The NDFD data can periodically vary somewhat in valid times and extent of coverage, probably because of its frequent updates, incorporating multiple sources, whereas the model output is rigorously consistent in time and coverage, which better suits optimum routing programs. Also, there is no pressure forecast in NDFD, which hinders analyzing any distinctions noted between forecasted winds and our own observations. And finally, the hi-res NDFD data (CONUS and Regional) are at present only available conveniently to a few navigation programs. In the meantime, we do have direct access to the National Blend of Models (NBM) forecasts that form the basis of the NDFD. The NBM may be the data of choice in the near future, as noted in Appendix 8.

Global Models

Global models are just that, they cover all the waters of the world, with possible exclusion of the polar regions. The U.S. Global Forecast System (GFS) is the most widely used internationally, due in part to its success and in part to its free availability worldwide. Essentially all navigation programs offer GFS forecasts in various detail, as do essentially every computer and every mobile device in the world. If you see digital weather data without any identification of its source, it is likely GFS data.

Besides the U.S. GFS, there are independent global models run by the U.S. Navy, Canada, United Kingdom, Japan, France, Australia, Korea, Brazil, the European Community, and likely others on some level. There are also combinations and variations of the model runs we discuss shortly.

Global models are typically run every 6 hrs, shortly after the synoptic times, as these are the common times that the world's weather community gathers observations and shares them worldwide amongst national weather services over the WMO's Global Telecommunication System (GTS) network. Each nation then pulls out the latest data to run their model, and in turn puts their results back onto the GTS network for other nations to consider for their own forecasts—some nations charge other nations and individuals a licensing fee for various uses of their data. All NOAA data are free to the public, worldwide.

Global models are characterized by extended forecasts over a fairly coarse grid (resolution), but including many parameters at various altitudes (levels). The GFS, for example, has data points only every 15 nmi, forecasting out to 16 days, covering more than 300 parameters, not just at the surface, but at multiple levels above the surface (often expressed in pressure units), including also such things as temperature of the soil one meter below the surface, which is indeed crucial to farming and other industries.

Table 7.5-1 lists a couple global models. The Global Deterministic Prediction System (GDPS) model is from Canada. The Navy Global Environmental Model (NAVGEM) model is from the U.S. Navy, which has its own weather service, completely independent from NOAA. Model data from the UK (UKMET) and EU (ECMWF) are not available publicly, only through third party commercial services, with a few exceptions given in Section 8.4 on sources.

For ocean routing, a data point every 0.25° (15 nmi) is usually more than adequate. In fact, for planning we might need only 0.5° or even 1° resolution, which would save a lot on download costs.

Section 8.4 describes more specifically how we make these requests by email. No matter when we send the request, the first "forecast" (h0) will correspond to the most recent synoptic time (effectively a surface analysis), keeping in mind that they are delayed by about 3.5 hr. Thus if you ask for a GFS set at 16z, your h0 would be 12z, but if you asked at 14z, your h0 would be 06z. It pays to know the delay as it varies with product and with how you are getting the product. Some third party sources require an extra delay to process the request. You can check when the product is truly available at the NCEP status link: nco.ncep.noaa.gov/pmb/

nwprod/prodstat, which includes the status of all NCEP models, global, regional, and ensemble. Compare a finish time there with when you can actually get the product from your provider to learn the real delay.

Model Ensembles

One way to evaluate the dependability of a model is to run it several times with slightly different input parameters, such as variations of the 500 mb surface. Sometimes small perturbations of the input can cause large changes in the forecast a few days out. Other times, we might find results are much less dependent on the details of the input, in which case we can think of that model forecast at that time as more dependable. For either outcome, the result we most commonly download and look at is an average of the various perturbed runs. These studies take longer, so ensemble forecasts generally use lower resolution and larger steps than the base model data. The runs at 00z and 12z might be most informative, as these are the synoptic times that sounding data (Section 3.4) are globally available.

Several nations run ensemble computations; two are listed in Table 7.5-2. GEFS is an ensemble of the GFS model; CMCE refers to ensembles of the GDPS model from the Canadian Meteorological Center, which includes varied physics as well as inputs. For use underway, the procedure might be to compare an ensemble average with a base forecast as a way to test the base, keeping in mind that a conclusion in one test might not represent what you see in a later one. Model results depend on the configuration of the atmosphere.

Although the average ensemble is the easiest to use in practice, we can also (in this Age of Information) download GRIB files of the *control* run as well as the results of each of the *perturbation* runs, typically 10 to 20 runs. This however wanders into diminishing returns for study on land, let alone a vessel underway. I just mention this so we are aware of the options when we see a forecast simply labeled "ensemble." With no further specification, we can assume we are getting the average result.

The ensemble concept of varying one model using different initial conditions is not the same as the NWS National Blend of Models (NBM). This promising program might instead be called "blend of national models," in that it hopes to coordinate the use of multiple U.S. *and* international models to create a consensus forecast, taking into account the known strengths of individual models in specific circumstances. Components of all models undergo updates every year or so, any one of which could affect the relative success of a model. Thus an ongoing blending concept seems a logical path to progress. NBM includes an expanded CONUS domain; and its oceanic domain covers most of the Pacific and Atlantic—both are larger than their NDFD equivalents (Appendix 8).

Table Notes: *See Section 8.4 for a list of sources, more models, and a discussion of parameters. "conus" = continental US; "na" = North America; "3h" is a forecast time interval; "h12" is the 12th forecast in a series; "HH" are the synoptic times. NBM has larger domains (+), see Appendix 8.*

Also looking ahead, the GFS will be updated in 2019 to the FV3 version, which promises notable improvements. See data1.gfdl.noaa.gov/fvGFS/fvGFS_products.php? Regions and products vary with initialization times. Try a 12z run for most options. Simulated radar is included.

Regional Models

It generally takes at least 5 or 6 grid points to get a fair representation of the model forecasts within that region, so looking at the best GFS at 15 nmi, we cannot expect the GFS to give any details within a 45 mile radius. A bay as large as 30 miles across that routinely has different winds than just outside the bay in the ocean could not be productively studied with a global model. Sea breezes and similar land effects

Table 7.5-1. Selected Global Model Datasets

| Model | Resolution | | | Updates every 6h. h0 valid at HH, then forecasts every... |
	km	nmi	deg	
GFS	28	15	0.3	1h to h120, 3h to h240, 12h to h384
GDPS	25	13	0.2	3h to h48, 6h to h96, 12h to h240
NAVGEM	32	60	1	3h to h48, 6h to h96, 12h to h144

Table 7.5-2. Selected Global Ensemble Datasets

| Model | Resolution | | | Steps and Range (Update interval) |
	km	nmi	deg	
GEFS	56	30	0.5	6h to h384 (6h)
CMCE	12	60	1	6h to h96, 12h to h240 (12h)

Table 7.5-3. Selected Regional Datasets

| Source | Resolution | | | Range | Steps | Updates |
	km	nmi	deg			
HRRR	3	1.6	0.03	18h 36h at HH	1h	1h
NAM (conus)	3	1.6	0.03	60h	1h	6h
NAM (na)	12	6.5	0.11	84h	1h	6h
RAP	11	6.0	0.10	21h	1h	1h
NBM (conus+)	2.5	1.4	0.02	264h	1h to h36, 3h to h192, 6h to h264	1h
NBM (oceanic+)	10	5.4	0.09	264h	3h to h192, 6h to h264	4h
NDFD (conus)	2.5	1.4	0.02	168h	1h to h18, 3h to h48, 6h to h96, 12h to h168	30m
NDFD (oceanic)	10	5.4	0.09	120h	3h to h48, 6h to h120	6h
HRDPS (upper na)	2.5	1.4	0.02	48h	3h	6h

would not show up at all. GFS winds will flow smoothly right across it (Figure 7.5-1), as they would for some even larger waterways, and certainly any smaller ones. If we want wind forecasts for more local waterways we need a regional model with much higher resolution. Even for coastal sailing, we can benefit from regional models as they treat the boundaries and adjacent waters more dependably.

"Regional model" here refers generically to what is often called *mesoscale* model, where that designation itself varies amongst contexts, but often means regions or systems that can be characterized within a few miles to several hundred miles. Regional models are therefore characterized by higher resolution, more frequent updates, limited extent in time, and generally restricted to specific areas. The HRRR model, for example, has resolution of 1.6 nmi, updates every hour, but extends out only 18 hr. It covers U.S. and near coastal waters. Table 7.5-3 summarizes several regional models. Generally speaking, if we have the option over a given waterway to use a regional or global model, the regional is likely more accurate. Most regional models incorporate their choice of global model as a starting point and as a way to treat the boundaries of the regional coverage.

To compare availability and specifications, available data sets from NDFD are included in Table 7.5-3. As noted several times, it will take practice and logged experience for mariners to determine which of these multiple sources of data best meet their needs.

Comparing Models

There are numerous reports online, and indeed in the daily news, that address the success of various models. Professional comparisons are typically presented in complex statistical terms, not easy to interpret, and newspaper claims that one model is better than another, tend to focus on specific events, without clarifying the nuances of such comparisons.

There are several ways to evaluate a forecast that we can consider, but the practical tests already covered are the ones that matter. Namely, has the model produced what we see on the water now and recently, and are the forecasts consistent going forward.

One way professionals look at this is to compare the surface analysis we see now to what it was forecasted to be 48 hrs ago, for each grid point over some region. Then we can keep doing this for 3 or 4 cycles in a row and average the differences. If the discrepancies between forecast and subsequent analysis are purely random, then they will average out to zero, some being plus, others minus. If they do not average to zero that model is said to have a *bias* value for that parameter in that region. Model biases for various parameters can then be compared amongst models, or for the same model in various conditions, and there is much of that data online (see Figure 7.5-2). These biases, however, are not necessarily a signature of the model, because they will change with the conditions of the atmosphere, and indeed with locations on earth. We do this underway by sequencing the weather maps (Section 7.2), focusing on the regions we care about.

We can also compare one model to another by just downloading different model forecasts we have access to and looking at the winds they propose over the route we want. When using optimized routing, we would compare the proposed routes from each of them, still keeping in mind how well each did in accounting for what we see now. A sample comparison from the Navy is shown in Figure 7.5-3, which shows both the model biases and actual errors compared to observations average over global data. We see that even though models can vary significantly in specific circumstances, on average they can be very similar for surface wind.

There are many ways to compare and evaluate models online. Beside the Navy link cited, there are also:

emc.ncep.noaa.gov/gmb/STATS_vsdb, and

wpc.ncep.noaa.gov/html/model2.shtml

But read the descriptions carefully. Sometimes the "observed" data the forecasts are compared to are actually the computed values of the corresponding analysis. The Navy presentations are clearer in this regard, referring specifically to observations from ships and buoys or ASCAT measurements. An interesting example of model verification is shown in Figure 7.5-4, which illustrates the subtleties in model verification.

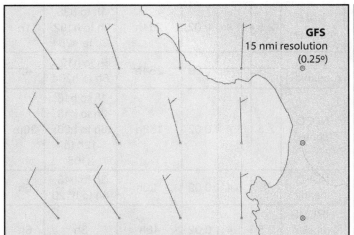 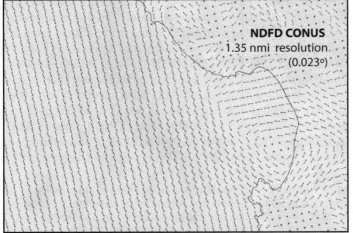

Figure 7.5-1. *Wind forecast for Monterey Bay (20 nmi across) from a global and regional forecast at the same time.*

With so much data and archived results, we can anticipate useful probabilities assigned to ocean forecasts, just as we have a probability of rain on land. The results are known to the professionals (discussed below), but we do not see this in standard sources. A step in this direction comes from scientists at Florida State University and the NWS who have collaborated on an interesting presentation of confidence levels for GFS ensemble forecasts (Figure 7.5-5). The usefulness of

these maps must be tested by mariners underway, which we could do by comparing ASCAT winds with GFS forecasts in the poor and good regions of confidence.

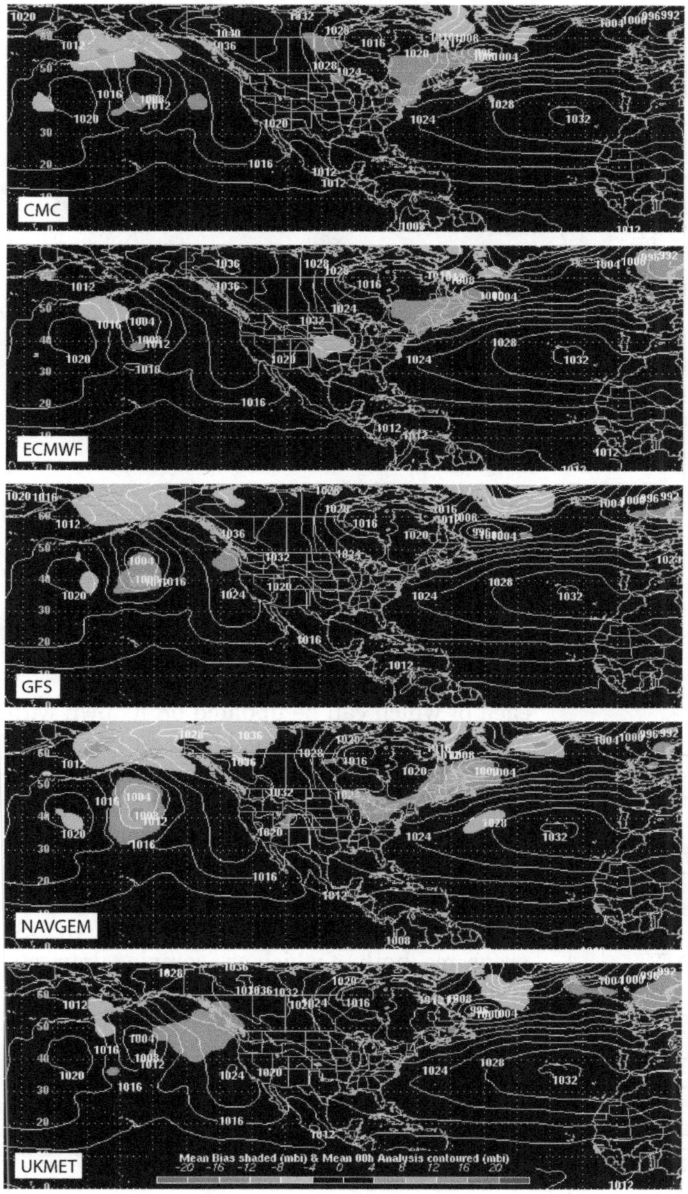

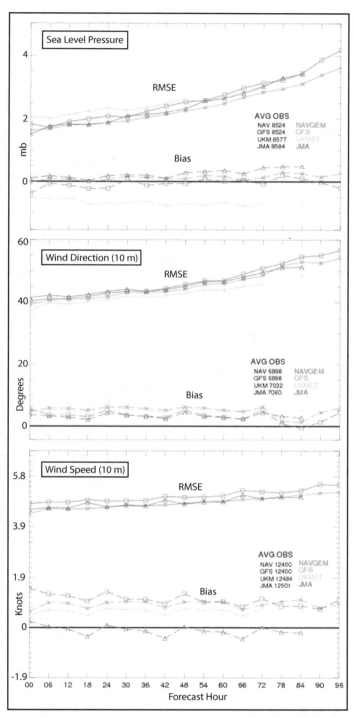

Figure 7.5-2. *SLP bias in 96-hr forecasts for several models over five 4-day cycles ending Dec 27, 2017. The background isobars are the individual averages of the five 00z reference analyses used. The isobars differ notably in this example in some locations; in other samples, they were remarkably similar for all models. In the 24-hr, 48-hr, and even 72-hr comparisons at this time, the biases were mostly under ±4 mb; only the 72-hr forecasts showed isolated patches of 4-8 mb. This comparison can be made at any time at* wpc.ncep.noaa.gov/mdlbias. *Note that a 0 to 4 mb bias, which could have a big effect on the wind, does not show up in this comparison.*

Figure 7.5-3. *Navy study (*fnmoc.navy.mil/verify_cgi/*) of global average model bias and root mean square error (RMSE) for SLP and 10-m wind for several models from Dec 5 to Dec 23, 2017. All are based on the 00z forecasts with 0.5° resolution. Bias reflects internal model consistency; RMSE are relative to actual surface observations. The models are fairly consistent giving wind speed to about ± (4 or 5) kts and wind directions to ± (40 to 50)°. Results vary somewhat for specific ocean regions compared to these global data.*

The confidence level maps are available by email request to Saildocs: "send http://moe.met.fsu.edu/confidence/images/current/wspd.1.png" (or /wspdtrop.1.png, for the Atlantic side.) The number "1" in the filenames is the h0 forecast (the analysis), then 2 = h6, 3 = h12, and so on. File wspd.9.png is the 48-hr forecast confidence map, Pacific side.

Which Model is Best?

We might read in a newspaper or blog post that the EU's ECMWF or UK's UKMET is superior to the U.S. GFS, or similar claims. Such statements are misleading and not productive. Any or all of the models can be wrong in some circumstances and any one could be superior to the others in special circumstances. National weather services of all nations use all models for their final products, although each does still offer the pure output of their own models—some for free; some for a fee.

In the US, we can see this process in action by reading the Model Diagnostic Discussions (nws.noaa.gov/data/WNH/PMDHMD) that show how professionals balance out the virtues of various models in the ongoing forecasts. There is a section called "Model Evaluation Including Preferences and Forecast Confidence" that is applied to each major feature on the current CONUS map. We get similar information of more practical application for high seas and coastal waters from the Forecast Discussions covered in the next section.

These dynamic model evaluations, nevertheless, remain misleading when it comes to the generic question, "Which model is best?" The GFS forecast that we get in GRIB format, for example, is a product of much more than just the GFS model physics; it is the result of several systems of analysis,

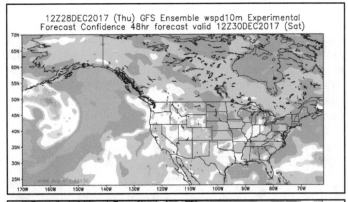
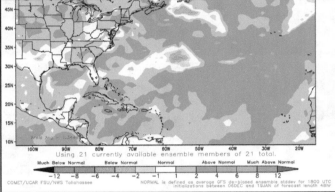

Figure 7.5-5. *Confidence levels for 48-hr forecasts of 10-m wind speeds by GFS Ensemble model. Maps are available for every 6hrs out to h180 from* moe.met.fsu.edu/confidence—*available by email from Saildocs. "Normal" is defined as the de-biased ensemble standard deviation averaged over archived verifications for this date range See also* ocean.weather.gov/windprob.shtml.

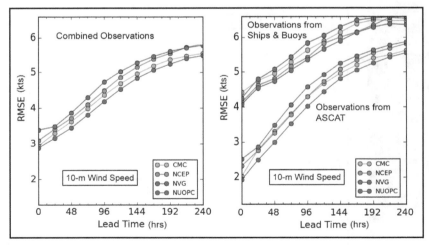

Figure 7.5-4. *Ensemble verifications from the Navy for 10-m wind speed, averaged over the globe for a 29-day period in October, 2016. Similar results are seen over specific oceans. The models agree with ASCAT data better than with buoy and ship reports. This could reflect the influence of the preponderance of ASCAT data over the oceans in the assimilation process. Also the model resolution (0.5° here) smooths out the wind forecasts over the coastal regions at the model boundaries. This can lead to large misses on the buoy comparisons, which are mainly in that region. In short, this is an indirect reminder that we cannot count on global models in near coastal waters. Data from* fnmoc.navy.mil/verify_cgi/

each of which can be updated on its own with notable impact on the final forecast skill of the GFS. In short, the way observations get assimilated into a model run is as important as the model itself when it comes to quality of the final product. The U.S. accomplishes this with their Gridpoint Statistical Interpolation (GSI) and Global Data Assimilation System (GDAS) programs, both of which are complex, intricate systems. In very broad terms, the GSI gathers the raw observations as they stream in continuously from global sources, applies complex quality control and statistical analysis, organizes the results in time and grid point space, and then stores the data to be used as scheduled by the GDAS.

The GDAS is an ongoing run of the GFS model that works with the GSI to prepare short term forecasts that will serve as the background for the next GFS analysis to be released. We get a GFS analysis run and forecast sequence every 6 hrs, but the GDAS works continuously with the GSI behind the scenes—entering data, interpolating missing points, testing its implications on other parameters and levels, balancing out fitting specific data with the perturbations that creates, and then running new short-term forecasts. It is an ongoing, circular process that prepares the GFS for its final run.

With that outline of the process in mind, it is important to remember when we compare specific results on the water, that the goal of NWP is to make the best overall analysis of the atmosphere, not to fit specific data.

Thus it is a subtle question to ask which model is best, implying some level of superiority now and in the near future, because modifications or updates to any one of these crucial processes in use by any model can effect its skill in predicting a specific parameter. One nation or agency might choose to include data that others do not, or to weigh it differently. Most of these tools are being updated every 6 months or so.

From the mariner's practical point of view, the best model is the one that at the moment is doing the best job in accounting for the wind we see, now and in the recent past. Tomorrow, or 12 hours from now, it could be a different choice.

With all that said, we standby for the new GFS in 2019 based on the Finite-Volume Cubed-Sphere engine (FV3), which they anticipate will provide state of the art global forecasting. Our practical definition of what is best for us remains unchanged. Google "FV3" for latest news.

7.6 Use of 500-mb Maps

Maps of the 500-mb pressure surface are used to indicate the flow of the winds aloft, as described in Section 3.3. That section, along with Section 4.3 on how 500-mb winds interact with surface winds, provide the background for this section.

Two 500-mb analyses (00z and 12z), two 48-hr forecasts, and one 96-hr forecast are available daily via radiofax or email request. Samples are shown in Figure 7.4-8, along with the accompanying surface analysis, and how both might evolve in time. For 500-mb maps, the analysis and forecast formats are essentially identical, in contrast to the surface maps, which use different conventions and scales for analyses and forecasts. From the OPC we get 500-mb maps of the full North Pacific and full North Atlantic. Southern Hemisphere maps are available from the Australian BOM.

These maps show winds in the upper atmosphere, at an altitude of about 18,000 ft (5500 meters) where the pressure is about 500 mb. Section 3.3 explains the formation and behavior of this important wind system. The ultimate wind we feel on the surface depends on what is taking place up here with these winds aloft: how fast it is, whether it is rising or sinking, whether it is diverging (spreading out or speeding up) or converging (focusing into a region or slowing down), as well as which specific direction the flow is proceeding across the globe, and how this pattern might be changing with time.

Lines on these maps are not isobars, they are the altitudes of the 500-mb surface expressed in decameters (10 meters). They are essentially topographical maps of the 500-mb pressure terrain. A line marked 564 means the pressure of 500 mb along that line is located 5,640 meters above the earth.

The general wind flow is west to east, with the higher 500-mb surface heights on the right with your back to the wind. Since it is these winds that steer the surface storms across the globe, it is the direction of these winds that tell us which precise direction weather will come from. Look, for example, at the several surface Lows in Figure 7.4-8. Their forecasted 24-hr motion is shown on the surface map (X to X), which can be compared to the direction of the winds aloft at that location. The 500-mb maps are computer generated with the short-wave troughs (dashed lines) periodically added by hand. Short waves and long waves are discussed in Section 3.3.

On the first map at the top of Figure 7.4-8 we see wind aloft flowing off the Pacific toward the NE and over the West Coast, with an intensifying Low also moving NE toward CA shown on the corresponding surface analyses. In the following maps of the figure (one every 12 hr), we see frontal waves forming, and can note that the isobars in the warm sectors of those waves are parallel to the winds aloft as discussed in Chapter 4. In the terminology of Section 3.3, this sequence of maps shows mostly-meridional (N-S) flow evolving into mostly-zonal (E-W) flow.

Wind speeds are marked in the usual conventions, barbs = 10 kts, flags = 50 kts, half-barbs = 5 kts. On 500-mb maps, only winds equal to or greater than 30 kts are shown (on surface forecasts, the lower limit is 33 kts). The steeper the surface (meaning the closer the contours), the stronger the winds. As discussed in Section 3.3, the steep surface means the temperature gradient below it is high. In other words, the larger the temperature differences on the surface, the higher the wind speeds aloft.

These winds meander around the globe in a serpentine pattern of waves (called Rossby waves) and these waves themselves slide slowly eastward with time. This change in pattern alters the direction of the storm tracks with time. Looking to the SW of the Aleutian Islands, we see the storm tracks evolving from toward the NE to toward the SE in just 36 hrs or so, which is rather faster than normal, indicating rapidly changing and complex patterns on the surface, which is confirmed in the surface analyses below this region.

North-south flow in these winds (pure meridional flow) is fairly rare. When the winds aloft kink to this extent they tend to slow down or stop the eastward progression of the waves. This pattern is called an *omega block,* since the wind path has bent into the shape of the Greek letter capital omega. Several times a year this happens in the Pacific Northwest. In the winter, this leads to a week or two of very cold weather on the coast coming down from the Canadian Arctic. For ocean sailing in the summer, this pattern (in either ocean) has a special significance as it can lock in the position of the surface High it surrounds. With an omega block, the High and wind flow around it can last for a week or more, whereas normally things are changing around more frequently. An example is shown in Figure 10.3-2. (In the map sequence of Figure 7.4-8 we are seeing the dissipation of a pattern that is almost an omega block.)

The 564 Line

Where the 500-mb surface is high, the air below it is warmer (lighter). The 5640-meter contour is drawn in bold on OPC maps since it can be used to identify the likely path of surface storms. There are several guidelines that have been proposed for this particular contour line by veteran OPC forecasters Joe Sienkiewicz (now Branch Chief, OPC) and Lee Chesneau (now in public teaching, marineweatherbylee.com). Their classic article from Dec., 2008 in *Mariner's Weather Log* expands on these.

(1) The surface storm track usually runs 300 to 600 nautical miles (5 to 10 degrees of latitude) north of this line and parallel to it.

(2) In the winter, this line marks the southern limit of Force 7 surface westerlies (28 to 33 kts). In the summer, the line marks the southern limit of Force 6 surface westerlies (22 to 27 kts). These surface westerlies are built from a convergence of the top circulation around the Atlantic or Pacific Highs and the bottom circulation around the Icelandic or Aleutian Lows. See related discussion of "centers of action" in Chapter 2.

The speed of the winds aloft tells us how fast the surface storms move across the globe and how intense their associated surface winds will be.

(3) Cold fronts and surface storm centers (Lows) move at about 1/3 to 1/2 of the wind speed of the 500-mb winds.

(4) Surface wind speeds on the cold-air side of moving Lows will be about 1/2 of the speed of the winds at 500-mb.

It is instructive to see how each of these guidelines is confirmed from the maps of Figure 7.4-8. The procedures of Section 2.4 on finding wind speed from isobars can be used for checking item (2). These consistent relationships show clearly how the winds aloft influence the surface winds.

Role of the 500-mb Maps in Route Planning

The atmosphere is a three-dimensional system. What happens on the surface is determined in large part by what happens aloft in the vicinity of these 500-mb winds. By studying these winds we get insights into which way surface storms are moving and how fast they are moving. The faster the winds aloft, the faster the winds on the surface. With the ideas presented in Chapter 4 we can also better understand why some systems are much stronger than others, and why they develop where and when they do.

But the ultimate question is how do we best use these maps underway? There are guidelines for this in the Sienkiewicz and Chesneau article, and there is even more detail on ship weather routing in the book by Captain Ma-Li Chen and Lee Chesneau called *Heavy Weather Avoidance—Concepts and Applications of the 500-mb Charts*. They cover well-tested procedures for ship passages at high latitudes that are derived almost exclusively from these maps. Their process includes the definition of surface zones below each part of each wave aloft that not only distinguish routing zones but

also gives a physical meaning to the space we sail through. After reading their book, you will not sail under one of these waves again without thinking of what is going on 18,000 ft overhead! A brief synopsis of their zones is in Section 10.5.

For small craft at sea, however, especially below latitudes of 50N or so, chances are the surface forecasts themselves will remain the main source of actual route decisions. Remember that if you have access to these 500-mb maps, then you also have access to the 24-hr, 48-hr, and 96-hr surface forecasts, not to mention even longer-term forecasts from the GFS. (As noted earlier, with the GRIB format we can overlay 500-mb winds and heights on top of the surface winds and isobars.) For our purposes, it is unlikely we will make a better surface forecast from the 500-mb maps than the ones the OPC makes for us. Nevertheless, as Sienkiewicz, Chen, and Chesneau have shown us, we gain much insight from studying these winds aloft.

Evaluating Surface Analysis Maps

Beyond the theoretical understanding of how winds aloft influence the formation and behavior of surface systems, our ongoing practical challenge remains how to evaluate the surface forecasts as best we can. We do this by checking the surface analysis isobars with our own barometer and wind measurements, and we also check by comparing surface analyses with plotted ship reports and ASCAT winds. As needed we can even look up reports that were not plotted.

Thus we have more faith in a forecast if the most recent surface analysis was right as far as we could check it. This level of checking we would do in most all circumstances where we are planning a route based on what the forecasts tell us. Recall too, that we are always sailing by the forecasts, not by the surface analysis. The four daily surface analyses are always in the past, at least 3 hrs old at best. For slower vessels, we have to look ahead as far as possible, especially on ocean passages, which means at least 48 hrs, maybe 96 hrs.

For day sails or overnight sails, it would be rare that we refer to the 500-mb maps at all. The cases we consider here are longer ocean or coastal passages, and in particular, those we want to optimize for some reason. And it is for this application that we propose a new way to look at these maps as a tool to help us evaluate the surface forecasts. Not make a better forecast, just apply some confidence level to the one we are given.

In most cases we analyze the surface forecasts as best we can based on recent surface analyses and make our decision. But there are some cases where the decisions we make have more at stake than others. This often happens in a yacht race where a wrong decision could lead to bad results, and a lot of preparation, expense, and the hopes of the entire crew would be compromised. In fact this level of decision making comes up at least once in most ocean yacht races. In sailboat races, a common decision is how close can you cut the corner of a High and not run out of wind; or whether or not to tack to meet and cross a front in a more favorable manner.

But similar crucial decisions are not limited to recreational racing. They could also come up in an emergency passage back to land, or in a search and rescue operation. Or it could come up any time at all that you simply decide you want to do the very best possible with what you have to work with. I have seen crucial weather decisions come up on a long coastal delivery where one of the crew members was on a tight schedule and the others were not. Although it continues to happen, it is a big mistake in the first place to have someone on board with an important deadline. It could well be that you do not have safe options to let them off once you start down the coast.

In such cases, you may have to decide to carry on to one port before the winds reverse, or turn around and head back to another port, taking every one out of their way. And so on. The right answer depends on the accuracy of the forecasts.

Again, we are not trying to make a better forecast, we are simply trying to evaluate the likely accuracy of the forecast we have.

In these cases we can look to the 500-mb map to add additional confidence (or maybe doubt) to the forecast we are going to depend upon. Remember our favorite phrase: there is always going to be a forecast, and they are not marked good or bad. We do know, however, that some are inherently better than others, and this is not just random. Some conditions of the atmosphere make predictions more difficult, and forecasts in these conditions are naturally not as good as others—we see that reflected on some level in the GFS confidence maps mentioned in the last section.

Needless to say, there are many aspects of the atmosphere that would enter into the question of what conditions lead to a good forecast and what makes for a poor forecast. One way to learn about this, even as non-professionals, is to read ongoing Forecast Discussions from the NWS and OPC. There are versions for coastal and offshore forecasts, but we are talking now about discussions of the high seas forecasts.

These discussions are available by FTPmail (Section 8.4) with this email request to nws.ftpmail.ops@noaa.gov:

```
open
cd data/raw/ag
get agpn40.kwnm.mim.pac.txt
get agnt40.kwnm.mim.atn.txt
quit
```

The first file is for the Pacific; the second is for the Atlantic; delete the line not needed. They are also available at the OPC website. These are not the same as the Model Evaluation Discussions mentioned earlier. These discussions are written by the actual forecasters who made the latest high seas forecast. Below is an extended sample to illustrate the broad value of this resource, including further demonstration that many models are being considered when preparing the official NWS forecasts.

```
The ASCAT pass from 04Z generally shows vari-
able winds 5-15 kt across much of the offshore
waters. The most recent observations as well
as an altimeter pass from 07Z indicate seas
across the waters 3-6 ft.
```

```
The current upper level pattern shows a ridge
across the offshore waters while a closed low
spins well W of the California waters. The key
to the forecast over the next week will be
how soon the low center kicks out and turns
NE towards the offshore waters. Over the first
few days the 00Z global models are in great
agreement with only minor differences between
them. The UKMET is a good compromise between
the faster GFS solution and the slower ECMWF.
I will populate the wind grids using the GFS
through 06Z Thu, then transition to the UKMET
through 03Z Sun, before finishing out the pe-
riod using the ECMWF.
```

```
Seas...Initially there isn't much difference
between the two main wave models, then sig-
nificant differences occur beginning on day 4
due to the position of the surface low. I will
populate the wave grids using the ENP through
06Z Thursday, then transition to the ENP for
the remainder of the period. I needed to do
some edits beginning Thursday in order to Bet-
ter represent the seas given that I populate
the wind grids using the UKMET.
```

These Forecast Discussions are almost always interesting reading. You learn a lot about the present state of the atmosphere and you get specific insights into the associated forecasts and model predictions. The 500-mb flow patterns are often referred to as a source of a doubtful or less-certain forecast—which is just the point we want to make now. Particular patterns in this category are strong zonal flows, split-flows, and cutoff lows. Schematic samples of these patterns are shown in Figures 7.6-3 to 7.6-6, followed by contrasting patterns that meteorologists might agree would lead to more confident forecasts.

The question of which patterns might lead to the best forecasts is almost as uncertain as which might lead to the weakest forecasts, because there are always other factors at play. But for a guess of the favorable or preferred winds aloft pattern we might guess that a smooth natural persistent flow around the known centers of action might be the best. These are shown for the Pacific and Atlantic in Figures 7.6-7 and 7.6-8.

Using these schematic patterns as guidelines, we can try to see if the winds aloft support a good forecast or one that might not be as good. Again, we are not trying to make a better forecast. We are just trying to assign some level of confidence to the forecasts given to us that might help us make crucial decisions. In most cases this is beyond the call of duty, but in some cases we want to do everything in our power to make the best decision.

This discussion is more or less limited to interactions with extratropical weather patterns. When it comes to negotiating tropical storms there are other, more direct rationales that come into play, and there are more frequent updates with statistical bounds provided.

Another Way to Look at It

Consider this very schematic situation: a bet between two professional forecasters about who can make the best ocean and coastal surface-wind forecast (Figure 7.6-1). They are given the same average state of the atmosphere that they both must work with. Then we ask one of them to sketch the pattern they want for their winds aloft at the time they are making this contest forecast. We would then call this their choice for favorable winds aloft pattern, because they conclude that with this pattern their forecast will be as good as possible, considering all the other average conditions that they cannot change.

Then we ask this same professional forecaster what winds aloft pattern would he want his competitor to have to work with. In other words, he wants to win, so he wants his competitor to have a poor forecast, and so he is wishing on him some winds aloft pattern that would make his job as difficult as possible. This we will call the unfavorable pattern.

So our job as navigators underway, having to make a crucial decision that depends on the winds, is to take a look at the winds aloft during the time of our passage and try to decide if they are more like a favorable pattern or more like an unfavorable pattern. If they are favorable we will put a higher probability on the forecast being true and be prepared to risk a bit more in depending on it to be right. On the other hand, if we conclude the pattern is more like an unfavorable pattern, we should be more conservative on our risks. If, ideally, we wanted to turn 90° at this point, then for now, we might just turn 45° (half of what we want to do) and wait for 6, or 12 hrs, whichever tells us more about what is going on.

Looking Ahead

Computer modeling is getting better everyday. Someday, NWP and all its related technologies will be so advanced that something like the NBM will be all we need, including the confidence levels we need to make our risk-versus-reward decisions. The NBM already includes probabilistic wind and pressure forecasts based on many ensemble runs, but the data are not yet readily available underway. See also ocean.weather.gov/windprob.shtml

But we are not there yet, and until that happens we have to do the best we can with what we have to make our own estimates of the probabilities. The forecasts are never going to be 100% guaranteed, no matter how sophisticated the analysis becomes. There will always be some uncertainty because it is such a complex system (the atmosphere) we are dealing with. It is hard enough in the open ocean, but along the coast, with land involved, it is even more difficult, yet we see data like HRRR, NDFD, and NAM adding new dimensions to our coastal and inland weather routing.

Weather Routing Decisions

We have discussed evaluating forecasts throughout the book, but have not yet specifically discussed Go or No-Go decision making. This comes up on all vessels, power or sail, on almost all voyages, on some level. We will use an example from sailboat racing, as it comes up more often in that setting, but it could just as well apply to a container ship, choosing a route in a dangerous situation or trying to make the most efficient run in normal conditions.

Suppose I have a forecast that says the wind is going to veer by 30° overnight, and I need to decide if I should jibe—the essentially ongoing decision when sailing downwind. If I jibe now, and the wind does veer 30° by tomorrow morning, I will gain relative to not jibing. But if I jibe now and the wind does not veer 30° by tomorrow morning, I will lose relative to not jibing. What do I need to know to decide if I should jibe?

We need numbers, or estimates of numbers, on all three factors involved: P, the probability of the wind veering as forecasted; Gain, the amount we gain (in hours or miles) if we jibe and the wind shifts as forecasted; and Risk, the amount we lose (in the same units) if we jibe and the wind does not shift as forecasted. We can figure the Risk and Gain numbers from our polar diagrams, so we are left with computing a "take-point probability" P for the forecast being correct. In other words, we need to calculate how big P has to be so that the chances of gaining are higher than the chances of losing.

That can be put into an equation form as:

$$P \times \text{Gain} \geq (1-P) \times \text{Risk}.$$

In words: the probability of the veer happening (P) times the Gain from the veer must be greater than the probability of no veer (1-P) times the Risk. If the probability of yes is 70% or 0.7, then the probability of no would be 30% or 0.3.

Now we can rearrange the terms to get:

$$P \geq \text{Risk} / (\text{Risk} + \text{Gain})$$

This is our working guideline. Table 7.6-1 is a way to get quick values, although the equation is easy to evaluate. The units can be anything, miles, minutes, hours.

Suppose you figure you would gain about 4 miles if the wind veers, but you would lose about 1 mile on the slightly slower jibe if it did not veer. Then, P = 1/5 = 20%. The forecast only has to be right 20% of the time and you come out ahead. A clear call to go for it.

On the other hand, suppose you face a more ambitious maneuver to catch up. You figure you will gain 2 miles if the forecast is right, but you would lose 8 miles if there is no veer,

Figure 7.6-1. *Shape of the winds aloft.*

Unfavorable upper level flow patterns that make surface forecasting difficult

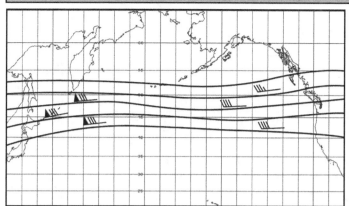

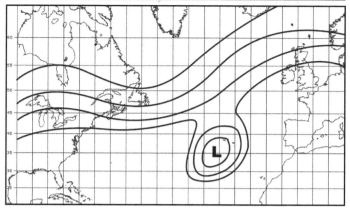

Figure 7.6-3. *Strong zonal flow aloft. This is an unstable pattern over either ocean, especially with stronger winds to the west. At any moment it could swoop into a large meridional wave, with dramatic influence on surface patterns that would be difficult to predict.*

Figure 7.6-4. *A cutoff low aloft. This low is about to break loose and carry on with a life of its own, making it difficult to predict its influence on the surface patterns. It is likely to remain more or less in place, but remains a loose cannon.*

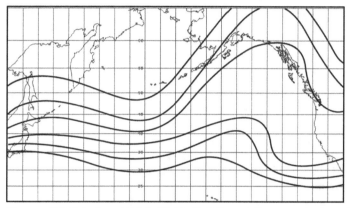

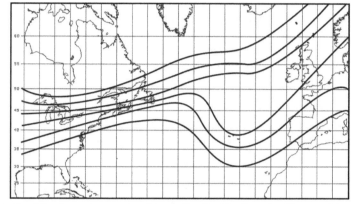

Figures 7.6-5. Left *and* **7.6-6.** Right. *Split flow aloft—around a trough in the Atlantic and around a ridge in the Pacific, though either could occur at any point along either ocean. It is easy to imagine that it could be difficult to predict which route a surface Low might follow when it hits the junction.*

Favorable upper level flow patterns that are more common to stable surface conditions

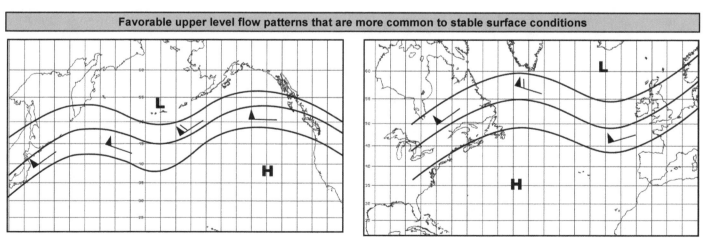

Figure 7.6-7. Left *and* **7.6-8.** Right. *Favorable wind aloft patterns. Winds aloft flowing in a smooth pattern for several days is a possible indicator for good surface forecasts. Especially if the winds are firm, say over 50 kts, and especially if they nicely wrap around the well known centers of action of the globe, namely, the Aleutian and Icelandic Lows and the Pacific and Atlantic Highs. This does not guarantee good forecasts, but chances are the surface forecast under one of these persistent patterns will be better than one underneath one of the changing patterns from Figures 7.6-3 to 7.6-6. We can, of course, also have very good forecasts without these particular shapes. This is just a very broad generalization, not taking into account what are indeed crucial details.*

i.e., the forecast is wrong. Then you have P = 8/10 = 80%. The forecast in this case has to have an 80% chance of being right, which makes you study the weather maps very carefully, look for ship reports, read the Forecast Discussions, etc. Do whatever you can to make some estimate of the probability that it will be right.

If the winds aloft were changing rapidly, and the present surface analysis did not match what you actually saw in pressure and wind, then you probably can't believe this is 80% likely—even though that is what they call for—and you might have to pass on this potentially winning maneuver. Or maybe jibe for just 3 hrs and then jibe back to wait another 3 hrs to get the next map. In other words, do half of what you want for the time being.

Table 7.6-1. Take-Point Probability

		RISK								
		1.0	*2.0*	*3.0*	*4.0*	*5.0*	*6.0*	*7.0*	*8.0*	*9.0*
GAIN	*1.0*	0.50	0.67	0.75	0.80	0.83	0.86	0.88	0.89	0.90
	2.0	0.33	0.50	0.60	0.67	0.71	0.75	0.78	0.80	0.82
	3.0	0.25	0.40	0.50	0.57	0.63	0.67	0.70	0.73	0.75
	4.0	0.20	0.33	0.43	0.50	0.56	0.60	0.64	0.67	0.69
	5.0	0.17	0.29	0.38	0.44	0.50	0.55	0.58	0.62	0.64
	6.0	0.14	0.25	0.33	0.40	0.45	0.50	0.54	0.57	0.60
	7.0	0.13	0.22	0.30	0.36	0.42	0.46	0.50	0.53	0.56
	8.0	0.11	0.20	0.27	0.33	0.38	0.43	0.47	0.50	0.53
	9.0	0.10	0.18	0.25	0.31	0.36	0.40	0.44	0.47	0.50

Needless to say, we will not be doing this level of analysis on every maneuver we make in response to the forecasts, but every navigator knows when a decision has some risk involved, and this is one way to think about it. There will always be nuances. Suppose it veers only 15°! Can you figure out what other boats might have done? And so on. If I am a container ship at sea, do I want to be influenced by what my sister ship has just done on the opposite route?

7.7 Ship Reports

Ship reports on OPC surface analysis maps have changed over the several editions of this book. Specific ship IDs were removed in 2008, and other data have subsequently been added, including SST. Their presentation, however, still could be much improved by seemingly simple graphic options. As it is now, it appears the reports are drawn first and then everything else is layered on top of them, rendering parts of the information illegible in frequent cases. With the new color maps, if the reports were on top, the fine lines of the reports would be visible without distracting from what is under them. On the other hand, as we see shortly, if we cannot read a specific report we need on a map, we can send an email to ask for the report in digital format, and actually learn even more.

The graphic layout of the reports are based on what is called a *station model*, but in the wake of recent sections, we should note that the word "model" in this application is unrelated to NWP models; it means here only a prescription for how to structure the report graphic. Ship reports use an abbreviated version of the full station model used on some land based maps, with the addition of SST. Examples with brief descriptions were introduced in Chapter 1 (Figure 1.6-1 and Table 1.6-1); the symbols are defined in Figure 7.7-1 with further elaboration. We see more of these reports on unified analysis maps since they cover land reports as well; OPC maps include only a few land based reports along the coast. Table 7.7-1 is an important reminder about wind symbols.

There is much to be learned from ship reports, so it can pay to study them carefully. If a crucial one is obscured by other symbols on the chart, we can get the numerical values of the report from the NDBC by email request as explained in Section 8.4.

Of particular interest is how well the reported pressure and wind agree with the isobars, which can call for referring to Section 2.4 on figuring the expected wind and interpolating isobars.

The reports occasionally include a present weather symbol (thunderstorm, fog, rain, and others) that can help interpret other data in the report. A full list of such symbols is in Appendix 11. Recent thunderstorm activity, for example, might explain why a wind report does not agree with the isobar spacings, and the nature of the rain might tell us where a front is located compared to where it is drawn on the map. More often, however, this weather symbol is missing, marked by an open circle at that location, which we might assume means no notable "weather" in effect (according to Appendix 11 options). Zoom in on the blank circle to look for tiny tick marks: top, bottom, or one on each side. These indicate clouds building, dissolving, or not changing. You will need a magnifying glass!

An often overlooked or under-used part of the report is the *pressure tendency*, PTDY, which is the change in mb over the past 3 hrs. Since the maps come every 6 hrs, this is intermediate to the last analysis we saw, so it can help us more precisely judge how the isobars are changing. When negotiating the corner of a High, this can be crucial information. Even more specific insight into this is in the *pressure tendency characteristic*, which is an even smaller symbol that is often obscured. They are defined in Table 7.7-3. Comparing these characteristics at several places around you, combined with the actual tendencies, gives a dynamic view of the pressure from a static map image. These can then be compared with your log or plot of recent pressures.

Ship and station reports on unified analysis maps are slightly different. The center section is a circle coded with cloud cover marked off in quadrants at 25% cover per segment. The color conventions are different, and there is no SST included. There is also more of them—sometimes too many, as seen in Figure 7.7-2—including reports with only

Table 7.7-1. Text Ship Reports Online or by Email														
	WDIR	WSPD	WVHT	DPD	PRES	PTDY	ATMP	WTMP	DEWP	VIS	TCC	S1HT	S1PD	S1DIR	HTSGW
	°T	kts	ft	sec	mb	mb	°F	°F	°F	nmi	8th	ft	sec	°T	ft
A	210	31.1	6.6	7	**998.4**	0.6	66.2	64.4	60.1	5	7	9.8	9	250	11.8
B	100	12	6.6	6	**1033.6**	-1.0	39.2	37.4	24.8	5	6	13.1	12	270	14.7
C	310	21	6.6	5	**1028.8**	1.5	66.0	64.4	48.9	11	6	9.8	12	270	11.8

Table Notes: *Section 8.4 on Sources explains several ways to obtain the reports in text format by email request.*

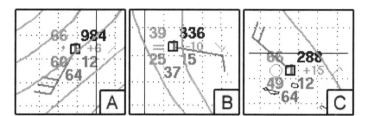

Figure 7.7-1. *Three ship reports, direct from a surface analysis, not cleaned up. These are actually fairly clean ones—there is usually obstruction on the symbols. The location of the report is inside the small square box at the tip of the wind arrow. Red is the air temp; green is dew point; blue is SST (WTMP), each in °F. Black is the last 3 digits of the pressure in mb. The blue arrow is the reported wind, see Table 7.7-2. It is best to use a protractor for the direction and not just guess it. The purple number is the SWH of the combined seas. This parameter (in WW3 called HTSGW) is not given in the text report directly. Here we added the column and computed it as HTSGW = SQRT(WVHT^2 + S1HT^2), using the SWH of the wind waves (WVHT) and the height of the dominant swell (S1HT). The smaller (±) orange numbers are ten times the pressure tendency (PTDY), which is how many mb the pressure changed in the past 3 hr. Compare values in Table 7.7-1. The small symbol to the right of PTDY is the pressure tendency characteristic code, explained in Table 7.7-3. Present weather symbols, when available, are on the left, below the air temp, but most reports do not have "weather," marked by an open circle, as in example C—the almost invisible tick mark at the bottom means clouds are dissolving. Tick at the top means clouds are developing. A tick on either side means no change in the clouds. A full list of these symbols is in Appendix 11. Dots mean rain; commas, drizzle; horizontal lines are fog.*

Table 7.7-2. Wind Symbols on Weather Maps			
Symbol	Nominal	Actual	Wind force ratio
⊢	5 kts	2.5 to 7.5	9.0
⊣	10 kts	7.5 to 12.5	2.8
⊣	15 kts	12.5 to 17.5	2.0
⊣	20 kts	17.5 to 22.5	1.7
⊣	35 kts	32.5 to 37.5	1.2

Table Notes: *The symbols are ± 2.5 kts. Wind force ratio is high end divided by low end, quantity squared. When displayed in a GRIB viewer or navigation program, we can read actual wind speed at a grid point with a mouse rollover at the tip of the arrow, and even read interpolated values between arrows.*

Table 7.7-3. Tendency Characteristic Symbols	
Description	*Map Symbol*
Increasing, then steady or Increasing, then increasing more slowly	╱‾
Increasing (steadily or unsteadily)	╱
Increasing, then increasing more rapidly Decreasing, then increasing Steady, then increasing	✓
Increasing, then decreasing	╱╲
Steady	—
Decreasing, then increasing	╲╱
Decreasing, then steady Decreasing, then decreasing more slowly	╲_
Decreasing (steadily or unsteadily)	╲
Decreasing, then decreasing more rapidly Steady, then decreasing Increasing, then decreasing	╲

one parameter, and indeed many report locations marked with no parameters given! These show just a circle with an "M" inside (it looks like an "H") meaning cloud coverage is missing, as is the other data normally shown.

Ship reports on radiofax maps are limited to wind and pressure, and an occasional weather symbol (Figure 7.7-2). When relying on just these radiofax versions it is useful to get the reports in text format when you need all the information you can get. That process and details of map file types is in Chapter 8.

These ship report examples near Hawaii happen to relate to earlier notes on how the OPC relies on more than just the GFS in making their analyses and forecasts. Figure 7.7-3 shows the GFS analysis overlaid on the OPC analysis. We notice that the OPC drew the 1020 isobar (orange) notably closer to the 1024 line above it, which would enhance the winds at these report sites. The GFS called for nominal 15 kts, whereas the reports were nominal 25 and 30. Both reports were also 1020 mb, which helps locate the isobar. The OPC

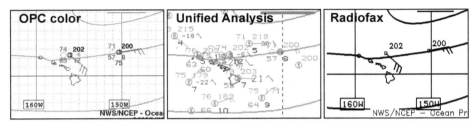

Figure 7.7-2. *Comparison of ship reports on three map types. The radiofax maps show only pressure, wind, and weather (missing in these samples). The extra reports in the UA map are congested and not used on the OPC map, but they are consistent with the three OPC isobars shown, 1016, 1020, and 1024, which supports moving the isobar.*

knows which ships have historically good reports. There are also ship reports we do not see.

But these reports were not alone in encouraging a shift—in my hypothetical reconstruction of the process! We happen to have ASCAT data over this region that did not make it into the GDAS in time to influence the 00z GFS analysis (Figure 7.7-4). It only covered one of the reports, but it shows solid 20+ kts of wind in the area, with almost 25 in the yellowish parts, which is more encouragement for the forecaster to tighten up the isobars. In short, experienced human forecasters who mind over the models remain a crucial step to getting the best forecasts.

Ship reports play a crucial role in both making the forecasts and then our interpretation of the forecasts. The system

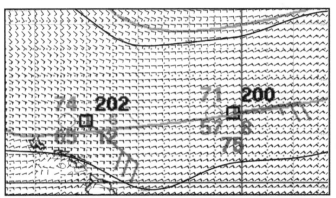

Figure 7.7-3. *GFS analysis (black wind and isobars) overlaid onto the OPC Analysis at 00z Jan 6, 2018. The GFS missed the pressure and wind speed at the two ship reports. It also very badly missed the winds on the leeward side of the islands, which is not surprising for a global model. NAM and HRRR, did a very good job in that region, as did the NDFD HI regional data.*

Figure 7.7-4. *An ASCAT pass over the region of Figure 7.7-3 just prior to the GFS analysis. The red dot marks the location of the 30-kt report, which at 2 PM local time could have been influenced by a squall.*

is not as convenient as we might like at the moment, but we can look ahead to new S-412/S-100 compliant displays that will present ship and buoy data in the same manner we now get data on aids to navigation using electronic navigational charts (ENC). Figure 7.7-5 is a hypothetical rendering of how this cursor pick display might one day look—with ENCs, we place the cursor over a charted object and left click to pop up a panel of attributes.

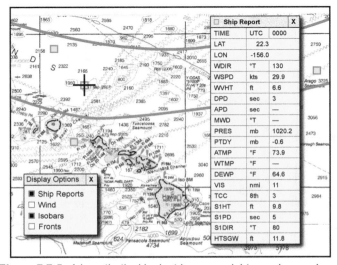

Figure 7.7-5. *A hypothetical look at how we might one day read ship reports and other weather data with the new S-412/S-100 standard on echart displays using a "cursor pick."*

Windy.com

The Czech website windy.com has become over the years an increasingly convenient and extensive global resource. Many parameters, at many levels, are animated with model forecasts from GFS, ECMWF, and NAM. This is one of the few places in public service where you can compare these models in detail—the popular commercial service PredictWind also offers this comparison. Windy.com also has spot reports that can be used for quick barometer checks, and versatile meteograms. You can overlay the 500-mb forecasts with the surface analysis to study this crucial interaction, or store buoy locations for quick checks on model accuracy.

Figure 7.7-6. *Windy.com logo on a small section of their global coverage.*

8.1 Overview

When we speak of sources, we benefit by making a couple distinctions. First, there is the vast set of resources we use when planning a trip, and second there are those real-time sources we use underway to choose our routes on a daily or even hourly basis.

To understand the real-time sources is the bigger task. We have to learn what types of products are available (maps, text, GRIBs...), and how each is used; we have to learn the communications options we have for obtaining these products underway (radio, fax, email...), and how to operate those systems; and finally we have to learn who provides these products (OPC, NOMADS, Saildocs, FTPmail...), and how we obtain them.

It is equally important to know and understand *both* resources: for planning and for use underway. It is fundamental, for example, that we do not head off on a voyage across hurricane prone waters right in the middle of the hurricane season. For many ocean passages it is these tropical storm seasons that dominate the planning, and the very first thing we need to look at.

Planning Sources

As we read in the newspaper and see on TV, there are indications of changes taking place on the statistics of tropical storms and global weather in general, but by and large we can count on established weather statistics for our ocean and coastal voyage planning—at least for sometime into the future (See a 1977 to 2017 comparison at starpath.com/wx).

Planning data are easy to find online, though frankly these data were also available prior to the internet. Good navigation supply stores had printed copies of the primary and even specialized references. But note the word "had." The early Navy Atlases, for example, are no longer available, and fewer outlets stock the printed references that are now readily available online.

The new, however, is not always better than the old. New electronic *Sailing Directions* available online are certainly more up to date than the older printed publications, but one thing they miss are the beautiful old sketches of the shorelines as seen from the water. These are rarely included any longer. Some may be outdated by new construction, but they could have been just deemed old-fashioned. So if you run across an old set of *Sailing Directions* for a region you might visit, it could be worth hanging on to them to add to your preparation for the approach. To be fair, the new ones do include many more actual photos of bays and harbors, but there remains appeal to the hand-drawn sketches. We can

still make our own after we get there, which will naturally highlight the features we want to note for a returning voyage.

Another feature missing from newer *Sailing Directions* is a list of typical radar ranges from which land can be detected. These too have been dropped, with the reasoning that radar is so different now than it was then that this data could be misleading. But this reasoning is not really applicable to typical yacht radar, and chances are we could benefit from this information on smaller vessels if we had it. Again, we make our own notes in the logbook.

There is a general tendency in all government publications toward less detail rather than more. *Planning Guides*, for example, contain much less climatic data than they used to in both meteorology and oceanography. On the other hand, the modern COGOW wind data are far superior to any historical data, so we have no reason to miss the older statistics.

Despite these few points mentioned, the *U.S. Coast Pilots*, *Sailing Directions*, and *Planning Guides* remain the primary references for ocean and coastal route planning, along with the counterparts to each of these publications from other nations around the world. Data from the *Coast pilot* for places like Chesapeake Bay, Puget Sound, the Great Lakes, and any other navigable waters of the U.S. are also used to plan a sailing vacation on purely inland waters as well. The regional climatic data they include are as good as any.

Section 8.2 on climatic sources outlines these publications and how to use them. These are mainly for longer term planning, such as best season or month for a specific voyage. A variation on climatic averages over many years is to look into, say, July conditions along a specific route over just the last few years. New access to archived data now allow this type of study.

Sources Underway

Once we leave the dock, we are dependent on wireless communications for updates on any weather preparation we made before leaving. Many of the products we would use underway have been discussed throughout the book, so this chapter focuses on details of obtaining them. In some circumstances (for example sailing in the trades), we might only need to check one source, once or twice a day; other times, when weather is changing or crucial decisions are needed, we would check as often as we can and as many sources as we can. Most ocean voyages include periods of heavy and lighter needs.

The way we get weather data underway is one of the areas that is changing the most quickly. We have new data sources and new communications options. On inland and coastal waters, NOAA Weather Radio over VHF (and its counterparts around the world) remains a main source for most mariners, but there are many supplements available, depending on our communications options. In U.S. ports, harbors, and marinas the traditional visual flags and light warnings of small-craft advisories, storms, and hurricane-force winds remain vital signs for many mariners not so engaged with the latest technologies.

The revolution in wireless communications invades the marine field just as it does all others. Where at one time we made telephone calls in coastal waters via the VHF radio operators, these services have all but vanished, being effectively replaced by cellphone communications. Likewise, offshore we once relied almost exclusively on HF (SSB) radio for both telephone communications and for weather, but this service for telephone calls is also long gone. There is still vessel-to-vessel voice communications, and some ham operators use HF for telephone patches to land lines, but most voice communications between vessels and between vessel and land is by satellite phone (satphone) these days. An exception to note are the several popular HF/SSB nets run by cruising sailors in various parts of the world. These groups keep each other informed of latest weather affecting their local regions with the opportunity to share observations.

In coastal waters, the VHF radio remains the primary means of communications amongst vessels. There are even cruiser's networks that meet at specific times to discuss weather and other matters on VHF. Ham operators have similar networks on 2-meters (VHF) devoted to local maritime affairs in some areas.

The big revolution that contributed most to the demise of HF voice high seas communications was the onset of easy to use free or inexpensive email via HF radio. Place a Pactor modem between your computer and your HF radio and you can communicate around the world, efficiently and inexpensively with email. My guess is this was more of a factor in the demise of HF phone calls than the availability of satphones, because the demise actually took place substantially before satphones became widely used. In fact it started at a time when the future of the satphones for recreational mariners was still in doubt. Now the use of satphones is more common than HF radios.

The other relevant change is the general use of computers onboard vessels underway. Most vessels nowadays have a computer onboard that is being routinely used in some capacity for communications or navigation. Electronic charting systems (ECS) are not only used for chart navigation; most of the systems are directly networked to sources of weather data that can be displayed on top of a navigation chart.

The previous edition of this book discussed smart phones and tablets as a potential revolution in marine navigation, but that is history now. Many vessels rely primarily on tablet navigation, as they are essentially compact laptop computers. Our first edition discussed use of "personal digital assistants (PDA)"—essentially a smartphone forerunner with apps, but no communications—as they were indeed one of the first versions of ECS. In the second edition, we were embarrassed about that, noting you could barely find that term in a Google search. But just like that old suit or dress you long put away that is now fashionable again, if you hear someone on the boat say "Alexa, get the latest surface analysis," you are using what the manufacturers call your personal "digital assistant." Things change, and then change again.

What has not changed, and likely will not change in the near future is the primary source of the data we use. Not considering international use of foreign weather services, the weather data we get, no matter the direct or apparent source, originates from the various Centers of the NWS. Third parties often provide very useful packaging and distribution of the data, but the primary source remains the NWS. Even the specialized services that do indeed add levels of scrutiny and evaluation to the products they distribute, rely themselves on primary data from NWS—or from the Navy's Fleet Numerical Meteorology and Oceanography Center (FNMOC) in Monterey CA. The U.S. is unique in having two complete, independent weather services, although they do collaborate on several crucial programs.

One could imagine a system where the distribution of NWS data was delegated entirely to third parties, or more to the point, that individuals or shipping companies choose to get all of their weather from a commercial provider, rather than from the NWS directly. For many years now there have been private, national and international, companies providing not just weather data but actual weather routing for commercial shipping and recreational sailing. This has proven very successful over the years, providing mariners with safe, efficient routing by true experts with sophisticated analysis tools of their own. Again though, the basic data they work with is from the NWS, or its international counterparts.

But there have been notable failures in the reliance on commercial weather delivery—each that I know of traceable to breakdowns in communications, not quality of information. Thus we return to the prudence of all mariners knowing what is available to them underway from readily accessible public sources, and the value of knowing how to incorporate what they are told about the weather with what they see on the water.

8.2 Climatic Sources for Voyage Planning

The obvious first step in planning any voyage is to be sure we are not headed off at a time when the weather is *expected* to be bad based on historical records. This is especially true when sailing in or across those parts of the tropics that are prone to tropical storms and hurricanes in certain seasons. It also applies to planning trips in many other waterways around the world subject to severe weather.

The statistics of tropical storms are doubly important to know because there is no indication of these storms in climatic wind data such as the COGOW data (See Section 10.6), which is usually the first check point for planning sailing voyages, coastal or ocean.

Without some research, for example, one might consider delivering a yacht from San Francisco to Seattle in December. And unless your insurance company stopped you before you left, you might learn very quickly why this is usually a bad idea. Not only can the winds be strong (hurricane force at times) and the seas huge, there are oftentimes few if any places to hide along the coast, and turning back against the southerlies is not often a choice either. The few ports along the coast that might otherwise give refuge are inside of river bars that are often very dangerous to cross, effectively closing the harbors for long periods of time (Section 8.7).

With winter bad for this trip, you might (still without research) choose August instead, only to find that it too might not be as good as you would guess. August could present you with very strong northerlies right on the nose along the whole route.

So what month is best on this route? Is it different on the East Coast? And should we sail right along the shoreline, or head offshore and follow the coast from much farther out? These are the types of questions we can answer by studying standard resources, which are readily available.

The same type of inquiry could apply to much shorter routes, even on inland waters. Is it better to cross the Strait of Juan de Fuca in the morning or in the afternoon? And why would that matter? (The answer is in the next subsection). If I am going to sail (or paddle) around an island today, which is the best direction to go as far as wind is concerned? Do tidal currents change that choice? And so on.

Needless to say, we sail in the weather, not in the climate—meaning what is really happening when we are there, and not the average for that time of year—but that should not dissuade us from choosing the optimum times to have the best chance for good conditions. It could be crucial to the planning of a charter sailing vacation. The boats may be available all year long, but the wind might be much better in one season than another, on average.

There are several primary sources for climatic data, and the most important one depends on the waterways involved. For U.S. inland and coastal waters the most important is almost always the *U.S. Coast Pilot*. Online archives and live data could be useful as well.

For planning offshore sailing and ocean passages, the CO-GOW wind data, Pilot Charts, *Planning Guides*, and *Sailing Directions* become the primary sources for the major crossings, but useful information might also be found in special sources, especially for individual harbors. And don't forget to check the hydrographic offices (iho.int) of the countries you plan to visit. Some are a real wealth of navigational information.

We cover sources individually below, but first a reminder about the timing of the planning we are talking about. The resources covered in this section are for longer term planning, meaning next month, or next season, or what month is

best for a particular voyage, or what route do I take across the ocean in July versus May, and so on. When it comes down to a short cruise of a day or so, to take place in the next few days, then we would use different resources. We now have access to GFS forecasts that extend out 16 days! And though we would not want to rely on these long-range data to any great extent once underway, chances are they are still better than relying on the averages accumulated over many years when it comes to short-range planning.

In other words, suppose the climatic data calls for a 15-kt northerly along this route for this time of year, which is just what we want, and in fact just what we have at the moment—in support of the climatic predictions. But we want to go early next week, not right now, and we have access to model forecasts that call for strong southerlies building in about 8 days. Not long ago, we would not have had this information. It used to be that a 96-hr forecast was the longest look into the future we had, which in some respects was a blessing, as it is likely as far as we dare look and hope to have any reliability. But now we can see what at least one numerical weather model thinks is going to happen well beyond that—based on all it knows about what is going on now. Chances are we are better off believing it, at least enough to wait a few days before choosing the week-from-now departure. Once we are within 96 hrs of the proposed departure time, we can start to see what OPC meteorologists think is going to take place, not just what one computer thinks. We may also have other independent model predictions to work with.

So the message is, we are covering longer-term planning here, not near-term planning, which is more of a tactics topic, covered in Chapter 9.

U.S. Coast Pilots

The *U.S. Coast Pilot* is a series of nine navigation reference books (in print, about 9" × 11" × 2") maintained by NOAA's Office of Coast Survey that cover a wide variety of information important to navigators of U.S. coastal and intracoastal waters, and waters of the Great Lakes. There are free PDF versions of each volume (nauticalcharts.noaa.gov). Most of their content cannot be shown graphically on nautical charts and is not readily available elsewhere. This information includes regulations, outstanding landmarks, channel and anchorage peculiarities, dangers, weather, ice, freshets, pilots, port facilities, notes on local currents, and more.

Having the appropriate *Coast pilot* on board (in some format) is fundamental to navigation; the General Information section is required reading for all navigators. These books are also the best sources of climatic marine weather data for all U.S. waters. The data include wind speed and direction, sea state, temperatures, visibility, and pressures. Areas covered by each volume are illustrated in Figure 8.2-1. *Coast Pilots* are updated once a year, but for most applications to small-craft navigation, having even an outdated *Coast Pilot* is much better than none at all. Each year there is a USCG Special Notice to Mariners that lists the past year's changes.

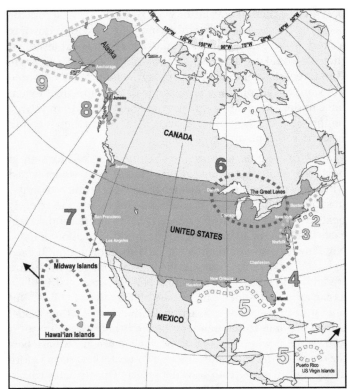

Figure 8.2-1. U.S. Coast Pilot *coverage by volume number.*

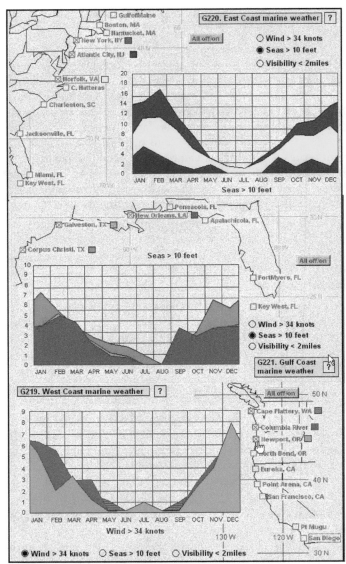

Appendix A to each *Coast Pilot* is a comprehensive list of addresses and phone numbers for all agencies that provide services related to marine navigation, weather, and communications. Some private agencies or commissions are also included.

Weather information is included in three separate locations in each *Coast Pilot*: (1) The Introductions to each section and each chapter include general discussions relevant

Figure 8.2-2. Below. *Sample climatic data from Appendix B of* Coast Pilot Vol. 2. *Even more specific data are shown for another sample location in Figure 8.2-4. Superscript (1) means percent frequency from ship reports, with the caution that ships tend to avoid bad weather so severe conditions are likely underestimates.*

Figure 8.2-3. Above. *Sample Coast Pilot data (as shown in Figure 8.2-2) converted to an interactive app display. The seasonal windows for coastal travel show up clearly with such a display. Similar plots could be made from an Excel graph of the Appendix B data.*

METEOROLOGICAL TABLE – COASTAL AREA SOUTH OF NANTUCKET, MA Between 40°N to 41°N and 66°W to 70°W													
WEATHER ELEMENTS	**JAN**	**FEB**	**MAR**	**APR**	**MAY**	**JUN**	**JUL**	**AUG**	**SEP**	**OCT**	**NOV**	**DEC**	**ANNUAL**
Wind > 33 knots [1]	8.1	7.2	5.7	2.8	0.6	0.3	0.2	0.4	1.2	2.9	4.9	7.4	3.2
Wave Height > 9 feet [1]	14.5	13.5	10.6	7.7	3.2	1.4	0.6	1.1	2.5	5.2	8.8	11.5	6.3
Visibility < 2 nautical miles [1]	6.6	8.8	9.9	13.6	23.5	27.5	27.8	17.2	8.9	5.0	4.7	4.2	14.3
Precipitation [1]	15.6	13.9	9.8	9.1	6.3	4.7	4.3	4.9	5.4	7.0	9.7	13.4	8.3
Temperature > 69° F	0.1	0.0	0.1	0.1	0.6	5.9	27.3	39.5	19.3	3.9	0.4	0.1	8.3
Mean Temperature (°F)	39.9	39.8	41.1	45.1	51.6	59.9	66.9	68.7	65.3	58.8	51.8	44.1	53.1
Temperature < 33° F [1]	17.2	19.2	7.8	1.2	0.2	0.0	0.1	0.1	0.0	0.0	0.3	6.3	4.0
Mean RH (%)	83	83	83	85	87	88	89	87	84	81	81	82	85
Overcast or Obscured [1]	45.5	42.4	37.8	35.7	38.6	36.9	34.9	27.6	25.8	26.1	35.2	42.2	35.6
Mean Cloud Cover (8ths)	6.0	5.7	5.2	4.7	5.0	4.9	4.9	4.5	4.3	4.5	5.4	5.9	5.1
Mean SLP (mbs)	1015	1015	1015	1015	1016	1016	1016	1017	1018	1018	1016	1016	1016
Ext. Max. SLP (mbs)	1044	1049	1054	1049	1047	1040	1037	1040	1050	1051	1047	1056	1056
Ext. Min. SLP (mbs)	962	965	967	961	976	983	987	987	986	972	972	963	961
Prevailing Wind Direction	NW	NW	NW	W	SW	SW	SW	SW	NE	W	NW	NW	W
Thunder and Lightning [1]	0.5	0.4	0.3	0.3	0.5	0.6	0.7	0.9	0.8	0.6	0.5	0.3	0.5

WEATHER ELEMENTS	JAN.	FEB.	MAR.	APR.	MAY	JUN.	JUL.	AUG	SEP	OCT.	NOV.	DEC.	YEAR	YEARS OF RECORD
KEY WEST, FL (24° 33'N, 88° 39'W) elevation = 20 feet (6 m)														
SEA LEVEL PRESSURE*														
Mean (Millibars)	1019.5	1018.6	1017.2	1016.3	1015.6	1015.8	1017.5	1016.1	1014.4	1014.7	1016.8	1018.9	1016.8	44
TEMPERATURE (DEGREES F)														
Mean	70.2	71.0	74.1	77.2	80.7	83.4	84.7	84.6	83.5	80.3	75.9	71.6	78.1	46
Mean Daily Maximum	74.9	75.8	78.8	81.8	85.2	87.9	89.4	89.5	88.2	84.6	80.0	76.1	82.7	46
Mean Daily Minimum	64.9	65.7	68.9	72.1	75.7	78.3	79.4	79.2	78.3	75.5	71.3	66.6	73.0	46
Extreme - Highest	86	85	88	90	91	94	95	95	94	93	89	88	95	46
Extreme - Lowest	41	45	47	48	64	68	69	68	69	60	49	44	41	46
RELATIVE HUMIDITY														
Average Percentage	70.0	60.6	47.5	37.6	31.0	33.3	49.7	35.8	19.5	21.7	43.3	64.0	42.7	46
CLOUD COVER														
Percent of time Clear	21.7	25.0	21.0	19.1	13.3	4.4	2.4	2.0	2.1	11.2	17.6	20.7	13.3	44
Percent of time Scattered	32.2	33.6	36.1	39.0	39.5	32.9	31.1	30.5	28.3	36.9	35.3	31.7	33.9	44
Percent of time Broken	23.2	23.0	23.4	24.5	27.7	33.4	40.4	41.6	40.9	28.5	25.1	24.2	29.7	44
Percent of time Overcast	16.5	13.1	13.6	12.0	12.9	20.1	15.9	15.3	18.6	15.5	14.9	16.1	15.4	44
PRECIPITATION														
Mean Amount (inches)	2.22	1.50	1.70	1.97	3.23	4.80	3.65	5.08	6.43	4.80	2.44	2.08	39.90	46
Greatest Amount (inches)	17.64	4.46	9.69	10.60	12.90	14.43	11.69	10.43	18.45	21.57	27.67	11.18	62.92	46
Least Amount (inches)	T	0.02	T	0.00	0.34	0.33	0.44	2.23	1.70	0.74	T	0.07	19.99	46
Maximum Amount-24 hrs (inches)	6.42	2.54	5.26	6.19	7.20	5.14	3.05	3.29	6.06	6.49	22.75	6.66	22.75	46
Mean Number of Days with Precipitation	11	9	9	8	11	16	17	19	21	16	11	12	160	46
WIND														
% of Observations with Gales	0.00	0.01	0.00	0.00	0.00	0.03	0.00	0.00	0.18	0.09	0.03	0.01	0.18	45
Mean Wind Speed (knots)	10.4	10.5	10.6	10.6	9.3	8.4	8.2	8.0	8.5	9.6	10.5	10.3	9.5	45
Direction (percentage of observations)														
North	9.5	10.4	8.0	7.0	4.9	2.6	1.6	2.4	2.8	6.6	8.1	9.2	6.1	45
North Northeast	11.2	9.6	6.5	4.8	3.4	1.9	1.4	2.1	2.7	8.7	11.8	12.9	6.4	45
Northeast	15.7	12.0	7.5	6.0	4.4	3.2	3.0	4.5	6.7	17.3	20.2	18.6	9.9	45
East Northeast	12.0	9.2	7.1	7.8	6.5	5.0	5.6	7.6	10.8	18.7	17.3	14.3	10.2	45
East	9.1	8.6	9.7	12.1	12.5	10.3	11.6	11.8	12.8	11.2	9.5	9.0	10.7	45
	10.0	11.1	14.8	18.8	20.5	18.6	23.8	19.8	18.4	10.0	9.2	9.4	15.4	45
	7.8	10.1	14.7	15.1	17.0	18.8	21.2	18.9	13.9	6.8	6.6	7.4	13.2	45
East		5.1	7.2	5.9	7.3	9.4	9.0	8.7	6.6	3.3	2.5	2.9	6.0	45
East Southeast			5.4	3.8	4.7	7.9	6.3	5.8	5.5	2.7	2.1	2.8	4.6	45
Southeast	10.2	1			2.5	4.8	2.9	3.1	3.4	1.8	1.2	1.3	2.5	45
South Southeast	9.1	9.6	10.2		.3	2.8	3.0	2.9	1.8	1.5	1.4	2.3	45	
South	9.5	9.6	9.3	9.1	7.9					1.1	0.8	1.1	1.4	45
South Southwest	9.1	9.6	9.3	9.2	7.4	8.7	7.4	7.1			0.7	0.8	1.0	45
Southwest	8.3	8.9	8.6	8.3	7.3	7.7	7.3	7.2	8.4	9		1.1	1.3	45
West Southwest	7.8	8.5	9.8	8.3	7.7	7.1	6.9	7.7	7.7	8.1	7.6		2.4	45
West	8.2	8.6	9.2	8.9	7.5	6.5	5.8	6.8	9.3	7.1	7.1		.5	45
West Northwest	10.3	11.5	10.3	10.0	7.9	6.2	6.3	6.5	6.8	6.8	8.7			5
Northwest	12.3	12.4	12.2	10.1	7.7	6.1	6.7	7.0	7.6	8.1	10.3	11.9	9.7	45
North Northwest	13.4	12.9	12.5	10.8	8.1	6.8	7.6	7.1	7.6	9.7	11.9	12.6	10.9	45
VISIBILITY														
Mean Number of Days with Fog	3	2	1	Miss	Miss	1	Miss	1	1	1	1	2	13	46
% Observations with Visibility <= ½ mile	0.17	0.16	0.03	0.01	0.01	0.01	0.02	0.02	0.05	0.03	0.02	0.13	0.05	45

Figure 8.2-4. *Sections of Climatology Tables for Key West, FL from Appendix B of* U.S. Coast Pilot, Vol. 5.

to the entire area covered. (2) In the individual sections as the book proceeds along the coast, local weather is discussed when significant. And (3), Appendix B includes statistics for major ports and sections of the coastal waters covered. Sample data are shown in Figures 8.2-2. Figure 8.2-3 shows one way to present the statistics, and Figure 8.2-4 shows another format they use for more specific data.

Referring back to the question posed on crossing the Strait of Juan de Fuca: *Coast Pilot Vol. 7* tells us that during the summer, the sea breeze in the Strait of Juan de Fuca gets strongly channeled in the late afternoon, building up to 25 kts routinely on clear days. Early morning winds in the Strait are often light or calm, though the region may be engulfed in thick sea fog. Thus you get a nice navigator's choice of crossing a strait that has a lot of ship traffic in light air and thick fog or clear weather and strong winds! It is about a 10-mile crossing, exposed to the open ocean to the west.

In a nutshell, I would think that every navigator would want a PDF copy of each Coast Pilot they might need right in their cellphones. These can be viewed in standard ebook readers, with all the search, bookmarking, and annotation features those apps offer. One way to do that is to download the PDF on a computer then email it to yourself and choose to open in one of the readers.

Similar navigation reference publications produced by the U.S. for foreign waters are called *Sailing Directions* and *Planning Guides*. They are published by the National Geospatial-intelligence Agency (NGA). Canadian coast pilots, on the other hand, are called "*Sailing Directions*" and British coast pilots are called "*Pilots*." Canadian and British versions are copyrighted print products only. *British Admiralty Pilots* are divided into smaller regional books, each very expensive, but also very comprehensive.

Pilot Charts

For inland and coastal routes the *Coast Pilot* is your first traditional reference for planning. For offshore sailing the relevant Pilot Chart has traditionally been the first resource to consider for overall weather and oceanographic data—not counting various commercial books that propose ocean routes and sailing seasons; we mention a few of these later on. Since 2010 or so, COGOW (See Section 10.6) would be the first place to check for wind data alone, but Pilot Charts include far more than just wind data.

Pilot charts are semi-permanent publications from the NGA based on data provided by the U.S. Naval Oceanographic Office and NOAA. They are charts of a major ocean area intended to be used in conjunction with regular navigational charts and other aids to navigation. The chart presents in graphic form averages obtained from data gathered over many years in meteorology and oceanography to aid the navigator in selecting the quickest and safest routes. Included are explanations on how to use each type of information depicted on the chart. A sample section is shown in Figure 8.2-5.

Pilot Charts are available in printed sets of months for each ocean from sellers listed at the end of this section. Most Pilot Charts are also online as free hi-res PDF files at the NGA website (under publications, at msi.nga.mil). The opencpn. org community has also converted each Pilot Chart into an RNC echart that loads into any ECS or ECDIS. These are super convenient, valuable resources. Find them in the chart

download section of their website. Pilot Charts are part of American maritime tradition, in use since before the Civil War—and of some historic interest in that the motivator of the project (Matthew Fontaine Maury) defected to the South when the war started.

Sailing Directions and Planning Guides

Sailing Directions Enroute and *Planning Guides* are NGA publications that cover information for foreign waters similar to that presented in the *U.S. Coast Pilots* for U.S. waters. The discussion of *Coast Pilot* content above applies to these books as well. The term *Sailing Directions* is used generically to describe any book or document that discusses navigational matters and related information for mariners. It also serves to some extent to be a compilation of tested local knowledge of the regions covered, along with various national and international legal matters related to navigation. *Sailing Directions Enroute* are online as free downloads from the publications section msi.nga.mil. Regions covered by individual volumes are shown in Figure 8.2-6.

Planning Guides are special editions of the *Sailing Directions* that cover broader areas (ocean basins) and more general information. They are intended to assist mariners in planning ocean voyages and eliminate duplication by consolidating useful information about countries adjacent to a particular ocean basin. They include extensive climatology and oceanography data, as well as legal procedures that apply in the adjacent countries. Available *Planning Guides* are indicated in Figure 8.2-6 by boxed numbers. Both of these valuable resources should be checked for international voyaging.

Mariners Weather Log

The *Mariners Weather Log* is a print and PDF publication of the NWS that contains articles, news and information about marine weather events and phenomena, storms at sea, and weather forecasting. It is a popular newsletter/ journal for the Voluntary Observing Ship (VOS) Program,

Figure 8.2-5. *Section of a U.S. Pilot Chart. August winds near Cuba are given for each 2° of Lat-Lon. In the top right corner, the wind has a 39% probability of being from the east and 32% from the southeast. When the probability is less than 29%, it is represented by the length of the line, which is relative to a printed scale not shown here.*

Predicted wind speeds are in Beaufort Force numbers, with each side of a feather being one number. In the top right the E and SE winds are Force 4 (11 to 16 kts), the much less likely NE wind would be Force 3 (7 to 10 kts).

The circled numbers are the percentage calms at each location. The current arrows on this chart are marked with speed in kts with a "steadiness" depicted by the line style: a heavy line means 50% steady, thinner lines means 25% to 50% steady, and a dashed current arrow means steadiness is less than 25%. See the steady Gulf Stream near Florida, and the weak unsteady back-stream south of Cuba. Other Pilot Charts do not have the steadiness data and some give the speeds in nmi drift per day instead of knots. Magnetic variation and a few segments of great circle routes with waypoints and leg distances are also visible.

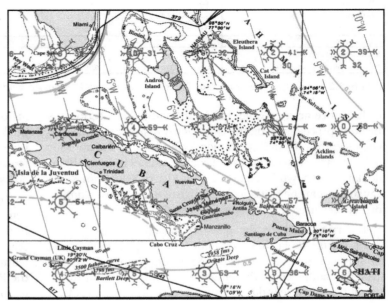

Port Meteorological Officers (PMOs), cooperating ships officers, and their vessels. It is a comprehensive chronicle on marine weather. The Log is currently published three times per year (April, August, & December). The online edition is free from vos.noaa.gov/mwl.shtml. Back issues are available online from 1998 on. Earlier editions that date from its inception in the early 80's can be found in libraries.

Each year they do a summary of both tropical and extratropical storm statistics in a convenient, easy to read format. There are other sources for the tropical storms (NHC among others), but this is a unique source for a discussion of extratropical storms, which are of far more interest to mariners. As pointed out elsewhere in the book, although hurricanes cause tremendous damage and suffering on land, they have less actual impact on mariners. They are so well forecasted and tracked that we can, and do, usually avoid them, whereas neither is true for giant extratropical storms of higher latitudes.

We also include a reference to the Log in Chapter 4 on strong wind systems, because in each issue they do a wonderful analysis of individual strong storms that took place since the previous issue, along with firsthand accounts from mariners who faced them. There is also usually an article or two of general marine weather interest in each issue. They are usually written on an informative, yet non-technical level.

Archived Weather Data

Periodically we need to look at marine weather conditions, somewhere on earth, sometime in the past. How we do this has changed recently as NOAA agencies were restructured. Now the primary source for historical data are the National Centers for Environmental Information (NCEI), formerly National Climatic Data Center (NCDC). This is the source for past weather maps, text observations and forecasts, and even GRIB files of model forecasts and ASCAT data. In short, we have a powerful resource for studying past conditions if needed for research or training.

For a text archive of conditions *at specific stations*, the most direct access is from the historical links at the bottom of any station report from the National Data Buoy Center (NDBC). This provides an hourly (or more frequently) list of all the data that the station offers, back many years in time. The data can be imported to a spreadsheet for further analysis.

For maps and other products we turn to NCEI (ncei.noaa.gov), but are quickly confronted with good news and bad news. The good news is there is an amazing amount of archived weather data available; the bad news is, it is not as easy to locate products we might want, such as OPC forecasts and analyses for past dates. The data are indeed there. For example, at the time of this writing, this is the key link to the maps: ncei.noaa.gov/thredds/model/ncep_charts.html. The top folders are the archived unified analyses and several oth-

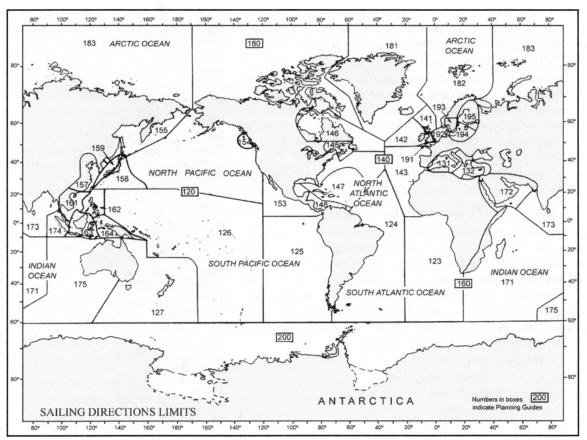

Figure 8.2-6. *Regions covered by Sailing Directions volumes and Planning Guides (boxed numbers).*

er formats; the OPC maps are at the bottom called "NCEP Charts Ocean Analysis" and "NCEP Charts Ocean Forecasts." Unfortunately, for now it is difficult to find a logical path of links to get there.

The problem is, at the moment, all the related agencies (OPC, NO-MADS, NCEI) are changing their websites and their policies on who does what—which is not uncommon. Every indication is these latest changes will be improvements, and we will eventually have better access to more products. In the meantime we wait for things to settle into place. We have articles and videos at starpath.com/wx that go over the ways to get to specific historical data, and we will update these as needed.

Another historical product of interest are model forecasts in GRIB format. These are also available (all NCEP models), but with new changes at NOMADS and NCEI, after Jan 1, 2018 we can no longer easily request data for a specific Lat-Lon window. The data are all there, but now we must download the full globe or full region for a model and work with that. These are large files and not all GRIB viewers will load them. For example, take archived GFS analyses at nomads.ncdc.noaa.gov/data/gfsanl. These are large files (50-60 MB) with hundreds of parameters. LuckGrib is one viewer that will show these files; otherwise a special viewer would be required such as the remarkable Panoply for Mac or PC (giss.nasa.gov/tools/panoply). There are examples and tutorials on accessing and displaying archived model data at starpath.com/wx.

When looking for recent model data, note that any GRIB file available via Saildocs can be accessed from their server for 30 days after its valid time with a custom request, as explained in Section 8.3

Archived copies of graphic ASCAT winds can be found at the OSWT website (manati.star.nesdis.noaa.gov/datasets/ASCATData.php) by simply selecting the date at the top of the page. This is a powerful tool for looking up actual ocean winds on specific days in the past. Thus if you do ever need to recreate a voyage or yacht race, you can go back and find the actual winds at the time.

When it comes to the tropics and the concern for tropical storms, the National Hurricane Center, NHC (nhc.noaa.gov) is pretty much one stop shopping. The Archives section gives full details of every storm, organized by year and region, and the Climatology section (under Educational Resources) has statistics such as those presented in Figure 8.2-7 on how formation zones and tracks change throughout the season. Tropical analysis and forecast maps, on the other hand, are found at the NCEI, as discussed above.

U.S. Navy Forecaster Handbooks

For this edition, we have moved forward and archived several older weather resources at starpath.com/wx. But there is one set of older sources that we should not overlook, so long as they are available, which are the remarkable *Forecaster Handbooks* from the Naval Research Laboratory (nrlmry.navy.mil/pubs.html). They include in-depth reports on marine weather in specific locations, including much data on European ports. Available volumes are listed below—several of which have been updated to modern information.

01. Japan and Adjacent Seas
02. Philippine Islands and Surrounding Waters
03. South Korea and Adjacent Seas
04. Arctic
05. Aleutians, Bering Sea and Gulf of Alaska
06. Central America and Adjacent Waters

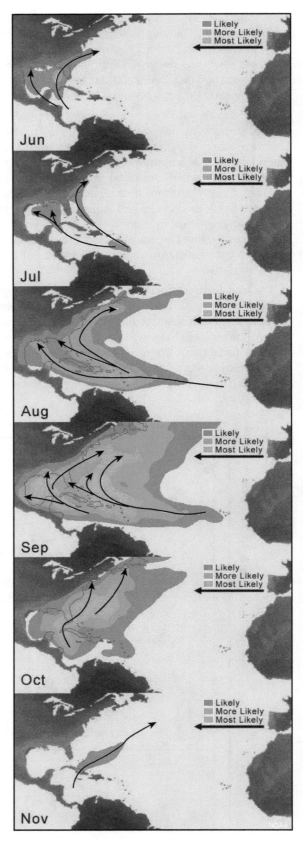

Figure 8.2-7. *Formation zones and tracks of SW Atlantic hurricanes by month. From the NHC web page.*

07. Middle East/Arabian Sea
08. Handbook for Forecasters in the Mediterranean
09. Regional Forecasting Aids for the Mediterranean Basin
10. Digest of Selected Weather Problems Mediterranean
11. European Severe Weather Port Guide
12. Sea Ice Analysis and Forecasting
13. Typhoon Havens Handbook, Pacific
14. Hurricane Havens Handbook, North Atlantic
15. Puget Sound Area Heavy Weather Port Guide
16. South Africa and Atlantic/Indian Ocean Transit
17. Bay of Bengal
18. Meteorological Phenomena Arabian Sea
19. Winter Shamal in the Persian Gulf
20. Indian Ocean
  Part 1 The Red Sea and Persian Gulf
  Part 2 The Gulf of Aden and West Arabian Sea
  Part 3 The Persian Gulf and Gulf of Oman
  Part 4 The Makran Coast from Gwadar to Karachi
  Part 5 West Coast of India with Notes on Bombay
  Part 6 East Coast of India and Ceylon
  Part 7 The Coast of Burma
  Part 8 The South Indian Ocean
  Part 9 Coast of East Africa
21. Tropical Cyclone Forecaster's Reference Guide

Clearly we have tremendous resources for knowing ahead of time what to expect for most waterways of the world. Prudent navigators will check these documented sources and not be surprised by known systems. The amount of research we do depends on the time we have to plan and the goals in mind. For U.S. coastal waters, we get prudent coverage from the Coast Pilots. For international waters, there is more work do to. Sailing in the tropics always calls for careful study of tropical storm statistics.

Racing sailors want to know all they can about a new race course, domestic or overseas. I am sure America's Cup weather consultants dig up every single piece of data available for a race course in the run-up to an event.

Where to Buy Printed Nav Pubs

These days the U.S. government is pretty much out of the printing business. They have passed on navigation publications to third party printers, while at the same time offering free PDF versions of most publications. Navigation suppliers typically have active online stores, so printed copies of key publications are easy to come by, which is good, because certain pubs are required on some vessels. Nautical chart dealers typically carry related navigation publications. A list is online at nauticalcharts.noaa.gov, but they have an unusual policy on who they include; many leading outlets are not included! See starpath.com/wx for additional sources.

8.3 Weather by Email

As time goes by, there will likely be more use of internet at sea, but for now this is still an expensive option. The affordable alternative is well established. We can receive all the working weather data we need by email request. It takes the form of a file attachment to an email received over HF radio or satphone—communications options are discussed in Section 8.5.

The official email source is the NWS program called FTPmail, which advertises itself as offering *all* NWS products by email request. The most popular unofficial source, which is the sole source for many mariners worldwide, is the extensive complimentary service offered by saildocs.com. Both have been discussed several places early in the book, as it is valuable to start using both as soon as possible. In this section we cross reference earlier discussion and add more specific notes on the use of each system.

FTPmail

A good way to understand FTPmail is to use a browser and go to this page: tgftp.nws.noaa.gov. This is the folder on the NWS computer that stores all the latest NWS weather data available by FTPmail, which includes the latest weather maps, text forecasts, discussions, and latest station observations. There are several folders there, but the files we need will all be in either the /fax or /data folders, or sub-folders of the latter. Viewed from a browser, you can just click a file to view it—PNG, JPG, GIF, and TXT files will open immediately, TIF files may have to be downloaded to view.

There are several advertised ways to learn about the program, but they are redundant and complex documents. The best approach is to skip them all, and use only the instructions in Appendix B (called A-8 in the Table of Contents) of this file: nws.noaa.gov/os/marine/rfax.pdf. If you have any version dated earlier than Sept 21, 2017, it should be updated at that link. This PDF not only explains the process, but provides interactive links for many of the products that create an email with the right format for the request. Don't be misled by the title, *Worldwide Marine Radiofacsimile Broadcast Schedules*; FTPmail has nothing to do with radiofax, but we might need those fax schedules for other applications (Section 8.5). As long as we know where the FTPmail info is located, we are covered. (Maybe some day they will add FTPmail to the title and fix the table of contents... And remove all the other help files.) New reference sources are being created. See Information/Product Guides at the OPC website.

The way FTPmail works is, we send an email to their server (nws.ftpmail.ops@noaa.gov) that includes actual command level instructions to their computer. We tell it to "open" a connection to the root directory (tgftp.nws.noaa.gov), then change directory ("cd") to either "fax" or "data," and maybe subdirectories of "data," and then we tell it to "get" the file we want. The get command means return a copy of the file to us by email. Then, so we do not leave their computer hanging, waiting for more commands, we must tell it to "quit," which closes the connection.

It is a systematic process, but since we are working with actual computer commands, no typos are allowed. Also such commands are case sensitive, so we must type the file name exactly as presented. The process reduces to knowing the file name of what we want, and the directory path to it. A sample request in Section 7.3 shows that you can ask for more than one file at a time, and even get files from one directory and then change to a new directory in the same string of commands, although these could also be sent separately.

Once you have an email set up that gets you what you want, you can then just re-send the same email later for updates. Graphic indexes of map files are in Figures 7.2-1 and 7.2-6; Appendix B of rfax.pdf lists all of the map files by name, most with a direct (mailto:) link to create the email in your default mail program. See also Table 8.3-1. In other cases, they give a prescription of how you create a request for specific text reports.

It is important to remember that FTPmail does not address any issues at all of file size. PYAA12.gif (latest western Atlantic analysis) is about 90 kB, whereas PYAA12.TIF downloads as about 35 kB, a notable factor in airtime. Saildocs, discussed next, offers the valuable service of reducing map files by a factor of two, sending us TIF version at a scant 18 kB. This feature favors using Saildocs for weather maps.

For completeness, although we do not get GRIB formatted model forecasts by FTPmail, we could in principle get the NDFD forecasts in GRIB format. But the files are too large for wireless transfer at sea. Articles at starpath.com/wx explain accessing these with an internet connection, but for use underway we need third party providers who package these for us in limited Lat-Lon windows.

Saildocs

This is an email weather service developed by Jim Corenman in 1999 for SailMail users (sailmail.com), but you can use it to obtain weather data even if you do not use SailMail for your high seas email service, though many using it do use both of these fine services. There is a modest cost per year for the SailMail program (as there is for all wireless email programs), but the Saildocs weather service is open to all at no charge who agree to their terms of usage. It is easy to use and popular among sailors worldwide.

Start by sending a blank email to info@saildocs.com, which will return the initial set of instructions. We request products from Saildocs by writing to query@saildocs.com, and in the body of the message list the items we want, each preceded by "send," one request per line. Like FTPmail, Saildocs can return any of the products listed at tgftp.nws.noaa.gov, but the protocol for requesting them is different, and they offer products from other sources, in particular, GRIB forecasts from several models, as well as oceanic NDFD. They also offer several unique services not available from other sources, such as sending outdated GRIB files (up to 30 days old) and providing custom image and data deliveries from outside of standard NOAA sources.

As when using any such broad resource, we have to learn how best to get what we want. We could, for example, send this message to query@saildocs.com:

send http://tgftp.nws.noaa.gov/fax/PYAA12.TIF

send PYAA12.TIF

This could be in one email, or two separate ones. The first fetches exactly what is online at 36 kB, but the second format is the Saildocs shortcut to ask for a weather map, and this one comes back at 18 kB—Saildocs has reduced the file size for us. In short, even though Saildocs will fetch any file we want from the FTPmail folder, we get best results using their prescribed shortcuts, which is always simpler than asking with a direct path, and usually simpler than using FTPmail itself.

A main task, however, remains up to us. We need to know the filenames for the maps we want, and for Saildocs we want to use the TIF version, when available. As noted earlier, several analyses map files are indicated in Figures 7.2-1 and 7.2-6, but Appendix B of rfax.pdf is a more complete source. Alternatively, you can request lists of file names by region as explained in Table 8.3-1.

We have also prepared a convenient way (Starpath Briefings) to request maps using interactive PDF files:

starpath.com/downloads/PacificBriefing.pdf

starpath.com/downloads/AtlanticBriefing.pdf

These files take advantage of the Saildocs email option for use offshore, or the FTPmail option with an internet connection. A sample is shown in Figure 8.3-1.

Although we stress the value of the graphic weather maps, in practice these maps are not the main product Saildocs distributes. Their distribution of model forecasts in GRIB format is the main service they provide to many mariners. They have a convenient, versatile way to request GRIB files by email; several navigation programs have even automated the Saildocs GRIB requests from within their own programs. When using one of those programs for standard products, we do not need to know the format for direct email request, but to access the full range and versatility of products available from Saildocs we do need to know the request format, which is explained clearly in their help files.

GRIB files we get from Saildocs originate from the NWS (largely from nomads.ncep.noaa.gov), but Saildocs fetches them for us with a tremendous added value—they select out from the very large global or regional files online, just the

Table 8.3-1. Indexes of Weather Map Filenames	
Region	*filename*
Pacific	rfaxpac.txt
Atlantic	rfaxatl.txt
Mexico	rfaxmex.txt
Alaska	rfaxak.txt
Hawaii	rfaxhi.txt
Foreign	otherfax.txt

Table Notes:

Using FTPmail:
    open
    cd fax
    send filename
    quit

Using Saildocs:
send http://tgftp.nws.noaa.gov/fax/filename

See also Appendix B of rfax.pdf.

Lat-Lon region we want, and just the parameters we want, at just the resolution we want, and sends just the forecasts we want. In principle, we could do this ourselves, this is public data, but it would be extremely tedious.

Samples of Saildocs GRIB file requests are in Section 2.1; details for making requests are found at saildocs.com/gribinfo and saildocs.com/gribmodels. Forecasts available include: GFS, NAVGEM, NAM (12km), COAMPS, HRRR, and NDFD (oceanic), as well as RTOFS, WW3, and OSCAR. A few model specs are in Section 7.5, but for a complete list of available models, forecasts, and products, check the "grib filter" links at nomads.ncep.noaa.gov. Alternatively, luckgrib.com/models has a concise description of commonly used models, including a graphic display of regional coverages.

If you miss a model forecast that you need for your analysis, you can get them from Saildocs for up to 30 days past the valid time. Suppose, for example, it is 0320z on Jan 22, 2018 and you wanted yesterday's 18z NAM forecast to check winds you have observations for. You could have gotten this with a normal request up to about 0315 or so on Jan 22, but about then, the 00z run becomes available, and that is what you would get with a normal request, i.e.,

send NAM:47N,49N,125W,122W|0.11,0.11|0,1..18|
WIND,PRMSL

At 0300z, Jan 22 this brings back the 18z forecast for Jan 21. But at about 0315z or later, this then brings the 00z analysis for Jan 22; you have missed yesterday's 18z version. But all is not lost. You can append to the request the time you want, going back as far as 30 days.

send NAM:47N,49N,125W,122W|0.11,0.11|0,1..18|
WIND,PRMSL|file=2018012118

This will get you the file you want. *Remember, there is a space after "send," but no spaces at all after that one.* If you do not get back what you expect, check carefully for spaces in the text of the request.

Section 4.2 describes how to use Saildocs to retrieve graphic images of ASCAT data; the same technique was used in Section 7.5 to obtain graphic GEFS confidence levels. We illustrate obtaining zone forecasts from Saildocs in Section 8.4.

Another option from Saildocs, "spot forecasts," can be useful in special applications. It is also a way to save airtime, with a few lines of text rather than a full GRIB file. Read about this option at saildocs.com/spotforecasts. The default spot forecasts use GFS and WW3 models for a specific Lat-Lon, every 6 hrs for 5 days; similar services from other sources call this "virtual buoy" data, but there are no buoys involved; it is all model data. There are several ways to customize the spot request, which can be made in steps as small as 3 hrs. You can ask for model forecasts at DR positions along a proposed route, but we can use it other ways. Consider this spot request:

send spot(NAM):38.072N,129.966W
send spot(GFS):38.072N,129.966W
send spot(COAMPS):38.072N,129.966W
send spot(NDFD):38.072N,129.966W

You will get back what is shown in Table 8.3-2. This is the location of buoy 46059, located 357 nmi west of San Francisco, so we have (on some level) a check of the forecasts with actual observations. The request was made at 04z on Jan 22, so these forecasts were based on the 00z model runs, including the NDFD Oceanic forecasts, which, in contrast to the NDFD CONUS, is only updated every 6 hrs. The buoy data were filled in the following day; only the 00z data existed at the time of request.

Figure 8.3-1. *Custom interactive weather map request form. Static thumbnails show samples of each. They are organized by category and valid times. Each has two options for download, via Saildocs or direction from FTPmail folder. Estimated file sizes and update times are shown for each. This pdf can be stored in a computer or tablet, which will in turn interact with your default browser or mail program. There is a similar Pacific version. Maps received via Saildocs are reduced in size by 50%. In each case the request brings back the latest version of the map requested.*

Table 8.3-2. Wind and Pressure Spot Forecasts from Saildocs												
	NAM			GFS			COAMPS		NDFD		Buoy 46059		
UTC	kts	°T	mb	kts	°T	mb	kts	°T	kts	°T	kts	°T	mb
0000	11.9	304	1021.3	12.9	313	1021.8	23.9	239	12.6	330	13.5	330	1021.6
0600	11.0	296	1025.5	10.9	310	1025.4	23.3	236	9.9	319	11.7	310	1025.6
1200	4.9	287	1027.0	4.3	311	1027.0	6.5	313	4.1	316	3.9	290	1027.2
1800	4.7	151	1029.2	7.5	144	1028.0	7.8	057	7.1	149	7.7	170	1028.8

Table Notes: *Spot forecasts for the location of Buoy 46059 on Jan 22, 2018 using several sources. Wind speed forecasts are given to us precise to 0.1 kt, although certainly not that accurate. Buoy reports are only recorded precise to the nearest whole m/s, which are then converted to kts with x1.93. Thus they are not as precise as indicated. The rounding alone introduces an uncertainly of about ± 1 kt (1.93/2). Buoy wind directions are reported in units of 10°, so these are uncertain by about ± 5°. (The 057 COAMPS wind dir is likely a numerical glitch in the system.)*

Table 8.4-1. Station 46059
38° 4.3' N 129° 58.0' W
10:00 AM AKST
1900 GMT 01/22/18
Wind: S (180°), 9.7 kt
Gust: 13.6 kt
Pres: 30.38 rising
Air Temp: 55.8°F
Water Temp: 58.1°F
Dew Point: 45.3°F
Wave Summary
9:40 AM AKST
1800 GMT 01/22/18
Swell: 11.2 ft
Period: 13.8 sec
Direction: WNW
Wind Wave: 1.3 ft
Period: 3.8 sec
Direction: WSW

This is an isolated, rough comparison, but the implication is we do indeed have good resources for 24-hr forecasts from a variety of sources. This type of comparison can be greatly extended using the Saildocs option for subscribing to a request for automated deliveries over a set period of time. We can also ask for the buoy reports as well, discussed below.

Table Notes: *A buoy report by email. Sometimes the degree signs do not transfer properly. NDBC notes the longitude of the buoy and assigns it to Alaska standard time (AKST), but that is frankly not good procedure.*

8.4 Real Time Observations

It is not uncommon for experienced mariners to give more credence to actual reports (observations) than to forecasts. We see, for example, at the interface between British Columbia and Alaska to the north and Washington state to the south, that Environment Canada tends to be more conservative with their forecasts, meaning they tend to forecast the higher end of a range of possible wind speeds than the NWS might do for the same regions. It is dubious, however, to incorporate such reasoning, or past experiences, into our decision making.

Likewise we confront a similar issue on sailing around the Pacific High or Atlantic counterparts. The forecast might call for no wind if we carry on in the present direction, but then we see ship reports of 10 kts or so ahead of us where the forecast maps show calm. In either situation, with crucial decisions at hand, we have to balance out all the information and reasoning we can put together—which has been the theme of this book throughout. In all cases, this starts with knowing what observations are available and how to access them.

VHF Weather Radio

In coastal waters, VHF weather (NOAA Weather Radio) is a primary source of reports. Observations are updated every 3 hrs. It is often beneficial to make a list of the reporting stations in the order given, so the next report is taken down more efficiently. Airport data might not be of prime interest, but they are often the only VHF reports with valuable pressure trend indicated. See discussion in Section 1.6.

Station Reports by Email

Each report in the radio broadcast is from a specific station (buoy or lighthouse) with a NDBC number, which means we can also obtain the reports by other means, usually up-

dated more frequently than the VHF broadcasts, sometimes nearly live. This is obviously better than every 3 hrs.

We can get individual station reports from FTPmail:

```
open
cd data/observations/marine/latest_obs
get 46059.txt
quit
```

We get back the data shown in Table 8.4-1. Wind and pressure are updated every 10 minutes; sea state every hour.

Dial-a-Buoy

Without email available, we can still get live buoy data with even a flip phone. The program is called *Dial-a-Buoy*; it is another resource of the NDBC. Just dial this number:

888-701-8992

Then enter the 5-digit station ID you care about. Station 46059 gives back the same data shown in Table 8.4-1, plus in the first section, a "wave height," which is the HTSGW defined in Table 7.7-1. It can be confirmed with the data they provide in the wave summary part of the report. For more practice, try 58283 for Station LTBV3 Lime Tree Bay, VI. Following any buoy report, a forecast is sometimes available.

Station IDs can be found on the graphic display at the NDBC web site; if you don't know the ID, press 2 when they answer, and you are prompted for a Lat-Lon. After you have been through the instructions, on the next call you can just press 1 and the ID, and not have to listen through again. The Dial-a-Buoy phone number is a good addition to the navigator's contact list.

Ship Reports

The content and presentation of ship reports are covered in Section 7.7. Selected reports are on the analysis maps, but these are often difficult or impossible to read. Text versions are more useful. Beyond viewing the text versions at the NDBC website, we can also get them by email request.

An easy way, with fixed format, is send a blank email to:

shipreports@starpath.com

with your Lat, Lon in the subject line as: 35.5N, 65.4W. You then get back by return email all ship reports within 300 nmi of that location over the past 6 hr. This does not have to be where you are, just the region you care about.

A more versatile, but complex, request can be made to Saildocs using this format:

send https://www.ndbc.noaa.gov/radial_search.php?lat1
=35.5N&lon1=65.4W&dist=300&ot=S&time=6

where lat1, lon1 is the center of a radial search within a radius (dist). The observation type (ot) can be S (ships), B (buoys) or A (all). The time specified can be a specific time in the past, i.e., time=-6, meaning 6 hrs ago, or you can use time=6, meaning over the past 6 hrs. This time specification (in whole hours) can be anywhere from 1 to 12.

Generally we want to know what is going on in specific regions in recent times, so the Starpath request might meet most needs—it also brings back the data in a neater format as it is custom-designed for this purpose. See starpath.com/shipreports.

ASCAT Winds

We have covered ASCAT wind data in depth in Section 4.2, including how to get graphic images of the wind data, as well as GRIB formatted versions, which are super convenient. For ocean sailing, these satellite wind measurements are the premier real time observations.

BuoyCAMs!

These are new real time resources that offer a great training opportunity. As of about 2014, NDBC has 360° cameras on over a dozen buoys, whose live images can be viewed online, updated every 15 minutes (Figure 8.4-1). This is a great way to see the ocean sky as well as study cloud progressions as fronts, squalls, or tropical storms approach. You can also watch tropical clouds throughout the early evening to see if they gang up into congestus piles, foretelling likely squalls for the evening, or flatten out into strato patches that just continue to flatten and disappear or break up into fairweather puffs for a nice night at sea. We can get these unique panoramas of ocean skies from the comfort of home. At higher latitudes you can check for visibility.

We missed the tropical storm season for this printing, but will watch for close encounters next summer. A related new training resource from NDBC is in Appendix 10, which presents recorded and plotted values of wind and pressure as past hurricanes approached and passed over a buoy.

8.5 Weather Communications at Sea

Throughout the book we refer to getting various weather products by email or directly from an internet connection. In a port or marina with internet, we do this the same way we do at home, using the vessel's computer or tablet. And indeed, most marinas do have internet available. In earlier editions we talked about rowing into shore with a thumb drive to find an internet cafe for weather data, but that is pretty much history in all but the remotest locations .

Once we pull away from the dock, we need some wireless means of communications—or better put, once we pull away from the coast. In many places, there is good cellphone connection between the dock and a few miles offshore. Many near coastal routes have cellphone service the whole way, and there are special antennas and amplifiers to enhance this. Using a cellphone as a hotspot, we can often make usable internet connections. The internet sources cited throughout the book are accessible for much of our sailing.

For connections to weather sources offshore we have several choices, and to be crass about it right up front, the choice depends on how much we can, or are willing, to spend. Costs vary from the bare minimum (a shortwave receiver) at about $300 for equipment and no monthly service charge, on up to internet connections similar to those on land (but significantly slower) for about $15,000 in equipment and some $2,000 per month service charge. And sure enough, there is an almost smooth continuum of options between these two extremes.

Figure 8.4-1. *Two samples of buoy cam images from Oct 12, 2017. Top is Buoy 41043, 170 nmi NE of San Juan, PR, local time 12:10 PM; bottom is Buoy 51004, 200 nmi SE of Hilo, HI, local time 7:10 AM. See the BuoyCAM link at the NDBC site.*

The absolute bare minimum would be a shortwave radio *receiver* and a simple long wire antenna. You could not communicate *from* the boat, but you could hear high seas voice reports, broadcast at specific times, and you could receive HF fax maps, also broadcast at specific times, that you interpret and display in your computer—all of which would have to be tested thoroughly before departure. HF radio reception can be sensitive to many variables. The radio's headset output goes to the computer's microphone input, and there are numerous software programs that interpret, adjust, and display the map images. This type of radio should be considered for all vessels, as it is a battery-operated backup to whatever system you have. Prior to 2019 we could have used such a SW radio to hear the hourly storm warnings over WWV or WWVH, but his has been discontinued (Figure 8.5-1).

The high-end internet options, besides being very expensive, are restricted by vessel size. At present, top of the line internet access at sea requires antenna domes of 2 to 3 ft diameter, which limits them to pretty large vessels, with exceptional power capabilities, essentially ships and large yachts. There are intermediate options that are manageable for smaller yachts with domes the size of a basketball. This equipment is in the range of $3,000 to $4,000, with usage

fees of several thousands of dollars per month (taking into consideration all weather data of interest, plus some limited general browsing and media activity). This level of access is common to high-end yachts and some racing sailboats. Monthly service can be turned off when not needed.

With those upper-end options mentioned, we can turn to the most common means of satellite communication, which is a handheld satphone or dedicated satellite data receiver and WiFi router, such as the Iridium Go or Iridium Glow. These latter devices serve as WiFi hotspots that transfer voice or data communications to your phone, tablet, or computer on your vessel. Any of these also allow judicious internet access, such as downloading weather data via a direct URL. With these data receivers, voice calls are made through your cellphone or tablet, as opposed to using the satphone, which is essentially a large cellphone to begin with. The generic term *satcom* is used to describe satellite communications, regardless of the receiver type. Iridium Go and Glow devices are also called *WiFi terminals*. See Figure 8.5-2.

Each company offers many airtime packages, so individuals need to balance out voice-time versus data-time requirements, as well as perhaps other usages. The satphone can be taken off the boat for other applications; this is more

Recent Developments

Storm Warnings. This place in the book had in recent printings been devoted to the HF radio storm warnings that were broadcast hourly on the National Institute of Standards (NIST) time-tick broadcasts over stations WWV and WWVH. These unique, dependable resources had been in place for decades, but fell to recent NWS budget cutbacks in 2019. Full high seas weather forecasts, including storm warnings, can still be received in voice over HF radio (see Table 8.7-1), but, unfortunately, these are at a broadcast power of 3 kW, whereas the previous HF storm warnings were at 10 kW, which were much easier to receive on an inexpensive SW radio. The radiofax signals also can still be received with a SW battery-operated radio and associated computer apps.

FV3 GFS. The main content upgrade at NOAA is from NCEP, who produce the GFS model. The GFS model was updated on June 12, 2019 to the new FV3 version (15.1.1), which, beyond promising to be an improved global model for surface wind, pressure, and precipitation, also now includes simulated radar reflectivity (REFC) for global waters. We discuss the parameter in Section 4.6. REFC is the best forecaster for squalls. Having this in the global GFS model extends this data to all waters, but we might still expect the squall forecasts to be better in short-term forecasting rather than long. The GFS extends out to 16 days! Rapid refresh and high-resolution data on REFC is referenced in Section 4.6.

OPC Map Conventions. Other recent changes to highlight are the new 72-hr forecasts from OPC, which are a welcome addition, and their decision to not track the movements of Highs on the surface analysis maps, which for ocean-going sailors is not such a welcome change. Lows are also now only tracked if they are developing.

The 500-mb maps have been mostly automated for some time, but are now fully automated; the manual annotations marking troughs and ridges are no longer added.

Figure 8.5-1. *New developments at NOAA that affect marine weather. Some of these are mentioned in the text; others are not.*

awkward with a WiFi terminal. There are wireless routers for satphones that turn them into WiFi hotspots, but the WiFi terminal plans offer better data rates than we get from satphone plans, which do not distinguish between voice-time and data-time.

In short, when it comes time to make this decision, we need to talk with a trusted seller of these products to have them help us best meet our needs. The hardware, software, and airtime options are changing continuously. At present, either of these options have equipment prices (including needed accessories) of $1,000 to $2000, with airtime charges of several hundreds of dollars at least, for bare minimum usage on an ocean voyage. Though easier to say then to buy, for extended voyaging, having both a dedicated receiver (Go or Glow) and a handheld satphone, would likely end up providing the best service, and likely the best operations cost. In any event, this equipment should be purchased close to departure time, to take advantage of the latest technology. The Iridium Certus system, for example, will become available in 2019-2020, with much higher speeds and more options.

We discussed satellite communication first, as is it the most popular choice these days, but traditional HF radio is still a completely viable option for high seas communication, especially if your vessel already has the radio installed. Once the radio is installed and working, the monthly costs are notably lower than using satellite phones or data receivers. An HF radio high seas email account, such as Sailmail, has a modest annual charge, and it can be used with satcom as well.

On the other hand, the HF radio installation is more expensive than a satphone or data receiver—actually quite a bit more. When we combine the cost of the radio, antenna and tuner, ground plane, installation, and Pactor modem (needed for email communications over the HF radio), it is some five times the cost of a satcom installation. The Pactor modem can cost as much as the radio itself (en.wikipedia.org/wiki/PACTOR). Furthermore, satcom connections are often easier to establish and accomplish, and not as dependent on time of day or weather conditions. Also, HF radio work is sensitive to electrical noise on the boat, so that has to be addressed, and also transmitting takes a lot of power. You might have to run the engine to charge the battery for an hour or so for each radio communication, depending of course on your electrical system.

With that said, if you already have an HF radio installed, it pays to have it tested and tuned up—it takes a professional with special meters to do this. Besides saving airtime for a lot of products and email, you can also take part in cruiser's network meet ups, or talk with other vessels at no charge versus roughly $1.50/minute on a satphone.

With satellites or radios, there are still learning curves to successful data transfer. In both cases we need a good connection to obtain larger files, and with both options we will find times when the connection is not good enough, and we have to wait. See starpath.com/wx for links to related articles on practical matters.

Experienced HAM operators can take their hobby to sea and likely have better success with HF radio than those with less radio training. They can choose HF radios that allow use of the HAM bands as well as standard marine bands, which gives them more options for communications. They can also take advantage of HAM HF email accounts that offer limited file transfer at no charge. These options require a General license, the next step up over the entry level Technician license.

The common requirement for high seas communications is a wireless email account. These provide an email service that can interface from the computer to the radio or satphone, and most are associated with a weather provider for GRIB files and other products. Since they are designed for high seas communications, they offer special treatment for large files and some level of compression for all communications. Others offer efficient means of establishing connections that can save time, and some offer fire wall protection for internet connections to limit background transfers that consume a lot of data. Other options include tracking functions, so your position, COG, and SOG are transmitted with every connection. Direct links to social media is a modern option to some systems.

Satellite providers offer their own connection programs that are popular, but they have various restrictions that have led many mariners to choose third party options to best meet their needs. Several we are familiar with are listed in Table 8.5-1. There are numerous others. Pricing structure and available services differ among them.

Figure 8.5-2. *Popular means of satcom connections, using a handheld satphone (left) or dedicated satellite receiver, such as the Iridium Go (top right) or Iridium Glow (center). Voice communications through those WiFi terminals are done with a phone or tablet. A satphone can also be connected to a WiFi router to reach mobile devices. Other NMEA instruments can be wired to the router for transfer to mobile devices.*

WEFAX and HF Voice

With an HF radio on board, be it a full functioning transceiver with an insulated backstay antenna and tuner, or just an inexpensive quality shortwave receiver with a long wire antenna, there are options for weather data at sea that do not require a high-seas email account nor Pactor modem. We can receive all weather maps by radiofacsimile, a process often nicknamed "WEFAX" by its practitioners. We can also hear voice broadcasts of the high-seas forecasts.

Both voice broadcasts and radiofax maps are broadcast at specific times, which may or may not be convenient considering other things going on with the navigation, but that is simply a limitation of this source. The NWS provides the data to the USCG and they do the broadcasting. Voice broadcasts for each ocean are given every six hours at fixed times. Broadcast times and frequencies are in Table 8.7-1 . Another source of information on this program is the USCG Navigation Center (navcen.uscg.gov).

Those who have had to rely on this source of information have learned that a tape recorder stationed near the radio can be a valuable aid, as are a set of headphones so the rest of the boat is not disturbed by late night broadcasts. They have also learned that it is much easier and dependable to obtain this data by email request when possible!

The main reference for radiofax is the rfax.pdf document we use for FTPmail instructions (nws.noaa.gov/os/marine/rfax.pdf). Broadcast times and frequencies for all worldwide radiofacsimile broadcasts are included. Since it takes some ten minutes to download a map, these broadcasts are going on essentially continuously throughout the day

The speaker output from the radio is plugged into the microphone input to the computer and then dedicated software interprets the signal and displays the maps or images. Text documents received in this format are images of the printed messages. There are several popular software programs for the decoding; JWX (arachnoid.com/JWX) and Fldigi (sourceforge.net/projects/fldigi) are a couple popular options with full functions and good online documentation. There is a learning curve to optimizing the images, but there are many help files and videos online. Some programs include options to control your radio, others focus on receiving the signal, once you have the radio set up properly and the signals are coming in. In most cases we must be on hand at least at the start of the download to make tuning adjustments as might be needed.

There are advertised phone apps that in principle just need to hear the radio in the background in order to translate a map. These are in the app stores. This, however, is a complex process, so all such alternatives should be tested.

Dedicated Radiofax Receiver

At the other end of the radiofacsimile spectrum using real radios, are the traditional marine radiofacsimile receivers, used worldwide in the shipping and fishing industry, as well as on government vessels. Many smaller vessels have

Table 8.5-1. Samples of Wireless Email Providers		
Mail Program	Source	Associated Weather
Mail & Web*	irridium.com	Predict Wind
Sat-Fi*	globalstar.com	Predict Wind
MailASail	mailasail.com	MailASail Teleport
OcensMail	ocens.com	Ocens WeatherNet
Sailmail	sailmail.com	saildocs.com
XGate	globalmarinenet.com	predictwind.com

Table Notes: *Services marked (*) are free for users of their products; some restrictions apply. Several satcom airtime providers also offer free web and email apps and services.*

switched to receiving maps and other products by email, but for the maps alone, it is hard to beat the dependability of these long-tested devices. I used them for many years on yachts before we ever dared bring a computer onto a boat. They are just dedicated HF radio receivers, with a one-foot wire antenna on the stern pulpit—it does not take much of a radio to just receive this fax signal. Inside they include their own WEFAX software tied to a printer.

Most are programmed with all the world's sources of radiofax stations and frequencies, and you just chose the ones

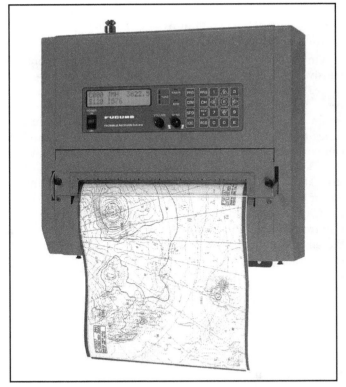

Figure 8.5-3. *Traditional marine radiofacsimile recorder. Shown here is Furuno model FAX410. These include their own radios, programed with the right frequencies worldwide. Their programming does not list specific maps, but rather you decide from the schedules what products you want, and when they are broadcast, then you program the units to come on at the right time, for the right duration, on the right frequency, which will then record the maps you want, unattended.*

you want, and when you want them, and be sure the roll of fax paper is full, and let it go. When you wake up in the morning there is a long ribbon of maps hanging from the device. With these programmed properly, you will always have the maps you want at hand and on time, more or less unattended—if there is a crucial map coming up, it is only prudent to be on hand to double-check all is working properly—otherwise, you will have to send an email and ask that the map be mailed back to you!

NAVTEX

There is another unattended source of weather data that is required on larger commercial vessels, although we have ready access to the service on any vessel, and this one is not just unattended, it is fully automated. It is a text service called NAVTEX, a part of the Global Marine Distress and Safety System (GMDSS) of the IMO and IHO. It provides navigational and weather information every four hours, at fixed times that depend on the station. NAVTEX is the primary means for transmitting urgent coastal marine safety information to ships worldwide. It is considered a coastal service, useful out to about 200 nmi from shore. The broadcasts are in English at 518 kHz worldwide, which is at the top of the low frequency (LF) band, just below the bottom of the AM band, so it takes a special radio to receive it. Individual nations can supplement the signals at 490 kHz in their native language, but the English versions at 518 kHz remain in place. There is also an HF broadcast of the information at 4209.5 kHz.

A sample NAVTEX disply is shown in Figure 8.5-4. Some models can relay the information to your ECS or ECDIS display. The key feature of this system is this information is always there. No matter how distracted you may be with other matters on the vessel, this report will show up automatically on the vessel, in many cases printed out as well as stored as digital text files.

Broadcast times for U.S. waters are listed at navcen.uscg. gov, along with other details of the system. NAVTEX includes much navigation safety information as well as weather. Each broadcast includes an alphanumeric header that is used to program the messages you want. The first character of the

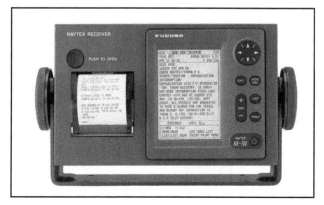

Figure 8.5-4. *Furuno NAVTEX model NX-700. There is also a small external unit and small mushroom antenna that makes up the full system. Other brands have only LCD or only print outputs.*

header is a letter ID for the station, the second sets the desired content, with options such as: A. Navigation warning, B. Meteorological warning, C. Ice report, D. Search and rescue plus piracy notices, E. Meteorological forecasts, and more. NWS NAVTEX forecasts are in section E; Special warnings are broadcast as needed in Section B.

Weather forecasts from U.S. NAVTEX stations are combinations of selected offshore forecast zones near the stations. We can read these custom NAVTEX zone forecasts online (nws.noaa.gov/om/marine/forecast.htm) or request them by email, as explained in Section 8.6.

Although these radio signals are described as more difficult to decode than WEFAX, similar software exists for doing this on our own using any standard radio that receives the signals in lieu of an actual NAVTEX receiver. JNX (arachnoid.com/JNX) and Fldigi (sourceforge.net/projects/fldigi) are two free ones with good documentation online. Note JWX and JNX are similar names for different programs. Fldigi is the same program for NAVTEX and WEFAX. There are other options for both NAVTEX and WEFAX decoding. See also related discussion of SafetyNET via Inmarsat in Section 8.7.

Commercial Weather Services

There are several companies, small and large, in the U.S. and Europe that offer weather products and routing services for a fee. Some distribute or use only NWS data; others collect data from several government agencies worldwide and offer their own interpretations of the products. All add value to the products to justify the service fee, either per product, per time period, or per voyage. The products offered vary from custom weather reports for specific waters, on up to day by day weather routing, meaning an actual proposed course to follow in the present conditions.

The latter companies are usually called *weather routing services*. The former might be called *data providers*. Weather routers vary from large international companies with a 24-hr staff of professional meteorologists serving shipping fleets worldwide, to individual professionals providing services to individual vessels from home or small office facilities. These days a trained individual has access through the internet to essentially all the data that are used by even the most sophisticated weather routers, so the choice of such services often boils down to the experience of the router, with the vessel type you care about, in the particular waters you care about, and how the data are delivered, and what it costs. A small company could well be the very best source for sailboat or other small craft routing.

Routing services can be found online, or better still from recommendations of friends who have used them. There are many high quality services, and even within these, there are numerous options for data delivery and extent of services.

Likewise there are many commercial data providers with a broad range of services and pricing structures. Some provide primarily NWS data, but offer the service of convenient data selection, packaging, and data compression. In some cases, the satcom airtime saved with compressed delivery (compared to FTPmail) compensates for the service fee. Others include international data, as well as their own in-house forecasts and model runs. Some services are integrated into navigation programs for even more convenience. GRIB files are a key component of some services, but others offer all forms of weather and ocean data. Several sources we know of are listed in Table 8.5-2. There are many more.

Commercial services for both delivering data and routing vessels are certainly the wave of the future. It is standard practice for large shipping companies and a key part of many sailing events where such outside assistance is allowed, and indeed routine for many yachts around the world. And this is not restricted to private commercial companies. The Canadian and British governments and several European nations have active commercial divisions of their weather bureaus from which you can purchase custom services and forecasts.

The value of learning the basics, and even more, about marine weather, however, is not diminished by such good services. A prudent mariner will always want the independence and security of being able to evaluate guidance provided, and to fill in on their own if that convenient support is lost. This is also why we have stressed *all* the sources of weather available to us, not just the best or easiest. The few cases we know of where professional services of highly respected consultants broke down were all tied to failures in communications. The vessels had good advice ready for them, they just could not get it, which is Murphy's-Law at its worst when this happens just after a major change in a storm's development or path, which brings up the next topic.

Practice with Communications

It is absolutely essential before setting off on an ocean passage to test all of your communications equipment. This sounds like a no-brainer, but we have seen these tests under done multiple times and the consequences of it—and not just by beginners. Even experienced people can let this slip when there seems to be so many other important things that must get done. And the more communications options available

Table 8.5-2. Samples of Weather Data Providers
adrena-software.com
clearpointweather.com
greatcircle.be
gribfiles.com
luckgrib.com
ocens.com
predictwind.com
sailflow.com
squid-sailing.com
theyr.com
wxworx.com

Table Notes: *These companies offer weather data (beyond just GFS forecasts) for a fee. There is a broad spectrum of services and products represented. Some provide data only, others provide software with data links incorporated in them. Some offer multiple products. These are samples only; there are many others..*

on the boat, the more likely that part of the system will get neglected.

None of these systems is plug and play. Your satcom and radio sales source should be good help, which favors buying from knowledgable specialists, rather than bargain shopping on Amazon. The service is everything. We should be 100% confident that we know how to email, text, and talk back and forth from and to the boat, and get all the weather products we want or might need. Radios, including a simple shortwave receiver, must all be practiced. HF (SSB) radio use requires many hours at the nav station going over manuals, programming channels, and practicing reception of voice and fax. See Mariner's Weather Checklist (Section 9.5) for a reminder.

8.6 Zone Forecasts by Email

One thing we miss the most from the now defunct MSC charts is the defining boundaries and names of the various forecast zones and categories used by the NWS. There are convenient graphic indices online, linked to the forecast texts, but that does not help offshore without internet. Furthermore, they are not always linked to the files we have access to by email—some forecasts are located multiple places online. However, we can indeed receive any of these forecasts by email, so long as we know what to ask for.

Unfortunately, looking at all U.S. waters, it is a complex system, so for efficient access it is valuable to learn the structure in use—at least in use for now. There are proposals for changing some of these. There are three basic categories of forecast zones: *coastal* (0 to 60 nmi off), *offshore* (60 to 250 nmi off), and *high seas* (>250 nmi off), and then these zones can be grouped into other categories, such as *coastal waters* (groups of coastal zones), *offshore waters* (groups of offshore zones), and *metareas* (groups of high seas zones).

Coastal Forecast Zones

Coastal zones are mostly in two bands, 0 to 20 nmi offshore and then 20 to 60 nmi off. Hawaii is an exception, as shown in the graphic index from the NWS in Figure 8.6-1. Figure 8.6-2 is our own compilation of the coastal zones for the Pacific Coast to show the overview. We can request these zone forecasts by email, either one or a few at a time, or we can request predefined groups of zones (coastal waters), indicated in Figure 8.6-2.

Coastal zones are grouped into what are called *coastal waters,* named by the nearest large city. These groups can include anywhere from 4 to 15 of the coastal zones, but more typically 4 to 6, as shown in Figure 8.6-2 for the Pacific Coast. To receive coastal waters group forecasts (CWF) by email, use the file names in Table 8.6-1, which includes both the Pacific and Atlantic Coasts. These file names are not obvious in the NWS online sources, but they are listed in the rfax.pdf document that explains FTPmail. The Saildocs request shortcuts for coastal waters are the first two components of the full file name, marked in green in Table 8.6-1.

Atlantic forecast zones are more complex, and some are pending changes. We leave the individual zones to be checked by users. All U.S. coastal zones are defined in a similar manner, with online links to the forecasts at:

nws.noaa.gov/om/marine/zone/usamz.htm

To request individual zones by email, the process is the same as shown in Figure 8.6-2. Atlantic coastal zone forecasts are stored in tgftp.nws.noaa.gov/data/forecasts/marine/coastal/an for Lats >31N, or in /am for Lats <31N, which, on some level, marks the division of responsibility between the OPC and the NHC. We see discontinuities there in several products.

On the other hand, despite the complexity of the individual zones, the Atlantic coastal waters forecasts (predefined groups of the individual zone forecasts) can be requested from Saildocs or FTPmail with the links in Table 8.6-1. For coastal routes (on either coast), these CWF are likely the easiest and most efficient way to request the data. Coastal waters forecasts also include a special file of the synopsis for the region. The synopses files are not indicated on any of the graphic images, but there is one for each region.

Note that the Saildocs shortcut for *individual* coastal zones (i.e., send pzz132) works for many, but not all US coastal zones. They do offer consistent service for coastal waters, which include the individual zones. See Figure 8.6-2 and Table 8.6-1.

Offshore Forecast Zones

The region of 60 to 250 nmi from the coast is covered by the *offshore forecast zones*. They are shown in Figure 8.6-3. The Pacific and Mid-Atlantic offshore zones are also in two bands: 60 to 150 nmi off and 150 to 250 nmi off. The Gulf of Mexico and the SW North Atlantic and Caribbean have custom zone definitions, as shown in the figure. Forecasts for these zones are all available by email, as indicated in the figure. In some NWS sources, they refer to this latter group as "Tropical Atlantic and Caribbean."

Groups of offshore zones are called *offshore waters*. They are named by the region they cover, such as "New England"

or "Bering Sea." These can consist of as many as 24 offshore zones ("SW North Atlantic and Caribbean") or they can be just one zone—"Hawaii" and "East Gulf of Alaska" are examples of offshore waters that only include one zone. Like the coastal waters, the offshore waters groups also include a synopsis file that covers the region. Thus requesting the HI

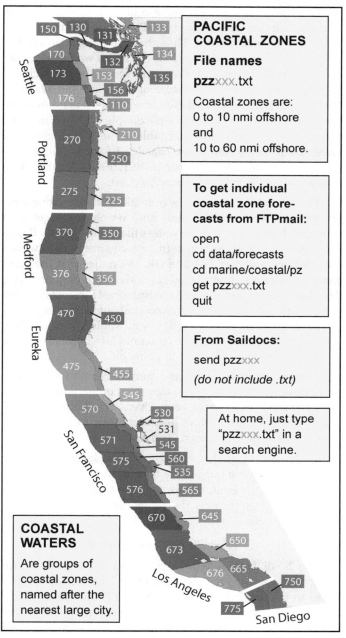

Figure 8.6-2. *Samples of coastal zone forecast file names and coastal waters groupings. Zone forecasts are all stored at tgftp. nws.noaa.gov/data/forecasts/marine/coastal/pz/. File names are pzzxxx.txt, where xxx are the numbers shown above. The coastal waters forecast (CWF) groups labeled by city names can also be requested by email as explained in Table 8.6-1. These files contain copies of the individual zone forecasts they cover. The Eureka forecast includes zones: 450, 455, 470, and 475. The CWF are stored in a different folder, so the FTPmail commands are different, but Saildocs has single-word shortcuts for the CWF as well as for the zone forecasts.*

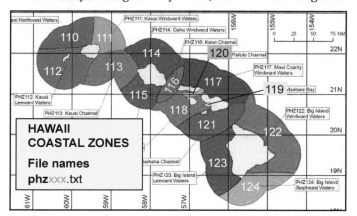

Figure 8.6-1. *Hawaii coastal forecast zones graphic index from the NWS. This graphic index online is interactive but difficult to read (we added the larger numbers). There is a text list of all U.S. zones at nws.noaa.gov/om/marine/textzones.htm.*

offshore waters (fzhw60.phfo.off.hfo.txt) gets you its one off-shore zone forecast (phz180.txt) as well as its synopsis file (phz105.txt). Other such requests, gets you forecasts of all of the included zones plus the synopsis file.

Offshore Waters Forecasts *versus* Radio Broadcast Versions

The NWS has a second version of each offshore waters forecast that they prepare for the USCG to broadcast over the radio in the voice reports. These have to be condensed, because the full report over each of the zones would be a long one. This calls for compromise on the forecasts. For each day they need to give some measure of the wind and sea state that is an average or compilation of what takes place over the entire combined set of zones. An example is shown in Table 8.6-3. The bottom row of that table is the Washington and Oregon offshore waters voice broadcast forecast, 60 to 250 nmi offshore, for Saturday night, PST, Feb 3, 2018. These files are online at fzpn35.kwbc.off.n35.txt.

The rows above that are the individual offshore zone fore-casts in that region for this same time, which we can get all in one report from the offshore waters file fzpn25.kwbc.off.pz5.txt. Figure 8.6-2 shows where these zones are located within the offshore waters of WA and OR. We notice that the summary broadcast is pretty good for zones 900, 905, and 910, but elsewhere in these waters, the broadcast forecast does not represent what the NWS really knows about what is expected. If you were in zones 810 or 815, you would get misleading advice from this information; you could falsely conclude that the NWS does not know what is going on.

This is, obviously, just one example, taken at random at the time of writing. You can make other comparisons like this from the full list of text forecasts given at nws.noaa.gov/om/marine/forecast.htm, which includes links to the offshore waters and to the condensed versions of each.

We have stressed that voice reports available by a battery operated shortwave radio are a backup to more sophisticated sources on the boat, but we see here that this is indeed a backup. When we can get the actual files by email, we have better information in this case.

High Seas Forecasts

The NWS *high seas forecast zones* are organized two ways, with some overlap between them. They are also duplicated in two subfolders of the NWS FTPmail folder (Table 8.6-4). Referring to Figure 8.6-4, we see the WMO metar-eas in solid color zones with roman numeral identifiers, and overlaid on these are the NWS high seas zones outlined in red lines. The metarea forecasts are part of the GMDSS program; they can be obtained online directly at gmdss.org. The NWS is the source of two metarea forecasts (IV and XII), with those files indicated in the figure and in Table 8.6-4.

There are a couple subtleties in the high-seas file structure. The Pacific metarea XII (hsf.epi) is a combination of three zones, whereas in the Atlantic, metarea IV is actually the same as hsf.at1. In other words, hsf.at1 includes hfs.at2

File Name	Coastal Waters Label
Table 8.6-1. Coastal Waters Forecast (CWF) Files at tgftp.nws.noaa.gov/data/raw/fz/	
Pacific Coast (0 to 60 nmi)	
fzus56.ksew.cwf.sew.txt	Seattle, WA • 49 N to 46.7 N
fzus56.kpqr.cwf.pqr.txt	Portland, OR • 46.7 N to 44 N
fzus56.kmfr.cwf.mfr.txt	Medford, OR • 44.1 N to 41.8
fzus56.keka.cwf.eka.txt	Eureka, CA • 41.8 N to 38.9 N
fzus56.kmtr.cwf.mtr.txt	San Francisco, CA • 38.9 N to 35.7
fzus56.klox.cwf.lox.txt	Los Angeles, CA • 35.7 N to 33 N
fzus56.ksgx.cwf.sgx.txt	San Diego, CA • 33.4 N to 32.5 N
fzhw50.phfo.cwf.hfo.txt	Hawaii • Out 40 nmi
Atlantic Coast (0 to 40 nmi)	
fzus51.kcar.cwf.car.txt	Caribou, ME • 45.2 N to 43.4 N
fzus51.kgyx.cwf.gyx.txt	Gray, ME • 44.5 N to 42.7 N
fzus51.kbox.cwf.box.txt	Boston, MA • 42.9 N to 40.5 N
fzus51.kokx.cwf.okx.txt	New York, NY • 41.3 N to 39.9 N
fzus51.kphi.cwf.phi.txt	Philadelphia, PA • 40.4 N to 38.3 N
fzus51.klwx.cwf.lwx.txt	Baltimore, MD • 39.5 N to 37.8 N
fzus51.kakq.cwf.akq.txt	Wakefield, VA • 38.4 N to 36.3 N
fzus52.kmhx.cwf.mhx.txt	Morehead City, NC • 36.3 N to 33.9 N
fzus52.kilm.cwf.ilm.txt	Wilmington, NC • 34.4 N to 32.8 N
fzus52.kchs.cwf.chs.txt	Charleston, SC • 33.2 N to 31.2
FL, Gulf of Mexico, and PR (0 to 60 nmi)	
fzus52.kjax.cwf.jax.txt	Jacksonville, FL • 31.3 N to 29.5
fzus52.kmlb.cwf.mlb.txt	Melbourne, FL • 29.5 N to 27 N
fzus52.kmfl.cwf.mfl.txt	Miami, FL • 27 N to 24.6 N
fzus52.kkey.cwf.key.txt	Key West, FL • 79.6 W to 83.3 W
fzca52.tjsj.cwf.sju.txt	San Juan, PR • 64 W to 68 W
fzus52.kmfl.cwf.mfl.txt	Miami, FL • 25.2 N to 26.4 N
fzus52.ktbw.cwf.tbw.txt	Tampa, FL • 26 N to 29.3
fzus52.ktae.cwf.tae.txt	Tallahassee, FL • 83.2 W to 86.5 W
fzus54.kmob.cwf.mob.txt	Mobile, AL • 86.5 W to 88.3 W
fzus54.klix.cwf.lix.txt	New Orleans, LA • 88 W to 91.3 W
fzus54.klch.cwf.lch.txt	Lake Charles, LA • 91.3 W to 94.4 W
fzus54.khgx.cwf.hgx.txt	Houston, TX • 94 W to 96.6 W
fzus54.kcrp.cwf.crp.txt	Corpus Christi, TX • 28.4 N to 27.2 N
fzus54.kbro.cwf.bro.txt	Brownsville, TX • 27.3 N to 26 N

Table Notes: *These files (CWF) are groups of coastal zone forecasts covering about 200 nmi along the coast. They are available from Saildocs, i.e.,* send fzus52.ktbw *for coastal waters around Tampa, FL. Use just the green part of the full file name. For FTP-mail use:*

    open
    cd data/raw/fz
    get fzus52.ktbw.cwf.tbw.txt
    quit

Alaska and the Great Lakes have an extensive system of individual coastal zones and coastal waters. See the nws.noaa.gov/om/marine/zone/usamz.htm *for the definitions.*

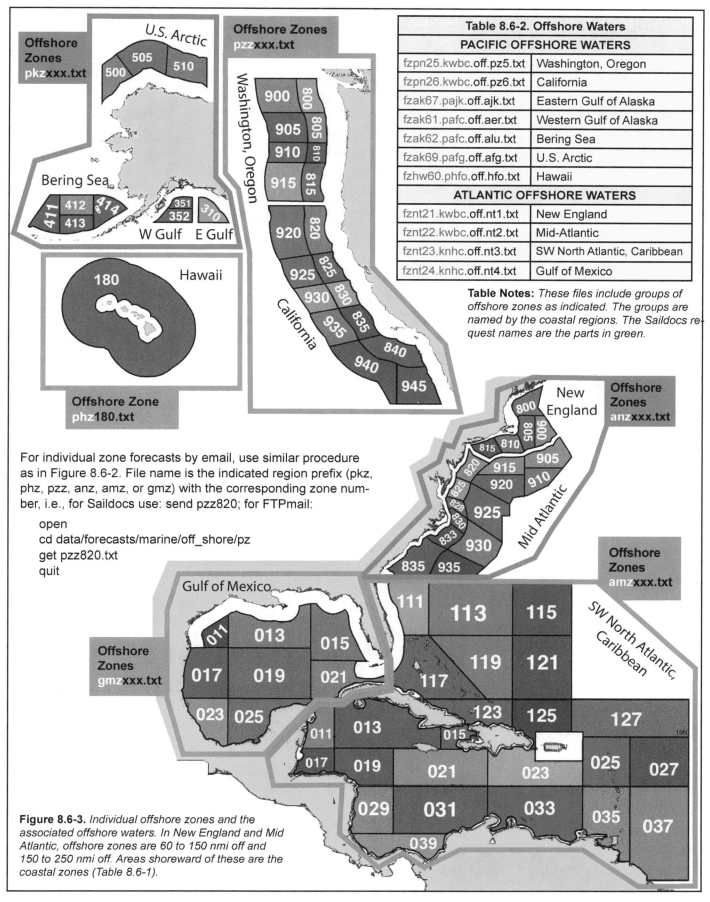

Table 8.6-2. Offshore Waters	
PACIFIC OFFSHORE WATERS	
fzpn25.kwbc.off.pz5.txt	Washington, Oregon
fzpn26.kwbc.off.pz6.txt	California
fzak67.pajk.off.ajk.txt	Eastern Gulf of Alaska
fzak61.pafc.off.aer.txt	Western Gulf of Alaska
fzak62.pafc.off.alu.txt	Bering Sea
fzak69.pafg.off.afg.txt	U.S. Arctic
fzhw60.phfo.off.hfo.txt	Hawaii
ATLANTIC OFFSHORE WATERS	
fznt21.kwbc.off.nt1.txt	New England
fznt22.kwbc.off.nt2.txt	Mid-Atlantic
fznt23.knhc.off.nt3.txt	SW North Atlantic, Caribbean
fznt24.knhc.off.nt4.txt	Gulf of Mexico

Table Notes: *These files include groups of offshore zones as indicated. The groups are named by the coastal regions. The Saildocs request names are the parts in green.*

For individual zone forecasts by email, use similar procedure as in Figure 8.6-2. File name is the indicated region prefix (pkz, phz, pzz, anz, amz, or gmz) with the corresponding zone number, i.e., for Saildocs use: send pzz820; for FTPmail:

    open
    cd data/forecasts/marine/off_shore/pz
    get pzz820.txt
    quit

Figure 8.6-3. *Individual offshore zones and the associated offshore waters. In New England and Mid Atlantic, offshore zones are 60 to 150 nmi off and 150 to 250 nmi off. Areas shoreward of these are the coastal zones (Table 8.6-1).*

but the latter covers only the area shown in the figure. Note that one of the metarea files ends in a "1" and the other ends in an "i"—this way they keep us on our toes!

We can request these files from FTPmail, in the manner described earlier using the directories shown in the table, or from Saildocs. The metareas have easy shortcuts at Saildocs The request is simply:

    send met.4
    send met.12

You can also get other metareas around the world from Saildocs in the same simple format. Check Saildocs help files for details.

For the other NWS high-seas zones we need to know the file names and a Saildocs shortcut. The file names and locations of zones are in Table 8.6-4. To get these from Saildocs, request only the green part of the file name, i.e.,

    send fznt01.kwbc

which happens to be an alternative way to get metarea IV. Sailing in the hsf.at2 zone you could save some 5 to 10 kB in file size using just hsf.at2, depending on the complexity of the report. On the other hand, this small savings in file size would only matter when combining several such requests in one satcom connection. For just one small file, the initial connection time could be notably larger than a small-file transfer time, which is why it is more efficient to queue up your weather and email transfers to all occur in a single connection.

Use of the High Seas Forecasts

Underway on an ocean passage we typically have the GFS GRIB forecasts, and we can request the corresponding graphic analysis maps from Saildocs. The value of comparing these has been covered. Now we can add to this the high seas text forecast, which, as explained in Section 7.3 on map reading, will inevitably tell you something about the map that you do not learn from the other two sources alone. Try this Saildocs request for a passage to Hawaii:

    send PYBA90.TIF
    send met.12
    send gfs:15N,60N,170w,115w|0.5,0.5|00,06|press,wind

This study package gets you the map, text report and GFS forecast, which can be compared.

For a passage from New England to Bermuda, try:

    send PYAA12.TIF
    send met.4
    send gfs:15N,60N,100w,40w|0.5,0.5|00,06|press,wind

The goal of the exercise is to compare all three and see how they complement your understanding of the winds at various parts of the map. These are each updated four times a day. You can also subscribe to them at Saildocs so they are sent automatically for practice at home. Underway, subscriptions must be used judiciously as they can ratchet up the airtime if not monitored.

Table 8.6-3. Sample of Radio Broadcast Summary					
Zone	Wind	Seas	Zone	Wind	Seas
900	W to SW 15-20	6'	800	W 15-20	6-7'
905	W 5-15 → W to SW 10-20	5-7'	805	W 5-15 → 10-20	5-6'
910	W 5-10 → W to SW 5-15	5-6'	810	NW <5 → W	4-5'
915	N to NW 5-15 → <10	4-5'	815	N 10-20	4-5'
Condensed summary			Wind		Seas
Washington and Oregon Cape Flattery to Cape Lookout			W to SW 10-20		5-8'

Use of Offshore and Coastal Forecasts

Figure 7.2-5 showed one example of when we need to know the winds well down the route in front of us. In that case we needed to know if the trades were easterly or northeasterly, and were they strong, medium, or light. Watching these winds ahead daily while still a long way from them, helps us make adjustments to our route so we meet them at a favorable angle.

You can discern trade winds roughly from the isobars on graphic maps, and we get precise predictions from the GFS. But those GFS values are the unvetted model predictions. We get much more dependable forecasts for the trades from the text forecasts, in this case actually made by the folks at the Honolulu Forecast Office (HFO). So a practice pack for this approach, from say halfway across, can be studied with this Saildocs request (*omit parts in italics*):

    send PYBA90.TIF
    send met.12 (high seas)
    send phz180 (offshore waters, 40 to 240 nmi)
    send http://tgftp.nws.noaa.gov/data/raw/fz/fzhw50.phfo.
    cwf.hfo.txt (coastal waters out 40 nmi, see notes)
    send gfs:15N,40N,160w,130w|0.5,0.5|00,06|
    send ndfd:18N,23N,161w,153w|0.1,0.1|00,06|

Notes: (1) The Saildocs default for GRIB parameters is wind and pressure. (2) The Saildocs shortcut for coastal waters listed in Table 8.6-4 does not work for HI, although it works for all others, hence the direct request.

Table 8.6-4. High Seas Forecasts Files at tgftp.nws.noaa.gov		
/data/forecasts/ marine/high_seas	/data/raw/fz/	Comment
east_pacific_1.txt	fzpn01.kwbc.hsf.ep1.txt	
east_pacific_2.txt	fzpn03.knhc.hsf.ep2.txt	Green part is the Saildocs shortcut.
south_hawaii.txt	fzps40.phfo.hsf.sp.txt	
north_hawaii.txt	fzpn40.phfo.hsf.np.txt	
—	fznt02.knhc.hsf.at2.txt	
north_pacific.txt	fzpn02.kwbc.hsf.epi.txt	Metarea XII
north_atlantic.txt	fznt01.kwbc.hsf.at1.txt	Metarea IV

Remember Saildocs is not an official provider. There are no guarantees. Glitches can happen. When we discover one, we can get the files from direct request (as above), or we can use FTPmail.

For any ocean passage we can prepare ahead of time the right email request for this sequence of forecasts, and then study them before and during the voyage, from departure to arrival: coastal waters, offshore waters, high seas, offshore waters, coastal waters.

Another valuable use of the coastal and offshore zone forecasts is to study the best route to transit a coast. On the West Coast, for example, there is at least one popular cruising guide that recommends sailors to transit the West Coast (San Francisco to Strait of Juan de Fuca, or vice versa) by heading straight out to 100 nmi offshore, and then do the run and come back in. Needless to say, we must always take into account present conditions and assure we have ample safe water, but in most cases, that proposed route is just a way to add two days to the trip in order to guarantee worst conditions. But we no longer have to take the word of experienced delivery skippers who would not go out like that, but rather follow the coast more close in. Now we can test this. Just watch conditions (day *and* night) for a week or so before departing, using the coastal waters and offshore waters along the route.

NAVTEX Forecast Zones

NAVTEX forecasts are expected to cover about 200 nmi offshore, all over the world, and be accessible within their coverage range. The formats are different from different nations. Samples can be seen at gmdss.org. Some use Beaufort force numbers for wind speed, but they are all in English, worldwide.

The NWS policy is to derive these forecasts from the offshore waters, and to exclude the coastal waters, referring the recipient to NOAA Weather Radio and "other sources" for those waters. The preceding pages covered these "other sources." Other nations include the coastal waters. In all cases, NAVTEX reporting zones are subdivided. In the U.S., they are subdivided as shown in Figure 8.6-5. Station W in Astoria, OR has two sections; station F in Boston, MA has three sections. In these cases they list the subregion forecasts in sequence.

These NAVTEX forecasts can be requested by email as indicated in Table 8.6-5. The key point to remember, however, is that these special forecasts are also condensed, just as the offshore waters are condensed for radio broadcast, discussed earlier. These are even more condensed as they cover larger areas. The big difference in these two condensations is the NAVTEX broadcasts are part of a safety at sea system, so they are meant as warnings. They are described as "highest conditions," probably meaning highest winds and biggest waves. In short, these are not tactical weather reports, they are warnings of what you might see in some parts of these large zones. For tactical weather routing we should use the offshore waters forecasts of Table 8.6-2 and the coastal waters forecasts of Table 8.6-1. The green parts are the Saildocs shortcuts.

8.7 Miscellaneous Sources

The NWS has a broad array of resources that we have not covered, and many existing ones are under development. There are extensive resources, for example, for the Great Lakes and for Alaska that we have only touched on. Others mentioned that are on the horizon, such as the S-412 program, are very exciting, and indeed could revolutionize how we do marine weather underway. After reviewing Section 8.6, imagine just cursor-clicking your chart and getting the option to view all related reports or forecasts for that location! Public weather services and products from the U.S. Navy are also expanding and adding to our tools. In this section we add two more well established crucial resources, along with notes on mobile access to some of what we have covered.

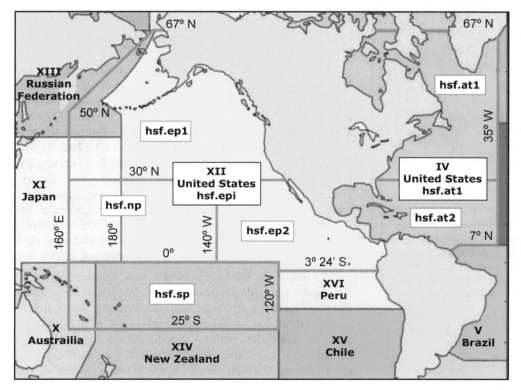

Figure 8.6-4. *NWS High seas forecast zone boundaries (red outlines) and WMO metareas (solid colors). They are broadcast four times a day, within an hour of 4:30 and 10:30, AM and PM, UTC.*

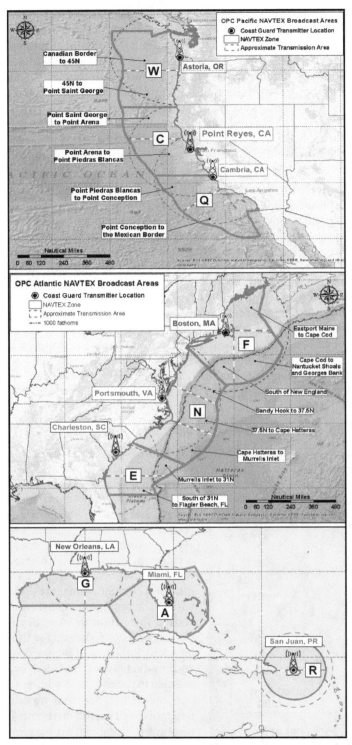

Table 8.6-5. NAVTEX forecast files		
ID	File name	Broadcast Station
F	fznt23.kwnm.off.n01.txt	Boston, MA
N	fznt24.kwnm.off.n02.txt	Portsmouth, VA
E	fznt25.kwnm.off.n03.txt	Charleston, SC
A	fznt25.knhc.off.n04.txt	Miami, FL
R	fznt26.knhc.off.n05.txt	San Juan, PR
G	fznt27.knhc.off.n06.txt	New Orleans, LA
W	fzpn24.kwnm.off.n09.txt	Astoria, OR
C	fzpn23.kwnm.off.n08.txt	Pt. Reyes, CA
Q	fzpn22.kwnm.off.n07.txt	Cambria, CA
O	fzhw61.phfo.off.n10.txt	Honolulu, Hi

River Bar and Inlet Crossings

Numerous river bars along the West Coast and breaker island inlets along the East Coast can have out flowing (ebb) currents that routinely reach 4 kts or more. When these currents happen to meet an onshore swell at the shoaling waters at the entrance, the waves can be very steep and breaking. Crossing these bars can be dangerous, and indeed in some cases should not be attempted at all in these conditions. The state of the tidal current and ocean swell are sometimes given in local coastal zone forecasts (i.e., pzz210.txt specifically for the Columbia River bar included in coastal waters of WA and OR, fzpn25.kwbc)—or this example from the coastal waters of California (fzus56.kmtr) on the San Francisco entrance: "ACROSS THE BAR... Combined seas 11 to 13 feet at 12 seconds. Maximum ebb current of 2.5 knots at 06:25 AM Monday and 2.6 knots at 06:43 PM Monday." This example (Feb 19, 2018) shows what this can be; these would be dangerous breaking waves at the ebbs, at an entrance that is more often passable with care. These waves were twice the average values. River bars farther north are more often closed.

And there are other special resources to check. On the West Coast, the status of the river bars are updated continuously at wrh.noaa.gov/pqr/marine/BarObs.php showing conditions and which ones are restricted or actually closed at the moment to certain classes of vessels. There is also this excellent document online from the USCG 13th District that describes each river bar and its navigation: D13_LNM_Special_Notice_to_Mariners_2015_Chapter_3_Guide_to_Hazardous_Bars.pdf. There do not seem to be direct counterparts of those two resources for the East Coast inlets, but this link mwp.secoora.org is a remarkable resource showing up to the minute tidal currents, winds, swells, and other data all along the coast from Norfolk, VA to Brownsville, TX.

We know the basics: the worst time to cross is with a strong ebb against a deep ocean swell. We would know about the swell as these are large area patterns, and we could see and feel it, and we could, in principle, look up the tidal currents on board. But without specific data in hand as we approach such a crossing on either coast, we can always call the USCG on the VHF to check conditions—remember you

Figure 8.6-5. *U.S. NAVTEX forecast zones. Subregions included in the reports are marked by red and white dashed lines. Contrary to this NWS presentation of the zone boundaries, these zones do not cover the nearest 60 nmi offshore, but since they are compilations focusing on the severest conditions, this has little practical significance. Alaska has five NAVTEX stations.*

cannot see the breakers when approaching from the back of them. There is good reason why there is usually a USCG station near each of these potentially dangerous entrances. Samples on the East Coast include Barnegat Inlet, NJ; Oregon Inlet, NC, and St. Lucie Inlet, FL, among others.

Weather by Mobile Device

Needless to say, there are tons of phone apps that tap into NWS resources, many going to the zone forecasts we have discussed. With the background presented here, you can judge if any of these meet your needs with the best data. In other words, if they are giving you just the NAVTEX file for offshore conditions, that is not the best data.

Some apps provide graphic views of high-resolution models such as the HRRR for inland waters, which could be very helpful, and some let you compare model forecasts, which is another useful feature. Others offer custom model computations of their own. There are many of these, and they vary and evolve too quickly to be more specific. They have to be checked individually. Some tablet apps provide versatile GRIB file sources and presentation and some even include optimum routing functions (Section 10.7).

The NWS has long offered their own mobile weather service that is very convenient for getting most of their products. The main marine mobile link is:

nws.noaa.gov/om/marine/cell/marine.htm

which has a wealth of data, with indices formatted for cellphone access. This is not an "app" but just a custom webpage. We can save this link to the home screen of our phones for quick access. Remember, the link weather.gov/marine is an index to most NWS products as well, but the mobile link has more convenient organization.

Tropical Storm and Hurricane Sources

Needless to say, the most intense of all marine weather systems demand the most care if we are anywhere near them. What is equally important to know is the GFS model forecasts we get for such systems are not at all adequate for safe navigation near these systems. The GFS is notoriously bad at predicting the strong wind speeds of these systems. We have seen many cases where they call for 30 to 50 kts of wind when indeed the system is a hurricane, with more than twice these wind speeds. This is especially hazardous when the systems are newly formed and you are using low-res GFS. After a day or two, the GFS is closer. This limitation should be considered basic knowledge for the use of GFS winds in the tropics, and indeed for any new, rapidly forming storm outside the tropics.

On the other hand, the GFS can indeed do a good job with the peripheral wind patterns and tracks of the systems, even when the peak winds are underestimated. So the forecasts remain valuable in that regard, but we cannot rely on those alone as we may not appreciate what is actually taking place. We must supplement the GFS with better data.

We have stressed how the graphic analysis and forecast maps from OPC help us interpret the GFS forecasts, but that also does not help much with tropical storms and hurricanes. The important thing these maps do tell us, however, is the actual nature of the Low we see on the GFS, and they tell us where to go to get the proper information. Figure 8.7-1 shows the GFS analysis of an intense Low, with reported patches of wind up to 71 kts. Thus we know this is a hurricane; the GFS winds were not too far off in this case, because this has been a hurricane for two days. Had we looked at the GFS winds several days earlier the peak winds would have been more in error. Even in this case, the actual sustained winds were over 90 kts, not 71 kts.

We do, however, see nicely from the GFS, the pattern of the strong winds, peaking as expected on the dangerous side. We also see the extent of 34-kt winds, that mark the area to be avoided according to the NHC's 34-kt rule (Figure 4.5-4).

Figure 8.7-2 is the OPC analysis map, showing a hurricane degrading into a tropical storm. We do not learn much about the wind pattern, but we do get the warning this is a hurricane with sustained winds of 90 kts, and the important advice to check the NHC Advisories. This is a deceptively simple map, compared to what we would see for a larger extratropical storm. The advisory referred to is shown in Figure 8.7-3 (see also Figure 8.7-4). A key part of these advisories are the precise location of the storm and the radii of the 34-kt wind pattern, which we are instructed to avoid. Individual advisories can be requested (see Saildocs and FTPmail help files), but the main information is also included in the simple Saildocs metarea requests (met.12 or met.4).

When sailing in the tropics in the hurricane season, it is fundamental to know of these resources and to practice with them. Underway we get tropical storm location and motion:

Every 6 hr from metarea reports

Every 3 hr from NHC advisories

Every 1 hr from WWV/WWVH HF radio storm warnings.

To create more study examples as we wait for the next hurricane season: archived OPC and NHC maps can be found at ncei.noaa.gov/thredds/model/ncep_charts.html and archived NHC advisories and details of any storm can be found at nhc.noaa.gov/archive. Archived GFS GRIB files are stored at nomads.ncdc.noaa.gov/data/gfs4, but they are large, global files, with 354 parameters! LuckGrib (Mac or iPad) or Panoply (Mac or PC) are two ways we know of to look at these large GRIB files.

HF Voice Broadcasts

On a modern vessel, the voice broadcasts over HF radio mentioned in Section 8.5 are now a backup source, because we can request these at any time by email, and do not have to wait for the specific broadcast times and hope the radio is properly tuned at that moment. Nevertheless, a prudent navigator will maintain some means of obtaining these, because they can be received by battery operated shortwave radios, even if all ships power is lost.

Needless to say, they are easier to receive with a proper HF SSB transceiver (if available), or higher quality HF receiver only, but the better receivers cost as much as a satphone. There are numerous intermediate-cost receivers that should do the job, but they must be practiced. Examples were mentioned in Figure 8.5-1 in the context of using them to receive the storm warnings that are broadcast with the time tics.

Broadcast schedules are given in Table 8.7-1. Recall that the offshore forecasts made for radio broadcast are compila-

tions of a large number of zones that might not give as full a picture as we would get from the individual offshore zone forecasts. See discussion of Table 8.6-3. For convenience in practicing reception, Table 8.7-2 compiles broadcast times sequentially from Table 8.7-1.

SafetyNET

SafetyNET is a GMDSS mandated satcom system using Inmarsat-C. Products and schedules are similar to NAVTEX. It is an unattended automated source of weather data. SafetyNET broadcasts use the WMO metarea forecast zones, with

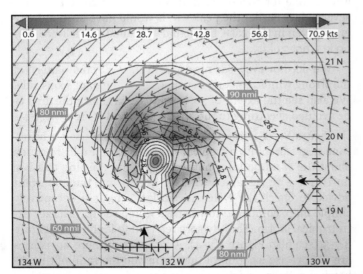

Figure 8.7-1. *GFS (0.5°) wind analysis for 06z, Aug 22, 2017. Thin black lines are wind-speed contours. This section includes GFS wind speeds from 0.6 kts to 70.9 kts. The yellow area marks the extent of 34-kt winds Green lines mark NHC forecasted 06z position and radii of 34 kt winds (Figure 8.7-3). This GFS central pressure at 06z was 1002.4, compared to NHC value of 960 for 9 hrs earlier. This archived GFS file is displayed here in the program Panoply. Part of the discrepancy between this GFS and NHC forecasts is the resolution of the GFS. Note in the Advisory the eye diameter (location of deepest pressure) was 10 nmi, and strongest winds are just outside that. A 30-nmi GFS grid averages out these extremes in wind and pressure. We would likely see closer agreement with the 15-nmi GFS, or better still the 5.4-nmi oceanic NDFD that extends out to 140W.*

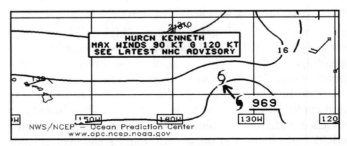

Figure 8.7-2. *OPC analysis 00z Aug 22, 2017 reports this is a hurricane with peak sustained winds of 90 kt, and direction to check the NHC Advisories.*

HURRICANE KENNETH FORECAST/ADVISORY NUMBER 14
NWS NATIONAL HURRICANE CENTER MIAMI FL
EP132017
2100 UTC MON AUG 21 2017

HURRICANE CENTER LOCATED NEAR 18.3N 131.6W AT 21/2100Z POSITION ACCURATE WITHIN 10 NM. PRESENT MOVEMENT TOWARD THE NORTHWEST OR 305 DEGREES AT 8 KT ESTIMATED MINIMUM CENTRAL PRESSURE 960 MB.
EYE DIAMETER 10 NM. MAX SUSTAINED WINDS 105 KT WITH GUSTS TO 130 KT.

AT 21/1800Z CENTER WAS LOCATED NEAR 18.0N 131.2W

FORECAST VALID 22/0600Z 19.4N 132.4W
MAX WIND 90 KT...GUSTS 110 KT.
64 KT... 25NE 20SE 15SW 20NW.
50 KT... 50NE 40SE 30SW 40NW.
34 KT... 90NE 80SE 60SW 80NW.

Figure 8.7-3. *Section of the NHC Advisory. The 06z was a 12-hr forecast; not shown are the included similar forecasts for: Aug 22, 18z (24-hr); Aug 23, 06z (36-hr); Aug 24, 18z (48-hr); and two extended forecasts for days 3 and 4. See a similar example in Figure 4.8-4.*

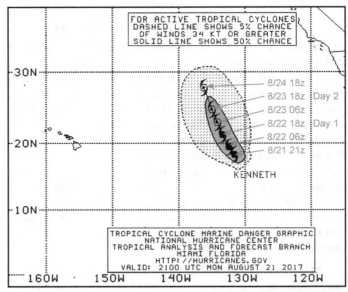

Figure 8.7-4. *Tropical cyclone warning chart (PWFK11.TIF). These charts show positions listed in the latest advisory, but do not label them. The Atlantic counterpart is PWEK11.TIF. The dashed line marks the area to be avoided, but we can see this better for a specific day by plotting out the 34-kt radii.*

coverage determined by the footprints of the four Inmarsat satellites and the four GMDSS Sea Area designations. All GMDSS participating nations provide SafetyNET broadcast data, although some do not offer NAVTEX. See GMDSS/SafetyNET at navcen.uscg.gov for details and references. As with NAVTEX, SafetyNET broadcasts are safety information, not tactical or full weather coverage. At present, mariners do not have access to SafetyNET broadcasts via an Iridium satcom system.

Table 8.7-1. High Seas and Offshore HF Voice Broadcasts								
New Orleans (NMG)								
4316, 8502, 12788	0330Z	0515Z	0930Z	1115Z	1530Z	1715Z	2130Z	2315Z
Offshore forecasts, hurricane information High seas forecast, hurricane information								

Chesapeake (NMN)						
4426, 6501, 8764	0330Z	0515Z	0930Z			
6501, 8764, 13089			1115Z	1530Z	2130Z	2315Z
8764, 13089, 17314				1715Z		
Offshore forecasts, hurricane information High seas forecast, hurricane information						

Pt. Reyes (NMC)				
4426, 8764, 13089	0430Z	1030Z		
8764, 13089, 17314			1630Z	2230Z

Kodiak (NOJ)		
6501	0203Z	1645Z

Honolulu (NMO)				
6501, 8764		0600Z	1200Z	
8764, 13089	0005Z			1800Z

Guam (NRV)				
6501		0930Z	1530Z	
13089	0330Z			2130Z

Table 8.7-2. Practice Times
0005Z
0330Z
0430Z
0515Z
0600Z
0930Z
1030Z
1115Z
1200Z
1530Z
1630Z
1715Z
1800Z
2130Z
2230Z
2315Z

Table Notes: 1. All frequencies in kHz, upper side band (USB). **2.** Broadcast of hurricane and other weather broadcasts from these stations may on occasion be preempted, as the frequencies are shared with other USCG stations. **3.** NMG, NMN, NMC can also be interrupted as they share the transmitters with the radiofax broadcasts. **4.** Bold numbers in Table 8.7-2 mean more than one frequency has broadcasts at that time.

Heinrich Wilhelm Dove (1803 – 1879) was a contemporary of FitzRoy and also referred to by professionals in his era as the "Father of Meteorology." FitzRoy ("Father of Marine Weather") translated his first edition of *Law of Storms* in 1857, and they both praised each other in subsequent books.

He was a Prussian physicist and meteorologist, with numerous accomplishments in both areas. He was praised for his lecture skills and a prolific scientist with over 300 publications in both experimental and theoretical studies. His PhD dissertation in 1826 was on the subject of atmospheric pressure.

Notable in practical marine weather was his climatic studies of global winds, temperatures, and pressures that led to his observation that tropical storms rotated counterclockwise in the NH and clockwise in the SH around a minimum in atmospheric pressure. He had many innovative interpretations of global wind flow and his compiled data were crucial to subsequent development of global wind theory.

He invented the concept of isotherms and indeed it could be argued that he made the first weather map or was at least crucial to its concept. He was the first to consider local weather as being the result of a global atmosphere and thus predicted and described seasonal weather patterns as well as diurnal variations in wind and pressure.

In 1847 he was appointed Director of the Prussian Meteorological Institute, which had just been founded by the renown Alexander van Helmholtz, thus making him a direct counterpart to FitzRoy, Maury, and Buys Ballot. He was criticized toward the end of the century for not keeping up with progress in the physics of the atmosphere, but his key role in the overall development of the science is clear.

The expanded second edition of *Law of Storms* translated by Robert Scott in 1863 is online as a pdf; it offers good testimony to his intellect and contribution. The online edition is from Harvard University, purchased for them with funds donated by Nathaniel Bowditch.

9.1 Instruments and Logbook Procedures

The primary instruments of marine weather are an anemometer and wind vane for wind speed and direction, a barometer for atmospheric pressure, and a thermometer for sea and air temperature.

For all instruments, the ideal system includes options for recording and displaying past data either in an attached computer or in the instrument console display, as in Figure 9.1-1. With more computer use, and most instruments using National Marine Electronics Association (NMEA) conventions for data transfer, these options are available in several navigation programs (Figure 9.1-2).

Barometers are discussed in Chapter 2. Refer to that section for background; more applications of this most crucial of marine instruments are given in this chapter, and in Chapter 10. Stand-alone electronic barographs show plots of the pressure, but we can also use low-cost USB barometer sensors and do the plotting in our navigation software. In any event, we should have the pressure recorded frequently in the log book as a backup.

Thermometer sensors for sea water temperature are most convenient when permanently in contact with the water, so the temperature can be read continuously. When sailing in the Gulf Stream or other regions where ocean current behavior might be detected by temperature, it is crucial to have a large prominent read out so you know immediately when the temperature changes. In regions where this matters, it can matter a lot. Also remember that hurricane development requires water of 80 °F or warmer, which is a reminder that we want the thermometer calibrated. We should always be very attentive to the weather when the water temperature gets much warmer than its climatic value shown on pilot charts. A handheld

infrared thermometer is a good back up. They are inexpensive and easy to use, but they must be calibrated. Standard calibration points of a thermometer are the equilibrium of water and ice at 32 °F and the boiling point of water, which is 212 °F for pressures 994 mb to 1032 mb. Several inexpensive thermometers can be calibrated to create a standard, which can then be compared in the 50 to 90 °F range we care about.

Strange as it may sound, air temperature is not often crucial to your understanding of the weather (wind and wind forecasting), but it does help with general life onboard. You will, for example, get documented proof that cabin temperatures get remarkably hot in the tropics, and how, even in the middle of summer, it can get very cold at night in the higher midlatitudes. There are also notable tactical uses. It can be useful to note the difference between air and sea temperature as that affects the stability of the air, and thus the likelihood of squalls or their severity. You will also notice air temperature changes at frontal passage, and usually the larger the change the more severe the frontal weather. Look for ship reports of air temperature on either side of a front on the surface analysis map. And for what it is worth, you can often detect the cooler air from downdrafts in squalls. Broadly speaking, the more data you are aware of, the more you are in tune with the environment, which will generally lead to the better use of it to your advantage.

Wind instruments are also crucial, but we need not say much here on them since they are usually adequately described as far as usage, installation, and calibration in their

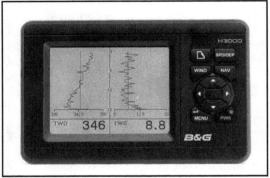

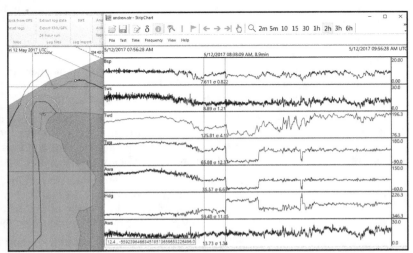

Figure 9.1-1. *Samples of graphic display of data in wind instruments. Compliments of B&G Instruments.* ockam.com *has an extensive online presentation of wind analysis for sailors using logged wind data.*

Figure 9.1-2. *Samples of logged and plotted instrument data viewed in Expedition. Compliments of Andrew Haliburton. When all parameters are recorded, inconsistencies can be spotted to detect influence of current or calibration errors, as well as comparisons and improvements to polar diagrams (Section 10.7).*

associated manuals. You also might find it instructive to read not only your instruction manuals, but those of other brands as well. Much like radar, GPS, and knotmeters, we find that different companies put emphasis on different aspects of the installation, calibration, and usage of their devices. This is even more likely with wind instruments. If you do not feel you are getting enough information from your manuals, go online and download some for similar devices from other companies, and check them out. Even though brands and features are different, the calibration procedures and tips on installation could be informative.

Wind direction is a pretty mechanical operation of just checking the physical alignment at the masthead. Some units then let you make offsets electronically as needed. It might be useful to take a big protractor to the masthead and check some of the wind angles by direct measurement. Wind speed is often first calibrated in dead calm air by motoring at fixed speeds to see if the apparent wind matches your knotmeter, or better your GPS SOG *in still water*. Make measurements on reciprocal headings to account for current if suspected.

Then there is the issue of how the sails might affect the wind speed and angle. The solution, if needed, might be an extension of the arm holding the instruments away from the masthead. Then check to see that you get the same wind angles and speeds on opposite tacks and jibes. You could also take your anemometer for a ride in your car and hold it out of the window to compare with speedometer for higher wind speeds.

The more subtle issue of heel angle affecting the apparent wind angle is addressed in Appendix 9. Some sophisticated wind instruments account for this, others do not, so we must correct for this ourselves if we choose to.

A sling psychrometer for measuring dew point might be included in a set of weather instruments, but the measurement procedures are more demanding for recreational mariners than the needs justify. Used properly, they are typically accurate to 1 or 2 F° using tables rather than the scales printed on the devices. Trained VOS mariners make the measurements and we see them in the ship reports.

Hygrometer is the generic name for relative humidity (RH) measuring devices, of which sling psychrometer is one type, probably the most basic. Mechanical synthetic hair hygrometers from Fischer Instruments are accurate to ±3% RH. Top of the line electronic instruments are ±1%. These measurements, however, are all extremely sensitive to the air temperature. The air temperature can change less than 1 degree and the RH may change 5%. The RH you measure can depend on how close you are to the sensor when you read it!

If you need to estimate the dew point, fill a shiny metal can (food can with label off) with water and let it come to equilibrium with the air temperature. Then slowly add ice cubes, stirring with a thermometer, until you see water vapor condense on the outside of the can. At that point, the water-can temperature should be the dew point. Precision instruments based on this method are called "metal mirror" devices.

Logbooks

It can be useful to have a separate logbook for weather notes, but the main data might be best in the primary logbook. Normal logbook data includes, time, date, log reading, course steered, COG from GPS, knotmeter speed, SOG from GPS, VMG to next way point, and perhaps also the tack or jibe you are on. This last record sounds pretty basic, and should in principle be deducible from all other data, but you will be surprised how often it is valuable to have this confirmation. Weather data would include apparent wind speed, apparent wind direction, (maybe record the tack here), barometer, plus maybe air and water temperature, some cloud description, and some sea state description.

The crucial data are wind and pressure. Try to estimate and record the pressure to the nearest tenth of a mb. The wind data would typically be apparent wind speed and apparent wind angle. If you have true wind instruments, and are sure they are working properly, then true wind angle and true wind speed would be better. In any event, it is very good practice to have another column where you compute the true wind angle and speed from the apparent data. Then add the true wind angle to your true heading to record in a column that will have true wind direction. This is the main column you are watching for weather warnings, and for tactics in general. A programmed calculator, smart phone app, or computer program that just takes the 3 inputs and gives back the true wind data (Section 2.5) is a must for this. It takes too long to plot it out each time.

True wind instruments are a blessing when they work, but they take careful maintenance to be right. Your knotmeter must be right on both tacks, as well as wind speed and direction. Also if you are using a heading sensor to get true wind direction (as opposed to true wind angle), then this heading sensor must be right as well. If anything is off, even just a little bit, you can get seriously wrong vector solutions for the true wind. Think of looking for the vector difference between two vectors that are almost the same. If one has even a small error, the difference has a big error. This same type of error can occur with mini-ARPA radar units with maladjusted inputs. You know that boat is not going 150 kts just by looking at it, but an important wind change might not be so obvious.

Good shipboard forecasting calls for frequent observations and logbook entries. During ocean races, it is common to enter the log every hour, but this could be extreme for cruising or deliveries. The traditional rule is to enter the log whenever anything changes, or every 4 hrs, or every watch change, regardless of any changes. If you later note something has changed, you can then go back to see when it first happened. If a tropical storm or depression is anticipated, we would want to record the pressure every hour, regardless of what the sky or wind looks like.

The meaning of "any changes" depends on the conditions at hand. A 5° change in the average course, for example, is a large change, even for a sailing vessel in a seaway where the heading is routinely swinging around through some 40° or more. It is easy to detect such changes in an average course when sailing to weather, even in rough conditions, but it takes more diligence to do so on a reach. But if the course changes this much, something did indeed change in the wind or seas. Likewise, any call for a change of trim indicates something has changed in the wind or seas and should signal a log entry.

Recall that a 6° error in course heading corresponds to a 10% cross track error, i.e., for every 10 miles you run on a course that is off by 6°, you will be off to the right or left of where you think you are by 1.0 nmi. An average knotmeter speed change of 10% is a notable difference.

Section 7.2 includes a section on sequencing weather maps. This could be done by pasting paper copies in a notebook along with transcripts or notes from voice broadcasts. Using a computer we can develop a file and folder naming system to organize these for study.

Generally we will be recording our tracks electronically, if not in a computer program, then in the graphic display of the console GPS unit. With this data, any change from a straight track line becomes very apparent and hopefully we will have a log entry to indicate what led to the change we observe. If not, go back and make a note of what happened with the track line and when, because otherwise we might lose this information if we change the track display.

In any event, it is most important that we make a special logbook entry at the synoptic times of 00z, 06z, 12z, and 18z. These are the times we need data to compare with the weather maps. The primary logbook is kept on ship's time, which will not be UTC as a rule, so you have to convert these synoptic times to ship time and make a note or set an alarm to remind you to record the data. In U.S. coastal waters you might also want entries at 09z and 15z as the Unified Analysis maps are also updated at these times.

9.2 Onboard Forecasting

Forecasting tips from our own onboard observations have been given throughout the book. Here we summarize these and expand on a few.

Shipboard forecasting can be thought of on two levels. One is making the best guess of what might happen based *solely* on what you can see and measure yourself. The second is the more productive approach of using your own observations to confirm or elaborate on an official forecast or map that you have from a professional weather service. The first approach might be called "seat of the pants" forecasting, the second is just plain prudent navigation, making the most of all resources available.

What you actually do forecasting-wise and how you do it are about the same for either purpose, but there are a few distinct differences. For example, outside of the tropics, the actual barometer reading is not of much value in seat of the pants forecasting. It is the barometer change that matters most in that case. But if we are trying to verify a recent weather map we have in front of us, then the real pressure

measured with a calibrated barometer becomes a valuable aid to interpreting the map.

Seat of the pants forecasters will certainly have more surprises to deal with than those with more resources at hand. But anyone in any vessel could end up with nothing more to go by, so it pays learn as much as possible about shipboard forecasting.

Important reminder: official surface analysis maps and forecasts are not necessarily right! The degree that we care which detail is right or wrong and to what extent, depends on our circumstance. A sailor cares very much if the wind is 12 kts or 16 kts, or if it is from the NW or the N-NW. A larger power driven vessel in the same conditions doesn't care about these distinctions at all.

As a general rule, details of mapped isobars in regions with good weather are not as reliable as those from areas with more severe weather. This is in part because ship reports of fair weather may be less precise than those from heavy weather, and in spite of all the wonderful satellite data we have on wind, actual ship reports still play an important role in the map production. Many times we have seen otherwise smooth isobars bend to match one or two ship reports.

Likewise, map details in areas with few ship reports—that is, in areas well away from great circle routes between major ports—may be more in doubt than those with many ship reports. The actual distribution of ship reports that go into a specific analysis can be observed on the surface analysis maps, and actually tracked down for more specifics by email request (Section 8.4).

The observations we care about most are:

- wind speed
- wind direction
- barometer
- clouds
- sea state
- water temperature

Usually, it is not the present value of these parameters that matter most, but rather the sequence of values that shows how they are changing. Hence, careful logbook records are crucial. Furthermore, it is generally a combination of these observations that means the most.

Sea state and clouds are pure visual observations; the others require some instrumentation. For rough observations, wind speed can be estimated with the Beaufort scale, wind direction relative to compass heading, and water temperature from a thermometer in a bucket of water—although this is more often just a way to lose a bucket. Barometric pressure, however, requires a proper instrument—shark oil barometers are the same as snake oil barometers. And though it sounds really harsh, many common barometers found on vessels could be replaced by a picture of a barometer when it comes to their practical value. To do the best job, we need calibrated instruments (see Appendix 5).

The following notes summarize and extend points made in earlier chapters as related to shipboard observations, that might help us make our own forecasts or validate ones given to us.

Forecasting with Wind

Changes in the wind are the main thing we want to forecast in marine weather—that is, large changes in the wind. Hence any small shift in true wind speed (TWS) or true wind direction (TWD) is an important sign to watch for. If TWS changes, the isobars have changed, and they are the map of the overall wind field around us. If the TWS goes up (away from squalls), the isobars have gotten closer together; if TWD changes, the isobars have rotated.

A change in the true wind can occur before or even without any change in barometer reading. Imagine sailing around the corner of a High along the 1020 isobar at a TWA of 150°. The pressure won't change, and the TWA won't change, your heading just changes as the TWD veers around the High as you proceed. The TWS could go up or down or stay the same, depending on what the isobars on either side of 1020 are doing.

The key to careful wind observation is recording TWD frequently and precisely. That is, record that the wind is, say, 280 rather than just "westerly," and if it changes (in average value by 5° or so) make a log entry. Generally we will be recording apparent wind in the logbook, but when watching for weather changes we must make the extra effort to convert these to true wind. We must also make an extra effort in general when entering the logbook—namely, you can't just look at the meter (compass heading, wind speed or wind direction) and write down whatever you see. You have to watch it awhile and take some average value.

When making an entry that covers the past watch, it is best to check with who was on watch to see if your recording is a realistic average for that period. If you are recording the present observations, then you still need to watch and average over a few minutes. Needless to say, instruments that record the data for you are an asset, but they do not remove the need for careful written records.

As with most onboard observations, the best understanding of what you see is obtained by combining a real forecast or map with what you can observe. Or at least to understand the prevailing (climatic) patterns of a given region and how they change. This type of preparation would be considered standard good seamanship. Such data is often given in *Planning Guides*, *Coast Pilots*, and Pilot Charts. Modern vessels would likely have the COGOW wind plots printed and at hand for the time of the passage.

We should understand, for example, that prevailing good weather in the summertime midlatitudes is usually associated with wind flow around the prevailing mid-ocean Highs and corresponding thermal Lows that build up over the coastal lands. Bad weather comes with an invading Low or front coming in from the west, which either rides up over these Highs or blasts through them. Occasionally, very strong winds result from a High packing up against an entrenched thermal Low or trough on shore.

The best prevailing winds are from COGOW; the best climatic description of world pressure patterns and their standard deviations is the *Mariner's Pressure Atlas* (Starpath Publications, 2014).

Wind Changes as First Signs

The West Coast of the U.S. is similar to the west coast of any continent. In fact, these guidelines apply to any midlatitude waters located to the east of mid-ocean Highs. In these locations, fair winds are from the NW quadrant. Foul weather comes with wind in the southerly quadrant. Remember that winds around Highs are usually fair winds and winds around Lows are often storm winds. Highs and Lows are compared in Section 2.3.

East of a High, fair NW wind evolves into a foul South wind by backing around. Hence, the first sign to look for in these circumstances is the onset of a backing shift in the wind—320 shifting to 310, for example.

The wind can begin this backing shift toward the south long before any barometer indications, and often before any real confirmation from clouds. Also, in a west coast situation (east of a High) this backing shift will generally start before the wind builds. This is different from the typical behavior one might expect on an east coast (west of an offshore High). Hence, when east of a High, a backing shift is the first key indicator of potential bad weather.

New clouds are a less reliable sign. We may see cirrus invade and begin to spread into cirrocumulus without bringing any bad weather at all. But if we see that cloud pattern start to develop (discussed later) and then see the wind start to back around, we have good evidence that something is happening. Then we might see the barometer start down. We must always look for combinations of signs, not rely on any one sign.

Figure 4.3-9 showed how wind backs around as a Low replaces a ridge of high pressure. Note in particular that in some cases the pressure actually went up as the wind started to back around. This shows that the wind shift can often be a much better sign than pressure alone.

On an east coast, fair weather summertime winds typically come from the S quadrant (SW to SE) as wind flows around the offshore High. In these cases, the wind that signals an approaching weather system is more likely to be a building wind than a shifting wind. The approaching Low (or more likely front) coming in from the west quadrant will bring with it wind that is already from the S quadrant so the first tendency of the local wind is to build rather than shift. In these cases, a simultaneous pressure drop might be more likely than it is in similar approaches on the west coast.

From the different generic behavior of changing winds on a west coast versus an east coast, we can see the value of looking at a map if we have access to one. It always pays to look at a map of the region you are in to see what is causing the wind you have and how it will likely change if a new system approaches from the western quadrant or from the south. What to expect as the first signs depends on what it is, Low or front, and where it is coming from.

Put another way, a prudent mariner will always know what pattern is causing the present wind and what should be the first signs of an approaching change shown in the forecast maps.

You get this information from a weather map, or from simply knowing how the wind behaves in your region with an approaching Low or front from various directions, and then listening to a weather report of what might be on the way. The first can be done by anyone in any part of the world after some practice with weather maps. The latter is called local knowledge. It is more work and takes longer to learn—and is generally less dependable, which I know sounds like heresy, but I must take the side of reality in this important matter.

Frontal Winds

On the east side of a High, frontal winds will tend to back around to the south as the front approaches, eventually building and then undergoing a sudden veer at the front itself. On the west side of a High, the winds will tend to build first and then begin to veer or back depending on the circumstances, but will nevertheless undergo a strong veer as the front passes. Generally the veer will take the frontal winds with a prominent cold front from somewhere in the south quadrant to somewhere in the west quadrant. What happens after the front depends on what kind of front it is and what is behind it.

Important Universal Rule on Fronts

When a NH front passes (any kind, any place), the wind will make a sudden veer. In the SH, wind always backs at a front. Cold fronts veer more than warm fronts. Cold fronts can be seen coming as a wall of tall dark clouds. Warm fronts are anticipated from a lowering of stratus clouds and a long period of light steady rain. It might get slightly warmer as a warm front approaches, but generally the main temperature change is felt after the front passes. A cold front is not felt until it passes. Cold fronts move faster than warm fronts and generally bring stronger and gustier winds with larger veers.

Sea Breeze as Forecaster

In the NH, a sea breeze generally builds in the onshore direction or from slightly to the left of it, and then proceeds to veer as it builds in the afternoon. If it starts out W it will move toward the NW. If E, it veers to the SE. In other words, in normal sea breeze conditions we expect a veer with a building sea breeze.

Some regions are well known for their sea breezes and this information is in the *Coast Pilots* or in *Sailing Directions*. If the sky is clear and there is no weather pattern over the region that dominates the wind flow—which means not much wind at night—then in the morning the sea breeze will build. It is dependable. In some coastal regions it is the dominant wind pattern for many months of the year. If conditions appear right for this to happen, but it does not happen, then something is taking place to prevent it, and this is a sign to us.

One possibility is that a low pressure is approaching that is canceling out the drop in pressure over the land as it heats leaving no gradient and no wind. Hence the absence of a sea breeze or a dying sea breeze is sign of some approaching low pressure. A dying sea breeze, by the way, will often back around to where it came from (NH).

Squall Winds

Wind changes are not going to tell us much about squalls that we can't get from seeing their clouds. As a rule, surface winds in the vicinity of a few miles from a developing squall are pulled in toward the squall. After and during the downburst, which is signaled by the rain, the local winds emanate out of the squall, much stronger in front and often weak or fluky behind it.

Note that very intense squalls can precede a fast moving cold front and they are common on the perimeters of tropical storms—in these special cases, squalls can come within the presence of strong winds. But away from such systems, in the general case of the vast majority of squalls, the cumulus cloud development that creates squalls takes place in relatively light air. Most squall pictures you will see show no white caps away from the squalls themselves. This occurs because strong winds interrupt the convective process that builds them. It stirs up the air too much so it can't get focused into individual clouds. Hence a good stiff wind at night will be less likely to bring squalls than a calm or light air night.

Wind Gusts

Well away from the influences of land, gusts are often just patches of higher air that swoop down to the surface. Thus we can expect them to be stronger than the surface winds (i.e., they are gusts!) and they will likely be veered relative to surface winds—you can test this hypothesis using the NDBC plots of wind speed and direction for ocean buoys. Gust speed increases are larger for light air (50 to 100%, say 2 kts gusting to 3 or 4, or 3 kts gusting to 6) but in stronger winds the percentage increase is lower (20 to 30%, say 20 kts gusting to 25, or 30 kts gusting to 39).

Often the helm can be assisted by someone watching the water surface to windward, as you might detect the gust patch approaching from the texture of the water.

Wind on Radar

For what it might be worth, though stretching the context of wind forecasting, if you are under power or reaching, or not aware of the true wind direction for any reason, you can often spot this direction very easily from the radar screen, because the sea clutter is more prominent in the windward direction. Sometimes this observation can be correlated with radar monitoring of squalls for a useful conclusion—keeping in mind that you are observing the direction of relative motion of the squalls, which depends on your speed and heading, whereas the wind direction observed this way depends only on your heading.

Role of Clouds

Cloud observations are an important contribution to our understanding of what is taking place with the weather, but these observations must be combined with other data to be useful. Without supporting information we may not be able to read as much as we like from the typical clouds and cloud changes we see so frequently. Some cloud patterns are indeed strong signs, while others are not at all dependable.

An approaching warm front or Low, for example, will usually have a distinct cloud sequence, and if you are in clear skies to begin with, it is an easily recognized sequence. But the state of the atmosphere might be such as to give this same sequence without the onset of a significant change in the wind—which is ultimately the main thing we care about in marine weather.

Likewise, a general change in the weather is often marked by what is called a "chaotic sky," meaning a prominent cloud display of many different kinds of clouds, all visible at once, moving in different directions at different altitudes. But although some changes in weather are indeed marked by this dramatic cloud pattern, I have seen several striking examples of this type of sky that just slowly dissolved into more of what we had weather-wise before the pattern developed.

It is my feeling that clouds are more valuable in confirming what is more or less already taking place than in actual forecasting of what might take place in the future. Naturally, there are special cases, and even if the signs are not conclusive so often, they are indeed warnings of what might be happening which we can combine with other observations to put the picture together.

On the other hand, there are cases where cloud observations are irreplaceable. Squalls on the high seas, for example, even very large ones, are usually not forecasted at all in official reports and maps (the exception is the HRRR model in U.S. coastal waters). The likelihood of these, and their stage of development, we must judge underway, on our own. And cloud observations are crucial to this. Squall lines are also not often forecasted. We must recognize them from the clouds and prepare accordingly. (Again, we miss the cloud symbol annotations for thunderstorms on tropical maps that used to be there. They were accurate and helpful.) Tropical storms also have distinct cloud patterns that can help in our understanding of where we are relative to them.

Away from prominent weather systems, layers of stratiform clouds usually imply stable air—meaning not gusty, and slow to change. In contrast, large cumulus clouds imply unstable air with large vertical updrafts. Gusty winds changing frequently. In fact, any cumulus structure implies some level of instability. Even way up high, when thick cirrostratus evolves into cirrocumulus, it is a sign that some new instability has entered the scene.

A reminder of the basics: a wall of tall dark clouds with low ceiling means strong gusty winds. The clouds would be a combination of nimbostratus and cumulonimbus. The systems would be either a cold front, large close squall, or squall line—or in hurricane zones, it could be the bar of a hurricane itself.

As a broad, general guide, any change in the clouds that is not toward fair-weather cumulus is a sign the weather *might* deteriorate. That is not at all a strong guideline and almost obvious, because strong wind almost always requires clouds, but a basic point to keep in mind when viewing the clouds.

Warm Fronts

Probably the most famous role of clouds in forecasting is their indication of a warm front approaching into clear skies—usually a more successful indicator in the summer than winter. There is a classic sequence to expect in the sky, which will typically proceed on schedule over a period of about 24 hrs plus or minus some 12 hrs.

From a cloudless sky, the first indication is the appearance of a ring around the sun or moon. This is proof positive that a thin layer of invisible cirrostratus (ice crystals) has invaded the sky. The ring is 22° in radius because that is the only angle light can escape from an ice crystal. Put a thumb on the sun and with an outstretched hand, the little finger will be roughly on the ring, see Figure 9.4-5. It is big, not like the small corona we see around the sun shining through the frosted-glass look of altostratus.

The next sign—or sometimes the first sign, when a ring does not appear—is the first appearance of cirrus clouds in an otherwise clear sky. These can start out as single isolated clouds that gradually grow more numerous, or as a more prominent invasion of a sheet of the clouds seen rising up over the western horizon. These cirrus, or the halo, mark the time of the "first signs" of the front. If the first sign is cirrus and they are very high and light, then it may indicate that the front will take longer to arrive than one that first shows up with a more dramatic appearance of more prominent cirrus.

Next, the cirrus will thicken into cirrocumulus or a denser cirrostratus. From here the clouds begin to lower, forming altostratus and then stratus. Somewhere along this sequence, the altostratus will become nimbostratus and start to rain. It will be a long steady light rain, as opposed to downpours or showers. The start of the rain very roughly marks the halfway time to the arrival of the actual frontal boundary on the surface. It will continue to rain until the front arrives, which will be roughly the time it took from first signs to first rain.

During this overall sequence, the barometer will be dropping and the winds will be changing. On the West Coast, the wind is most likely to be backing around as it builds, or maybe even start to back around before it builds. On the East Coast, the wind is more likely to build in speed with less change in direction as the front approaches.

At the front itself, the winds will become more gusty and will undergo a sudden veer. Once veered into the warm sector wind, the wind speed and direction should remain fairly steady. The barometer could rise or remain steady, depending on your course relative to the straight isobars in the warm sector.

Later we discuss estimating the speed of the winds aloft, which adds to the interpretation of the high cloud patterns first seen in the warm front sequence. These observations can warn of severe fronts as opposed to weaker ones.

Cloud-wise, Lows also often approach into clear skies much as a warm front does. Winds also back around and build, and also veer back to where they were as it passes. But the veer is gradual with an isolated Low, not sudden as when a front passes.

Cold Fronts

Cold fronts typically follow a warm front in a day or so. The air mass between the two is called the warm sector. Its most characteristic clouds would likely be patches of stratocumulus, or general broken sky cover, with scattered showers. Generally the wind and pressure are steady within the warm sector.

The cold front can be seen approaching as a wall of tall dark clouds. Near the front, gusty wind will increase quickly, typically with thunderstorms and heavy rain. As the front passes, the wind will suddenly veer, and following the passage the skies will gradually clear, maybe with patches of stratocumulus. Often there is a noticeable freshness and clarity to the air after a prominent cold front passes—providing there is no other system hot on its tail.

Cold fronts can travel around on their own, without a preceding warm front. This happens much less often with warm fronts (at least on the U.S. West Coast).

Occluded fronts approach much as warm fronts do, but what happens at the frontal surface is typically some combination of the two (cold and warm). Plain bad weather. Clouds and rain, light and heavy, building gusty winds.

Clouds in Light Air

As a rough rule, there is wind under cumulus clouds. If you are a sailor, stuck in a mid-ocean High, in very light and fluky wind—or on a large inland lake—then look for clouds and inch your way toward them. For isolated clouds that are not raining, the general wind flow is in toward the base of the cloud. For a raining cloud, the wind flow is out of the cloud. Generally, low clouds are moving downwind at a direction that is slightly veered from the surface winds. Wind speed and direction at 850 mb (available in some GFS sources) is a way to estimate cloud or squall movement. In light air, clouds can be everything. Even being on the best side of them can matter a lot, so keep records of what you learn.

Also in these circumstances it can pay to climb to the spreaders or get as high as you can with binoculars. Sometimes there are patches of wind that can be seen as dark texture on the surface even though there are not any clouds present. For a while it was standard procedure in America's Cup races to try to judge if the left or right side of the course is favorable from what could be seen from the masthead—that is, after paying 6-digit fees to get the best guess before they went out on the race course!

Squall Clouds

Squalls require big cumulus clouds, which in turn requires warm moist air and vertical instability. At sea in warm water, this often occurs at night when the air temperature drops below the water temperature. If we watch the clouds at sunset, we can often get some idea of what kind of night it will be—squally or not squally.

If we do have squalls, we are likely to have many of them, or at least see many around us, though we might not go through many ourselves. It is rather rare to have just one. If conditions are right, they will be all around. If not, there won't be any. Without adequate instability in the air, at sunset the cumulus clouds of the day generally spread out into stratocumulus and maybe even into stratus or evaporate.

In contrast, when squalls are imminent, at sunset the cumulus don't flatten out, but seem to gang up, or coalesce into individual bigger clouds. Then you can watch them develop, if it is still light enough. Or you can sometimes see this during the day as well. The thing to look for is the vertical development (cloud base to cloud top), relative to the distance from cloud base to sea level. If the vertical development of all the clouds stays well less than the height of their base, then you just get big cumulus (cumulus congestus), but there is not enough instability for them to go all the way to cumulonimbus.

On the other hand, if vertical development starts to become equal to or much greater than base height, then they are well on their way to becoming thunderstorms. These signs are not always crisp and clear, but sometimes they are very noticeable and even useful for planning what might take place. Keep in mind that distant squalls will be over water that is below your horizon, so they will appear lower than they are. This observation on development is for the nearby ones. See Figure 8.4-1 for a possible way to study squall development in the tropics from home.

To judge the severity of an approaching squall from its clouds, the indicators are the vertical development (how high it is), its base height (how low it is) and its color (from white to black—the darker it is the more rain it has in it, which likely means it has not started its downburst). As a rule, very tall, very low, and very dark mark the worst kind. The best way to put quantitative values on these parameters is to start taking mental or even written notes on ones you see. After sailing through the first one, you have a standard, which will improve as more squall days (and nights) are experienced. We have to "go to school" on the squalls at hand.

Obviously, at night it is difficult or impossible to see the cloud structure and color, but on clear nights you can often see them outlined on the horizon. Sometimes during the day, cloud heights are obscured by stratus layers, but more often than not, the full clouds are visible as isolated events. Also don't forget radar. Night or day, radar shows very well which squalls are more intense than others. Cellphone photos of the radar screen may help in ranking these as well.

The anvil top to cumulonimbus clouds is a clear sign of a severe squall, so big it rose all the way up to the winds aloft which blew its top off into the anvil pattern (incus). On the other hand, once it has built to that level, it is most likely past its worst conditions on the surface. This is a sign that the cloud has reached full maturity and by now has started to decay. A surface downburst is most likely under clouds with a well developed anvil top. Unfortunately, you can't see the tops of the ones you really care about, because they are too close or already overhead. If you see them you do know you are in an air mass capable of producing giant squalls.

Sea Breeze Clouds

Sea breezes are onshore breezes, and when the coastal topography is elevated they can run up the slopes of near coastal mountains and hills. By midmorning this updraft in normal conditions generally starts the formation of small cumulus cloud caps. The appearance of these cloud caps is a good sign of a developing sea breeze, which might not yet be felt offshore. These winds generally peak in late afternoon.

Likewise, the absence of these clouds might forewarn the lack of a sea breeze to come, which in turn signals that some low pressure has moved in to cancel out the sea breeze gradient.

Trade Wind Cumulus

Trade wind cumulus are a good sign that you have reached the trade wind belt in normal conditions. Trade wind cumulus are small low puffy cumulus that fly along with the trades, especially prominent at night with a crystal clear starry sky behind them. On the other hand, if you know you have been in the trades and one day these clouds disappear, or they start to thicken, it is likewise a sign that something is disturbing the normal flow of the trade winds. An easterly wave is one possibility or a tropical disturbance is another. Or it could be just an instability of the atmosphere that could lead to one of these disturbances. In any event, it is time to start watching the barometer carefully and noting wind changes when these clouds change. Recall, too, that in the tropics you will usually have to unfold the real barometric trend from its semidiurnal variation—discussed later and in Figure 9.3-1

Direction of Winds Aloft from Cloud Patterns

We care about the direction of the winds aloft because that tells us where the next weather is coming from, either SW, W, or NW. The path of winds aloft is sometimes called the *storm track*, because these winds aloft pull the surface Lows along with them as they cross the midlatitudes of the globe (see notes on the 564-line in Section 7.6). The direction and speed of the winds aloft can be read from the contours of the 500-mb maps, but without these, we can read this direction and make a rough estimate of the speed of the winds aloft from cloud patterns of high clouds. These clouds would be either cirrus, cirrocumulus, or sometimes altocumulus. Clouds are a fluid (of either water droplets or ice crystals), and wind blowing across this fluid makes waves in it just as it does in fluid water, or fluid-like sand in the desert.

The wind direction is perpendicular to the wave pattern just as in water waves (see Figure 9.2-1). Sometimes, however, the clouds are blown into broad bands or *cloud streets* which run parallel to the wind. In these cases, the short wavelength pattern is built within the bands, still perpendicular to the wind. When many such streets are formed, they themselves make up a broad wave pattern of many streets running parallel to the wind.

Waves in cirrocumulus or thick cirrostratus look like rippled sand. Waves in altocumulus look more like sheep lined up in rows.

Direction of Winds Aloft from Fallstreaks

The mare's tails, called fallstreaks, of cirrus clouds are caused by the ice crystals falling out of the fast-moving air into the slower winds below. The heads of the cirrus clouds point in the direction of the upper winds; the tails are streaming back in the opposite direction of the upper winds (Figure 9.2-2). This is sometimes (maybe most of the time) a difficult way to estimate the direction of the winds aloft, since the perspective is difficult to unravel, but it sometimes works quite well. In other cases, the shear of the two wind speeds does not line up with the wind direction so this method does not work as well.

Speed of Winds Aloft

There is a correlation between strong winds aloft and the severity of the storms they bring with them, so it is helpful to

Figure 9.2-1. *Waves In cirrocumulus and altocumulus clouds. Winds aloft make waves in clouds below them just as surface winds make waves in water. The direction of winds aloft is perpendicular to the waves and parallel to the bands or streets of waves. Cirrocumulus waves are more delicate, like waves in sand, than the more common altocumulus waves, which appear as rows of sheep. Both patterns are transitory, forming, dissipating, and reforming again, perhaps in another part of the sky. Reproduced from the author's book* Emergency Navigation

make an estimate of the upper wind speed. We can get the direction from the clouds, as mentioned above. That tells us which way to look for approaching weather (SW, W, or NW). If we can now estimate their speed, then we have a gauge of what might be coming with them. There are several ways to do this.

Generally we cannot perceive the motion of typical cirrus clouds flying along with the winds aloft. But when these winds are strong (70 or 80 kts or more) then we can indeed see them move by just watching carefully. Hence, if you can see them move, any storm or front they bring with them is likely to be a severe one. Assuming they are at 20,000 ft, a motion of 2° per 10 seconds (about a finger width) corresponds to about 40 kts. This is perceptible from land with a steady tree branch or other reference. Without a reference they must be moving at least twice this speed or so in order to detect the motion.

Another gauge is the shape of cirrus clouds themselves. The very existence of mares tails, for example, or prominent cloud waves, are indications of strong winds, and the more torn and stretched they are, or the more prominent and persistent the waves, the stronger the winds.

Even without mares tails or waves, however, individual cirrus in the presence of strong winds appear ragged and torn, as opposed to the fluffy white cotton swaths or patches of cloud that they normally are.

Crossed Winds Rule

This is a phrase Alan Watts uses in some of his popular books on marine weather. It implies combining the observations just discussed on locating the direction of the storm track from high clouds with Buys Ballot's Law for locating the direction to the low center from your location. The idea is il-

lustrated in Figure 9.2-3. It is a simple way to tell if a Low has passed you or is headed toward you.

Barometers

Barometric pressure has two important functions in weather work underway. One is to evaluate weather maps or professional forecasts that you have from a wireless broadcast, and the other is to warn you of impending changes in the weather if you do not have such forecasts. If you do not have the official forecasts, the barometer is a key part of your own private forecasting. When you do have a map or forecast, the barometer is one of the ways you tell if the forecast is correct and on time, or not.

The first application of forecast evaluation requires a calibrated barometer, the second is aided by a good calibration, but you can learn something at least from any functioning barometer. Barometer calibration is discussed in Section 2.2 and Appendix 5.

Barometer as Forecaster

The general guideline we have used over the years we denote as "4-5-6," meaning that when you are in fair weather to begin with, any pressure drop of 4 or 5 mb in a 6-hr period is a definite warning of the possible approach of a Low or frontal system (Table 9.2-1). We proposed that guideline 25 years ago in the first version of the Weather Trainer software, and have not come up with a better one yet. It is not gospel. Pressure can go up or down for multiple reasons. It is simply a way to convey numerically a "pay attention" rate for pressure drops. Now that the NDBC offers such a nice plot of overlaid wind and pressure for many of their stations, we have an easy

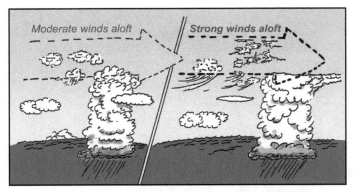

Figure 9.2-2. *Cirrus clouds as signs of the winds aloft. Fallstreaks of cirrus cloud usually stream back, in the opposite direction of the winds aloft, particularly when the winds are strong. This sign, however, can be difficult to read, unless they stream in the same direction in all parts of the sky, and there is also some indication of cirrus bands in line with the tails. Strong winds aloft are indicated by jagged, torn cirrus and prominent swept-back tails, and perhaps even noticeable motion to the clouds. Weaker winds aloft have puffier, smoother, apparently stationary cirrus, without tails. Strong winds aloft generally mean the midlatitude weather patterns they carry have strong surface winds. Reproduced from the author's book* Emergency Navigation

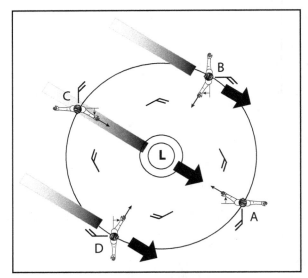

Figure 9.2-3. *Crossed winds rule. Four mariners have determined from high cloud patterns that the winds aloft (the storm track) are flowing from NW to the SE. Buys Ballot's Law tells us to put our back to the wind, left arm out and slightly forward (30° or so) and it will be pointing to the Low. Thus A knows the Low center is headed straight toward him; B knows it is passing to the south at the moment, D knows it is passing to the north at the moment, and C knows it is past and getting farther away. The reasoning can be applied at any location, not just these four points.*

way to test this, and get some statistics on its value. In doing so, we have seen cases where we can get strong winds at a slower drop, but this guideline covers more cases than it misses, even including the enhanced complexity of pressure trends on inland and near coastal waters.

On the other hand, once the barometer starts down faster than 4-5-6, or continues this rate of drop for more than 6 hrs, you are almost certainly past the forecasting stage, and just watching the extent and degree of the system as it approaches. Our goal with the guideline is not to describe how the pressure drops in a storm (it can often drop much faster than that), but rather how to detect a storm on the way that is not there yet.

As mentioned, drops of a slower rate can also be significant if they persist, so we need to keep an eye on the barometer at all times and record its value in the logbook frequently—once a watch at minimum, or every hour if anticipating some change. Don't forget the set needle that most aneroids have to mark the last reading.

This guideline applies to looking for bad weather coming to replace good weather. If you are already in 20 or 30 kts of wind, it could well be that things will get worse when the pressures starts back up, without dropping at all. It is the gradient across the map that causes the wind, not the direction of its trend over time at any one place. If you are caught in the "sting of the scorpion's tail" you will often see that happen, as discussed in Section 4.4.

In the tropics, be aware of the important semidiurnal variation in pressure and take this into account when watching the barometer. We can also see this effect outside of the tropics with good instruments or analysis, as shown in Figure 9.2-4. Also within the tropics the actual value of the pressure takes on new significance for forecasting. Both of these points are covered in Section 9.3 on Tropical Storm Forecasting.

Wind, Pressure, and Weather Maps

We have discussed barometer use for checking maps and monitoring progress throughout the book. Chapters 2 and 7 contain much on the subject. We stress the value of doing the comparisons carefully (Tables 2.4-1, 2) and the need for a calibrated device. We strive to do pressure comparisons at ± 1 mb—that is one quarter of the distance between isobars. Realistically, this level of precision cannot always be achieved.

When our recorded pressure, wind speed, and wind direction all agree with the h0 model analysis, we have more confidence in the following forecasts. When they do not agree, we first try to figure out what the discrepancies might mean.

This takes some detective work.

(1) When wind speed agrees, the forecasted isobar spacing is about right.

(2) When wind direction agrees, the isobars are oriented properly on the map.

(3) When the pressure agrees, the isobars near us may be right, but strictly speaking we only know that the right isobar crosses our position.

Table 9.2-1.	
"4-5-6" Guideline to Pressure as Wind Forecaster	
Likely Significance	*Steady pressure drop over 6 hrs*
Alert	Less than 3 mb
Caution	3 to 4 mb
Definite Warning	4 to 5 mb
Too late for forecasting	More than 5 mb

(4) When the wind is about right, but the pressure on the map is lower than you observe, it could mean the High is closer to you than map implies, or the High is higher than the map knows. These observations are crucial when cutting the corner around the High or its ridge.

By looking at these and the actual pressure we observe, we might be able to judge that the Low or front is closer or farther away than shown on the map. It is instructive work to piece together your best guess at why the map and observations do not agree. Sometimes, after doing this, you will

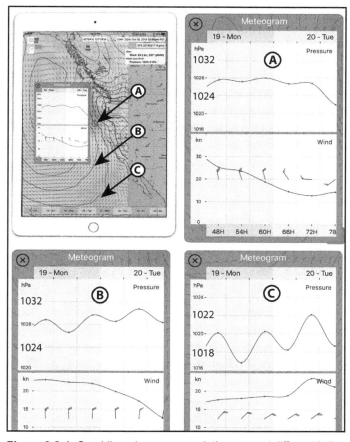

Figure 9.2-4. *Semidiurnal pressure variation seen at different latitudes in a GFS forecast. Off northern CA, the effect is barely visible with amplitude under 1 mb. It increases going south, and just into the tropics we see the normal average amplitude of ± 1.7 mb with peaks at 10 AM and PM, and minima at 4 AM and 4 PM local time. From the meteogram feature of the LuckGrib iPad app. At higher latitudes the effect can also be masked by the auto-scaling function of electronic barometers because the pressure changes so much.*

notice that in the next analysis the discrepancy has been corrected.

As noted early in the book, more often than not, when sailing, we will be using our forecast evaluation not so much to evade bad weather as to find more wind in fair weather. This will often take the form of concern about how close the High is, which will shut off our wind if it gets too close. In these cases, the absolute pressure will be crucial.

When making these decisions, actual ship reports on the map can be valuable. The isobars on the shortest route ahead, for example, might not imply enough wind, based on their spacings, but you see numerous reports in the region with plenty of wind for you. In this case you might be justified in carrying on till the next map comes out. On the other hand, the isobars might imply there should be plenty of wind, but the reports are all light. In this case you might want to drive away from the High somewhat till you see that next map.

Rain

The nature of rain can tell us much about what is taking place at the moment and what is likely to occur in the near future. By nature of the rain, we mean simply: rain or no rain, heavy or light, short or long lasting. There are details of rain terminology in Appendix 7. Frontal system rain is discussed earlier under Fronts and Lows.

Rain and squalls are discussed earlier in several sections. The summary is the strong winds come with the first rain. If not yet raining, the worst may be yet to come,; if already raining the worse may be past—and we cannot be reminded too often that behind a squall the wind can be very light an fluky. If a squall is going to outrun you, try to get away from it as best you can.

Visible rain under distant clouds might tell us something about the wind there if we can discern the slant of the rain. If the rain is straight down, there is little cloud motion and hence weak winds below it. If the rain angle is steep, it implies fast clouds and stronger winds on the surface. As a rule, there is a correlation between the speed of low clouds and the surface wind speeds. Look around in these cases to see if there might be differences in different directions. Also be careful not to confuse sunlight streaking through a cloud as a rain pattern (praecipitatio). Check the angle of the sun if there is any doubt. Also, the nature (color and texture) of the sea surface under a cloud might be some indication of the wind. Stronger winds make rougher surfaces which appear darker. Again, though, we must not confuse shadows with wind.

Again, radar is a huge help for studying squalls, and a stabilized display using a heading sensor makes this much more effective than a basic heads-up display.

Sea State

Sea state means swells, waves, and ripples. There is something to be learned from all of them, and any seaway is most often a combination of all of them.

Swells

Swells tell us about far-off storm systems, because waves generated in a storm generally build to speeds that are faster than the storm itself. When these outrun a storm they organize into swells that can travel a thousand or more miles from the storm and still be detectable as long, low swells. The farther they go, the lower and longer they become. Low refers to the height, trough to crest. Long refers to the wavelength, crest to crest. (The transverse widths of swells are always very long, often stretching across the horizon.)

We will be in some form of swell more often than not, so our job is to sort out the ones that might tell us something about forthcoming changes in the weather.

Swells from a cyclonic storm radiate outward from the center, but distant ones are only felt from the forward side of the moving Low. In the NH, swells are longest and highest in the right forward quadrant of a slow moving Low, with the weakest swells coming from the left rear quadrant. A fast moving Low, however, can bring storm seas with it, without prior warning from advancing swells.

Typical wind waves have periods of 3 to 7 seconds, except for very strong winds with fully developed seas. Swells blend into the sequence with periods of a half a dozen or so seconds for close storms and some 10 to 13 seconds or so for typical distant storms, and even longer in rare cases.

Only storm force systems can develop significant swells with periods over 13 seconds or so, and periods longer than 20 seconds rarely develop for even the largest storms. Hence, the arrival of a new swell with periods in the range of 10 to 20 seconds whose direction does not change with time, indicates you are in the dangerous sector of a major storm.

Periods longer than this imply a large storm, but one that is very remote from you that probably won't affect you. Swells from close storms can be up to 10 or 20 ft high. Ones from a distant storm may only be a few feet high.

Remember we are discussing swells here, not waves. So the first task is to be sure you are indeed looking at swells. The key feature of swells is uniform height from one to the next and a very broad width. Waves on the other hand, have many heights and are not wide. The transverse extent of wind waves (their width) is only a few times their length from crest to crest.

A steady swell direction, with an increase in swell height and a decrease in swell period indicates a storm approaching.

If the swell reaches a peak height and then decreases, the storm either died off or turned in direction. Likewise, if the direction noticeably changes in a steady way, the storm is passing to the side of you—veering, it is going to the pole-side of you; backing, it is going to the equator-side of you.

When a new swell appears and remains constant in swell height and swell period for some 6 hrs or more, then it is possibly from a remote system that won't affect you. The flag is up, however, to pay attention.

With weather maps at hand, it is generally instructive to try to identify the source of any new long, low swell that is detected. It is your laboratory homework underway. It is also instructive to try to identify the wave and swell directions in the ww3 sea state forecasts if you have access to them.

When you feel an unusual swell go by, seemingly isolated from the regular wave train, as if someone just dropped a giant rock into the ocean somewhere, then take note of it immediately and try to spot its direction of travel. And then wait for the next. Without special attention, you might miss them since they can be well separated. If you note it immediately, however, you may be able to spot it since they are very wide waves, stretching across the horizon, as opposed to wind waves which are only some several times their length in width.

The wavelength (L) of swells is given by $L = 5T^2$, where L is in feet and the period (T) in seconds. A period of 13 seconds would correspond to a wave that is 5×169 or 845 ft long or roughly some 300 yards. Think of looking for the next wave 3 football fields away. Generally you can't see the pattern, just feel them individually. Try timing the period to clinch the identification. Remember too that wave speed is determined by wavelength. These long waves will be fast, they will go right by. Remember that wave speed is the same as *hull speed*, equal to $1.34 \times$ square root (L), or something like 3T in knots. At a 13-second period, the wave is moving at about 39 kts. It is like driving a car over a speed bump when they go by, if not masked by the prevailing wind waves.

Since we have excellent wave and swell forecasts online as well as global weather maps, the behavior of swells as they propagate across the ocean cane be studied at home. The links needed are all at the OPC website (see Figure 5.4-3).

Waves

Waves, meaning wind waves, build with increasing wind and time, assuming they are not limited by fetch or water depth. When we have wind, we have waves, and when we have waves, we have waves of many heights, lengths, and speeds. Hence we always describe waves in terms of statistical properties, such as *significant wave height (SWH)*, being the average height of the highest one third of all waves. This is the usual height reported in observations and forecasts, though it is often not identified as such. Properties of waves and related notes are in Section 5.4, which includes notes on forecasting wave properties.

The Beaufort Scale (Section 5.4) is the traditional way to relate wind speed and sea state. It pays to practice with it. Bigger waves than expected for a given wind speed, especially steeper waves, is a good sign that you might be in a current flowing against the wind. Likewise, the lack of seas for a given wind, implies the current is flowing with the wind.

Ripples

Ripples are the "fish scales" or "cat's paws" seen on the surface of waves and swells. At lower wind speeds you have to look carefully to see them; at higher winds they are promi-

nent. They are capillary waves that respond to the instantaneous wind direction. They are your best gauge of wind direction, and tell of approaching gusts because you can watch the patch of cat's paws approaching you.

If you have lost your orientation for some reason, and are steering by the seas and not the wind, ripples also provide the earliest way to detect that the wind direction has changed. Generally the wind waves flow in the direction of the prevailing wind. But when the wind shifts, the waves have too much inertia to change instantly; they take an hour or more to begin to respond. So when the ripples are lined up diagonally across the wave direction (consistently), you know the wind has shifted.

When the wind shifts in direction, it generally beats down the existing waves before they can rebuild in the new direction. A big shift in the wind can be a blessing if the seas have been a problem, but it might only be a temporary blessing, because the waves might then build up in the new direction. The duration guidelines in Section 5.4 help set a time scale to both events, though a contrary wind or big shift seems to beat down the waves much faster than it takes to build them.

In firm winds of say over 17 kts or so, watch the peaks of the waves for signs of spray. Real spray does not start much till 30 kts of wind, but wisps of it occur at lower speeds. You can sometimes spot this spray blowing off at an angle when the wind has shifted but the seas have not yet had time to respond. At higher wind speeds it becomes more obvious.

9.3 Onboard Forecasting of Tropical Storms

Tropical storms and hurricanes are certainly the best forecasted weather systems afloat, and the main resource (for U.S. adjacent waters) is the National Hurricane Center (NHC) in Miami, FL (nhc.noaa.gov). As soon as clouds or wind starts moving in a circle (apparent in satellite photos and wind data), there is a team of scientists watching its every movement and feeding these observations into various hurricane computer models to predict its behavior. Scientists may feel that the models are not as good as they would want, but from a mariner's point of view, we are told every hour or so where the system is located and a best guess of what it is likely to do next. And these predictions get better and better each year.

Figure 4.5-4 shows the "Mariner's 1-2-3 Rule" from the NWS, which is the key to prudent application of their forecasts. Even if we do not have the forecasts, we should be aware of this diagram and how the position uncertainty increases, as well as remembering their guideline of avoiding the forecasted 34-kt wind region around the storm center. Again, however, it would be rare to not have the forecasts. Even an inexpensive shortwave radio brings the storm location, course, and speed every hour, and the 34-kt radii.

Furthermore, these storms occur in specific places during specific seasons, which are well documented and readily available. The NHC also has links to the RSMC (Regional Specialized Meteorological Centers) sites that watch the other hurricane zones around the world. Nevertheless, as with all weather phenomena, their occurrence and behavior are spread over some statistical range of space and time, so despite precautions we might end up in the neighborhood of one. And despite other precautions, we might also end up without access to the official reports, which puts us onto the topic at hand of doing the best we can to detect such systems and to monitor their progress relative to our own position and maneuvers.

Even with these excellent official reports readily available to us when all our equipment is functional, we are dealing here with the most severe systems mariners might encounter, clearly life threatening to any vessel. But the appearance of such a system in our proximity does not at all foretell inevitable doom. These are usually small systems that we can indeed maneuver away from. Just getting some 100 miles away from the center can make a tremendous difference in the force of the wind and seas. And since they are so well tracked, we are, with prudence, more likely to get away from it than to get caught right in it.

The key point to avoiding hurricanes within a hurricane zone is to treat each tropical disturbance as a potential hurricane—although only some 10% of such disturbances actually develop into hurricanes. Start your reckoning immediately regarding your chances of encountering it on your present course, based on known behavior of tropical systems, and then if you have any chance at all of running into the forecasted 34-kt wind region, immediately maneuver to avoid it as discussed in the next section, or go back if that is an option, or go to some other destination that might offer some shelter.

Keep in mind also that if you are anchored in some partial shelter (nothing is complete shelter from such systems), then your biggest hazard might well be other anchored boats breaking loose, crashing into you, and tearing you loose. It is not uncommon to maintain power into the wind to relieve stress on the anchor cable during the encounter. It is prudent to look around, to the extent you can, to see that others are being as careful as you are.

Once the thing has developed into a tropical storm or hurricane, it does not move around very secretively. The very strong winds are tightly located, but the signs of these usually extend far ahead of the system. They can be tracked by just about any kind of satellite looking at the ocean.

The goal is to get as much distance as possible between you and the passing storm and to go for the navigable side if you have that choice. Proper action, however, cannot be taken until you know where the storm is relative to you, and which way it is moving. For tropical storms, predicting the location and motion of the storm are the only goals of forecasting—you do not have to guess whether or not it will be bad. You also have to have some feeling of what progress you might be able to make in the present and anticipated winds and sea state.

Some or all of the following signs will be evident as a tropical storm approaches.

Swells in the Tropics

As mentioned for all storms above, this could be prominent for developed tropical systems. The onset of a new long, low swell coming from the direction of the storm could be the first sign, provided you are in deep water—long swells are deep swells, so in shoal water they can be reflected and refracted from the slope of the bottom and change direction. This swell is typically the earliest natural sign, although the sea state you do have might mask this in some cases. If you happen to be somewhere in deep water within some 1,000 miles of a hurricane, look for this sign as a learning experience, even when there is no threat from that particular storm. Alternatively, you might try virtual research by following the NHC internet site to spot the development of a tropical storm that they believe is going to become a hurricane, and then watch the wave and swell maps (WW3) to see if you can detect any indication of the effect of the storm.

You might also find it interesting to zoom in on tropical island groups on Google Earth to see how waves refract around the islands. It can be a very interesting exercise—these are static pictures of past waves; not live data.

Barometers in the Tropics

Hurricanes occur in the tropics, and often at very low latitudes of the tropics. Careful barometer use in this region has an important difference from use at higher latitudes because of the relatively large daily variations of the pressure due to an atmospheric tidal action. The tides are caused by solar heating and cooling, which creates three cycles having periods of 4, 12, and 24 hrs. The 12-hr cycle has the largest amplitude being in the range of 1 to 2 mb.

The dominant 12-hr cycle gives rise to two highs and two lows, which in analogy to tidal cycles, would be called a semidiurnal pattern. Several traditional marine weather textbooks, Navy training manuals, and USCG exam questions, refer to this effect as "diurnal" pressure variation, which implies they are using the word to mean simply "daily" without reference to tide cycles—which keeps us on our toes as this is a semidiurnal tidal effect.

This semidiurnal variation can also occur to a lesser extent at higher latitudes (Figure 9.2-4), but this is often masked by the typical small variations in pressure due to the normal shifting around of the isobars, which is not so prevalent in the tropics. Also the Coriolis effect dampens the rate of pressure change, whereas the Coriolis effect is much weaker at lower latitudes—but even within the tropics this effect causes the semidiurnal variation to be strongest near the equator and grow weaker with increasing latitude. The effect is stronger over land than over water.

The peaks are usually at about 10 AM and PM local time, with minimums at about 4 AM and PM. Local time of 10 AM means 2 hrs before local apparent noon, when the sun is at its peak height in the sky. See Figure 9.3-1 for a schematic reminder. Four PM local time is 4 hrs after local noon. The effect of the 24-hr and 8-hr cycles is to make the morning peaks slightly larger than the nighttime peaks, while the afternoon minimum is slightly lower than the early morning minimum. Since the highs and lows are caused by solar heating, the range of this effect can depend on the local cloud cover and humidity.

This daily variation must be taken into account when monitoring pressures in low latitudes to watch for approaching systems. A sample is shown in Figure 9.3-1. These days this type of data can be readily obtained from the NDBC. Average barometric pressure drops near an approaching hurricane are shown in Table 9.3-1. See also the pressure profile shown in Figure 4.5-5, which extends out some 300 nmi. Real hurricane profiles are shown in Appendix 10.

The following discussion covers signs that might be evident while still far enough from the storm to avoid its worst impact—with a lot of assumptions here about average speeds of storm motion and your motion, average changes in the actual central pressure of the storm, etc.

Within the tropics we learn to live with the daily pressure variation. With the exception of this daily variation, pressures in typical hurricane regions are generally fairly stable, with standard deviations of just 2 or 3 mb. Hence any deviation from the average pressure should be regarded with suspicion. With an accurate barometer and knowledge of the average pressure for your month and location, along with the standard deviation from that average pressure, you can be very specific about your observations and what they might

Table 9.3-1. Average Pressure Drops	
Barometer	*Distance to eye*
steady or pumping	500 to 400 miles
rise of a few mb	400 to 300 miles
4 to 5 mb/6hr	350 to 250 miles
1 to 2 mb/hr drop	250 to 150 miles
2 to 3 mb/hr drop	150 to 100 miles
3 to 4 mb/hr drop	100 to 80 miles
4 to 6 mb/hr drop	80 to 50 miles
6 to 12 mb/hr drop	wall of the eye

imply—especially valuable if you have lost wireless contact with your forecast sources.

The swells mentioned earlier might show up in the range of well over 500 miles off. At about 500 miles away, we might expect the disappearance or irregularity in the semidiurnal variation of barometer readings. Also a slight rise in average pressure might be detected while still in fair weather somewhere near the edge of the cirrus clouds (Table 9.2-2).

At about 300-150 miles away, we might detect a slowly falling barometer, with the rate of fall increasing from 1 or 2 mb/hr, with perhaps the semidiurnal variation still evident but fading. Traces of real hurricanes are given in Appendix 10.

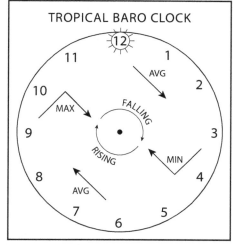

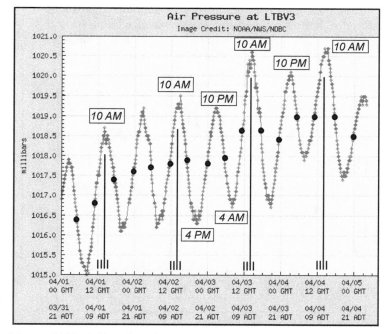

Figure 9.3-1. *Daily pressure variation in the tropics. Left. A schematic clock face as a reminder of the pattern in local time: daily maxima at 10; minima at 4 (AM and PM). Readings near 1 or 7 would be close to a median value. Right. Data from Lime Tree Bay, VI, 17.70° N, 64.75° W. To figure the proper local time, take the longitude divided by 15 to get the time zone and then subtract that from GMT. In this case, 64.75/15 = 4.3 so Local time = GMT - 4. Note they show it at 3h, which means they must be on daylight saving time. The predicted local times are shown on the plot. Halfway points between the full range on each cycle shows how the actual ambient pressure is changing over these 5 days—slowly rising from about 1016.5 to 1019.0 mb, with an indication of a downturn taking place. Note that the expected difference between morning and nighttime peaks (about 0.5 mb) is masked on Apr 2 by the rise in the ambient pressure over that period. To watch for an approaching tropical storm, we need to extract an actual pressure drop from a pattern like this one. Knowing ahead of time how much of a change is due to diurnal fluctuations lets you discover the real drop, which could be masked during its initial hours unless you correct for this. Using the NCDC resource referenced at the end of Section 8.2, we can learn that the average for March at this location is 1016.7 with a standard deviation (SD) of 1.7 mb. Thus this pressure of 1019 is about 2 SD higher than normal, making it a rare occurrence (about 3% probability).*

Warning: once the barometer gets down to, say, 5 or 6 mb below the normal for the region, season, and time of day, (after perhaps a slight rise) then you have a clear sign of the likely presence of a tropical cyclone, even if a cloud bar (discussed below) is not discernible. In other words, when sailing in hurricane zones, it is crucial that you record the barometer even in fair weather so that you can indeed learn what is normal behavior and average values. Five mb down from average is something like 2 SD, which means you have about 98% chance of this coming from a storm and not from typical statistical pressure variations—discussed below.

Paying careful attention to the natural signs around you, including your barometer, you are still in a position to increase the closest point of approach significantly using the methods outlined in Section 4.8. Proper action at this stage could be crucial.

At about 120 to 60 miles away, a typical drop rate might increase to about 5 or 6 mb/hr. The role of forecasting is over, though you may still be able to run away, depending on where you are. At some point soon however, the barometer will undergo a real plummet of 10 to 30 mb/hr. At this stage or even earlier, running from the system is no longer practical and the goal is to take whatever course you can to move away from its center and minimize the interaction time.

Tropical Pressure Statistics

Atmospheric pressures in the low latitudes where tropical storms form and travel for most of their lives are significantly more stable than corresponding pressures at higher latitudes. At higher latitudes there are more systems coming by with larger and more varied pressure changes taking place. At Long Island Sound, NY, for example, in the month of March,

the average pressure is 1016.3 mb with a standard deviation of 9.7 mb, based on an average of 8,111 observations over the past 10 years. For comparison, in San Juan, PR in September, peak of the hurricane season, the average pressure is 1013.5 mb with a standard deviation of 1.7 mb.

The key factor here is the *standard deviation*. Studies show that an extended set of pressure measurements for the same location follows what mathematicians call the normal distribution (bell curve). This curve describes much of what we see in nature that stems from more or less random distinctions. The heights of American women, for example, between ages of 18 and 24 follows a normal distribution with a mean value of 65.5 inches and a standard deviation (SD) of 2.5 inches.

Figure 9.3-2 shows three examples. Atmospheric pressures in the tropics are like the tall narrow example with small SD, whereas at higher latitudes the pressure distributions are more like the lower, spread-out curve. In fact the difference between New York and Puerto Rico mentioned above is even more dramatic than shown in this figure.

In normal distributions it is easy to predict the probability of values that differ from the mean (average) value of the data set, as shown in Figure 9.3-3. From this we can make Table 9.3-2 that tells us about the pressures we might observe and what they can mean. For example, if the mean pressure within a tropical storm zone is 1014 for the time we are there, with an SD of 2 mb, and we observe a pressure of 1010 mb, then that is 2 SD below the average, and that modest pressure drop means a lot. It has only a 2.3% chance of being part of the normal pressure fluctuation at this location, and more like a 98% chance of being a tropical system approaching.

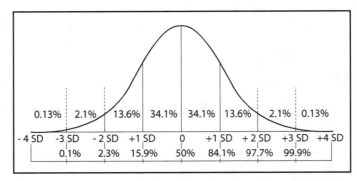

Figure 9.3-3. *Probabilities related to any normal distribution of observations. In a normal distribution, 68% (2x34)of the values are within 1 SD of the mean, half above and half below; 95% are within 2 SD of the mean; and 99.7% fall within 3 SD of the mean. If we carefully figured all the areas under the sections, we would learn that the probability of a value being less than the mean by 1 SD is 16%; less than 1.5 SD is 7%; and less than 2 SD is about 2%, which is summarized in Table 9.3-2.*

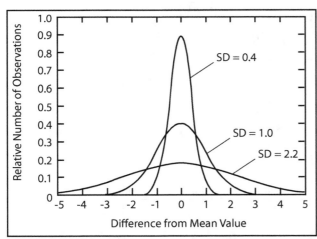

Figure 9.3-2. *Three "normal" distributions of (say) 100 measurements with 3 different standard deviations (SD). When SD is small, the values are all near the mean value (like monthly pressures in the tropics); when it is large they are more spread out (like pressures at high latitudes). To find the SD of a set of numbers, first find the average, then make a list of all the differences between each value and the average, then square each difference (to cancel its sign), then find the average of these squared differences, and then take the square root of that. In this sense, the SD is the average difference from the mean for the full set.*

Table 9.3-2. Normal Pressures	
Observed pressure	Probability
1.0 SD below average	16%
1.5 SD below average	7%
2.0 SD below average	2.3%

With tropical SDs of just 2 or 3 mb, you do not have to be much below average before the (mental) flag should be up to alert you. Note this is another valuable application of a calibrated barometer that you can trust to give the right pressure.

This behavior, and even this approach to tropical storm warning, is not newly recognized, but I venture to guess that it has not been used much, at least by small-craft mariners. The reason is, they did not have accurate barometers in the past and they did not have the crucial data: accurate average values *and* the standard deviations. This is all possible now, and it is something easy to watch when sailing in tropical waters without a wireless contact that would give proper warnings of such systems.

The pressure statistics (standard deviations) show why this is useful knowledge in the tropics, but not at higher latitudes. If the pressure drops 4 mb below the average in, say, San Francisco or Annapolis, it does not tell us anything at all about the weather, but this identical drop on St. Croix or Mauritius is essentially a red flag that alerts us to pay attention.

The crucial data are the standard deviations. We can get average monthly pressures from pilot charts, but not the SD. Accurate SD values are included in the *Mariners Pressure Atlas* (Figure 9.3-4), but sailing in the tropics without that resource you could assume the SD = 2.5 mb, as an average for hurricane zones and seasons.

Again, we are describing an observation that is most valuable when you have lost wireless contact with your forecast sources. Otherwise you know almost hourly where the storms are located and how they are moving.

Tropical Clouds, Sky, and Rain

The first cloud signs of a tropical storm are similar to those of a warm front or extratropical Low. First signs are the invasion of cirrus into a clear sky or high above the normal trade wind cumulus of the tropics. These cirrus, however, might very early show distinct bands radiating from the distant horizon.

If the storm actually comes your way, the cirrus are followed by cirrostratus, cirrocumulus and then altocumulus with a bank of black cloud (bar of the storm) on the horizon. The bar is made up of thick nimbostratus and regions of intense cumulonimbus squalls.

Note that the whole thing, cirrus down to bar, might be clearly evident on the horizon while you are still in fairly light air and moderate or calm seas—see Figure 4.5-7. Such might be the case if one is passing you some 300 miles off. See Figure 9.3-5 for a very schematic representation of the difference in cloud motion when one is passing versus coming at you. Before the wall, which is when you enter heavy squalls and torrential rain, you might have sporadic spells of rain, but could have otherwise reasonable weather with at least patches of clear sky.

Wind

Careful wind observations are also crucial to forecasting the location and motion of tropical storms. These storms bring with them well defined, tightly circulating wind fields so the direction and change in direction tell us very clearly what side of its path we are on.

Warning: an increase in speed or change in direction of the trade winds, especially with an unsteady or dropping barometer, is good indication that a tropical storm is approaching.

To encounter a hurricane, you will most likely be sailing in the tropics in trade wind conditions beforehand—E to NE winds in northern tropics, E to SE in the southern tropics. In the northern latitudes, the storm will likely be coming out of the east bringing with it counterclockwise circulating winds. Its path can be erratic and the actual approach to you could be from any direction, hence it is not clear what direction the first winds of the storm will actually be. But there will

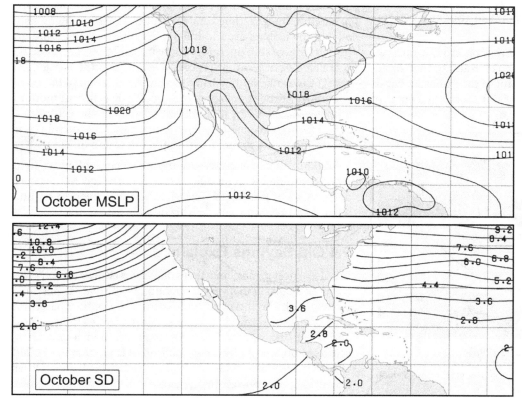

Figure 9.3-4. *Samples of global monthly average pressures (MSLP) and standard deviations (SD) from* Mariner's Pressure Atlas *(Starpath Publications, 2014). Also available as inexpensive ebooks.*

likely be three stages to the wind. The present normal trade winds, a transition period with shifting winds or even calms, and the entrance into the actual circulating wind field of the cyclone. Just building trade winds may be the first wind sign, but there are other transitions possible.

If you had access to real reports or model forecasts, you could anticipate the behavior of the transition winds, but if making all observations unaided, this transition is uncertain. It will take place somewhere about 300 to 200 miles from the storm center. In other words, typically at 200 miles off, you will be in the circulating winds of the storm—still, in many cases, with plenty of time to get out of its worst conditions.

Remember the NHC's guideline for what it means to avoid the system. They recommend avoiding the region around the center that has winds greater than 34 kts. You can go online to study a few hurricanes from the past. Daily position reports, including 34-kt radii, are archived so you can note their sizes and how they change. Hurricanes cover a vast range of sizes from 100 miles across to 1,000 miles across.

To figure the direction to the storm, you must be within the circulating wind field of the storm, in the new wind. You should get the new wind well before you get into the squalls. The first step is to recognize that you are in the new wind (the barometer would be starting a slow, steady drop), and then use this wind direction to figure the direction to the storm.

Use Buys Ballot's Law: with back to the wind and left arm out, rotate it 22° forward to point to the low. This is equivalent to standard recommendations (i.e., Bowditch), which state the storm center is 10 points (112°) to the right of the wind direction. If the wind is northerly at say 010, the center of the storm is located in direction 010 + 112, or 122°. Using Buys Ballot, your left arm would point to 100, and 22° forward is also 122°.

For confirmation, this is the direction from which we might have first seen swells appear (or roughly that direction), and this would be the focal point of the radiating bands of cirrus clouds, and if a bar were visible, also the center of the black bar of clouds on the horizon.

Figure 9.3-5. *(Very) schematic appearance of a storm bar, coming toward you, left, and going by you, right.*

If you are already into the region of squalls, then first, you must be sure you are not in squall winds that distort the ambient wind direction when doing this, and then use just 9 points instead of 10 (rotate left arm forward just 11°). The closer-in winds of the storm follow the isobars more closely.

The next step is to figure if you are to the right, left, or center of the storm's track. You need this information to determine which way to go. This is determined by which way this new wind shifts as the storm moves towards you, or past you.

Figure 4.7-3 showed these wind shifts. In the NH, if the new wind veers (i.e., 045 goes to 050 goes to 055) then you are on the right-hand side of the storm. This is the dangerous side, which will ultimately have the strongest winds and seas with winds tending to push you onto the path of the storm.

If the new wind backs (i.e., 045 goes to 040 goes to 035), then you are on the "navigable" left side of the storm. On this side, getting away from the storm's track will be a downwind course. Again, we stress that this method of figuring the side of the storm you are on assumes you are within the closed isobars of the storm. If this is done much before then, it could give very wrong information.

Radar is always helpful for monitoring squall motion, but typical X-band yacht radars might only see associated storm squalls out to 25 miles or so, often much less (the antennas are also not very high). A ship's S-band radar, on the other hand, could, in principle, see squalls out twice that far or more. S-band is inherently less sensitive to rain, but tropical squalls have intense (called *violent*) rain rates with large droplets, so they can be seen at some distance off.

The squalls around a tropical storm could be as much as 250 nmi from the storm center (Figure 4.5-5), and as we see in satellite images, they rotate with the storms, moving parallel to the isobars around it, so radar observations could, in principle, give ship operators some information that could be correlated with weather reports. Plotting (on the navigation chart) the range and bearing to your best estimate of squall center over time could show the squall's direction of motion. Sometimes, however, it is difficult to identify the center of a squall from its radar image, not to mention that the rain center often appears to move within the full squall image.

Again, all these observations are clearly of most help when combined with an official report of the location, speed, and course of the storm. The goal here has been to outline what might be done without this outside assistance.

9.4 Old Sayings Explained

From earliest times, mariners have generalized about the weather resulting in a very large number of weather maxims, usually with the intent of forecasting the weather based on time of year or some observation. "March comes in like a lion and leaves like a lamb," is a common, more or less useless, one used on land. A long compilation of these maxims called *Weather Lore* was made in 1893 by Richard Inwards. Other accounts go back even further, to Aristotle's *Meteorologica* (around 330 BC) and to the compilation of maritime weather by Aratus a generation later.

Strangely enough, Inwards' book, presented as a definitive compilation of weather lore to date, gives no specific acknowledgment to the pioneering work on weather by Robert FitzRoy (Captain of the *Beagle,* that Darwin made famous), who was the first director of the British equivalent of the NWS and in many senses the inventor of weather forecasting. FitzRoy's book (*Weather Manual*) preceded his by 20 years.

A modern book on weather lore (*The Weather Companion* by Gary Lockhart) fails in turn to mention Inwards' classic treatment at all and grossly underestimates the significance of FitzRoy's work, while doing just the opposite for Christopher Columbus!

Unfortunately, very few of these maxims from general weather lore (past and present) are true. Some contain partial truths; others are completely wrong. There is clear evidence in such matters that one tends to remember the hits and forget the misses.

Mariners have tended to be more discretionary in their use of such maxims, for the obvious reason that they have more to lose if they are wrong. The earliest useful compilation for mariners was the *Weather Manual* (1866) by Robert FitzRoy, who might well be considered the father of scientific marine weather. There are not many such sayings in use by sailors, but those that remain have a definite value. We must remember, though, that even these are just guidelines to educated guesses.

The very use of such guidelines, however, is a key part of practical marine weather. It is difficult to separate good maxims from practical knowledge of what to expect on the basis of sound observations. It's mostly a matter of expression. If it rhymes or sounds good, it is a maxim. If it is a dry statement of circumstance, it is not. The latter might be called rules. In any event, we have taken the liberty to expand on the literature of maritime weather lore by adding a few rules and editing a few maxims. We have just a few of these rules stated here. Most are in Section 9.2 that covers onboard forecasting.

To simplify presentation we have occasionally just made into rules what is generally known. For example, in this book we call this Rule No. 1: A tall, mean-looking black cloud with low base most likely brings strong gusty winds! (Figure 9.4-

1). It doesn't rhyme, but it is a widely accepted good rule throughout the world for squalls, cold fronts, or worse... and you will recall we have a second Rule No. 1! Namely, double and triple check all your vessel's communications systems before leaving the dock.

In any event, we need such rules and maxims because they are easy to remember. The most effective approach to large-scale marine weather is to have weather maps available and know how to interpret them. In this mode, maxims play a limited role, but we don't always have these maps. Also, rules and maxims about local systems (squalls, etc) and about the interaction of wind and terrain are especially valuable because no map will ever have information about these problems. For example, I would rather have a weather map to tell if things will improve tomorrow than rely on "red sky at night," but I flat out need to know that the downburst winds of a squall come with the rain, or that wind is backed over land, relative to over water, and so on, because these details are not shown on maps.

The maxims listed here are probably useful some 60 to 70% of the time, with the higher success more likely in the summer. We would hope that the "rules" would have a higher success rate, but it would be difficult to speculate that even the best would be as high as 90% right without setting some conditions.

"Red Sky at Night, Sailor's Delight."

The reference is mostly to the high sky looking west, since in any fair weather situation the sky is to some extent red to the west lower in the sky (Figure 9.4-2). With a red sky overhead—meaning the clouds overhead or to the west are red—it means first that you do indeed have some clouds around as you would if you have been in a period of bad weather (most likely stratocumulus, or at least these will typically give the most dramatic red skies). In the midst of bad weather, on the other hand, with another day or more of it to come, the sky will not be red, but gray all day, including sunset which may not be discernible at all.

Hence a red sky means the overcast is breaking to the west and weather comes from the west. In other words, had there still been clouds to the west, the sunlight would not have gotten through. With no clouds to the west, we can expect the weather to improve during the night. The actual color red, however, has no significance. Low sunlight is more reddish

Figure 9.4-1. *Rule No. 1. A tall mean-looking cloud with a low black base usually means strong gusty wind.*

Figure 9.4-2. *Red sky at night usually means clearing in the offing. The clouds involved are usually stratocumulus.*

Figure 9.4-3. *Mackerel skies are waves or clusters in cirrocumulus clouds, meaning the winds aloft are strong.*

because it travels through more of the atmosphere to get to us, and the blue end of the spectrum is very much more likely to be scattered away than is the red. (Scattering along this extra path length is the same reason why all stars fade as they descend toward the horizon.)

This maxim can be traced back to biblical times (Matthew 16:2). It also implies that sailors will be delighted with less wind, which is clearly not always true.

"Red Sky in the Morning, Sailors Take Warning."

This is often tacked onto the previous one, above. It is separated here because it is not very useful as a forecaster—it wouldn't even be here if it were not so often added to the other, which is a good one. Again the sky in question is overhead and we are looking east. The clouds and weather to the east, which is now clear, is what we had, but now we have clouds (which came from the west), so things must be getting worse.

But we could have known this quite well from the presence of the clouds alone. This is just a nice red goodbye to the fair weather we had. It doesn't help with forecasting.

"Mackerel Sky and Mare's Tails Make Tall Ships Set Low Sails."

Again, this is an old one, which in various forms goes back to early seafaring literature. Mackerel skies are waves (billows) in cirrocumulus (see Figure 9.4-3) indicating strong winds and shear aloft, and mare's tails are fallstreaks from cirrus clouds. Again, the fallstreaks indicate strong winds with distinct wind shear aloft. Mares tails are shown in Figure 9.4-4.

The value of the maxim lies more in the sequence or combination of both clouds rather than the appearance of either alone. Bad weather of a warm front or Low usually approach into fair skies with a leading edge of cirrus clouds which thicken into cirrocumulus and then on into stratus forms as they lower. This sign alone, without waves or tails, indicates an approaching system. The waves and tails indicating strong winds aloft imply that the surface system will be a strong one. There is generally a correlation between the strength of the winds aloft and the severity of the surface winds it might bring with it.

Hence it is valuable for mariners to recognize these cloud forms and to appreciate their significance. The tall ships re-

ferred to are the old square riggers which had to reduce sail to *courses* (lower mainsails) in strong winds.

Note that this sign is best if the clouds do indeed thicken into stratus and begin to lower. Some weather transitions will bring this cloud pattern and then be followed by clear skies, i.e., the maxim did not work. It should be looked at as a first sign that something might happen, and then further believe so when the cirrostratus thickens and starts to lower.

"Long Foretold, Long to Last, Short Notice, Soon Past."

This is another of the good ones—from a statistical point, probably the best of the lot. It refers to a general property of various weather systems. Long coming and long lasting, refers to warm fronts or large isolated Lows in general, which can take a half a day or up to a day or two to arrive from the first sign of its possible approach. This first sign is usually the first appearance of cirrus in an otherwise clear sky, or it could be the onset of a slow backing-around of the wind. Earlier we offered this guideline: On approaching warm fronts, from the time of first cirrus to the time of first rain is how long it will be until the front itself reaches you. This is the long foretold part.

The "short notice, soon past" part of the full couplet refers to squalls and cold fronts. Squalls appear out of otherwise moderate weather and last only a very short time (minutes to an hour or so) with heavy rain and strong gusty winds. The same is true of cold fronts, which appear out of the warm sector of a frontal system or in isolation, generally in at least partially clear sky and stable winds. And they also come with short-lived, heavy rain and strong, gusty winds. Both systems bring on their conditions rapidly or even suddenly, although both can typically be seen on the horizon from some distance off as they approach.

"First Rise After the Low, Can Portend a Stronger Blow."

This refers to a rising barometer after it has reached its minimum value with a passing Low. The strongest, gustiest wind often does not occur until the barometer reaches it's lowest value and begins to rise. This is a characteristic of intense, well developed storm systems with a "bent-back

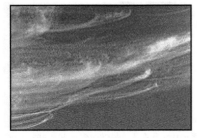

Figure 9.4-4. *Mare's tails are fallstreaks from cirrus clouds indicating strong winds aloft.*

Figure 9.4-5. *A ring around the sun or moon is one of the best natural signs of potential bad weather, especially in the summer, when first appearing in an otherwise clear sky. With your thumb on the sun or moon, the little finger of your outstretched hand will be roughly on the ring. It is 22° scattering of sunlight from ice crystals of transparent cirrostratus, new to your neighborhood. We still, however, need follow-up signs to confirm this prediction.*

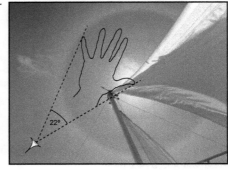

occlusion." Pressure gradients behind the low center in such a pattern can be very strong. This is often called the "sting in the scorpion's tail"—a phenomena that was recognized by mariners long before it was named or understood by meteorologists.

"Rain Kills the Wind."

Said of squalls and other raining isolated clouds. It's a good sounding phrase but must be interpreted carefully. Indeed, with large squalls, the strong wind comes with the rain—is even, to an extent, born of the rain—but when the rain is over, so is the strongest wind, and hence the phrase.

It's better perhaps to convert this one into a dry rule, such as: The strong gusty winds of a squall come with its first rain. If a squall approaches not yet raining, its worst is yet to come. If it approaches already in steady light rain, the worst of its downburst gusty winds is likely over.

This is not a good jingle for warm front rain, since in that case the rain continues on steady as the wind builds. At the front passage, rain and strong wind stop together.

"Fog (or Frost) Nips the Tide."

This is the early 19th century expression of the *inverse barometer effect*, namely that higher than average atmospheric pressure can reduce the maximum tide height. This remains important to mariners whose draft allows them in and out of certain ports only at high water. The magnitude of the effect is 10 cm of tide below the predicted tide for each 10 mb of pressure difference above the average pressure of the time and place. (This was quoted in the old books as 1 ft of tide for 1 inch of pressure, which is just 11% low.). See Figure 9.4-6.

Early mariners knew the effect well but not the cause, which is not related to fog or frost, but to the pressure, which is normally higher than average when fog or frost occur, because the associated clear skies allow for large overnight temperature drops. All else being equal, the only thing that changes from one tide cycle to the next is the weight of the air the tide must lift when rising. Thus in exceptionally high pressures the tide rises less.

In modern times this effect is more in the news in the opposite direction of adding to storm surge when the pressure is very low. When the pressure is lower than average, the tides are higher than average by the same amount. In the case of the 2012 Sandy surge into New Jersey and New York, the record low pressure of 945 mb added about 2.7 ft to the surge that caused so much damage.

We might just reword this one to say whenever you care about the precise level of the tide, remember the inverse barometer effect.

"A Fair Wind Follows the Sun."

This saying applies to the midlatitudes of either hemisphere. It is a trick phrase that generalizes different behavior in the NH and the SH. The sun moves everywhere from east to west. In the NH we see this sun motion as from left to right, but in the SH we see this same motion as right to left—as long as we rule out the tropics, where that is not always true, and this maxim would not apply anyway. (When we are in the tropics, the sun could be well north of the equator, as high as 23.4° N, and we could be just north of the equator, so we would be in a N Lat looking N to the noon sun. In this special circumstance we see the sun move right to left.)

When a High approaches to replace past poor weather of a Low, the wind will veer (shift right) in the NH and back (shift left) in the SH. Thus the wind direction is shifting in the direction the sun is moving.

This is a valuable point because the opposite is also true. Bad weather approaches in the NH with backing winds, and in the SH, with veering winds, both being "away from the sun."

Thus "follow the sun" means a veer in the NH and a backing shift in the SH. The concept of describing the asymmetry of wind behavior above and below the equator in terms of the common descriptor of the sun's motion is a pretty idea that dates to the times of early sea faring when much time was spent on long voyages around the capes. Useful ideas like this evolved even before the rotary nature of storms was fully understood.

In celestial navigation we use the phrase "elevated pole" to mean North in the NH and South in the SH. We could use "follow the sun" in a similar manner in marine weather to mean veer in the NH and back in the SH. Then some descriptions become more tidy, such as: when a front passes, the wind will follow the sun. When you go up in the atmosphere, the wind will follow the sun, no matter where on earth you are. When a sea breeze builds, it will follow the sun.

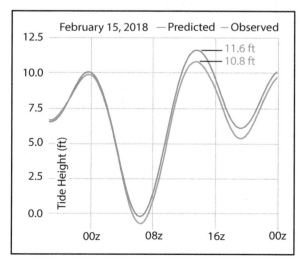

Figure 9.4-6. *Inverse barometer effect at Seattle, WA. Get water levels from tidesandcurrents.noaa.gov. Get corresponding pressures from NDBC and get climatic averages from the Coast Pilot, Appendix B. At 00z the pressure was about average and we do not see an effect. At about 14z the pressure was about 17 mb above average and we see the observed water level lower than predicted—but frankly even lower than expected by this effect alone (we see 24 cm and predict 17). The red curve is labeled preliminary, so perhaps with better analysis it would be closer. But this is the general effect that can be studied with the listed resources.*

Sometimes, however, if we generalize too much we risk getting left with a nice forest and no trees when we are trying to find firewood. See how awkward the generalization might be when we are trying to figure out which way the wind shifts along a low flat shoreline, discussed in Section 6.1. It is probably for good reasons that the usage has not survived.

On the other hand, with regard to use of old-school generalizations, we have found the concept of *centers of action* that we use throughout the book to be very valuable, even though it seems to have fallen out of most recent textbooks.

Many good rules have not found their way into a popular maxim, but are nevertheless important forecasters. A ring around the sun or moon, for example, is one of the very best natural forecasters (Figure 9.4-5). The fact that the wind will veer at every passing front in the NH (back in the SH), is another.

Local Knowledge

Local knowledge is often cast into the form of a maxim. Many exist for local winds and could well be worth note. "Tacking north you get a lift at Jefferson Head and a knock at Summit point," might be the way such things are formulated in some hypothetical waterway. Pay attention to who is sharing the maxim. If they are themselves responsible, knowledgeable sailors, then chances are their weather lore is valuable. But simply hearing the same advice from many people does not add validity to a maxim. We must hear it from someone we are certain has the credentials and experience to authenticate it, and then ideally experience it ourselves.

It is the task of the prudent mariner to separate anecdotes from valid local knowledge. One minimum test is just comparing what we can learn from standard resources such as the *Coast Pilot*, as well as comparing it with our own basic knowledge, which is another good reason to learn more.

In Section 8.6, we briefly discussed published "local knowledge" that recommends transiting the U.S. West Coast at 100 nmi offshore, and we proposed readers check actual coastal and offshore reports to show this is not in general good advice. We might also have recommended checking the *1853 Coast Pilot* for the West Coast. In the section Monterey to Columbia River, they recommend staying within 15 miles of land to avoid the strong winds offshore. That, too, has to be studied. Decisions must be based on both dependable sources and good knowledge.

9.5 Mariner's Weather Checklist

It is fundamental to safe efficient weather work at sea that these items be checked off and tested before departure. Having it all onboard without prior testing is not enough! Each of these items are discussed throughout the book.

#1. Barometer. Aneroid or electronic, they should be calibrated as outlined in Section 10.6. Remember your phone may likely have in it the most accurate barometer on the boat. See Section 2.2.

#2. Wind instruments. Calibrate apparent wind speed and angle. (A backup to barometer and wind is the small handheld Kestrel 5500. The barometers in these that we have tested have been excellent. You can check the wind speed driving along in a car, holding it out of the window.

#3. Knotmeter and compasses. Calibrate all. These have to be right for proper true wind data.

#4. True wind from apparent. We need a mobile or computer app that solves this, and we need to understand the solution. Even if our wind instruments compute this for us, we need a way to check it, and we need to practice enough that we would not hesitate to do it underway.

#5. Laptop computer. There are certainly ways to do safe weather work without one, but a computer makes everything related to weather tremendously easier, more versatile, and better. I would consider it a required item since so many of our best resources are obtained via the computer. In fact since computers (on the level needed here) are so inexpensive these days, it is not unreasonable to set up one with all your navigation and weather software and connections, and then just clone it to another one which you take as a back up. The clone could be owned by a crewmember. Tablets are an option, but they do not have the full functionality of a computer.

#6. Communications. This would be either a satphone, satellite data receiver, or an HF radio with Pactor modem. Users of HF radio are more accustomed to knowing there is a lot of prep and testing to be done. This is also true of the satcom solutions. External antennas are usually required for satphone or data terminal. Both have to be integrated into the computer, which can call for custom drivers and software.

#7. Email connections. We need software for the computer or mobile device to send and receive email by satcom or HF radio. Once an option is selected, test it extensively, sending email back and forth from boat to land. Send and receive attachments. Check how large files are handled, plus how to queue up a batch of mail to send and receive in one connection. Make a contacts list that includes tech support and the addresses for requesting weather files (FTPmail and Saildocs). An email can be resent to get the same file at different times. Practice getting weather maps, text reports, and GRIB files.

Much of the testing for (6) and (7) can be done by internet connection, but at some point actual satcom connections need to be tested. Even with the best equipment, we must have good signals to download larger files by satcom, else we get almost done, lose the connection, and the airtime has been wasted.

#8. Data viewers. We need a dependable versatile GRIB viewer, and it is often valuable to have a stand-alone program, even if we can view GRIB files in our nav programs. For PC viewing, the free ViewFax from Saildocs (which includes a convenient interface for requesting GRIBS—under *Get Data* in the File menu within the program) or XyGrib are good options. There are also enhanced commercial products such as GRIB Explorer from ocens.com for PC, and the popular Squid from greatcircle.be for Mac and PC. For Macs, the LuckGrib viewer does this job nicely, including the download and display of all types of GRIB2 map projections. It includes a unique Model Explorer that tells all about each data set available. There are many tablet apps that display third party GRIB files.

So the task at hand is pick which programs work best for you and practice loading and displaying the files, both received from within the apps and received from other sources. They all have many display options to be learned.

There is also the question of a graphic image viewer to consider. New computers include viewers for all image formats, but they might not allow for annotations, cropping etc. Microsoft Paint or Apple Preview are system options that will do the basics needed, but if you are familiar with Adobe Photoshop or its open-source counterpart Gimp, they could prove useful for special projects, as they work with layers.

#9. Text forecasts. Practice receiving with the various text forecasts: coastal, offshore, high seas, and especially the tropical cyclone advisories if headed to waters with them.

#10. HF (shortwave) receiver. Voice forecasts (offshore and high seas), radiofacsimile, NAVTEX, and storm warnings can all be received by relatively inexpensive HF (shortwave) receivers. These, however, take practice to be useful. They are not like the high-quality SSB transceivers that many vessels carry, which have insulated backstay or long whip antennas. Times and frequencies for radiofax are in the rfax.pdf document; the voice broadcast schedules are in Table 8.7-1. If a radio like this is to be considered as a back up to the main communications, then these sources should all be tested using an external long wire antenna. There are online videos on this.

#11. Sea surface temperature (SST). When sailing in the Gulf Stream or other strong current systems, or when sailing in the tropics in general, it is crucial to have a through-hull seawater temperature measurement, or some other permanent way to continuously read and display SST. A plot of SST versus time is helpful. For ocean currents, the water temperature marks the boundaries of various features, and for the tropics, the water temperature is a measure of storm potential, i.e., hurricane formation usually requires SST > 80 °F. Like all instruments, it should be checked to see that the output is correct.

#12. References. With the use of PDF documents, we can carry an extensive library of references. Opening these once in a standard ebook reader and saving to the associated library makes them easier to access, organize, and annotate. To transfer a PDF from computer to phone or tablet, email it to yourself, then open the attachment in one of the ebook readers. Navigators have to decide which publications merit a printed copy.

• Charts, *Coast Pilots, Sailing Directions, Light Lists, Tide and Current Tables, USCG Navigation Rules Handbook, Pub. 102 International Code of Signals,* and *Pub. 117 Radio Navigation Aids* are basic navigation requirements, not specifically weather, though each can enter in to weather related navigation decisions.

• Pilot charts (available as PDF and as RNC)

• COGOW screen caps for voyage.

• Broadcast schedules for WEFAX and voice

• Universal Plotting sheets

• *Mariner's Pressure Atlas*

• Base maps for weather plotting

• Images defining Coastal and Offshore zones

• Broadcast schedules for radiofax maps (these times tell us when the direct download products will be available.)

• Printed forecasts for wind, seas, and currents for the first 4 days (96h) of the voyage.

• Make a personal timeline for when various products will be available. This is a big, crucial job, but starting it before departure will help home in on a working version more quickly.

• Polar diagrams. These are needed by sailing vessels even if computed routing will not be used.

• Plots or GPX files of the route that would be followed based on known statistics for the season.

• Plots or GPX files of the route that would be followed if winds remained as they are at the start.

• Double check that manuals are available for all instruments, with correct phone numbers and email contacts to support for each that might be needed.

• HF frequencies and phone numbers for USCG contact. The former are the same as used for high seas voice reports; the latter are in the Coast Pilot.

• A copy of this book! (The ebook editions include live internet links.)

This chapter presents several special topics that support or expand the content of earlier chapters. There is no particular order to the presentation.

10.1 Southern Hemisphere Weather

There are two ways to get into Southern Hemisphere waters. You can sail there from the Northern Hemisphere, or you can fly to somewhere in the South and start your voyage cold-turkey in these new winds and waters. The first option is preferable. It gives you a nice long voyage with slowly evolving changes in weather patterns making life a bit simpler. Similarly it is easier on the celestial navigator to follow the stars across the globe, rather than being faced, all of a sudden, with an all new sky—with Orion standing on his head, for crying out loud! In fact, what's Orion even doing out in the sky when it is warm at night, in the middle of summer?

I speak from cold-turkey experience. Once flying to Australia from Seattle for the Sydney to Hobart Race (Boxing Day, December 26, each year) and a couple times flying from Seattle to the Society Islands to teach courses. The latter destination is not much of a shock, weather-wise. There are rainy seasons to consider, and the trades are from the SE and not the NE, but all in all, the stars are more of a challenge than the weather, if that is all the farther south you go (16° S to 18° S). Going on down to SE Australia (34° S to 43° S), on the other hand, the winds are starting to crank up, and the surprises come on more fast and furious.

The two main factors that cause winds to be different in the South are the reversal of the Coriolis force (things bend to the left, instead of to the right) and the much different geography. In the North, we have continents stretched along this latitude belt, but in the South there is much more open water. This gives wind systems longer range to intensify into deeper pressures, and to accelerate on their march to the east. As a result, when you get to the middle and higher latitudes of the Southern Hemisphere, you do not find bland "Prevailing Westerlies" like we have in the North, but instead you get the notorious winds of the "Roaring Forties" and "Furious Fifties."

The goal of this section is to highlight some of the differences and similarities of wind patterns and behaviors between the Northern Hemisphere (NH) and Southern Hemisphere (SH), so you are prepared when you get there. We make these comparisons and then suggest good sources for Southern weather data that you might not have used in the North. If you are taking the cold-turkey approach, it is best to start planning ahead of time and practice with the sources and study the maps before you get there. Unlike before the internet, now you can view all the products from Southern sources while still at home in the North.

For those who want to learn more about Southern Hemisphere weather, see the excellent "Learn About Meteorology" resource at the Australian Bureau of Meteorology (bom.gov.au/lam) and "Aviation Meteorology for Australia" an excellent online course at recreationalflying.com/tutorials/meteorology. A popular set of printed notes and resources is the *Mariners Met Pack* by Bob McDavitt (about.metservice.com/our-company/learning-centre/mariners-met-pack).

What Is the Same?

Generally speaking, basic weather behavior is the same in both hemispheres, before we account for the effects of the Coriolis force and the open waterway. Lows are the source of strong winds, clouds, and rain; Highs are usually characterized by lighter winds and clear skies—unless interacting with another system; close isobars mean strong winds, wide isobars mean weak winds; wind flow is parallel to isobars above the boundary layer, but wind crosses isobars to flow some two points (22.5°) into the Low at the surface; and so on. Systems also move generally from west to east outside of the tropics. And it is important to stress that the definitions of wind shifts are the same in the SH. A "veer" is a shift to the right. A "backing" shift is to the left. Other terminology and map symbols are also the same.

Though I may be one of the few people who was ever puzzled by this, the season name "summer" refers to the warm months in both hemispheres. June, July, and August are summer months in the North. December, January and February are the summer months in the South. The date of the "summer solstice," therefore also depends on the hemisphere.

Although there are differences in how the wind shifts and dangerous-side designations, there is a symmetry to the motion of tropical storms. Generally, they move west and somewhat poleward, and then curve more poleward and on back to the east.

What Does the Coriolis Force Reverse?

Because the Coriolis effect is reversed, SH winds flow counterclockwise and out of Highs and clockwise and into Lows. At this point we might realize that in the North wind bends right, and in the South wind bends left, so at the equator it does not know what to do! Which is correct. There is no Coriolis effect at the central belt of the earth (lower tropics, N and S) and as a result, weather patterns there do not move toward the east as they do in the higher latitudes of both hemispheres. In fact, as we noted in Chapter 4, tropical storms and easterly waves move generally to the west within the tropics.

This reversal of the Coriolis force also has several important practical consequences, beyond the way wind flows around Highs and Lows. As you go up in the atmosphere the SH wind backs instead of veering as it does the NH. This in turn has its own consequences. Low clouds and squalls in SH come from the left of the surface wind; open water gusts in the SH are usually backed; sea breezes back as they build in the SH, and near shorelines we expect the winds to veer as they flow onto low land and back as they leave it.

The dangerous side of a tropical storm is on the left in the SH, whereas it is right side in the NH; and building wind on the dangerous side veers as the storm approaches in the NH, whereas it backs on dangerous side in the SH.

What is Different that is Not a Direct Result of the Coriolis Effect?

The goal here is to separate the simpler distinctions (e.g. Coriolis Force changes, such as clockwise versus counter-clockwise flow around a Low) from ones that might not be as obvious (e.g. lack of occluded fronts). In some of the cases below, the effect of the Coriolis force is still relevant, though not dominant nor direct.

A fundamental difference between NH and SH weather is the seasons are reversed. June and July are (cold) winter months in the SH; Dec and Jan are warm summer months. Winter stars of the North (e.g. Orion) are summer stars in the South. Summer stars in the North (e.g. Scorpio) are seen in the winter in the South.

Possibly the most important difference between the hemispheres is the open water between latitudes 35° S and 55° S that gives rise to the Roaring Forties, Furious Fifties, and on to the Screaming Sixties of the Southern Ocean—the only ocean that circumscribes the globe. The names refer to the latitude ranges.

We might get our own circumpolar ocean in the North if the water keeps warming and the ice thawing, but it will be too far north to have similar influences on the wind. The Canadian Coast Guard is already planning new stations in their Arctic waters in anticipation of global shipping through the Northwest Passage within the decade. We have watched the waters of the Northeast Passage (Northern Sea Route over the top of Russia) open more and more each year.

Contrary to what we might guess from the names and locations of these SH winds, it is not so much that the Roaring Forties and Furious Fifties have continuous strong winds blowing at high speeds, like our prevailing westerlies on steroids, but rather it is a much enhanced propensity for strong wind systems to come flying by, bringing winds up to 60 kts and chaotic seas with them.

Fronts and pressure systems move across the open belt of water in the SH at speeds very much higher than in the NH, giving rise to sudden and severe systems. On the south coast of New South Wales, Australia, these systems are called "Southerly Busters," and every ocean-going sailor in the region has their own stories about interacting with them. Southerly Busters are more frequent in warm months; they are also seen along the east coasts of South America, South Island of New Zealand, and South Africa.

It is not uncommon to have cold fronts moving at 50 kts. At these speeds, a front that is not even on the latest surface analysis could be on top of you by the time the next analysis comes out. Or, looking at the most recent 24-hr forecast, you might see a front that has already passed you that you cannot even identify on the latest surface analysis map. Thus you have some figuring to do.

Another unique difference is much of the strong wind of the sailing waters of the SH is caused by frontal systems, as opposed to circular Lows. Sometimes there are half a dozen or more distinct frontal lines indicated between New Zealand and the east and southeast coasts of Australia. In some of these cases, the Lows are just at higher latitudes, but in many cases, the fronts do not appear to have Lows associated with them at the valid time of the map. Often there are many short segments of fronts identified, which is not such a common feature in NH maps.

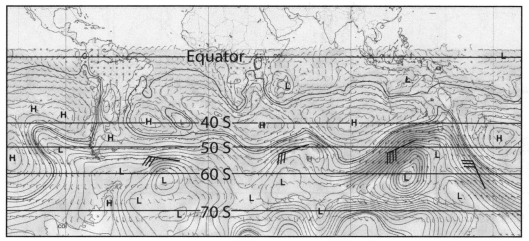

Figure 10.1-1. *The Roaring Forties, Furious Fifties, and Screaming Sixties of the Southern Hemisphere make up a global land-free track along which fast moving Lows and fronts bring strong winds frequently. Highs form in the oceans as shown. Sequences of Highs in the Southern Indian Ocean create intense cold fronts between them, which are a common source of strong winds over Australia and New Zealand. This GFS example is from March 14, 2018, viewed in LuckGrib.*

Another distinction is, of the many fronts in the SH, you see very few occluded fronts, whereas in the NH occlusions are very common. This may be due to the way the fronts form, or it might be that they are simply not analyzed or displayed in the same way, and thus not indicated on the maps.

The behavior of subtropical Highs is notably different. They do not stay in place as long in the SH summer as they do in the NH, and thus they are not as well known in the SH as "centers of action." Highs are more active in the SH. They form in southern Atlantic, Pacific, and Indian oceans and then move east, as often as once a week or so. Fronts form in the troughs between successive Highs, which are much like segments of a polar front (See Appendix 6). That is, air flowing south from the equatorial regions along the trailing edge of the leading High in a sequence of highs, is very warm compared to the cold air coming north along the leading edge of the trailing High, thus creating an active cold front moving east. Therefore, you might expect strong winds along the perimeters of Highs in the SH, which is not a guiding concept in the NH.

This pattern of Highs forming in three roughly equally-spaced ocean basins and being deposited into a strong, steady westerly flow, leads to a certain level of periodicity to SH weather patterns (at least in some regions), that does not have a counterpart in the NH. It is dependable enough in some cases that it is pointed out in sailing directions, so that mariners might plan a voyage based on timing of these systems. Unlike "every 7th wave is the big one," however, which is not true at all, there can in fact be a gap between these periodic severe systems that you can sail on, with some rough

level of confidence in how long you have to get there before the next might arrive, even over time periods that extend beyond the forecasts. Check with local sailing directions and sources mentioned here for details.

Another difference that takes some adapting to for NH navigators—at least it did for me—is the orientation of fronts relative to their associated Lows. In the NH, fronts "hang down from the Lows" as they march eastward around the globe, but in the SH the fronts are somehow "suspended above the Lows" as they move east, which looks very strange to northern navigators! Obviously in both cases the Lows are poleward of the front, so it is all perfectly consistent, but after a lot of work with NH maps you will have to think on this some to adapt.

Special Sources for SH Weather

The main sources of data for the SH that you might not have used while sailing in the NH are: Bureau of Meteorology in Australia (bom.gov.au), Meteorological Services of New Zealand (metservice.co.nz), Meteorological Services of Fiji (met.gov.fj), Japan Meteorological Agency (jma.go.jp), South African Weather Service (weathersa.co.za). Plus you might check for individual reports from the World Meteorological Organization (worldweather.wmo.int).

Radiofax analyses, forecasts, 500-mb, and wave maps are available from the BOM. A sample is shown in Figure 10.1-2. Hand drawn analysis and forecast maps are available from several nations. See samples in Figures 10.1-3 and 10.1-4. Unfortunately, some of these files are very large for downloading underway. The list of radiofacsimile broadcasts we have dis-

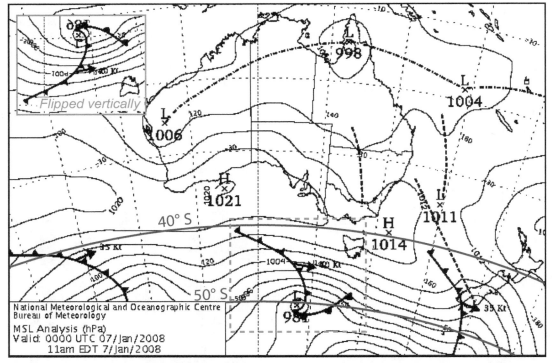

Figure 10.1-2. *Surface analysis from the BOM. This snapshot shows a sequence of three fronts moving rapidly to the east (35 to 40 kts) with associated tight isobars generating strong winds in the Roaring Forties and Furious Fifties (blue lines added).*

BOM radiofax maps do not show wind barbs, so Table 2.4-1 will be valuable. A SH frontal wave is shown in the center, with the cold front "suspended" above the low. (For comparison, it is duplicated in the top corner and flipped over to show the symmetry with the NH.)

The warm fronts often move south, leaving a sequence of cold fronts marching east. The troughs (dashed lines) could also develop into fronts and may even be drawn as fronts when looking at later maps or maps from other services. These maps are available from BOM by email request to Saildocs. Use: send http://www.bom.gov.au/difacs/ IDX0102.gif, where the last part is the file name. Get a full list of file names and available times at tgftp.nws.noaa.gov/fax/otherfax.txt. The file sizes are a tidy 50 kB. Other map regions, including many informative color maps are available at bom.gov.au.

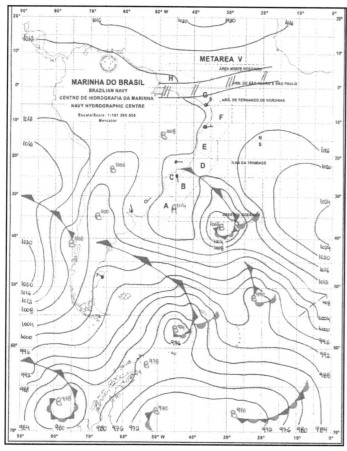

Figure 10.1-3. *Surface analysis from the Brazilian Navy (an active participant in the S-412 program). We can request maps from any past time with* send https://www.marinha.mil.br/chm/sites/www.marinha.mil.br/chm/files/cartas-sinoticas/c18031700.jpg, *where the file name is cYYMMDDHH, with hh =00 or 12. The file size is ~990 kB, which is very large for delivery underway. View them online at* marinha.mil.br/chm/dados-do-smm-cartas-sinoticas/cartas-sinoticas.

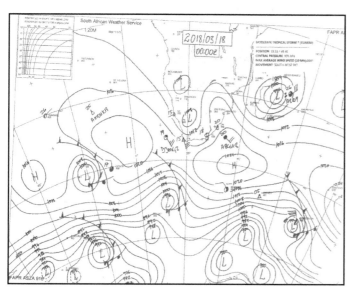

Figure 10.1-4. *Latest surface analysis from the South African Weather Service. It can be requested from Saildocs:* send http://www.weathersa.co.za//media/data/observation/synoptic/ma_sy.gif. *It is updated at 00z and 12z, but the file size is ~970 kB.*

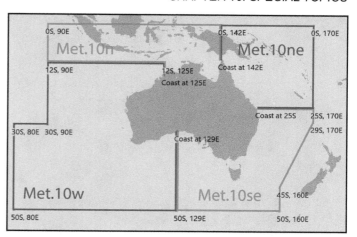

Figure 10.1-5. *Metarea zones that can be requested individually from Saildocs. The request is simply:* send Met.10ne. *The metarea help file at saildocs.com lists other metareas in the SH that can be requested this way.*

cussed earlier (rfax.pdf) tells which nations produce radiofax maps, and chances are they have the files available for email request.

Many coastal waters in the SH have NAVTEX broadcasts, but Australia and New Zealand do not. Both have an intricate network of VHF coastal stations reporting local observations and forecasts. Offshore forecasts provided to the GMDSS SafetyNET are available by email request from Saildocs as described in Figure 10.1-5.

You will find there are parts of the SH that are not covered well by maps from these main agencies listed, so you must fall back on standard model forecasts such as GFS. These are global models, so you can just select the region you care about and get the same data and format you are used to. All the standard precautions we have discussed apply, with an extra uncertainty in the SH, because there are fewer ship observations than in the NH.

10.2 Monsoons

Monsoons are probably the world's most famous seasonal winds. They blow over the Arabian Sea and adjacent waters of the subcontinent of India for six months from the northeast (northeast monsoon) and for six months from the southwest (southwest monsoon). They have been crucial to maritime trade and cultural exchange since the beginning of seafaring history.

Though a full theory is still under study, they are in effect a giant sea breeze, caused by the much greater annual variation of temperature over large landmasses compared with the neighboring oceans. This creates giant Highs over Eurasia in winter (Siberian High) and prominent Lows in summer (Asiatic Low). The shape of the terrain also has a considerable effect. The process is illustrated in Figure 10.2-1

Monsoons are strongest on the southern and eastern sides of Asia, but monsoons also occur on other coasts when the prevailing atmospheric circulation is not strong enough

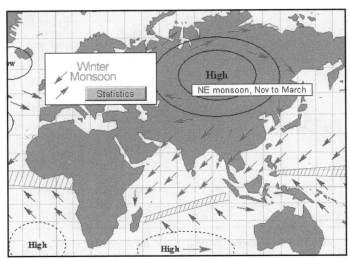
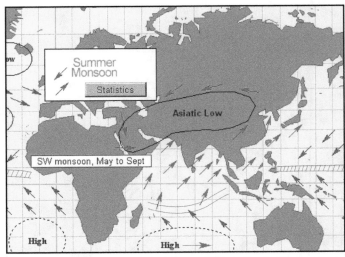

Figure 10.2-1. *Left.* The NE monsoon generated by the Siberian High pushes the doldrums (crosshatched zones) into the Southern Hemisphere. *Right.* In the summer, the Asiatic Low develops, which pulls the winds of the Indian Ocean North, pulling apart the ITCZ (doldrums) and forming a *monsoon trof* (no crosshatch)—the origin of that term used elsewhere around the globe. From the Starpath Weather Trainer. You can use climatic data tools of Section 10.5 to see more specific wind patterns. See also Mariner's Pressure Atlas.

to inhibit them. Global winds (prevailing westerlies, trade winds, etc.) are generally distinguished from local winds (Tehuantepecer, Mistral, etc.), but monsoons must be considered hybrids of sorts.

In the NH winter, an intense High develops over the cold Eurasian continent (centered over Siberia) and from around October or November to March a persistent NE monsoon wind blows over the North Indian Ocean and South China Sea, a direct consequence of the clockwise circulation around the High. Over the Western Pacific Ocean the wind is NNE. The winds are generally moderate to fresh, but can reach gale force locally as surges of cold air move south and par-

ticularly where funneling occurs (Taiwan Strait, Palk Strait, etc.). Weather is generally cool, fair, and with well-broken clouds, though the coasts of South China and Vietnam are frequently affected by extensive low clouds and drizzle. The NE Monsoon winds may extend across the equator, changing direction to N or NW off East Africa and W or NW over Northwestern Australia.

In the NH summer pressure over Asia falls, with lowest pressure near the West Himalayas. The counterclockwise circulation around the Asiatic Low gives persistent SW Monsoon winds from May to September or October over the Northern Indian Ocean and South China Sea, and SSW or S

Table 10.2-1. Monsoon Statistics		Jan	Feb	Mar	Apr	May	Jun	Jul	Aug	Sep	Oct	Nov	Dec
South China Sea	NE	5-6	4-5	4	—					—	—	5-6	5-6
Eastern China Sea	NE-N	5	5	4	—					—	4-5	5	5
Yellow Sea	N-NW	5	5	4	—					—	4-5	5	5
Japan Sea	N-NW	5	5	4	—					—	4-5	5	5
North Indian Ocean	NE	4	4	4	—					—		4	4
South China Sea	SW				—	3	4	4	4-5	—			
Eastern China Sea	SW-S					—	3-4	3-4	—	—			
Yellow Sea	SW-SE					—	3-4	3-4	—	—			
Japan Sea	SW-S-E					—	3-4	3-4	—	—			
North Indian Ocean	SW				—	—	5-6	6	6	5	—		
Indonesian waters	W-NW	3	3	3	—						—	—	3
Arafura Sea	NW	5	5	3-4	—							—	3-4
N and NW Australia	W-NW	4-5	4-5	—								—	
Indonesian waters	SE				—	—	4-5	4-5	4-5	4-5	—		
Arafura Sea	SE			—	—	4	4	4	4	4	—		
N and NW Australia	SE-E			—	3-4	4-5	4-5	4-5	4-5	3-4	—	—	

Table Notes:
Wind speed in Beaufort force numbers:
3 = 7 to 10 kts,
4 = 11 to 16 kts,
5 = 17 to 21 kts,
6 = 22 to 27 kts,
— means variable wind.

winds over the Western Pacific Ocean. Winds are generally fresh to strong and raise considerable seas. Warm humid air gives much rain and clouds on windward coasts and islands.

The seasons of the principal monsoons and their average strengths are shown in Table 10.2-1. Sailing directions throughout the monsoon regions and especially the China Sea have been well known since the early 1800s due to extensive China trade. They are well documented in all modern resources.

In each type of monsoon heavy weather is experienced at times, with sudden and severe squalls and torrential rain. But the most severe weather of the region is, of course, from typhoons—a Chinese word meaning great wind, the regional name for what is elsewhere called hurricane. They occur chiefly between May and October or November.

10.3 Blocking Highs

Throughout the book we have discussed how many ocean-going sailing routes end up being planned around large subtropical Highs. These center-of-action Highs are often planted right in between where we are and where we want to go. Since we typically want wind behind us, there is usually an obvious route around them, namely clockwise in the NH and counterclockwise in the SH. A frequent tactical decision to be made is how close can you cut the corner, saving distance to your destination, but risking getting too close to the higher pressure and running out of wind. Refer back to Figure 7.2-2 to see an illustration.

Some sailors use the 1020 isobar for a guideline around the Pacific High in the summer, and sure enough that works out to be about right for a typical central pressure. But the peak of the Pacific High (and Atlantic Highs) can vary significantly—anywhere from under 1030 to over 1040. A better guideline might be to stay two full isobars off the peak—if you put your position on the map, you see two closed isobars between you and the center. This means the 1020 line is about right for 1028 to 1030 or so, but if the High is really high then you can cut closer. Also, of course, keep an eye on the forecasts. It is the pressure when you get to the corner that matters, not what it is now.

The basis of this analysis is the assumption that the High will have about the same shape when you get there. Fortunately there are pretty good guidelines for this based on the shape of the surface High at the moment, and of course, we always gain more insight with a look to the 500-mb flow over the top of it. A stable High usually means the winds aloft are wrapping around it to some extent. In ideal cases the surface High is under a nice ridge in the winds aloft.

The phrase *blocking High* means (from the perspective of the surface map) that it is firm enough that it will fend off Lows and fronts banging on it from the west. This means the flow aloft is up and over the north side of the surface High so it takes systems around the High rather than through it. If we have only one look at a surface map—which could happen

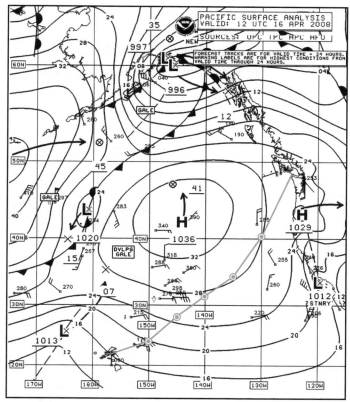

Figure 10.3-1. *A nice blocking High. Note we could go around the SE corner with a target pressure of 1028 or so, and still have wind. The center of this High is slightly NW of its climatic home, but close enough. The route shown from WA to HI is discussed in Section 10.4.*

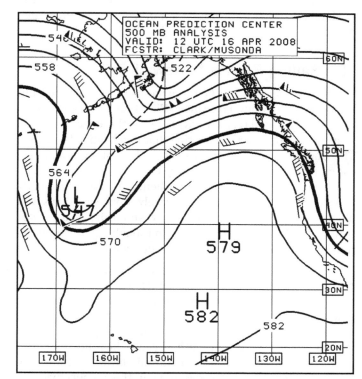

Figure 10.3-2. *The 500-mb winds aloft at the time of the map above it, showing a nice omega block wrapping around the surface High. We can count on this High sitting in place for a while.*

if we lost our communications underway—we can judge the stability of the High from three factors:

Factors contributing to a Blocking High

(1) Is the High in the right place for this time of year?

(2) Is it 1030 mb or more at the center?

(3) Does it have at least 2 nearly-round isobars around it?

If these three conditions are met, then chances are very good this High will look about the same tomorrow. Then tomorrow, you can look and make the evaluation again. At some point, one of these criteria will fail, and at that point, we can no longer have faith that things will be the same. If the High starts to look like a croissant, or falls down to 1028 mb or so, then the first Low or front along the way will blast right through it.

We of course have the official forecasts of the shape and location of the isobars, but it might just help your interpretation of the maps to think of the High as a thing protecting you from assault, as long as it remains strong. The first of the criteria requires some climatic data, which you can get from a Pilot Chart. More specific statistical data on monthly pressures, including standard deviations, are included in the *Mariner's Pressure Atlas* from Starpath Publications.

Figure 10.3-1 shows a good blocking High, and Figure 10.3-2 shows even better news about this High. In this case not only is the surface High under a ridge in the winds aloft, the ridge is an omega block (Figure 3.3-9). The normal easterly migration of the Rossby waves is interrupted, and the High might sit in this location for 4 or 5 days, or even a week or more.

10.4 Sailing Routes to Hawaii

Every 2 years since 1966 there has been a yacht race from Victoria, BC to Maui, HI (called "Vic-Maui") in the first part of July. It is a good race for navigators as there are lots of options for weather tactics covering that much latitude change. There are several stages to the tactics. The first one is an interesting result of the Mercator projections we use on nautical charts, and one to keep in mind whenever sailing diagonally across large latitudes changes. Namely, if you sail due south along the west coast from the Canadian border, you are not getting much closer to Hawaii, even though without analysis it might look like you are on a Mercator chart.

Thus the well known route down and around the High can be started too soon. If two boats enter the ocean together at the Strait of Juan de Fuca, and one heads south and the other takes the great circle route to Hawaii (which is north of the rhumb line), then just about every mile the higher boat sails it gains on the one headed south, because the route due south does not bring it any closer to Hawaii—or at least not very much. (A Mercator map is deceptive in this perspective. Los Angeles to HI is only about 100 miles farther than Strait of Juan de Fuca to HI, 1,000 miles to the north.)

But the direct route can't go on very long. You do have to turn south in time to get around the High, because if you wait too long you won't be able to do it, meaning the wind angles will be terrible. So that is step one to sort out. Something similar can happen on other long voyages, in other parts of the world that cover large latitude changes.

Then comes the rounding of the corner of the High as outlined in the last section, where guidelines are proposed. However, looking at the recorded tracks of all the winning boats in all divisions for all past Vic-Maui races, one sees a regular pattern. Essentially all of these winning boats passed within 100 nmi of these way points:

(1) 40° 30'N, 130° 00' W

(2) 34° 30'N, 135° 00' W

(3) 31° 30'N, 140° 00' W

(4) 28° 30'N, 145° 00' W

(5) 24° 30'N, 150° 00' W

This does not count a few exceptional flyers, and unusual weather patterns, but it covers most all of the winning tracks by far. These waypoints are plotted out in Figure 10.3-1 as a red line.

Thus we have a simple rule on how to sail to Hawaii from the Pacific Northwest. Enter those waypoints into your GPS and go that way. Put another way, if you do not pass within 100 nmi of each of these waypoints you should have a very good reason why.

There are lots of ways to get stuck while sailing to HI if one does not consider the above notes. For example, tropical storms to the SE of the High, packing up the isobars so you think you can sail more directly there. So you take that higher, shorter route, and then the tropical storm curves back to the east or dissipates completely, taking all pressure off the High, which in turn explodes into a giant sea of no wind. In that case you will wish you did not try to cut the corner, even though there was no significant change in the location or intensity of the central High.

The key point here is a cross ocean race like this takes 10 to 15 days and the only dependable forecast extends out 4 days, at best. So there is no long-term forecast good enough to tell you what the winds will be like when you get halfway there, at the crucial turning point. So even if the winds are very favorable at the start, and it looks like you could sail straight to HI, you must try to overcome this temptation and take the statistically safe route. Or at least be aware of these factors, as you watch what your competitors are doing, what the 48-hr and 96-hr maps are saying, what your barometer is showing, what the ship reports are saying, and so on. You just have to cut it closer than your competitors to win.

Once you get around the corner, you have to apply the tactics discussed in Figure 7.2-5. Do this better than your competitors and you have another opportunity for gain.

The equivalent basic routes from San Francisco (Pacific Cup Race) or from Los Angeles (TransPac Race) are essentially rhumb lines, which you then modify to account for the precise shape and location of the SE corner of the High (or it's ridge) and the state of the trade winds. Again, with the tactics of Figure 7.2-5 playing an equally important role, and maybe coming into play a bit farther out.

10.5 Chen-Chesneau 500-mb Routing Zones

In Section 7.8 we discuss the use of the 500-mb maps as a way to evaluate the confidence level we might put on the surface forecasts. This we can do without much underlying knowledge of how surface Lows actually interact with the flow aloft. But we do, in fact, already know basic elements about this interaction that might let us take the analysis a bit farther.

In particular, we know that the divergence downstream of a prominent trough aloft is the key to deepening the surface Low, as discussed in the text related to Figure 4.3-12. There is a lot of practical knowledge to be gained from understanding this relationship between the winds aloft and surface Low formation.

The subject was first brought to the broader attention of mariners by Sienkiewicz and Chesneau in their frequently quoted articles in the *Mariner's Weather Log* (December, 2008). Since then, Lee Chesneau has joined forces with Captain Ma-Li Chen to produce a new, in-depth book on the subject: *Heavy Weather Avoidance—Concepts and Applications of the 500-mb Charts* (Figure 10.5-1).

In that book they present, among many new and useful concepts, a way to think about the wind flow aloft that we see on the 500-mb maps. It is valuable to understand for all mariners, not just professional ship routers. It has been used in practice by Capt. Chen for many years.

They consider the band of wind at the 500-mb level, between 5400 and 5700 meters altitude, as the storm track we can use to plan surface routes around. They point out that surface Lows often form near the base of the trough aloft— that is, on the surface, below this point overhead—and then they deepen as they move diagonally toward the top of the

ridge, as shown in Figure 10.5-2. They define zones in this pattern as shown in the figure that we can use as guidelines as to what we might expect.

The safest place to travel is within the A-zone, below the 570 line. If you do encounter Lows or fronts below this line in the "available" zone they would be expected to be moderate.

The D-zone is called the "difficult" or dangerous zone. This is where the surface Lows are developing rapidly and can be quite intense.

The C-zone is the "cautious" zone, because it could be perfectly good sailing until a Low coming rapidly up the D zone spins out on top of you. Most of such Lows will be dissipating at that time, so they might not be super intense, but once spun out of the westerly wind flow they could sit there for some period of time generating high seas over a large area that could not be avoided.

Behind the trough is called the B-zone. It is the place to "be careful." They suggest that you can travel in that region, but you must be careful because the Rossby waves that make up these troughs and ridges are slowly sliding to the east, and right behind every B-zone is a D-zone.

Needless to say, their book covers much more sophisticated applications of these concepts and many others as well. It merits careful study for maximum benefit. In the meantime, this simple description of theirs helps us stay aware of our location on the surface relative to this primary driving force of Low development that is overhead. Looking at the 500-mb maps with these concepts in mind helps us better appreciate what we see on the 48-hr and 96-hr surface forecasts, and gives us some insight to details that we might have otherwise overlooked.

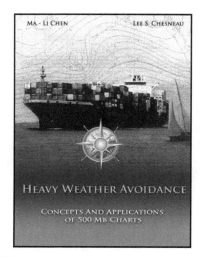

Figure 10.5-1. *Available from marineweatherbylee.com.*

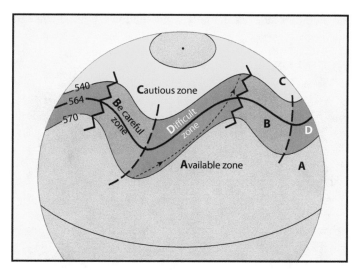

Figure 10.5-2. *Schematic display of a 500-mb chart showing the Chen-Chesneau routing zones. The 5640-m elevation (564 line) is marked with a bold line on OPC maps of these winds. Surface Lows often move NE along the "Ma-Li Diagonal" (dashed line) from the base of the trough to the tip of the ridge. They deepen over the 1 or 2 days it takes them to reach the top, where they often spin out into the C zone and dissipate. Whenever possible, it is best to plan routes that remain in the A zone.*

10.6 Modern Pilot Chart Data

Pilot charts have been our go-to source for global climatic marine weather since the 19th century. The latest versions are online at msi.nga.mil as PDFs and as raster navigation charts (RNC) at opencpn.org. Samples from pilot charts are in Figures 3.6-6 and 8.2-5. The climatic data on these charts are very good, despite being quite old—it seems that the magnetic variation data are the main things updated every decade or so. Climate change is indeed real, and some statistics are bound to evolve, but this remains a minor factor in our choice of which sails we need and what time of year and what route is best for an ocean passage.

COGOW

We do, however, have new data, and, more important, easier, more precise ways to access these data. Climatic wind data took a giant step forward with the work of Craig Risien at Oregon State University. His program is called Climatology of Global Ocean Winds (COGOW) and the data are available to the public at:

numbat.coas.oregonstate.edu/cogow

His compilation of QuikSCAT satellite wind measurements from 1999 to 2009 marked the state of the art in global climatic wind data for route planning and other applications, such as oil spill analysis, global heat distribution, and offshore wind power generation. All of the prevailing wind features discussed throughout this book show up beautifully in this data. It is semi-monthly, worldwide coverage of the wind streamlines that FitzRoy, Maury, Sadler, and others over scores of years could only have dreamed of. The data are presented as graphic map sections, with corresponding wind roses at each grid point as shown in Figure 10.6-1. Gap winds at Tehuantepec and Papagayo show up nicely—the darker areas on either side are actually wind shadows. Online you can just click through other months to see when these winds are strongest. We also see a minor gap wind (on average) at the Canal Zone, which we did not know of before seeing this.

The strong enhancement of the trade winds along the NW coast of Colombia is only hinted at in pilot charts, but is clearly seen in the COGOW data. This is an interesting wind system that appears be to due to semidiurnal pressure variations over Northern Colombia. When active, the NWS refers to the winds as "pulsing" but does not mention the pressure variation. The ITCZ between the trade winds show up nicely at about 8N, and we see that the NE trades start to build in January west of about 112W. We also see an unusual reversal of the flow south of Panama.

We can also see unusual effects like *tip jets* at the southern tip of Greenland and north tip of Madagascar. These are unique large-scale land effects that have been much studied by meteorologists.

SV *Pitufa* Ocean Winds

Although all the data are available at the COGOW site (both graphically and digitally as NetCDF files), sailor Christian Feldbauer (SV *Pitufa*) noted that the interface to this valuable resource could be made more convenient to fellow sailors, which he set about to do. His presentation is at pitufa.at/oceanwinds. The resolution is a lot lower (2° x 2°), so we do not see the details mentioned earlier, visible in the COGOW presentation, but it is adequate for ocean planning. The interface is fast and easy to use. Wind statistics at any point can be displayed with a mouse click.

Even more valuable, he has compiled the data into a KML file that can be downloaded, then opened in Google Earth and saved, so that future inquires do not require an internet connection. This is a valuable addition to the ocean navigator's computer. A sample is shown in Figure 10.6-2. (Note that all

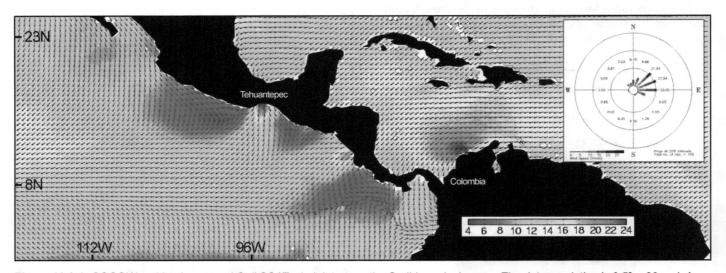

Figure 10.6-1. *COGOW archived averaged QuikSCAT wind data over the Caribbean in January. The data resolution is 0.5° = 30 nmi. Arrows show wind direction; speed is from the colorbar. Any point can be clicked for a wind rose of probabilities. The inset example is for Great Inagua Island, just above the Windward Passage between Cuba and Haiti. Tabulated wind data are also available, as is a list of all the data points that went into the averages at each grid point. This picture is a combination of two adjacent images from the COGOW site.*

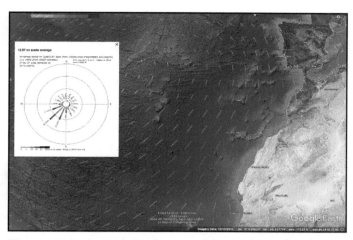

Figure 10.6-2. *Sample of the SV Pitufa Ocean Winds KML file displayed in Google Earth. All twelve months can be stored in your computer for easy access as needed.*

US navigation charts can also be stored in Google Earth on your computer, which could be a valuable backup for those who do not use electronic charting routinely.)

Recall that KML is a GIS format consistent with the planned S-412 format, so looking ahead we can anticipate data like this overlaid on our navigation charts as well.

It is important to remember that the winds shown in the plots of the COGOW data, wherever it is shown, represent a weighted average of all data at that point. In the trades, for

example, an arrow showing 15 kts from the NE could be 80% likely; but in higher latitudes with more changing winds, an arrow showing 15 kt from the NE could be representing something that takes place only 30% of the time, with another 30% being from the N-NW and the W-NW. It is always important to look at the wind roses to see the statistics in both speed and direction.

OpenCPN Climatology Plugin

The open source navigation program OpenCPN, conceived of by lead developer David S. Register, has evolved into a valuable aid to navigation and marine weather analysis with the help of numerous supporters. Weather related plugins by Sean D'Epagnier is one example. His Climatology_pi is a unique tool for presenting digital values of climatic data with adjustable display options. The data he uses is listed in Table 10.6-1. This is clearly a look into the future of route planning. Indeed, you can run his WeatherRouting_pi (Section 10.7) using climatic wind and current data for any date, globally. Examples are shown in Figure 10.6-3.

Needless to say, we sail in the weather, not in the climate, so we have to interpret the results accordingly. Also, like all elements of the OpenCPN project, this one is evolving, and will just improve with extended usage and feedback.

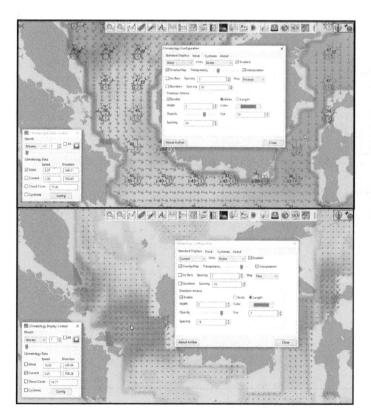

Figure 10.6-3. *Sample outputs from the OpenCPN Climatology plugin. Wind above; current below. There are other climate parameters available, including tropical cyclone tracks. See Table 10.6-1.*

Table 10.6-1. Climate Data in the OpenCPN Climatology Plugin	
Parameter	*Source*
Wind	ftp://eclipse.ncdc.noaa.gov/pub/seawinds/SI/uv/ (1987 to 2013)
Current	http://podaac.jpl.nasa.gov/dataset/OSCAR_L4_OC_third-deg (1992 to 2012)
Air Temp	ftp://ftp.cdc.noaa.gov/Datasets/ncep.marine/air.mean.nc
Precip	ftp://ftp.cdc.noaa.gov/Datasets/cmap/std/precip.mon.mean.nc
Relative Humidity	ftp://ftp.cdc.noaa.gov/Datasets/icoads/1degree/global/enh/rhum.mean.nc
Cloud	http://www.jisao.washington.edu/data/coads_climatologies/cldccoadsclim5079.nc
Sea Level Pressure	http://www.jisao.washington.edu/data/coads_climatologies/slpcoadsclim5079.nc
SST	http://www.jisao.washington.edu/data/coads_climatologies/sstcoadsclim6079.1deg.nc
Lightning	ftp://ghrc.nsstc.nasa.gov/pub/lis/climatology/HRMC/data/LISOTD_HRMC_V2.3.2013.hdf
Sea Depth	https://www.esrl.noaa.gov/psd/data/data.nodc.woa98.html
Cyclone Tracks	http://unisys.com
El Nino Years	https://www.cpc.ncep.noaa.gov/products/analysis_monitoring/ensostuff/ensoyears.shtml

Table Notes: *From the "About" tab of the OpenCPN Climatology plugin. These are all modern, excellent sources, many updated daily. The winds used include the COGOW data and more. The OSCAR currents reflect accurate locations of average current bands, but the predicted speeds most likely underestimate what we can expect. Latest updates of all of these data can be found at the links given, but it will take a program like Panoply to view them.*

10.7 Optimum Sailboat Routing

Computer calculations of optimum ocean routing were initiated by the US Navy as soon as computers were available, sometime in the early 50s. The process has evolved continually since then. It is widely used in commercial shipping to optimize time and safety of ships and cargo.

Applications of numerical routing to sailing across a GRIB forecast, based on vessel performance (polar diagram), have been in use for over 20 years. We did not cover this in the last edition, just five years ago, despite its having been routine practice in ocean sailboat racing for many years.

The reason then was that this technology takes special care to be productive. Those experienced racing navigators who were routinely using it spent very many hours learning the nuances of the process and software they used. They were (and remain) prepared to continually update the route throughout the race, not to mention spending many hours devoted to accurate calibrations of all instruments, which is crucial to effective results. Also, at that time, only the high-end navigation programs offered routing computations, including the crucial function of continually measuring and updating the polar diagram data for the vessel.

These reasons to leave this topic to other specialized books and training materials (referenced later) have not changed!

What has changed is computed sailboat routing is now ubiquitous, readily available, and promoted by many sources. It is now important to know how the process works so you can judge its applicability to your needs and understand the factors that enter into it. Before, we knew that the experts used it, but we did not have the tools to do so in our own sailing. Now we can push a button and have the "best route" emailed back to us, which means we need to know what is going on.

Sailboat navigation has been a matter of weather routing since the earliest days of seafaring when knowledge of wind patterns were first recorded. This knowledge was codified and expanded globally by Maury and others in the mid 1800s. Now we have amazing environmental data (wind, sea state, and currents) and computers and navigation programs that can do extensive complex computations in seconds. But we also need to know the performance of the boat in all the possible variations of these environmental parameters. In short, there are three basic components to numerical weather routing: the environmental data (GRIBs), the vessel data (polar diagrams), and the routing computation itself (navigation programs or services capable of it).

It is fundamental to deeply understand that if either of these first two inputs are wrong—meaning they do not adequately reflect the true environment or the true performance of your boat—then the computed route is unlikely to be effec-

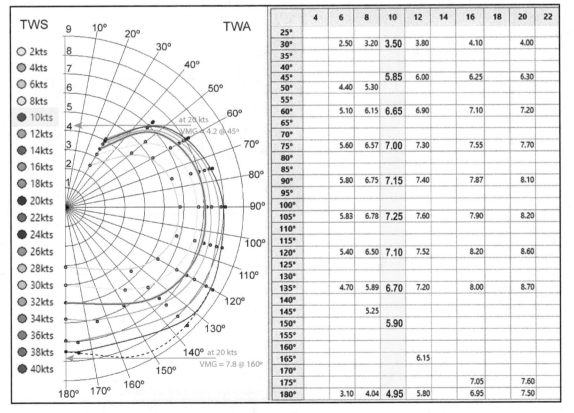

Figure 10.7-1. *Example of vessel performance data ("polars"). This polar manager is from OpenCPN. All routing programs include a polar manager, with varying levels of data collection and manipulation functionality. The routing computation must interpolate the table, so more data is better. This one is missing low and high wind values, with only sparse data in the aft quadrant. The dashed line, for example, shows what might be a better 20-kt curve, with notably different downwind performance than given by the existing data. The 10-kt data highlighted in yellow are used in the isochrone examples. Boats can't sail at 30° TWA; those entries are only used to interpolate optimum upwind angles. Although they can be interpolated from what is given in the polars, it is best to have specific upwind and downwind optimum VMG entries for each wind speed. Polar data are saved in various file formats: TXT, CSV, POL, and others, but differences in formatting (sometimes subtle) must be addressed to use them in different programs. Some vessels use separate diagrams for different sail combinations. Some also maintain alternative polars for various sailing conditions.*

	4	6	8	10	12	14	16	18	20	22
25°										
30°		2.50	3.20	3.50	3.80		4.10		4.00	
35°										
40°										
45°				5.85	6.00		6.25		6.30	
50°		4.40	5.30							
55°										
60°		5.10	6.15	6.65	6.90		7.10		7.20	
65°										
70°										
75°		5.60	6.57	7.00	7.30		7.55		7.70	
80°										
85°										
90°		5.80	6.75	7.15	7.40		7.87		8.10	
95°										
100°										
105°		5.83	6.78	7.25	7.60		7.90		8.20	
110°										
115°										
120°		5.40	6.50	7.10	7.52		8.20		8.60	
125°										
130°										
135°		4.70	5.89	6.70	7.20		8.00		8.70	
140°										
145°			5.25							
150°				5.90						
155°										
160°										
165°							6.15			
170°										
175°								7.05	7.60	
180°		3.10	4.04	4.95	5.80		6.95		7.50	

(Polar diagram labels: TWS — 2kts, 4kts, 6kts, 8kts, 10kts, 12kts, 14kts, 16kts, 18kts, 20kts, 22kts, 24kts, 26kts, 28kts, 30kts, 32kts, 34kts, 36kts, 38kts, 40kts. TWA angles 10° through 180°. Annotations: "at 20 kts VMG = 4.2 @ 45°" and "140° at 20 kts VMG = 7.8 @ 160°")

tive and could even be misleading, regardless of how good the routing software might be.

Polar Diagrams

We have spent much of this book on the options and quality of the environmental data, including ways to evaluate it underway. So to understand the numerical routing process, we look first to the vessel data, illustrated in Figure 10.7-1 that shows a sample tool for collecting and adjusting polar diagrams, often nicknamed "polars." Yacht designers provide polars for their designs, but these are more for comparing one model to another. They are not realistic predictions of what you actually see on the water. Racing organizations also run *velocity prediction programs (VPP)* to rate vessels for competition. Many polars from the Offshore Racing Congress (ORC) are given at jieter.github.io/orc-data/site. Routing software programs typically include a large number of polars for various yacht types, each in their own preferred format—the polar formatting becomes an issue when you wish to compare results from two different programs; you may have to rebuild it in the second router's polar manager.

The basic polar is a table of expected boat speeds for various true wind speeds (TWS) and true wind angles (TWA), usually with an accompanying polar plot of the data, which makes it easier to visualize the optimum upwind and downwind sailing angle for each wind speed. It assumes flat water with no current, the best sail choice made, and in the best trim. (Usually the routing program references another table of your best sail choices for combinations of TWS and TWA.) In Figure 10.7-1 we see that at TWS = 10 kts, the best angle

to weather is TWA = 47°, which should yield a boat speed of 5.85 kts, assuming the boat is "sailing her polars." The best VMG downwind at TWS = 10 kts, in the specified conditions, would be 5.9 kts at TWA = 151°.

Isochrones

An isochrone is a curve on the chart connecting all places you could sail to in a specific time interval. These points are figured from the polar diagram for a specific TWS. The diagram tells you what your speed would be, depending on which TWA you start on. A sample is shown in Figure 10.7-2 for a TWS of 10 kts. Figure 10.7-3 shows a sequence of isochrones, each generated from a node on an earlier one. The figure shows only a few options, from a few nodes, but many thousands of possible routes emerge very quickly (exponentially), and it is up to user settings and the navigation program's math routines to prune these down to a reasonable set of choices. The isochrone interval is a common input, because once plotted, isochrones help the navigator interpret the proposed optimum route. Another option is to limit how far off the rhumb line you are willing to diverge looking for the potentially fastest route.

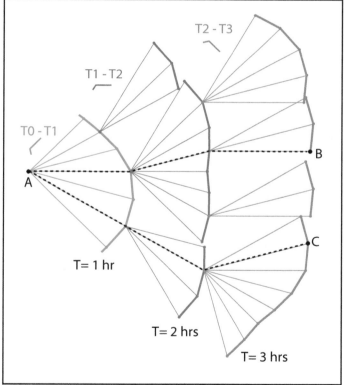

Figure 10.7-3. *Examples of sequential isochrones computed from selected nodes on the previous one. These mark possible routes that are used to find the optimum one across changing winds. Just two examples are shown as dotted lines. If all options were shown it would be a maze of crossed lines. The programmer must use several logics and approximations to prune out those that cannot win and concentrate on promising ones. The goal is to get each succeeding isochrone as far from the previous one as possible. If wind and current remain constant, successive isochrones will be parallel curves.*

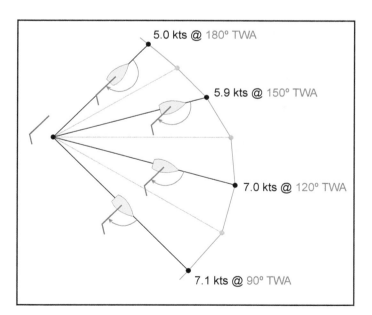

Figure 10.7-2. *Isochrone (red line) for a 1-hr time interval in a 10-kt wind, assumed uniform over the region. How far the boat proceeds depends on the polars (Figure 10.7-1). When computing the isochrone, the nav program must interpolate the tabulated polar data, and if there are not enough data points, the interpolation may not represent the true performance.*

The routing program then looks at all possible routes (node to node) to the destination and finds the fastest. It must use various mathematical means to prune the choices down to manageable numbers and make logical decisions on viable routes. Procedures for doing this are fairly well documented, which accounts for the increasing number of routing opportunities—that step, however, is not the only key to the most successful programs. This process leads to the fastest route across a maze of isochrones, but we have to check the winner to see if an option just slightly longer looks a lot more reasonable!

Remember the program is just crunching numbers; it is not thinking about tactics, seamanship, or general good practice. Champion navigator Stan Honey, for example, has pointed out that computed optimum routes often take you too close to a High you are rounding, considering the practical matters of sailing. Inevitable sailing adjustments in variable conditions near a High often call for short turns into the wind for more speed or control, which takes you bit-by-bit closer to the High, where such corrections are needed even more. His analogy on this is very clear: a routing program would take you around the Grand Canyon right on the edge, but a practical person would give themselves a safety margin. (Sections 10.3 and 10.4 discuss practical guidelines for rounding Highs, which can help with this evaluation.)

Figure 10.7-4 shows a computed optimum route with isochrones. Such a route can then be converted to a GPX file for an actual route to navigate. Although the concept of isochrones is key to most computations, navigation programs differ significantly on how they implement the analysis, and equally importantly how they create and interpolate the polars. Programs also differ in the tools they offer to analyze the routes once created.

Waves

When all is working properly, this type of routing is state of the art navigation, but there are many factors that must be right. The polars are the key issue. They must be right, which means a key working tool is a way to continuously measure true wind speed, true wind angle, and boat speed and then use this data to update your polars. But even the best polars made on inland sailing will be wrong when we get into ocean waves. Flat water polars need to be duplicated and saved to be modified as wave polars for different wave heights and wave angles. Then the navigator can look at the wave forecasts (WW3) to decide when to use which polar. It is not uncommon to have to remove all weight from the bow when encountering big waves, and this change of trim can affect the polars.

Sailing downwind in following seas we will likely be faster than flat water; sailing into the seas, slower. Usually the wind and waves are in the same direction so there is hope for a useful codification of these effects. On the other hand, even top navigators were challenged trying to route across the seas in the 2016 Pacific Cup (San Francisco to Oahu) with a storm in Alaska and two hurricanes and a tropical storm in the offing creating big confused seas across much of the race course. Even without big storms looming about, as soon as one jibe is much favored because of the waves (i.e., combined seas not in line with the wind), we see the problem. Handling the sea state properly is a big challenge in routing.

One way to approximate the effect of waves, which is available in most programs, is just scaling the whole polar diagram. Thus in favorable following seas, we might just raise the boat speeds of all TWA by x 1.2, knowing that for the next leg of this route we are going downwind. Likewise, we could scale them x 0.8 going into the waves, or some appropriate factor. This is not as good as real wave polars, but it is a minimum correction we can make. The main idea is to gather your experience on these actual corrections and build them into a polar.

Wave data can be used to help shape a route, even if corrections to polar speeds are not optimized or even included. Most programs let us set a maximum wave height we want to avoid. Thus a forecasted region of high waves becomes a prohibited zone that must be routed around. The same constraints can be put on winds over a selected maximum speed.

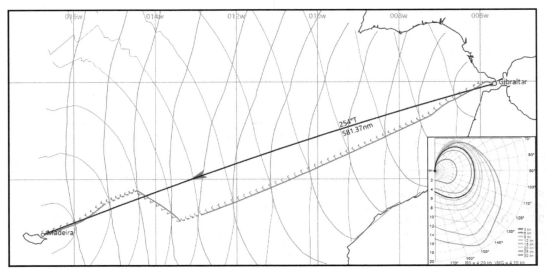

Figure 10.7-4. GFS route from Gibraltar to Madeira computed by Expedition using the polars shown in the insert. No current or wave corrections applied. Blue lines are 6-hr isochrones from the start; red lines are Expedition's reverse isochrones, marking equal times to the destination. The latter are helpful for comparing competing routes or sides of a race course; combined with the isochrones, we get a good picture of how the suggested route won out.

Study the Results

A key factor in the successful use of computed routing is to have ways to test or reason through the proposed routes. This might start by making your best guess of the route yourself—the old fashioned way. In other words, make your own isochrones by setting, for example, a day's run on a pair of dividers and walking off across the weather map what seems the best route, keeping the corresponding forecast under the dividers. With digital GFS forecasts you can take even smaller steps if needed as you advance the forecast to match your step size. Generally, the key issues of the route will become clear, and you will have a feel for the range of possibilities.

Now you can run the router to see what the computer thinks, knowing the wind and boat speed more precisely at each step than we could do by hand, and testing possible variations. Your previous analysis could spot the "flyers" you know are unlikely. For example, suppose the polars are wrong or inadequately defined at a particular TWA and they lead the boat off to a place you cannot in fact achieve with your actual performance data, and then the winds turn all favorable from that location, which makes that the "optimum" route, but not the right one. That is just one way to see how crucial the polars are.

Ways to test such things might be to scale the polars down by some factor to see how much that changes the route. Another test might be to block off that route you know is not right. Most routing programs offer a way to create a boundary region that is off limits in the route selection. This is a common tool near land, where for example, you want to rule out going through one pass and not another. Just block off the pass you don't want, even though it is a shorter route and the program would have taken if it could. On an ocean route, you could just sketch in a blocked region to rule out heading off in that direction.

We can also compare the computations with what we know are the seasonally average successful routes for a particular crossing. In Section 10.4, for example, we have the waypoints that mark the average winning route of the July Victoria to Maui Race. If you were routing that passage, it would be interesting to compare what the computer proposed to that climatic average. Differences would be expected as winds of course vary, but if the computed route were dramatically different from that, then we should study it carefully to understand why it is different, and is that source of difference dependable. All of the popular ocean races have archived statistics of winning routes, and these are just as valuable to cruisers as to racers.

Another approach is to remember that shorter term forecasts (< 4 days) are notably better than longer term ones—the GFS offers data out 16 days! To see the full route across the ocean we are forced to use the long term forecasts knowing they grow weaker with time. Once we see the computed optimum full route, we can then look at where that puts us at the end of 3 or 4 days, and then run a route just out to that point.

If short term and long term agree we have more confidence in the longer runs. If notably different, we have to think about it.

Wind Data

Then we face the ongoing question of, "is the model wind forecast correct?" We cover ways to analyze this throughout the book, but this reduces to the nitty-gritty when we start routing computations. With most programs, it is a simple task to load one model forecast, run the route, and then load another model forecast and run it again for another route. If the wind forecasts are very similar looking, then chances are the routes will be similar, but after 4 days models will likely diverge and different routes emerge. All the above tests still apply to every model used, but we can also try other things.

Most programs allow for some level of forecast modification. The most basic is to just scale and rotate the full set of wind forecasts to match what we measure at the moment. If the wind we saw at h0 was 10 kts at 070, but we were seeing 12 kts at 090—and this is still true now some 4 hrs later—then we just turn on a universal correction that scales the wind up by x 1.2 and rotates the winds to the right by 20°, and run the route again. In principle, this has to be an improvement; but we have to adjust again and re-compute the route if they fall out of agreement.

Very light air is a special challenge. All models will likely differ, and polars are likely to be more uncertain, and you could be faced with vastly diverging routes. In such conditions, chance encounters with clouds or squalls could be the determining factor on actual progress. On the other hand, if you could be convinced that one model is indeed right in such conditions, it could pay off. Or as noted before, we could get convinced that wind will for sure build in a particular location, and we force the program to find the best route to it.

Ocean Currents

On some passages, ocean currents can dominate the choice of optimum route. Sailing across the Gulf Stream is just one example. But even on routes not dominated by currents, the forecasted currents (RTOFS) can have a notable influence on the outcome. Consequently, unlike the wave forecasts, which have difficult, subtle corrections, the currents have a simple, direct effect on our route. The corrections are easy to make mathematically in the routing program, it is just a matter of knowing if the current forecasts are correct or not.

We are not totally helpless to answer this question. We can measure the current we are in fairly accurately—and any program sophisticated enough to do routing must be able to compute the set and drift of the current (the vector difference between COG-SOG and HDG-BSP)—if they cannot compute the current, they cannot compute the proper true wind. Our instruments have to be right, or the current will be wrong, but we count on accurate instruments and analysis in general if we want to be successful with computer routing. So we can compare the RTOFS currents with what we observe, and keep these records in the logbook. Then we have a feeling for the validity of the RTOFS predictions.

That is important to know because the currents can be 1 or 2 kts or more in wild, mesoscale eddies, even in waters not famous for strong currents. Also in the tropics, approaching Hawaii for example, currents can be strong enough to influence a route. There are a few ocean buoys that report current speed, which would be helpful. It is also important to appreciate that the current forecasts can be wrong. They are not in general as good as the wind forecasts.

So we need to experiment with the influence of the currents on the route in similar ways we do with wind. (Expedition, for example, lets users scale the currents, just as they might scale the winds.) To ignore the currents could be a big mistake, but to overrate them could be big mistake as well. Think of a case in the Gulf Stream where using full currents follows a meander of strong current along a longer route, but 75% current strength cuts across the meander in favored wind angles. Keep in mind too that wind against current makes *steep* waves, which can slow us down more than the height alone might indicate.

Note that even though RTOFS could be off on midocean eddies, it is generally very good in the Gulf Stream, as the model focuses on that current system. For inland waters, good tidal current data are crucial to successful routing.

Figure 10.7-5 shows effects of current routing, which looks good (longer but faster), providing the current predictions are correct, which is not as certain in that location as it can be in the Gulf Stream. We need direct evidence if we are to go out of the way chasing currents.

Basic Check Points

It is not uncommon to run across snags when first running a routing program. They are complex computations that expect input in specific kind and format.

• What chart to use. Routing can generally be done while viewing any chart format in most programs, but due to the complexity of the output you might find it easier to route on the base map of the program. There are high-res base maps available to most programs, and these vector maps are typically what is determining where the land boundaries are located that must be avoided in routing. This is probably true in most cases, even if you load an ENC that has more accurate vector boundaries. In any case, custom made boundaries are often the best choice to avoid land and the shoaling approaching it. A computed route can always be saved as a navigational route of way points.

• Enough data. We need environmental data to cover the full route we are asking for, using the speeds in the polars. If a passage would take 12 days and we only have 10 days of data we cannot run the full route—or may not be able to run it at all. Different programs have different tolerances. Some will let you just extend the last day's data as a fixed wind field for the remaining days. Others will just not run. Hi-res data extend out only 2 or 3 days. The same behavior could apply to wave and current data that do not cover the route.

• Synchronized data. Sometimes wind, current, and wave data do not start at the same time, and could have different update intervals. Some programs take this in stride and interpolate as needed. Others could have a problem with this, so you would have to manipulate the start times to an overlap in valid data times. An option for currents is to use the global OSCAR data for the region of the route. Then this same single 8-day average current file could be used for every day of the route. These tend to be on the low side, so they might be scaled up some.

• Data resolution. For ocean work we can get by with the 0.25° GFS, but for coastal or inland routing we need higher resolution—at least 4 or 5 grids across a region to have hopes for routing. Some of the 3-km data (i.e., HRDPS, NAM, NDFD-CONUS) are only available in Lambert or stereographic projections that few navigation programs can read at the moment. This will likely change.

• Multiple GRIB files. Some programs allow you to load multiple GRIB files (i.e., wind, current, and waves) for the routing, others allow only one. In the latter case, we need to combine the three files externally into one GRIB file for the program. Starpath.com/wx has instructions on combining GRIB files.

• Polars cover forecasted winds. If the forecasts along a route call for, say, 25-kt winds at times, but your polars only

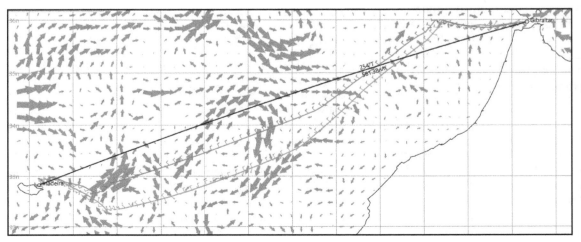

Figure 10.7-5. *Same route as Figure 10.7-4, but a day earlier. Red is the route without currents data; green is the route using RTOFS (gray arrows). The no-current route (red) went right across a contrary eddy against 1.5 kts of current. The green route took advantage of favorable current part way across and avoided the adverse eddy.*

have curves up to 20 kts, then the routing program has to deal with this. Some interpolate more extensively than others. If there is a snag, this might be something to check. Interpolation of the polars is a key part of the computations, which differs amongst the programs.

• Comparing the same route for various polar percentages can reflect on its sensitivity to performance. Likewise, vary the weight of the ocean current, keeping in mind that the actual locations of strong current bands may not be where they are forecasted to be. RTOFS may overestimate current speeds and OSCAR currents will likely underestimate them.

• Comparing different routing programs. Besides starting at the exact same time and place, using identical wind data, a fair comparison between two different programs requires that the polars be *identical*. Because the format of different polar managers differ, this is sometimes difficult to achieve. Key points are having the upwind and downwind optimum VMG values be the same, and to use the same wind speed entries.

• Multi-leg routes. Generally we route from A to B in one leg, even if that crosses islands or headlands. We count on the program to have an adequate vector base map to account for this and avoid the land. Sometimes there are hi-res base maps we can load to fine tune this process. If this is not working as expected, we can force the issue by manually setting prohibited boundaries to keep the boat off the land. A multi-leg route could possibly be handled with such boundaries, but if not, then you might have to make one computation for each leg of the route.

• Motoring or reaching. In a sailboat race the engine is not allowed, but when cruising we can incorporate engine use in routing if the boat speed under sail falls below a declared value. Routing programs that have this option, however, do not know all that you know about this situation. They will effectively create isochrones in all forward directions using your designated motoring speed seeking the fastest net route to the destination. What they don't know is, there could be directions you want to go for other reasons whenever you could. When the wind goes light, you might, for example, prefer to work your way farther south toward the trades that you know you can count on, even though that might not be mathematically fastest route to your destination based on forecasts.

This type of decision can also happen under sail, in a race. You might, for example, decide it is best to set a head sail at night during strong winds in lieu of a spinnaker. This can give you a broader range of headings, and you might again have a preferred direction to go that is contrary to the computed route. Likewise new temporary winds from clouds or squalls might give you the freedom to make miles in a direction you would prefer at the moment, which might not be along the computed route.

In short, there can be beneficial deviations from the "optimum route" that will require new route computations once they are achieved.

Summary

The goal in this short overview of optimum routing is to highlight a few factors that might lead us astray, but once these factors have been addressed, this process is a very powerful tool for ocean navigation, and indeed something that sailors should consider for extended voyages. It is, however, distinctly not a shortcut for the navigator; it is a way to find an optimum route proposal providing the time can be spent to do it judiciously. Solutions using generic polars could provide valuable starting points to study, but all proposals should be viewed in light of the issues raised.

There is a list of selected programs that offer these tools in Tables 2.6-1 and 2.6-3, amongst others. In some commercial products, you just email end points and a start time to a service that keeps a polar on file for you, and they email back a computed route. Predictwind.com, fastsail.com, squid-sailing.com are examples offering that service. The resulting gpx files can be used in any program.

Looking only at stand alone routing programs for computers (there are many for tablets alone), Expedition (expeditionmarine.com) is an advanced solution written by Nick White. It is considered the gold standard by the majority of racing navigators. There are two valuable Kindle ebooks devoted to that program by Will Oxley: *Expedition Navigation Software: A "Gentle" Introduction* (2017) and *Modern Race Navigation: Expedition Software in Action* (2014). America's Cup sailor Peter Isler (islersailing.com) has a series of video courses on Expedition that he offers through the North Sails training program (northu.com).

Stan Honey, who is not just a top practitioner of the art, but made fundamental contributions to the development of the concept, has numerous articles and videos online that discuss ocean racing navigation and routing. See, for example, original.livestream.com/pacificcup.

MaxSea-Nobeltec's TimeZero (mytimezero.com) offers versatile routing options that also have a rich history and racing record behind them. The program evolved from the MaxSea founder Brice Pryszo's first ever stand-alone PC navigation program to do isochrone computations. TimeZero is available in 13 languages and is feature-rich with an easy interface.

On the open source side, Sean D'Epagnier has developed a series of powerful plugins for OpenCPN that provide versatile weather work including optimum routing. These include: Grib_pi, Weatherfax_pi, Polar_pi, and Weather_routing_pi. Together they provide the key elements needed to execute the full process on a Mac or PC. His Climatology_pi (Section 10.6) lets you route across climatic average winds on any date, globally, without live data—or use it to fill in wind, current, and waves if the live data runs out. OpenCPN has a large international following (available in 21 languages, plus many dialects), which contributes to the ongoing development of each component. A sample route computations is shown in Figure 10.7-6.

Many sailors have found it productive to follow major international races online such as the Volvo Ocean Race (volvooceanrace.com) and Vendee Globe (vendeeglobe.org) to make their own real time routing computations for favorite boats using their own routing tools. The environmental data and polars are readily available. Sydney-Hobart, Marion-Bermuda, TransPac, Victoria-Maui, and Pacific Cup are other options to analyze in real time with excellent live tracking.

We can learn the fundamentals of the process as outlined above, but successful optimum routing on the water ultimately depends on accurate integration of wind and navigation instruments with the routing software, specifically the parts that record data for the creation and updates of the polars. These require TWA and TWS. We have assumed this is all in order, but this takes a lot of work to get right. See Appendix 9, on true wind computations. Accurate instrumentation is also needed to monitor progress relative to the polars. If we are not sailing to our polars, we will not make the route. We may have to scale down the polars to better match actual performance.

Figure 10.7-6. Right. *Routing display from OpenCPN, Naples to Tunis, using 3.6 km winds from the DWD ICON model. The alternating colored lines are the isochrones. The yellow "cursor route" can be used to see how various points on an isochrone were achieved. This and other methods of route analysis are included. All programs provide their own unique tools for this study. The winds shown correspond to the time the vessel was at the circled position along the route. Openskiron.org includes very nice 4-km WRF data for this region. The smaller regions used can be loaded simultaneously in OpenPCN.*

Christoph Hendrik Diederik Buys Ballot (1817-1890) was a Dutch chemist and meteorologist after whom Buys Ballot's Law is named, as he was the one of the first scientists to make the association of wind flow roughly parallel to isobars rather than simply from high to low pressure—American William Ferrel (of Ferrel cell fame) was also aware of this at the same time.

Buys Ballot was a contemporary of FitzRoy in the UK and Maury in the US, and reading his original papers you see that he had the same dedication to careful measurements and documentation, with a keen sense of the value of barometric pressure. He founded the Royal Dutch Meteorological Institute in 1854 and he remained its chief director until his death. (This is the same agency that brings us the ASCAT wind analysis today.)

He developed forecasting methods similar to FitzRoy and he was one of the first to see the need for international cooperation. In 1873 became the first chairman of the International Meteorological Committee, a precursor of the World Meteorological Organization (WMO).

Like other great contributors to meteorology in those days he was accomplished in many fields, including chemistry, mineralogy and geology, as well as being a professor of physics and mathematics.

Appendix 1. Abbreviations

> or <	greater than or less than	ITCZ	Intertropical Convergence Zone	SH	southern Hemisphere
~	approximately	k	kilo	SLP	sea-level pressure
ASCAT	Advanced Scatterometer	kB	kilobyte	SOG	speed over ground
ATL	Atlantic Ocean	KML	keyhole markup language	SSB	single sideband
BA	British Admiralty	KMZ	a zipped KML file	SST	sea-surface temperature
BOM	Bureau of Meteorology	kt	knot	STNY	stationary
CMCE	Canadian Meteorological Center	M	mega	SWH	significant wave height
COG	course over ground	m	meter	TD	Tropical Depression
COGOW	Climatology of Global Ocean Winds	METAR	"airport weather report"	TROF	trough
CONUS	Continental US	MB	megabyte	TRPCL	tropical
CPA	closest point of approach	mb	millibar	TSTM	thunderstorm
DLR	dry lapse rate	MLR	moist lapse rate	UK	United Kingdom
DSIPT	dissipate	MSLP	mean value of SLP, or same as SLP	UKMET	UK Met Office
DVLPG	developing	NAVGEM	Navy Global Environmental Model	URL	uniform resource locator
DWD	Deutscher Wetterdienst	NBM	National Blend of Models	USCG	United States Coast Guard
ECMWF	European Community Medium Range Weather Forecast	NCDC	National Climatic Data Center	USNO	United States Naval Observatory
ECS	electronic charting system	NCEI	National Centers for Environmental Information	UT	Universal Time
ELR	environmental lapse rate			UTC	Coordinated Universal Time
EU	European Union	NDBC	National Data Buoy Center	VHF	very high frequency (30 to 300 MHz)
F2, F5...	Beaufort force 2, 5, etc	NDFD	National Digital Forecast Database	VMG	velocity made good (to wind or course)
FTP	file transfer protocol	NGA	National Geospatial-Intelligence Agency	VOS	Voluntary Observing Ship
GDAS	Global Data Assimilation System	NH	Northern Hemisphere	VSBY	visibility
GDPS	Global Deterministic Prediction System	NHC	National Hurricane Center	WMO	World Meteorological Organization
GE	Google Earth	NIMA	National Imagery and Mapping Agency	WRF	Weather Research and Forecasting
GEFS	Global Ensemble Forecast System	NIST	Nat. Inst of Standards & Technnology	z	zulu, as in 12z = 1200 UTC
GFS	Global Forecast Model	nmi	nautical mile	**Cloud Abbreviations**	
GIS	Geographic Information System	NMEA	National Marine Electronics Association	CL	Low clouds
GMT	Greenwich Mean Time	NM, nmi	nautical mile	Sc	Stratocumulus
GPS	global positioning system	NOAA	National Oceanic and Atmospheric Administration	St	Stratus
GRIB	gridded binary (data format)	NCOM	Navy Coastal Ocean Model	Cu	Cumulus
GTS	Global Telecommunication System Network	NWP	numerical weather prediction	Cb	Cumulonimbus
HF	high frequency (3 to 30 MHz)	NWS	National Weather Service	CM	Middle clouds
HH	synoptic times, 00z, 06z, 12z, 18z	OPC	Ocean Prediction Center	Ac	Altocumulus
HRDPS	High Resolution Deterministic Prediction System	PMO	Port Meteorological Officer	As	Altostratus
HRRR	High Resolution Rapid Refresh	POS	position	Ns	Nimbostratus
hr	hour	PTDY	pressure tendency	CH	High Clouds
h0, h1...	forecasts in a GRIB dataset	OSCAT	OceanSat scatterometer	Ci	Cirrus
HTM(L)	hypertext mark up (language)	OSWT	Ocean Surface Winds Team	Cc	Cirrocumulus
HURN F	hurricane force winds	RMSE	root mean square error	Cs	Cirrostratus
hPa	hecto Pascal (same as mb)	RSMC	Regional Specialized Meteorological Center		
HYCOM	Hybrid Coordinate Ocean Model	RSS	really simple syndication		
ICON	Icosahedral Nonhydrostatic model	RTOFS	Real Time Ocean Forecast System		
IHO	International Hydrographic Organization	sat	satellite		
		SD	standard deviation		

For a list of GRIB parameter abbreviations used in model forecasts see:

nco.ncep.noaa.gov/pmb/docs/on388/ table2.html

Appendix 2. Standard Atmosphere—Pressure and Temperature vs. Altitude

Feet	Meters	Pa/Po	Pa	Po-Pa	Ta F°	Ta C°	Feet	Meters	Pa/Po	Pa	Po-Pa	Ta F°	Ta C°
0	0	1.0000	1013.3	0.0	59.0	15.0	1200	366	0.9574	970.1	43.2	54.7	12.6
5	2	0.9998	1013.1	0.2	59.0	15.0	1250	381	0.9556	968.3	44.9	54.6	12.5
10	3	0.9996	1012.9	0.4	59.0	15.0	1300	396	0.9539	966.5	46.7	54.4	12.4
20	6	0.9993	1012.5	0.7	58.9	15.0	1350	411	0.9522	964.8	48.5	54.2	12.3
30	9	0.9989	1012.2	1.1	58.9	14.9	1400	427	0.9504	963.0	50.2	54.0	12.2
40	12	0.9986	1011.8	1.5	58.9	14.9	1450	442	0.9487	961.3	52.0	53.8	12.1
50	15	0.9982	1011.4	1.8	58.8	14.9	1500	457	0.9470	959.5	53.7	53.7	12.0
75	23	0.9973	1010.5	2.7	58.7	14.9	1600	488	0.9435	956.0	57.2	53.3	11.8
100	30	0.9964	1009.6	3.7	58.6	14.8	1700	518	0.9401	952.5	60.7	52.9	11.6
150	46	0.9946	1007.8	5.5	58.5	14.7	1800	549	0.9366	949.1	64.2	52.6	11.4
200	61	0.9928	1005.9	7.3	58.3	14.6	1900	579	0.9332	945.6	67.7	52.2	11.2
250	76	0.9910	1004.1	9.1	58.1	14.5	2000	610	0.9298	942.1	71.1	51.9	11.0
300	91	0.9892	1002.3	10.9	57.9	14.4	3000	914	0.8962	908.1	105.1	48.3	9.1
350	107	0.9874	1000.5	12.8	57.8	14.3	4000	1219	0.8637	875.1	138.1	44.8	7.1
400	122	0.9856	998.7	14.6	57.6	14.2	5000	1524	0.8320	843.1	170.2	41.2	5.1
450	137	0.9838	996.9	16.4	57.4	14.1	6000	1829	0.8014	812.0	201.3	37.6	3.1
500	152	0.9821	995.1	18.2	57.2	14.0	7000	2134	0.7716	781.9	231.4	34.1	1.1
550	168	0.9803	993.3	20.0	57.0	13.9	8000	2438	0.7428	752.6	260.6	30.5	-0.8
600	183	0.9785	991.5	21.8	56.9	13.8	9000	2743	0.7148	724.3	289.0	27.0	-2.8
650	198	0.9767	989.7	23.6	56.7	13.7	10000	3048	0.6877	696.8	316.4	23.4	-4.8
700	213	0.9750	987.9	25.4	56.5	13.6	11000	3353	0.6614	670.2	343.1	19.8	-6.8
750	229	0.9732	986.1	27.2	56.3	13.5	12000	3658	0.6360	644.4	368.8	16.3	-8.8
800	244	0.9714	984.3	29.0	56.2	13.4	13000	3962	0.6113	619.4	393.8	12.7	-10.7
850	259	0.9697	982.5	30.7	56.0	13.3	14000	4267	0.5875	595.2	418.0	9.2	-12.7
900	274	0.9679	980.7	32.5	55.8	13.2	15000	4572	0.5643	571.8	441.4	5.6	-14.7
950	290	0.9661	978.9	34.3	55.6	13.1	16000	4877	0.5420	549.2	464.1	2.0	-16.7
1000	305	0.9644	977.2	36.1	55.4	13.0	17000	5182	0.5203	527.2	486.0	-1.5	-18.7
1050	320	0.9626	975.4	37.9	55.3	12.9	18000	5486	0.4994	506.0	507.3	-5.1	-20.6
1100	335	0.9609	973.6	39.6	55.1	12.8	19000	5791	0.4791	485.5	527.8	-8.6	-22.6
1150	351	0.9591	971.8	41.4	54.9	12.7	20000	6096	0.4595	465.6	547.6	-12.2	-24.6

Table Notes: *The standard atmosphere has a surface temperature of 59 °F (15 °C) and a lapse rate of minus 3.56 °F/1000 ft (1.98 °C/1000 ft). The standard surface pressure is 1013.25 mb and the pressure drops at a rate that can be computed from Pa = Po [1 - (6.87535*H/1,000,000)]^5.2561, where Pa is the pressure at altitude H (given in feet), and Po is the base or surface pressure, 1013.25 mb. The notation x^y means × raised to the power of y.*

If you live at an elevation of 1100 ft, your pressure will read 39.6 mb lower than reported at sea level if your barometer is properly calibrated. If the barometer in your boat is 10 ft above sea level, your barometer reads 0.4 mb lower than it should if not corrected to sea level. To record barometer offsets for calibration at some elevation (say 1,100 ft), record with the time and date of observation your barometer reading (say 953.6 mb), along with the proper sea level pressure at your location for that time obtained by interpolating Internet data (say it is 990.0 mb). Then compute the expected pressure at your elevation if the barometer were exact (Pa/Po × your reading), which in this example would be 0.9609 × 990.0 = 951.3 mb, so we see that our barometer reads too high by 953.6 - 951.3 = 2.3 mb at an instrument pressure of 953.6 mb.

Appendix 3. Sea Sate Definitions

		\<No Swell\>	\<low\>		\<moderate\>			\<heavy\>			\<Confused Swell\>

Table A3-1. Douglas Combined Sea and Swell Scale

Seas		No Swell	low		moderate			heavy			Confused Swell
			Short or Average	Long	Short	Average	Long	Short	Average	Long	
		0	1	2	3	4	5	6	7	8	9
0	calm	00	01	02	03	04	05	06	07	08	09
1	smooth	10	11	12	13	14	15	16	17	18	19
2	slight	20	21	22	23	24	25	26	27	28	29
3	moderate	30	31	32	33	34	35	36	37	38	39
4	rough	40	41	42	43	44	45	46	47	48	49
5	very rough	50	51	52	53	54	55	56	57	58	59
6	high	60	61	62	63	64	65	66	67	68	69
7	very high	70	71	72	73	74	75	76	77	78	79
8	precipitous	80	81	82	83	84	85	86	87	88	89
9	confused	90	91	92	93	94	95	96	97	98	99

Table A3-3. WMO Swell Descriptions

Lengths	Heights
Short < 100 m	Low < 2 m
Average 100 - 200 m	Moderate 2-4 m
Long > 200 m	Heavy > 4 m

Table A3-2. WMO Sea State Code

Code	Significant Wave Height				Description
	Range (m)	Range (ft)	Mean (m)	Mean (ft)	
0	0	0	0	0	Calm (glassy)
1	0 - 0.1	0 - 0.3	0.05	0.2	Calm (rippled)
2	0.1 - 0.5	0.3 - 1.6	0.3	1.0	Smooth (mini-waves)
3	0.5 - 1.25	1.6 - 4.1	0.875	2.9	Slight
4	1.25 - 2.5	4.1 - 8.2	1.875	6.2	Moderate
5	2.5 - 4.0	8.2 - 13.1	3.25	10.7	Rough
6	4.0 - 6.0	13.1 - 19.7	5.0	16.4	Very Rough
7	6.0 - 9.0	19.7 - 29.5	7.5	24.6	High
8	9.0 - 14.0	29.5 - 45.9	11.5	37.7	Very High
9	> 14.0	> 45.9	> 14.0	> 45.9	Phenomenal

Table Notes:

The Douglas Sea State Scale was created by H.P. Douglas in 1917, while he was the head of the British Meteorological Navy Service. It offers a unique way to describe the combined seas of wind waves (seas) and swells.

The Douglas and WMO scales do not agree on code numbers, i.e., moderate is 3 in the former and 4 in the latter. Furthermore, the Douglas scale does not include quantitative measures, i.e., code 35 is "moderate" seas with "long," "moderate" swells, which remain undefined.

We can use WMO definitions (A3-2 and A3-3) to clarify this, as has been needed in court cases when commercial weather providers made contracts using Douglas scale terms that were not clearly defined, and the charter party could not make desired vessel speeds due to sea state. See Lloyd's Maritime Law Newsletter, 826, 2017.

Appendix 4. Historical Note on the Use of Calibrated Barometers in the Tropics

The following is from *The Mercantile Marine Magazine, Vol 1*, January, 1854, page 8. It relates to Section 9.3.

"The slightest deviation from the barometric mean between the tropics demands on the part of the commander immediate attention. And how is this barometric mean to be obtained? Simply by all vessels that will co-operate, reading their barometers every two hours, on the voyage out and home."

"...Let no commander be deterred from making the observations because he has not a 'compared' barometer on board [*this means calibrated*]; if he have one, so much the better, but if he have not, any observations he can furnish us with, are better than none. Besides, if he discuss his own observations or any portion of them, he will soon determine the value of his instrument, and if it don't please him, he will get a better."

Three months later in the April issue, they bring up this point again in an article that compares the new aneroid barometers with the traditional mercury barometers. They speculate that the aneroids may not be linear over their full range—a fact we have pointed out elsewhere in this book—and call for a careful study before pressure observations will be useful.

This is exactly what happened. Traditional mercury barometers were tedious to use at sea, but they were accurate once known corrections were applied. But *common* aneroids were not, and before the internet came about, it was very difficult for mariners to calibrate an aneroid device. So this type of observation fell out of modern teaching (as the aneroids replaced mercury devices)—nevertheless, the proposal is mentioned in *Bowditch* throughout the years. Now with good electronic barometers and accurate aneroids, and good pressure statistics from NCEI, it is back in our toolkit for weather watching. We have also located accurate and easy to use worldwide mean monthly pressures and their associated standard deviations from early U.S. Navy data. The data are presented in the *Mariner's Pressure Atlas.*

Appendix 5. Barometer Calibration

Setting a barometer to read the proper pressure once only assures that it is right at that pressure. This is not a calibration. A calibration means we know the instrument is right at all pressures it might read, or we have a table or graph that tells us how much to correct the reading at each indicated pressure. Over a period of time, you can make a very good calibration of your barometer as outlined here.

Table A5-1 shows sample data collected over a 7-month period, which was used to calibrate four barometers, although data are shown for only one of them—a good marine barometer we have had since the 80s. This is about a third of all points taken over that time period; we missed a couple good opportunities at high pressure.

Columns A, B, and C are the times the barometer read the pressures listed in D, always read at the same elevation, at my desk, in the office. Column F is the actual SLP at that time, and E is the difference between those two shown on the left in Figure A5-1.

The reference station was WPOW1 (NDBC), 1.5 nmi to the SW. Column G is the reference pressure reported at date I, time J. Column H is the reported pressure tendency (PTDY), which is the mb change over the past 3 hrs. Thus the values in F that match our time of reading are figured as: F = G + [(C/60) x (H/3)]. For example, at 1748, June 8, our barometer read 1005.2. Checking WPOW1, the latest report was at 1700 with a PTDY of +2.9, so the correct SLP we should compare to is: 1005.2 +[(48/60) x (2.9/3)] = 1005.2 + 0.8 = 1012.0.

You have now learned the relative errors in the device. Moving it to the boat and setting it to the right pressure once, shifts the correction scale to be 0.0 at that pressure. In an earlier calibration of this same barometer, we had set it to be correct at 983 mb. We see some scatter in A5-1, but the average curve is pretty good. In some barometers, this test will reveal errors ten times those seen on this one. See starpath.com/wx for more resources.

Figure A5-2. *Calibration of the same barometer 10 years earlier, using our NIST-traceable pressure standards and pump-out tank. We see trends here that were only indicated in the short homemade calibration, but the general results are the same.*

A	B	C	D	E	F	G	H	I	J
Date	Hr	Min	Baro	Diff	SLP	WPOW1	PTDY	Date	Time
7-Jun	13	58	999.5	6.3	1005.8	1006.6	-2.4	7-Jun	1300
8-Jun	08	51	998.3	5.6	1003.9	1003.8	0.3	8-Jun	0800
8-Jun	16	33	1004.0	6.7	1010.7	1010.2	2.9	8-Jun	1600
8-Jun	17	48	1005.2	6.8	1012.0	1011.2	2.9	8-Jun	1700
8-Jun	20	28	1006.8	6.6	1013.4	1013.1	1.9	8-Jun	2000
9-Jun	08	20	1005.8	6.5	1012.3	1012.4	-0.7	9-Jun	0800
12-Jun	08	39	1009.5	6.8	1016.3	1016.2	0.6	12-Jun	0800
24-Jun	09	05	1014.0	6.9	1020.9	1020.9	0	24-Jun	0900
23-Oct	10	20	1030.5	6.9	1037.4	1037.3	1.2	Oct 23	1000
13-Nov	13	35	997.5	6.5	1004.0	1004.4	-1.9	13-Nov	1300
15-Nov	16	50	995.9	6.1	1002.0	1002.4	-1.5	15-Nov	1600
20-Dec	17	40	1022.0	7.0	1029.0	1028.4	2.6	20-Dec	1700
21-Dec	10	20	1024.0	6.9	1030.9	1030.9	-0.3	21-Dec	1000
24-Jan	17	10	995.0	6.3	1001.3	1001.4	-1.2	24-Jan	1700

Table A5-1. Sample Barometer Calibration Data

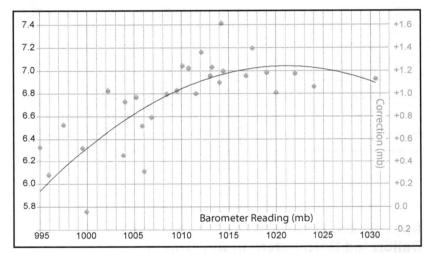

Figure A5-1. *Homemade calibration using local pressure reports (Table A5-1). Left scale is uncorrected for elevation. Right scale corrects for elevation and assumes the barometer is correct at 983 mb to match earlier calibration, Figure A5-2.*

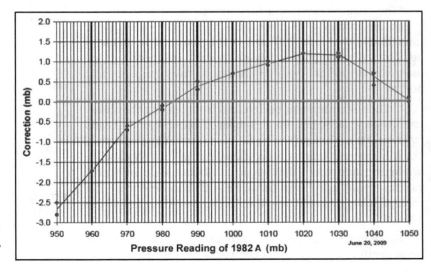

Appendix 6. Global Air Masses, Polar Fronts, and Centers of Action

Snapshots of the sources of the world's winds can be seen from a summer and winter plot of the typical cold and warm air masses, the semi-permanent fronts between them, and the resulting pressure centers that guide the flow of the winds around the earth.

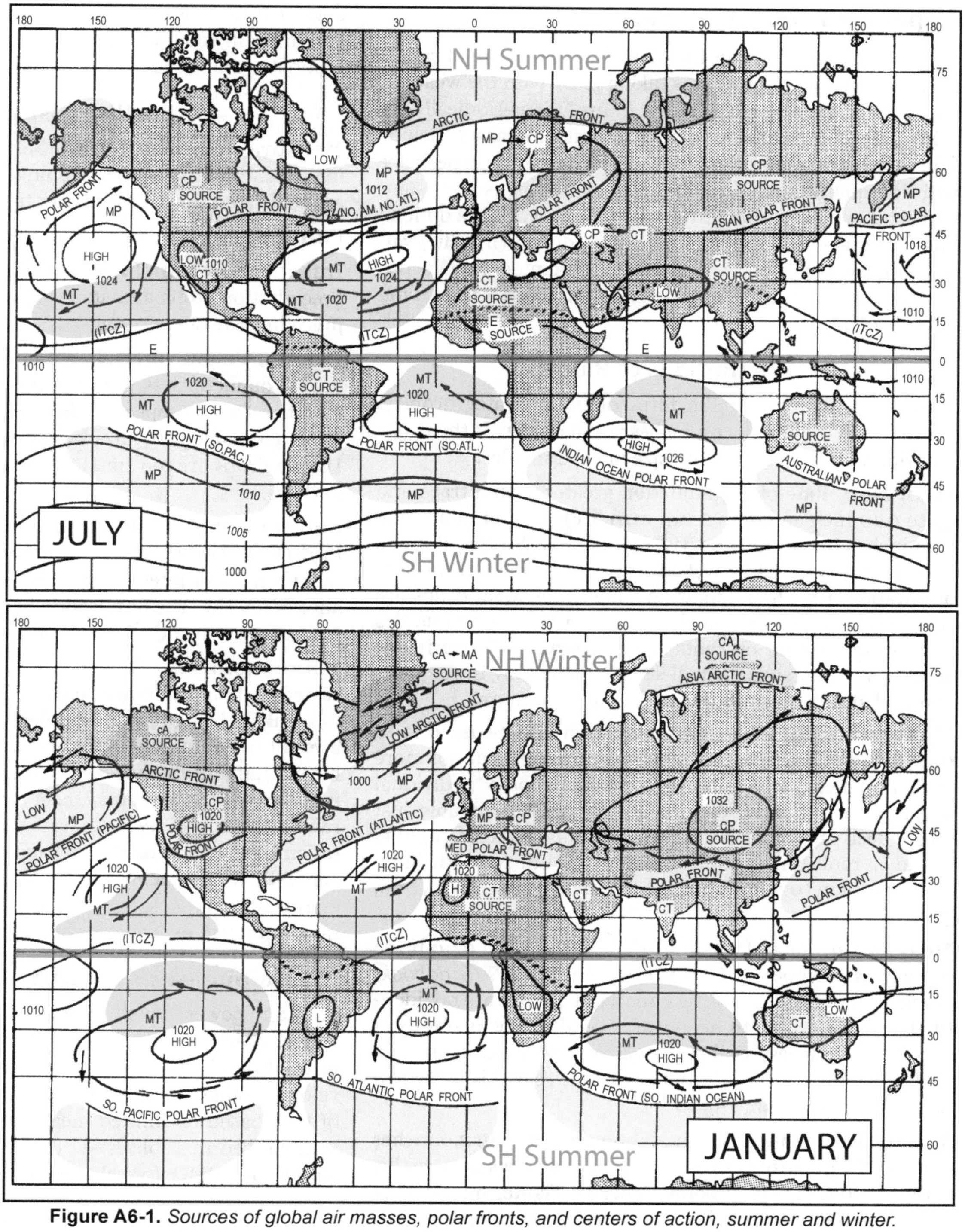

In NH summer we see the Pacific and Atlantic Highs, well defined with closed isobars, have pushed the polar fronts north, up against the Aleutian and Icelandic Lows. We also see the Asiatic Low over India that pulls in the SW monsoon. The doldrums (ITCZ) are running from about 5N to 15N around the globe.

In the SH winter (still top picture) we see the weak mid-ocean Highs have let the polar fronts across each ocean come up to the relatively low latitudes of some 30 to 45S, which are the source of many spin-off fronts and Lows passing across the Roaring Forties to the Screaming Sixties, which we see as a band of isobars spanning the globe. The polar fronts follow roughly along the extensions of the warm flow of the Brazil, Mozambique, and East Australia Currents.

In the NH winter, bottom picture, the Highs weaken and the polar fronts move farther south, following roughly along the warm Gulf Stream and Kuroshio Currents. The Aleutian and Icelandic Lows become more prominent centers. The Siberian High develops over Russia, which drives the NE monsoon clear across the Indian Ocean. Notice that the doldrums are a bit farther south.

In the SH summer, the polar fronts are pushed south to some 60S and the Highs in each ocean are better defined, though rarely as well defined as their NH counterparts.

These maps are from the excellent Navy training manual called *Aerographer's Mate, Module 5—Basic Meteorology*, (Naval Education and Training Professional Development and Technology Center, 2001).

Figure A6-1. *Sources of global air masses, polar fronts, and centers of action, summer and winter.*

Appendix 7. Notes on Rain

We have seen throughout the book that the nature of rain is a valuable indicator of what is taking place with the weather, and what might take place in the future. We periodically get rain information from ship reports, and forecasts include rain information. Many of us, however, have little experience with the quantitative description of rain. This is consistent with what we learn from PMOs; they confirm this is a difficult observation—even they do not attempt digital (mm/hr) values, but use only generic descriptors (light, moderate, heavy; continuous or intermittent), defined in the *NWS Observing Handbook*.

Definitions of Rain

Rain. Precipitation in the form of liquid water droplets greater than 0.5 mm (0.02 inches) in diameter. If the drops are widely scattered, the drop size may be smaller.

Light rain. Rate of accumulation greater than a trace and up to 0.10 inch an hour (**≤ 2.5 mm/hr**), but not more than 0.01 inches in 6 minutes. *NWS Handbook*: "Scattered drops that do not completely wet an exposed surface, regardless of duration, [up] to a condition where individual drops are easily seen; slight spray is observed over the decks; puddles form slowly; sound on roofs ranges from slow pattering to gentle swishing; steady small streams may flow in scuppers and deck drains. Visibility 1 km (0.5 nmi) or more."

Moderate rain. Rate of accumulation is between 0.11 to 0.30 inch per hour (**2.5 mm to 7.6 mm/hr**), but not more than 0.03 inches in 6 minutes. *NWS Handbook*: "Individual drops are not clearly identifiable; spray is observable just above deck and other hard surfaces; puddles form rapidly; sound on roofs ranges from swishing to gentle roar. Visibility less than 1 km (0.5 nmi) but not less than 0.5 km (0.25 nmi, 550 yds)."

Heavy rain. Rate of accumulation greater than 0.30 up to 2.0 inches per hour (**7.6 to 50 mm/hr**). *NWS Handbook*: "Rain seemingly falls in sheets; individual drops are not identifiable; heavy spray to height of several inches is observed over hard surfaces; visibility is greatly reduced; sound on roofs resembles roll of drums or distant roar. Visibility less than 0.5 km (0.25 nmi, 550 yds)."

Violent rain. Rate of accumulation greater than 2.0 inches per hour (**> 50 mm/hr**). *NWS Handbook* does not use this classification; they go up only to heavy. The term is used by the UK MetOffice, which has slightly different categories (<2, 2-10, 10-50, >50 mm/hr), which they call "showers" rates, with a lower set of rates for "rain."

I believe there is a value to the term Violent rain, even though any level of Heavy rain is *really heavy*. Mariners who might sail in squalls, especially those on the fringes of a tropical storm will definitely see Violent rain. I have seen this a couple times, once very dramatically. It was in a tropical system near Hawaii, and in one squall we were standing in the cockpit of a 40-ft boat and, without exaggeration, we could not see the bow! It was like standing under a faucet. We were dumb struck as we stood there laughing at such an amazing demonstration of nature—plus, we were in 30+ kts of wind, and this rain had totally beaten down the waves till they were a smooth rolling sea of swells alone .

Further Distinctions

Measurable precipitation. Means a total of at least 0.01 inch (i.e., the first tip of a tipping bucket rain gauge, which are calibrated in 0.01 inches per tip).

Continuous rain. Intensity changes gradually, if at all.

Intermittent rain. Intensity changes gradually, if at all, but precipitation stops and starts at least once within the hour preceding the observation.

Drizzle. Uniform precipitation composed exclusively of fine drops (diameter less than 0.5 mm or 0.02 inch) very close together. Drizzle appears to float while following air currents, although unlike fog droplets, drizzle falls to the ground. Drizzle drops are too small to appreciably disturb still water puddles.

Showers. Precipitation from a convective cloud (cumuliform) that is characterized by its sudden beginning and ending, changes in intensity, and rapid changes in the appearance of the sky. The implication here is that *rain,* in contrast, comes from stratiform clouds (nimbostratus).

Thunderstorms. Though thunderstorms are often forecasted without reference to rain, it is implied that they will most likely bring heavy or violent rain. Thunderstorms are a result of cumulonimbus clouds, which by their vary name means rain. There are, of course, smaller squalls with only moderate rain, or you may meet a squall stage with just light rain left over, and there is a category of squalls (low-precipitation supercells) that do not have much liquid rain at all, but generally we can safely assume that a forecast with thunderstorms means that somewhere in the region it will have heavy rain, but it will be just underneath these cumulus clouds.

Rain Intensity Gauged by Windshield Wipers

Many power-driven vessels have windshield wipers, and when in use they offer a semi-quantitative way to judge rain intensity underway. It is also a way for all mariners to develop a feeling for rain intensity when on land. Our summary of this, based on limited measurements and discussions, is summarized in Table A7-1. Thanks to Matthew Thompson, Seattle area PMO, for valuable discussions on this topic.

Coverage vs. Probability

Although we tend to gloss over the wording in forecasts about rain and thunderstorms, it can pay to read this part carefully. These are very specific forecasts, even though they can sound very similar. First, there is a big difference between rain and showers, as noted above. Then we need to notice if they refer to a probability of occurrence anywhere over an understood area, or the percentage of an area covered by the forecasted precipitation type. These are two different forecasts, often distinguished only by the descriptor used, or by the lack of a descriptor. See definitions in Table A7-2.

Table A7-1. Rain Intensity and Windshield Wipers		
Intensity	*Wipers*	*Observation*
Light	On Intermittent	Keeps up easily, but at high end of Light, windshield just covered at sweep time
Moderate	On full time, Slow to Fast	Keeps up at slow for low Moderate, but at high end of Moderate windshield covered completely at sweep time on Fast
Heavy	On full time, Fast	Keeps up on Fast for low end of Heavy, but cannot keep up for long as rain increases.

Table A7-2. Showers and Thunderstorms		
Coverage	*Percentage*	*Probability*
isolated (few)	10 to 20%	slight chance
scattered	30 to 50%	chance
numerous	60 to 70%	likely
categorical	> 80%	categorical

Showers are effectively squalls, but less severe than those called thunderstorms. Both are characterized as moderate or strong, based on satellite cloud images, from which they can interpret the height and density of the systems. Thus we have forecasts such as: "Scattered moderate to isolated strong tstm within 120 nmi of front, E of 78W," which describes the percentage of the area covered, and the intensities. Compared to: "Showers likely and slight chance of thunderstorms," referring to the probability of the events over the forecast area. A forecast of "showers and thunderstorms" without a descriptor is *categorical*, which is >80% by either definition.

Rain on Radar

Rain rates are presented on a decibel scale in NOAA weather radar images. These images are readily available in cellphones, so they offer a good way to get a feeling for rain rate classifications: mobile.weather.gov, enter zip, press Go, choose Radar. An example is shown in Figure A7-1, with decibels to precipitation rates shown in Table A7-3. Archived radar images are at gis.ncdc.noaa.gov/maps/ncei/radar

Rain in Model Forecasts

GFS has two common rain parameters, precipitation rate (PRATE) and accumulated precipitation (APCP). Both are available from Saildocs using those names—the generic request for "rain" gets PRATE. There is some subtlety to the use of either of them, however. The GFS data for both parameters use "mixed accumulation intervals" of 0 to 3 hrs, followed by 0 to 6 hr intervals. If you ask for GFS rain (PRATE) plus,

say, wind, you get no rain data in h0. Ask for just rain, and h3 is the first forecast delivered, meaning 3 hrs past the most recent model run. PRATE at h3 is the average rate of rainfall between h0 and h3 in units of mm/hr. At h6 we see the average rate of rainfall from h0 to h6, again in mm/hr.

This appears seamless in most viewers; we see units of mm/hr for each forecast as we step through them. But the presentation is a bit misleading, in that the rate we see at h6 could be describing rain that all fell between h3 and h4, in which case the h3 rate would be zero.

The same applies to the presentation of accumulated rainfall (APCP), which should be in units of just mm, with the understanding that this is the total that fell over the past 3 hrs, alternating with the total that fell over the past 6 hrs. This display would then pulse the accumulated rain as we step through the forecasts. To avoid that, most viewers scale the accumulations to the time intervals. Thus, with this parameter as well, we need to keep in mind this averaging out of the actual accumulations when we compare forecasts to what we observe (using observation methods described earlier to judge intensities). Several viewers will not display ACPC and count on PRATE as the rain parameter. A few viewers use mm/hr for APCP units, but that is technically incorrect.

From this point, things get briefly easier, then harder. Hourly rain forecasts in HRRR use a fixed 1-hr interval—the easy one! NAM forecasts, like GFS, use mixed accumulation intervals. Hourly rain forecasts in 3-km NAM use a 1 hr, 2 hr, 3 hr sequence of accumulation intervals, and 12-km NAM has a complex interval sequence that repeats every 12 hr. In short, rain data are complicated.

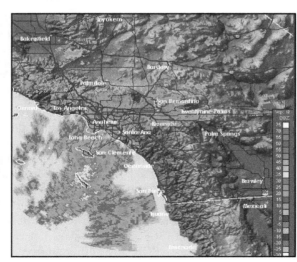

Figure A7-1. *NOAA weather radar image as can be seen at mobile.weather.gov. Rates are in decibels. Table A7-3 relates the colorbar to precipitation rates. The NAM and HRRR models offer a simulated radar parameter (REFC) in these same units. Not all reflected signals are from rain that reaches the ground at the places indicated, or at all, so the values reported by radar will likely be higher than observed.*

Table A7-3. dBZ vs. Rain Rate			
dBZ	*(mm/h)*	*(in/h)*	*Intensity*
65	421	16.6	Violent / large hail
60	205	8	Violent / moderate hail
55	100	4	Violent / small hail
50	48.6	1.9	Heavy
45	23.7	0.92	Moderate to heavy
40	11.53	0.45	Moderate rain
35	5.6	0.22	Moderate rain
30	2.7	0.1	Light to moderate
25	1.3	0.05	Light
20	0.6	0.02	Very light
15	0.3	0.01	Mist
10	0.15	< 0.01	Light mist
5	0.07	< 0.01	Hardly noticeable

Appendix 8. National Blend of Models (NBM)

This is a new source of data for mariners, with the potential of being the source of choice when available from popular providers. See descriptive links at weather.gov/mdl/nbm_home. We will post news and procedures at starpath.com/wx. NBM resolution and frequency structure is similar to NDFD, but it has expanded domains, especially in the oceanic sector (Figure A8-1). The present version is 3.0, with 3.1 expected in August, 2018. The output is a blend of NCEP models (global, regional, and ensemble) with Canadian, ECMWF, and FNMOC models and ensembles.

The NBM CONUS data include 10-m wind and direction, but no MSLP; the oceanic sector includes probabilistic winds and pressures: 10th, 50th, and 90th percentiles, based on 63 ensemble runs. Ver. 3.1 will also include simulated radar in hourly steps out to 36 hrs. Optimum routing with the various wind probabilities should be instructive. NBM GRIB files are available at tgftp.nws.noaa.gov/SL.us008001/ST.expr/DF.gr2/DC.ndgd/GT.blend and at NOMADS. (Graphic wind probabilities are at ocean.weather.gov/windprob.shtml.)

NBM predicts conditions at buoys across U.S. waters out several days at weather.gov/mdl/nbm_text. Use the "NBH" set (hourly, out to 25 hrs) to compare overnight forecasts as discussed in Section 6.3.

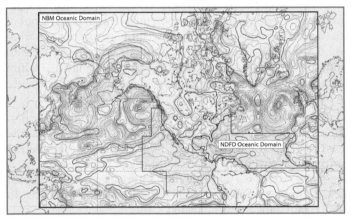

Figure A8-1. *NBM v3.0 oceanic sector winds, probabilistic percentiles displayed as contours at 5-kt intervals; bold is 10 kts: black is the 50th percentile (mean value); red is the 90th percentile (highest 10%); green is 10th percentile (lowest 10%). See starpath.com/wx for ways to interpret this and other displays.*

Appendix 9. Nuances of True Wind

Routing computations can go wrong if the true wind is not determined as accurately as possible. This requires calibrated instruments and proper procedures. Here we look at two small factors that affect true wind determination: heel angle and anemometer height.

Heel Angle and Leeway

Heel angle affects the measured value of the apparent wind angle (AWA) and apparent wind speed (AWS). Heel in turn causes leeway, which affects the vector solution for the true wind (TWA, TWS) needed to compare with, and contribute to, polar data. Wind instruments measure, for example, AWA ($34.3°$) and AWS (14.5 kt), and digital inclinometers measure heel angle ($-23°$). With the boat heeled, the AWA measured (AWA^m) must be corrected to reflect the angle relative to the horizontal (AWA^c):

$$AWA^c = atan[\,tan(AWA^m)/cos(heel)\,]$$
$$= atan[\,tan(34.3)/cos(23)\,] = 36.5$$

Likewise, the AWS is affected and must be corrected:

$$AWS^c = AWS^m \times cos(AWA^m)/cos(AWA^c)$$
$$= 14.5 \times cos(34.3)/cos(36.5) = 14.5 \times 1.03 = 14.9$$

These are both small changes, but they all add up, and these are the values that must be used in the final wind computations. (For quick estimates, heel narrows the correct apparent wind angle by just under a factor of cos(heel), which at $20°$ heel is 0.94 or 6%.)

There are sophisticated instruments for continuous real-time digital leeway (LWY) measurements, but for this wind analysis most vessels compute a theoretical leeway based on heel angle. A common formula for that is:

$$LWY = K \times heel / BSP^2,$$

where K varies between 10 and 13 or so; it has to be measured for your boat at several knotmeter speeds (BSP). Measuring individual values of LWY to determine K at specific speeds takes care but can be done with normal instruments. Whenever SOG = BSP, but COG ≠ HDG, then that difference is a measure of LWY at that BSP and heel angle. There are other procedures that let you do this in current with prescribed maneuvers to remove the effects of current, although early into a new wind without current is a better time to study this.

Using K = 12.4 at a BSP of 5.70, we get a LWY = 12.4 × $(-23)/5.7^2$ = $-8.8°$, which is shown in Figure A9-1 for HDG = 040.0 T; BSP = 5.70; SOG = 5.70; COG = 031.2 T, showing true wind values before and after correcting apparent wind for a heel = $-23°$. The corrections are small, but significant in optimum route computations. Polar diagrams from yacht designers and VPP programs include leeway in TWA values, and the route computations takes TWA from the polars.

[For more on these corrections see: David Pedrick and Richard McCurdy, *Yacht Performance Analysis with Computers*, Chesapeake Sailing Yacht Symposium, January 1981.]

Ground Wind vs. Water Wind

Polar diagrams refer to a true wind flowing over the boat as it sits dead in the water, with apparent wind equal to true wind. Polars do not know, nor do they care, if the water itself is moving, which would in fact contribute to that "true wind." Thus true wind to a polar diagram is water referenced, sometimes called "water wind." Meteorologists, on the other hand, care about true wind relative to the fixed earth, which a sailor would then have to call "ground wind." Ground wind is easy to compute. It is the vector difference between (AWS, AWD) and (SOG, COG). It does not care what might have caused (SOG, COG) to be different from (BSP, HDG). It also does not

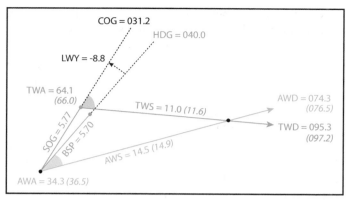

Figure A9-1. *Vector solution for TWS and TWA with known leeway, but without correcting the apparent wind for the effects of heel. Numbers in italics are the corrected values. Wind angles change about 2° and wind speeds about 5%. This example assumes no current. The slightly larger SOG reflects the fact that knotmeters read very slightly low when slipping to leeward. With no current, SOG is just speed through the water (STW), which is approximated as STW = BSP(knotmeter)/Cos(leeway). In this example true wind is the same as ground wind.*

use AWA, but assumes we have computed AWD (apparent wind direction) properly, usually HDG + AWA^c.

Figure A9-2 shows the vector solutions for these two types of true wind. It is up to the combination of the wind instrumentation and navigation software to sort out these parameters from the measured data. Some wind instruments include inclinometers and make the heel corrections to apparent wind before sending out the data. We can approximate these differences for general weather tactics in weaker currents, but when it comes to optimum routing these differences can have a notable influence.

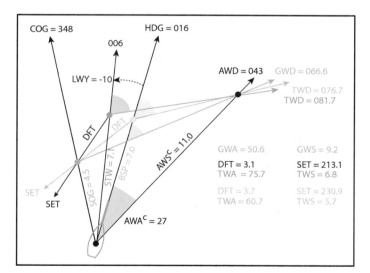

Figure A9-2. *Vector solution for "water wind" (TWS, TWA), with and without leeway corrections, and for "ground wind" (GWS and GWD). With measured heel input, navigation programs will solve for set, drift, and leeway based on the other inputs and use them to solve for the wind data. Recall that leeway is actual motion through the water. This picture assumes AWA and AWS have been corrected for heel, which is often done within the wind instruments. If we ignore leeway (light gray values), it implies a different current and notably different true wind results, but ground wind is not affected.*

Anemometer Height

Wind speeds we get from model forecasts, as well as AS-CAT, ships, and buoys, are all normalized to be valid at 10 m (33 ft) above the water—called 10-m wind. A sailboat's anemometer, on the other hand can be located at 25 m above the water, or more. Thus if we are next to a weather buoy reporting 10 kts of wind, we will read a higher wind on our anemometer (11 kts or so), because wind speed generally increases with height above the water. This does not imply that either measurement is accurate to this level of precision, but just that there will be this consistent difference.

Again, this is a small correction, but routing computations are a continual interplay between what wind we measure and what is reported, so we have to account for this correction in that process, and we would like to do so as best we can.

A common procedure is to scale up the forecast winds to match the anemometer height using an empirical factor based on the formula in Figure A9-3. The correction could be anywhere from 5 to 15%, and, frankly, it can depend on just about everything, but mainly on wind speed and stability. Like other fine tuning in this process, we have to gain experience to see what works.

This semi-permanent wind-height adjustment is not the same as the almost continual adjustments to the forecast winds we need to make to compensate for what we actually observe—now comparing winds at the same height. In other words, we can't ask the program to give us the *optimum* route from A to B, when the GRIB forecasts have NE 10 kts at A and we know the wind is actually E-NE 13 kts at A. We have to fix that before pushing the compute button. If we are requesting a third party to tell us the best route, we have to somehow tell them the present forecasts are not exactly right.

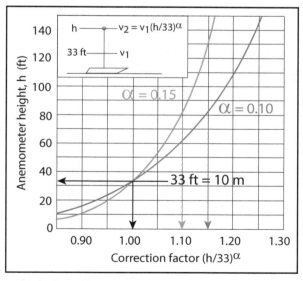

Figure A9-3. *Guidelines for estimating wind speed as a function of height above the water. The exponent (alpha) is usually in the range 0.10 to 0.15, which for an 80-ft mast height changes the correction from 1.15 to 1.10—the symmetry in numbers is a coincidence. The correction can depend on wind speed and stability, with most uncertainty in light air or gusty conditions.*

Appendix 10. Hurricane Profiles

Figure A10-1 is a copy of Figure 4.5-5, which is an estimate of typical hurricane properties we put together years ago, based on statistical data available at the time. Now we have tremendously more specific information. One new source is the Hurricane Data link at the NDBC. It shows examples of hurricanes that have passed over one of the buoys they monitor, yielding measured wind, pressure, and sea state data during their approach and departure from the buoy sites.

Examples showing the actual eye passing over a buoy are shown in Figures A10-2 and A10-3. We have added a miles scale to the pictures by looking up the storm speeds from the NHC archives. The distances are asymmetric, because these storms speeded up at recurvature.

We notice that the wind speeds measured from the buoys are significantly lower than the archived values listed in the NHC archives, which they determine accurately by several means. The reason is partly due to definitions. NHC winds are one-minute averages, whereas the buoy data are 8-minute averages, which lowers the peak values. Furthermore, the reference level for surface winds is 10 m, and the anemometer heights of both buoys are only 4 m above the sea surface. This is normally an easy correction to make to the wind speeds, but not when the waves are 10 to 15 m high. In the troughs, these buoys are shielded from the wind much of the time, which again would reduce the average values.

No two hurricanes are the same, and there is a broad range of characteristics, but our schematic of what we called "average properties of a large system" seems to scale reasonably with these actual measurements.

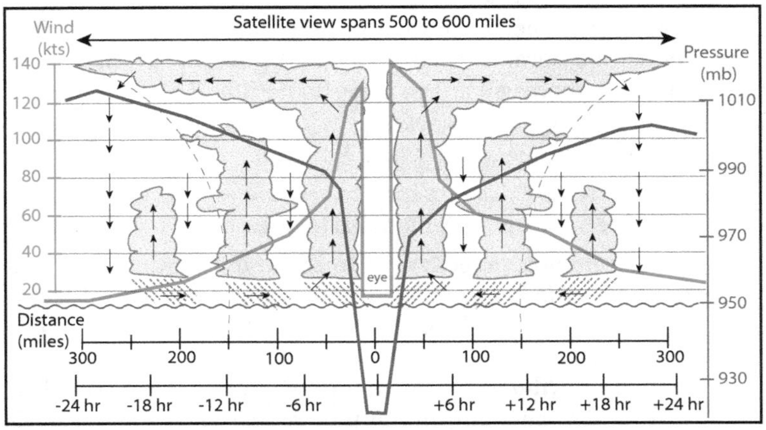

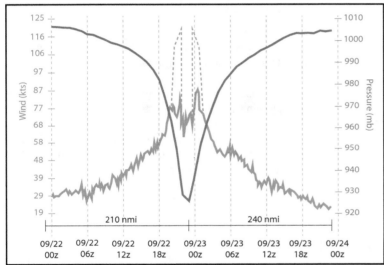

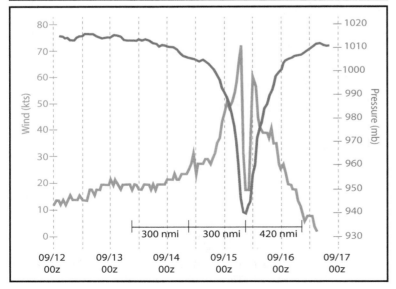

Figure A10-1. Top. *Reproduction of Figure 4.5-5, representing average properties of larger systems. This is a schematic, made up of average statistics. The following figures are real data.*

Figure A10-2. Middle. *Wind and pressure data from Hurricane Rita passing over buoy 42001 in 2005 (ndbc.noaa.gov/hurricanes/2005/rita). Rita was a major hurricane at this time, with sustained winds of 120 kts at 00z, 9/23. In this case the eye (~20 nmi diameter) passed over the buoy, just 2 nmi off the centerline. We added the dashed red lines to indicate the NHC archived wind speeds, discussed in the text.*

Figure A10-3. Bottom. *Wind and pressure data from Hurricane Floyd passing over buoy 41010 in 1999 (ndbc.noaa.gov/hurricanes/1999/floyd.shtml). According to the NHC archives, the peak sustained wind at 06z, 9/15 was 110 kts, with a central pressure of 935 mb. The wind speed discrepancy is discussed in the text.*

Appendix 11. Present Weather Symbols
(i.e., code 64 is intermittent heavy rain; code 3 is clouds forming.)

	0	1	2	3	4	5	6	7	8	9
00	Cloud development not observed or not observable during past hour	Clouds generally dissolving or becoming less developed during past hour	State of sky on the whole unchanged during past hour	Clouds generally forming or developing during past hour	Visibility reduced by smoke	Haze	Widespread dust in suspension in the air, not raised by wind, at time of obs	Dust or sand raised by wind, at time of obs	Well developed dust devil(s) within past hour	Duststorm or sandstorm within sight of station or at station during past hour
10	Light fog	Patches of shallow fog at station not deeper than 6 feet on land	More or less continuous shallow fog at station not deeper than 6 feet on land	Lightning visible, no thunder heard	Precipitation within sight, but not reaching the ground	Precipitation within sight, reaching ground, but distant from station	Precipitation within sight, reaching the ground, near to but not at station	Thunder heard but no precipitation at the station	Squall(s) within sight during past hour	Funnel cloud(s) within sight during past hour
20	Drizzle (not freezing, not showers) during past hour, not at time of obs	Rain (not freezing, not showers) during past hour, not at time of obs	Snow (not falling as showers) during past hour, not at time of obs	Rain and snow (not falling as showers) during past hour, not at time of obs	Freezing drizzle or rain (not showers) during past hour, not at time of obs	Showers of rain during past hour, but not at time of obs	Showers of snow, or of rain and snow during past hour, but not at time of obs	Showers of hail, or of hail and rain during past hour, but not at time of obs	Fog during past hour, but not at time of obs	Thunderstorm (with or without precip) during past hour, but not at time of obs
30	Slight or moderate duststorm or sandstorm, has decreased during past hour	Slight or moderate duststorm or sandstorm, no appreciable change during past hour	Slight or moderate duststorm or sandstorm, has increased during past hour	Severe duststorm or sandstorm, has decreased during past hour	Severe duststorm or sandstorm, no appreciable change during past hour	Severe duststorm or sandstorm, has increased during past hour	Slight or moderate drifting snow, generally low	Heavy drifting snow, generally low	Slight or moderate drifting snow, generally high	Heavy drifting snow, generally high
40	Fog at distance at time of obs but not at station during past hour	Fog in patches	Fog, sky discernable, has become thinner during past hour	Fog, sky not discernable, has become thinner during past hour	Fog, sky discernable, no appreciable change during past hour	Fog, sky not discernable, no appreciable change during past hour	Fog, sky discernable, has begun or become thicker during past hour	Fog, sky not discernable, has begun or become thicker during past hour	Fog, depositing rime, sky discernable	Fog, depositing rime, sky not discernable
50	Intermittent drizzle (not freezing), slight at time of obs	Continuous drizzle (not freezing), slight at time of obs	Intermittent drizzle (not freezing), moderate at time of obs	Continuous drizzle (not freezing), moderate at time of obs	Intermittent drizzle (not freezing), thick at time of obs	Continuous drizzle (not freezing), thick at time of obs	Slight freezing drizzle	Moderate or thick freezing drizzle	Drizzle and rain, slight	Drizzle and rain, moderate or heavy
60	Intermittent rain (not freezing), slight at time of obs	Continuous rain (not freezing), slight at time of obs	Intermittent rain (not freezing), moderate at time of obs	Continuous rain (not freezing), moderate at time of obs	Intermittent rain (not freezing), heavy at time of obs	Continuous rain (not freezing), heavy at time of obs	Slight freezing rain	Moderate or heavy freezing rain	Rain or drizzle and snow, slight	Rain or drizzle and snow, moderate or heavy
70	Intermittent fall of snowflakes, slight at time of obs	Continuous fall of snowflakes, slight at time of obs	Intermittent fall of snowflakes, moderate at time of obs	Continuous fall of snowflakes, moderate at time of obs	Intermittent fall of snowflakes, heavy at time of obs	Continuous fall of snowflakes, heavy at time of obs	Ice needles (with or without fog)	Granular snow (with or without fog)	Isolated starlike snow crystals (with or without fog)	Ice pellets (sleet, U.S. definition)
80	Slight rain shower(s)	Moderate or heavy rain shower(s)	Violent rain shower(s)	Slight shower(s) of rain and snow mixed	Moderate or heavy shower(s) of rain and snow mixed	Slight snow shower(s)	Moderate or heavy snow shower(s)	Slight shower(s) of soft or small hail, with or without rain, and/or snow	Moderate or heavy shower(s) of soft or small hail, with or without rain and/or snow	Slight shower(s) of hail, with or without rain and/or snow, not assoc with thunder
90	Moderate of heavy shower(s) of hail and/or rain/snow, not associated with thunder	Slight rain at time of obs; thunderstorm during past hour not at time of obs	Moderate or heavy rain at time of obs; tstm during past hour not at time of obs	Slight snow and/or rain/hail at time of obs; tstm during past hour not at time of obs	Moderate or heavy snow and/or rain/ hail at time of obs; tstm past hour not at obs time	Slight or moderate thunderstorm without hail but with rain and/or snow at obs time	Slight or moderate thunderstorm with hail at time of obs	Heavy thunderstorm without hail but with rain and/or snow at time of obs	Tstm combined with duststorm or sandstorm at time of obs	Heavy thunderstorm with hail at time of obs

About the Author

David Burch is a Fellow of the Royal Institute of Navigation in London as well as a Fellow of the Institute of Navigation in Washington, DC, from which he received the Superior Achievement Award for outstanding performance as a practicing navigator. He has logged more than 70,000 miles at sea, including twelve transoceanic yacht races, with several first place victories and a passage record for boats under 36 feet that lasted 16 years. He also navigated the only American entry in the storm-ridden 1993 Sydney to Hobart Race.

On the academic side, he is a former Fulbright Scholar with a PhD in physics. As Founding Director of Starpath School of Navigation in Seattle he has designed courses and taken part in the teaching of marine weather and navigation for more than 30 years. He continues to work on the development of online training materials, which are presented at starpath.com. His articles on special topics in navigation and weather appear at starpath.com/articles.

Other books by the author

Weather Workbook
The Barometer Handbook
Mariner's Pressure Atlas
Introduction to Electronic Chart Navigation
Celestial Navigation
Inland and Coastal Navigation
Radar for Mariners
Fundamentals of Kayak Navigation
Sailor's Logbook
Emergency Navigation
The Star Finder Book
Hawaii By Sextant
How to Use Plastic Sextants

CPSIA information can be obtained
at www.ICGtesting.com
Printed in the USA
BVHW011047221022
650025BV00006B/46

9 780914 025580